T0224003

Lecture Notes in Computer Science 9100

Commenced Publication in 1973
Founding and Former Series Editors:
Gerhard Goos, Juris Hartmanis, and Jan van Leeuwen

Editorial Board

More information about this series at http://www.springer.com/series/7410

Peter Y.A. Ryan · David Naccache
Jean-Jacques Quisquater (Eds.)

The New Codebreakers

Essays Dedicated to David Kahn
on the Occasion of His 85th Birthday

 Springer

Editors
Peter Y.A. Ryan
Université du Luxembourg
Luxembourg
Luxembourg

Jean-Jacques Quisquater
Université Catholique de Louvain
Louvain-la-Neuve
Belgium

David Naccache
Ecole normale supérieure
Paris
France

ISSN 0302-9743   ISSN 1611-3349 (electronic)
Lecture Notes in Computer Science
ISBN 978-3-662-49300-7   ISBN 978-3-662-49301-4   (eBook)
DOI 10.1007/978-3-662-49301-4

Library of Congress Control Number: 2016933242

LNCS Sublibrary: SL4 – Security and Cryptology

Printed on acid-free paper

This Springer imprint is published by Springer Nature
The registered company is Springer-Verlag GmbH Berlin Heidelberg

Foreword

Midway through the second decade of the twenty-first century it is quite clear that we are living in a world of cryptographic abundance. Increasingly the stability of our information-based world depends on trusted, reliable communications between all elements of the interconnected societies in which we live. As we live our lives more and more through digital transactions, be they e-mail, financial management, social media publication, home security, personal fitness and healthcare, or video entertainment, we rely on sophisticated cryptographic mechanisms operating silently in the background to keep us and our personal data safe. Cryptography provides techniques to keep information secret, preserve its integrity, and validate its source but few citizens know the extent to which they depend on it, and even fewer will have ever considered studying it.

From its first routine adoption by the Spartans in the fifth century BC, cryptography has been the domain of the military, governments, and spies. Governments throughout the ages have strived to control the dissemination of information relating to cryptology (encompassing both cryptography, the creating of codes and ciphers, and cryptanalysis, the solving or "breaking" of codes and ciphers) and its widespread usage. This control meant that even as late as the 1960s there was little material published relating to the field and there had been no attempt made by the "open" research community to compile a definitive account of the history of the subject.

It was against this background that in the 1960s David Kahn set out to write a serious history of cryptology. His book, *The Codebreakers – The Story of Secret Writing*, published in 1967 was the result of over four years of painstaking research compiling its content from interviews with cryptologists, unpublished documents in archives, and scientific papers. The result was an outstanding achievement that for the first time presented the whole scope of the subject in a readily understandable form. The dustjacket on my copy proudly proclaims that it is, "The first comprehensive history of secret communication from ancient times to the threshold of outer space." While it is always hard to measure the impact of a book, this unprecedented tome became a reference work for those of us entering the emerging commercial cryptologic community in the 1970s and 80s. Its blend of technical thoroughness and flowing prose made it fascinating to read cover to cover – although I confess it took me a considerable time to make it through the 1,000 plus pages. Of particular importance to me was how it provided the context of both the cryptographic and cryptanalytic elements of the field – it highlighted what we now see as the adversarial game played by those who wish to protect our data and those who wish to subvert it. A good cryptographer will try to analyse their techniques from all the perspectives of their adversary, both technical and human. The lessons of *The Codebreakers* are as relevant today as when David first compiled his book nearly 50 years ago.

Since its publication, David has continued to contribute to the field. In 1977 he was a founding editor of the journal *Cryptologia,* in 1982 he was an original committee member of what became the International Association for Cryptologic Research

(IACR) that now has in excess of 1,400 members worldwide and exists to promote research in cryptology and related fields. In 1995 David was selected to become scholar-in-residence at the National Security Agency (NSA), the very institution that sought to stifle publication of *The Codebreakers* 30 years earlier.

In 2010 I was privileged to be invited to speak at a Fest in Luxembourg organised to honour David's 80th birthday. It was a fascinating occasion with contributions from a wide variety of speakers with backgrounds from academia, commerce, and government. David closed the event with a talk entitled "My Life in Cryptology." It occurred to me at the time that David didn't just document cryptologic history, he earned his place in that history back in 1967.

Andrew J. Clark

Visiting Professor, Information Security Group,

Royal Holloway University of London

Past President IACR

Preface

Nowadays cryptography permeates our lives, even if it is largely transparent and most people are blissfully unaware of its crucial role. Cryptography, and in particular "modern cryptography," forms one of the foundations of the information society. It is thus hard to imagine that only a few decades ago cryptography was the sole preserve of governments, spies, diplomats, and the military. In the 1960s, when David Kahn conceived the idea of penning a history of secret writing, it was virtually impossible to find an account of the subject, let alone a readable one. Virtually no research was conducted in the "open," academic world and no university offered courses on cryptography. Of course, work went on in the making and breaking of codes in secret in the world's intelligence agencies: NSA, GCHQ, the KGB etc., but none of this saw the light of day.

Thus, Kahn's idea to write a major history of the subject was audacious and ambitious, and indeed prescient. It is hard to gauge the impact of the book, but it seems clear that many people who went on to contribute to the development of modern cryptography had their appetite whetted by reading *The Codebreakers*; certainly this is true of many of the contributors to this book. Kahn's book is remarkable in having a blend of technical detail mixed with tales of daring and adventure. It is a superb piece of scholarship, minutely researched but without the dryness that so often comes with scholarship.

In 2010 David turned 80 and a number of us decided to arrange a Fest in Luxembourg to honour the event (http://www.codebreakers2010.uni.lu/index.html). The event was highly successful and enjoyable, with talks by many of the world's leading cryptographers and security experts. Several of the talks resulted in chapters in this Festschrift. A highlight of the event was a fine banquet in Luxembourg's Chateau de Bourglinster.

Since the publication of *The Codebreakers*, the world has changed dramatically: We learnt of the breaking of the German Enigma, which heralded the age of the computer, and witnessed the advent of public key cryptography and enabled the Internet to become the medium of social and commercial interaction it is today. Cryptography and information assurance now form major academic disciplines with thousands of researchers and a proliferation of conferences and courses. The discovery in the 1970s of public key cryptography revolutionized the subject and brought it out of the shadows. The realization that the ability to encrypt does not necessarily entail the ability to decrypt overturned (implicit) assumptions that had held sway for centuries. Arguably this insight is comparable in its impact on cryptography as that of Einstein's Theory of Relativity, with the realization that space is not absolute, on physics.

We felt it appropriate therefore to call the present Festschrift *The New Codebreakers* to pay homage to Kahn's groundbreaking contribution and to carry the story forward into the new era.

It is now five years since the Fest in 2010, and David is now 85, so this Festschrift serves to honour this later anniversary. We are delighted to have been able to gather 33 chapters from distinguished members of the cryptography, security, and history of intelligence communities. The chapters cover a wide range from theoretical cryptography to security applications and from the history of intelligence to recreational applications. We hope you will all enjoy reading this as we enjoyed reading David's book all those years ago.

We would like to thank again all those who attended David's Fest in 2010, especially those who gave talks, and all those who contributed chapters to this volume.

November 2015

David Naccache
Peter Y.A. Ryan
Jean-Jacques Quisquater

Contents

History

Mary of Guise's Enciphered Letters

Valérie Nachef[1]([✉]), Jacques Patarin[2], and Armel Dubois-Nayt[3]

[1] CNRS(UMR 8088) Et Département de Mathématiques,
Université de Cergy-Pontoise, 2 Avenue Adolphe Chauvin,
95011 Cergy-pontoise Cedex, France
`valerie.nachef@u-cergy.fr`
[2] Laboratoire de Mathématiques de Versailles, UVSQ CNRS,
Université de Paris-Saclay, 78035 Versailles, France
`jpatarin@club-internet.fr`
[3] CEARC, Observatoire de Versailles Saint-Quentin-en-Yvelines,
11 Boulevard D'Alembert, 78280 Guyancourt, France
`dubois-nayt@iut-velizy.uvsq.fr`

1 Introduction

In this paper, we will present the decryption of letters that were written in code by the secretary of the queen of Scotland, Mary of Guise (Mary Queen of Scots' mother), in 1553 (one letter of 25 August 1553) and in 1559: one letter of January 1559, that we will call "the big letter", one letter of August 1559, that we will call the "key letter", and one letter with no date but encrypted with the same Table. These letters only exist in manuscript form and are preserved by the archives of the Quai d'Orsay (French Ministry of Foreign Affairs) in a collection entitled Mémoires et Documents, Angleterre, XV. The documents in this Library collection have different origins. They were compiled at the end of the 19th century when the French minister of Foreign Affairs, Louis Decazes (1873–1877) decided to allow public access to diplomatic records. The documents relating to the period from the origins to 1830 were filed chronologically and inventoried in 1892. The correspondence of Mary of Guise was part of that first batch of documents. On the basis of the emblems decorating the book covers of this volume, it is possible to assume that its binding dates from the July Monarchy. The volume does not vary in format and writing from beginning to end. It contains exclusively 16th century copies and a table of contents of the same period[1].

The letters were written in Middle French (the French language used during the sixteen century) by the queen. Several letters that passed between Mary of Guise, after she became regent of Scotland, and the Noailles brothers, French ambassadors to England, were encrypted. The encryption method, which was the standard method at that time, was based on a secret nomenclator, that we will call encryption table.

---

[1] We are grateful to Grégoire Eldin, Archivist at the Archives of the Foreign Ministry, who provided us with information on this volume.

© Springer-Verlag Berlin Heidelberg 2016
P.Y.A. Ryan et al. (Eds.): Kahn Festschrift, LNCS 9100, pp. 3–24, 2016.
DOI: 10.1007/978-3-662-49301-4_1

The paper codex of 184 folios kept by the French Foreign Office's archives also contains plain text letters written by Mary of Guise to M. de Noailles.

When we first embarked on the study of these letters, we did not know if there were pairs of plain texts / cipher texts among the letters. Moreover, we noticed that Mary's secretary used two different encryption tables. The first one served around 1553 and the second one around 1559. As we will see, the second one is much more sophisticated than the first.

The paper is organized as follows. In Sect. 2, we briefly introduce Mary of Guise's life and the historical context of the letters. In Sects. 3 and 4, we provide a detailed description of the letters found at the Quai d'Orsay. We also explain our decryption work and provide the Tables. In Sect. 5, we compare these tables with the one used by Mary Queen of Scots twenty years later. The conclusion is given in Sect. 6.

2   Mary of Guise and the Historical Context of the Letters

2.1   Mary of Guise

Mary of Guise was the eldest daughter of Claude of Lorraine, duke of Guise. She was born in 1515 in Lorraine and she died in 1560 in Scotland. She was first married in 1534, to Louis II d'Orleans, Duke of Longueville, who died in 1537. She became queen of Scotland after marrying the Scottish king, James V, in 1538. This second union for both spouses produced three children. The first two, James and Arthur, had died in infancy, when their daughter Mary (Queen of Scots) was born on 8 December 1542. King James passed away six days later in the wake of the humiliating defeat against the English at Solway Moss (24 November 1542), making the infant Mary queen regnant of Scotland.

Mary of Guise only assumed the regency twelve years later once she had worked to enhance her political status both in Scotland, France and England. She then convinced the incumbent regent, The Duke of Châtelherault, who had been in office since 1542, to surrender the Regency on 12 April 1554.

Therefore on 25 August 1553, when our first encrypted letter was written, Mary of Guise was not the regent of Scotland yet. Still, she was exchanging thoroughly on that possibility with her French correspondents as it was a matter of debate at the French Court. The French king and her brothers, the duke of Guise and the Cardinal of Lorraine, supported the idea enthusiastically while Henry Cleutin, the representative of France in Scotland, amongst others, expressed serious reservations.

The summer of 1553 was however far more critical for the female claimant to the English throne, Mary Tudor. Her brother Edward had died on 6 July that year after altering the succession and excluding both her and Elizabeth, her half-sister, in favor of Henry VII's great niece, the Protestant Lady Jane Grey. This decision precipitated a succession crisis that lasted most of July but by 3 August, thanks to the support of prominent men, Mary was triumphantly entering London as the new English queen. By the end of the month, she was accepting the apologies of some of those who had supported Lady Jane Grey's claim to create a government. Mary Tudor's experience and English events at the time were bound to be of great interest to the aspiring Scottish regent. Now that Catherine of Aragon's daughter was on the English throne, Englands relationship with France was jeopardized as Henry II was a long-standing enemy of Charles V's Holy Roman Empire. Besides, as a woman who was considering taking command, she must have been interested to know how the first English reigning queen managed to assert her authority over her councilors, Parliament, and more generally her subjects.

2.2 The Regency

Her authority was however soon challenged by the Scots who resented her over-reliance on French men and by the Protestant Lords who supported the Reformation of the Kirk[2]. In the first three years of her rule, her main objective was to support the king of France, Henry II, in his war against Spain, that was allied with England. To do so, she fought the English who kept raiding the borders and as she was struggling on that front, she led a policy of religious tolerance towards the new religion that was spreading in Scotland.

Protestantism was first introduced in Scotland in the 1520s by Lutheran preachers, but by the 1550s, the Scottish reformers were mostly disciples of John Calvin who were to build a reformed church, closer to the Dutch or French ones than to the English Anglican church.

In the winter 1558–1559, however, Mary took a tougher line on Protestantism as the Protestants multiplied their religious demands. This is when Scottish Reformer John Knox started to attack her bitterly. He had just returned from Calvin's Geneva, which he considered as "the most perfect school of Christ" ([2], pp. 240–241) . Mary of Guise's authority had first been seriously challenged a year earlier when a group of Scottish Lords, known as the "Lords of the Congregation" drew up a covenant to "maintain, set forth, and establish the most blessed Word of God and his Congregation" ([1], p. 273).

To confront them, she benefited from the military and financial aid of the French king, Henry II, but had two fierce opponents in Mary Tudor (queen of England from 1553 to 1558) and Elizabeth Tudor (queen of England from 1558 to 1603). As an ally of the French king and an enemy of the English queen's husband, Philip II of Spain, she had nipped in the bud any possible help from her coreligionist counterpart south of the border. As for the Protestant Elizabeth, she was her religious enemy from the beginning.

The new English queen brought fresh hope to the Scottish Protestants who were eager to gain her support in their fight for religious freedom and national sovereignty. For several months, she did not play fair with her Scottish counterpart as illustrated by the second encrypted letter studied here, in which Guise

---

[2] Name given to the Church of Scotland.

made it abundantly clear that she was no fool and that she could see what Elizabeth was up to. On the advice of her secretary William Cecil, Elizabeth was in fact preparing to make a decisive move by agreeing to military action. Cecil was determined that it was high time to build a British state and to unite England and Scotland. He saw the violent turn taken by the Scottish Reformation as an opportunity to achieve a higher goal and threatened Elizabeth to resign if she did not follow his views on that issue. Elizabeth, on the other hand, was still hesitating at the time Guise wrote the letter dated January 1560 under scrutiny in this paper. Her call for clarification on the English queen's intents is therefore genuine and gives vivid evidence of the dramatic tension that was building up at the time. It shows Guise facing an agonizing wait while the indecisive Elizabeth was making up her mind. Things became clearer a month later on 27 February 1560 when the treaty of Berwick was signed between James, Duke of Châtelherault, in the name of Mary Queen of Scots, and Elizabeth I. It affirmed and legitimated the military and political interference of the English Queen in Scottish affairs officially to protect Scotland's ancient rights and liberty.

Party as a result, religious disturbances intensified in the first half of 1559, which led to the queen outlawing the Protestant leaders and to their taking arms against her (one of our encrypted letter is of January 1559). They were spurred on by John Knox whose passionate sermon against idolatry sparked a riot in Perth and led to violent acts of iconoclasm. Following several unsuccessful attempts, a peace agreement between the queen regent and the Lords of the Congregation was concluded on Leith Links on 23 July 1559. Mary granted the Protestants freedom of worship and agreed to send the French soldiers away. In return, the Protestant Lords would obey the queen and stop all form of intimidating against the Catholic Church. During the military campaign, Mary had successively sought refuge in the palace of Falkland and the castle of Dunbar, avoiding the capital as much as possible.

After a truce that soon turned out to be a sham, she eventually returned to Edinburgh. Mary breached the Leith Agreement by welcoming French reinforcements in August and September 1559 (one of our encrypted letter is of August 1559) while the Lords of the Congregation were engaged in secret negotiations with the English queen and eventually convinced her, with the assistance of her Secretary, William Cecil, to fight a preventive war against the French troops that were arriving by sea. To be successful, the enterprise required the support of the second person of the realm, the Duke of Châtelherault, which they obtained relatively easily as the latter was greatly offended by the presence of French garrisons in Leith. Hence, on 19 September 1559, the former regent, who was also concerned about the dynastic future of his family, second in line for the throne, joined the Congregation and led them in their campaign against Mary of Guise's government. The military struggle that mostly took place in Fife was turning to the disadvantage of the Congregation in the last months of the year when English intervention completely reversed the situation. The French retreated to Leith while the Congregation and the queen of England signed the Treaty of Berwick on 27 February 1560. This guaranteed further English assistance to get rid of the French. Fighting between the two armies was still going on when Mary died in Edinburgh Castle on 11 June 1560.

2.3 The Treaty of Edinburgh

A month later, England and France made peace and concluded the Treaty of Edinburgh, which sealed the withdrawal of their respective troops from Scotland. In that same summer, on 11 August 1560, the Kirk was officially reformed by the Scottish Parliament, which abolished the old faith and adopted a new confession. Mary of Guise's body would have to wait for nine months before her coffin was shipped to France, and buried in July 1561 in the Benedictine Convent of Saint Peter in Rheims, where her sister Renée was an abbess.

2.4 Mary of Guise's Correspondence

Mary of Guise's encrypted letters are all addressed to M. de Noailles but, in fact, three brothers hide behind a single name. The first was Antoine de Noailles who, thanks to the patronage of Anne de Montmorency, was appointed ambassador to England in April 1553. With this nomination, the French king, Henry II, was also rewarding the efficiency with which Antoine de Noailles had helped first d'Essé and Termes ship their troops to Scotland in 1548 and 1549. Once in England, however, Antoine de Noailles, struggled with his new assignment. He did not manage to prevent Mary Tudor from marrying the king of Spain and got involved into two plots against the English queen: the Wyatt rebellion (1554) and the Dudley conspiracy (1556). As a result, he was forced to leave England in June 1556. He was replaced successively by his brothers François and Gilles.

When the war between France and Spain broke in 1557, the French resident ambassador was withdrawn and Gilles de Noailles only returned to London as such in May 1559. He is the second addressee of Mary of Guise's coded letters. He was in London during the wars of the Congregation (1559–1560). In March 1561, he travelled to Edinburgh to speak on behalf of Mary Queen of Scots who was preparing her return home and wanted to reassure the Scottish Parliament about her benevolent state of mind.

The succession of two brothers as French ambassadors to England probably explains why we have two different encryption tables. We can assume that the first one was used with Antoine de Noailles and the second one with Gilles de Noailles.

3 Enciphered Letters with Table 1

In the records held in the archives of the Quai d'Orsay, there are only two documents encrypted with Table 1: a complete letter and a fragment of another letter. They were written in 1553.

3.1   The Context of the Letter

In the full letter, Mary of Guise used the code to confirm that the person who passed along the message was the rightful messenger. This was meant to allow further safe exchanges with M. de Noailles.

When Mary wrote the letter of the 25th of August 1553, she had not yet been invested with the regency but she was working on it and gently trying to convince the duke of Châtelherault to give up his office. The letter is addressed to the French ambassador Antoine de Noailles who had been appointed to this position in April 1553 after a brilliant military career.

This letter was written at a sensitive time in English history. Mary Tudor had just managed to recover her crown that had first been denied to her by her Protestant brother, Edward VI and his coreligionists. Edward VI had died in the previous month on 6 July 1553 after excluding his half-sisters, Mary and Elizabeth from the succession and naming Lady Jane Grey as his heiress. To recover the English crown, Catherine of Aragon's daughter had to raise an army and fight her challenger's supporters. She eventually secured her rights on 19 July 1553 when Lady Jane Grey stepped down from the English throne following the weakening of her army. By the time this letter was written, Lady Jane Grey was in jail along with the Protestant leaders who had engineered her succession to the throne, the first of which being her father-in-law, the Duke of Northumberland. He was executed on the 22nd, hence Mary of Guise's heightened interest in English matters a few days later. Guise was also concerned with the rumors circulating across Europe, of a possible marriage between the English queen and the son of Charles V, Philip of Spain. This marriage was considered potentially dangerous for national sovereignty in both England and Scotland. Mary of Guise in fact dreaded an invasion from a hostile England, just as she was concerned that if Mary and Philip had children, they would take her daughter's place on the English line of succession. Hence, the importance for Mary to get safe and reliable information from Noailles. The latter would learn at his expense a year later the usefulness of coded letters. He supported the popular uprising that tried to prevent the Spanish marriage in the first months of 1554. This rebellion, which was given the name of its leader, Thomas Wyatt, also compromised the French through their ambassador who offered aid to the rebels in writing. The missives that betrayed him were seized by the English and Noailles was caught red handed. Yet, he was not recalled and continued to serve the interest of Henry II and, when he could, those of the Scottish regent-to-be.

3.2   The Letter

In Fig. 1, we show the full letter encrypted with Table 1. It was written in 1553 to Antoine de Noailles.

On the same page, we have the cipher text and above the plain text. The cipher text was written by Mary's secretary. The plain text is probably written by M. de Noailles's secretary.

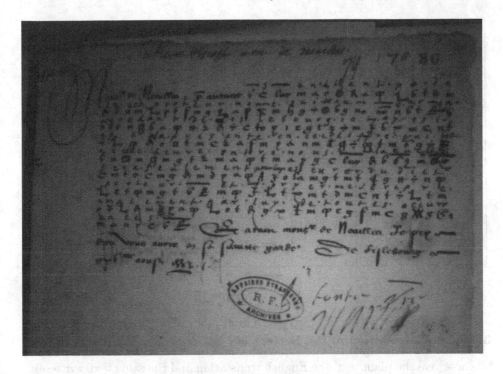

Fig. 1. Letter with plain text and cipher text, 25 August 1553

3.3 Table 1

We now provide Table 1 (Fig. 2). To recover Table 1, we used the letter above and also another document which is a contains a fragment of a letter. Still on the same document, we have the plain text and the cipher text.

Since we had only two documents to establish this table, we were unable to recover the complete table. For instance, we do not know how "f" and "x" were coded. This may be one reason for which Table 1 appears simpler than Table 2. However, we do not know, if at least for most letters of the alphabet, Table 1 is complete. For example, in Table 1, there are three different symbols to code "a". We can suppose that the cryptographer was careful and varied the different symbols very often to code "a". If this is the case, there are no additional symbols to code "a" in Table 1. In Fig. 1, we also observe that the same symbol was used for "q" and "null". The secretary first chose it for "null" and later he used it again for "q". In this table 1, we did not manage to establish the symbols used for countries and people but we succeeded with Table 2. In Table 1, there is a symbol for the French word "es" (is in English). This symbol is used in two different ways: first to represent the word "est" and second as part of an other word, like "estre", where it is used together with the symbols representing "r" and "e".

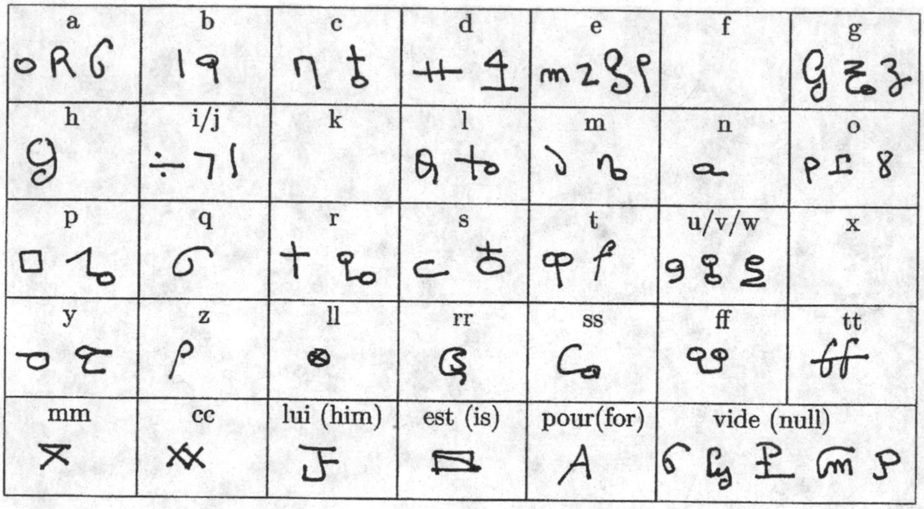

Fig. 2. Table 1 (Around 1553)

3.4 The Translation of the Letter

We now give the plain text, the English translation and the same text written in Modern French. As we can see the Middle French is significantly different from modern French and therefore is not easy to read and to understand: the form of the letters, the spelling and some words are different (Fig. 3).

4 Enciphered Letters with Table 2

Among the documents, there are three letters encrypted with Table 2. They were written in 1559. At that time, Gilles de Noailles was the ambassador of France to England. Initially, we did not know if the corresponding plain texts were to be found in the records.

4.1 The Key Letter (of August 1559)

We began with a letter divided into 3 parts, the second one being the only encrypted section (see Fig. 4).

Fortunately, this part, where Mary of Guise complains about the Protestants, is deciphered in another document (see Fig. 5).

Even the clear text is not easy to read. We have the following text:

"Que cognoisses monsieur de Noailles si j'en ay ma part de tous coustes et comme de *cestuiez* je suys tormentee de ces gens enragez desquelz vous entendres les depportemens par les lettres de monsieur Doysel et comme les choses sont passees pardeca despuys noz dernieres qui me gardera"

La Reine d'Escosse à M. de Noailles	La Reine d'Écosse à M. de Noailles	The Queen of Scotland to M. de Noailles
Monsieur de Noailles, s'en allant par delà ce porteur nommé Guillaume Ara Marchant de Lislebourg Je luy ay escfripte la presente en ce chiffre qui est a cette heure entre nous laquelle sera seulement pour luy asseurer du Dit porteur et lui pryer m'escrire amplement par luy de toutes occurrences, Et a Tans Monsieur de Noailles je prie Dieu vous avoir en sa sainte garde. De Lislebourg ce 25e aougt 1553. La toute votre Marie	Monsieur de Noailles, comme ce porteur Guillaume Ara, marchant d'Edimbourg va vous voir, je vous ai écrit cette lettre avec le code que nous utilisons actuellement pour vous faire savoir que vous pouvez lui faire confiance et vous demander de m'écrire plus longuement au sujet de tout ce qui se passe. Entre temps, Monsieur de Noailles, je prie Dieu de vous garder sous sa sainte protection. D'Edimbourg, le 25 Août 1553. Bien à vous. Marie	M. de Noailles, as this bearer, a merchant from Edinburgh who goes by the name of Guillaume Ara, is coming over to you, I have written the present letter in the code we currently use to let you know that the said bearer can be trusted and to ask you to write to me at length through his intermediary about all that happens. In the meantime, I pray God to keep you in his holy protection, From Edinburgh, August 25th 1553, Yours truly, Mary.

Fig. 3. Letter in Middle French, Modern french and English

We were not sure that this text is completely correct, especially the term in italics. We now explain how we proceed to find Table 2. Figure 6 shows the cipher part of the text.

We did not know if the symbols represented letters, syllables, words or parts of words. After looking carefully at the cipher text, we remark that the group of symbols "╫ ╫╫" appears twice just separated by one symbol Ꝓ on the fifth line. On the plain text, we notice that the group "en" appears exactly the same way (we mark them in bold above).

Thus we made the hypothesis that there was a matching: "╫" to encrypt **e**, " ╫╫" to encrypt "**n**, and "Ꝓ" to encrypt "**s**. Then using the clear text and the cipher text, we began to build Table 2. Moreover, we obtained the following plain text:
"vous comgnoisserez Monsieur de Noailles si j'en ai ma part de tous costez et comme dez cestuy cy je suis tourmente de ces gens enragez desquelz vous entendrez les depportemens par les lettres de mosieur Doysel et comme les choses sont passées par deça depuis noz dernieres".

We now give in Fig. 7 the beginning of the table that we obtain with this first document.

4.2   The Decryption of the Other Documents

Relying on that first version of Table 2, we were able to decrypt partially all the other encrypted letters. This allowed us to guess new symbols for letters but also for words like "qui" (who), "faict" (fact), "dict" (said). At that time we obtain a improved version of Table 2. But there were some symbols for which we did not have the meaning. For us these symbols were representing words rather than

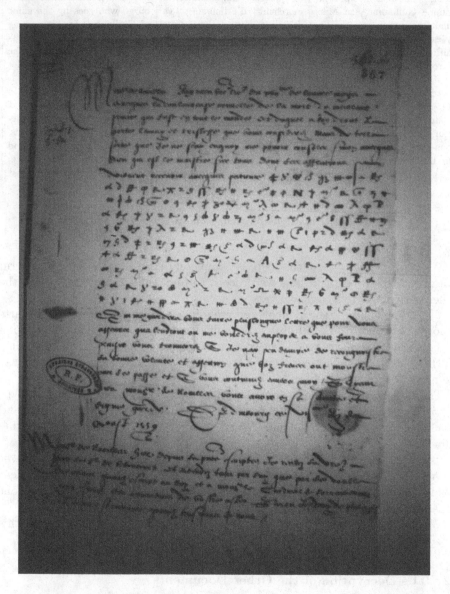

Fig. 4. Letter with plain text and cipher text: our "key letter" of August 1559

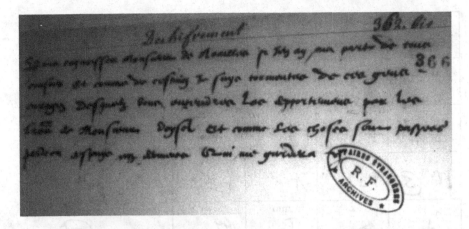

Fig. 5. Deciphering

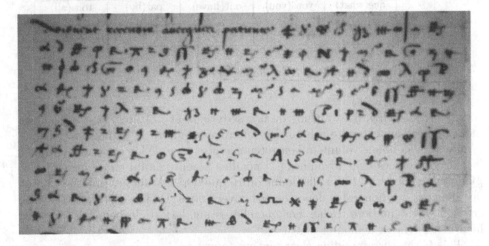

Fig. 6. Encrypted part of the key letter

letters and by the context of the texts we were pretty sure that these symbols
were used to name people or countries.

Then we look at all the documents in the codex and although we have only
partial decryption, we found a clear text that matched with one of our decrypted
texts.

Here is the partial decryption we had:

"Este advertie que a la dernière assemblu des guardiens des deux fronttières
le comte de northomberland demanda au conte boihuil s'ile ne seroit pas bien aise
que le [...] fust [...] des [...] ainsi que l [...] se trouvoit des [...] danantagre que sire
Henry Persy frere du dict conte a dict a ung autre gentilhome de pais que si les [...]
voloient avoir [...]ecour [...] d [...] pour le faict de [...] ilz le auroient et de faict ung
serviteur familier du dict conte et des frere est depuis naguere venu secretement

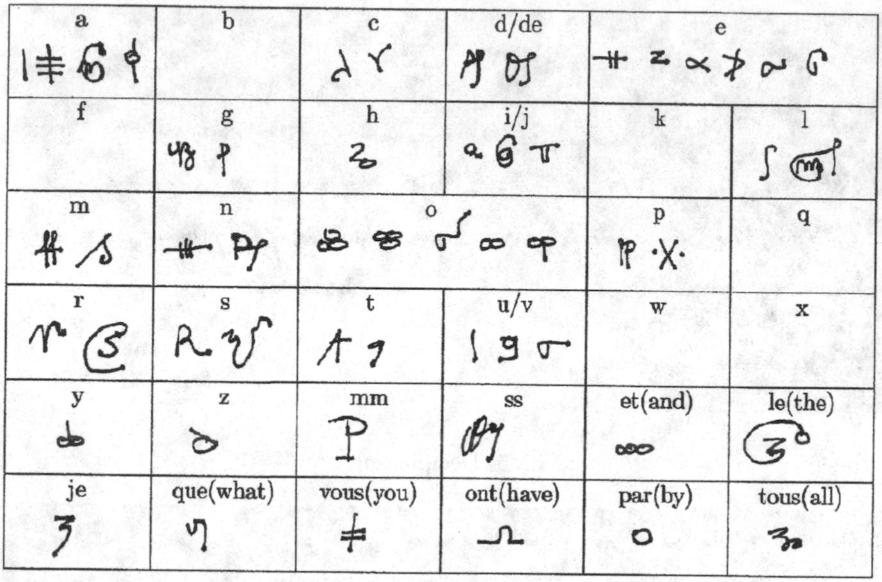

Fig. 7. Beginning of Table 2

communicquer et parlera aucuns de noz sedytieux et [...] dont la praticque ne me semble pouvoir tendre a bonne fin ni correspondre a la demonstration que [...] faict de sa bonne volunte a l entretenement et bien de la commune amitié et intelligence de ces trois royaumes [...] noailles aceepte de lui en de ouvertire et plaincte de ma part a ce qu elle donne ordre que doresnavant ses ministres usent de eilleur et [...] honnestes deportemens envers nous. De [...] coste j ne scaichse envoi ils aient matiere d cher her querelle estant le fort de heimuth [...]de ce heure entierement demoli et abatu.

This is the corresponding clear text we found:

"esté advertie que la dernière assemblée des Gardiens des deux frontières, Le Comte de Northonberland demanda au comte de Bothwell s'il ne seroit pas bien aise que l'Escosse fust quicte des Françoys ainsi que l'Angleterre se trouvoit d'Espaignolz. Davantaige Ser. Hernry Persy frère du D Comte a dict à ung aultre Gentilho de ce pays que si les Escossoys voulloient avoir secours d'Angleterre pour le faict de la Relligion Ils l'auraoient, et de faict ung ser viteur familier du Dt Comte et d'un frère Syen, est depuis naguères venu secrètement communiquer et parler a aulcuns de Noz séditieux et perdez dont la pratique ne me semble pouvoir tendre a bonne fin ny correspondre à la démonstration que la Royne d'Angleterre faict de sa bonne volonté et l'Entretenement et lien de la commune amytié et Intelligence de ces trois Royaumes vous priant Monsr de Noailles a ceste occasion luy en faire ouverture et plaincte de ma part a ce qu'elle donne ordre que doresnavant ses ministres usent de meilleurs et plus honnestes dèportements envers Nous, et estre asseuré que de Notre cousté je ne say chose en quoy Ils ayent matiére de chercher querelle estant le fort de Heymondz suyvant ce que je vous ay cy devant escript de ceste heure entieremt desmoly et abattu"

With these two texts, we were able to find the encryption of words rather than alphabet letters: terms that were missing are symbols used for countries and people (France, England, Scotland, Scottish people, the king, the queen of England for example) or words like "plus" (more).

Then we found in the codex the clear texts corresponding to all the encrypted documents and we completed Table 2.

As far as we know, this code has never been broken so far and the tables were not known either. Table 2 is given below.

4.3   The Difference Between the Decryption and the Clear Letters

We then compared our decryption with the plain text. We found minor differences: for instance some letters were missing in the encrypted text. It happened with the word "contrary", which is "contraire" in French, and which reads as "cotraire" in the deciphering. It seems therefore that the person who decrypted the text added the missing letters. There are about 20 examples like that. In these examples, letters are missing in the encrypted text and the secretary who decrypted the texts added the missing letters. We have another example with the word "rebels" which was written "rbelles" instead of "rebelles". Another example is given above: the word "ouverture" (opening) is decrypted in "ouvertire".

4.4   A Letter Encrypted with Table 2

We now give an example of a letter encrypted with Table 2. This letter is dated 2- January 1559 (we could not read the second digit) but it actually corresponds in our calendar system to January 1560 as from 1155 to 1751, the English year began on the 25th of January. It gives first-hand information on the way the new English queen, the Protestant Elizabeth, managed to give military support to the Congregation without making it official for a long time. She was chiefly advised on this matter by her secretary William Cecil who was keen to end the auld alliance between France and Scotland and to replace it with an Anglo-Scottish one (Fig. 9).

4.4.1   The Context of the Letter

The aim of the sea war the English started unofficially in 1559–1560 was to blockade the Forth and its estuary, the Firth, to prevent the French troops from landing. Cecil was also the architect of Châtelherault's "double treason", as described in the letter, who both turned against the French alliance and joined the protestant cause. His presence on the Congregation's side meant that the Protestants had a suitable and legitimate candidate to replace Guise if she proved tyrannical to the commonwealth.

Fig. 8. Table 2 (Around 1559)

Monsieur de Noailles pour vous faire entendre les deportemens de la Royne d'Angleterre bien cotraires a ce qu'elle vous a tant defoy dict et que m'avez excript elle a hui vaisseaux dedans ce feyrth qui font la guerre ouvertement et usent de depredations contre les subjects de ce royaume et ont pris deux petits vaisseaux du roi que j'avoys fait mettre sus pour la seurete de feyrth avecques ung heu charge de quelques pieces et munitions de mal dypogoce que l'on faisoit trajecter de l'autre coste pour les forces que roy y a pour le reduction des rbelles et d'autant que infraction de paix qui ne procede que de la part de la royne d'angleterre comme dieu scayt qui juge toutes choses je vous a fait ceste lettre afin qu'en puissiez parler seuremen j envoyay mecredy ung herault et ung trompete pour scavoir a quelle ocasion ilz estoient la. Il parlerent a ung jeune homme nomme Woter qui dict estre vicc admiral d'Angleterre donne lequel respndict que par connandement de la royne s maistresse il estoit venu visiter les portz d'Angleterre et voant le tem beau ils estoit mys en ce feyrih et leur avoi ion tire de lisle comme s ilz este ennemys luy fut remontre qu'il avoit prins les deux vaysseaux de Ferande et Culancl lontemps auparavant dont les deux capitaines qui estoient assis auprès de lui pouroient bien tesmoigner et qu'il faloit que ceulx de lisle tirassent puysqu'ilz se declaroient ennemys et pour empescher leur descente qu'ilz vouloin faire pour la surprise de lisle et aussi qu'ilz devoient saluer les forteresses comme s'est la coustume en passant. Le dict herault leur dict quelle responce vounez vous que je face a royne qui vous estes nous rccongnoisson bien des vaisseaux de la reine d'Angleterre respondict Wonter dictes a la roine sa maistresse que voyant qu'on m avo tire j'ay entrepris de secourir ceulx de l congregation contre les François et ceulx qui preignet leur part et de les assister des forces que j'ay par de ca et autres plus grandes qui se preparent toutefoy sans en avoir nul commandement de la royne ma maistresse

Monsieur de Noailles, to let you know the misdeeds of the queen of England which clearly contradict what she has told you many times and what you wrote to me. She has eight vessels in the Forth, which openly wage war and wreak havoc among the subjects of this kingdom. They captured two of the king's small ships which I had ordered in haste to the Forth for protection along with a flat-boat, freighted with a few artillery pieces and ammunition that were being transported across to the opposite coast and destined for the reinforcements sent by the king to repel the rebels. Since this a breach of the peace which is of the queen of England's own making, as God, who is the judge of all, knows, I am writing this letter to you so that you can speak about what happened with certainty. On Wednesday, I sent a herald and a trumpeter to find out the reason for their presence. They spoke to a young gentleman called Winter who said he was an English vice-admiral and answered that he had been ordered by the queen, his mistress, to visit some ports in England and that, when he saw the nice weather, he sailed up the Forth and that we opened fire on them from the isle as if they were enemies. He heard in reply that they had captured two vessels long before, those of Fernando and Cullen, something that thc two captains who were sitting next to him could attest to and that the troops on the isle had had to open fire since they had declared themselves enemies to prevent their surprise landing on the isle. He was also told that they should have saluted the fortresses as they were sailing past as is the custom. The said herald then asked : "what answer do you want me to make to the Queen who asked about your identity". Winter answered that they admitted they were vessels of the queen of England. Tell the queen, your mistress, that when we saw we were being shot at, I undertook to rescue those of the Congregation from the French.

Fig. 9. Letter in Middle French and English

Tel mas que comme cela est trop aise de descouvrir que ung simple subject et officier eust la volunte et encore moins le povoir de faire la guerre sans le commandement et vouloir tres expres de la royne et que l'on face la guerre aux depens d'un prince sans qu'il en sache riens aussi que c'est une expresse contravention aux ordonnances et et traictez d'entre ces deux royaumes d'Ecosse et d'Angleterre par lesquels les subjectz d'une part et d'autre ne peuvent entrer sans sauf conduict par terre n par mer si ce n'est par fortune de temps et lorsqu'il y sont arrivez le vent contraire pour venir icy et se sont servis des marées et mis en lieu ou la rade n'est aucunement bonne et ou ils n'ont accoutume de venir qu'en temps de guerre sans se vouloir faire congnoistre a personne que aux particuliers rebelles avecques lesquels ils ont eu commumication leur donnant cofort et aide et courent sus aux subjectz du roy et n'ont vounu saluer ny abaisser voiles a nule des places royales de ce royaume Par les moindres se peult commencer la guerre mais les plus grans et sages sont bien empeschez a happoyncter s'il y a quelque subjectz alienez par de deça il s'en trouvera beaucoup de bons pour s'emploier a la defence de leur patrie et si les roys d'Ecosse ont bien sceu faire la guerre au temps passe celluy qui est aujourd'huy n'a moins de moyen d'y faire bien pourvoir Toute la chestiente congnoistra que nous n'avons poinct cherche la querelle et s trouvera trop mal fondee sur la deffence de telz rebelles qui ne laisseront pour cela en recevoir la recompense qu'ilz ont desservy comme il y en a déjà bon commencement et le congnoistrez par ce pacquet

It is easy to see behind this masquerade that a mere subject and officer could not have the will and even less the power to wage war without the expressed order and wishes of the queen and that war cannot happen at the expense of a prince without his knowledge. This is a clear breach of the ordinances and treatises concluded between the two kingdoms of Scotland and France, according to which the subjects on both sides cannot cross over by land or by sea without a safe-conduct except when the vagaries of the weather forbid. When they arrived, the wind was against them so they used the tides and they docked in a harbor that is hardly safe and where they only come in times of war. They did not want their presence to be known by anyone but the very rebels with whom they communicated and to whom they gave support and aid. They then rushed to attack the king's subjects and refused to salute or to drop the sails in front of any of the royal strongholds of the kingdom. Wars can be declared for far less but the greatest and wisest lords will think things through before making that decision. If there are a few hostile subjects here, there will also be many good ones who will devote themselves to the defence of their country and if the kings of Scotland were able to fight wars in times past, the incumbent has no less means to do so. The whole of Christendom will know that we did not start the quarrel and will not find good reasons to take the defence of such rebels. They are bound to get the reward they deserve as it has already been the case and as you will learn from this parcel. It seems to me that you should give that part to Monsieur de Candale to play. He will be a past master at it without the help of anyone else, after or before you speak to the queen whichever you think best.

Fig. 9. (continued)

Il m a semble que ferez fort bien de faire jouer ce persnage a monsieur de candale scaura s'y conduire bien dextrement comme de lui mesmes apres que aurez parlé a la roine ou devant comme adviserez pour le mieulx avecques toutes les protestations qu'il fauldra faire a la royne devant les lettres missives et le blanc seler de son seau pour se remetre a la miserycorde du Roy que si elle veult secretement il le monstrera qui est pour luy faire congnoistre combien il y peu defiance aus dict rebelles et que le conte d arguil est après pour en faire autant elle aura ass de raison par ce moen d en trer en suspition cotre eulx et le langage qu'elle tiendra nous en advertir incontinent et avecques ceste presente envoie le tout au Roy lequel par cela entendra bien la fin sans que pour ce l on face autre estat d duc pour le moyen que l'on a de le bien chastier il m'a semblé que veu le bon visage que a monsieur d candale d'elle luy dire comme de lui mesmes que estant ostage il aura grani regret de venir commencer une guerre qui imorte tant que cesty et qu'il a pens que devant die et devant le monde il ne scauroit estre accuse de descouvrir la desloaulte et double trahison du duc et néanmoons si vous trouveez meylleur de manier cela vous mesmes je remectz le toute a votre discretion et me semble que devez parle ouvertement a la roine de ceste infraction et combien dieu qui fait les vengencas des guerres injusies est a craindre et autres chses que vous scaurez tres bien de vous mesmes adjouster et que est marri d'estre contrainct de entendre au Roy une telle nouvelle encores que d'ailleurs il en soit adverti et le ou vous congnoistrez qu'elle vouldra fort desa avouer faictes quelle escripve et par de ça lettres qui pourront veoir avecques bonne demoniration de punir les infracteurs si comme elle dict ilz n ont poict de commandement d'elle et aussi de faire prendre les ministres des rebelles qui sont a la solecitation pres d'elle n'y faire aussi instance d'un valet de chambre du Roy

He must protest to the queen about the missives and white seings that are stamped with her seal and for which she should ask for the mercy of the king, and tell her that if she wants he will show her in secret what will make her recognize that the rebels can hardly be trusted, something which the earl of Argyl will confirm later. She will then have enough reason to become suspicious of them. Inform us right away of what she says, and along with the present letter, send the lot to the king, who will understand the outcome without having to mention the duke with whom we can deal on our own. It seems to me that as Candale will receive a warm welcome from her, he will be able to tell her that being a hostage, he would greatly regret to see a war of such significance break out and that he thinks that before God and before the world, he should not be blamed for disclosing the disloyalty and double treason of the duke. Nonetheless, if you think it best that you should handle the affair yourself, I leave it all at your discretion. And it seems to me that you should speak openly to the queen about the breach of the law and tell her that God who avenges unjust war is to be dreaded, and other things that you will be perfectly able to add yourself and that you are most aggrieved at having to break such news to the king even though he has already been informed of the matter. And when you find out that she is willing to severely reprimand this offence, ensure that she writes letters to Scotland that clearly show that she is eager to punish the law-breakers if, as she claims, they did not act at her command. And also ask that she have the ministers of the rebels who are submitting their requests to her arrested. Also complain about the king's servant who was robbed as he was leaving Berwick by some Scots and English who acted together. Please warn of this problem the couriers and other people who will travel across not to go through Berwick without first informing Dunbar.

Fig. 9. (*continued*)

20 V. Nachef et al.

qui a este destrousse au partir de bar- vic par quelques Excossoys et Anglois qui estoient ensemble et a ceste caus fault bien advertir les courriers qui viendront et autres personnes de ne passer barvic qu'ilz n aient premierement adverti a dom- barre afin qu'il soit donne escorte pour leur personne et seurete de pacquets ou y sera pourveu promtement il i a tro lotemps que je congnoys les incommodites de la guerre et que pour l'honneur de dieu premiere- ment je desire en eviter les moiens et aussi pour avoir tousjour dieu de notre coste si ceste declaration passe plus avant je prie dieu vous avoir Monsieur de Noailles en sa sainte et digne garde. D'Edimbourg, Jan- vier 1559	This way they will swiftly be provided with an escort for their safety and that of their parcels. I have known the torment of war for too long and for the honor of God I wish to avoid resorting to such means and also to keep God on our side for ever, if this declaration of war goes any further. On that note, I pray God (will keep you under his holy protection [4]). From Edimn- bourg, January 1559

Fig. 9. [4](This is how Guise ended all her letters to Noailles.) (*continued*)

Mary tried to have the former regent prosecuted for attempting to usurp the Scottish Crown and treason but she failed. The letter refers to other people by names starting with the Admiral Winter who led the English fleet and was sighted off Fife Ness in January 1560. He had been bolder than the French reinforcements sent by François II, Mary Queen of Scots' first husband, who stayed in their ports because of the bad weather. His presence in the Forth meant that the French could not reach Saint Andrews where the Congregation had settled and were forced to retreat to Leith, the only safe haven that Guise had time to fortify.

The indirect testimony given here through the voice of Guise confirms what comes up in other sources, namely that Winter pretended to enter the Firth of Forth "accidentally". Yet as other letters prove, starting with that written by the Governor of Berwick, Sir James Croft to Admiral Winter on 21 January 1560, the sea invasion had been authorized at the highest level and he was ordered "that as wind and weather will serve, he should sail into the Firth for the impeachment of the French, according to his instructions; and after conference with the Earl of Arran, the Prior of St. Andrews, or such as they shall direct, should act to the most annoying the French, and furthering the Congregation".

Part of the "annoying" consisted in capturing enemy ships. Winter himself reports the incident mentioned in Guise's letter to the Duke of Norfolk in a message dated 25 January 1560. He recounted that "he took two of their vessels of war; the captain of one was Fernando Santandero, a Spaniard, and of the other James Cullen, gent., the hoy laden with their ordnance and munitions and part of their barks laden with victuals, and ran the rest aground on Fife side, where they were destroyed by the Scots; as the bearer hereof shall inform him more fully" [3].

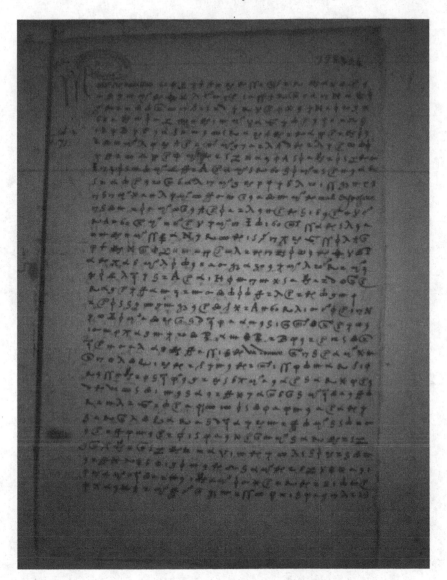

Fig. 10. Cipher text

This was clearly a breach of the Peace Treaty that was supposedly still bounding England and its queen.

The letter displays Guise's reluctance to enter a war with England and her clear overdependence on the French without whom she could hardly pretend to scare off the English and their queen.

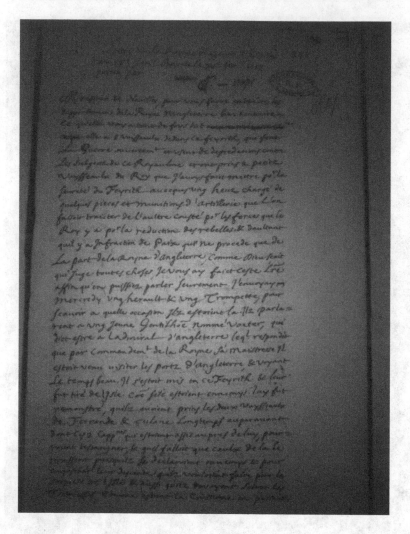

Fig. 11. Deciphering

We give the beginning of the encrypted letter. We also provide the plain text from the archives, the plain text we obtained and the English translation[3].

4.4.2   The Letter and Its Translation

As we can notice, punctuation marks are not encrypted. This does not help fro the decryption (Fig. 9).

---

[3] We are grateful to Eliane Viennot who guided us through the most difficult passages in middle French and to Nicole Dufournaud whose skills in palaegraphy have been used her to our benefit.

In Figs. 10 and 11, we provide the cipher text and the deciphering (from the archives) of the beginning of this letter.

5 Some Comments on the Encryption Method

As mentioned earlier, in her correspondence with M. de Noailles, Mary of Guise made use of a nomenclator. If we compare Tables 1 and 2, we see that some symbols appear in both tables but they do not represent the same letter in the alphabet. We can compare both these tables with the nomenclator employed by her daughter Mary Queen of Scots (Fig. 12).

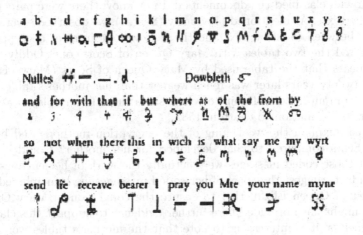

Fig. 12. Mary Stuart's table

We can see that this table is far less sophisticated than her mother's tables since there is only one symbol for each letter in the alphabet. As a result, it was possible to use the frequency method to recover the table. This kind of encryption method was widely used during the sixteenth and seventeenth centuries. More solid encryption schemes were used during the eighteenth century. For example, Marie-Antoinette, queen of France during the Revolution, adopted a poly-alphabetic system which was considered to be (and is still) more difficult to break [4].

6 Conclusion

In this paper, we explain how we decrypted Marie of Guise's enciphered letters, which are kept by the French Foreign Office archives in Paris. These letters were written between 1553 and 1559 by the regent of Scotland in order to communicate with the French ambassadors in England, the Noailles brothers. Unfortunately, it turned out at the end of our work that the clear texts were already known and contained in the paper codex. However, this research was worth conducting for several reasons. First, we were able to recover two secrete encryption tables. The first table was probably used to communicate with Antoine de Noailles and the second one with Gilles de Noailles. Since we had only two documents it is difficult to know if Table 1 was as elaborated as Table 2. However, if we consider all the information that we have, it is very likely that Table 2 was more sophisticated. This choice may be accounted for by the greater need to protect the secrecy of her communication. As far as we know, these tables have never been published. We were also able to establish the link between plain texts and cipher texts. This was not obvious, since in the archives, the classification of the documents do not follow an exact order. This may result from the fact that the person who classified the documents did not know there were pairs of plain texts/ciphertexts. As mentioned previously (Sect. 4), we observed several minor differences between the clear text and the text we obtain after decryption. We also compared the two tables with Mary Queen of Scots' one. Oddly enough, it also appears that the table used by Mary Queen of Scots (Mary of Guise's daughter) twenty years later was much weaker than her mother's table. This is important from an historical point of view, since those letters played a decisive role in her condemnation to death in 1587.

What can explain the weakening of the encryption method used by Mary Queen of Scots compared to that developed for her mother? Could it be evidence that those coded messages were actually the work of her enemies? Some sources, in fact, suggest that part of her coded messages were enciphered by the cryptologist of Queen Elizabeth I to ensure the conviction of Mary Queen of Scots. We might have provided here further evidence to support this claim.

Nevertheless, it is interesting to note that the mother's tables were significantly more complex than those assigned to his daughter.

References

1. Laing, D. (ed.): John Knox, Works, vol. 1. James Thin, Edinburgh (1895)
2. Laing, D. (ed.): John Knox, Works, vol. 4. James Thin, Edinburgh (1895)
3. Calendar of State Papers Foreign, Elizabeth, vol. 2, p. 645 (1559–1560)
4. Nachef, V., Patarin, J.: I shall love you until death. Cryptologia **34**(2), 104–114 (2010)

About Professionalisation in the Intelligence Community: The French Cryptologists (*ca* 1870–*ca* 1945)

Sébastien-Yves Laurent[✉]

Université de Bordeaux, Pessac, France
sebastien.laurent@u-bordeaux.fr

Abstract. Social Sciences and especially Sociology and History are very useful to understand how the Cryptographic Field has been shaped in France in 19th and 20th centuries. This paper tackles this issue explaining how and why this Field has been influenced in-depth by a strong process of 'Professionalism' under the Ecole Polytechnique rule.

Being neither a Mathematician nor a Cryptologist, but a Social Scientist I belong to a minority in this book: nevertheless I will try to demonstrate how precious were and are Dave's books for Historians and Political Scientists interested in the study of the Hidden side of the State. I would like to plead for the use of more Sociology in the Intelligence Studies Field. Social Scientists interested in Intelligence or Cryptology often conduct their research studying either the structures or the heroes (that is to say for instance Masterspies or Defectors). Some use the two approaches, but rather rarely. I am personally convinced that the combined use of the study of the structures and that one of some Individuals actors that played a major role – there are many in Cryptography from Herbert O. Yardley[1] to Alan Turing via Marian Rejewski[2] – can find advantages to be completed by the study of a third level, the professional groups (or the Bodies). However that may be, I would consider as an assumption the fact that, broadly speaking, in the Cryptologic field the role of some Individuals is more important that in Intelligence. Dave demonstrated the role of successive Genius that improved Secrets Writings, Ciphers and the use of Mathematics. Until now despite the growing role of Softwares and computing, the importance of Inventors remains. Be that as it may, I would plead not for taking into account the "masses" in the study of cryptology but to promote the study of the collective actors. Indeed, the case of France at the crossroads of 19th and 20th Centuries shows a main transformation, the blossoming of Bodies among those of the Officials who where in charge of Intelligence within the State.

---

[1] See David Kahn, *The reader of gentlemen's mail: Herbert O. Yardley and the birth of American codebreaking*, New Haven-London, Yale University Press, 2004, 318 p.
[2] See *Marian Rejewski 1905–1980. Living with the Enigma secret*, Bydgoscz, Bydgoscz City Council, 2005, 287 p.

© Springer-Verlag Berlin Heidelberg 2016
P.Y.A. Ryan et al. (Eds.): Kahn Festschrift, LNCS 9100, pp. 25–33, 2016.
DOI: 10.1007/978-3-662-49301-4_2

1   The Lack of Tools to Study the Collective Actors

No Historian can face the study of collective Actors without being confronted immediately to the notion of "Intelligence Community" (IC). Unfortunately these two words written together create the illusion of an Intelligence Body that would be homogeneous. In fact, all the academic literature using this expression does not define the notion, nor try to explain it[3]: in this way the IC is only the addition of several Agencies or of several Bodies. Actually it's a fuzzy expression. The second consequence is that if most of the structures, the organs or the bureaucracies have been studied, this is not the case of the collective Actors like the Officers, Analysts or the Cryptologists that were employed in these structures. From my point of view it is the consequence of a lack of a sociological approach. In appearance the use of Sociology can introduce some complexity but at the end it provides more light because the past is not only the combination of Individual Actors and of Structures.

As the "IC" the term of "Professionnalisation" has been used by Historians of Intelligence without being firstly carefully defined[4]. Implicitly again, most Histories of Intelligence conclude that at the end of 19th Century many European IC were on the way of Professionnalisation. This is not my stance and I would begin considering this as an assumption that must be confirmed. Professionnalisation has been in fact used by Historians and political Scientists as a synonym for skills. But one thing are the skills of Individuals, another one is the capacity of a Body to train its members. Incontestably, the latter is a sign of a modernisation Process in a State. I would also use the recent definition of Martin Rudner who insists on some features: the management of human capital and the teaching of knowledge to new entrants in the Body[5].

In dealing with the study of French Cryptologists under the Third Republic (1870–1940), I would have also to consider if these peculiar men, most of them coming from the Army or from the Navy, behaved only as Individuals or if they were strictly linked to the Bodies that appeared at the end of the 19th Century. It could help us to understand if the French Intelligence Apparatus based partly on the quality of Cryptography at the beginning of the 20th Century was the result of some Individuals or of the renewal of the French Army after the 1870 Defeat.

2   The French "Intelligence Community" as a Battlefield

During the first half of 19th Century there was two unique Official Bodies in charge of Intelligence, the Diplomats and the Police Body. From the beginning of the 19th Century until today, the history of Intelligence in France - and abroad - is a story of permanent

---

[3] See for instance: Jeffrey T. Richelson, *The US Intelligence Community*, New York, Vetwiew press, 2008, 592 p.

[4] Christopher Andrew and David Dilks (ed.), *The missing dimension. Governments and Intelligence Communities in the Twentieh Century*, London, Macmillan, 1985, p. 6 et 7.

[5] See Martin Rudner, "Training and educating US Intelligence Analysts", *International Journal of Intelligence and Counter Intelligence*, 2009, 22: 1, p. 139 et 142.

rivalries, sometimes of turf wars between the bodies that were in charge of Intelligence. At the beginning of the 19th Century there was a balance between Diplomats abroad and Police in the domestic Area, each of these actors being alone and powerful in its respective field. If there is a natural tendency for organisations belonging to the same field to fight each other there was ideological and political reasons as well that explain such attitudes. Despite the trend of a dual dominance (both Police and Diplomatic) on Intelligence activities, officers who played an important role in Intelligence during the Napoleonic period – on battlefields of course, but also to a lesser extent in domestic Intelligence - tried to emerge on the Intelligence scene.

Three times some Officers attempted vainly in 19th Century to create Intelligence organs within the Army.

Under the July Monarchy, in 1826, a so-called "section de statistique"[6] was created within the "Dépôt de la Guerre". There, Staff Officers and "ingénieurs-géographes"[7] gathered theoretically every kind of knowledge that referred to Foreign Countries in which the French Army campaigned or would have to. But the "section" was only a board created for a publishing aim without any specific staff abroad to gather information and the other parts of the French administration refused to cooperate with the "Dépôt de la Guerre". The section slowly vanished after mid-19th Century. The second attempt by officers to play a role in State Intelligence was more successful but was not a French specificity. In January 1860, Napoléon the Third, decided to appoint four Military Attachés[8] in Saint-Petersbourg, Berlin, London and Vienna[9]. Like in Prussia[10] these officers were closely linked to the Emperor and they collected not only military Intelligence but political information as well. Nevertheless, these first Intelligence Officers were less numerous than Diplomats.

Finally, after the Prussian Sadowa Victory in Austria, Napoléon the Third and the French High Command impressed by Prussian Strength decided to implement a profound Military Reform. For the first time since 1815, Intelligence was a part of the Military Agenda. Marshall Niel, the minister of War, decided to (re-)organise the collection of Military Intelligence that relied only at this time on the Military Attachés. Napoléon the Third and Niel decided to transform the new 2nd Bureau in a structure that would gather Open Source Intelligence and Covert Intelligence. They undertook, under lieutenant-colonel Jules Lewal's[11] command, head of the new Second bureau, specific and covert missions devoted to the collection of Intelligence

---

[6] *Mémorial du Dépôt général de la Guerre*, Paris, Ch. Picquet, 1828, p. xvij.

[7] A special Military body created at the end of 18th Century in order to draw maps.

[8] The first French Military Attachés (to Embassies) appeared in fact after 1826 thanks to the 1826 ordonnance that allowed (chap. II, art. 14, al. 2, see *Journal militaire officiel*, 2e semestre 1826, n° 16, p. 609) the French General Staff to appoint Officers to Embassies. The first were sent to Madrid and to Constantinople.

[9] See *Mémoires du Maréchal Randon*, Paris, Typographie Lahure, 1877, tome II, p. 49. Randon was the Minister of War in charge of implementing the new Military Attachés.

[10] See Gordon A. Craig, « Military diplomats in the Prussian and German service: the attachés, 1816–1914 », *Political Science Quarterly*, vol. LXIV, 1949, pp. 65–94.

[11] SHD, DAT, 7 Yd 1616 (personnel file).

in the North German Confederation[12]. Before their departure the Staff Officers for whom covert activity was not in their habits received precise instructions to dissimulate their work. From Spring 1868 to December 1869 about 30 Officers were sent as spies on the other side of the border for 30–40 days far-reaching missions[13]. The High Command decided to end the covert missions in December 1869 because some officers had been arrested and their names published in the Press. The absence of global coordination with the Foreign Office was another weakness of the State Intelligence organisation. Moreover it occurred too late. With regards to the attempt as establishing an Intelligence Military Organ in peace time, the third one, that occurred just before the 1870 War, was again a failure.

French military defeats in 1870 like later in 1940 have always been a strong spur used to implement far-reaching Reforms. During the first decade of the Third République, the High Command rebuilt a new army, partly drawing inspiration from the German Army. Among the mid-level officers who played a discrete but effective role was Emile Vanson[14], who was one of Lewal's officers sent for spying in Germany in 1868. Vanson was the real inventor of the modern French General Staff in 1874 with its partition into 4 bureaus[15]. So he created the "2nd Bureau"[16] (a "G-2") and also a "section de statistique"[17] at its margin. He was the first official in France to understand that it was crucial to separate the collection of Intelligence from its analysis and to set up these two tasks in two different organs and to entrust them to two different kinds of officers. From 1874 to 1914, the 2nd Bureau comprised on average between 20 and 30 officers to centralise and to analyse Intelligence and the "section" never more than three officers. The section had two different tasks: collecting by covert means abroad - that is to say spying - and running the counter-espionage on the French territory as well. With Vanson's 2nd Bureau and "section de statistique" two specific bureaus emerged, designed to be the core of the Intelligence State - in fact the first modern Secret Services[18]. In 1874 the formalisation of Public Intelligence activities was achieved and so the very quick uprising of the Military Body within the State completed. Moreover from the

---

[12] SHD-AG, M.R. 1577, Memo for the Minister of War with regards to the Mission on the Rhine, December 12th, 1867, 5 p.

[13] Reports and maps done during the mission are in SHD-AG, M.R. 1577 to 1581.

[14] See his personnel file: SHD, DAT, 10 Yd 114.

[15] Decree n° 91 (March 12th, 1874) on the reorganisation of the General Staff, *Journal Militaire officiel*, 1er semestre 1874, p. 230–231. On the direct role played by Vanson in this Reform, see général Vanson, « Deux documents concernant la réorganisation de l'armée en 1873 », *Carnet de la sabretache*, 1896, 4e volume, p. 148–159.

[16] This 2nd Bureau was different from that one created at the end of the 1860 s in the Dépôt de la Guerre. One of the major difference was that the new one was part of a General Staff that did not exist before 1870.

[17] Who became in 1899 « section de renseignements », then « service de renseignements ».

[18] The main part of the 2nd Bureau archives remained and are today in SHD (7 N 653–677). The archives of the « section de statistique » were partly destroyed, partly disseminated after the Dreyfus Affair. One can find some hints and traces of them in the « police spéciale » archives (Archives nationales, F7) and in the archives of the Préfecture de Police.

beginning of the 1870s the Officers obtained to have a part of the French Police Body under their command for the counter-espionage task. A major step in the History of French Intelligence was taken. It was a real Triumph for the Military Body.

3   The Uneven Professionalisation of the Civil Servants in Charge of Public Intelligence

Among the three Official Bodies that were in charge of Intelligence, the Professionalisation Process was rather uneven.

The Diplomatic Corps was the oldest one. Based for two centuries and a half on social and cultural criteria – the diplomats being recruited in the Aristocracy – the situation evolved from mid-19th Century. From then on the French Foreign Office set up entrance examination. The most important criterion was the proficiency and not the social origin and the background. The recruitment was enlarged to the upper middle-class but it remained elitist. Nevertheless it was only a consequence of the better education received in these classes. The democratisation of the Diplomatic Corps was reinforced from the 1880s thanks to a proactive policy implemented by the French Republicans[19]. Moreover a growing part of the Diplomats were educated in a private University, the « Ecole libre des sciences politiques » founded in 1872[20] as a response to the 1870 Defeat. There the young men learned everything that was necessary to succeed at the Quai d'Orsay's entrance examination. In no more than a decade the Ecole libre obtained the best results and a quasi monopoly on all entrance examination of the French Civil Service. Incontestably, in the second half of 19th Century the Diplomatic Corps was one the most professionalised in France compared to other high ranking civil servant Bodies.

A short sociological overview of the Police Body – the second one to be in charge of Intelligence, that is to say political Surveillance and Counter-espionage – shows a very different case. This Police (called « police spéciale ») had been created in 1855 and had never been abolished thereafter. This part of the Police was not the most important quantitatively. Yet the Police Body experienced at the end of 19th Century a process of professionnalisation: one began to recruit Policemen trying to take into account Proficiencies and specialised schools were set up[21]. Among the numerous parts of the Police Body, the police spéciale – the one in charge of Intelligence - was aside because of its specific missions. That is why the French Home Office paid attention to its recruitment. This is the reason why on average, these Policemen and Police Officers, these Constables had a better background than the other. But there was not any School, not any kind of education or training for the « Police spéciale ». This Police activity, including counter-espionage, was a practice

---

[19] See Isabelle Dasque, *Monsieur de Norpois: les diplomates de la République (1871–1914)*, thèse de doctorat d'histoire contemporaine sous la direction de Jean-Pierre Chaline, Université Paris IV, 2005, 960 p.

[20] See S. Laurent, *L'École libre des Sciences Politiques de 1871 à 1914*, Institut d'études politiques de Paris, 1991, 180 p.

[21] See Jean-Marc Berlière, « La professionnalisation de la police en France: un phénomène nouveau au début du XXe siècle en France », *Déviance et société*, XI-1, mars 1987, p. 67–104.

learned « on-the-job ». Moreover one should remind the fact that the « Police spéciale » was the most important Body in charge of Intelligence: the total strength of this Police was by far the most numerous compared with the two other Bodies. Moreover it played a strategic role by its presence on all the French Territory.

With regards to the Military Officers the most recent entrant on the Intelligence scene the situation is more complex. Indeed the existence of entrance examination for specialised schools was ancient: the Ecole Polytechnique (called « X » here-after) had been created in 1794 and the Ecole spéciale militaire (or « Saint-Cyr ») in 1802. There the military cadets were trained and they chose after the graduation a second School were they received a more specialised training (Cavalry, Infantry, Engineering or Artillery). Later in their career they had the opportunity to apply for a third School: the Ecole supérieure de Guerre created in 1876. To enter into this *Kriegsakademie* they had to take an examination whose result was to select those who were able to become Staff Officers and who could have access to the highest ranks. Undoubtedly among the three Bodies, the military one was the most special-ised. Nevertheless the situation was very different for the Officers who chose after 1870 the path to Intelligence. As the « police spéciale » the emerging Intelligence Officers learned « on-the-job ». The unique skill that was required to be appointed in Intelligence organs was the ability to speak another Language that was most of the time German or Italian. The situation evolved after the World War I, when the French General Staff decided to send the applicants for Intelligence careers to a School created in 1921 by the University in Mayence[22], the Centre d'études germa-niques (CEG). This School disappeared in 1940 but in April 1942 the French General Staff created a more specialised School than the CEG, an « Intelligence School » located in Lyon were Intelligence Constables and Intelligence Officers met and received a common training. The School disappeared with the German Occupa-tion of Southern France in November 1942. But one must recall that the Intelligence Officers had not been proactive in 1921 like in 1942 in this process and had not been at the origin of the Training structures. They were reluctant to accept the idea that Intelligence could be learned in Schools or through Courses. If professionalisation was a reality for Officers broadly speaking, it was less right for the very few who chose Intelligence.

4   The Belated Uprising of the Military in State Decyphering Activity

At this Time cryptography could be considered as a sub-field in Public Intelligence. The Decyphering activity was splitted into three Ministries. The oldest one was the Ministry of Foreign Office (*Quai d'Orsay*), then came the Home Office and later the War Office.

The Civil servants in charge of cryptography inside the Ministry of Foreign Affairs had ties with the Intelligence Officers because the most skilled experts came from the Army or from the Navy. The Civil cryptologists in the Quai d'Orsay were also connected

---

[22]Located in german occupied territories by the French Army, then after 1930 in Strasbourg.

with some independent experts in the Cryptographic field. The cooperation with Officers began in second half of the 19th Century. As David wrote it in 1967 the Marquis de Viaris, a former Navy Officer who had become cryptologist, was employed by the Quai d'Orsay to reorganise the « bureau du chiffre » in the 1880s[23]. But after that Viaris remained one of the most important expert whose advice was important in case of difficulties[24]. The Quai d'Orsay relied also on the capitaine Bazeries, an Officer that had been appointed to the Quai for ten years[25] and who continued to work free-lance for the Diplomats after being retired[26].

The Home Office became an actor of Public cryptography with the development of the Telegraph. Regulations (two laws in 1837 and in 1850 and a decree in 1851)[27] gave this Office the monopoly on the Telegraph network and the right to monitor all the telegrams whatever they come from. The strong Public Surveillance on the communication[28] and, in a broader extent, of all political or social activities allowed the Home Office to dispatch the intercepted Telegrams between the Foreign Office, the War Office and to keep for itself all the material concerning the political militants[29]. The Home Office tried to train its experts but used also Military Officers that were in advance on Decyphering.

5   The Growing Professionalisation of Military Cryptologists: The "X" Path

The Military surge within the State Decyphering Activity is not an hasard. This fits into a broader process that is to say the emergence of the Military Officers Corps in the French Intelligence Community. As it has been said, in less than one decade (from 1870 to 1880) the Military succeeded, first, in building modern Intelligence organs inside the General Staff and then, in obtaining from the Political Authority to have the "police spéciale" under their command. It's evident that the Military cryptologists benefited from the new situation.

The role played by Officers in the State Cryptographic Activity especially as experts for the Home Office and for the Foreign Affairs highlights the fact that they belonged

---

[23] David Kahn, *The Codebreakers. The Story of secret writing*, New York, Macmillan publishing, 1967 [rééd. 1996], p. 242.

[24] S.H.D.-A.G., 1 M 2352, lettre du ministère des Affaires étrangères ou au ministre de la Guerre, 27 décembre 1900.

[25] SHD, DAT, 6 Yf 5578 (Bazeries personnel file).

[26] On Bazeries see Octave Homberg's memoirs (*Les Coulisses de l'histoire. Souvenirs 1898-1928*, Paris, Librairie Arthème Fayard, 1938, p. 39). Homberg was head of the bureau du chiffre in the Quai at the end of 19th Century. See also S.H.D.-A.G., 1 K 842, Marcel Givierge, *Etude historique sur la section du chiffre des origines à 1921. Historique I*, s.l.n.d., p. 16.

[27] Law from May, 6th 1837; November, 29th 1850 and a decree from December, 27th 1851.

[28] See S. Laurent, *Politiques de l'ombre. État, renseignement et surveillance en France*, Paris, Fayard, 2009.

[29] Cf. Commandant Cuignet, *Souvenirs de l'Affaire Dreyfus. Le Dossier Trarieux-Tornielli-Reinach*, Paris, Société anonyme d'édition Belleville, 1911, p. 13, footnote 1 and Marcel Givierge, *Etude historique sur la section du chiffre des origines à 1921. Historique I*, s.l.n.d., p. 16 (S.H.D.-A.G., 1 K 842).

to professionalised bodies in which the recruitment was based on skills and proficiencies. Despite the fact that some of the experts like Bazeries were men who entered the Army as privates that is to say with a basic education, other like Valério and Viairis came from Military Schools. This was a sign of the forthcoming evolution. Indeed, from the last quarter of 19th Century Officers coming from the Ecole Polytechnique ("X") with specific knowledge in Mathematics established themselves as leaders in the Cryptographic Field. They were strongly helped by the new dominance of Officers in the Intelligence Field, even if they were not at this time considered by their *camarades* as real Intelligence Officers but as technical experts. These men have been scholars from our current point of view, but at this time they were only considered as such experts.

Nevertheless, as quickly as the Intelligence Officers thirty years before they succeeded in becoming recognized as experts by the other parts of the so-called Cryptographic Community. One man, François Cartier (1862–1953), played a major role in the building of new cryptographic organs inside the General Staff and inside the Minister of War. Thanks to the highest quality of his work in Cryptography he succeeded in establishing the specialised Military Officers in the Cryptographic Community. François Cartier came from the X and has been then specialised in Artillery and Military Engineering in a time, of course, during when all calculation was a mental work. He was appointed in 1900 in the Military Wireless Telegraphy and the same year as secretary of the Military Cryptographic Committee. Besides being the first Officer to have excellent skills in Cryptography, he was also the first to have understood the necessity to built permanent organs. In 1908 despite being only a captain he met the minister of War[30] and outlined the necessity to create an interdepartmental committee on ciphers. This committee created only six months later was used by Cartier as a tool to establish the Officers position in the State Cryptographic Field, despite the Foreign Office's refusal to join[31]. With regards to Cryptography, this Committee was the main tool used by the Military to dominate the Home Office and the Colonial Office. Cartier was the first secretary of this committee and was helped by a younger polytechnicien, Marcel Givierge (1871–1931). From 1912 to 1920, Cartier was head of the minister of War Cipher's section (« section du chiffre »). He was at the origin of the first courses in Cryptography in the Ecole supérieure de Guerre implemented in 1913[32]. Moreover during all the First World War he ran the Cryptographic Department of the French General Staff. During the WWI Cartier appointed many alumni from the Ecole Polytechnique in the Cryptographic Department. During and after the World War I reserve Officers like Georges Painvin (1886-1980), for instance, played a very important role in helping their eldest *camarades* from the Ecole Polytechnique and who had chosen after a military career. This shows that the Ecole Polytechnique became very discreetly and slowly the privileged access to the Cryptographic field. In this successful evolution some talented and clever Officers like Cartier and Givierge used their command of

---

[30] S.H.D.-A.G., 1 K 193, fonds privé du général Toutée.

[31] S.H.D.-A.G., 1 K 842, Marcel Givierge, *Etude historique sur la section du chiffre des origines à 1921. Historique I*, s.l.n.d., p. 18.

[32] Cf. S.H.D.-A.G., 1 K 842, Marcel Givierge, *Etude historique sur la section du chiffre des origines à 1921. Historique I*, s.l.n.d., 3e époque, p. 3.

Cryptography but also their ability to use institutions. Thanks to the growing role of Mathematics in Cryptography, from Cartier on the Ecole Polytechnique was implicitly recognized as the unique School for the training of future Cryptologists. During the main part of 20th Century Officers graduated from Polytechnique remained at the core of the Decyphering Public Activity even if the Ecole normale supérieure competed with Polytechnique after WWII. This evolution that shows that professionalisation became more marked for Cryptologists compared to Intelligence Officers does not mean than a specific Body appeared. The first time this Idea appeared was in January 1942: at this time Admiral Darlan, commander-in-chief of the French Army wanted to create a specific Body and a Decyphering School. The project vanished with his assassination that occured at the end of the year.

The end of the 19th Century is a real break in the Building Process of the French Public Surveillance and Intelligence Machinery: from 1870 on the Army established itself at the core of it. This situation lasted until the end of the WWII but had long-time effects. In the Military shelter built by Intelligence Officers, the cryptologists settled. Among them, the Officiers graduated from the Ecole Polytechnique prevailed, by far. Their skills and an actual professionalisation process explain for the most part this achievement but the esprit "de corps" matters also a lot. It would be narrowing to reduce the evolution of Cryptology in France to some key persons: social and cultural reasons had a main role in the rise of the peculiar French codebreakers.

Myths and Legends of the History of Cryptology

Sophie de Lastours[✉]

Paris, France
sophiedelastours@hotmail.com

« Pandore[1] avait l'Ancêtre, et le chiffre a la Fille,
Ce dernier rejeton de l'illustre Famille
Des boîtes d'où jaillit l'espoir du lendemain,
L'inconnu convoité, souci du genre humain.[2] »

1 Introduction

The State, no matter its form, is constantly exposed to countless threats. These threats range from the most intense, such as war, to the most subtle such as treason, terrorism, spying and economic pillaging. All these call for the taking of appropriate defence measures. Since the days of antiquity, States used fortifications to protect their territories. While doing so, States preserved the secrecy of their communications using cryptology, often called *"the invisible power"*. Cryptology is one of the pillars of the intelligence world. As such it played and continues to play a primordial role. Cryptology is nonetheless a double-edged sword present at the heart of our societies.

2 The Secret of Secret

Cryptography has an ancient history, as old as writing itself. Humans counting with their fingers could elaborate codes, and their imagination helped them draw, create symbols and ultimately invent writing. Writing in itself became a code in a context in which literacy was limited. Literate persons became, in a way, decipherers. During a long period, literacy was the monopoly of the clerical class. Such was the case in Egypt and in Babylon.

According to Flechter Pratt[3], Greeks invented transposition and Romans invented substitution. Transposition and substitution remain, until today, the two main building-blocks of encryption systems. A digit is a symbol. The difference between a digit and a number is, by analogy, similar to the difference between a letter and a word. Since the

---

[1] *Pandora was born from Zeus' resentment. Zeus wanted to punish mankind for receiving re as a gift from Pometheus. Hephaistos modelled Pandora from clay. Athena breathed life into her, Aphrodite gave her beauty and Apollo gave her musical talents.*

[2] Claude Ducellier, « B.211 », Aux Armées, of October 9, 1939, Bulletin de l'ARCSI, #2 and #3, June to September 1955. B.211 was a cipher machine bought by the French Army from its inventor, the industrialist Boris Hagelin, at the end of the 1930s.

[3] Flechter Pratt, Histoire de la cryptographie, *Les écritures secrètes depuis l'Antiquité jusqu'à nos jours*, Payot, 1940.

© Springer-Verlag Berlin Heidelberg 2016
P.Y.A. Ryan et al. (Eds.): Kahn Festschrift, LNCS 9100, pp. 34–39, 2016.
DOI: 10.1007/978-3-662-49301-4_3

Roman counting system uses Latin letters. The words "cipher" and "code" are frequently used as synonyms whereas they are not. Similarly, the terms "digit" and "number" are also frequently used as synonyms while they are not. The French national lottery, « *La Française des jeux* » is itself guilty of this confusion. In different civilisations, different digits and numbers are different destiny indicators: the digits four[4], seven, twelve[5], thirteen, and seventeen[6]… without forgetting the celebrated golden ratio[7]. The myth of the digit stems from the power of the enigma that constitutes any existence: Wasn't the forbidden fruit given by Eve to Adam a means to break the code protecting knowledge?

The myth of the original sin is one of the Bible's foundations[8]. Since times immemorial, it is believed that the Bible's text contains a hidden structure abiding by mathematical rules. The advent of computers allowed deepening this research. Three Israeli researchers[9] published in 1994 a detailed article on this topic. They evaluate the probability that their demonstration is owed to the sole effect of chance to around 1 in 2.5 billion. These researchers claim that the discovered coded messages form a coherent corpus of messages intentionally embedded in the text by a superior form of intelligence[10]. In particular the holocaust, the creation of the state of Israel and the murder of Rabin are prophesized in the text. The above does not necessarily prove that, if these codes are indeed present in the text, God introduced them. This publication triggered a controversy of experts where proponents of the theory and sceptics exchanged heated arguments[11]. This is where the journalist Michael Drosnin got into the picture. Interestingly, Drosnin defined himself as an agnostic Jew. Drosnin published « *The Bible, the secret code*[12] ». Drosnin attributes the would-be presence of messages in the text to an extra-terrestrial form of intelligence, thereby scorning the myth.

At that point, many researchers, Christians and Jews, practicing and non-practicing decided to confront the challenge. Their studies severely shook Drosnin's claims and demonstrated that "*secret codes*", identical or similar to those found in the Bible were present in any intelligible language with a probability greater than in a random meaningless collection of letters. Researchers found in Moby Dick the coded prediction of

---

[4] 4 brings bad luck in Asia because the pronunciation of the word 4 can mean « death » in Chinese.

[5] 12 is a divine number: 12 Gods in the Olympus, 12 tribes of Israel, 12 zodiac signs, 12 Apostles….

[6] 17 brings bad luck in Italy.

[7] Matila Ghika (1881–1965), *Le nombre d'or*, Gallimard, 1931. Prince, diplomat and Romanian naval engineer.

[8] Specialists agree that the text of the Hebrew Bible was written between the 8th and the 2nd centuries BC.

[9] Dorson Witztum, Eliahu Rips and Yoav Rotenberg, respectively physicist, mathematics professor and a computer science student.

[10] These coded messages are only present in the Bible's canonic Hebrew text (aka Masoretic). This version is due to copyist scribes who reproduced the texts faithfully. These copyists were called the "Lords of tradition".

[11] The sceptics were Brebdan McKay, mathematician; James D. Price, engineer and professor of Hebrew and Barry Simon a mathematician orthodox Jew.

[12] Michaël Drosnin, *La Bible : le code secret*, Laffont, 1997.

the death of Lady Di, along with the name of her lover, Dodi and even the name of their chauffeur! Contradicting (also called negative) codes were also found in the Bible. For instance sentences such as "*God is a despicable entity*" as well the sentences "*God exists*" and "*God does not exist*". The conclusion was that, if in the case where the Bible would happen to be a book inspired by God, God did not embed in the Bible any secret message.

Committed partisans of the existence of hidden messages in the Bible still continue the fight. These are of the opinion that if contradicting codes exist in the Bible, this is a trial of our faith: making mankind believe that the existence of hidden messages in the Bible is an effect of randomness is a test of the reader's faith[13]. As is written in 1 Peter 1:8: « *Though you have not seen him, you love him; and even though you do not see him now, you believe in him and are filled with an inexpressible and glorious joy!* » [14].

According to Herodotus, who is unanimously recognized as the « *Father of History* », the legend of Iliad was written between 850 and 750 BC, i.e. about 4 years after the mythical war that it narrates. A fragment of the Iliad mentions that Bellerophon had chased from Argos by king Proetus because queen Anteia have falsely accused him of harassment. Because tradition considered that the execution of a host is an unforgivable crime, Proteus sent Bellerophon to his father in law in Lycia, giving him a tablet of clay covered with unknown signs and asking him to deliver this tablet to his father-in-law. These symbolic engraved signs were letters of an alphabet different from Greek and demanded that Bellerophon be executed. Recognized as a being of divine essence, this grandchild of Sisyphus who had to fight other wars[15] was not executed.

3   The Cipher: A Cornerstone of History

Cryptology, a multi-millenary-old discipline is today at the forefront of human history. One of its faces defends our individual freedom, its other face protects the others' individual freedom. Cryptography is two-faced like Janus the God of doors: the closed door of peace and the open door of war. Just as cryptography, Janus faces both past and future. A sculpture symbolizing cryptology is currently present at the entrance of the headquarters of the CIA in Langley (VA). Hundreds of letters forming a ciphertext are engraved on this sculpture. Only the artist who created the sculpture and the CIA's director allegedly knows the plaintext. Is the key transmitted from director to director as is the case for the transmission of nuclear codes from president to president? It seems that this ciphertext was decrypted a few years ago. Let us hope that this secret message advocates peace and tolerance between nations.

In politics, diplomacy and economy, cryptology is a weapon of prime importance. The hackers who infiltrated the French ministry of Economy belonged to a digital protest movement, a sort of "*digital alter-globalization*" after the expression coined by Eric

---

[13] http://jewsforjudaism.org/response.html.
[14] In this verse, Christ talks to the Apostle Thomas.
[15] Allusion to his end and to the end of his mythological destrier Pegasus.

Filiol[16]. Does the myth of cryptology collapse when the most protected State's site is successfully attacked? How many thefts and intrusions occurred? How many capital pieces of information or documents are forever lost? The biblical myth of the forbidden fruit is back: cryptology was since ancient times under the control of military. Now it also represents great dangers. It facilitates condemnable acts, mafia activities, money laundering and terrorism.

The importance of controlling the power of cryptology cannot be disregarded. On the contrary, following the example set by South Korea, it is necessary to establish cyber defence units. The existence of decryption as a source of intelligence and the explanation that has been given of this tool by the intelligence services, when it has been disclosed, has often been confined to a limited circle. That was the case with the radiogram announcing victory in June 1918, the work of Ultra carried out by the British and that of Magic by the Americans.

It may even be said that the civil and military authorities remain, for the most part, unaware of the role played by cryptology in conflicts.

Vassili Mitrokhin[17] claims that the CIA was not made aware before the end of 1952 of the revelations that were decrypted by the US Army Security Agency (ASA) from 1948 onwards. That information was kept from President Truman out of fear that he might mention it to the Director of the CIA. It was only in 1945 that it became possible for the defection of a cipher clerk with the Soviet Embassy in Ottawa, Igor Gouzenko, to be fully exploited and the extraordinary extent of the espionage carried out by the USSR on Allied nuclear secrets revealed.

Instances of decryption that have changed the course of history appear to be few and far between, which means that many remain unknown and that the secret of their success has been well kept, but, when they were disclosed, the reality was astounding.

The supreme achievement of cryptology over the course of time has been to remain secret, a *tour de force* in a society that today worships transparency. Antoine Rossignol[18] relentlessly repeated that, for a military cipher to be effective, it must delay decryption until the order had been executed or until the information became valueless. This principle remains fundamental in the use of that science, even though all aspects of our life are becoming dependent on cryptology, with computers, bank cards etc.

Not to have any secrets is a sacrifice. If, for Madame de Staël *'Glory is the brilliant mourning of happiness'*, can it not be said by way of riposte that *'Facebook is the brilliant mourning of secrecy'*?

There have been numerous espionage cases of all kinds in which cryptology has played a key role in our daily lives since that discipline was first developed. Satellites and surveillance and decryption systems have been criss-crossing the planet for a long time, hackers – or a better term may be 'crackers'[19] – becoming younger and younger

---

[16] Who defines himself as a « buccaneer » of information security. He is currently heading the ESAT's virology and cryptography lab and teaches at ESIEA Laval.

[17] Russian renegade who wrote with Christopher Andrew the "Mitrokhin Archives".

[18] Antoine Rossignol (1600–1682) had the title 'Adviser to the King', and his son Bonaventure and his grandson were also eminent cryptologists.

[19] The term used by Eric Filiol.

and more successful. Will this constant pushing back of the limits not end by giving rise to some kind of balance of terror, as nuclear weapons did in their day?

Let us conclude by considering the expression '*cipher key*' – those two words which are a twofold '*open sesame*' at the heart of cryptology, where everything hinges on the secret held by those words. Consider the richness of vocabulary in this field:[20] '*avancer un chiffre*' (to give a general figure'), '*doubler un chiffre*' (double a figure) or '*gonfler un chiffre*' (inflate a figure); in those examples the word is in the singular, but it may also be used in the plural, as in '*être fâché avec les chiffres*' (to be no good at maths), '*jongler les chiffres*' (juggle the figures), '*maquiller les chiffres*' (massage the figures) and '*falsifier les chiffres*' (falsify/forge the figures).

The word 'code' has equally widespread use: code of conduct, civil code, post code, penal code, highway code, genetic code and, last but not least, code of honour.

The myth of cryptology in history resists all attempts at deductive reasoning as it exists in the realms of the divine, whereas daily reality calls everything into question and seeks to falsify everything.

We are plunged into a vicious circle in which time speeds up and becomes digital time, one piece of information driving out another within the space of a second. At the same time, there has been a commensurate increase in the cipher-power while the power of decipherers has increased equally – if not more so?

The human being is the weak link: Mary Queen of Scots, the Chevalier de Rohan, Marie-Antoinette, General Pichegru, Murat died as a result of ciphers for different reasons – treachery, simply being forgotten, boastfulness, dishonest compromise. Painvin[21] fell ill as a result, Olivari[22] suffered terrible headaches, Betty Pack's health never improved. Some of them must have been driven insane!

The head of British intelligence Stewart Menzies was trapped by ciphers to such an extent that he could not refer to the Enigma machine in putting forward his defence.

Fletcher Pratt recalls that an officer of the English Cipher Bureau calculated that one third of the encrypted messages processed by his department during the First World War were incorrect owing to errors made in encryption.

Where a piece of information is secret, the adversary will do everything in his power to obtain it. Francis Walsingham, spy master of Elizabeth I insisted as a matter of principle that the kingdom's archives containing the messages of encoders be destroyed.

Let us go back to Pandora, referred to above. While she had many qualities, she also had a number of flaws: Hermes taught her how to lie and Hera provide her with the gift of curiosity.

This is why she was unable to resist and opened the famous box that Zeus had given her upon her marriage, while at the same time warning her of the danger of opening the lid. The ills of humanity were thus set free: war, sickness, famine, poverty, deception,

---

[20] Translator's footnote: the word '*chiffre*' in French may be translated, *inter alia*, as 'figure', 'number' or 'cipher'. The play on words intended by the author is somewhat lost, therefore, in translation.

[21] Captain Georges-Jean Painvin, who decrypted the victory telegram in June 1918.

[22] Colonel Henry Olivari was a member of the cipher team during the First World War. He was sent on overseas mission to Russia for six months.

vice, destructive passion, as well as Hope; Pandora, overwhelmed, wanted to put back the lid, but, alas, it was too late, only Hope remained.

It is no coincidence that Pandora that, according to Hesiod[23] the bard who, who legend says, locked horns with Homer in a dialectic contest, 'such beautiful evil'.

Concerning for the sibylline stanza that introduces this article to decrypted by any member of ARCSI, [24] although different interpretations may sping up …

From the Song of Songs (the '*Cantique des Cantiques*') to the Quantum of Quanta (the '*Quantique des Quantiques*'), not to mention the possibility of the Song of Quanta (the '*cantique des quantiques*') … the history of ciphers is mythical. For a long time, quantum cryptology was presented to us as opening the gates of Paradise. We have now learned that it is not invulnerable.[25]

Sir Charles Napier, when conquering the Indies, telegraphed from the front from which he was commanding the Sindh campaign the shortest message in the history of ciphers: PECCAVI (I have sinned). That is not a myth.

---

[23] Greek poet, 8th century B.C.

[24] ARCSI: Association des Réservistes du Chiffre et de la Sécurité de l'Information (Association of Cipher and Information Security Reservists).

[25] A conclusion that the professor of quantum computing, Hoi-Kwong Lo of Toronto summarized concisely as follows: '*We need quantum hackers as much as we need quantum cryptographers*'. Le Monde, Internet, Actu.net, 26.06.2009.

Vernam, Mauborgne, and Friedman:
The One-Time Pad and the Index of Coincidence

Steven M. Bellovin[✉]

Columbia University, New York, USA
`smb@cs.columbia.edu`

Abstract. The conventional narrative for the invention of the AT&T one-time pad was related by David Kahn. Based on the evidence available in the AT&T patent files and from interviews and correspondence, he concluded that Gilbert Vernam came up with the need for randomness, while Joseph Mauborgne realized the need for a non-repeating key. Examination of other documents suggests a different narrative. It is most likely that Vernam came up with the need for non-repetition; Mauborgne, though, apparently contributed materially to the invention of the two-tape variant. Furthermore, there is reason to suspect that he suggested the need for randomness to Vernam. However, neither Mauborgne, Herbert Yardley, nor anyone at AT&T really understood the security advantages of the true one-time tape. Col. Parker Hitt may have; William Friedman definitely did. Finally, we show that Friedman's attacks on the two-tape variant likely led to his invention of the index of coincidence, arguably the single most important publication in the history of cryptanalysis.

1 Introduction

The one-time pad as we know it today is generally credited to Gilbert Vernam and Joseph O. Mauborgne [26]. (I omit any discussion of whether or not the earlier work by Miller had some influence [2]; it is not relevant to this analysis.) There were several essential components to the invention:

- Online encryption, under control of a paper tape containing the key.
- The requirement that the key be random.
- The requirement that the key be non-repeating, across not just a single message but across all messages.

It has always been clear that Vernam invented the first element, though some of his colleagues made notable contributions; in particular, Lyman Morehouse devised the variant that used two looped tapes with relatively prime lengths. This is well-attested by contemporary memos, Vernam's patent (US 1,310,719), etc.

The origin of the other two elements, though, has always been rather murkier. Drawing on letters, interviews, and documents, David Kahn concluded that Vernam came up with the randomness requirement, albeit without full understanding of the cryptologic requirement (he noted—incorrectly, as it transpires—that

© Springer-Verlag Berlin Heidelberg 2016

P.Y.A. Ryan et al. (Eds.): Kahn Festschrift, LNCS 9100, pp. 40–66, 2016.

DOI: 10.1007/978-3-662-49301-4_4

the word "random" did not occur in the patent and in fact was not mentioned until Vernam's much-later paper [40]), and that Mauborgne—possibly drawing on earlier work with Parker Hitt—realized that absolute security could only be obtained if no portion of the key was ever repeated. Ralzemond Parker, Vernam's manager, strongly disagreed; he has long claimed that Vernam alone invented the one-time pad; see, e.g., [28], [1, Parker to Kahn, 21 Nov 1962], [1, Parker to Kahn, 3 Apr 1963] and [1, Parker to *Scientific American*, 26 Jul 1966].

To try to resolve a problem he himself called "the most difficult [he] faced in [his] research" [1, Kahn to *Scientific American*, 6 Aug 1966] Kahn suggested to me that we reexamine the relevant files in the AT&T archives. Unfortunately, despite diligent efforts by AT&T archivist George Kupczak, we could not locate them all; the folder numbers have been changed in the 50 or so years since Kahn's original efforts, and many keyword searches across three visits were futile. We did find one crucial folder; I also relied on papers in the William Friedman Collection at the George C. Marshall Foundation Library and in the Dr. David Kahn Collection at the National Cryptologic Museum. Those papers include Kahn's own notes on the missing AT&T folder; I re-analyzed them.

My conclusions are different than Kahn's. I believe that Vernam (possibly alone, possibly with the help of his AT&T colleagues) was primarily responsible for the idea of a non-repeating tape. Furthermore, he and/or his colleagues at AT&T did indeed know that the key needed to be random, though it is unclear when and how they concluded this. Mauborgne was likely the person who codified the non-repetition requirement, but his conclusion was rather later in coming, and was based on not just his own work, but also that of Parker Hitt and William F. Friedman. He may also have had the original insight behind Morehouse's two-tape variant. Friedman (and possibly Hitt) were the first to realize the true security of the non-repeating, random tape. Finally, I believe that attacking the Morehouse scheme is what led Friedman to invent the index of coincidence.

1.1   The Morehouse Scheme

Per [26] and numerous other sources in the various archives, the original AT&T proposal was for a true one-time tape system: a character from a key tape was XORed with a plaintext character to encrypt, or with a ciphertext character to decrypt. Mauborgne doubted its feasibility for production use. For example (and using the paper tape specifications given in [38]), a key tape that held 1,000,000 characters would require a reel over two meters in diameter. Even 100,000 characters—the bare minimum for a day's traffic—would require a reel about .6 meters across. On top of that, the problems of secure key tape manufacturing, distribution, destruction, and accounting were daunting.

The solution was Morehouse's two-tape system. Two tape loops, of relatively prime lengths, were used; a character from each tape was XORed to produce a key character. The effective length of the key stream is the product of the length of the two tapes. Using the notional lengths of 999 and 1,000 characters, the loops would be be about 2.5 m in circumference; this is easy to handle. The tapes could even droop onto the floor.

2   The Problem

2.1   Kahn's Reasoning

Kahn's reasoning, based on an analysis of the sometimes-conflicting information from different sources, is presented in a long endnote to the section of his book discussing Vernam's invention. A somewhat longer version is in [1, Kahn to *Scientific American*, 6 Aug 1966]. Unless otherwise noted, information in this section is taken from the endnote.

The attribution of the invention of randomness to Vernam is, according to Kahn, due to the lack of any other claims. Kahn does assert that AT&T never mentioned randomness until Vernam's 1926 paper [40] and notes that Mauborgne was the one who was aware of the dangers of coherent running keys [1, Kahn to *Scientific American*, 6 Aug 1966]; however, since Maubornge never claimed credit for randomness of the key, he is content to let the AT&T claim stand.

The difficult question has always been about non-repetition. The strongest evidence Kahn has for his conclusion is a categorical statement by Mauborgne [1, Mauborgne to Kahn, 5 Mar 1963]:

> The answer to the question contained in the third paragraph of your letter "who invented this"? (referring to the non-repetitive cipher key tape) you have already deduced—yes, I did it.

When Kahn questioned him further, after Parker's continued disagreement, Mauborgne seemed rather miffed that Kahn did not consider the question settled [1, Mauborgne to Kahn, 25 Oct 1964], : "So far as I am concerned the case is closed. Many thanks."

Kahn also relied on a letter from Donald Perry [1, Perry to Kahn, 1 Jul 1963], which states that the Army didn't like AT&T's two-tape system, so AT&T came up with the one-time system. This sequence—the two-tape version coming first—is at variance with all other claims; furthermore, it is contradicted by the patent history and various memos in the AT&T archives. Accordingly, I do not attach much weight to it.

Finally, Kahn cites Hitt's statement that keys for the Larrabee must be as long as the plaintext. Hitt was a friend and colleague of Mauborgne's; Kahn speculates that Mauborgne helped Hitt develop the notion, and hence was long aware of the notion of very long keys.

2.2   Organizational Structures

It is impossible to follow this without understanding the organizations each party represented and perhaps spoke for. Most obviously, when a request was sent to George Fabyan or a result was announced by him, it was really Friedman who was doing the work. Fabyan was egotistical and apparently wanted his name on any publications [3]. However, he was not a cryptanalyst; he was a businessman. It is likely that the more bombastic (and, on occasion, apparently ignorant) comments were by Fabyan, while the technical meat was supplied by Friedman.

Friedman himself had disclaimed some of Fabyan's more outlandish claims [21, Friedman to Parker, 16 May 1944], such as the assertion that any enciphered message could be broken [4, Fabyan to Gherardi, 31 Mar 1919].

Mauborgne was in the Office of the Chief Signal Officer in the Signal Corps. As such, and despite his abilities as a cryptanalyst, his responsibility was what today would be called "information assurance": he was responsible for keeping U.S. communications secure. He was *not* charged with reading other countries' traffic, and thus was not "officially" a cryptanalyst. He was, however, the only senior cryptologist in the Signal Corps; when the Chief Signal Officer, Gen. George Squier, opined on the security of a scheme, it was almost certainly Mauborgne's technical opinion that was being cited.

Herbert Yardley, on the other hand, headed the Military Intelligence Division's (MID) Cipher Bureau, i.e., what we would call the COMINT function. His superior, Gen. Marlborough Churchill, had great confidence in Yardley's abilities; cryptologic statements from Churchill should be understood as Yardley's statements. Friedman certainly thought that Yardley was responsible for MID's opinion of the two-tape solution [21, Friedman to Parker, 16 May 1944].

Hitt had no official role in the goings-on; he was, however, a skilled cryptanalyst and had served as Chief Signal Officer for the U.S. 1st Army during World War I. He was a friend of Mauborgne's, and knew Friedman and Yardley; most likely, his opinion was sought by all concerned.

At AT&T, Bancroft Gherardi and John Carty, as high-level managers, had the primary communications responsiblity; the technical work was done by Vernam, Ralzemond D. Parker (his manager), and Morehouse, among others.

AT&T knew that Vernam's online encryptor was an interesting invention, and notified the military [26]. Mauborgne worked with them, and suggested that they contact Fabyan, who had a lab that did research in many fields including cryptology. Friedman led a team that did the technical analysis and tried to crack the system. Mauborgne probably could not adopt a cryptographic device without buy-in from the Cipher Bureau, the official cryptanalysts. Most likely, he was the one to bring Col. Hitt in, though this was apparently done with Fabyan's knowledge and consent. Fabyan, in turn, seemed to value Hitt's role as a neutral party; he was not formally charged with either attacking the AT&T machine or defending it.

3   The Opposing Viewpoints

Vernam, who died in 1960, did not leave any known documents with his side of the story. Instead, we must rely on Parker as Vernam's advocate, as opposed to Mauborgne. Friedman, who was the independent evaluator of the scheme, worked for Mauborgne shortly thereafter, and became good friends with Parker in later years, is the nearest we have to a neutral observer who nevertheless was intimately familiar with the technology and the organizations concerned.

3.1   The Case for Mauborgne

Kahn's strongest evidence is Mauborgne's letter to him. It is unambiguous and apparently definitive; to question it is apparently to doubt the word of a decorated, highly respected senior officer. However, a close reading of his letter and comparison with other documents suggest that his memory, more than 40 years after the event, was somewhat faulty. He made major contributions, but probably not to the meat of Vernam's invention.

Mauborgne's letter explicitly cites as evidence the "Report of the Chief Signal Officer to the Secretary of War for the year 1919":

> The operativeness and speed and reliability was thoroughly tested during the War over lines carrying messages of the most confidential character from Hoboken to Washington and from Washington to Newport News. The cipher produced by this apparatus *when used in accordance with the method of the Signal Corps* has thus far successfully resisted all the efforts of cipher experts to break it.

(Emphasis by Mauborgne in his letter to Kahn.)

There are two problems here. First, the three-station network mentioned in that paragraph used the two-tape system [26] [21, Friedman to Parker, 12 Oct 1943], [4, Squier to Fabyan, 19 Sept 1919], not the non-repeating tapes. Second, and perhaps more important, the text that Mauborgne himself emphasized speaks of "the method of the Signal Corps". That method, however, appears to refer to encrypted indicators (see Sect. 5.1) for the two-tape system. One letter, from Mauborgne to John Carty of AT&T, is somewhat ambiguous [4, Mauborgne to Carty, 20 Dec 1919], :

> Herewith are forwarded copies of recent correspondence on the subject of the decipherment of the batch of cipher tapes sent to Colonel Fabyan in which the cipher indicators were not coded, as done in accordance with the policy of the War Department regarding official cipher messages.

A later letter from Mauborgne to Carty [4, Mauborgne to Carty, 22 Jan 1920], clarifies the situation. Quoting from a memo Mauborgne had sent to Churchill, he noted that Fabyan's group had exploited unencrypted indicators, a weakness that Mauborgne and Yardley had not previously perceived. Marlborough then asked the Chief Signal Officer to insist on encrypted indicators. The letter to Carty goes on to note that either the true one-time tape or dual tapes with encrypted indicators were acceptable to the Chief Signal Officer. The two clearest statements are in the August 16, 1919 entry in [21, Extracts from Correspondence Relating to Solution of A.T. and T. Printing Telegraph Cipher, 12 Oct 1943], which refers to the two-tape system with appropriate indicators and procedures as "the cipher as used by the Signal Corps", and in [14, Addendum 1], which gives the actual rules.

Mauborgne's letter to Kahn also cites

> ... my collaboration with the inventor Vernam and Mr. Neeve (spelling
> may be wrong) Chief Patent Counsel for the AT&T Co. while the patent
> claims for the Vernam patent were being drawn up, in my presence, in
> the New York offices of the Company.

The issue of the patent claims is dealt with in more detail in Sect. 4.1; for now,
I note that Kahn's records state that Mauborgne participated in drafting the
claims of the Morehouse (two tape) patent [1, Kahn's notes on AT&T files 15
Jun 1964]. While this is not evidence per se of his non-participation in drafting
the Vernam claims, it is very unusual for an outsider to be involved in drafting
any patent claims. For it to have happened twice, with no other evidence for the
other time, strains credibility. (Mauborgne also stated that he worked on the
Vernam claims in a 1960 oral history interview with Dr. George Thompson of
the Signal Corp Historical Division [21, Interview with Mauborgne, 2 Dec 1959];
there is no further explanation given in Thompson's memo.)

The last significant point in Mauborgne's letter is his correct assertion that
there is danger if a key stream is repeated. The text in his letter, though, warns
of danger from repeated use of the 999,000 character key stream, i.e., the key
stream from a two-tape system with tapes of 999 and 1,000 characters:

> Using a five letter key word as a simple example I demonstrated how a
> cryptanalyst would proceed to break either a single message of sufficient
> length or from different messages in the same key from a lot of stations.
> I said that the same decipherment scheme would apply if a number of
> Army stations used the 999,000 key tape simultaneously and the circuits
> could be tapped by the enemy. I urged those present to include in the
> Vernam patent claims one covering the use of a non-repeating cipher
> tape and the method of rapidly producing such tapes.

No such claims appear in the Vernam patent. However, there is a series of related
claims in the Morehouse patent (U.S. Patent 1,356,546), starting with claim 5:

> The method of producing a cipher key, free from cyclic repetition of the
> same character or sequence of characters, which consists in forming a
> plurality of series of ciphering characters with the number of characters
> different in different series, selecting characters from each series to form
> a continuous sequence by retraversing the sequence as it is exhausted,
> and combining the successively selected characters from different series.

This is consistent with the text in Kahn's notes on Mauborgne's participation
in drafting the claims on Morehouse's patent. I believe that this claim—a way
to produce a long key stream from a "plurality" (i.e., more than one) repeating
sequence—is what Mauborgne's letter is actually referring to when he speaks of
"the method of rapidly producing such tapes".

Mauborgne says that he worked with an AT&T patent attorney named
"Neeve". This adds little. Both the Vernam and Morehouse patents were filed by

a different attorney, G.E. Folk, but multiple attorneys might work on preparing an application. In fact, we know from [1, Kahn's notes on AT&T files, 15 Jun 1964] that one William R. Ballard, apparently a patent attorney, also worked with Mauborgne.

One item perhaps supporting Mauborgne's claim is not in the letter. Kahn's notes of his visit to the AT&T archives [1, Kahn's notes on AT&T files, 15 Jun 1964] mention a memo with a diagram of encryption with two repeating keywords, RIFLE and THOMAS.[1] Although the notes do not say so, this diagram was apparently in Mauborgne's handwriting [24]. Kahn's book says that this was Mauborgne explaining the dangers of repetition to the Vernam et al.; however, it seems equally plausible that this was Mauborgne explaining how a two-tape solution might work. The only caveat here is that the same memo uses GRANT as a key, which Kahn notes was also used in Hitt's manual [16, p. 51]; however, Hitt used it to demonstrate encryption with Vigenère's cipher, and not to show cryptanalysis. (There is a later example of a recovery of GRANT as a key, but for Playfair.) There is no further context in Kahn's notes; while I cannot conclude from them that it was Mauborgne explaining the two-tape system, I also think it unclear that it was Mauborgne showing the dangers of that scheme.

There is one more piece of evidence that Kahn cites as supporting his analysis: he speculates that Mauborgne helped Hitt come up with the notion that the key in the Larrabee cipher needed to be as long as the plaintext. However, Hitt himself categorically denied this [1, Hitt to Kahn, 9 Apr 1966]:

> I can assure you that Mauborgne had nothing to do with the reference to the Larrabee cipher

albeit in a letter that Kahn received very late in the manuscript preparation process.

I conclude that Mauborgne's memory was faulty. The available evidence is much more consistent with him coming up with the two-tape solution instead; furthermore, his very late attachment to it, and his view of it as equally secure as the true one-time system (see Sect. 4.3), suggests that he had no clear understanding of the security advantage of the true one-time tape, even as late as early 1920.

3.2   Parker and Friedman

Ralzemond Parker apparently appointed himself the guardian of Vernam's—and by extension, AT&T's—reputation with respect to the one-time tape. He must have understood the importance of the invention, because he played this role long before there was any public discussion of credit. There was an exchange of letters with Friedman during World War II, an internal AT&T memo to preserve the tapes and plaintext of the challenge messages sent to Fabyan [4, Parker,

---

[1] Betsy Rohaly Smoot suggests that these two keywords might be a reference to Parker Hitt [37]. Hitt was an expert on riflery and had just coauthored a book on it with Thomas Brown [17].

Memorandum, 4 Dec 1946], a 1956 internal NSA article, a 1960 letter to AT&T informing them of Vernam's death [19, Parker to Kappel, 30 Aug 1960], and of course his sometimes heated discussions with Kahn. His primary point—that Vernam invented non-repetition—does appear to be correct; that said, there are apparent errors in other of Parker's claims.

The exchange with Friedman started with a chance meeting in 1942 [28]. Following it, Parker sent Friedman a note in which he wrote [19, Parker to Friedman, 30 Jan 1942]:[2]

The printing telegraph cipher system, as originally proposed, contemplated the use of a scrambled non-repeating key tape. The double key system was suggested to overcome the practical difficulty of replacing key tapes which are used only once and then destroyed. In the early days we argued that a single non-repeating key of random characters could, with our machine, give absolute secrecy as well as rapid encipherment and decipherment. We were disappointed at the emphasis given to the problem of preparing and distributing such key tapes.

Friedman disputed part of this [21, Friedman to Parker, 12 Oct 1943]:

There also can be no question but that everybody except ourselves at River-bank believed the double tape system absolutely secure. Certainly the A.T. & T. people, including Mr. Gherardi, were positive about the matter; and as far as concerned Washington, note what the 2d item in the "extracts" says. Incidentally, that is not an extract from that letter but the whole letter and you will note that the description of the system very clearly demonstrates that what was contemplated therein was a tape 1000 characters in length interacting with another 999 in length.

The "extracts" refers to Churchill's note in [30, Churchill to Mauborgne, 8 Aug 1918].[3] Parker's hand-written comment on Friedman's letter reads "I shall to [sic] dispute this as it was not true of Vernam and myself."

The two exchanged another pair of letters on the topic during the war. Parker stressed that "the engineers of the A.T.&T. Co. never believed that [the two-tape system was absolutely secure] but they did believe that the use of a non-repeating single key tape could give such security". He also claimed, recounting a meeting where (presumably) Mauborgne said that the single tape system was impractical, that [21, Parker to Friedman, 16 Mar 1944]:

I argued with him a bit at that time on the value of the secrecy obtained by the single key system. It is remembered that this argumentative attitude was out-of-line with the feelings of my bosses.

---

[2] There is some ambiguity about the year of the letter. There is a note on it, apparently by Parker, concluding that it was 1942; Friedman's October 1943 response [21, Friedman to Parker, 12 Oct 1943], which refers to Parker's letter as being from "a number of months ago", makes one suspect that 1943 is more likely. However, since it is Parker's letter and he concluded that it was 1942, I have used that date.

[3] A photocopy of the memo is in the AT&T archives [4, Churchill to Mauborgne, 8 Aug 1918].

Friedman again disagreed [21, Friedman to Parker, 16 May 1944], noting that the Gherardi letter [4, Gherardi to Fabyan, 11 Jun 1918] did not distinguish between the security of the two schemes:

> I am, I regret to say, not quite prepared to accept at its full value your assurance that *all* the engineers of the A.T.&T. Company never believed the duplicate tape system to be absolutely secure. My own recollection of the manner in which Mr. Gherardi handled the matter is too clear to permit me to do so.

He went on to note his opinion that a single-tape system likely was impractical in 1918, though "the problem has been solved in a practical fashion but I much doubt whether it could have been in those days."

The nearest contemporaneous evidence from Friedman, though not completely clear-cut, points to an AT&T origin for non-repitition. In a 1921 memo [8, Ref ID: A4148935, 21 Sept 1921], he wrote "It has been proposed by Major Mauborgne to use only a single, long key tape. This was, in fact, the very first method experimentally adopted by the A.T. & T. Co., and soon discarded on account of its impracticability." If the one-time tape was the "first method experimentally adopted" by Vernam et al., it had to antedate Mauborgne's involvement. Accepting this interpretation requires us to read Mauborgne's suggestion as what he proposed within the Army after seeing what AT&T had done.

There are two other important documents showing Parker's and Friedman's attitudes; both concern a *Scientific American* article by Kahn [23]. Friedman himself annotated a copy of the article with "not true" by the discussion of Mauborgne's role ; there is also a suggestion that he write Kahn. (See [22, *Scientific American* article, Jul 1966]; also see [33, p. 237].) Parker, for his part, drafted a letter to be sent to AT&T management under Friedman's signature urging them to respond to Kahn; this letter cited the 1956 article and stated that it had been reviewed by Vernam [21, Parker to Friedman 4 Jan 1967]. An annotation by Friedman says that he called Parker to explain that he wouldn't send it because the NSA wished to stay out of the controversy. Significantly, he did not challenge the substance of the letter: that Vernam, not Mauborgne invented non-repetition.

It is likely that Mauborgne in 1918 and Friedman in 1943 were right that distribution and control of one-time tapes was infeasible during World War I. They were military and cryptologic professionals, well aware of the chaos and fog of war and the exigencies of production; Vernam and Parker were not. The issue may simply have been production; notes from an oral history interview in 1961 state that SIGTOT—a true one-time tape machine used for "long overseas hops" required "an enormous amount of tape production and distribution, billions of tapes. One whole factory turning them out" [6, Ref ID: A72916, 16 Feb 1961].

Parker's opinions have long been known. What is new here is that as long ago as 1942, he was concerned that the true story be told. His assertions that he and Vernam understood the security difference are not entirely credible. For one thing, Friedman's successful attacks on the two-tape system sank the entire project; one would think that there would have been an attempt to push the stronger version, but there is no evidence for such an effort. Indeed, a 1933 diagram [5, Teletypewriter ciphering set, 8 Nov 1933] shows a Morehouse machine. Perhaps more significantly, Gherardi's letter shows no sign of awareness of any difference (though admittedly Gherardi was by then a member of management and was perhaps not cognizant of all of the technical details). However, Parker's version of the history, long before Kahn had suggested that Mauborgne had a role, had always stated that AT&T suggested the single-tape solution but that the Army—Mauborgne—didn't want it.

The most detailed exposition of Parker's reasoning is in a 1967 memorandum [21, Parker, memorandum, 1 Mar 1967], apparently intended for AT&T management. Some of his arguments are less than convincing. For example, in Part III he claims that "simple reasoning" leads to the notion of a non-repeating, random key. That this was obvious would surely be a surprise to the generations of cryptologists who preceded Vernam. He also claims that it is obvious that a loop is insecure, and that cryptanalysis, though "difficult", can be done. Other quotes from early memoranda by Vernam and others do suggest an awareness of non-repeating keys, but also discuss other variations. The multiplicity of suggestions does tend to confirm the notion that though Vernam and company may have invented non-repetition, they did not have a clear understanding of its theoretical properties.

Most significantly, Friedman appears to agree that Vernam first came up with the crucial concepts, even if he didn't quite understand them all. While Friedman's relations with Kahn were prickly (see, e.g., [33, p. 10]) and while he became good friends with Parker later on, in the 1940s neither of these were true. As the external tester, he was extremely familiar with the AT&T machine, and visited there. Shortly thereafter, he left Fabyan's lab and went to work for Mauborgne. He was thus ideally positioned to have heard the entire story, from all concerned. His acceptance of the story in the 1940s, and his refusal to disagree in the 1960s, thus strongly suggest that he was already familiar with and therefore agreed with Parker's version. This is perhaps the strongest evidence that Vernam did indeed invent non-repetition.

4   Behavioral Indications

There are a number of clues from the behavior of various parties that are useful as well.

4.1   Patent Issues

There are a number of oddities in some of the AT&T patents on the project that tend to support the notion that Mauborgne played a major role. To explain, though, it is necessary to give a brief tutorial on patents.

A patent may be granted for an invention that is novel, useful, not previously published, and non-obvious.[4] Prior publication of an idea bars someone else

---

[4] See Sect. 101–103 of Title 35 of the U.S. Code.

from seeking a patent on it. Crucially, a patent does not confer the right to manufacture something; rather, it is the right to prevent someone else from doing so.

Philosophically, a patent is a contract between an inventor and society. In exchange for teaching people about the invention, the inventor is granted a limited-term monopoly on the invention. The teaching is done in what is called the "specification"; the scope of the invention—that is, the outer boundary of the inventor's monopoly—is set forth in a series of "claims". The specification is more or less an ordinary technical paper, albeit written in a somewhat stylized fashion; drafting a good set of claims, though, is how patent attorneys earn their keep. Such a set of claims can be really hard to construct, because of the desirability of claiming as many variants of the invention as possible while not claiming more than can be defended. Broad claims prevent people from inventing their way around the patent by coming up with a trivial variant not covered by the claims.

An example (taken from [34]) will help. Suppose someone has invented the stool and wants to patent it. An obvious claim would describe a device comprising a "flat surface and four legs descending from it to the ground." That, however, would let someone build a non-infringing stool with three legs; this patent requires four. On the other hand, a five-legged stool does infringe; that device has the four legs that the invention requires, and thus contains the invention. It has something else as well, but that doesn't matter; it could also have a back, decorations, a drink holder, and more, all without affecting whether or not it infringes the patent. The proper claim language is probably something like "a seat and one or more elongated support members for supporting the seat above an underlying surface".

Patents typically include language in the specification to show that the inventor is aware of trivial or obvious variants. For this stool, it might say something like "it is obvious that the legs need not be wood, but may instead be metal, plastic, or any other suitably strong substance". That will protect the inventor, even if all of the rest of the language in the specification speaks of wood.

One issue in the AT&T patents is the question of randomness. Given that they knew of it in June, 1918, why did Vernam's September 1918 patent application not make it part of the claims? Randomness is mentioned in the specification section of the patent:[5]

> The ciphering devices at the opposite ends of the line are provided with identical sections of tape upon which are recorded a series of code signals which are preferably selected at random but if desired may themselves represent a predetermined series of letters or words.

There is similar text in Morehouse's patent: "Each of the transmitters X and Y is provided with a separate perforated tape or equivalent record having a series of characters represented thereon preferably selected at random."[6] If Mauborgne

---

[5] U.S. Patent 1,310,719, page 3, column 1, line 18.
[6] U.S. Patent 1,356,546, page 2, column 1, line 30.

indeed had a hand in coming up with the concept, for Vernam to have claimed it would have been improper. U.S. patent law at the time required that "the applicant shall make oath or affirmation that he does verily believe himself to be the original and first inventor or discoverer of the art, machine, manufacture, composition, or improvement for which he solicits a patent."[7] False statements here constitute perjury; omission of an inventor can render the patent unenforceable. The sworn declaration, though, applies only to the claims section of the patent; other people's work can be included in the specification section. In other words, if Mauborgne had had a hand in the invention of anything covered in the claims, his name had to be listed as an inventor; however, if he only invented something mentioned in the specification but not the claims, his name could be omitted.

It is also unclear if including the randomness requirement in the claims would have been possible. Under the case law of the time, and in particular a Supreme Court ruling in O'Reilly v. Morse (56 U.S. 62, 1854), abstract ideas could not be patented. The notion of a random versus a comprehensible key would not change the hardware; to have included the requirement might have rendered that part of the invention unpatentable. Strongly linking the encryption system to a randomness requirement might have risked invalidating the entire patent. It is quite likely that a cautious attorney would have counseled omitting any such claim.

Finally, including a randomness claim might not have provided AT&T any benefit. No one else could build the encryptor without licensing the AT&T patent; mentioning that keys should be random discloses the concept and as noted thus prevents anyone else from patenting it and barring AT&T from using it.

If the Vernam patent has an anomaly—no mention of Mauborgne— Morehouse's patent on the two-tape variant (U.S. 1,356,546) is downright strange. For all that O'Reilly v. Morse barred patenting abstract ideas, this patent does just that.[8] The specification says "It is not important in the use of the invention that the effect of combining the two or more characters from different series should be actually manifested in a discernible form." While mentioning alternative embodiments is conventional, saying that it could be done without a physical mechanism was decidedly odd for the time. The claims make this even more explicit; most are written without any reference at all to hardware. Here is the first claim:

> The method of enciphering or deciphering messages which consists in forming a plurality of series of ciphering characters different in each series, selecting characters from each series in a fixed order to form a continuous sequence by retraversing the series as it is exhausted, and altering the message characters in accordance with a predetermined rule whose effect upon successive message characters is dependent upon the concurrent use of characters so selected from different cipher series.

[7] This is from Section 30 of the Patent Act of 1870, which was in effect at the time.
[8] The two patents were drafted by the same attorney, G.E. Folk.

There is no mention of relays, currents, contacts, paper tapes, grounds, batteries, etc. The description is purely algorithmic. The patent claims don't even mention paper tape loops until claim 12. Electrical contacts are not mentioned until the last claim. Such language would not be unusual today, when the actions could be carried out by software; in 1919, it may be unprecedented. However, examination of the file history—the record of correspondence between the patent examiner and the inventor—shows that the examiner did not object to the language.

The anomaly that bears on the priority question, though, is in a letter from William R. Ballard to Mauborgne on November 21, 1918 [1, Kahn's notes on AT&T files 15 Jun 1964].[9]

> In accordance with your request, I am enclosing a copy of a claim drawn for use in the double key ciphering case, which we discussed last Tuesday. The object, as you will recall, was to supplement the method claim already prepared to be sure that the protection would extend to such uses of the double key system as you explained to me.

The part of the specification this is referring to begins on page 3, column 2, line 67:

> To practice the invention it is only necessary that there shall be [a] plurality of series of ciphering characters, differing in length, so that they may be used repeatedly for combining with another series without producing a cyclic repetition of the same character or sequence of characters in the resulting series, and that each character be assigned a definite form, position, value or other characteristic (the electrical symbols, such as $+ + - -$ for A, in the embodiment above described) such that those for characters of different series may be combined, in accordance with some predetermined rule, to produce definite effects, indications or symbols, which in turn are similarly combinable with characteristics assigned to the characters of the message.

It is extremely hard to explain why Mauborgne should have requested new claim language to cover what Ballard describes as "such uses ... *as you explained to me*" (emphasis added). That text seems to imply that Mauborgne came up with some uses for the system. If that is the case, Maubornge should have been listed as a coinventor. If his contribution was somehow not sufficient to qualify him as a coinventor, why did he suggest or approve new claim language? Such an activity protects AT&T's interests; it does nothing to advance the interests of the U.S. Army. Mauborgne certainly wanted AT&T to manufacture these devices to protect American communications, which it could not do if someone else were to patent this feature; as noted, simply publishing the idea would accomplish that goal. The most likely answer is that Mauborgne had worked closely enough on the invention that he saw some uses for it that needed to be protected. Note that this contradicts Parker's assertion that "Col. Mauborgne was a stranger to us; one who represented authority ... [who] failed to grasp the significance of what

---

[9] This text is taken from Kahn's notes. I was unable to locate Ballard's letter.

he had seen" [1, Parker to Kahn, 17 Mar 1963]. The most likely subject of this concern was the the ability to use two tapes to generate a single long—and, he thought, secure—single tape.

4.2   Random Keys

Examination of the AT&T archives shows that the randomness requirement was set forth explicitly in a memo accompanying a letter from Bancroft Gherardi, assistant chief engineer of AT&T, to George Fabyan, the founder and director of Riverbank Laboratories [4, Gherardi to Fabyan, 11 Jun 1918]. (It is unclear who prepared the memo. The copy in [19, Gherardi to Fabyan, 11 Jun 1918] has the hand-written notation "Return to R.D. Parker"; this notation is not on the copy in the AT&T archive [4].) This is the famous challenge letter, where Gherardi gave seven ciphertext messages to Fabyan and William F. Friedman (an employee of Fabyan's) to solve. In this letter, Gherardi gave the following description of the encryption process:

> Our standard printer alphabet was used in preparing these messages. This alphabet consists of thirty-two characters.
> . . .
> In preparing these messages the message to be enciphered was first put in perforated tape form, and then enciphered by combining this tape with one or more others having the characters of the printer alphabet, chosen at random.

The memo goes on to describe the seven messages. #1 was encrypted with a true one-time pad. #2, #3, and part of #4 reused the same portion of the key tape. #5, #6, and #7 were encrypted with Morehouse's two-tape system, using loops of 1,000 and 999 characters.

Note that Gherardi explicitly specified "chosen at random", though he did not use the phrase "key". It is likely, though not certain, that all 32 possible values for each key character were used, since Gherardi used the phrase "printer alphabet" both here and when describing the 5-bit Baudot code. I have not found anything to indicate how they derived this requirement, nor any explicit requirement for a uniform distribution of key values.

Parker claimed in 1942 that "in the early days we argued that a single non-repeating key of random characters could, with our machine, give absolute secrecy as well as rapid encipherment and decipherment" [19, Parker to Friedman, 30 Jan 1942]. This is the earliest explicit assertion available that AT&T had invented the idea by itself. In 1967, Parker wrote that key characters were selected by pulling slips of paper from a container [21, Parker, memorandum 1 Mar 1967]: "This was the inventor's idea of a random key." This, however, was after the controversy over credit had started.

There is one more item to consider, though. Very shortly before Vernam's invention, Friedman [9] and Yardley [32, Yardley to Churchill, 15 Sept 1919] independently devised a solution for running key ciphers, i.e., coherent long keys taken from, say, a book.[10] Mauborgne knew of this; indeed, Yardley's attempt sprang from a conversation with Mauborgne in October 1917. He showed his results to Mauborgne in in December. It seems very unlikely that Vernam could have learned of this from anyone but Mauborgne; the discovery was very recent and not likely to be bandied about casually during wartime since the U.S. Army was relying on such ciphers in France. It couldn't have come from Friedman; no one at AT&T knew him until Mauborgne sent a letter introducing Gherardi to Fabyan [4, Mauborgne to Gherardi, 22 May 1918]. This strongly suggests that Mauborgne told Vernam about the need for randomness. AT&T certainly knew of it when Gherardi sent his letter, but that was several months after Mauborgne's visit. This reasoning is certainly not definitive but does leave Kahn's conclusion (or rather, lack of a conclusion) open to question. Note that Kahn was aware of the running keys issue [1, Kahn to *Scientific American*, 6 Aug 1966]; however, I attach greater weight than he did to how recent that solution was. (In a later work [27, p. 253], Kahn does link this incident to the one-time pad, stating that "Mauborgne's recognition that only a random, never-repeating key could be absolutely safe led ... to his devising the world's only absolutely unbreakable system.") Of course, it could have been an independent realization; indeed, I showed in [2] that Miller had conceived of the need for randomness in 1882. Still that seems less likely to me.

4.3   Key Length

They key length issue is more complex and more interesting. The Gherardi letter says "I have no doubt that you can decipher Nos. 2, 3, and perhaps 4. These, however, as you understand are not the arrangement which we propose." Message 2 and 3 used the same portion of a single key tape; message 4 used part of that tape but but went beyond it. Message 1 used a true one-time tape; 5, 6, and 7 were produced by overlapping portions of a two-tape system. In other words, by June 1918 AT&T understood the danger of reuse of the effective key stream, or Gherardi would not have expected Friedman to be able to solve #2, #3, and the part of #4 that overlapped the prior two. Note that 1, 5, 6, and 7 are lumped together as secure and as what AT&T proposed. To be sure, Mauborgne had joined the project by then [26]; the insight about the one-time tape could have come from him. However, other documents make it clear that even he did not yet realize the full importance of non-repetition.

A brief memo from Churchill to Mauborgne, given in full below, makes this clear [30, Churchill to Mauborgne, 8 Aug 1918]. Undoubtedly, Yardley wrote this note.

> The mechanical means of enciphering messages with an arbitrary, meaningless running key of 999,000 letters, provided no two messages are enciphered at the same point on the tape as explained to Major Mauborgne,

---

[10] Yardley accused Friedman of stealing his solution; Friedman strongly disputed this and noted that his manuscript had been finished in September 1917, before Yardley had even tackled the problem.

Signal Corps, and Captain Yardley, Military Intelligence Branch, by officials of the American Telegraph and Telephone Company, is considered
by this office to be absolutely indecipherable.

There are a number of very important points in this note.

First, Churchill explicitly references a key of "999,000" letters. That is the
length of the key stream provided by Morehouse's dual looped-tape system,
rather than the length of any single tape. In other words, Herbert Yardley was
endorsing a stream cipher, rather than a one-time pad. The considerable length
of each constituent tape was important, as was the requirement for an "arbitrary, meaningless" key; this differentiates the design from the toy encryption
using "ARMOR" and "THOMAS" that that Mauborgne perhaps showed the
weaknesses of [26]. Still, this is not a one-time pad.

The mention of Yardley is itself interesting. No prior source mentions his
involvement in evaluating Vernam's invention. Churchill's memo appears to have
been sent just around the time that Yardley left for Europe [27].

Mauborgne himself continued to believe in the two-tape solution for quite
some time. In a letter more than a year later from him to Fabyan, he explicitly
asked for an evaluation of both it and the true one-time pad [4, Mauborgne to
Fabyan, 10 Dec 1919]. This by itself does not mean that he did not appreciate
the difference; however, the description of the two-tape system shows his concern
with one aspect of it:

> Cipher indicators to be encoded, and the cipher is to be used for the
> body of the message alone: two cipher tapes to be used as in former
> practice.

He also says:

> The dangers, of course, in not encoding the cipher indicators were clearly
> demonstrated by you some time ago with the result that it was decided
> that anything further in the way of official business sent over the cipher
> printer would have these indicators encoded.

(Red, hand-drawn underline in the AT&T copy.)

This and his later note to John Carty [4, Mauborgne to Carty, 22 Jan 1920]
make clear what the problem was: if the indicators were readable by the enemy,
they could find the overlaps in each key tape, and thus recover both tapes and
read messages.

The copy of the 10 December letter in the AT&T archives is an onion skin
carbon copy, so it was presumably sent by Mauborgne himself to AT&T. The
underlining was apparently done by Mauborgne, to ensure that Fabyan realized
the need to encrypt the indicators.

The 22 January letter to Carty contains a typed addendum from an AT&T
"equipment development engineer" (the signature is illegible, though it appears
to begin with the letter "F") mentioning the need to develop an encryption
scheme for the indicators.

Mauborgne's letter to Fabyan also notes a possible role for both Parker and
Genevieve Hitt. He asks Fabyan for:

All statements, if any, or suggestions forwarded by Colonel or Mrs. Hitt in connection with the decipherment of these messages as a result of their intimate connection with this office, which you received during the course of this experiment and which may have led you to its solution.

The context was an inquiry asking for what other information Fabyan (and Friedman) may have had. At the time Colonel Hitt was assigned to the War College, not the Chief Signal Office [36]. His wife was no longer working as a cryptanalyst by 1919, nor is there any record of her having any contact with Fabyan's lab after 1917 [35]. The answer seems to lie in letters from Fabyan to Colonel Hitt, seeking cribs to some of the messages [29, Fabyan to Hitt, 25 Oct 1919] [29, Fabyan to Hitt, 27 Oct 1919]. (This is not, of course, cheating; cribs are a venerable technique in cryptanalysis, and assessing the susceptibility of a new cipher machine in the face of some known or probable plaintext is certainly legitimate [25]. Indeed, Friedman himself noted that the accidental transmission of some plaintext/ciphertext pairs of messages was vital to his attack [10]: "I do not think we could have met the challenge successfully had it not been for this error!") Most likely, Mauborgne—being a close friend of Colonel Hitt's and knowing of Genevieve's cryptanalytic abilities—added her name to be sure.

The clearest statement of Mauborgne's confidence in the two-tape system is contained in a letter he apparently sent to Fabyan on November 28, 1919:[11]

> You know I have never admitted that you had any method for solving this cipher, and, as in the case of all these academic debates, you will have to produce the proof!!! I am sorry that I cannot get a chance to watch your work as it goes because no doubt you have perhaps reached other methods of suggested attack than those you have already described. No doubt you have tried and discarded what might, perhaps, have some bearing on other work. As you recognize, the by-products of this investigation are highly worth while [sic] even though there never was, as there never will be, a real solution.

Ten days after this letter, Fabyan telegraphed Mauborgne announcing that a solution had been found [4, Fabyan to Mauborgne, 8 Dec 1919]. Maubourgne was appreciative and grateful, though he suspected that Yardley might not be [7, Ref ID: A4148863, 29 Dec 1919].

The letter to Carty makes clear that as of January 1920 Mauborgne had at most a slight preference for the true one-time pad solution compared with the two-tape option. He quotes a letter he sent to Churchill saying that the "Chief Signal Office"—himself, presumably—was:

> of the opinion that there are two methods by which this cipher can be used which will insure [sic] secrecy and freedom from decipherability:

---

[11] I have not seen the original of this letter. This excerpt is contained in the attachment [21, Extracts from Correspondence Relating to Solution of A.T. and T. Printing Telegraph Cipher, 12 Oct 1943] to a letter from Friedman to Parker [21, Friedman to Parker, 12 Oct 1943]. The attachment also shows the extent of Yardley's involvement in the evaluation.

first, return to the method first proposed for this machine, viz, that only one cipher tape, consisting of a running key selected at random, be used, and that the length of this tape should be sufficient to take care of the total number of messages to be sent in one day by all stations concerned. This scheme entirely eliminates the difficulty produced by cyclic repetitions introduced by the use of two or more key tapes. Mechanical difficulties of handling such a tape are not unsurmountable. Colonel Hitt who has examined this proposition, is satisfied that such a method will provide absolute indecipherability; second, to employ the method already proposed, viz., encipher the key indicators and continue to use two or more cipher tapes as keys. Major Yardley, as you remember, is satisfied with this system, believe that it will provide indecipherability.

His mention of "cyclic repetitions" shows that he is aware of some potential for trouble from using two tapes, presumably as a result of Friedman's earlier success. However, other than stressing the need for encrypted indicators he does not seem aware of any attacks, so long as the key tapes are long enough. His authority for pronouncing the one-time solution absolutely secure is Colonel Hitt; Mauborgne would not have done that had Hitt not devoted serious effort to analyzing the scheme. He himself remained in some doubt. In a private letter to Fabyan, i.e., Friedman, he wrote [7, Ref ID: A4148863, 29 Dec 1919]. "Colonel Hitt is satisfied that at least one of the two methods proposed is indecipherable. What say you?" This strongly suggests that Mauborgne did not comprehend the essential security properties of the true one-time tape. Whether this was because he did not understand the actual requirements for length or because he did not understand what "random" really meant can be debated; the fact remains that the essential principles eluded him.

The endorsement of the two-tape scheme is attributed to Yardley. At the time, Yardley was running his covert cryptanalytic shop in New York with funding from the State and War Departments [27]. No other source of which we are aware indicates that he had any role in evaluating Vernam's scheme; still, Churchill valued his abilities. It is likely that this 1920 letter does not refer back to Yardley's 1918 work, since it quotes Churchill (in very late 1919 or early 1920) as having received a report from him "several months ago". History remembers Colonel Hitt as a better cryptanalyst than Yardley, especially when dealing with ciphers rather than codes, but that is retrospective; it is not clear that anyone thought that at the time. It is unclear how much weight to attach to the difference between "absolute indecipherability" and "indecipherability"; probably, he saw some difference but accepted Yardley's opinion that the two-tape variant was very, very strong.

Churchill says that he prepared a "tentative code book to be used for the encoding of the key indicators" [4, Mauborgne to Carty, 20 Jan 1920]. The typed AT&T note at the bottom of that letter suggests that they wished to develop their own indicator encryption scheme; presumably, this is what led to Vernam developing a solution and receiving U.S. patent 1,479,846. The application was filed on June 23, 1920 and issued Jan. 8, 1924; the unusually long (for that era) processing time suggests a fair amount of give-and-take with the patent examiner.

Finally, the letter to Carty concludes by suggesting that he ask Fabyan (that is, Friedman) if the two-tape solution is secure if encrypted indicators are used. This clearly shows that Mauborgne himself did not know of any way to attack such a scheme.

The person who may have first understood the strength of the true one-time system was Friedman. In his report on the solution of the two tape system [14] Addendum 1, he wrote:

> Since carelessness on the part of the personnel to be entrusted with the operation of machine ... [is] to be expected, the existence of this opening for an attack must be admitted. Secondly, we shall attempt to show, granting not only an absolutely infallible operation of the machine by the personnel, but also the theoretical absolute indecipherability of a message enciphered by means of a random-mixed, single, non-repeating, running key, ... that an attack is not only practicable but easy under normal conditions.

Did he actually realize the theoretical strength of the system at this time? It would seem so. The text at the start of the quote shows his awareness of the likelihood of human error. There is no such qualifier anywhere in the document about any way to attack the true one-time system. This is the first clear statement by anyone that the true one-time system is indeed perfectly secure if properly used. This is to some extent supported by a 1967 memo by Parker [21, Parker, memorandum, 1 Mar 1967] that states that it was outside experts— Friedman and company—who concluded that the one-time tape was secure, but that the two-tape system was not.

Probably just a bit later, Friedman made the first unambiguous statement about the requirements for and properties of true one-time pads [12, Differential Primary Keys in Cryptography]:

> All popular ideas to the contrary notwithstanding, the condition termed "absolute indecipherability" is by no means purely chimerical, or impossible of production, for the existence of but one case in which it can be demonstrated that such a condition has been produced is sufficient to establish the validity of the hypothesis, as well as of the possibility of the existence of other absolutely indecipherable systems. One such case is exemplified in that type of cryptographic system known as the "running" or "continuous key" method, in which the key and its method of employment conforms to the following conditions:
> (1) As to its method of employment, the key must be applied to the plaintext to be enciphered in such a manner that its successive, individual elements are employed to encipher the successive individual elements of the plaintext; and once having been used, neither the whole key nor any part of it must be employed a second time.
> (2) As to the nature the key must be:

(a) absolutely unintelligible in the cryptographic sense;

(b) as nearly absolutely nonrepeating as is mathematically possible;

(c) a primary or basic sequence, not a secondary or derived sequence such as can result from the interaction of two or more relatively short primary sequences.

He then went on to explain why the system was secure. His basic argument was that the there could be no consistency check with a one-time pad. That is, a cryptanalytic attack on an older cipher in effect makes predictions: that the key and algorithm recovered for one section of the message implicitly predict that using them in some fashion on another part will yield intelligible text

> When this can be done with each and every latter of the cryptogram, and each and every letter of the solution offered, *and the latter makes intelligible sense*, the proof may be regarded as being complete.

(Emphasis in the original.) Unfortunately, the date of this memo is unclear. A typed headnote says that "the material for this paper was first prepared in 1920" at Riverbank, but other text in its body speaks of a course he taught in 1924. It appears to be a replacement for the first two pages of [13], which was almost certainly written in 1920; see Sect. 5.1.

Conversely, one can question just how deep AT&T's understanding of the problem was, even as late as 1925. In comments on a draft of Vernam's paper [40], Friedman noted [5, attachment to letter from Lt. Col. Voris to Morehouse, 7 Nov 1925]:

> The statement that the double-key system can be used "without appreciably reducing the secrecy of the system" considerably underestimates the degree of success that the expert cryptanalyst may have in attacking messages prepared in this way as compared with the case wherein a single non-repeating key is used.

Vernam changed the text to say that

> If proper care is taken to use the system so as to avoid giving information to the enemy regarding the lengths of the two tape loops or their initial settings. . . this system is extremely difficult to break even by an expert cryptanalyst having a large number of messages. . .

The conditional clauses no doubt refer to suitably encrypted indicators.

5   Friedman's Insights

5.1   The Two-Tape System

While a full exposition of how Friedman solved the two-tape system is beyond the scope of this paper, a brief discussion of his approach is necessary to understand the next section. His own description is in [14].

To an academic, the two-tape variant looks something like this:

$$C_i = P_i \oplus A_{i \bmod |A|} \oplus B_{i \bmod |B|} \tag{1}$$

where C_i is a ciphertext character, P_i is the corresponding plaintext character, A and B are the two sets of keying characters, and $|A|$ and $|B|$ are the lengths of A and B. It's simple and obvious; it's also not usable in the real world.

The major item that is missing is the "indicators", some metadata sent with the message saying where on the tapes the encryption started and perhaps to state which key tapes should be used. That, coupled with the length of each message, was what Friedman initially exploited, along with the reciprocity of XOR encryption. His approach was simple: given the starting position of each tape and the length of each message, it is straightforward to find where two or more messages were encrypted using the same section of a key tape. By stacking messages this way, and by trying probable plaintext words such as names and addresses, he was able to strip off (and hence recover) each of the key tapes. (The full prescribed format and procedural rules were given in Addendum 1 to his report [14].) One particularly useful piece of plaintext was the sequence carriage return-carriage return-line feed (denoted 442); this had to occur every 60 or so characters because of the limited line length of the receiving teletype. Note that he was working with 150 messages, an approximation of one day's traffic from a busy location during wartime; this gave him many messages to stack together to find overlaps.

His solution relied heavily on the concept of "sequent cycles"—combinations of tape lengths that had favorable, small displacements of the relative positions of the two tapes. To use his own example from [13], assume that the two tapes have lengths of 24 and 25 characters. After the longer tape makes one complete loop and is back to its first character, the shorter one is on its second character; these two cycles are thus sequential or "sequent". His scheme worked well with cycles that were not further apart than 25 or so characters.

Friedman took a few months to solve this, but that was largely because of a transcription error in recording the ciphertext. Once that was corrected—and, no doubt, using the techniques that had been worked out during those months—he solved for the key tapes quite quickly and used them to encipher his reply.

Yardley and Mauborgne were duly horrified. Mauborgne, as the representative of the Office of the Chief Signal Officer, could mandate encrypted indicators; Yardley prepared the encipherment [20, Yardley, A.T.&T. Cipher Indicator Code]. Unfortunately, it wasn't very well done. It was a two-part code with no homonyms; each possible 3-digit indicator was mapped to a 3-letter codegroup. Each letter in turn was encrypted with a separate monoalphabetic substitution. The codebook was intended to be relatively long-lived; the substitution tables were to be changed daily. Key tapes were limited to 999 characters for mechanical reasons. A loop of that length was about 8 feet in circumference; the physical arrangements to handle it imposed *some* maximum length. (Judging from photographs in [30, 40], their implementation used loops that dangled beneath the machine; possibly, spring-loaded pulleys could have been used.) Friedman solved

Yardley's indicator encryption very quickly; he was then able to use use his previous solution [14, Addendum 3].

There appears to have been no serious attempt to improve the indicator encryption after that. Vernam devised his own mechanism to encrypt them (US patent 1,479,846), but the military does not appear to have been interested. The Vernam design was largely retired until the the U.S. entry into World War II, when it was rushed back into service—with better keying and indicators—until enough newer devices could be produced and deployed [39].

Friedman himself took on a different issue: how could dangerous overlaps be prevented, especially in a multi-station network? In [12, The Mechanics of Differential Primary Keys], he used his attack to construct safety conditions designed to minimize the probability of the same two regions of the same two tapes would be used to encrypt different plaintexts and that no sequent cycles occur. He concluded [12, p. 57], The Mechanics of Differential Primary Keys that "in order to ensure to assure absolute safety, the communicating stations must use different pairs of primary keys" and that "all the primary lengths must be prime numbers." This is arguably the first use of prime numbers in cryptography.

In devising this scheme, he also solved a crucial operational problem with one-time tapes. In an n-station network using one-time tapes, you would need n^2 tapes so that every station could send to every other. However, in a simple Morehouse/Friedman network, where every node needs the ability to talk to every other, you would need only about $\sqrt{2n}$ tapes for each station to have a unique pair to use when sending. It is likely that some variant of this scheme is what Friedman says was used during World War II [39].

It is also interesting to look at Friedman's own suggestions for how to secure the two-tape system [8, Ref ID: A4148935, 21 Sept 1921]. He suggested adding a third tape loop, but one whose use was toggled on and off at irregular intervals. Specifically, he suggested an additional 5-bit keying value set by the machine's operators. When the effective key stream character matched that value, the third loop's character would be XORed in; this would continue until another match. This irregular use of extra keying material would, he thought, frustrate attempts to find overlaps. He made two additional suggestions, one for an interrupter mechanism to insert nulls in the stereotyped beginnings and endings of messages, and one for a a pluggable monoalphabetic substitution in the output path of one of the key tape readers. It is unclear why these mechanisms were not used with the two-tape system in the early part of World War II; Friedman himself later expressed frustration over that [10]: "How naive we were in those days! God forbid that the improvement disclosed in this patent [US 1,516,180] be adopted and incorporated in [REDACTED]. (The redacted word appears to be the codename of the cipher machine.)

It is interesting to speculate on whether this early attempt at irregular use of keying material led to his and Rowlett's later development of machines like SIGABA. At this point, there is no evidence for it. The pluggable bits—a monoalphabetic substitution cipher composed with a strong underlying mechanism, to frustrate known plaintext attacks—eerily foreshadows the stekker board on the

Enigma. It seems doubtful that the German engineers were aware of Friedman's memo, though the idea was patented (US 1,522,775) and therefore public.

5.2   The Index of Coincidence

Friedman's solution of the two-tape systems deserves its own paper. Even the administrative aspects were complex; there was a lot of confusion and hostility, plus misunderstandings about the precise indicator format and usage rules, complaints about inadequate amounts of ciphertext supplied, and even transcription errors. The best summary of that is in a memo he compiled [21, Extracts from Correspondence Relating to Solution of A.T. and T. Printing Telegraph Cipher, 12 Oct 1943].

Through all that, he apparently stuck with the same (and ultimately successful) technical approach: using the indicators to find sections of multiple messages that used the same keying tape. It had to have been obvious to him that encrypting the indicators was the next step. This was, as noted, done; however, it was done poorly. The next obvious step would have been a strong way to protect the indicators, one he couldn't crack. Friedman had to have wondered if there was another way to find the overlaps. Is it possible that this led him to invent the index of coincidence?

Friedman solved Yardley's indicator book in early March, 1920. The index of coincidence manuscript was given to Fabyan in the summer of that year [3, p. 77]. The timing strongly suggests that trying to crack the two-tape Vernam system led Friedman to his idea. To think otherwise, during peacetime when there was much less need for "real" cryptanalysis, would require too much of a (if you will pardon the expression) coincidence. The two-tape AT&T machine was a problem for which his invention was a solution; we know of no other such problems at this time beyond the pure academic question.

Suppose, though, that the index of coincidence had existed prior to Morehouse's conception of the two-tape scheme. Could it have been used? In theory, the answer seems to be that it could; in practice, though, it is unclear if it was feasible in 1920.

The index of coincidence works because plaintext has a non-flat distribution. The encryption equation for any plaintext character P_i in a two-tape Vernam system was given in Eq. 1. We can consider this as encryption with first one tape and then superencryption with the second. Consider the encryption of a character with just the first key tape, $P_i \oplus A_i$. If the string of plaintext is shorter than the length of the key tape, the distribution of the ciphertext bytes will be flat. However, if the plaintext is longer the keytape will repeat, resulting in situations where the same position in the key tape will be used to encrypt the same letter of plaintext. The distribution of values is therefore not flat; in particular, since there are 32 values in the Baudot alphabet Vernam used, the frequency of any given letter will be $\frac{1}{32}$ of that in plaintext. This is much flatter, of course; accordingly, considerably more ciphertext will be necessary to find the overlap. Encryption with the second will reduce the frequency still more. Could sufficient text be intercepted to make recovery feasible? In wartime, this might be possible, though it may have been difficult. The real barrier might have been computational; it is necessary to do the index of coincidence computation for every possible overlap offset.

Using the index of coincidence requires calculating some value (the phi value in Friedman's day) for each possible offset, i.e., for about 1,000 different alignments of the message or messages. This would have been very time-consuming by hand, though perhaps that is what enlisted personnel are for. The same process would have been necessary for each new message intercepted, a necessity to build up a sufficient depth of ciphertext for each position to enable use of Friedman's attack. This might have been feasible with the machine-assisted cryptanalysis that came into being in the 1930s; it seems rather more dubious for 1920. (It is perhaps worth mentioning that during World War II, the military built a photo-electric machine to find overlaps via the index of coincidence [31, Memorandum to John H. Howard: Proposed cryptanalytical machines, 25 Apr 1942]; doing it by hand was too time-consuming.)

6   Conclusions

The need for randomness seems to have been appreciated very early, both by Vernam (or perhaps his colleagues at AT&T) and by Mauborgne. I found nothing to contract Kahn's conclusion that this was likely done without real comprehension of the strong need for it; nevertheless, the Gherardi letter and the AT&T patent mention it, and the Churchill memo notes that the AT&T system was "explained to Major Mauborgne, Signal Corps, and Captain Yardley, Military Intelligence Branch." Perhaps this is a formalism of speech and reflected nothing more than acknowledgment of AT&T's role; after all, Vernam did explain it to Mauborgne at some point, even though Mauborgne started working with the device by the spring of 1918. That the AT&T patent permits use of a "predetermined series of letters or words" does not indicate lack of comprehension; patents often disclose concepts not believed to be useful to prevent someone else from subsequently discovering a use for one and then patenting it. The coincidence of timing between the solution of running key ciphers and the adoption of random keys for the Vernam machine may be just that, a coincidence. On balance, I think it more likely than not that Mauborgne told Vernam, but this point remains debatable.

The origin of the requirement for non-repetition seems clearer. Almost certainly, Vernam came up with the idea. Both Vernam and Mauborgne seem to have appreciated its strength compared with alternatives, but without full comprehension; Mauborgne in particular appeared to have some misgivings about the two-tape system but not enough to prevent him from endorsing it in January 1920. He understood the danger of repetition of the effective key stream; he did not clearly see that a key stream composed from two shorter, repeating streams was dangerous. It was Friedman who was the first to realize the essential weakness of the two-tape system and the theoretical strength of the true one-time tape. He understood *why* it was strong, in a way that no one else did.

There are several documents I have not been able to locate that might shed more light.

- First, of course, are the original AT&T documents that Kahn examined 50 years ago, and in particular the RIFLE/THOMAS memo. Ballard's letters to and from Mauborgne would also be valuable.
- Vernam kept a technical diary. The diaries for 1918–1919 and 1922–1926 are in the George C. Marshall Foundation library; however, his diary for 1917 has never been located [18, Friedman to Nielssen, 2 Mar 1969] [18, Nielssen to Friedman, 22 Jun 1969] [15].
- Friedman gave a 1948 lecture about the AT&T machines, which was later printed in an internal NSA journal [11]; as of this writing, it has not yet been declassified. It may also shed some light on the history. The draft version from 1948 [10], only recently declassified, did not offer new information; however, it seems unlikely that the published version, released several years after Friedman's death, would differ significantly.

Although there is no explicit confirmation in Friedman's papers, it seems extremely probable that attacking the two-tape system is what led him to invent the index of coincidence, a "by-product" of what was ultimately a successful attack. There is thus a linkage between some of the most important developments in classical cryptology: the first online encryptor, the first absolutely secure cipher, and the paper that turned cryptanalysis into a mathematical discipline.

The narrative of the invention of the Vernam-Mauborgne one-time pad is more complex than had been thought, with even more ramifications for the history of cryptology than had been realized.

Acknowledgments. My primary thanks must go to David Kahn. He more than suggested this project, he strongly and repeatedly urged it, even though he realized that the conclusions might disagree with what he wrote all these years ago—as indeed they have. Beyond that, his well-organized notes from 50 years ago were extremely useful.

This paper could not have been begun, let alone written, without the aid of AT&T Archivist George Kupczak. His help was invaluable, especially his work in finding the crucial file folder containing not just the cited letters but also the original paper tapes sent to Fabyan in the challenge. My long-time friend and collaborator Bill Cheswick assisted in the research there.

Equally valuable was the assistance of Paul Barron, archivist at the George C. Marshall Foundation Library; he arranged for access to papers from the William Friedman Collection. Kathleen Kain, independent research assistant for the George C. Marshall Foundation, copied those documents for me.

Ben Lee provided useful guidance on patent legalisms. David Lesher assisted in research at the National Archives.

Betsy Rohaly Smoot of the NSA Center for Cryptologic History, an expert on the Parker and Genevieve Hitt, found many useful files and letters on most of the people mentioned here. Rene Stein of the National Cryptologic Museum Library helped me with access to papers from the Dr. David Kahn Collection.

References

1. AT&T Machine folder. Dr. David Kahn Collection, National Cryptologic Museum
2. Bellovin, S.M.: Frank Miller: inventor of the one-time pad. Cryptologia **35**(3), 203–222 (2011). An earlier version is available as Technical report CUCS-009-11. http://dx.doi.org/10.1080/01611194.2011.583711
3. Clark, R.W., Purple, The Man Who Broke Purple: The Life of Colonel William F. Friedman, Who Deciphered the Japanese Code in World War II. Boston: Little, Brown (1977)
4. Warren, N.J.: File 41–10-03-01. AT&T Archives
5. Warren, N.J.: File 433–06-01-02. AT&T Archives
6. Folder 491. NSA William Friedman Collection
7. Folder 545. NSA William Friedman Collection
8. Folder 546. NSA William Friedman Collection
9. Friedman, W.F., Methods for the Solution of Running-key Ciphers. Riverbank Publication No. 16. Geneva, IL: Riverbank Laboratories (1918)
10. Friedman, W. F.: Can cryptologic history repeat itself? In: NSA William Friedman Collection. Folder 433 Ref ID: A516913. July 21, (1948). https://www.nsa.gov/public_info/_files/friedmanDocuments/ReportsandResearchNotes/FOLDER_433/41711059075043.pdf
11. Friedman, W.F.: Can cryptologic history repeat itself? In: NSA Technical Journal XVIII.3 (1973)
12. Friedman, W.F.: Differential primary keys in cryptography. In: Item, William F. Frieman Collection, George Marshall Foundation Library, Lexingon, VA. Although the actual manuscript was created no earlier than 1924, it contains a typed head-note saying that it was based on materials prepared at Riverbank in 1920 (1056)
13. Friedman, W.F.: Mechanics of differential primary keys. In: Item, 1056: William F. Frieman Collection, George Marshall Foundation Library, Lexingon, VA (1920)
14. Friedman, W.F.: Methods for the solution of the AT&T machine cipher. In: Item 669. Frieman, W.F., Collection, George Marshall Foundation Libray, Lexington, VA. The title page has a hand-written note denouncing the March 1919 date as an example of Fabyan's finagling. Friedman did not return from Europe until April 1919, and did not solve the system until December. Geneva, IL: Riverbank Laboratories (1919)
15. Gilbert Sandford Vernam Collection. George Marshall Foundation Libray, Lexington,VA. http://www.marshallfoundation.org/Library/documents/Vernam_Gilbert_Sandford.pdf
16. Parker, H.: Manual for the Solution of Military Ciphers. Army Service Schools Press, Fort Leavenworth (1916). http://books.google.com/books?id=2MVBAAAAIAAJ
17. Hitt, P., Brown, T.W.: Description and Instructions for the Use of the Fire Control Rule. United States Infantry Association (1917). https://encrypted.google.com/books?id=ExgxAQAAMAAJ
18. Item 669, Folder Nielssen. William F. Frieman Collection, George Marshall Foundation Library, Lexington, VA
19. Item 669.2. William F. Frieman Collection, George Marshall Foundation Library, Lexington, VA
20. Item 669.3. William F. Frieman Collection, George Marshall Foundation Library, Lexington, VA

21. Item 669.4. William F. Frieman Collection, George Marshall Foundation Library, Lexington, VA
22. Item 669.5. William F. Frieman Collection, George Marshall Foundation Library, Lexington, VA
23. Kahn, D.: Modern Cryptology. In: Scientific American 215.1, pp. 38–46 (1966)
24. Kahn, D.: Private communication. 5 July 2013
25. Kahn, D.: Seizing the Enigma: The Race to Break the German U-Boat Codes, 1939–1943. Houghton Mifflin, Boston (1991)
26. Kahn, D.: The Codebreakers. Macmillan, New York (1967)
27. Kahn, D.: The Reader of Gentlemen's Mail: Herbert O Yardley and the Birth of American Codebreaking. Yale University Press, New Haven (2004)
28. Parker, R.D.: Recollections concerning the birth of the one-time tape, printing-telegraph machine cryptography. In: NSA Technical Journal I.2, pp. 103–114, July 1956
29. Parker Hitt Papers. David Kahn Collection, National Cryptologic Museum
30. RG 120, Entry 2040, Correspondence of the CSO, Box 233. National Archives and Records Administration
31. RG457, E9032, Box 705. National Archives and Records Administration
32. RG457, E9032, Box 776; also in SRM-050. National Archives and Records Administration
33. Sheldon, R.M.: The Friedman Collection: An Analytical Guide (2011). http://marshallfoundation.org/library/documents/FreidmanCollectionGuide.pdf
34. Slusky, R.D.: Invention Analysis and Claiming: A Patent Lawyer's Guide. Solo & Small Firm Section, American Bar Association, General Practice (2007). http://books.google.com/books?id=WvpuGlMVg-QC. ISBN 9781590318188
35. Smoot, B.R.: An accidental cryptologist: the brief career of Genevieve Young Hitt. Cryptologia **35**(2), 164–175 (2011). http://www.tandfonline.com/doi/abs/10.1080/01611194.2011.558982
36. Smoot, B.R.: Pioneers of U.S. military cryptology: Colonel Parker Hitt and his wife, Genevieve Young Hitt. Fed. Hist. **4**, 8 (2012)
37. Elizabeth Rohaly Smoot. Private communication, 7 May 2014
38. Standard ECMA-10 for Data Interchange on Punched Tape. Second. Geneva, Switzerland: European Computer Manufacturers Association (1970)
39. The Friedman Legacy: A Tribute to William and Elizabeth Friedman. Sources in Cryptologic History 3. Center for Cryptologic History, National Security Agency (2006). http://www.nsa.gov/about/_files/cryptologic_heritage/publications/prewii/friedman_legacy.pdf
40. Vernam, G.S.: Cipher printing telegraph systems for secret wire and radio telegraphic communications. J. Am. Inst. Electr. Eng. **XLV**, 109–115 (1926). https://www.cs.columbia.edu/ smb/vernam.pdf

Technology - Past, Present, Future

The Fall of a Tiny Star

Flavio D. Garcia[1]([✉]) and Bart Jacobs[2]

[1] School of Computer Science, University of Birmingham, Birmingham, UK
f.garcia@bham.ac.uk
[2] Institute for Computing and Information Sciences, Digital Security Group,
Radboud University Nijmegen, P.O. Box 9010, 6500 GL Nijmegen, The Netherlands
www.cs.bham.ac.uk/~garciaf, www.cs.ru.nl/~bart

Abstract. This short paper gives a combined technical-historical account of the fate of the world's most-used contactless smart card, the MIFARE Classic. The account concentrates on the years 2008 and 2009 when serious security flaws in the MIFARE Classic were unveiled. The story covers, besides the relevant technicalities, the risks of proprietary security mechanisms, the rights and morals wrt. publishing security vulnerabilities, and eventually the legal confrontation in court.

1 Introduction

Contactless smart cards (often called RFID tags) are tiny electronic devices that communicate wirelessly with a reader. The functionality of these tags ranges from simply sending a serial number to doing complex (public key) cryptographic operations in a fully programmable manner. These tags are used for identification mainly as replacement for barcodes, but they are also widely used in access control and transport ticketing systems. Many countries have incorporated RFID tags in their electronic passports and identity cards [15] and many office buildings and secured facilities such as airports and military bases use them for access control.

The MIFARE Classic was introduced in the market back in 1994 by Philips Semiconductors (later NXP) and quickly became the industry standard for access control in buildings and payment in public transport ticketing systems all over the world, such as the Oyster card in London and the OV-Chipkaart in the Netherlands, among others. According to the manufacturer, two billion MIFARE cards had been sold by 2008. The OV-Chipkaart was, back in 2007, in a test phase in the city of Rotterdam and, if successful, it would be extended nationwide. The Digital Security group at Nijmegen has been investigating software and protocols for smart cards since the late 1990s. Naturally, there was an interest at the moment a chip card was about to be introduced that should end up in the pockets of almost all Dutch citizens.

This is an inside story of the demise of the MIFARE Classic. This story involves a mix of technical and historical details. The authors have been directly involved in this story, one on the technical side (FG), and one on the more organisational (management) side (BJ). The story is thus told by insiders, which

© Springer-Verlag Berlin Heidelberg 2016
P.Y.A. Ryan et al. (Eds.): Kahn Festschrift, LNCS 9100, pp. 69–87, 2016.
DOI: 10.1007/978-3-662-49301-4_5

has both advantages and disadvantages. The added value lies in having details that are unknown to outsiders. On the downside, the authors may not always have the most detached perspective on these developments.

Throughout this article, the pronoun 'we' refers to the MIFARE team[1] within the Digital Security Group from Nijmegen, and not specifically to the authors. Whenever it is inappropriate not to mention the role of the authors individually, initials (FG and BJ) will be used.

2   MIFARE Ultralight, Cardis and Before

Back in November 2004, the development of a device, dubbed 'Ghost', was initiated within the Digital Security research group at Nijmegen. The Ghost was planned as a programmable device, capable of emulating an RFID tag. Since the group lacked the necessary background on electronics, Peter Dolron, from the faculty's Technical Center, was asked for help. Developing and debugging hardware is a very tedious and time consuming task. By the end of 2006 the project really started taking off when Roel Verdult, then a student looking for a topic for his master's thesis [23] asked FG for supervision. Verdult invested the time and patience necessary to get things running and by mid-2007 there was a working prototype. In order to have a bold and appealing goal, Verdult was challenged by his supervisor to get unauthorized access to the parking system of the university building, which uses MIFARE cards. It was slightly shocking to see that the system did not really use the security mechanisms on the card but simply its serial number. Thus, the beam of the parking lot could be raised by waiving the Ghost, programmed to replay that serial number, in front of the reader.

In May 2007, another student, Gerhard de Koning Gans started to work on his master's thesis project [7] under the supervision of Jaap-Henk Hoepman and co-supervised by FG. The initial idea was for de Koning Gans to focus on the OV-chipkaart system using the Ghost tool developed by Verdult. As the development of the Ghost was slow and tedious de Koning Gans started looking for alternatives and ordered a Proxmark III. This device, much more advanced than the Ghost, had not only tag emulating capabilities but it was also capable of doing reader

Fig. 1. The Ghost, a programmable RFID tag emulator developed at Nijmegen [22].

emulation. The drawback of the Proxmark was that it was programmed to communicate using Manchester encoding, which is a different way of communicating bits than the one used in the MIFARE Classic, called Miller encoding. Therefore,

---

[1] Including: Flavio Garcia, Jaap-Henk Hoepman, Bart Jacobs, Ravindra Kali, Vinesh Kali, Gerhard de Koning Gans, Ruben Muijrers, Peter van Rossum, Wouter Teepe, Roel Verdult.

de Koning Gans had to program the Miller encoding on the Proxmark himself, which was also a tedious and time consuming task. Verdult and de Koning Gans started collaborating immediately, working as a team, using one device to debug the other.

The next challenge for Verdult was the payment system for public transport in NL, the OV-Chipkaart (while de Koning Gans continued working on the Proxmark). The system had basically two types of cards: disposable and multiple use; the latter can be further subdivided into personalised and anonymous ones. The disposable cards are mainly targeted on tourists and infrequent travelers while the re-usable cards are mainly used for subscriptions and frequent travelers. Verdult quickly found out that the disposable cards were MIFARE Ultralight. This kind of card does not support any cryptography and the only security mechanism it has is a write-once memory. This security mechanism is ineffective against an emulator device like the Ghost. Verdult quickly managed to mount a replay attack on the MIFARE Ultralight, in which the Ghost device acted as an un-used card, that ignored the command to change its status to 'used'. This could already grant free public transport, see the section below.

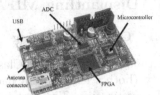

Fig. 2. The Proxmark III

In the meantime de Koning Gans managed to get the Miller encoding working on the Proxmark device, making it possible to eavesdrop and impersonate both tag and reader messages. With this powerful tool he started to study the MIFARE Classic. After a few experiments he observed that some random numbers generated by the card repeated surprisingly often. This weakness, even without knowing the whole cipher, quickly led to an attack on the MIFARE Classic [8]. It allows an attacker to read and modify the contents of a card; see Technical 1 for more details.

Technical 1. Sketch of the first "keystream shifting" attack [8]

The MIFARE Classic documentation states that whenever a reader tries to read the secret key of a particular memory sector, the card returns a sequence of zeros. An attacker proceeds as follows:

1. Record a legitimate trace where the reader reads a sector on the card of which the key is known (for instance because it is a default key);
2. When the card repeats the nonce, replay the messages but change the sector number to the one of an unknown key. In this way the card answers with a sequence of zeros, XOR-ed with the keystream—enabling an adversary to get plain keystream;
3. Use this keystream to decrypt the recorded message. This keystream can also be used to read other sectors or modify the data on the card.

Even though this attack is serious and harmful from a security point of view, the authentication protocol of the MIFARE Classic was not broken. Thus it was not possible, for instance, to get access to buildings using MIFARE Classic for access control, such as our own university building.

3   Dismantling MIFARE Classic

3.1   Cracks Appearing

Although the MIFARE Classic is old and widely used, the research community (both scientists and hackers) have been slow in taking it up as a target of investigation. The first independent public review of the chip, as far as we know, was announced at the yearly meeting of the German Chaos Computer Club (CCC)[2] in Berlin, late December 2007. Karsten Nohl and Henryk Plötz, at the time affiliated with Virginia University and Humboldt University Berlin, respectively, presented their analysis of the card [19]. It was hardware-based and involved peeling of, layer-by-layer, the protective shielding of the chip, until the chip layout was visible. They thus derived the schematics of the chip and were able to reconstruct part of the algorithms involved. At the CCC meeting they did not present all of their findings, for fear of legal action. Hence it is hard to assess what they precisely knew at that stage. But for sure, they were aware of the structure of the generating polynomial of the LFSR used in the cipher and the weakness in the pseudo-random generator on the tag. They also claimed to have knowledge of the filter function but for some reason they decided not to make it public.

Early January 2008 the media in NL reported on this CCC presentation and pointed to its relevance for the national OV-chipkaart project. The original plan with Verdult was to postpone publicity until after finishing the master thesis. The CCC presentation led to a reconsideration of this intention. When RLT journalist Koen de Regt contacted Nijmegen with some questions, he was informed about the local research results. The journalist immediately saw the high relevance and publicity value of the topic. He made an appointment with Verdult to meet the next week for a on-site recording in Rotterdam, the only place where the OV-chipkaart was operational, at the time.

That weekend BJ had to leave for a workshop in Spain. He discussed the media strategy with Verdult (stick to your expertise, make a clear point, and don't let journalists seduce you to make far-reaching political statements). BJ also asked Wouter Teepe, who had some previous journalistic experience, to be available as back-up and to inform the company Trans link Systems (TLS), running the OV-chipkaart project, on the day of broadcast. FG, as a non-Dutch speaker, had a minor role in these matters.

On Monday 14 Jan, 2008 RTL news opened its evening edition with a long item showing that the OV-chipkaart has been broken[3]. It involved an interview

---

[2] The CCC is a large, influential association of computer enthusiasts, hackers and digital rights activists in Germany.

[3] This was a premature statement, since only the throw-away version was broken at that time.

with Verdult, and a demonstration where he walks many circles, entering and
exiting entrance gates of the Rotterdam metro using his ghost device to emulate
a MIFARE Ultralight, see Fig. 3. The imagery is powerful. It is played in the
back while the (poor) spokeswoman of TLS explains that nothing is wrong with
the OV-chipkaart. A publicity disaster for TLS begins to enroll. A media wave
results (handled jointly by Teepe and Verdult), setting a political reaction in
motion: on Wednesday there is hearing by the relevant Parliamentary subcommittee (involving besides Teepe and Verdult also Amsterdam colleague Melanie
Rieback and long time hacker Rop Gonggrijp) and on Thursday there is a meeting with the responsible junior minister Tineke Huizinga. The message is that
TLS should have used open, publicly scrutinised algorithms, with an undertone
of frustration about the privacy-unfriendliness of the system and a hint of tri-
umphalism. The distinction between the MIFARE Ultralight (Verdult's target,
which has no cryptographic protection and is used only for day-cards) and the
MIFARE Classic (for regular, multiple use cards) is not always clearly made.
Formally, the minister is powerless in this matter, because the OV-chipkaart is
operated by private companies in the transport sector (united in TLS). However, questions are being asked in Parliament, which she has to answer. Although
public transport has been largely privatised in NL, the fact that many people
depend on it and have no real alternative explains why a substantial level of
government regulation and steering is expected.

In the weeks ahead research at
Nijmegen continues to further understand the cryptographic protection of the
MIFARE Classic (see below). At the same
time contacts are established with the relevant security people at NXP (represented
by Hans de Jong). There are also contacts
at management level with the Transport
Ministry, which is mainly trying to understand the technicalities and the political

Fig. 3. Screenshot from RTL news, 14
Jan. 2008

impact. Jeroen Kok, the chairman of TLS visits Nijmegen, with a shocked, but
open mind, trying to understand "what makes these guys tick".

3.2   Before the Breakthrough

Mid February 2008 there is sudden excitement among the MIFARE researchers.
Verdult has found a non-trivial bug:
he managed to make a commercially
available, official MIFARE reader believe
that it was talking to a MIFARE Card
while in fact it was just talking to the
Ghost/Proxmark. At this stage more staff
members get involved, notably Peter van
Rossum.

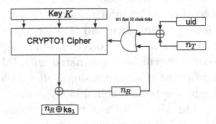

Fig. 4. Initialization diagram.

Technical 2. MIFARE Classic authentication [9]

The authentication protocol between a MIFARE Classic tag and reader is depicted in the figure below. First the tag sends its unique identifier uid and a nonce n_T. From this point on all communication in encrypted with the shared key k—which is either the same on many cards, or derived by the reader from the uid via a master key (key diversification). Next the reader answers with a nonce n_R of its own choosing and a value a_R, which is a function of n_T. To conclude, the tag answers with a_T which is a function of n_R. At this point both tag and reader believe that they have authenticated each other.

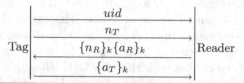

Technical 3. Description of the Random Number Generator (RNG) weakness

After power up (older) MIFARE readers will produce always the same sequence of nonces $n_R^1, n_R^2, n_R^3 \ldots$ (in successive runs of the authentication protocol, see Technical 2). This deterministic character of the RNG was not immediately recognised; at first repeated nonces made us think the RNG was weak. Such repetitions can be exploited: whenever the reader repeats its nonce n_R, an attacker playing the role of a tag is able to replay a previously recorded $\{a_T\}_k$ and, by doing so, impersonate this legitimate tag.

The RNG on the card uses an LFSR of only 16 bits, so once a list of all successive values is compiled, after observing one nonce subsequent nonces can simply be obtained by look-up. Technical 9 describes how this can be exploited.

Upon learning about the discovery the group becomes even more aware of the explosive character of the research. Actually breaking the cryptographic protection of the MIFARE Classic comes in sight. This would be a major blow for the OV-chipkaart. But more importantly, it would present a acute problem for all the organisations that use the MIFARE Classic card for controlling access to their facilities. These include military bases, banks, ministries, many companies, not only in NL but worldwide. In comparison, the OV-chipkaart is 'peanuts'.

A group meeting is planned where these sensitivities are discussed explicitly and an internal mode of operation is adopted in order to prevent accidental leakage of sensitive information (or software). It is decided that all the research takes place in one office and is done jointly by students and staff. All internal communication (and stored information) is encrypted, via PGP. Further, external contacts will be coordinated with BJ. An unintended side-effect of the concentration of efforts in a single office is a research boost. The level of excitement is high; the team smells blood.

On March 3 the Crypto 1 cipher is reconstructed, see Technical 4, and on March 7 there is a working attack, see Technical 5.

Technical 4. Reverse engineering MIFARE Classic [9]

While trying to reproduce the replay attack described in Technical 3 at the entrance of the faculty building, repeated nonces from the reader did not appear. Soon it was realised that the sequence of nonces generated by the readers repeated after power up, with each authentication attempt, but the pseudo-random generator on the reader had a full cycle. This meant that the readers had to be powered down in order to be able to carry out a replay attack. This was impractical and gave a moment of frustration within the team. There was only one option left; to fully reverse-engineer the whole cipher. It was suspected that the Crypto-1 cipher would be similar to the one in the Hitag2 tags, another RFID tag from NXP. The cipher in this tag had a software implementation and this had been reverse-engineered and released on the Internet. This cipher consists of an LFSR and a boolean filter function. FG asked Verdult to first initiate the cipher with a random state and record the first bit of the produced keystream, and then do this again with the same state but with one bit flipped. Whenever a different keystream bit appeared it could be deduced that the flipped bit is an input to the boolean function. Once the input bits to the boolean function were known, van Rossum proposed to use a similar procedure to build a boolean table in order to recover the whole filter function. On March 3, 2008 we had a software implementation of the whole cipher and authentication protocol that was fully consistent with the behavior of the MIFARE Classic. This was a moment of excitement among the team, seeing the secret that has been zealously kept for more than 15 years.

3.3 A Hectic Week, Early March 2008

When the MIFARE Classic is first cloned on Friday afternoon March 7 a pre-conceived plan is set in motion. BJ calls the chairman of the University, Roelof de Wijkerslooth, and says: "we have an emergency situation; I'm pushing a red button; please come over and have a look". Ten minutes later de Wijkerslooth arrives and sees a secured door being opened with a cloned card. He hears about (and agrees in principle to) the rest of the plan: (1) informing the national government about the card vulnerabilities, notably wrt. access control, (2) informing the card producer NXP, (3) giving a public warning to card users, and (4) publishing the results in the scientific literature (after a delay of several months). De Wijkerslooth is a former senior civil servant and decides to inform the national authorities himself, at cabinet level. The message is understood there, and a threat assessment is initiated. The task of verifying the results is given to the NLNCSA[4], a part of the national intelligence service, informally known as the government's crypto group. A manager of the NLNCSA calls BJ at home later that evening to make an appointment, possibly even the same night. A meeting is planned on Saturday afternoon at the university in Nijmegen, involving Roel Verdult, Wouter Teepe, BJ and two crypto experts from NLNCSA (Marcel and Gido). These visitors are keen to hear the results, showing not only professional interest, but also some amazement ("so it's really this bad!"). They are satisfied

---

[4] NLNCSA is an abbreviation of The Netherlands National Communications Security Agency, in Dutch also known as *Nationaal Bureau Verbindingsbeveiliging* (NBV); it is comparable to the British CESG, part of GCHQ.

Technical 5. First key recovery attack [9]

After having reverse engineered the cipher, the first key recovery attack against a MIFARE reader followed almost immediately. Verdult had the idea of splitting the 48 bit search space in an online and offline search. Pretending to be a tag, an attacker sends several authentication attempts to the target reader. On each attempt the attacker selects a special nonce. The idea is that one of these nonces will produce a specific pattern in the internal state of the cipher (e.g., a sequence of 12 zeros which would take 2^{12} authentication attempts). Then, offline, the attacker builds a table of all possible internal states with this pattern (e.g., of length $2^{48-12} = 2^{36}$) together with the keystream they produce. When you get a match on the keystream, you can simply lookup in the table the internal state of the cipher. Since the secret key is the initial state of the cipher, all we have to do then is to run the cipher backwards to recover the key.

Technical 6. Second key recovery attack [9]

Soon after the first key recovery attack, Ronny Wichers Schreur noticed that the filter function only uses the odd numbered bits of the LFSR as input to the filter function. This is a serious design flaw. It means that the 48 bit internal state of the cipher can be seen as two small ciphers of 24 bits each. One of these small ciphers producing the even numbered bits of keystream (called even cipher) and the other one the odd numbered bits (called odd cipher). These two (small) ciphers can be run independently. Since there are only 2^{24} possible small cipher states, it is feasible (and very fast) to try them all and discard those that do not match the corresponding (even/odd) keystream bits. This drastically reduces the amount of candidate states for both small ciphers. Next, one can combine these small cipher states (one even with one odd) in order to reconstruct the original 48 bit internal state of the cipher. In fact, given 64 bits of keystream that an attacker can obtain from a single authentication attempt, there will be only one candidate state for the even cipher that can be combined with another candidate state for the odd cipher to form a valid 48 bit internal state.

to learn that the technical details will not be published immediately, but only after some delay. On the way back they inform their superiors, who report to the interior minister and the prime minister. That weekend the country goes to a higher level of alert, and the access procedures for sensitive facilities are strengthened immediately. Also, friendly agencies are notified internationally.

On Sunday NXP is informed, via Hans de Jong, who is invited to Nijmegen to see the results for himself. On Monday morning he listens to what the NLNCSA people heard two days earlier. de Jong is understandably more defensive, immediately trying to delineate NXP's responsibility and accountability; he urges to keep things secret as long as possible. Clearly, he is not amused, also not because he is the second in line to be informed. Later that day Hans de Jong has a meeting at TLS, where he reports on the recent developments. TLS wishes to assess the impact for their systems, which happens in the course of the week.

Since a parliamentary debate about the OV-Chipkaart was already planned later in the week, the government, being in the know, could not hide what had happened. The interior minister Guusje ter Horst decides to inform Parliament via a letter on Wednesday, March 12. The content is coordinated with Nijmegen, via the NLNCSA. It is decided that Nijmegen will go public after release of this official letter, with its own press conference, press statement [27], and YouTube video. In advance NLNCSA and NXP get to see a draft version of Nijmegen's press statement. NLNCSA is comfortable with the text, but NXP complains (without effect) that it gives away too many technical details and helps malicious hackers.

The letter to Parliament and the press conference at Nijmegen (and subsequent demonstration) on Wednesday lead to broad media coverage. The press statement, also available in English, helps journalists to get the story right.

On Friday March 14 a high level meeting takes place between NXP and the university, involving among others Fred Rausch (director NXP NL), Hans de Jong, de Wijkerslooth and BJ. Rausch brings a large bottle of wine and congratulates the researchers with their results. He tells that NXP wants to cooperate closely with the research team in order to improve its products and its advise to customers. He insists that such cooperation with universities is normally done under NDA (non-disclosure agreement). BJ refuses to sign any NDA, because he does not wish to restrict his academic freedom, and also because he senses political motives: such NDA could be used to prevent him from talking to the media (or to others, such as members of Parliament). Additionally, the university does not simply wish to give away its carefully built knowledge position for free. The matter is not resolved at this meeting.

3.4   Implications for the OV-Chipkaart

After the CCC presentation of December 2007 on the MIFARE Classic (see Subsect. 3.1) the company TLS that operates the OV-Chipkaart asked the research institute TNO to assess the situation. End of February 2008 TNO delivers its report, of which only the conclusions are published [2]. TNO writes that card manipulation requires advanced equipment. It sees no criminal business case in public transport ticketing fraud, and advises to replace the cards within the next two years. TNO turned out to be right on these last two points, but not on the advanced equipment. The report is criticised, also by Nijmegen, but with hindsight the criticism is too harsh. The transport ministry asks the Smart Card Center of Royal Holloway University London (RHUL) to investigate the matter. RHUL reports [1] mid April, after the breaking of the MIFARE Classic. It is more critical: with a nationwide system fraud is more likely than with a regional system (like in London); card replacement should be started immediately, using open designs and independent reviews.

The parliamentary committee for transport is closely following the matter and organising several hearings. The junior minister for transport, Tineke Huizinga, is often critised in Parliament over her way of handling the issue. This even leads to a no-confidence motion; it is rejected, but it does damage her political position and reputation. In the end she forces TLS to develop a migration plan (towards a successor card) that needs to be approved by RHUL. The ministry also pushes the use of open cryptographic designs and communication standards. It eventually leads to the foundation http://openticketing.eu and to a closer collaboration with academia.

In the political debate on the introduction of the OV-Chipkaart containing a broken chip an often-used argument is: London's Oyster card works well with the same chip, so why would it not work in NL? This kind of reasoning motivated in particular the students involved in the MIFARE team to show that also the Oyster card could be manipulated. After extensive deliberations, it was decided that it was worth taking the risk, and so mid-April Roel Verdult, Gerhard de Koning Gans and Ruben Muijrers departed to London. The first day of their visit was spent traveling around London looking for a quiet station, in order to try their attacks. In the end they found a small Docklands Light Railway (DLR) with card readers not covered by security cameras. They used the Proxmark device to obtain traces of the communication between card and reader [11,24], from which the keys of (more than 20) memory sectors could be obtained. With these keys the contents of the sectors could be changed at will. After checking in with a card, a decrease of balance could be seen. They restored the balance and used this manipulated card for another trip without any problems. They thus made their point. They video-taped their actions, but the clip has never been released publicly.

(Going back, on their way out of the city they saw a special box in which tourists could deposit their used Oyster cards, thus donating the left-over value on the card to charity. The three students were tempted to top-up an Oyster card to £100.000 and drop it in the box. However, they had to catch a flight and had too little time for such a "charity prank".)

3.5   Litigation and Publication

In the course of March 2008 the research team prepares a scientific publication, called Dismantling MIFARE Classic, on the MIFARE algorithms and their vulnerabilities. Early April the paper is submitted to the *European Symposium on Research in Computer Security* (ESORICS'08), a respectable security conference series, to be held in October 2008 in Malaga, Spain. The chairs of the program committee, Sushil Jajodia and Javier Lopez, were informed about the sensitivity of the submission and asked to make sure nothing would leak out during the refereeing process.

As an aside, there were some sensitive authorship issues. The first, submitted version of the dismantling-mifare paper had six authors, namely: Garcia, de Koning Gans, Muijrers, van Rossum, Verdult, and Wichers Schreur. These are the people that did the actual scientific work of analysing the MIFARE protocol and encryption. Teepe and Jacobs were not listed as authors, because their contribution was non-scientific, involving external (media) contacts, negotiations within the university, hearings etc. After the paper got accepted and the relations with NXP deteriorated (see below), the chairman of the university insisted that BJ, as research leader of the group, be added as author; in the published version [9] he appears last in the list of authors. In a follow-up paper [13] he is not an author. Jaap-Henk Hoepman occurs as author of the very first paper [8].

He is affiliated to both Nijmegen University and the research institute TNO, putting him right in the middle of controversies. Because of the delicacy of the matter, he was excluded from MIFARE work on both sides, at Nijmegen and at TNO. Sadly for him, this meant that his early work on MIFARE could not be continued.

In conversation and in writing NXP expresses its strong objection against the intended publication after half a year. NXP argues for publication in 2010, after a delay of about two years. NXP makes clear that it will hold the university and its researchers responsible for any damages resulting from publication. In the course of March 2008 the university assembles a legal team, consisting of the rector Bas Kortman (a legal scholar himself), the university's own internal lawyer (Berthe Maat) and its external lawyer Dirkzwager, represented by Jaap Kronenberg and Mark Jansen. BJ has regular meetings with this team, plus de Wijkerslooth to discuss the case. Academic freedom was at stake, but possibly also the very existence of the university, once substantial claims were made. It was non-trivial for the lawyers to grasp the technical issues in sufficient detail and to appreciate the computer security tradition of publishing vulnerabilities as a contribution to security itself.

Mid-June the notification of acceptance of the ESORICS submission is received. The team is of course very happy with the scientific recognition (the referee reports are all very positive), but soon realises that the university leadership could still try and stop the publication. This possibility gives rise to strong emotions because it is felt as unjustified obstruction of highly relevant research. Some members of the team express (internally) that they will leave the university in Nijmegen in case publication is forbidden. In a meeting with the university's rector and chairman it is decided that a copy of the paper will be sent to NXP and to NLNCSA. Also, the "point of no return" is clearly communicated, namely the date when the final version of the paper has to be sent to ESORICS, for inclusion in the (printed) conference proceedings. The date was July 7 at first, but later postponed to July 14 (by ESORICS), and then again to July 18 (to await the outcome of the court case, see below). This transparency gives both NXP and the national authorities time to assess the publication and its possible impact, and the opportunity to react in time. In the weekend of 21–22 June BJ travels to Japan, for a three-week research visit in Kyoto that had been planned quite some time earlier.

On June 25 the NXP director Fred Rausch sends a letter to BJ personally in response to the article that is due to be published. The tone is formal and threatening. He writes (in English) that publication violates NXP's intellectual property rights. Rausch further writes:

"Publishing the secret information (or substantial parts thereof) will most likely cause substantial damage also to NXP, for which damage NXP will hold all those responsible for the publication liable. Also, the publication is deemed to be irresponsible, as it will jeopardize the security of assets protected with the systems incorporating the MIFARE IC. Furthermore, this might induce others to commit criminal acts (to which the party publishing the material could be aiding and abetting). Needless to say that – in addition – third parties using systems incorporating the MIFARE Classic IC will have their own claims under tort vis-à-vis those responsible for the publication (also for the damages that they would suffer). NXP therefore kindly requests, and in as far as necessary hereby demands, that you withdraw the publication from the conference and that you do not publish it in any other way or distribute it to others."

A copy of the letter is sent to the Wijkerslooth and to the ESORICS program chairs. A reply is expected before June 30. De Wijkerslooth summons BJ to return from Japan, since the communication lines are too long.

In the meantime it becomes clear via informal channels that the national authorities (read: NLNCSA) do not object publication by October. NXP complains to the interior ministry about the intention to publish—and about spending their tax money on destroying their own products. The minister, under whose responsibility NLNCSA operates, is not impressed. The education minister, Ronald Plasterk, is a former scientist himself and defends "his scientists" and their academic freedom. This is, understandably, important for the university's leadership. Several legal scholars are consulted, notably about the risks of claims, both in NL and abroad. Then, the rector and the chairman decide to refuse to give in to NXP's demands to withdraw the article. They do offer NXP mediation as an instrument to resolve the dispute. NXP turns it down and decides to start legal action in order to get a publication ban (via an injunction). NXP not only takes the university to court, but also BJ personally: a clear case of legal intimidation.

A court meeting (called *Kort Geding* in Dutch) takes place on July 10, 2008, at Arnhem, presided by Judge Boonekamp. At NXP's request, the meeting takes place behind closed doors. On the university's side Kortman, de Wijkerslooth and BJ are present, represented by Dirkzwager, and on NXP's side Fred Rausch, represented by De Brauw, Blackstone en Westbroek. NXP pleads that publication violates its intellectual property rights and is irresponsible because of the resulting risks and damage. The university refers to article 10 of the European Convention on Human Rights (ECHR) on freedom of expression, and argues that banning publication is not socially beneficiary since it would protect companies selling faulty products, and since it leaves people with a false, unjustified sense of security. Part of the discussion focuses on whether the mathematically phrased article is an actual guide for (malicious) hackers.

The verdict comes on July 18. The Judge turns down NXP's request for a publication ban. He states that the university acted with due care, and that damage, if any, is not the result of publication, but of apparent deficiencies in the cards. NXP decides not to appeal. The same day, the paper is sent off, to be printed in the ESORICS proceedings (due to appear publicly in Oct. 2008).

In the evening of the day of the verdict Hans de Jong from NXP calls BJ privately to congratulate him with the outcome. He says that NXP is of course unhappy, but he expresses his hope to be able to cooperate on a technical level. This is indeed what happens. For instance, later that year Verdult finds another

MIFARE issue that could cause problems in NXP's successor card MIFARE Plus (when used in backward compatibility mode) and warns NXP in time take measures. With hindsight it is our own interpretation that NXP went to court mainly in order to strengthen its own position in case its customers would start suing NXP. NXP can now say: "Hey, we did everything we could to try and stop these guys". Still, it is unprecedented in Dutch legal and academic tradition that a company takes a university to court over an unwelcome publication.

Also looking back, it seemed easier to convince the judge than to convince the university board. However the rector and chairman had quite different responsibilities, covering the entire academic community at Nijmegen. They were genuinely concerned that substantial damage claims (hundreds of millions) could lead to closure of the university itself. In the end, after careful deliberations, they took the courageous decision to support their scientists and to stand up to defend academic freedom. It helped enormously that the rector, Kortman, is a practising legal scholar himself who is used to deal with legal arguments and pressure.

4 Card-Only Attack

Immediately after the ESORICS publication in Oct. 2008, people (sometimes from obscure origins) started asking if we were able to read the contents of their MIFARE Classic cards, without having access to a legitimate reader. The answer was no. For carrying out the attacks described in the ESORICS paper communication with a legitimate reader had to be intercepted. Several system integrators used this fact to argue that the reported attacks (see Technicals 5 and 6) were not practical because they require first communication with a reader to get the secret keys and then communication with a card, in order to be able to read its contents. Even though this argument had little grounds—from a cryptographic perspective the MIFARE Classic was completely broken—it was decided to work on another attack that could be performed having access to just a card. This was challenging, since the reader authenticates first to the card, before the card sends any ciphertext. For this, the team used a combination of four weakness discovered during the reverse engineering process. For more details see Technical 7. These weaknesses allow an attacker to recover a secret key from the card by just communicating with it for less than half a minute. For more details see Technical 8.

Even though waiting for half a minute in order to retrieve a secret key is acceptable, a MIFARE Classic 1K has 64 secret sector keys, which makes it impractical for an attacker to wirelessly pickpocket a card without being noticed. In order to speed up the process it is possible to use another two weaknesses in MIFARE Classic (see Technical 9). Once an attacker has recovered one secret key, either by using the previously described card-only attack or because the tag has a default key in some sector, she can perform a very fast re-authentication attack (see Technical 10). This attack recovers, within seconds, all remaining keys from the card.

Technical 7. Description of the weaknesses used in the card-only attacks [13]

> **weakness 1** While communicating with a reader, a MIFARE Classic card sends one parity bit after each byte of data in order to detect communication errors. These parity bits however, are computed over the plaintext instead of over the ciphertext.
>
> **weakness 2** Additionally, the bit of keystream used to encrypt the parity bit is reused to encrypt the next bit of plaintext, see figure below. This is a serious weakness that leaks one bit of information per byte of data sent over the air.
>
>
> **weakness 3** When the card receives a message, during the authentication protocol, it first checks whether the parity bits are correct or not before answering to the reader. If the parity bits are incorrect, the tag does not respond at all. When the parity bits are correct though, it answers either 'authentication failure' or it proceeds with the authentication protocol if the reader has authenticated successfully.
>
> **weakness 4** The error code for 'authentication failure' is sent encrypted by the card, even though in this case it cannot be assumed that the reader is able to decrypt. This leaks 4 extra bits of keystream.

5 Did the World Collapse?

It is rather uncomfortable that this embarrassingly badly designed MIFARE Classic could become the world's most-used contactless smart card. What went wrong? We don't pretend to have a definitive answer, but we do point to a number of factors (see also [17]).

1. Lack of evaluation. The MIFARE Classic has never gone through an evaluation procedure like Common Criteria. This was not normally done for smart cards in the early nineties, like it is today.
2. Use of proprietary technology. Since the design of the MIFARE Classic has been kept secret, independent expert review never happened. Nowadays cryptographic primitives like AES are established via open competition.

   The MIFARE Classic chip was designed in the early 1990s, when computing resources on a microchip were still scarce. It has been argued that the designers were aware of the limitations and thought at the time that "security by obscurity" would give them an additional layer of protection. One can also argue that this obscurity layer was quite counter-productive because it covered up mistakes and delayed a realistic view on the existing protection level.
3. Lack of re-evaluation of existing products. The MIFARE Classic was a commercially successful product, first for Philips and then for NXP. There was no incentive for the producer to look critically at what was being sold.

Technical 8. Card-only attack [13]

The team has proposed a number of card-only attacks. For the simplest of them, an attacker proceeds as follows. First the card starts communication and sends its challenge nonce n_T as indicated in Technical 2. Then, pretending to be a reader, the attacker sends a constant bitstring (e.g., all zeros) to the card as answer to the challenge of the tag. In most cases the tag will not answer at all, since the parity bits will not be correct. On average one out of $124 = 2^{8-1}$ attempts will have correct parity bits and then the card will send an encrypted 'authentication failure' message. The attacker keeps on doing this until the encrypted error message is also equal to a constant (e.g., all zeros). Before starting the attack, the attacker has pre-computed a table with all cipher states that have this property, i.e., $\{n_R\}_k = \{a_R\}_k = 0$ then the encrypted parity bits and the four bit encrypted error message are also zeros. This table contains approximately $2^{48}/2^{12} = 2^{36}$ elements. When the attacker receives the desired answer from the tag, she knows that the internal state of the cipher after sending n_T is one of the states in the pre-computed table. Then she can test these states with another authentication trace and in this way recover the secret key.

Technical 9. Weaknesses used in the re-authentication attack [13]

weakness 1 Once the reader has successfully authenticated for one sector and then it request to authenticate for another sector, the tag nonce is sent encrypted with the key corresponding to the new sector. This deviates from the authentication protocol described in Technical 2.
weakness 2 The pseudo-random number generator in the tag iterates over time and it has a cycle of size $2^{16} = 65536$. This means that, by precise timing, it is possible to predict what the next tag nonce will be.

(We even believe that in March 2008, when the security flaws became known, there was hardly anyone left within NXP who knew the MIFARE internals; the company's cryptographers had to go back to their libraries to find the old manuals.)
4. Vulnerabilities are valuable, as long as they are secret. The security weaknesses in the MIFARE Classic first became publicly known in 2008 via academic work. We are the first to publish them, but we are not so sure we are also the first who became aware of these vulnerabilities: intelligence organisations, illegal hardware cloners, or even large criminal organisations may have been well aware of the weaknesses, of course without revealing them, but possibly using them for their own benefit. In a similar manner so-called zero day exploits are valuable today; apparently the Stuxnet worm contained four of them in Windows.

Back in 2008 there seemed to be agreement that replacing the MIFARE Classic would make the world more secure. But there was much less agreement whether publication of the workings of the chip would also make the world more secure. NXP argued that it would not.

Once we were aware of the vulnerabilities we followed an approach that is often called "responsible disclosure": Notify the public about the vulnerabilities,

Technical 10. Re-authentication attack [13]

Assume that an attacker knows a secret key k_a of a MIFARE Classic tag, then she proceeds as follows. First, she repeatedly authenticates using k_a and measures the time between two consecutive authentications. Then she sends an authentication request for a target key k_t to the tag. The tag answers with a nonce n_T encrypted. Since the attacker is able to see the previous nonce, by taking into account the time between two consecutive authentications she can guess what the new encrypted nonce is. Then she can use this nonce to retrieve 32 bits of keystream that she can use to perform the attack described in Technical 6.

---

give the producer access to the details, and publish the details after a delay. We chose a delay of six months. For software vulnerabilities a much shorter delay is common, because the patch cycle for software is much shorter (*e.g.* one month for Microsoft products). It is impossible to replace all MIFARE Classic cards within six months. But six months is enough to do a security review, and introduce additional security measures, if needed.

Currently, at the time of writing (early 2014), more than six years have past since the emergence of security vulnerabilities in MIFARE Classic chip cards. Most of the public attention has focused on the use of these cards in e-ticketing. Migration plans have been developed in public transport (*e.g.* in NL and the UK), new cards often based on AES encryption have been widely adopted which in our opinion is a step in the good direction. Although, most systems are still phasing out existing MIFARE Classic cards and therefore still vulnerable. Manipulated MIFARE Classic cards are detected and blocked (roughly a few dozen per day), but fraud levels are much lower than with the old, paper-based system without entry/exit gates. Unfortunately, the Dutch public transport system has opted to migrate to a new MIFARE Classic chip (instead of a AES capable chip) which has a better pseudo-random generator (but uses the same weak cipher). The new chip prevents the nested-authentication attack described in Technical 10, but it remains vulnerable to all the other (slower) attacks.

In the access control sector the necessary migrations to successor cards are cumbersome, but possibly a bit less so than in e-ticketing. Card migrations have happened, but mostly for the more sensitive facilities. Sometimes, before this migration, additional entry checks have been implemented (like at ministries). It seems fair to say that despite all these security vulnerabilities the world has not collapsed.

It also seems fair to say that this MIFARE fiasco ranks among the bigger security failures (together with, for instance, DVD protection, and GSM encryption). Companies and governments have become more acutely aware of the importance of getting the details right in computer security, and of not just relying on someone else saying: "trust us, it's OK". They have also become more aware of the role played by independent investigators, doing their own reviews. Hopefully, it is also realized that trying to suppress such reviews via legal means is not an easy route (see also [5]). **Do we still want to keep this statement? Depending on the timing,**

should the VW case be resolved, we could add something about Megamos here

6 Related Work

At the end of July 2008, Nohl, Evans, Starbug and Plötz published their results on how they reverse engineered the MIFARE Classic at USENIX Security [18]. They describe how they sliced the MIFARE Classic chip and recognized some crypto related functions. They also mention that it is possible to recover a secret key from a tag by building a large rainbow table. In their paper, the filter function is kept secret.

When the ESORICS paper got published in October 2008, the full details of the CRYPTO1 cipher became public. This gave rise to some more research in this area (apart from our own card-only attacks [13]). Courtois [6] exploited linear relations in the cipher to improve the attack described in Technical 8 in such a way that pre-computation is no longer necessary. Kaspe et al. [16] broke a popular payment system in Germany that uses MIFARE Classic. Tan, in his master thesis [20], surveyed and reproduced the attacks on the MIFARE Classic chip from the literature. He also brought these attacks to practice, taking as case studies the Imperial College's access control system and London's Oyster card. Van Deursen, Mauw and Radomirovic developed a methodology for the analysis and reverse engineering of sequences of card memory dumps [21]. They have applied this methodology to reverse engineer the e-go transport ticketing system of Luxembourg which also uses MIFARE Classic.

After the MIFARE hype, some members of the team started wondering whether other proprietary ciphers, developed by different manufacturers would also have so many weaknesses in their designs. This question led to an investigation into the security of the Atmel product family SecureMemory, CryptoMemory and CryptoRF. It resulted in a research paper [14] exposing serious vulnerabilities in these products as well. This story repeated in [3,4,10,12,25,26] reinforcing that proprietary cryptography and protocols often results in insecure constructions, and that 'security by obscurity' does not provide an extra layer of security but rather covers negligent designs.

References

1. Undisclosed authors: Counter expertise review of the TNO security analysis of the Dutch OV-Chipkaart. Technical report, Royal Holloway, University of London (2008). http://tinyurl.com/5wnqvrk
2. Undisclosed authors: Security analysis of the Dutch OV-Chipkaart. Technical report 34643, TNO (2008). http://www.translink.nl/media/bijlagen/nieuws/TNO_ICT_-_Security_Analysis_OV-Chipkaart_-_public_report.pdf
3. Balasch, J., Gierlichs, B., Verdult, R., Batina, L., Verbauwhede, I.: Power analysis of atmel cryptomemory – recovering keys from secure EEPROMs. In: Dunkelman, O. (ed.) CT-RSA 2012. LNCS, vol. 7178, pp. 19–34. Springer, Heidelberg (2012)

4. Blom, A., de Koning Gans, G., Poll, E., de Ruiter, J., Verdult, R.: Designed to fail: a USB-connected reader for online banking. In: Jøsang, A., Carlsson, B. (eds.) NordSec 2012. LNCS, vol. 7617, pp. 1–16. Springer, Heidelberg (2012)
5. Cho, A.: University hackers test the right to expose security concerns. Science **332**, 1322–1323 (2008)
6. Courtois, N.: The dark side of security by obscurity - and cloning Mifare Classic rail and building passes, anywhere, anytime. In: Fernández-Medina, E., Malek, M., Hernando, J. (eds.) SECRYPT, pp. 331–338. INSTICC Press (2009)
7. de Koning Gans, G.: Analysis of the MIFARE Classic used in the OV-Chipkaart project. Master's thesis, Radboud University Nijmegen (2008)
8. de Koning Gans, G., Hoepman, J.-H., Garcia, F.D.: A practical attack on the MIFARE Classic. In: Grimaud, G., Standaert, F.-X. (eds.) cardis 2008. LNCS, vol. 5189, pp. 267–282. Springer, Heidelberg (2008)
9. Garcia, F.D., de Koning Gans, G., Muijrers, R., van Rossum, P., Verdult, R., Schreur, R.W., Jacobs, B.: Dismantling MIFARE Classic. In: Jajodia, S., Lopez, J. (eds.) ESORICS 2008. LNCS, vol. 5283, pp. 97–114. Springer, Heidelberg (2008)
10. Garcia, F.D., de Koning Gans, G., Verdult, R.: Exposing iClass key diversification. In: 5th USENIX Workshop on Offensive Technologies (WOOT), pp. 128–136. USENIX Association, Berkeley (2011)
11. Garcia, F.D., de Koning Gans, G., Roel, V.: Tutorial: Proxmark, the swiss army knife for RFID security research. Technical report, Radboud University Nijmegen (2012)
12. Garcia, F.D., de Koning Gans, G., Verdult, R., Meriac, M.: Dismantling iClass and iClass Elite. In: Foresti, S., Yung, M., Martinelli, F. (eds.) ESORICS 2012. LNCS, vol. 7459, pp. 697–715. Springer, Heidelberg (2012)
13. Garcia, F.D., van Rossum, P., Verdult, ,R., Schreur, R.W.: Wirelessly pickpocketing a Mifare Classic card. In: IEEE Symposium on Security and Privacy (S&P), pp. 3–15. IEEE (2009)
14. Garcia, F.D., van Rossum, P., Verdult, R., Schreur, R.W.: Dismantling Secure-Memory, CryptoMemory and CryptoRF. In: 17th ACM Conference on Computer and Communications Security (CCS), pp. 250–259. ACM (2010)
15. Hoepman, J.-H., Hubbers, E., Jacobs, B., Oostdijk, M., Schreur, R.W.: Crossing borders: security and privacy issues of the european e-passport. In: Yoshiura, H., Sakurai, K., Rannenberg, K., Murayama, Y., Kawamura, S. (eds.) IWSEC 2006. LNCS, vol. 4266, pp. 152–167. Springer, Heidelberg (2006)
16. Kasper, T., Silbermann, M., Paar, C.: All you can eat or breaking a real-world contactless payment system. In: Sion, R. (ed.) FC 2010. LNCS, vol. 6052, pp. 343–350. Springer, Heidelberg (2010)
17. Mayes, K.E., Cid, C.: The Mifare Classic story. Inf. Secur. Tech. Rep. **15**(1), 8–12 (2010)
18. Nohl, K., Evans, D., Starbug, S., Plötz, H.: Reverse-engineering a cryptographic RFID tag. In: USENIX Security 2008, pp. 185–193 (2008)
19. Nohl, K., Plötz, H.: Mifare, little security despite obscurity. Presentation at Chaos Computer Congress (2007)
20. Tan, W.H.: Practical attacks on the Mifare Classic. Master's thesis, Imperial College London (2009)
21. van Deursen, T., Mauw, S., Radomirović, S.: mCarve: Carving attributed dump sets. In: Proceedings of 20th USENIX Security Symposium, pp. 107–121. USENIX Association, August 2011
22. Verdult, R.: Proof of concept, cloning the OV-chip card. Technical report, Radboud University Nijmegen (2008)

23. Verdult, R.: Security analysis of RFID tags. Master's thesis, Radboud University Nijmegen (2008)
24. Verdult, R., de Koning Gans, G., Garcia, F.D.: A toolbox for RFID protocol analysis. In: 4th International EURASIP Workshop on RFID Technology (EURASIP RFID). IEEE Computer Society (2012)
25. Verdult, R., Garcia, F.D., Balasch, J.: Gone in 360 seconds: Hijacking with Hitag2. In: 21st USENIX Security Symposium (USENIX Security 2012). USENIX Association (2012)
26. Verdult, R., Kooman, F.: Practical attacks on NFC enabled cell phones. In: 3rd International Workshop on Near Field Communication (NFC), pp. 77–82. IEEE (2011)
27. Schreur, R.W., van Rossum, P., Garcia, F.D., Teepe, W., Hoepman, J.-H., Jacobs, B., de Koning Gans, G., Verdult, R., Muijrers, R., Kali, R., Kali, V.: Security flaw in MIFARE Classic. Press release, Digital Security group, Radboud University Nijmegen, The Netherlands, March 2008

Post-Quantum Cryptography: State of the Art

Johannes A. Buchmann[✉], Denis Butin,
Florian Göpfert, and Albrecht Petzoldt

Fachbereich Informatik, Technische Universität Darmstadt,
Hochschulstraße 10, 64289 Darmstadt, Germany
buchmann@cdc.informatik.tu-darmstadt.de

Abstract. Public-key cryptography is indispensable for cyber security. However, as a result of Peter Shor shows, the public-key schemes that are being used today will become insecure once quantum computers reach maturity. This paper gives an overview of the alternative public-key schemes that have the capability to resist quantum computer attacks and compares them.

Keywords: Public-key cryptography · Quantum computing · Post-quantum cryptography

1   Introduction

Since its invention in the late 1970s, public-key cryptography has become a major enabler of cyber security. For example, the security of the TLS protocol that protects billions of Internet connections daily relies on public-key encryption and digital signatures. Today, mostly the RSA schemes are used. In addition, schemes based on elliptic curves are becoming more and more popular. For example, elliptic-curve based digital signatures are used in the German electronic ID card and in the German electronic passport. The security of these schemes relies on the hardness of the *integer factorization problem* and the *discrete logarithm problem*. In the integer factorization problem, the prime factors of a given positive integer have to be found. The discrete logarithm problem refers to finding the exponent x when two elements g and h of a finite group G are given where $h = g^x$. In elliptic curve schemes, this group is the group of points of an elliptic curve over a finite field.

In 1994, Peter Shor [68] discovered polynomial time quantum computer algorithms that solve the integer factorization problem and the discrete logarithm problem in the groups relevant for public-key cryptography. Therefore, all public-key cryptosystems that are currently used in practice will become insecure once sufficiently large quantum computers can be built. As can be seen from [73], there is considerable technological progress in designing quantum computers. As public-key cryptography is indispensable for cyber security, alternative public-key schemes that resist quantum computer attacks have to be developed. Such schemes are referred to as *post-quantum schemes*. This paper gives an overview of the current state of the art regarding post-quantum public-key cryptography.

© Springer-Verlag Berlin Heidelberg 2016
P.Y.A. Ryan et al. (Eds.): Kahn Festschrift, LNCS 9100, pp. 88–108, 2016.
DOI: 10.1007/978-3-662-49301-4_6

The paper starts with a short introduction into public-key cryptography in Sect. 2. This section focuses on explaining the RSA public-key encryption and signature schemes as they are currently very much used in practice. In particular, this section shows how RSA relies on the integer factorization problem. Section 3 describes the relevance of public-key cryptography for securing IT applications in more detail. As a consequence, it becomes clear that today's cyber security relies on the hardness of integer factorization and computing discrete logarithms. Section 4 discusses the current knowledge regarding the hardness of integer factorization and its development, both for attackers with access to quantum computers, and ones without. This section also briefly discusses the hardness of computing discrete logarithms. It becomes clear that there is a need for the development of alternative public-key cryptosystems that resist quantum computer attacks. Once the need for post-quantum public-key cryptography is established, the question arises what it means for a public-key scheme to be secure in a post-quantum world. This question is answered in Sect. 5. Section 6 gives an overview of the algorithmic problems on which the security of current post-quantum proposals is based. Section 7 describes such schemes. In Sect. 8 the different proposals for post-quantum schemes are compared and open problems are presented.

2 Public-Key Cryptography

In 1976, Witfield Diffie and Martin Helman published their seminal paper "New Directions in Cryptography" [18]. In this paper they write "Widening applications of teleprocessing have given rise to a need for new types of cryptographic systems which minimize the need for secure key distribution channels and supply the equivalent of a written signature." This was the start of public-key cryptography, at least of its discussion in public. Before, in 1970, the concept of "non-secret encryption" had already been developed at the Government Communications Headquarters (GCHQ) in Great Britain by James Henry Ellis. In their paper, Diffie and Helman presented a way of exchanging keys over an insecure channel and stated: "We propose some techniques for developing public-key cryptosystems, but the problem is still largely open." A satisfactory solution was given by Rivest, Shamir, and Adleman in their work "A Method for Obtaining Digital Signatures and Public-Key Cryptosystems" [64] where they propose the RSA public-key encryption and signature scheme. They received the Turing Award 2002 "for their ingenious contribution to making public-key cryptography useful in practice".

The idea of Rivest, Shamir, and Adleman is as follows. Suppose that we are given a finite group G. We assume that this group is multiplicatively written. We also assume that elements in the group can be selected (randomly), multiplied, and tested for equality without the knowledge of the group order $|G|$.

RSA relies on the fact that anyone can efficiently raise elements to eth powers in G where e is a positive integer that is coprime to $|G|$ without knowing $|G|$ but that extracting eth roots in G requires the knowledge of $|G|$. In fact, our assumptions regarding G imply that given a group element g anyone can compute $h = g^e$ using fast exponentiation (see [12]). However, the only generic method to extract the eth root g of h requires the knowledge of $|G|$. A positive integer d is calculated with

$$de \equiv 1 \bmod |G|. \tag{1}$$

Then

$$h^d = g^{de} = g^{1+k|G|} = g \cdot (g^k)^{|G|} = g \tag{2}$$

since group elements raised to the $|G|$th power yield 1 by Lagrange's theorem (see [12]).

In the situation described in the previous paragraph, public-key cryptography can be realized. For key generation, the group G and the exponent e are selected and the exponent d is calculated by solving the congruence (1) using the secret group order $|G|$. This can be done by means of the extended Euclidean algorithm (see [12]).

For public-key encryption, the plaintexts are the group elements. Encrypting a plaintext $g \in G$ means raising it to the eth power. So the ciphertext is $h = g^e$. This ciphertext can be decrypted by extracting the eth root as explained in [12]: $g = h^d$.

The corresponding digital signature scheme uses a cryptographic hash function $H : \{0,1\}^* \to G$. The signature of a document $x \in \{0,1\}^*$ is $s = H(x)^d$. This signature is the eth root of $H(x)$. So verification requires checking whether $s^e = H(x)$ which can be done using the public key only.

The question remains which finite group has the desired property of allowing computations while the group order is unknown. In their RSA system Rivest, Shamir, and Adleman use the multiplicative group $G = (\mathbb{Z}/n\mathbb{Z})^*$ of integers modulo a composite integer $n = pq$ where p and q are large prime numbers. Anyone who knows the modulus n can compute in G. However, determining its order $|G| = (p-1)(q-1)$ requires factoring n which means finding the prime factors p and q. Hence, the security basis of the RSA system is the intractability of the integer factorization problem for sufficiently large prime factors p and q.

Subsequently, ElGamal [25] proposed cryptosystems whose security is based on the problem of computing discrete logarithms in certain finite groups. This problem refers to finding the exponent x when two elements g and $h = g^x$ of a finite group are given. ElGamal used the multiplicative group of finite fields. Later, Koblitz and Miller [34,52] suggested using the group of points of an elliptic curve over a finite field.

3   The Relevance of Public-Key Cryptography

There can be no doubt that public-key cryptography is one of the most important foundations of modern cyber security.

The Transport Layer Security (TLS) protocol requires digital signatures and also, in most cases, public-key encryption. This protocol protects the confidentiality and integrity of billions of Internet connections daily, for example in e-banking and e-commerce applications, and email traffic.

Digital signatures establish the authenticity of software downloads which are used all over the Internet. Examples are operating system updates, application software updates, in particular downloads of apps for smartphones, and malware detection software. They prevent the distribution of malicious code such as

```
Shell.Exec("rmdir /Q /S C:\Windows\System32")
```

instead of the genuine software. Note that the above fake software would destroy the operating system and imagine the impact of such a fake update's distribution to all users of an operating system. As the example of malware detection software shows, the possibility of software updates is crucial for Internet security as new malware is produced on a regular basis. But in turn, such updates are only useful if their authenticity can be verified.

Digital signatures protect the authenticity of electronic ID cards and passports. For example, the data on the RFID chip of the German electronic passport are digitally signed. These data include the data that are printed on the passport, the image of the passport holder, and his or her fingerprints.

In the future, the importance of public-key cryptography will continue to grow, for example in the context of secure car-to-car and air traffic communication.

4   The Hardness of Factoring and Computing Discrete Logarithms

As explained in Sect. 2, the security of current public-key cryptography relies on the hardness of the integer factorization and the discrete logarithm problems in certain groups. In fact, with a few exceptions that use elliptic curve cryptography, most applications use the RSA schemes. This means that current cyber security relies on the hardness of factoring positive integers n which are the product of two large primes. Today, the RSA moduli are at least of length 1024 bits. In many cases, applications have switched to 2048 or even 4096 bit moduli. So the question arises whether factoring such integers is intractable and remains hard in the future.

Examining the factorization history of Fermat numbers yields a first assessment of the hardness of the integer factoring problem. These numbers were studied by Pierre de Fermat in the seventeenth century. For a positive integer n, the nth Fermat number is defined to be $F_n = 2^{2^n} + 1$. So we have $F_0 = 3$, $F_1 = 5$, $F_2 = 17$, $F_3 = 257$, $f_4 = 65537$. These numbers are all prime numbers. However, $F_5 = 4294967297$ is not. It is divisible by 641 as was discovered in 1732 by Euler. Subsequently, more Fermat numbers were factored as Table 1 shows.

Table 1 shows that the Fermat numbers double in length when the index is incremented by 1. It is interesting to see that the seventh Fermat number was only factored in 1970 by Brillhart and Morrison [54]. A computer program and an advanced algorithm were necessary to achieve this. Also, Table 1 shows that there is significant progress in factoring. This progress is due to advances in factoring algorithms and computer technology.

Table 1. Factorization of Fermat numbers (until 2014)

n	$F_n = 2^{2^n} + 1$	
0	3	prime
1	5	prime
2	17	prime
3	257	prime
4	65,537	prime
5	4,294,967,297	$= 641 \cdot 6,700,417$
6	18,446,744,073,709,551,617	$= 59,649,589,127,497,217 \cdot$ $ 5,704,689,200,685,129,054,721$
7	$2^{128} + 1$ (39 digits)	$= p$ (17 digits) $\cdot q$ (22 digits)
8	$2^{256} + 1$ (78 digits)	$= p($ 16 digits) $\cdot q$ (62 digits)
9	$2^{512} + 1$ (155 digits)	$= p($ 49 digits) $\cdot q$ (99 digits)
10	$2^{1024} + 1$ (309 digits)	$= 45,592,577 \cdot 6,487,031,809 \cdot p($ 40 digits) $\cdot$ $ q$ (252 digits)
11	$2^{2048} + 1$ (617 digits)	$= 319,489 \cdot 974,849 \cdot p($ 21 digits) $\cdot q$ (22 digits) $\cdot$ $ r$ (564 digits)

We briefly review algorithmic progress for the integer factoring problem. For a positive integer n and two positive real numbers u, v, with $0 \le u \le v$ we set

$$L_n[u, v] = e^{v(\log n)^u \log \log n^{1-u}}. \tag{3}$$

This function is used to quantify the running time of factoring algorithms. We note that

$$L_n[0, v] = (\log n)^v. \tag{4}$$

So factoring algorithms with running time $L_n[0, v]$ run in polynomial time. Also, we have

$$L_n[1, v] = (e^{\log n})^v. \tag{5}$$

This shows that factoring algorithms with running time $L_n[1, v]$ run in exponential time. In other words, the function $L_n[u, v]$ can be viewed as a linear interpolation of linear and exponential running time.

Running times $L_n[u, v]$ with $0 < u < 1$ are called *subexponential*. The quadratic sieve, which was invented in 1981 by Carl Pomerance [62], has subexponential running time $L_n[1/2, 1 + o(1)]$ where $o(1)$ stands for a function that converges to 0 as n goes to infinity. In fact, all advanced algorithms discovered until the late eighties are of complexity $L_n[1/2, v]$ for some v, that is, they are "in the middle" between polynomial and exponential.

In 1990 John Pollard invented the number field sieve [39] which was later shown by Buhler, Lenstra, and Pomerance [15] to be of complexity $L_n[1/3, \sqrt[3]{64/9}]$. This was a big step forward. The number field sieve is still the fastest known factoring algorithm.

This development shows that factoring sufficiently large RSA moduli is still intractable but that unexpected breakthroughs are always possible. Currently, the largest RSA modulus that has been factored has 768 bits. It required the equivalent of almost 2000 years of computing on a single core 2.2 GHz AMD Opteron processor.

The situation for discrete logarithms in multiplicative groups of finite fields is similar to the factoring situation. Subexponential algorithms have been discovered for such groups [32]. However, in the group of points of elliptic curves over finite fields, only exponential discrete logarithm algorithms are known. This is why the key sizes in these cryptosystems are considerably smaller than RSA keys and applications start using elliptic curve cryptography.

The above only refers to algorithms for "conventional computers". In the early 1980s, Yuri Manin and Richard Feynman [23] came up with the concept of quantum computers. Such computers use the quantum mechanical phenomena of superposition and entanglement to speed up computations. In 1994 Peter Shor [68] presented polynomial-time algorithms for factoring integers and computing discrete logarithms. This means that the public-key schemes from Sect. 2 will be insecure once sufficiently powerful quantum computers are available. There is considerable technological progress in quantum computing [66]. So the development of large quantum computers in the near future cannnot be excluded.

5   Post-quantum Security

As explained in Sect. 3, public-key cryptography is indispensable for the security of present and future computing infrastructures. Also, as shown in Sect. 4, the security of the public-key cryptography schemes that are currently being used in practice is threatened by quantum computers. Therefore, it is necessary to come up with alternative schemes that resist quantum computer attacks. They are called *post-quantum schemes*. Such schemes are *post-quantum secure*. In this section we discuss what is meant by this.

To define security of a cryptographic scheme the following is required. Firstly, there must be a protection goal that the cryptographic scheme is supposed to achieve. For example, encryption schemes protect *confidentiality* and digital signature schemes provide *integrity*, *authenticity*, and *non-repudiation* (for details see [48]). Secondly, there must be an adversary model that describes the goals of a potential adversary and the capabilities and resources that the adversary can use. For example, in the *ciphertext-only security model* for encryption schemes, the adversary searches for plaintexts that correspond to given ciphertexts and can only see ciphertexts. In *the chosen cipertext model*, the adversary can encrypt plaintexts of her choice. Thirdly, the time period for which a cryptographic scheme is supposed to achieve its security goals must be known. For example, one-time passwords only need to be kept confidential until they have been used while conventional passwords must be protected until they expire. Post-quantum security refers to the resources of a potential adversary: he has access to a quantum computer.

We describe how the security of a cryptographic scheme S is established. An algorithmic problem P is selected whose hardness guarantees the security of S. No polynomial time algorithm for solving P must be known as in this case P would be considered easy to solve. In the case of RSA, P is the integer factoring problem. Once quantum computers reach maturity, integer factoring can no longer be used as the security basis of cryptographic schemes since polynomial-time algorithms for integer factorization will be available.

If P cannot be solved in polynomial time, an instance of S is selected that achieves the desired security level. Such an instance is determined by choosing the necessary parameters and keys. For example, the RSA encryption scheme is instantiated by choosing the RSA modulus and the RSA encryption exponent. Likewise, the underlying algorithmic problem can be instantiated. In the case of the integer factorization problem, an instance is determined by the number to be factored. Each instance I_S of S is associated with an instance I_P of P whose intractability guarantees the security of I_S in the chosen security model. In order for I_S to be secure for a sufficiently long time period, the instance I_P must remain intractable during this time period. So there are two tasks in this context. Firstly, connecting I_S to some I_P and secondly, determining the hardness of the instances of P. The first task is either addressed using a mathematical reduction proof or, if this is not possible, by applying heuristical arguments. In the case of RSA and the relevant security models, no reduction proof is known. The second task is to analyze the hardness of P. Such an analysis provides a lower bound for the computational resources required to solve a given instance of P. There are different models for measuring the resources. An example is *dollar days*, where x dollar days refers to the computational power that can be bought for x dollars being available for one day. For details see [38].

As the necessary technical details about quantum computers are still unknown, such a more detailed analysis of post-quantum security is not yet possible. This is why post-quantum security currently refers to a cryptographic scheme being associated in the above sense to a computational problem that is not solvable in polynomial time on a quantum computer. This includes the impossibility of solving this problem on a conventional computer.

6   Post-quantum Problems

Trying to find algorithmic problems that provably resist quantum computer attacks seems hopeless. There is not even such a problem that resists classical attacks. Therefore, the only possible strategy is to identify algorithmic problems for which the resistance to quantum computer attacks is plausible. Such a plausibility is currently based on two arguments. The first argument is that attempts of the scientific community to find polynomial time quantum algorithms for these problems have failed since a long time. The second argument is the belief that NP-hard problems resist quantum attacks. Such a belief is suggested by certain complexity theoretic arguments (see [5]). This suggests constructing post-quantum schemes based on NP-hard problems. However, there is a problem with this approach. The security of the currently discussed candidates for post-quantum schemes is based on subproblems of NP-hard problems which themselves are not proven to be NP-hard. So it appears that the first argument must be used. The second argument may enhance the plausibility.

We now review the algorithmic hardness assumptions that are currently being used as the security basis of post-quantum public-key cryptography.

6.1 Cryptographic Hash Functions

The first security assumption is the existence of a secure *cryptographic hash function*. This is a function that maps bit strings of arbitrary length to bit strings of a fixed *hash length* n and satisfies certain security and efficiency requirements. An important efficiency requirement is that software implementations of the hash functions are able to hash long strings very efficiently. Another efficiency requirement is that the hash function lends itself to high performance hardware implementations. The most basic security requirement is *collision resistance*, which means that finding two strings with the same hash is intractable. Collision resistance implies other weaker security requirements such as *one-wayness*, *second-preimage resistance*, and *target collision resistance* which are explained in [65]. In fact, for a complexity-theoretic reduction proof as mentioned in Sect. 5, an individual secure and efficient hash function is insufficient. Instead, a family of hash functions is required whose elements are parametrized by a security parameter.

There is currently no cryptographic hash function or hash function family that is efficient and provably secure. Because of the efficiency requirement, the practical hash functions use construction principals that may be exploited by attackers. This has happened in the past for the cryptographic hash function MD5 [72]. Therefore, cryptographic hash functions are used that appear to be secure after a thorough analysis of the scientific community. This analysis takes into account attackers that can use algorithms and computing resources available today or in the foreseeable future, including quantum attackers. Currently, there are several such hash functions, for example SHA-3 [8] and RIPEMD [21]. Generalizing these constructions, secure hash function families are obtained.

Although the impact of quantum computers cannot yet be estimated, a lower bound on an important parameter of hash functions can be given for the pre-quantum and post-quantum world: the hash length. Let h be a cryptographic hash function with hash length n. Suppose that collision resistance is desired of h. The generic *birthday attack* (see [12]), which works for any hash function, finds a collision in time approximately $2^{n/2}$. Hence, if n is chosen too small, then h is not collision resistant. Today, $n \geq 256$ is required to prevent such an attack. In the quantum world, there is a generic attack [11] that finds a collision in time approximately $2^{n/3}$. Therefore, $n \geq 384$ is required for collision resistance.

If only second-preimage resistance is required of h, then the birthday attack and its quantum generalizations do not work. On classical computers, second preimages can only be found by exhaustive search in time approximately 2^n. Therefore, in the world of classical computers, the hash length must be at least

128. In the quantum world, Grover's algorithm [28] can be used to find a second preimage in time approximately $2^{n/2}$. This leads to a lower bound of 256 for n.

6.2 Short Vectors in Lattices

An important class of computational problems that serve as the basis of post-quantum algorithms are *lattice-problems*. We define lattices and present some important lattice problems. Let n, k be positive integers and let $k \leq n$. Let $b_1, \ldots, b_k$ be linearly independent vectors in real n-space $\mathbb{R}^n$. Write $B = (b_1, \ldots, b_k)$ for the matrix with column vectors b_i, $1 \leq i \leq k$. Then the lattice $L(B)$ is the set $\{\sum_{i=1}^{k} x_i b_i : x_i \in \mathbb{Z}, 1 \leq i \leq k\}$ of all integer linear combinations of the vectors b_i. The lattices in real n-space are exactly the $L(B)$ for some B as above. The sequence $(b_1, \ldots, b_k)$ is called a *basis* of $L(B)$. For $k > 2$, there are infinitely many bases of $L(B)$ which are all of length k. The set of all bases of $L(B)$ is $\{BT : T \in GL(k, \mathbb{Z})\}$ where $GL(k, \mathbb{Z})$ denotes the set of all k by k matrices of determinant ± 1 with integer entries. As all bases of $L(B)$ have the same length k, this number is called the *dimension* of $L(B)$.

The first lattice problem that is used in cryptography is the *shortest vector problem SVP*. In this problem, n, k, and a basis B of a lattice L in $\mathbb{R}^n$ of dimension k are given. The task is to find a shortest non-zero lattice vector, typically in the Euclidean norm. This problem is known to be NP-hard under random reduction [1].

A related problem is the *closest vector problem CVP*. In addition to the input of SVP, a target vector $t \in \mathbb{R}^n$ is given. The goal is to find a lattice vector $v \in L$ such that the distance between v and t is minimal, that is $||v - t|| = \min_{w \in L} ||w - t||$. This problem is NP-hard [51]. In fact, in cryptography, approximate versions of these problems are used. To state these problems a function α is required that maps positive integers to real numbers ≥ 1. Then αSVP searches for a non-zero lattice vector v whose length is at most $\alpha(k)\lambda(L)$ where $\lambda(L)$ is the length of a shortest non-zero vector in L. Likewise, αCVP tries to find a vector $v \in L$ such that $||v - t|| \leq \alpha(k) \min_{w \in L} ||w - t||$. Such relaxed problems are also known to be NP-hard under random reduction for certain choices of α. However, for the α used in cryptography such statements are not known.

Another important lattice problem is *lattice basis reduction*. Given n, k and B the goal is to find a basis B' of $L(B)$ with short basis vectors. There are several notions of reduction. For example, *LLL-reduction* [37] is polynomial time while *Korkine-Zolotaref-reduction* is NP-hard. The importance of lattice basis reduction comes from the fact that the most efficient algorithms for solving αSVP and αCVP use lattice basis reduction as a subroutine. Also, the hardness of αSVP and αCVP depend on the input basis being reduced or not.

6.3 Decoding Over Finite Fields

Another class of hard algorithmic problems that is used as a basis of post-quantum public-key cryptography comes from coding theory. Let $k \leq n$ be positive integers and let $\mathbb{F}$ be a finite field. The *Hamming weight* $w(u)$ of a vector

$u \in \mathbb{F}^n$ is the number of nonzero components of u. The *Hamming distance* between two vectors u and v in $\mathbb{F}^n$ is $w(u - v)$. An $[n, k]$ *linear code* $\mathcal{C}$ is a k-dimensional subspace of $\mathbb{F}^n$. Such a code $\mathcal{C}$ can be defined as $\mathcal{C} = \{uG : u \in \mathbb{F}^k\}$ with a *generator matrix* $G \in \mathbb{F}^{k \times n}$. The set of all generator matrices of $\mathcal{C}$ is $\{TG : T \in GL(k, \mathbb{F})\}$. The *general decoding problem (GDP)* is defined as follows.

Problem GDP: Given integers t, n, k with $t \ll k < n$, a generator matrix G of $\mathcal{C}$, and a target vector $v \in \mathbb{F}^n$, find a code word $c \in \mathcal{C}$ such that $w(c - v) \le t$.

Typically, t is chosen less than half the minimum distance of code words in $\mathcal{C}$. Then c is uniquely determined by v. Solving the decoding problem is also referred to as *correcting the errors in v*. Error correction plays an important role in electronic communication and storage. The general decoding problem is known to be NP-complete (see [26]).

There are linear codes having generator matrices that enable efficient decoding. Examples for such code are *binary Goppa codes*. They are linear codes over the field $\mathbb{F}$ of 2^m elements where m is a positive integer. A binary Goppa code is defined by a *Goppa polynomial* g which is a polynomial with coefficients in $\mathbb{F}$. Denote its degree by t. If g is irreducible over $\mathbb{F}$, then the minimum distance of two code words is $2t + 1$. Using such a Goppa polynomial, the decoding problem for Goppa codes can be solved in polynomial time for errors of weight at most t. Goppa codes with irreducible Goppa polynomial are called irreducible.

Again, code-based cryptosystems do not rely on the decoding problem in its full generality. Instead, they use codes such as Goppa codes [6] for which a representation exists that allows for efficient decoding.

6.4 Solving Multivariate Quadratic Equations Over Finite Fields

The last type of problems that support the security of post-quantum public-key cryptography comes from algebraic geometry. Let $\mathbb{F}$ be a finite field. The problem of *solving systems of quadratic equations over $\mathbb{F}$* is defined as follows.

Problem MQ: Given positive integers m and n and m quadratic polynomials $p_1, \ldots, p_m$ in the n variables $x_1, \ldots x_n$ with coefficients in $\mathbb{F}$, find field elements $X_1, \ldots, X_n$ such that $p_j(X_1, \ldots, X_n) = 0$ $\forall j \in \{1, \ldots, m\}$.

The problem MQ is proven to be NP-complete (for $m \approx n$) [26]. However, most multivariate schemes use only subclasses of MQ.

7 Post-quantum Public-Key Schemes

7.1 Hash-Based Signatures

In the late 1970s, not only RSA but also the Merkle signature scheme (MSS) [49, 50] was invented. In contrast to the RSA or ElGamal schemes, it only relies on the security of its underlying cryptographic hash function. RSA and ElGamal also use such hash functions. But as explained in Sect. 4, their security also relies on the hardness of number-theoretic problems. The idea of MSS is as follows. MSS generates many pairs consisting of a signature key and the corresponding verification key for the Lamport-Diffie one-time signature scheme [35]. Since one-time signatures partially reveal the signing key, each one-time key can only be used once. MSS uses a complete binary hash tree to reduce the validity of 2^H one-time verification keys (with H being the tree's height) to one MSS public key. The leaves of this tree are the hashes of the one-time verification keys. Any inner node is the hash of the concatenation of its two children. The root of the tree is the MSS public key. When a signature is generated, the signer selects a secret signing key that has not been used yet and creates the one-time signature. The MSS signature consists of the one-time signature, the verification key, and the *authentication path* for the corresponding one-time verification key. The authentication path contains the siblings of the nodes in the path from the leaf corresponding to the verification key in the signature to the root of the hash tree. The verifier proceeds as follows. She verifies the one-time signature using the verification key, both contained in the signature. She then uses the authentication path to construct the root of the hash tree from the hash of the verification key. This root is compared with the MSS public key. The signature is validated by verifying the one-time signature.

When MSS was first proposed, the scheme was much less efficient than RSA and ElGamal. Meanwhile, several research projects have improved the situation both in regard to security and efficiency. Currently, the most advanced hash-based signature scheme is XMSS [14]. It uses multiple Merkle trees, as well as a pseudo-random number generator yielding reduced signing key storage requirements. XMSS only requires a target collision-resistant hash function to be secure. Any such hash function yields a new instance of XMSS. More generally, it is shown in [14] that there is a secure instance of XMSS as long as there is any secure signature algorithm. This means that XMSS has minimal security requirements. It also forward secure, i.e. signatures generated before a key compromise remain valid. Instead of Lamport-Diffie one-time signatures, it uses a variant of the more efficient Winternitz scheme [13]. Furthermore, XMSS is very efficient in practice as its implementation on different platforms shows. For details see [14].

The fact that an IETF Internet-draft for hash-based signatures [46] exists demonstrates their readiness for practical application. For their practical use, a major challenge is to deal with the most important difference between hash-based and other signature schemes: statefulness. This refers to the fact that hash-based signatures rely on many one-time key pairs, making it necessary to keep track of key usage. At any time the signing device must know the state of the scheme: which of the one-time signature keys have been used and which have not. If several signing devices are used, it is necessary to synchronize them on a regular basis or to partition the set of signing keys into disjoint subsets: one per device. Key storage demands special care in the case of statefulness, since new attack vectors may surface. Another challenge is the issue of optimal parameter selection, which is not obvious. This problem has been partially addressed in a recent generalization of XMSS [31].

7.2 Code-Based Public-Key Cryptography

In this section we show how to construct public-key encryption and digital signature schemes based on coding theory. The public-key encryption schemes are very efficient except for the large key sizes. The digital signature schemes still require more research.

An important example of a code-based public-key encryption scheme is the McEliece scheme [45] invented in 1978. This scheme is still considered to be secure, even in a quantum world.

To generate a key pair for this scheme, one selects a generator matrix G for a binary $[n, k]$ code $\mathcal{C}$ such that G can be used to efficiently correct t errors for some t much less than the minimum distance of $\mathcal{C}$. Also, a non-singular matrix $S \in \mathbb{F}^{k \times k}$ and a permutation matrix $P \in \mathbb{F}^{n \times n}$ are selected randomly with the uniform distribution. They are used to hide the special generator matrix G by computing the generator matrix $G' = SGP$ of the permuted code $\mathcal{C}'$. Then, the public key of the scheme is (G', t). The secret key consists of S, G and P.

To encrypt a message $m \in \mathbb{F}^k$, one chooses randomly a vector $z \in \mathbb{F}^n$ of weight t. The ciphertext of the message m is $c = mG' + z \in \mathbb{F}^n$.

To decrypt the cipertext c, one proceeds as follows. First, we observe that

$$x = cP^{-1} = (mG' + z)P^{-1} = mSG + zP^{-1}. \tag{6}$$

Since P is a permutation matrix and the weight of z is t, the weight of zP^{-1} is also t. Furthermore, mSG is a codeword in $\mathcal{C}$ since G is a generator matrix of $\mathcal{C}$. This shows that the distance of x from $\mathcal{C}$ is t. Hence, by our assumption, x can be decoded, the result being the codeword

$$y = mSG. \tag{7}$$

Next, m can be calculated by solving the linear system (7). The original McEliece scheme uses binary Goppa codes.

Encryption and decryption in the McEliece scheme can be performed very efficiently [9]. However, the keys are quite large. There are variants of McEliece which deal with the problem of large key sizes, for example the scheme of Sendrier et al. [53] which allows fast hardware implementations [29].

For the McEliece scheme to be applicable in practice, a semantically secure conversion is needed. The idea of Persichetti [56] is going into the right direction.

Code-based signatures still require more research. There is the scheme of Courtois, Finiasz, and Sendrier [36]. In this scheme signing is quite slow and public key sizes are very large. Also, no security reductions are known. There are also signature schemes that follow the Fiat-Shamir paradigm (see [12]) and are based on the Stern identification protocol [70], such as [2,47]. This scheme has security proofs which reduce hard coding problems to the security of the schemes. Still, there are several efficiency issues with these schemes, for example the signature length.

7.3 Lattice-Based Public-Key Cryptography

Lattice-based cryptography is similar to code-based cryptography. The similarity comes from the fact that the knowledge of an in some sense reduced lattice basis allows computing closest vectors while this problem becomes intractable when an unstructured basis is given. This suggests making the reduced basis of a lattice $L \subset \mathbb{R}^n$ for some n the secret key and some other unstructured basis the public key. Encryption would mean to select a lattice vector v as plaintext and to hide it by adding some small error vector e: $c = v + e$. Decryption would be done by solving the closest vector problem with input c. The closest vector is the plaintext v. Likewise, a message d would be signed using a hash function $h : \{0,1\}^* \to \mathbb{R}^n$. The signature of a message d would be the closest vector s to $h(d)$. Verification would be performed by checking that s is a lattice vector that is close to $h(d)$.

Unfortunately, this straightforward approach does not yield secure schemes. It requires substantial modifications. Recent examples of lattice based public-key encryption schemes are [40,69] and of lattice-based signature schemes are [3,22]. As a result, schemes are obtained that do not directly rely on the hardness of lattice problems. Instead, they rely on the *learning with errors problem (LWE)* [63] and the *shortest integer solution problem (SIS)* [1]. In turn, the hardness of these problems is based on the hardness of lattice problems.

Lattice-based public-key cryptography is very promising. On the one hand, the schemes appear to be very efficiently implementable. If schemes are selected that rely on hard problems in *ideal lattices* [42,43] then the required storage space and computing time is very limited, at least asymptotically. On the other hand, many lattice-based schemes have very strong security properties: they allow a worst-to-average case security reduction. This means that an instance of the scheme under consideration is secure as long as the worst case of a large class of lattice problems is intractable. Why is this important? For other schemes such as RSA, code-based, hash-based, and multivariate schemes it can only be shown that an instance of a scheme is secure as long as a related computational problem is hard. So in order to guarantee security it is necessary to select the instance of the scheme in such a way that the corresponding instance of the computational problem is hard to solve. For RSA, it is known how to select hard instances: the RSA modulus is constructed as the product of two big random prime numbers. However, for the other types of schemes, it is not so clear how to construct hard instances of the underlying problem. Worst-to-average circumvents the necessity to generate hard instances.

However, when worst-to-average case reduction is used, the lattice-based schemes loose their efficiency. In order to make them more efficient, reductions to random instances of the LWE or SIS problem can be used. This results in very efficient schemes [22]. Another alternative is the NTRU public-key encryption scheme [30] which has no security proof whatsoever but very good performance.

In addition to the advantages explained in the previous sections, lattice-based cryptography allows for the implementation of many advanced schemes, most notably fully homomorphic encryption [27]. This is not known for the other classes of public-key schemes mentioned in this paper.

7.4 Multivariate Public-Key Cryptography

In this section we explain how public-key schemes based on the hardness of solving systems of nonlinear multivariate equation over finite fields work in principle.

Let $\mathbb{F}$ be a finite field and m, n be two positive integers. One chooses a *central map*, which is a quadratic map $\mathcal{Q} : \mathbb{F}^n \to \mathbb{F}^m$, $x = (x_1, \ldots, x_n) \mapsto (q_1(x), \ldots, q_m(x))$. The map $\mathcal{Q}$ must be easily invertible in the sense that it is easy to find a preimage for every image x under $\mathcal{Q}$. To hide the structure of this central map in the public key one composes it with two affine linear maps $\mathcal{S} : \mathbb{F}^n \to \mathbb{F}^n$ and $\mathcal{T} : \mathbb{F}^m \to \mathbb{F}^m$. The result is the quadratic map $\mathcal{P} = \mathcal{T} \circ \mathcal{Q} \circ \mathcal{S}$ which is the public key of the corresponding public-key schemes. $\mathcal{P}$ is supposed to look like a random system and therefore is assumed to be difficult to invert. The secret key of the scheme consists of $\mathcal{Q}, \mathcal{S}$ and $\mathcal{T}$ and therefore allows to invert the public key.

To sign a document d one uses a hash function $\mathcal{H} : \{0, 1\}^* \to \mathbb{F}^m$ to compute a hash value $h = \mathcal{H}(d)$ of the message. To compute a signature of the document d, the signer computes recursively $x = \mathcal{T}^{-1}(h)$, $y = \mathcal{Q}^{-1}(x)$ and $z = \mathcal{S}^{-1}(y)$. The signature of the document d is $z \in \mathbb{F}^n$. Here, $\mathcal{Q}^{-1}(y)$ means finding a preimage of y under the central map $\mathcal{Q}$.

To verify the authenticity of a signature $z \in \mathbb{F}^n$, the receiver of a message checks if $\mathcal{P}(z) = \mathcal{H}(d)$.

There exists a large variety of practical multivariate signature schemes. The best known of these are UOV [33], Rainbow [19], and pFlash [20]. Additionally, there exist multivariate signature schemes from the HFEv- family, which produce very short signatures (e.g. 120 bit). The most promising scheme in this direction is Gui [61]. Signing and verifying with all of these schemes is very fast, presumably much faster than RSA and ECC [10,16].

In the last years, there have been several attempts to decrease the key size of multivariate signature schemes [58,59]. However, despite of this work, the key sizes of multivariate signature schemes are still much larger than those of classical schemes such as RSA.

To construct a public-key encryption scheme on the upper principle the central map $\mathcal{Q}$ must be injective. In particular, we therefore need $m \geq n$. To encrypt a plaintext $x = (x_1, \ldots, x_n) \in \mathbb{F}^n$, one simply computes $c = \mathcal{P}(x) \in \mathbb{F}^m$. Since the owner of the secret key can invert the central map $\mathcal{Q}$ and knows the two affine linear maps $\mathcal{S}$ and $\mathcal{T}$, she can determine the plaintext by computing $x = \mathcal{S}^{-1} \circ \mathcal{Q}^{-1} \circ \mathcal{T}^{-1}(c)$.

The currently most promising multivariate encryption scheme is the SimpleMatrix (or ABC) encryption scheme [71], which allows very fast en- and decryption. However, decryption failures occur with non-negligible probability. Furthermore, the key sizes of this scheme are quite large.

A major problem of all multivariate public-key schemes is their security, which is somewhat unclear. Many of the proposed multivariate schemes have been broken in the past (e.g. MI [44] and Oil and Vinegar [55]). The above mentioned schemes are all quite young (some less than 10 years), which means that they have not yet been subject to extensive cryptanalysis. Furthermore, there exist no security proofs for multivariate public-key schemes.

However, similarly to the case of code-based cryptography, there exists a provable secure multivariate identification scheme [67]. Via the Fiat-Shamir transform [24] it is possible to extend this scheme to provable secure (yet ineffi-cient) multivariate (ring) signature schemes [60].

8   Conclusion

In this section we evaluate and compare the proposals for post-quantum public-key cryptography that are described in this paper.

Firstly, we compare the required hardness assumptions. From a structural point of view, the general decoding problem, the lattices problems, and the problem of solving multivariate systems of quadratic equations over finite fields are similar. These problems are NP-hard. However, the computational problems that support the security of the post-quantum schemes are in subclasses that are not known to be NP-hard. As for the integer factorization problem, it may happen that algorithms are discovered that solve the relevant problems in poly-nomial time. In this case the corresponding cryptographic systems can no longer be considered to be secure. Therefore, thorough research is required to establish the hardness of these problems. In fact, in order to enable the selection of secure parameters for required security levels, such research must determine quanti-tatively the resources necessary to solve a given instance of the computational problems.

In code-based security, solving the general decoding problem for Goppa codes can be considered to be hard. Detailed studies investigate this hardness in details (see [7,57]). In contrast, structured codes such as quasi-linear codes must be studied in more detail. Lattice-based cryptography uses a multitude of different computational hardness assumptions such as LWE, ring LWE, SIS, ring SIS, αSVP, etc. Therefore, more research is required to establish the hardness of the most relevant of these problems in detail even though there is much research on the general lattice problems such as SVP (e.g. [4,17,41]). In multivariate cryptography, new research is required whenever a new central map is introduced or a sub-problem that allows for smaller keys.

The problem of coming up with a secure hash function appears to be quite different from the problems discussed in the previous section. Firstly, the only relevant security parameter is the hash length while the other problems have many more parameters. Secondly, experience shows that it is not hard to come up with a secure alternative if a cryptographic hash function is broken. Typically, an easy way of enhancing the security of a given hash function is to increase the number of rounds in the insecure hash function at the expense of reducing its efficiency. But also new constructions are possible. Thirdly, assuming that there is a secure hash function is much more basic than the problems from the previous section. For example, all signature schemes require such hash functions if long documents are to be signed.

Next, we compare the post quantum schemes that have been presented in this paper. The most advanced scheme is the hash-based signature scheme XMSS [14]. Furthermore, it provides the strongest security guarantees as it can be shown that there is a secure instance of XMSS as long as there is any secure signature scheme. This is due to the flexibility of XMSS: any secure cryptographic hash function can be used to construct a secure instance of XMSS. These properties support the quantum-resistance of XMSS. If a cryptographic hash function turns out to be vulnerable to quantum attacks — which has never happened so far — an alternative quantum-resistant hash function can be used to make XMSS quantum-resistant again. XMSS is also very efficient and there is even a related standard draft [46]. There are no hash-based public-key encryption schemes.

The fact that a practical and secure post-quantum signature scheme exists is consequential. In order to prepare computing systems for the quantum computer era, a quantum-immune trust anchor is needed for potential updates. XMSS can serve as such a trust anchor. Now is the time to integrate XMSS into standard protocols such as TLS or S/MIME and to develop concepts to deal with its statefulness.

A good alternative for hash-based signature schemes are multivariate signature schemes such as Rainbow [19]. Multivariate schemes offer fast signature generation and verification and produce significantly shorter signatures than RSA. However, the key sizes of multivariate signature schemes are still relatively large. Furthermore, there are no security proofs for the efficient multivariate signature schemes.

As for post-quantum public-key encryption schemes, currently the code-based McEliece scheme appears to be the most reliable choice. McEliece and RSA were proposed roughly at the same time and remain secure since then although there are no formal security proofs for them. The drawback of the McEliece scheme are its large keys. It is therefore not applicable in all contexts, for example, when there are limited computing resources. The usefulness of code-based signature schemes is unclear as they are still much too inefficient.

From a research and development point of view, lattice-based cryptography is very promising. There are very interesting proposals for signature and public-key encryption schemes. In addition, in lattice-based cryptography there are several special-purpose schemes for example for fully homomorphic encryption, blind signatures, ring signatures, and group signatures. Such schemes admit the strongest security proofs: worst-to-average-case reductions. The ring variants promise high efficiency as their time and space requirements are quasi-linear in the security parameter. However, lattice-based schemes still require more research before becoming practical. The hardness of the underlying problems, in particular of the relevant ideal-lattice problems, requires more research. There is still a gap between security and efficiency. The efficient versions do not yet take advantage of the strong reduction proofs. In many cases, reduction proofs would profit from becoming tighter.

How far is post-quantum cryptography? There are many promising proposals some of which are rather close to becoming practical. In view of the importance of public-key cryptography explained in Sect. 3, a joint effort is necessary to make the promising proposals ready for practice. Such an effort provides quantitative predictions of the hardness of the relevant problems and tight security proofs leading to trustworthy parameters. It also provides optimized implementations and standards.

References

1. Ajtai, M.: Generating hard instances of lattice problems (extended abstract). In: Proceedings of the Twenty-Eighth Annual ACM Symposium on Theory of Computing, STOC 1996, pp. 99–108. ACM, New York (1996)
2. El Yousfi Alaoui, S.M., Cayrel, P.-L., Mohammed, M.: Improved identity-based identification and signature schemes using Quasi-dyadic Goppa codes. In: Kim, T., Adeli, H., Robles, R.J., Balitanas, M. (eds.) ISA 2011. CCIS, vol. 200, pp. 146–155. Springer, Heidelberg (2011)
3. Bai, S., Galbraith, S.D.: An improved compression technique for signatures based on learning with errors. In: Benaloh, J. (ed.) CT-RSA 2014. LNCS, vol. 8366, pp. 28–47. Springer, Heidelberg (2014)
4. Bai, S., Galbraith, S.D.: Lattice decoding attacks on binary LWE. In: Susilo, W., Mu, Y. (eds.) ACISP 2014. LNCS, vol. 8544, pp. 322–337. Springer, Heidelberg (2014)
5. Bennett, C.H., Bernstein, E., Brassard, G., Vazirani, U.: Strengths and weaknesses of quantum computing. SIAM J. Comput. **26**(5), 1510–1523 (1997)
6. Bernstein, D.J., Buchmann, J., Dahmen, E. (eds.): Post-Quantum Cryptography. Springer, Heidelberg (2008)
7. Bernstein, D.J., Lange, T., Peters, C., Schwabe, P.: Faster 2-regular information-set decoding. In: Chee, Y.M., Guo, Z., Ling, S., Shao, F., Tang, Y., Wang, H., Xing, C. (eds.) IWCC 2011. LNCS, vol. 6639, pp. 81–98. Springer, Heidelberg (2011)
8. Bertoni, G., Daemen, J., Peeters, M., Assche, G.V.: The KECCAK reference, January 2011. http://keccak.noekeon.org/
9. Biswas, B., Sendrier, N.: McEliece cryptosystem implementation: theory and practice. In: Buchmann, J., Ding, J. (eds.) PQCrypto 2008. LNCS, vol. 5299, pp. 47–62. Springer, Heidelberg (2008)
10. Bogdanov, A., Eisenbarth, T., Rupp, A., Wolf, C.: Time-area optimized public-key engines: MQ-cryptosystems as replacement for elliptic curves? In: Oswald, E., Rohatgi, P. (eds.) CHES 2008. LNCS, vol. 5154, pp. 45–61. Springer, Heidelberg (2008)
11. Brassard, G., Hoyer, P., Tapp, A.: Quantum algorithm for the collision problem. arXiv preprint quant-ph/9705002 (1997)
12. Buchmann, J.: Introduction to Cryptography. Springer, Heidelberg (2004)
13. Buchmann, J., Dahmen, E., Ereth, S., Hülsing, A., Rückert, M.: On the security of the Winternitz one-time signature scheme. In: Nitaj, A., Pointcheval, D. (eds.) AFRICACRYPT 2011. LNCS, vol. 6737, pp. 363–378. Springer, Heidelberg (2011)

14. Buchmann, J., Dahmen, E., Hülsing, A.: XMSS - a practical forward secure signature scheme based on minimal security assumptions. In: Yang, B.-Y. (ed.) PQCrypto 2011. LNCS, vol. 7071, pp. 117–129. Springer, Heidelberg (2011)

15. Buhler, J.P., Lenstra Jr., H.W., Pomerance, C.: Factoring integers with the number field sieve. In: The Development of the Number Field Sieve, pp. 50–94. Springer, Heidelberg (1993)

16. Chen, A.I.-T., Chen, M.-S., Chen, T.-R., Cheng, C.-M., Ding, J., Kuo, E.L.-H., Lee, F.Y.-S., Yang, B.-Y.: SSE implementation of multivariate PKCs on modern x86 CPUs. In: Clavier, C., Gaj, K. (eds.) CHES 2009. LNCS, vol. 5747, pp. 33–48. Springer, Heidelberg (2009)

17. Chen, Y., Nguyen, P.Q.: BKZ 2.0: better lattice security estimates. In: Lee, D.H., Wang, X. (eds.) ASIACRYPT 2011. LNCS, vol. 7073, pp. 1–20. Springer, Heidelberg (2011)

18. Diffie, W., Hellman, M.E.: New directions in cryptography. IEEE Trans. Inf. Theory $22(6)$, 644–654 (1976)

19. Ding, J., Schmidt, D.: Rainbow, a new multivariable polynomial signature scheme. In: Ioannidis, J., Keromytis, A.D., Yung, M. (eds.) ACNS 2005. LNCS, vol. 3531, pp. 164–175. Springer, Heidelberg (2005)

20. Ding, J., Yang, B.-Y., Dubois, V., Cheng, C.-M., Chen, O.: Breaking the symmetry: a way to resist the new differential attack (2007). http://eprint.iacr.org/2007/366

21. Dobbertin, H., Bosselaers, A., Preneel, B.: RIPEMD-160: a strengthened version of RIPEMD. In: Gollmann, D. (ed.) FSE 1996. LNCS, vol. 1039, pp. 71–82. Springer, Heidelberg (1996)

22. Ducas, L., Durmus, A., Lepoint, T., Lyubashevsky, V.: Lattice signatures and bimodal gaussians. In: Canetti, R., Garay, J.A. (eds.) CRYPTO 2013, Part I. LNCS, vol. 8042, pp. 40–56. Springer, Heidelberg (2013)

23. Feynman, R.: Simulating physics with computers. Int. J. Theor. Phys. $21(6–7)$, 467–488 (1982)

24. Fiat, A., Shamir, A.: How to prove yourself: practical solutions to identification and signature problems. In: Odlyzko, A.M. (ed.) CRYPTO 1986. LNCS, vol. 263, pp. 186–194. Springer, Heidelberg (1987)

25. El Gamal, T.: A public key cryptosystem and a signature scheme based on discrete logarithms. In: Blakely, G.R., Chaum, D. (eds.) CRYPTO 1984. LNCS, vol. 196, pp. 10–18. Springer, Heidelberg (1985)

26. Garey, M.R., Johnson, D.S.: Computers and Intractability: A Guide to the Theory of NP-Completeness. W.H. Freeman, New York (1979)

27. Gentry, C.: Fully homomorphic encryption using ideal lattices. In: Proceedings of the Forty-First Annual ACM Symposium on Theory of Computing, STOC 2009, pp. 169–178. ACM, New York (2009)

28. Grover, L.K.: A fast quantum mechanical algorithm for database search. In: Miller, G.L. (ed.) Proceedings of the Twenty-Eighth Annual ACM Symposium on the Theory of Computing, pp. 212–219. ACM (1996)

29. Heyse, S., von Maurich, I., Güneysu, T.: Smaller keys for code-based cryptography: QC-MDPC McEliece implementations on embedded devices. In: Bertoni, G., Coron, J.-S. (eds.) CHES 2013. LNCS, vol. 8086, pp. 273–292. Springer, Heidelberg (2013)

30. Hoffstein, J., Pipher, J., Silverman, J.H.: NTRU: a ring-based public key cryptosystem. In: Buhler, J.P. (ed.) ANTS 1998. LNCS, vol. 1423, pp. 267–288. Springer, Heidelberg (1998)

31. Hülsing, A., Rausch, L., Buchmann, J.: Optimal parameters for XMSS^{MT}. In: Cuzzocrea, A., Kittl, C., Simos, D.E., Weippl, E., Xu, L. (eds.) CD-ARES Workshops 2013. LNCS, vol. 8128, pp. 194–208. Springer, Heidelberg (2013)
32. Joux, A.: A new index calculus algorithm with complexity l (1/4+ o (1)) in very small characteristic. IACR Cryptology ePrint Archive 2013:95 (2013)
33. Kipnis, A., Patarin, J., Goubin, L.: Unbalanced oil and vinegar signature schemes. In: Stern, J. (ed.) EUROCRYPT 1999. LNCS, vol. 1592, pp. 206–222. Springer, Heidelberg (1999)
34. Koblitz, N.: Elliptic curve cryptosystems. Math. Comput. **48**(177), 203–209 (1987)
35. Lamport, L.: Constructing Digital Signatures from a One Way Function. Technical report, SRI International Computer Science Laboratory (1979). http://research. microsoft.com/en-us/um/people/lamport/pubs/dig-sig.pdf
36. Landais, G., Sendrier, N.: Implementing CFS. In: Galbraith, S., Nandi, M. (eds.) INDOCRYPT 2012. LNCS, vol. 7668, pp. 474–488. Springer, Heidelberg (2012)
37. Lenstra, A., Lenstra Jr., H.W., Lovász, L.: Factoring polynomials with rational coefficients. Math. Ann. **261**(4), 515–534 (1982)
38. Lenstra, A.K.: Key lengths. Technical report. Wiley (2006)
39. Lenstra, A.K., Lenstra Jr., H.W., Manasse, M.S., Pollard, J.M.: The number field sieve. In: Ortiz, H. (ed.) Proceedings of the 22nd Annual ACM Symposium on Theory of Computing, Baltimore, Maryland, USA, 13–17 May, pp. 564–572. ACM (1990)
40. Lindner, R., Peikert, C.: Better key sizes (and attacks) for LWE-based encryption. In: Kiayias, A. (ed.) CT-RSA 2011. LNCS, vol. 6558, pp. 319–339. Springer, Heidelberg (2011)
41. Liu, M., Nguyen, P.Q.: Solving BDD by enumeration: an update. In: Dawson, E. (ed.) CT-RSA 2013. LNCS, vol. 7779, pp. 293–309. Springer, Heidelberg (2013)
42. Lyubashevsky, V., Micciancio, D.: Generalized compact knapsacks are collision resistant. In: Bugliesi, M., Preneel, B., Sassone, V., Wegener, I. (eds.) ICALP 2006. LNCS, vol. 4052, pp. 144–155. Springer, Heidelberg (2006)
43. Lyubashevsky, V., Peikert, C., Regev, O.: On ideal lattices and learning with errors over rings. In: Gilbert, H. (ed.) EUROCRYPT 2010. LNCS, vol. 6110, pp. 1–23. Springer, Heidelberg (2010)
44. Matsumoto, T., Imai, H.: Public quadratic polynomial-tuples for efficient signature-verification and message-encryption. In: Günther, C.G. (ed.) EUROCRYPT 1988. LNCS, vol. 330, pp. 419–453. Springer, Heidelberg (1988)
45. McEliece, R.J.: A public-key cryptosystem based on algebraic coding theory. Deep Space Network Progress Report **44**, 114–116 (1978)
46. McGrew, D., Curcio, M.: Hash-Based Signatures. Internet Engineering Task Force (2014) (Internet-Draft)
47. Melchor, C.A., Cayrel, P., Gaborit, P., Laguillaumie, F.: A new efficient threshold ring signature scheme based on coding theory. IEEE Trans. Inf. Theory **57**(7), 4833–4842 (2011)
48. Menezes, A.J., Van Oorschot, P.C., Vanstone, S.A.: Handbook of Applied Cryptography. CRC Press, Boca Raton (2010)
49. Merkle, R.C.: Secrecy, authentication and public key systems. Ph.D. thesis, Stanford University (1979)
50. Merkle, R.C.: A certified digital signature. In: Brassard, G. (ed.) CRYPTO 1989. LNCS, vol. 435, pp. 218–238. Springer, Heidelberg (1990)
51. Micciancio, D.: The hardness of the closest vector problem with preprocessing. IEEE Trans. Inf. Theory **47**(3), 1212–1215 (2001)

52. Miller, V.S.: Use of elliptic curves in cryptography. In: Williams, H.C. (ed.) CRYPTO 1985. LNCS, vol. 218, pp. 417–426. Springer, Heidelberg (1986)
53. Misoczki, R., Tillich, J., Sendrier, N., Barreto, P.S.L.M.: MDPC-McEliece: new McEliece variants from moderate density parity-check codes. In: Proceedings of ISIT, pp. 2069–2073. IEEE (2013)
54. Morrison, M.A., Brillhart, J.: A method of factoring and the factorization of F7. Math. Comput. **29**(129), 183–205 (1975)
55. Patarin, J.: The oil and vinegar signature scheme. Dagstuhl Workshop on Cryptography, September 1997
56. Persichetti, E.: Secure and anonymous hybrid encryption from coding theory. In: Gaborit, P. (ed.) PQCrypto 2013. LNCS, vol. 7932, pp. 174–187. Springer, Heidelberg (2013)
57. Peters, C.: Information-set decoding for linear codes over $\mathbf{F}_q$. In: Sendrier, N. (ed.) PQCrypto 2010. LNCS, vol. 6061, pp. 81–94. Springer, Heidelberg (2010)
58. Petzoldt, A., Bulygin, S., Buchmann, J.: CyclicRainbow – a multivariate signature scheme with a partially cyclic public key. In: Gong, G., Gupta, K.C. (eds.) INDOCRYPT 2010. LNCS, vol. 6498, pp. 33–48. Springer, Heidelberg (2010)
59. Petzoldt, A., Bulygin, S., Buchmann, J.: Linear recurring sequences for the UOV key generation. In: Catalano, D., Fazio, N., Gennaro, R., Nicolosi, A. (eds.) PKC 2011. LNCS, vol. 6571, pp. 335–350. Springer, Heidelberg (2011)
60. Petzoldt, A., Bulygin, S., Buchmann, J.: A multivariate threshold ring signature scheme. In: AAECC (2012)
61. Petzoldt, A., Chen, M.-S., Yang, B.-Y., Tao, C., Ding, J.: Design principles for HFEv- based multivariate signature schemes. In: Iwata, T., Cheon, J.H. (eds.) ASIACRYPT 2015, Part I. LNCS, vol. 9452, pp. 311–334. Springer, Heidelberg (2015). doi:10.1007/978-3-662-48797-6_14
62. Pomerance, C.: The quadratic sieve factoring algorithm. In: Beth, T., Cot, N., Ingemarsson, I. (eds.) EUROCRYPT 1984. LNCS, vol. 209, pp. 169–182. Springer, Heidelberg (1985)
63. Regev, O.: On lattices, learning with errors, random linear codes, and cryptography. In: Proceedings of the Thirty-Seventh Annual ACM Symposium on Theory of Computing, STOC 2005, pp. 84–93. ACM, New York (2005)
64. Rivest, R.L., Shamir, A., Adleman, L.M.: A method for obtaining digital signatures and public-key cryptosystems. Commun. ACM **21**(2), 120–126 (1978)
65. Rogaway, P., Shrimpton, T.: Cryptographic hash-function basics: definitions, implications, and separations for preimage resistance, second-preimage resistance, and collision resistance. In: Roy, B., Meier, W. (eds.) FSE 2004. LNCS, vol. 3017, pp. 371–388. Springer, Heidelberg (2004)
66. Saeedi, K., Simmons, S., Salvail, J.Z., Dluhy, P., Riemann, H., Abrosimov, N.V., Becker, P., Pohl, H.-J., Morton, J.J.L., Thewalt, M.L.W.: Room-temperature quantum bit storage exceeding 39 minutes using ionized donors in silicon-28. Science **342**(6160), 830–833 (2013)
67. Sakumoto, K., Shirai, T., Hiwatari, H.: Public-key identification schemes based on multivariate quadratic polynomials. In: Rogaway, P. (ed.) CRYPTO 2011. LNCS, vol. 6841, pp. 706–723. Springer, Heidelberg (2011)
68. Shor, P.W.: Polynomial-time algorithms for prime factorization and discrete logarithms on a quantum computer. SIAM J. Comput. **26**(5), 1484–1509 (1997)
69. Stehlé, D., Steinfeld, R.: Making NTRU as secure as worst-case problems over ideal lattices. In: Paterson, K.G. (ed.) EUROCRYPT 2011. LNCS, vol. 6632, pp. 27–47. Springer, Heidelberg (2011)

70. Stern, J.: A new identification scheme based on syndrome decoding. In: Stinson, D.R. (ed.) CRYPTO 1993. LNCS, vol. 773, pp. 13–21. Springer, Heidelberg (1994)
71. Tao, C., Diene, A., Tang, S., Ding, J.: Simple matrix scheme for encryption. In: Gaborit, P. (ed.) PQCrypto 2013. LNCS, vol. 7932, pp. 231–242. Springer, Heidelberg (2013)
72. Wang, X., Yu, H.: How to break MD5 and other hash functions. In: Cramer, R. (ed.) EUROCRYPT 2005. LNCS, vol. 3494, pp. 19–35. Springer, Heidelberg (2005)
73. Wikipedia: Timeline of quantum computing – wikipedia, the free encyclopedia (2014). http://en.wikipedia.org/w/index.php?title=Timeline_of_quantum_computing&oldid=613219069. (Accessed 25 September 2014)

What is the Future of Cryptography?

Yvo Desmedt[1,2](✉)

[1] Department of Computer Science,
The University of Texas at Dallas, Richardson, USA
Yvo.Desmedt@utdallas.edu
[2] Department of Computer Science, University College London, London, UK

Abstract. To predict the future one should study the past. Kahn has documented the 2000 years of history of cryptography. However, have cryptographers learned their lesson? To answer this question we will take an optimistic as well as pessimistic viewpoint.

1 Introduction

Predicting the future is always very difficult. Indeed, who in 1930 could have predicted that mechanical computers, such as mechanical sorting machines, would be obsolete 50 years later. Moreover, reality has shown that science fiction writers often wrongly estimate the time to develop certain technologies. Another example can be found in the 1960's TV science fiction series "Star Trek." Mobile phones and laptops should have been a 23rd century technology! To avoid such pitfalls we will try to answer the question "What is the future of cryptography" from different angles. Before we can start to answer this question, we need to state what we mean by cryptography.

As documented by Kahn [29], for centuries the goal of cryptography was to protect the *privacy when communicating*. In the 1970's Simmons suggested Gilbert, MacWilliams and Sloane (see [24]) to study the problem of *authenticity*. This new security goal was quickly followed by the first work [15] on *non-repudiation*, provided when using digital signatures.

Although cryptography is often associated with communication security, this characterization is incorrect. First of all communication security has to deal with many issues cryptography usually[1] ignores. The goal of availability, in the presence of an adversary, is an important topic and this requires, e.g., connectivity and anti-jamming techniques when the communication technology being used is point-to-point or wireless respectively. Moreover, since 1978 cryptography is also interested in the topic of storage security [6,49]. As pointed out by Shamir [49]

A part of this text is based on a presentation given by the author at Catacrypt 2014. Some parts of text are copies of the unpublished slides. The author thanks Jean-Jacques Quisquater for inviting him for the Catacrypt presentation.

[1] The work by Dolev-Dwork-Waarts-Yung [16] has attracted some rather limited interest in the topic of combining the requirements of availability with these of privacy.

P.Y.A. Ryan et al. (Eds.): Kahn Festschrift, LNCS 9100, pp. 109–122, 2016.
DOI: 10.1007/978-3-662-49301-4_7

the problem of secret sharing goes back to the mechanical world[2]. Besides the problem of secure storage, since Yao's work on the millionaire's problem and his work on secure multi-party computation [54,55], cryptographers also work on privacy issues involved in computations, in particular when multiple parties are involved. To give a description of what modern cryptography is, we use the "definition" given in [13]

> Cryptography is the science and study of the (abstract) security aspects of data against a malicious adversary. Cryptographic systems (i.e., schemes and protocols) are being and have been developed to protect some of these security aspects of the data. Cryptanalysis is the study of methods used to break such cryptosystems.

Above definition contains several aspects worth discussing in further details. We will start by clarifying what "security aspect" means. Moreover, in above, cryptography is defined as a science. We wonder whether this characterization is premature and if so, what will be needed to make it a science in the future (see Sect. 4.2). When considering the extensive research that is happening in cryptography, we could conclude that the future of cryptography is bright. However, one could argue that cryptography may have achieved its peak. Whether the relevance of cryptography will increase or weaken is discussed in Sect. 4.8. Finally, we conclude in Sect. 5.

2   The Evolution of Security Goals

Anonymity, authenticity, availability, non-repudiation, privacy, etc., can be regarded as security goals, or security aspects of data. As mentioned in the introduction, in the beginning cryptography was only interested in privacy (sometimes called confidentiality and/or secrecy). We have seen that since 1974, the security goals cryptography wants to protect have evolved. This brings several questions, which we now pose and analyze. Note that this discussion is heavily influenced by Meadows [40][3] whose work was in the context of computer security.

2.1   Rights and Duties Induce Security Goals

Meadows' 1993 understanding of cyber security can be summarized as following.

> The goal of cyber security is to protect *the rights and expectations associated with data* and to protect the processes involved in the data.

---

[2] Shamir cites Liu's 1968 book on combinatorics. It is not clear from Liu's book [35, pp. 8–9] the source of the problem of mechanical secret sharing. It might be an interesting problem for historians to find out more about the history of mechanical secret sharing. In this context, note that Simmons in one of his lectures mentioned that Ingemarsson had told him about mechanical safes in which two keys were needed to be combined to open the lock.

[3] Some of the material cited was mentioned during the presentation, but did not appear in the text.

Meadows [40] also stated that:

- rights and duties induce security goals,
- rights are country and time depended, and differ for corporations, individuals, and governments.

We now briefly survey some of the expectations and rights associated to data today.

2.2   Areas of Research

To each of the expectations and rights often corresponds a security goal. Examples worth mentioning include: anonymity, authenticity, authorized wiretapping, availability, censorship, confidentiality, copyright, delegation, freedom of speech, identification, integrity, privacy, revocation, timestamping, traceability, and witnessing. To achieve these security goals technical means have been developed. These technical means make assumptions on the availability of certain techniques. Public key encryption and conventional encryption are nothing more than two different techniques, often combined, to achieve privacy of communication.

Research in cryptography has developed techniques that enable privacy at such a level one would never have suspected to be possible. Indeed, the work on Secure Multiparty Computation allows, for example, a borrower and a bank to decide jointly whether the borrower is qualified for a loan from the bank without the need for the borrower to reveal in the open (i.e., in plaintext) to the bank the assets of the borrower. Moreover, the bank does not have to reveal their criteria. Data usually required by the bank would be provided encrypted and never be decrypted. At the end the only information that the bank will learn is whether the borrower qualifies or not.

3   An Optimistic Viewpoint

In the last decades we have seen an explosion of research in cryptography, both in the number of papers and in the number of venues that accept papers in the area. So, one may conclude that the area is doing well and that funding agencies regard it as being quite important.

Moreover, over the last decades, we find that there are quite many cryptographers who believe that our field has a good foundation. Indeed, some say:

Statement 1: we understand factoring well and we recommend RSA keys of 2048-4096 bits,

Statement 2: Shamir has stated AES will be the last block cipher (according to Bart Preneel)

Statement 3: having moved from heuristic security to "proven secure" security, we understand cryptography better than ever!

Statement 4: practical security is well understood when using the "random oracle model,"

Statement 5: the Snowden revelations have encouraged Google and others to switch to http*s* instead of http.

Statement 6: the use of secure multiparty computation solves the problem of dealing with untrusted platforms (assuming at most t are untrustworthy).

Statement 7: fully homomorphic encryption and attribute based cryptography, may one day play a big role to help achieve computer security.

We will look critically at the aforementioned statements in Sect. 4.

4   A Critical Look

To make progress, it turns out, that a critical look often enables a better under-standing of strengths and weaknesses. The goal of this section is to consider some of the aforementioned statements and consider them from a different perspective.

We start by considering a historic viewpoint. Kahn [29] teaches us that during World War II, both Japan and Nazi Germany were very confident about the strength of the ciphers they were using. So, one could wonder whether today's optimistic viewpoint has a good foundation and/or is scientifically justifiable.

4.1   Lack of Cryptanalytic Efforts

When we look at Statements 1 and 2, we wonder whether these optimistic view-points are just a consequence of a self fulfilling prophecy. Indeed, at the first Crypto conferences we had 33–48 % of the papers on cryptanalysis. At Crypto 2012 it was only 6 %.

Related to Statement 1 on RSA [46], a problem we have is that essentially no new algorithms — at least ignoring quantum computers — have been developed since 1990 on factoring (see [31]). Imagine that today we would still be using 25 year old hardware to do our computation, but that is in essence, from an algorithmic viewpoint, what we do when factoring numbers!

Related to AES [10], the argument many have made is that it was very carefully designed, and so, there is nothing to worry about. Such an attitude can not be justified when studying the history of cryptanalysis. From Kahn [29] we learn that the longest a cryptosystem withstood cryptanalysis was for roughly 300 years. None of our modern cryptosystems, such as AES, have been around for so long.

The research on the security of conventional cryptography faces another prob-lem. Even though most of our data is transmitted using conventional cryptosys-tems, standards have primarily been developed based on work only presented at workshops, such as FSE, instead of at the flagship conferences such as Asi-acrypt, Crypto and Eurocrypt. Moreover, the emphasis is on developing systems that can only withstand some specific attacks, such as "linear" and "differential cryptanalysis."

From the Snowden leaks it seems NSA is using hacking techniques. Some have concluded that NSA today is unable to break most modern cryptosystems. Unfortunately this conclusion could be wrong for at least two reasons. First, the lawyers at the Guardian stopped the editor of publishing a lot of documents from the Snowden leaks and only a very small fraction has been published [43]. Secondly, NSA might have protected better what algorithms they can break and the algorithms they use, and so Snowden might have failed to access that information. From Kahn and later also Bamford [4] we learn about the efforts NSA has made to hire graduates with PhD degrees in mathematics. As speculated by Quisquater at Catacrypt, NSA might have developed mathematics that has not yet been reinvented in the open domain. Since NSA also is involved in breaking secret military algorithms, it sees many more cryptosystems than the typical academic. Finally: who in academia will "waste" years trying to break some cryptosystem? At NSA such an effort might be of national importance! So, one should not underestimate the understanding of NSA of cryptanalysis.

4.2   Learning from Other Disciplines

We should realize that cryptography as a science is in its infancy. The history of science teaches us that other disciplines were first in a pre-scientific stage. Indeed:

- alchemists believed they would succeed in transforming lead into gold. Newton's work involved a lot of research on alchemy. It took until Mendeleev before we had chemistry.
- astrologists believed they could predict the future by looking at the movement of the stars. Wikipedia even states that:

> Kepler's primary obligation as imperial mathematician was to provide astrological advice to the emperor [Rudolph II].

Today astrology has fallen into disbelief (at least for scientists) and has been replaced by astronomy.

Modern cryptographers believe that the gap between encryption (signing, etc.) and cryptanalysis is superpolynomial (in the security parameter), but we have no proof! So, one could wonder whether cryptology should, one day, be replaced by "cryptonomy"[4].

It is interesting to observe that Gisin [25] recently referred to conditionally secure cryptography as "Belief Based Cryptography."

4.3   Can We Trust Implementations?

For cryptography to be useful, it must be implemented. But without secure implementations, the use of cryptography might not achieve the promised result.

---

[4] "Nomy" stands for "A system of laws governing or a body of knowledge about a specified field.".

We start with giving an historic example. In their 1979 survey paper Diffie-Hellman [15] stated that one of the first electronic implementation of the one-time-pad suffered from a side channel attack. In electronics a "1" corresponds to a voltage between two thresholds and the same is true for a "0." Although the logic in the aforementioned implementation worked correctly, from a logical viewpoint, the voltage of the signal leaked the plaintext. Although some countries, such as India [51] have switched to typewriters for their most secure data, one should not forget that mechanical cryptographic devices have side channels too. Indeed, such machines make noise. A lot of research today is focusing on avoiding such side-channels, however, side-channels are not the only implementation problem, as we now discuss.

The software security we find on many platforms is problematic to say the least. Insecure computers (e.g. laptops and smart phones) could make even the best security on the communication level insignificant [48]. The saying of Spafford, professor at Purdue University, USA, seems to sum up the situation nicely [32],

"Using encryption on the Internet is the equivalent of arranging an armored car to deliver credit card information from someone living in a cardboard box to someone living on a park bench."

Although a lot of e-commerce takes place using the web, browsers are very vulnerable. In the context of both e-voting [19] and internet banking [2] the author co-authored work showing how to bypass cryptographic protection. Although a lot of research is taking place on side channels, very little is happening on guaranteeing that cryptographic security cannot be bypassed on such applications as the web, in particular when the operating system has been hacked.

In Statement 6 we mentioned that secure multiparty computation has been suggested as a solution to deal with untrusted platforms. Independently Yung [57] and the author in co-authored work on e-voting [11] (see also [17]) realized that this statement is incorrect. The author was inspired by something that has already been realized in the reliability community for a long time. It goes as follows. When servers are replicated (without privacy concerns), using, e.g., different platforms manufactured by different companies in different countries on which we run software, ideally based on different algorithms programmed by different programmers, at the end one still needs an electronic vote, to decide, when having $2t + 1$ outputs, what the majority outcome is (assuming at most t platforms are in error). The hardware/software used for this voting has to be 100 % reliable! Otherwise, reliability fails.

Yung [57] proposed as a solution that each country develops their own trusted Lagrange interpolation hardware (which needs to be replaced by a trusted Reed-Solomon decoder when dealing with malicious servers when using outsourcing). The solution to rely on human computation, proposed in the context of voting [11] (see also [17]) allows to deal with countries that cannot develop such hardware or in situations one does not trust the vendor.

4.4 The Bigger Picture

The recent work on fully homomorphic encryption [23] has been received extremely enthusiastically. It is regarded by many as the best solution to deal with privacy when using untrusted servers (see Statement 7). Unfortunately, this is only a part of the total picture, as we now discuss.

Users and customers have forgotten that companies often disappear, e.g. are bought up. Indeed, DEC and Sun, that were the 2nd and 3rd largest computer corporations in the 1980's, no longer exist! The use of a single cloud provider should therefore be questioned. Alternatives, as secure multiparty computation, might be better in including availability, business continuity, reliability as design criteria.

In general, we should try to look at the bigger picture and see what security requirements we need. Earlier on we mentioned that these requirements evolve and so, the bigger picture may not always be easy to specify.

4.5 Wrong Proofs

Koblitz and Menezes in [30] gave a very negative picture of Proven Security.

We regard that during the course of the several decades of research on cryptography, proven security can be viewed as one of the biggest scientific successes of cryptography. Shannon is regarded as the first to have proven a cryptosystem secure by proving that the one-time-pad can provide privacy against a passive adversary [50]. This proof has probably been checked thousands of times and is actually a nice homework in an undergraduate course on Discrete Mathematics for Computer Scientists. The fact that no error has been found in Shannon's proof demonstrates that security proofs are possible.

Many decades after Shannon's security proof, the concept was extended to a *computational* (conditional) setting by Rabin in 1979 [44], in a rejected paper. Note that Rabin's paper lacked a good security model (or definition). A chosen text attacks broke Rabin's scheme. Only after formal definitions were introduced by Goldwasser-Micali in 1982 did the area start to flourish [26].

A criticism sometimes expressed is that Shannon's proof was in the context of unconditional security and that many other proofs are not. Two issues need to be addressed to answer such a criticism:

– *If* it turns out that none of the conditional assumptions are scientifically valid, *then* only unconditionally security will remain. This means that care is needed with Statement 3.
– As long as no major break has been made on proving some of these conditional assumptions to be correct, the use of security proofs assuming unproven assumptions is the most scientific approach to cryptographic security, at least from an abstract viewpoint.

The fact that the cryptographic community has published incorrect security proofs can *not* be used as an argument that they are useless. However, the community should address this issue.

4.6   Research Versus Deployment

As the author already pointed out in 2005, we have a growing gap between theory and practice in information security, in particular in cryptography. We only briefly survey some of the points made by the author then. The 2005 paper mentions that:

> The cryptographic applications a typical user comes in contact with are SSH (or VPN) and SSL. Very few other cryptographic protocols, schemes are implemented and widely deployed. There are several reasons for this. First of all, the road from a great idea to a successful implementations is a bumpy one. Theoreticians tend not to be aware of this. One needs to carefully match theory with needs. Often standards and prototypes are developed. To become a successful product issues as user-friendliness and marketing are important.

The author also pointed out that:

> Although Usenix is interested in implementations, it does not focus on software which is commercially deployable.

For more details and a general discussion about gaps between theory and practice in information security, their potential impacts, and corrective measures, consult [14].

There are many examples where cryptography should have been deployed, where it is not. The use of authentication in such settings as SCADA was already recommended in 1983 [12]. Many politicians are confusing the cryptographic protection of authenticity with the use of encryption. Out of fear that deploying authentication techniques (without privacy) will promote encryption, we are in a situation today that communication between a control tower and an airplane is not authenticated.

4.7   Applications with Security Flaws or Broken Remain in Use

Although it was already pointed out in 1997 [45] (see also [1,8]) that the currently used PKI is very vulnerable to hacking, and although its feasibility was demonstrated with the attack against DigiNotar [18,27], the PKI system used on the WWW has not been improved!

Another example is Tor[5], which is still being promoted although several very serious security problems have now been identified. In this paper, we only mention that Egerstad was able to obtain the log-in and password information of about 1000 officials of foreign embassies, by being a Tor exit node [52].

Many more examples can be given such as the use of WEP on wireless networks.

Updating software and removing an application as WEP, installed on billions of machines is far from trivial. However, if never done, then the same vulnerability can be exploited by others. It shows the need to ensure that original design

---

[5] https://www.torproject.org/.

has been done very carefully, with keys long enough to deal with future progress on cryptanalysis.

4.8   Will Cryptography Become Irrelevant?

What one might regard as the biggest threat to cryptography, is that the new generation of young people has a very different viewpoint about privacy. We briefly discuss this viewpoint and its different dimensions that correspond to this viewpoint.

One can wonder what the meaning of privacy is in a world in which users of Facebook are revealing on their Facebook profile such information as that they are going out for the night. Unfortunately, some users find out the cost of not understanding the importance of privacy. Indeed, a woman in Indiana (US) who posted exactly this information, was robbed by a Facebook friend [42].

Although stories on such robberies are widely disseminated in the media, users are still sharing potentially self harming data. There are many examples of information people should regard as private and protect as much as possible. Indeed, one such an example is religious belief, as Alexander found out in Malaysia after being imprisoned expressing his atheist views on Facebook [38].

To have an understanding of the pervasive nature of today's web services that leak personal information and personal thoughts, consider the fact that over 900 million users are sharing various aspects of their personal and professional lives on Facebook every month [20]. Almost 230 million users are exposing some of their spontaneous thoughts as tweets on Twitter [53], 280,000 meetings of like minded people are arranged by 9 million users of Meetup [41], 4 billion videos are watched on YouTube on a daily average [56], 80 million users are flicking through pictures uploaded by 51 million registered users of Flickr [21], around 15 million users have shared their 1.5 billion locations using Foursquare [22], over 90 million users can hangout on Google+ [5], and almost 150 million users are sharing their resumes and being connected to their professional contacts on LinkedIn [33].

As another example, we consider the decision of University College London (UCL) to host its students' and staffs' email on the Microsoft system. Considering the fact that the majority of users do not use encryption for their emails and users' emails normally contain personal and professional content, UCL is trusting Microsoft with such content. So, if our threat model now considers Microsoft as a potential adversary then Microsoft could mine a lot of information about a user. It can find the social network of a user, the strength of their ties with particular correspondents, the level, etc. For a researcher working at UCL's Institute of Archeology, the impact of UCL's decision might be minimal. However, people at the Department of Computer Science might have contracts with a competitor of Microsoft, lets say HP. Imagine UCL jointly with HP applying for a patent, while Microsoft is independently applying for a similar patent. Obviously, one will be suspicious. Unfortunately non-encrypted email is the de-facto standard in reality, so cryptography does not help with such a problem.

While the cloud is regarded by many users and managers as the solution for inexpensive data storage and computing, the lack of proper computer security further endangers privacy. Indeed, cloud servers might be compromised by a third party or there may be a flaw in the design. Personal data of millions of users has been compromised due to regular security breaches of reputable organizations, this includes hacks of Gmail accounts, of Sony's database, public sharing of LinkedIn passwords, and of IMF's computers (see e.g., [28,34,39,47]).

To make matters worse, several of the cloud based web services encourage users to provide them with more and more personal data. This includes their promotion to save users' data on servers like Microsoft's SkyDrive[6], Apple's iCloud[7], or Google's Drive[8]. These drives on the cloud are supposed to be kept private and the data will be shared only with the owner's consent, except when required for advertisements and other uses by the service provider. Similarly, some services encourage users to share their personal data with their friends, for example, in the "About" section of personal information, Google+ encourages its user to provide the names of cities the user lived in and other names. For the potential negative impact of this sharing and other examples, consult [36].

As is well known, search engines are a potential threat to the privacy of the users. For example, Zuckerberg, CEO of Facebook, stated [37],

> I think that these companies with those big ad networks are basically getting away with collecting huge amounts of information ...

Finally, most modern smartphones and laptops contain cameras that can be turned on by web applications! One could argue that when some cameras are turned on, a LED will go on. Unfortunately, the control of these LEDs might be software, such as is the case for "power switches" on many devices, which do not actually switch the power off[9].

In all applications, *once a user, willingly or not, reveals private information in the open, cryptography, unfortunately, can no longer help users regain their privacy.*

5   Conclusions

Predicting the future is impossible. While protecting privacy by using encryption was the main topic for centuries, since the work on authentication [24], we have seen a wide range of different topics under research in cryptography. When and whether they will be deployed and how widely remains to be seen.

The work on unconditionally security does not need to rely on unproven assumptions, except that we must assume randomness can be extracted from

---

[6] https://skydrive.live.com/.

[7] www.apple.com/icloud/.

[8] https://drive.google.com/start.

[9] The following note is out of context. Several renowned scientists have worried about the use of automatic weapons, robots equipped with advanced AI software. Maybe such devices should have real power switches!

nature. Unfortunately, unconditionally secure solutions are not often deployed. For long term security, one should strongly encourage the use of unconditionally secure cryptography.

From history we should have learned the lesson that the loss of privacy is extremely dangerous. Unfortunately, the temptations offered by social media, cloud servers and the like, have undermined privacy to an extend never seen before. Even if cryptography is being used by such servers, it seems that we have lost a lot of privacy, either due to the user's own decisions or due to the ones of some manager to use cloud servers and the like. Since security expectations are time depended, it is not clear how this trend will evolve, or whether users will rebel. An extreme viewpoint is the one expressed by Brin's in his book "*The Transparent Society*" [7], in which privacy is almost abolished.

Regardless whether privacy will vanish, or its importance restored, there are enough other security goals, such as authenticity, availability, traceability, etc., that the role of cryptography will not vanish.

The future will show us what parts of the extensive research done in the last 40 years on cryptography turned out to be useful and which ones were hype.

From a quantum computer perspective, both discrete logarithm and factoring have been broken. The slow progress on making a "large" quantum computer a reality, has been used as an excuse to continue using these assumptions. To be on the safe side, post-quantum cryptosystems should be used, but they have not been widely deployed in such applications as SSL.

Most of the above conclusions are related to the use of cryptography. One could wonder what the future will bring from a research viewpoint. We first focus on the imbalance between cryptography and cryptanalysis.

It is good to see the cryptanalysis of integer based multilinear maps [9]. The development of AES by academics was regarded as a major success story (see Statement 2) and regarded as an improvement over having algorithms developed in secret. However, we could argue that many academics have not put in the effort needed to carefully analyze the security of AES. Indeed, many regard the research in this area as not sufficiently challenging to pursue it. As long as such an attitude persists, one should wonder whether putting trust in academics to develop such systems is actually a good idea. Indeed, since most of our data transmitted is encrypted using conventional cryptography, its security should be a primary research topic. Hopefully, the future will convince a broader community to start having a much more fundamental understanding of block ciphers, in the same way as the understanding of the security of public key cryptography.

One of the biggest challenges is to prove or disprove assumptions on which we base proven secure cryptosystems. From the history of astronomy and chemistry we learn that sometimes a better understanding only comes after centuries of research.

Whether the work on secure multiparty computation, fully homomorphic encryption, attribute based cryptography, etc., will play a key role in computer security depends heavily whether the community will develop dedicated solutions to some specific computer task problems.

Finally, future security goals may imply new tools, which will keep researchers in cryptography busy.

The question whether cryptography will eventually be regarded as a success, or as a failure (see e.g. the viewpoint in [3]), might depend on whether we restore the balance that used to exist between cryptanalysis and cryptography. Kahn [29] teaches us that it is quite dangerous to be too optimistic!

Acknowledgment. The author thanks Amos Beimel, Yuval Ishai, and Eyal Kushilevitz for a discussion, at the 2013 Workshop on Mathematics of Information-Theoretic Cryptography at Leiden, on the history of secret sharing. Their viewpoint has influenced the discussion in Foonote 4.

The author also thanks Bunyamin Sari for an invited seminar lecture in his department of mathematics. This made the author realize, yet again, the influence of the work by Koblitz-Menezes [30], and the impact it has on how several mathematicians regard the area of modern cryptography.

The author thanks Catherine Meadows for e-mail discussions on her 1993 paper. The author thanks Shah Mahmood for the many discussions on whether social networks will make privacy and cryptography irrelevant and for some of the references on this topic. (see Sect. 4.8).

References

1. Adams, C., Burmester, M., (moderator), Y.D., Reiter, M., Zimmermann, P.: Which PKI (Public Key Infrastructure) is the right one? (panel). In: Proceedings of the 7th ACM Conference on Computer and Communications Security, 1–4 November 2000, pp. 98–101 (2000)
2. Adham, M., Azodi, A., Desmedt, Y., Karaolis, I.: How to attack two-factor authentication internet banking. In: Sadeghi, A.-R. (ed.) FC 2013. LNCS, vol. 7859, pp. 322–328. Springer, Heidelberg (2013)
3. Anderson, R.: Why cryptosystems fail. In: Proceedings of the 1st ACM Conference on Computer and Communications Security, 3–5 November 1993, pp. 215–227 (1993)
4. Bamford, J.: The Puzzle Palace. Penguin Books, New York (1985)
5. Barnett, E.: Google+ hits 90 million users. The Telegraph (2012)
6. Blakley, G.R.: Safeguarding cryptographic keys. In: Proceedings of National Computer Conference, AFIPS Conference Proceedings, pp. 313–317 (1979)
7. Brin, D.: The Transparent Society: Will Technology Force Us to Choose Between Privacy And Freedom?. Perseus Books, Cambridge (1999)
8. Burmester, M., Desmedt, Y.G.: Is hierarchical public-key certification the next target for hackers? Commun. ACM **47**, 68–74 (2004)
9. Cheon, J.H., Han, K., Lee, C., Ryu, H., Stehlé, D.: Cryptanalysis of the multilinear map over the integers. In: Oswald, E., Fischlin, M. (eds.) EUROCRYPT 2015. LNCS, vol. 9056, pp. 3–12. Springer, Heidelberg (2015)
10. Daemen, J., Rijmen, V.: AES proposal: Rijndael. http://csrc.nist.gov/encryption/aes/rijndael/Rijndael.pdf
11. Desmedt, Y., Erotokritou, S.: Making code voting secure against insider threats using unconditionally secure MIX schemes and human PSMT protocols. In: Haenni, R., Koenig, R.E., Wikström, D. (eds.) VoteID 2015. LNCS, vol. 9269, pp. 110–126. Springer, Heidelberg (2015)

12. Desmedt, Y., Vandewalle, J., Govaerts, R.: Cryptography protects information against several frauds. In: Proceedings of the International Carnahan Conference on Security Technology (Zürich, Switzerland, 4–6 October 1983), pp. 255–259. IEEE (1983)
13. Desmedt, Y.: A definition of cryptography. In: Proceedings of the Tenth National Conference on Information Security, pp. I-VII (2000)
14. Desmedt, Y.G.: Potential impacts of a growing gap between theory and practice in information security. In: Boyd, C., González Nieto, J.M. (eds.) ACISP 2005. LNCS, vol. 3574, pp. 532–536. Springer, Heidelberg (2005)
15. Diffie, W., Hellman, M.E.: Privacy and authentication: an introduction to cryptography. Proc. IEEE **67**, 397–427 (1979)
16. Dolev, D., Dwork, C., Waarts, O., Yung, M.: Perfectly secure message transmission. J. ACM **40**, 17–47 (1993)
17. Erotokritou, S., Desmedt, Y.: Human perfectly secure message transmission protocols and their applications. In: Visconti, I., De Prisco, R. (eds.) SCN 2012. LNCS, vol. 7485, pp. 540–558. Springer, Heidelberg (2012)
18. Essers, L.: Dutch government struggles to deal with DigiNotar hack. PC World (2011)
19. Esteghghari, S., Desmedt, Y.: Exploiting the client vulnerabilities in internet e-voting systems: hacking helios 2.0 as an example. In: 2010 Electronic Voting Technology Workshop/Workshop on Trustworthy Elections (EVT/WOTE 2010), 9–10 August 2010 (2010)
20. Facebook statistics: http://newsroom.fb.com/content/
21. Flickr: http://advertising.yahoo.com/article/flickr.html. Accessed 20 February 2012
22. Foursquare: https://foursquare.com/about/. Accessed 20 February 2012
23. Gentry, C.: Fully homomorphic encryption using ideal lattices. In: STOC, pp. 169–178. ACM (2009)
24. Gilbert, E., MacWilliams, F., Sloane, N.: Codes which detect deception. BELL Syst. Tech. J. **53**, 405–424 (1974)
25. Gisin, N.: CROSSING Workshop: Where Quantum Physics, Cryptography, System Security and Software Engineering meet, Darmstadt June 2 (2015)
26. Goldwasser, S., Micali, S.: Probabilistic encryption and how to play mental poker keeping secret all partial information. In: STOC, pp. 365–377 (1982)
27. Hacking in the Netherlands took aim at Internet giants. The New York Times, 5 September 2011 (2011)
28. Jolly, D., Minder, R.: Spain detains 3 in playstation cyberattacks. New York Times (2011)
29. Kahn, D.: The Codebreakers. MacMillan Publishing Co., New York (1967)
30. Koblitz, N., Menezes, A.: The brave new world of bodacious assumptions in cryptography. Not. Am. Math. Soc. **57**, 357–365 (2010)
31. Lenstra, A.K., Lenstra, Jr. H.W., Manasse, M.S., Pollard, J.M.: The number field sieve. In: Proceedings of the Twenty Second Annual ACM Symposium on Theory of Computing, STOC (14–16 May 1990), pp. 564–572 (1990)
32. Lieberman, D.: Securing web servers with SSL. http://www.infosecisland.com/blogview/15874-Securing-Web-Servers-with-SSL.html. Accessed 12 September 2012
33. Linkedin: http://press.linkedin.com/about. Accessed 20 February 2012
34. Linkedin passwords leaked by hackers. BBC (2012)
35. Liu, C.L.: Introduction to Combinatorial Mathematics. McGraw-Hill, New York (1968)

36. Mahmood, S., Desmedt, Y.: Poster: preliminary analysis of google+'s privacy. In: ACM Conference on Computer and Communications Security, pp. 809–812 (2011)
37. MailOnline: Zuckerberg defends Facebook. by saying Microsoft, Google and Yahoo! are even worse at ignoring user privacy. Daily Mail (2011)
38. Malm, S.: Indonesian man jailed for two-and-a-half years for writing 'god doesnt exist' on his Facebook page. Daily Mail (2012)
39. Markoff, J., Barboza, D.: F.B.I. to investigate Gmail attacks said to come from China. New York Times (2011)
40. Meadows, C.: An outline of a taxonomy of computer security research and development. In: Michael, J.B., Ashby, V., Meadows, D., (ed.) Proceedings on the 1992–1993 Workshop on New Security Paradigms, pp. 33–35. ACM (1993)
41. About Meetup. http://www.meetup.com/about/. Accessed 20 February 2012
42. Henderson, M., Melissa de Zwart, D.L., Phillips, M.: Will u friend me? Legal Risks of Social Networking Sites. Monash University (2011)
43. Only 1%. http://www.bbc.com/news/uk-25205846
44. Rabin, M.: Digitalized signatures and public-key functions as intractable as factorization. Tech. rep. Massachusetts Institute of Technology Technical Report MIT/LCS/TR-212 Cambridge, Massachusetts, January 1977
45. Reiter, M.K., Stubblebine, S.G.: Path independence for authentication in large scale systems. In: Proceedings of the 4th ACM Conference on Computer and Communications Security, pp. 57–66, April 1997
46. Rivest, R.L., Shamir, A., Adleman, L.: A method for obtaining digital signatures and public key cryptosystems. Commun. ACM **21**, 294–299 (1978)
47. Schneider, H., Nakashima, E.: IMF investigates suspected attack on its computers. Washington Post (2011)
48. Schneier, B.: Why Cryptography is Harder than it Looks. Counterpane Systems, Minneapolis (1997)
49. Shamir, A.: How to share a secret. Commun. ACM **22**, 612–613 (1979)
50. Shannon, C.E.: Communication theory of secrecy systems. Bell Syst. Techn. Jour. **28**, 656–715 (1949)
51. Sridharan, V.: Edward Snowden NSA scandal: India's diplomatic mission in London uses typewriters to beat snoopers. http://www.ibtimes.co.uk/articles/509532/20130927/nsa-snooping-snowdenindia-typewriter-embassy-delhi.htm. 27 September 2013
52. Taylor, C.: Tor researcher who exposed embassy e-mail passwords gets raided by Swedish FBI and CIA. Wired (2007)
53. Taylor, C.: Social networking 'Utopia' isn't coming. CNN (2011)
54. Yao, A.C.: Protocols for secure computations. In: 23rd Annual Symposium on Foundations of Computer Science (FOCS), pp. 160–164. IEEE Computer Society Press (1982)
55. Yao, A.C.: How to generate and exchange secrets. In: 27th Annual Symposium on Foundations of Computer Science (FOCS), pp. 162–167. IEEE Computer Society Press (1986)
56. YouTube: YouTube statistics. http://www.youtube.com/t/press_statistics. Accessed 16 May 2012
57. Yung, M.: Panel at Intrust, Beijing

Efficient Cryptographic
Implementations

Bitsliced High-Performance AES-ECB on GPUs

Rone Kwei Lim, Linda Ruth Petzold, and Çetin Kaya Koç[(✉)]

Department of Computer Science,
University of California, Santa Barbara, CA 93106, USA
{rklim13793,petzold,koc}@cs.ucsb.edu

Abstract. In order to perform high-performance Monte Carlo simulations of fracture in certain composite materials, we needed fast methods for generating deterministic random numbers. We made several design choices, and due to the fact that the entire simulation was to be done on both CPUs and GPUs, we designed new methods for fast implementation of the AES in the ECB mode on such architectures. This paper describes our algorithms and summarizes the performance results. In our implementation we were able to produce a speed of 78.6 Gbits per second on the GeForce GTX 480, which was 31–62 % faster than the fastest implementations reported in the recent literature on similar devices.

1 Introduction

The purpose of this study was to develop fast methods for generating deterministic random numbers using the AES in the ECB mode. The resulting random numbers were intended to be used in high-performance Monte Carlo simulation of fracture in certain composite materials [10]. The simulations for this study were done both on CPUs and GPUs to obtain the fastest implementations, and thus, to compare the speedup gain. We were motivated to develop high-speed implementations of the 128-bit AES-ECB on the NVIDIA GTX 480 GPU, and subsequently obtained significantly faster implementations of the AES. The present paper reports our implementations along with comparisons to recent results found in the literature.

2 CPU Versus GPU Architectures

A general-purpose CPU generally has several cores to run multiple threads, and a large cache for immediate access to the data, and also, sophisticated flow control mechanisms such as branch prediction, data and instruction prefetching, and out-of-order execution. The availability of floating-point ALUs make such CPUs very suitable for scientific computing tasks, achieving double-precision floating-point arithmetic at the rates of 40-160 GFlop/second at their peak performance. In the context of the research on Monte Carlo simulations of fractures [10], we worked with Intel Core 2 Quad Q6600 CPU at 2.4 GHz and Intel Core i7 2600 CPU at 3.4 GHz. The latter CPU has 4 physical cores and 8 MB cache.

© Springer-Verlag Berlin Heidelberg 2016
P.Y.A. Ryan et al. (Eds.): Kahn Festschrift, LNCS 9100, pp. 125–133, 2016.
DOI: 10.1007/978-3-662-49301-4_8

In contrast, a GPU, such as NVIDIA GTX 580, has a large number of execution units to process data in parallel. The original intention for designing GPUs was to create hardware that performs 3D graphics processing, however, the GPU architectures have evolved, coupled with a sophisticated computational model and a platform of computation called CUDA (Compute Unified Device Architecture). This new platform offered a C-like programming language, while the hardware provided integer, logical and floating-point instructions to support a wide range of computational needs in scientific computing. The present implementation was done on the NVIDIA GTX 580 which has 16 SMs (Streaming Multiprocessors) where each SM has 32 SPs (Shader Processors). Each SM executes independent streams of instructions while the SPs within each SM execute instruction in an SIMD fashion. The NVIDIA GTX 580 has 64K L1 cache and 768K L2 cache.

There are no sophisticated control flow mechanisms similar to CPUs, however, GPUs run large numbers of threads, providing large parallelism. If a program can be broken up into many threads all doing the same computation on different data (ideally, executing arithmetic operations), a GPU will probably be an order of magnitude faster than a CPU. On the other hand, applications with complex control flow, a CPU is going to be faster many orders of magnitude.

Figure 1, reprinted from [10], makes a comparison of the "silicon budget" (silicon area or number of transistors) for a CPU versus a GPU. The CPU uses most of its transistors for the control logic, the ALUs and the cache. On the other had GPUs spend nearly all of its available silicon area for its simple processors (ALUs).

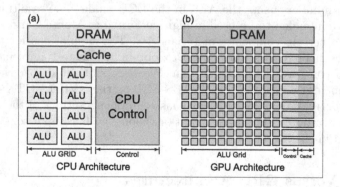

Fig. 1. The silicon area for a CPU versus a GPU [17].

2.1   GTX 480

We have implemented our algorithms on the NVIDIA GTX 480 GPU, which is based on the Fermi architecture. It has 15 SMs (Streaming Multiprocessors), where each SM has 32 SPs (Shader processors). Each SM can execute independent streams of instructions, whereas the SPs within each SM execute instructions in a SIMD (Single Instruction Multiple Data) manner. The NVIDIA GTX

480 has a 64K L1 cache per SM and a 768K L2 cache shared over all SMs. It also has 32768 registers per SM and 1.5 GB of global GPU memory. GPUs lack the sophisticated flow control mechanisms that are present on CPUs, such as branch predictor. Instead, GPUs have more transistors devoted to execution units and are designed to run large numbers of threads, which makes them suited for problems with a high degree of parallelism [22,24]. Figure 2 shows a schematic illustration of the Fermi architecture.

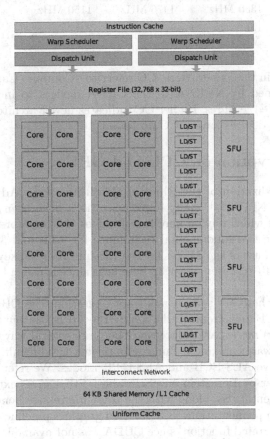

Fig. 2. Fermi architecture diagram [22].

2.2   Comparing GPUs

The GTX 285 has 30 SMs, each with 8 SPs. It has 16K L1 cache per SM and no L2 cache. It also has 16384 registers per SM and 1 GB of global GPU memory. In comparison, the 8800 GTX has 16 SMs, each with 8 SPs. It has 16K L1 cache per SM and no L2 cache. It also has 8192 registers per SM and 768 MB of global GPU memory.

We find it useful to make a comparison of various GPUs that we are referencing in the context of our AES implementations. Table 1 compares various

Table 1. Comparison of various GPUs.

	8800 GTX [18]	GTX 285 [19]	Tesla C2050 [21]	GTX 480 [20]
Bus bandwidth	4 GB/s	8 GB/s	8 GB/s	8 GB/s
Memory size	768 MB	1024 MB	3072 MB	1536 MB
Mem bandwidth	86.4 GB/s	159.0 GB/s	144 GB/s	177.4 GB/s
SP count	128	240	448	480
SP clock	1350 MHz	1476 MHz	1150 MHz	1400 MHz
CC	1.0	1.3	2.0	2.0

GPUs referenced in this paper. Here, CC refers to "Compute Capability", which is an index assigned by NVIDIA to the CUDA devices to indicate its set of computation-related features. Higher CC indicates newer architectures, and the NVIDIA's newest devices have a CC up to 3.5 [16].

3   AES Encryption on CPU and GPUs

Since the standardization of the Rijndael algorithm as the Advanced Encryption Standard by NIST [14], many implementations have been reported in the literature, most of which rely on known techniques. The creators of the Rijndael algorithm describe two fundamental techniques for 8-bit and 32-bit CPUs [4]. The most common use of the AES is for the 128-bit (16-byte) key; it is projected that AES will be 40 % slower [1] for 32-byte keys since it uses 14 rounds, instead of 10.

Furthermore, there are several modes of operation: the CBC (cipher-block chaining), the ECB (electronic code-book), the OFB (output feedback), and the CTR (counter) modes, etc. Moreover, there are several ways of benchmarking the AES software, making a fair comparison very difficult. Most common comparisons involve AES-ECB and AES-CTR modes. We refer the reader to a highly useful paper by Bernstein and Schwabe [1] that gives extensive analyses of various implementations, along with the most impressive benchmark results.

Earlier GPU implementations [3,5,28] used graphics pipeline and OpenGL to compute the AES round function, since CUDA was not available back then. The availability of CUDA made sophisticated high-speed implementations possible.

Another point of discussion that is relevant to the present paper is bitsliced AES implementations on various CPUs. There are several papers of interest: Rebeiro et al. [27], Matsui [12], and Matsui and Nakajima [13]. Bitsliced implementations are not as competitive with word-level implementations on CPUs due to the cost of transpositions of the ciphertext.

4   AES-ECB on the GPUs

Our implementation starts with the CPU-based bitsliced implementation of the AES by Kasper and Schwabe [8]. Their implementation processes 8 16-byte blocks at a time. A direct conversion to a GPU implementation results in poor performance, due to an insufficient number of registers. The 8 blocks alone take up 32 registers per thread, and each thread is limited to 63 registers maximum. The result is that the compiler spills variables into memory instead of keeping them in registers.

We restructured the algorithm to process 4 16-byte blocks at a time to improve performance. The sections below describe the performance improvements we made to various parts of the AES algorithm.

4.1 Bit Ordering

In our bitslicing implementation, bits from multiple blocks are collected together, i.e., bit 0 of row 0, column 0 from blocks 0, 1, 2, 3 are grouped together, as shown in Figs. 3 and 4. Each bitsliced state variable has 64 bits; there are 8 of these state variables.

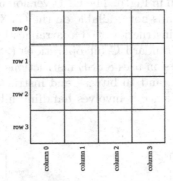

Fig. 3. The state of one block.

row 0				row 1				row 2				row 3			
column 0	column 1	column 2	column 3	column 0	column 1	column 2	column 3	column 0	column 1	column 2	column 3	column 0	column 1	column 2	column 3

Fig. 4. The bitsliced state.

4.2 Load and Store

On GPUs, the performance of global memory is improved when it is accessed contiguously. When reading the input blocks, we first load the blocks contiguously from global memory to shared memory, and then distribute them among individual threads. Similarly, when writing the output blocks, we first write the blocks to shared memory from individual threads, and then collect them together and store to global memory contiguously.

4.3 SubBytes

The AES algorithm defined in [14] used a table lookup for the S-box. In the bitsliced implementation, the table lookup is replaced by a series of Boolean operations (xor, or, and) [8]. Kasper and Schwabe [8] used 163 CPU SSE instructions. In our implementation, since we restructured the algorithm to process 4 blocks at a time, extra registers are available that we use to store intermediate values, thus reducing the instruction count to 117×2. The doubling of the instruction count arises from the fact that the GPU registers are 32 bits, thus, each 64-bit bitsliced state requires 2 operations to process. Since the two halves can be processed independently, we utilize ILP (instruction level parallelism) to increase performance.

4.4 ShiftRows

In this step, the bytes in a block are shifted by a variable amount for each row, as shown in Fig. 5. In the bitsliced state, this operation becomes a rearrangement of nibbles (4-bits), as shown in Fig. 6. The CPU version used the pshufb instruction [8], but this instruction is not available on the GTX 480. Instead, we found the GTX 480 has a prmt instruction that rearranges bytes [23]. We combined this instruction with the standard C bit operations (>>, <<, &, |, ^) to improve performance. The CPU version uses 8 SSE instructions [8], while our GPU version uses 32 prmt, 16 shift, and 16 bitwise and instructions. The GPU version requires more instructions since it involves handling nibbles (4 bits) instead of whole bytes (8 bits).

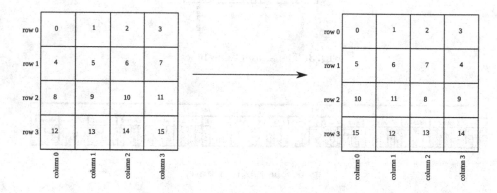

Fig. 5. The ShiftRows step.

Fig. 6. The ShiftRows step for the bitsliced state.

4.5 MixColumns

This step involves a matrix multiplication over the AES finite field, as specified in [14] (see Fig. 7). Using Boolean operations, the matrix multiplication becomes a sequence of shifts and xor operations. The CPU version of Kasper and Schwabe uses 16 pshufd and 27 xor instructions [8], while our GPU version uses 27×2 xor and 8×2 prmt instructions. The 2 factor is explained in the SubBytes section.

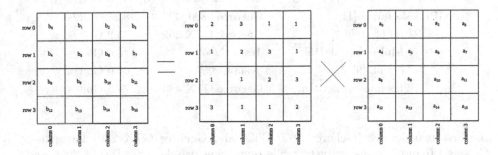

Fig. 7. Matrix multiplication in MixColumns.

4.6 AddRoundKey

This step requires only xor operations. Our GPU version loads the 10 round keys into shared memory to improve performance when processing multiple blocks. By loading the round keys into shared memory, we avoid having to read the round keys from GPU global memory repeatedly.

4.7 Resistance to Timing-Attack

The CPU-based algorithm of Kasper and Schwabe is resistant to timing side channels due to the use of constant time operations [8]. By using a bitslicing approach, our algorithm is also resistant to timing side channels. All operations that involve key or data use bitwise operations whose execution time does not depend on the values of the data. In contrast, other GPU-based AES implementations use lookup tables whose execution time depends on the data, i.e., these operations are not constant time. Furthermore, the bitsliced implementations are also inherently immune to the cache-timing attacks, as discussed in [1, 2, 26].

5 Results and Conclusion

We summarize all recent results in Table 2, along with our result in the last row. This table shows we have the fastest GPU implementation among all reported results.

Considering that CC (Compute Capability) of these devices is a good indication of their architectural richness and computational power, we notice that

Table 2. Comparing recent implementations. CPU speeds are per core.

CPU	Bernstein and Schwabe [1]	Core 2 Quad Q6600	1.82 Gbit/s
	Kasper and Schwabe [8]	Core 2 Quad Q6600	2.06 Gbit/s
		Core 2 Quad Q9550	2.99 Gbit/s
		Core i7 920	3.08 Gbit/s
	OpenSSL 1.0.1e [25]	Core i7 2600	0.98 Gbit/s
		Core i7 2600 (AES-NI)	5.78 Gbit/s
GPU	Manavski [11]	GeForce 8800 GTX	8.28 Gbit/s
	Iwai et al. [6,7]	GeForce GTX 285	35.2 Gbit/s
	Nishikawa et al. [15]	Tesla C2050	48.6 Gbit/s
	Li et al. [9]	Tesla C2050	60.0 Gbit/s
	This implementation	GeForce GTX 480	78.6 Gbit/s

the first two devices (GeForce 8800 GTX and GeForce GTX 285) have their CCs as 1.0 and 1.3, respectively, while remaining two devices (Tesla C2050 and GeForce GTX 480) are both 2.0, however, our AES-ECB implementation on a device with the same CC is 62 % faster than that of Nishikawa et al. [15] and 31 % faster than that of Li et al. [9].

Moreover, our implementation is quite practical; it is used in the deterministic RNG portion of a successful Monte Carlo simulator for fracture computation in certain composite materials, as described in [10].

References

1. Bernstein, D.J., Schwabe, P.: New AES software speed records. In: Chowdhury, D.R., Rijmen, V., Das, A. (eds.) INDOCRYPT 2008. LNCS, vol. 5365, pp. 322–336. Springer, Heidelberg (2008)
2. Bernstein, D.J.: Cache-timing attacks on AES (2005). https://cr.yp.to/antiforgery/cachetiming-20050414.pdf
3. Cook, D.L., Ioannidis, J., Keromytis, A.D., Luck, J.: CryptoGraphics: Secret Key Cryptography Using Graphics Cards. In: Menezes, A. (ed.) CT-RSA 2005. LNCS, vol. 3376, pp. 334–350. Springer, Heidelberg (2005)
4. Daemen, J., Rijmen, V.: The Design of Rijndael: AES - The Advanced Encryption Standard. Springer, Heidelberg (2002)
5. Harrison, O., Waldron, J.: AES encryption implementation and analysis on commodity graphics processing units. In: Paillier, P., Verbauwhede, I. (eds.) CHES 2007. LNCS, vol. 4727, pp. 209–226. Springer, Heidelberg (2007)
6. Iwai, K., Kurokawa, T., Nishikawa, N.: AES encryption implementation on CUDA GPU and its analysis. In: 2010 First International Conference on Networking and Computing (ICNC), pp. 209–214. IEEE (2010)
7. Iwai, K., Nishikawa, N., Kurokawa, T.: Acceleration of AES encryption on CUDA GPU. Int. J. Netw. Comput. 2(1), 131–145 (2012)
8. Käsper, E., Schwabe, P.: Faster and timing-attack resistant AES-GCM. In: Clavier, C., Gaj, K. (eds.) CHES 2009. LNCS, vol. 5747, pp. 1–17. Springer, Heidelberg (2009)

9. Li, Q., Zhong, C., Zhao, K., Mei, X., Chu, X.: Implementation and analysis of AES encryption on GPU. In: 14th IEEE International Conference on High Performance Computing and Communication and 9th IEEE International Conference on Embedded Software and Systems, HPCC-ICESS 2012, pp. 843–848 (2012)
10. Lim, R.K., Pro, J.W., Begley, M.R., Utz, M., Petzold, L.R.: High-performance simulation of fracture in idealized 'brick and mortar' composites using adaptive Monte Carlo minimization on the GPU (Manuscript, in preparation, November 2014)
11. Manavski, S.A.: CUDA compatible GPU as an efficient hardware accelerator for AES cryptography. In: IEEE International Conference on Signal Processing and Communications, 2007, ICSpPC 2007, pp. 65–68 (2007)
12. Matsui, M.: How Far Can We Go on the x64 Processors? In: Robshaw, M. (ed.) FSE 2006. LNCS, vol. 4047, pp. 341–358. Springer, Heidelberg (2006)
13. Matsui, M., Nakajima, J.: On the power of bitslice implementation on Intel Core2 processor. In: Paillier, P., Verbauwhede, I. (eds.) CHES 2007. LNCS, vol. 4727, pp. 121–134. Springer, Heidelberg (2007)
14. National Institute of Standards and Technology: Advanced Encryption Standard (AES), FIPS 197, November 2001
15. Nishikawa, N., Iwai, K., Kurokawa, T.: High-performance symmetric block ciphers on multicore CPU and GPUs. Int. J. Netw. Comput. 2(2), 251–268 (2012)
16. NVIDIA: CUDA GPUs. https://developer.nvidia.com/cuda gpus
17. NVIDIA: CUDA Toolkit. https://developer.nvidia.com/cuda-toolkit
18. NVIDIA: GeForce 8800 GTX Specifications. http://www.nvidia.com/page/geforce_8800.html
19. NVIDIA: GeForce GTX 285 Specifications. http://www.geforce.com/hardware/desktop-gpus/geforce-gtx-285/specifications
20. NVIDIA: GeForce GTX 480 Specifications. http://www.geforce.com/hardware/desktop-gpus/geforce-gtx-480/specifications
21. NVIDIA: Tesla C2050 Board Specifications. http://www.nvidia.com/docs/IO/43395/Tesla_C2050_Board_Specification.pdf
22. NVIDIA: Next Generation CUDA Compute Architecture: Fermi, v1.1. (2009)
23. NVIDIA: Parallel Thread ISA, Version 2.3 (2011)
24. NVIDIA: CUDA C Programming Guide, Version 6.5, August 2014
25. OpenSSL Group: The OpenSSL Project. http://www.openssl.org
26. Osvik, D.A., Shamir, A., Tromer, E.: Cache attacks and countermeasures: the case of AES. In: Pointcheval, D. (ed.) CT-RSA 2006. LNCS, vol. 3860, pp. 1–20. Springer, Heidelberg (2006)
27. Rebeiro, C., Selvakumar, D., Devi, A.S.L.: Bitslice implementation of AES. In: Pointcheval, D., Mu, Y., Chen, K. (eds.) CANS 2006. LNCS, vol. 4301, pp. 203–212. Springer, Heidelberg (2006)
28. Yamanouchi, T.: AES encryption and decryption on the GPU. GPU Gems 3, 785–804 (2007)

Buying AES Design Resistance
with Speed and Energy

Rodrigo Portella do Canto, Roman Korkikian, and David Naccache[✉]

Département d'informatique, École normale supérieure,
45, rue d'Ulm, 75005 Paris, Cedex 05, France
rodrigoportella@gmail.com,david.naccache@ens.fr

Abstract. Fault and power attacks are two common ways of extracting secrets from tamper-resistant chips. Although several protections have been proposed to thwart these attacks, resistant designs usually claim significant area or speed overheads. Furthermore, circuit-level counter-measures are usually not reconfigurable at runtime. This paper exploits the AES' algorithmic features to propose low-cost and low-latency protections. We provide Verilog and FPGA implementation details. Using our design, real-life applications can be configured during runtime to meet the user's needs and the system's constraints.

Keywords: AES · Power scrambling · Power attack · CPA · Fault attack · Half size memory

1 Introduction

The Advanced Encryption Standard (AES) algorithm, also known as Rijndael, is a widely used block-cipher standardized by NIST in 2001 [1]. Compared with its predecessor DES [1,2], the AES features longer keys, larger plaintexts and more involved basic binary transformations [3].

Despite the fact that AES is mathematically safer than the DES, straightforward AES *implementations* are not necessarily secure and several authors [4–6] have exhibited ways of exploring information that leaks from AES implementations. Such leakage is typically power consumption, electromagnetic emanations or the time required to process data. Additional constraints such as fault-resistance, chip technology, performance, area, power consumption, and even patent compliance further complicate the design of real-life AES coprocessors.

This article addresses resistance against two physical threats: power and fault attacks. The proposed AES architecture leverages the algorithm's structure to create low-cost protections against these attacks. This allows very flexible runtime configurability without significantly affecting performance.

The remaining of the paper is organized as follows: Sect. 2 recalls the AES' main features and proposes an architecture for implementing it. Section 3 explains how to add power scrambling and fault detection to the proposed implementation. The result is a chip design allowing 29 different software-controlled

© Springer-Verlag Berlin Heidelberg 2016
P.Y.A. Ryan et al. (Eds.): Kahn Festschrift, LNCS 9100, pp. 134–147, 2016.
DOI: 10.1007/978-3-662-49301-4_9

runtime configurations. Section 4 introduces an idea of reducing the memory required to store *state keys* in the decryption mode. Section 5 compares simulation and synthesis results between an unprotected AES and our protected implementations. While Sect. 6 concludes this article, Sect. 7 proposes further research about a novel type of attack.

2   The Proposed AES Design

The AES is a symmetric iterative block-cipher that processes 128-bit blocks and supports keys of 128, 192 or 256 bits [1]. Key length is denoted by $N_k = 4, 6,$ or 8, and reflects the number of 32-bit words in the key. At start, the 128-bit plaintext P is split into a 4×4 matrix S of 16 bytes called *state*. The *state* goes through a number of rounds to become the ciphertext C.

The number of rounds N_r is a function of N_k. Possible $\{N_r, N_k\}$ combinations are $\{10, 4\}$, $\{12, 6\}$ and $\{14, 8\}$. A particular round $1 \leq r \leq N_r$ takes as input a 128-bit *state* $S^{[r]}$ and a 128-bit *round key* $K^{[r]}$ and outputs a 128-bit state $S^{[r+1]}$. This is done by successively applying four transformations called *SubBytes*, *ShiftRows*, *MixColumns* and *AddRoundKey*.

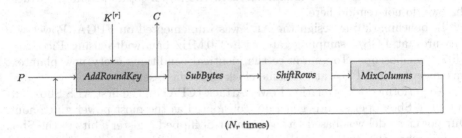

Fig. 1. AES encryption flowchart.

AES encryption starts with an initial *AddRoundKey* transformation followed by N_r rounds consisting of four transformations, in the following order: *SubBytes*, *ShiftRows*, *MixColumns* and *AddRoundKey*. *MixColumns* is skipped in the final round $(r = N_r)$. If during the last round *MixColumns* is bypassed, we can look upon the AES as the 4-block iterative structure shown in Fig. 1.

Decryption has a similar structure in which the order of transforms is reversed (Fig. 2) and where inverse transformations are used (Note that *AddRoundKey* is idempotent). In both designs, a register barrier at the end of each transformation block is used to save intermediate results. Therefore the intermediate information that eventually yields $S^{[r]}$ is saved four times during each AES round. It takes $4N_r + 1$ clock cycles to encrypt (or decrypt) a data block using this design.

Figures 1 and 2 show that, during each clock cycle, only one block of the chain actually computes the *state*, while the other three blocks are processing useless data. This is potentially risky, as the three concerned blocks "chew" computationally useless data related to P (or C) and $K^{[r]}$ and thereby expose

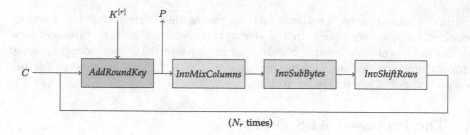

Fig. 2. AES decryption flowchart.

the design to unnecessary side-channel attacks.[1] This computation is shown in Fig. 3 where red arrows represent the path of usefully active combinatorial logic.

3   Energy and Security

3.1   Power Analysis

We assume that the reader is familiar with the power [6] and fault [7] attacks that we do not remind here.

To benchmark our design the AES was implemented on FPGA. Power was measured at $1\,GS/s$ sampling rate with $250\,MHz$ bandwidth using PicoScope 3407 A oscilloscope. To guarantee the identical conditions every new plaintext was given to the FPGA at the same clock after the reset.

We performed a Correlation Power Attack (CPA) on the first AES Sbox output since Sbox operation is generally considered as the most power gluttonous. Our power model was based on the number of flipped register's bits in the Sbox module when the initial register's barrier R_0 is rewritten with the Sbox output as follows:

$$\mathrm{HD}(Sbox[P \oplus K_0], R_0) = \mathrm{HW}(Sbox[P \oplus K_0] \oplus R_0) \tag{1}$$

where R_0 is the previous register's state; P is a given plaintext; K_0 is the AES master key.

The value R_0 was assumed to be constant since all the encryptions were performed at the same clock after the reset. When R_0 could not be computed then all possible 256 values were tried. Pearson correlation coefficient was used to link the model and the genuine consumed power.

The following section presents a reference evaluation of the unprotected AES implementation showing its vulnerability compared to two (LFSR and tri-state buffers) side-channel countermeasures introduced later.

---

[1] In that respect see our open question in Sect. 7.

3.2   Power Scrambling

It is a natural idea to shut down unnecessarily active blocks. To do so, each block receives a new 1-bit input named *ready* activating the block when $ready = 1$. If $ready = 0$, the block's pull-up resistors are disconnected using a tri-state buffer connected to the power source. This saves power and also prevents the circuit from leaking "unnecessary" side-channel information.

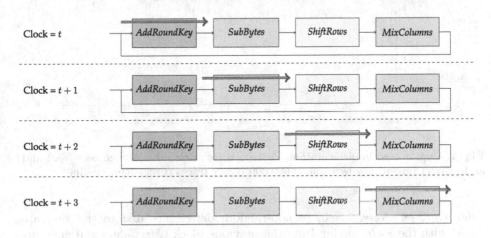

Fig. 3. Flow of computation in time.

Logically the pipeline architecture that we have just described has to be less vulnerable against First Order DPA attacks. Its four register barriers introduce additional noise, so we expect that the correlation shall be at least smaller that for the AES design with one round per clock computation.

To asses the security of each proposed design, we will compare an incorrect key byte correlation to a correct key byte correlation. Figure 4 shows these two coefficients. As expected, the correct key is correlated to the power traces, however even for 500,000 traces Pearson correlation coefficient is smaller than 0.015. Anyway, this implementation is vulnerable.

To exploit the unused blocks to hide the device's power signature even better we propose two modifications. The first consists in injecting (pseudo) random data into the unused blocks, making them process that random data. Subsequently, three of the four blocks will consume power in an unpredictable manner. Note that because we use the exact same gates to compute and to generate noise, the expected spectral and amplitude characteristics of the generated noise should mask leakage quite well. Although any random generator may be used as a noise source, we performed our experiments using a 128-bit LFSR. An LFSR is purely coded in digital HDL, making tests easier to implement.

Figure 5 shows that a multiplexer controlled by the *ready* signal selects either the useful intermediate *state* information or the pseudo-random LFSR output. For the *AddRoundKey* block, LFSR data replaces the key. Therefore when

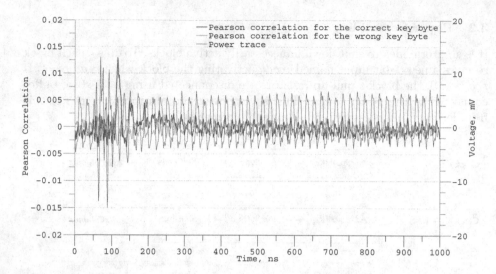

Fig. 4. Unprotected implementation: Pearson correlation value of a correct (red) and an incorrect (green) key byte guess. 500,000 power traces (Color figure online).

AddRoundKey's *ready* = 0, pseudo-random data (unrelated to the key) are xored with the *state* coming from the previous block (*MixColumns* if encrypting, *InvShiftRows* if decrypting). For the other blocks, the pseudo-random data replaces the *state* when *ready* = 0.

Attacks performed on this implementation revealed that this countermeasure increases key lifetime. Figure 6 is the equivalent of Fig. 4 for the protected implementation using an LFSR. The correct key correlation can not be distinguished from the incorrect key correlation even with 1,200,000 traces. However, we assume that this implementation still might be vulnerable if more traces are acquired or if Second Order DPA is applied.

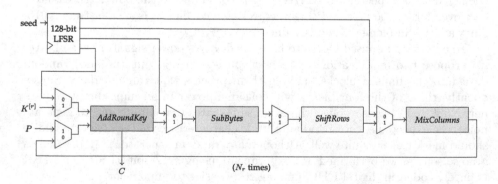

Fig. 5. Power Scrambling with a PRNG.

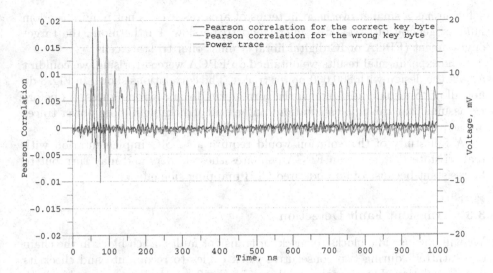

Fig. 6. LFSR implementation: Pearson correlation value of a correct (red) and an incorrect (green) key byte guess. 1,200,000 power traces (Color figure online).

Real-life implementations must use true random generators. Indeed, if a deterministic PRNG seed is used the noise component in all encryptions becomes constant and cancels-out when computing differential power curves.

A second design option interleaves tri-state buffers between blocks to hide power consumption. By shutting down the three useless blocks, we create a scrambled power trace where one block computes meaningful data while the other three "process" high impedance inputs, which means that these blocks "compute" leakage current coming from their inputs.

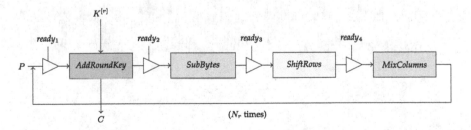

Fig. 7. Power scrambling with tri-state buffers.

As illustrated in Fig. 7, the input signal $ready_i$ determines which blocks are tri-stated and which block is computing the AES *state*. In other words, the $ready_i$ signal "jumps" from one block to the next, so that only one block is computing while the other three are scrambling the power consumption. Although this solution has a smaller overhead in terms of area (as it does not require random number generation) tri-state buffers tend to be slow. Furthermore, the target environment (FPGA or IC digital library) must offer tri-state cells.

The experimental results we obtained on FPGA were surprising, we couldn't attack the design with 800,000 power traces. The correlations shown in Fig. 8 do not allow to visually distinguish the correct key from a wrong guess. As before we assume that this implementation can be still attackable if more power traces are acquired or if Second Order DPA is applied.

A full study of this solution would require an ASIC implementation with real tri-state buffers, as an FPGA emulates these buffers and may turn out to be resistant because of an undesired CLB mapping side effects.

3.3   Transient Fault Detection

We will now use idle blocks to check for transient faults. Each block in the chain can "stutter" during two consecutive clock cycles to recompute and check its own calculation. For instance, as shown in Fig. 9, at clock t, a given block B_i receives a $ready_i$ signal, computes the $state$ and saves it in the register barrier R_i. At clock $t + 1$, the result enters the next block $B_{i+1\text{mod}4}$ which is now working, while B_i reverts to checking, $i.e.$, B_i recomputes the same output as at clock t and compares it to the saved B_i value. This process is repeated for the other blocks in the chain. If any transient fault happens to cause a wrong result at the output of any block, the error will be detected within one clock cycle.

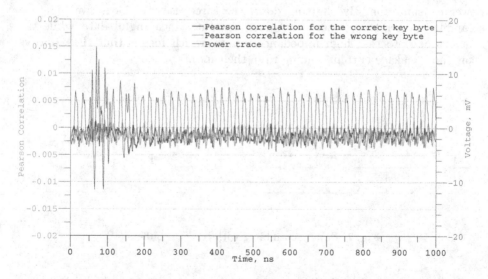

Fig. 8. Tri-state buffers implementation: Pearson correlation value of the correct key byte (green) and a wrong key byte guess (red). 800,000 power traces (Color figure online).

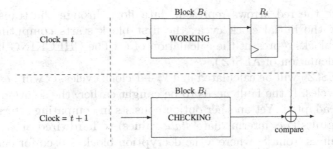

Fig. 9. Transient fault detection scheme for AES.

3.4   Permanent Fault Detection

The AES structure of Sect. 2 also allows us to use one block of the chain to compute a pre-determined plaintext or ciphertext. The encryption (or decryption) of a chosen input (*e.g.* the all-zero input Z) is pre-computed once for all and hardwired (let $W = \text{AES}(Z)$ denote this value). While the system processes the actual input through one block (out of four) during any given clock cycle, another block is dedicated to recompute W. One clock after the actual C emerges, $\text{AES}(Z)$ can be compared to the hardwired reference value W. If $W \neq \text{AES}(Z)$, a transient or a permanent fault occurred.

In this scenario, the system starts by computing $\text{AES}(Z)$ in the first clock cycle, followed by the actual computation of C. This allows the implementation to check up all the blocks during the execution and make sure that no permanent fault occurred. In the last clock cycle, while C is being processed in the last block, the correctness of $\text{AES}(Z)$ is compared with the hardwired value before outputting C.

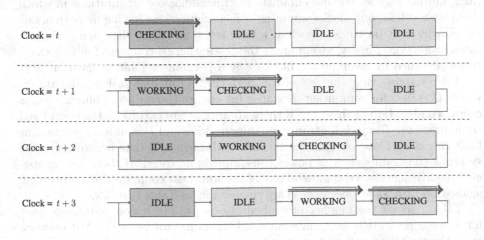

Fig. 10. Permanent fault detection scheme for AES (Color figure online).

In Fig. 10, the red arrows represent data flow through the transformation blocks. After the initial clock cycle, the first block starts computing C. The WORKING blocks represent the calculation of C. The CHECKING blocks represent the calculation of AES(Z).

While AES(Z) will be calculated in $4N_r + 1$ clock cycles, C will be calculated in $4N_r + 2$ cycles. If the fault needs to be caught earlier, the solution described in [8] can be adapted. Yet another option consists in comparing intermediate Z encryption results (*i.e.* intermediate *state* values) to hardwired ones. Note that our design differs from [8] where a the decryption block is used for checking the encryption's correctness [3].

3.5   Runtime Configurability

The proposed AES architecture is a 4-stage pipeline where each stage can be used independently of the others. As already noted, blocks can perform five different tasks:

- Compute a meaningful state;
- Be in idle state to save energy;
- Scramble power consumption;
- Check for transient faults by recomputing previous calculation;
- Check for permanent faults by computing a known input.

To explore all possible combinations, we proceed as follows: first, we generate all $5^4 = 625$ combinations (5 operations for 4 transformation blocks). We can consider a subset of these combinations if we work with 4 operations only, and remember that each E entry represents two actual options (tri-state or idle). This reduces the number of combinations to $4^4 = 256$. We eliminate all configurations that are circular permutations of others, *i.e.* already counted configurations shifted in time. We also eliminate the meaningless configurations in which there isn't at least one block computing. All configurations having more than one permanent fault protection block at a time are removed as they don't add any extra protection. Finally, we eliminate the cases where a transient fault checking is not preceded by a computing block or by a permanent fault verification.

Table 1 shows that the design can perform 29 different task combinations, where C stands for computing, E stands for energy (power scrambling, idleness or any combination of these two if there are more than two Es in the considered configuration), T stands for transient fault checking and P stands for permanent fault checking. These options can be activated *during runtime* according to the system's constraints such as power consumption or speed. If there are no specific requirements, we recommend any of the four best configurations protecting against all attacks at once. These are singled-out in Table 1 by a $\star$.

Table 2 shows the number of configurations per protection goal. Note that for a given protection goal, different configurations can be alternated between executions without any performance loss.

Table 1. 29 possible configurations.

Block 1	Block 2	Block 3	Block 4
C	C	C	C
C	C	C	E
C	C	C	T
C	C	C	P
C	C	E	E
C	C	E	T
C	C	E	P
C	C	T	T
C	C	T	P
C	C	P	E
C	C	P	T
C	E	C	E
C	E	C	T
C	E	C	P
C	E	E	E
C	E	E	T
C	E	E	P
C	E	T	T
★ C	E	T	P
C	E	P	E
★ C	E	P	T
C	T	C	P
C	T	T	T
C	T	T	P
★ C	T	P	E
C	T	P	T
C	P	E	E
★ C	P	E	T
C	P	T	T

Table 2. Number of configurations.

C	E	P	T	Configurations
4				1
3	1			1
1	3			1
3		1		1
3			1	1
1		3		1
2		2		1
1	1	2		1
1	2	1		1
2	2			2
1		1	2	2
2	1	1		3
1	2	1		3
1		1	2	3
2		1	1	3
1	1	1	1	4

4   Halving the Memory Required for AES Decryption

As we have seen, it takes $4N_r+1$ clock cycles to encrypt or decrypt an input. The first block of the chain, *AddRoundKey* xors the *state* with the *subkey*. Therefore, the *key expansion* block is designed to deliver a new 32-bit *subkey* chunk at each clock cycle.

When decrypting, the AES uses *subkeys* in the reverse order, so all *subkeys* need to be expanded and stored in memory before decryption starts. For that, decryption requires a $128N_r$-bit buffer. These $128N_r$ bits are stored in a register having N_r records of 128 bit each. Nevertheless, it is possible to halve the number of records by using the following idea: let sk_{N_r} be the *subkey* required at round N_r. All *subkeys* are computed but only the last $N_r/2$ *subkeys* are stored in memory. After the first 4 clock cycles, *AddRoundKey* block uses sk_{N_r} (the first

AddRoundKey uses the initial *key* sk_0 which we assume to be already recorded). After 4 more cycles, sk_1 is saved in the record previously occupied by sk_{N_r}. The buffer continues to be used in such a way that each previously used (*i.e.* read) *subkey* is replaced by a new *subkey* of rank smaller than $N_r/2$. By the time that AES decryption requires $sk_{N_r/2}$, the *subkeys* sk_1 to $sk_{N_r/2-1}$ would have already been replaced *subkeys* sk_{N_r} to $sk_{N_r/2}$.

Fig. 11. Memory Halving for AES Decryption When $N_r = 10$ (Color figure online).

As shown in Fig. 11, only 5 records are required when $N_r = 10$. Analogously, $\{6, 7\}$ records are required for $N_r = \{12, 14\}$. The red positions are *subkeys* being used at each *AddRoundKey* operation, from left to right. Note that we assume that the initial *key* sk_0 is known and does not need to be stored.

The algorithm is formally defined as follows: Create a buffer of $N_r/2$ records denoted $r[0], \ldots, r[N_r/2 - 1]$. Place in each $r[i]$ the *subkey* $sk_{i+1+N_r/2}$.

Define the function:

$$f(i) = \frac{|2i - N_r - 1| - 1}{2}$$

When sk_i is needed, fetch it from $r[f(i)]$. After this fetch operation update the record $r[f(i)]$ by writing into it sk_{N_r-i+1}.

5   Implementation Results

A 128-bit datapath AES encryption core was coded and tested in Verilog and compiled using Cadence *irun* tool. Cadence *RTL Compiler.* was used to map the design into a 45 nm *FreePDK* open cell digital library. Figure 12 represents the inputs and outputs of the AES core. The module contains a general clock signal called *CLOCK_IN*, an asynchronous low-edge reset called *RESET_IN* and a *READY_IN* signal that flags the beginning of a new encryption. Plaintext is fed into the device *via* the 128-bit bus *TEXT_IN*, while the 128-bit key is fed to the system through the input called *KEY_IN*. The module outputs two signals: *TEXT_OUT*, which contains the resulting plaintext and *READY_OUT*, that represents a valid output.

Table 3 compares an unprotected AES core to the countermeasures described in this paper. The increase in terms of area is ~6 % for the LFSR implementation and ~4 % for the tri-state design. The LFSR implementation showed almost no

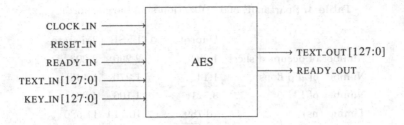

Fig. 12. AES design's inputs and outputs.

increase in terms of power consumption. Since tri-state buffers shut down three out of four blocks per clock, we expect a reduction in the power consumption. The tri-state design saves roughly 20 % of power compared to the unprotected AES. As tri-state buffers tend to be slower, this design lost 20 % in terms of clock frequency and throughput, while the LFSR version showed no speed loss, as expected.

Table 3. Unprotected AES, LFSR and tri-state buffer designs synthesized to the 45 nm *FreePDK* open cell library.

	Unprotected	LFSR	Tri-state
Area (μm²)	61,581	65,194	64,243
Number of cells	10,643	11,035	11,162
Sequential	783	911	787
Inverters	1,483	1,614	1,493
Logic	8,375	8,506	8,368
Buffers	2	4	2
Tri-state buffers	0	0	512
Total power (mW)	2.10	2.16	1.68
Leakage power	1.20	1.28	1.26
Dynamic power	0.89	0.87	0.41
Timing (ps)	645	645	806
Frequency (GHz)	1.55	1.55	1.24
Throughput (Gbit/s)	4.84	4.84	3.87

Table 4 shows the three designs benchmarks in FPGA. They were coded in Verilog and synthesized to the Spartan3E-500 board using the Xilinx ISE 14.7 tool. LFSR and tri-state designs showed an area overhead of ~15 % compared to the unprotected AES implementation. In terms of performance, LFSR design showed no loss, while the tri-state core lost ~7 %.

Table 4. Spartan3E-500 utilization summary report.

	Unprotected	LFSR	Tri-state
Number of occupied slices	1,994	2,290	2,296
Number of flip flops	1,142	1,270	1,146
Number of LUTs	3,521	4,106	4,031
Timing (ns)	10.789	10.714	11.580
Frequency (MHz)	92.68	93.33	86.35
Throughput (Mbit/s)	289.3	291.3	269.6

6   Conclusion

We described an unprotected AES implementation sliced in four clock cycles
per round. Making use of this approach, we built on top of the unprotected core
two power scrambling ideas to thwart side-channel attacks, such as CPA. We
also demonstrated how the design can also prevent fault injection by recomputing its internal *state* values or by compromising one out of four blocks at
each clock to compute the encryption of a known plaintext. We then exhibited
simulation results and showed the comparison of the unprotected against the
protected cores. The results confirm that the overhead in terms of area, power
and performance is small, making this countermeasure attractive.

Moreover, the proposed AES architecture provides different options to tune
the design into the user's need. Among 29 different configurations, examples
include: to make the proposed AES a 4-stage pipeline (*i.e.*, compute four different
plaintexts per execution), to use three blocks to generate noise against power
attacks, or to use one inactive block in the chain to recompute for encryption
correctness. In addition to the proposed AES implementation, we presented a
simple scheme to halve the number of memory positions required for storing
subkeys when AES is performing decryption.

7   Further Research: Ghost Data Attacks?

The footnote in Sect. 2 raises an interesting question: is it possible to exploit
leakage from uselessly active circuit blocks to infer information about P, C or K?
In this model the attacker is not allowed to access the side-channel information
resulting from the actual computation of the active block (that we can assume
to be ideally protected or not leaking) but only the side-channel information
leaked by the three uselessly active blocks. To the best of our knowledge such
attacks, that we call *ghost data attacks*, were never considered in the literature.

Acknowledgments. The authors thank Ms. Natacha Laniado (natacha@laniado.fr)
for proofreading and correcting this paper.

References

1. National Institute of Standards and Technology (NIST): Announcing the Advanced Encryption Standard (AES), November 2001
2. Akkar, M.-L., Giraud, C.: An implementation of DES and AES, secure against some attacks. In: Koç, Ç.K., Naccache, D., Paar, C. (eds.) CHES 2001. LNCS, vol. 2162, pp. 309–318. Springer, Heidelberg (2001)
3. Bertoni, G., Breveglieri, L., Koren, I., Maistri, P., Piuri, V.: Error analysis and detection procedures for a hardware implementation of the advanced encryption standard. IEEE Trans. Comput. **52**(4), 492–505 (2003)
4. Kocher, P.C.: Timing attacks on implementations of Diffie-Hellman, RSA, DSS, and other systems. In: Koblitz, N. (ed.) CRYPTO 1996. LNCS, vol. 1109, pp. 104–113. Springer, Heidelberg (1996)
5. Kocher, P.C., Jaffe, J., Jun, B.: Differential power analysis. In: Wiener, M. (ed.) CRYPTO 1999. LNCS, vol. 1666, pp. 388–397. Springer, Heidelberg (1999)
6. Mangard, S., Oswald, E., Popp, T.: Power Analysis Attacks - Revealing the Secrets of Smart Cards. Springer, New York (2007)
7. Joye, M., Tunstall, M. (eds.): Fault Analysis in Cryptography. Information Security and Cryptography. Springer, Heidelberg (2012)
8. Bertoni, G., Breveglieri, L., Koren, I., Piuri, V.: Fault detection in the advanced encryption standard. In: Proceedings of the 4th International Conference on Massively Parallel, Computing Systems, pp. 92–97 (2002)

Double-Speed Barrett Moduli

Rémi Géraud, Diana Maimuţ, and David Naccache[✉]

Équipe de Cryptographie, École Normale Supérieure,
45 rue d'Ulm, 75230 Paris Cedex 05, France
{remi.geraud,diana.maimut,david.naccache}@ens.fr

Abstract. Modular multiplication and modular reduction are the atomic constituents of most public-key cryptosystems. Amongst the numerous algorithms for performing these operations, a particularly elegant method was proposed by Barrett. This method builds the operation $a \bmod b$ from bit shifts, multiplications and additions in $\mathbb{Z}$. This allows to build modular reduction at very marginal code or silicon costs by leveraging existing hardware or software multipliers.

This paper presents a method allowing to double the speed of Barrett's algorithm by using specific composite moduli. This is particularly useful for lightweight devices where such an optimization can make a difference in terms of power consumption, cost and processing time. The generation of composite moduli with a predetermined portion is a well-known technique and the use of such moduli is considered, *in statu scientiæ*, as safe as using randomly generated composite moduli.

1 Introduction

Modular multiplication and modular reduction are the atomic constituents of most public-key cryptosystems. Amongst the numerous algorithms for performing these operations (*e.g.* [3,4,9,12]), a particularly elegant method was proposed by Barrett in [1]. This method assembles the operation $a \bmod b$ from bit shifts, multiplications and additions in $\mathbb{Z}$. This allows to build modular reduction at very marginal code or silicon costs by leveraging existing hardware or software multipliers. For a very detailed comparison of the principal modular reduction strategies, we refer the reader to [3].

This paper presents a method allowing to double the speed of Barrett's algorithm by using specific composite moduli. This is particularly useful for lightweight devices where such an optimization can make a difference in terms of power consumption, cost and processing time. The generation of composite moduli with a predetermined portion is a well-known technique [6,10,17] and the use of such moduli is considered, *in statu scientiæ*, as safe as using randomly generated composite moduli.

Related Work: Douguet and Dupaquis [5] describe a modified Barrett modular reduction algorithm whose purpose is the acceleration of this type of operation in certain (elliptic curve) groups of known moduli. Thus, the approach they

© Springer-Verlag Berlin Heidelberg 2016
P.Y.A. Ryan et al. (Eds.): Kahn Festschrift, LNCS 9100, pp. 148–158, 2016.
DOI: 10.1007/978-3-662-49301-4_10

consider implies moduli with a given form, *e.g.* the recommended ones from
[13]. Estimations of the speed-ups are not provided, but the resistance of various architectures to different physical attacks is discussed. A general form of
the Barrett constant and of the quotients (when certain moduli are used) are
described. As an example of the proposed techniques, the Elliptic Curve Digital
Signature Algorithm (ECDSA) [14] is taken into account.

We stress that no specific modulus generation algorithm is presented in [5].
The approach of [5] is rather a practical one, whereas our goal is to provide formal
mathematical models for moduli with a predetermined portion generation.

Knežević et al. [7] propose two sets of moduli for which Barrett's modular
reduction algorithm can be implemented by avoiding the precomputation of the
Barrett constant. The types of moduli considered throughout this paper do not
fall into those sets.

Structure of the Paper: Section 2 starts by introducing notations and describing Barrett's original algorithm. Section 3 recalls background concerning composite moduli a predetermined portion. Section 4 introduces our core idea, that
leverages Sect. 3 to generate Barrett-friendly RSA moduli. In Sect. 5, we apply
this idea to other cryptographic primitives, such as DSA [14].

2   Barrett's Algorithm

For a given a, let $\|a\| = 1 + \lfloor \log_2 a \rfloor = \lceil \log_2 (a+1) \rceil$. That is, $\|a\|$ will denote
the bit-length of a throughout this paper. $a|b$ will represent the concatenation
of the bit-strings a and b.

$x \gg y$ will denote binary shift-to-the-right of x by y places *i.e.*:

$$x \gg y = \left\lfloor \frac{x}{2^y} \right\rfloor$$

Barrett's algorithm (Algorithm 1) approximates the result $c = d \bmod n$ by a
quasi-reduced number $c + \epsilon n$ where $0 \le \epsilon \le 2$. We denote $N = \|n\|, D = \|d\|$
and set a *maximal bit-length reduction capacity* L such that $N \le D \le L$. The
algorithm will function as long as $D \le L$. In most implementations $D = L = 2N$.
The algorithm uses the pre-computed constant $\kappa = \lfloor 2^L / n \rfloor$ that depends only
on n and L. The reader is referred to [1] for a proof and a thorough analysis of
this algorithm.

Work Factor: $\|c_1\| = D - N + 1 \simeq D - N$ and $\|\kappa\| = L - N$ hence their
product requires $w = (D - N)(L - N)$ elementary operations. $\|c_3\| = (D - N) + (L - N) - (L - N + 1) = D - N - 1 \simeq D - N$. The product nc_3 will
therefore claim $w' = (D - N)N$ elementary operations. All in all, work amounts
to $w + w' = (D - N)(L - N) + (D - N)N = (D - N)L$. The goal of this paper
is to halve this work factor.

Algorithm 1. Barrett's Algorithm

Input: $n < 2^N, d < 2^D, \kappa = \left\lfloor \frac{2^L}{n} \right\rfloor$ where $N \leq D \leq L$

Output: $c = d \bmod n$

1   $c_1 \leftarrow d \gg (N-1)$;
2   $c_2 \leftarrow c_1 \kappa$;
3   $c_3 \leftarrow c_2 \gg (L - N + 1)$;
4   $c_4 \leftarrow d - nc_3$;
5   **while** $c_4 \geq n$ **do**
6 | $c_4 \leftarrow c_4 - n$;
7   **end while**
8   **return** c_4

---

3   Moduli with a Predetermined Portion

RSA [15] moduli with a predetermined portion are used to reduce storage requirements or computations. As mentioned before, such moduli are presently not known to be cryptographically weaker than randomly chosen ones. The first techniques for generating composite moduli were proposed by Vanstone and Zuccherato [17] who presented various ways of specifying $N/4 \leq \ell \leq N/2$ bits of n. Lenstra [10] proposed more advanced techniques for specifying up to $N/2$ bits. Based on Lenstra's algorithms, Joye proposed new techniques in [6]. Further works in the area include, for instance, [8,11,16]. We will hereafter recall the folklore method described by Joye (Algorithm 2), that perfectly fits our purpose[1].

Folklore Method. The purpose of the folklore technique recalled by Joye is to obtain an RSA modulus n with a predetermined leading part n_h. Letting $\|n_h\| = H$, we have:

$$n = n_h 2^{N-H} + n_\ell, \text{ for some } 0 < n_\ell < 2^{N-H} \tag{1}$$

The algorithm uses the function NextPrime(x) that returns the prime following x (if x is prime then $x = $ NextPrime(x)). Note that because the gap between x and NextPrime(x) is unpredictable, the algorithm may fail to return an n of the form $n = n_h 2^{N-H} + n_\ell$ and will have to be re-launched. We refer the reader to [10] for a more formal analysis of this process.

Lemma 1. (Bounding n and ω) *Consider the parameters used in Algorithm 2 and let $m = q - \omega$. Then, $n < n_h 2^{N-H} + (1+m)(2^{N-H} - 1)$ and $\omega < 2^{H+1} + 1$.*

Proof. By definition:

$$\omega = \left\lceil \frac{\eta}{p} \right\rceil \Rightarrow \exists \alpha < p \text{ such that } \omega = \frac{\eta}{p} + \frac{\alpha}{p}$$

---

[1] For the sake of clarity we remove all tests meant to enforce the condition $\mathrm{GCD}(e, \phi(n)) = 1$.

Substituting the value of η, we get:

$$\omega = \frac{n_h 2^{N-H}}{p} + \frac{\alpha}{p} \Rightarrow q = \omega + m = \frac{n_h 2^{N-H}}{p} + \frac{\alpha}{p} + m$$

Thus:

$$n = pq = n_h 2^{N-H} + \alpha + mp < n_h 2^{N-H} + (1+m)p < n_h 2^{N-H} + (1+m)(2^{N-H} - 1)$$

And upper bounding ω we get:

$$\omega < \frac{\eta}{p} + 1 = \frac{n_h 2^{N-H}}{p} + 1 < \frac{n_h 2^{N-H}}{2^{N-H-1}} + 1 = 2n_h + 1 < 2^{H+1} + 1$$

Note that the most significant bit of p must be set to 1, *i.e.* $2^{N-H-1} < p < 2^{N-H} - 1$. $\square$

It follows directly from Lemma 1 that:

$$q = \text{NextPrime}[\omega] \leq \text{NextPrime}[2^{H+1} + 1].$$

Applying the Prime Number Theorem, we find that $m \simeq \ln(2^{H+1} + 1) \simeq 0.7(H+1)$. In other words, the $\log_2(m+1) \simeq \log_2(0.7H + 1.7) < \log_2 H$ least significant bits of n_h are likely to get polluted. We hence rectify the size of n_h to $H - \tau - \log_2 H$ where $\tau \in \mathbb{N}$ is a parameter allowing to reduce the failure probability of Algorithm 2 at the cost of further shortening n_h. For the sake of clarity, we do not integrate these fine-tunings in the description of Algorithm 2 but consider that n_h is composed of a "real" prescribed pattern $\bar{n}_h$ of size $H - \tau - \lceil \log_2 H \rceil$ bits right-padded with $\tau + \lceil \log_2 H \rceil$ zero bits. Various success rates for $N = 1024, H = 512$ are given in Fig. 1. Based on those we recommend to set $\tau = 0$ or $\tau = 1$ and re-launch the generation process if the algorithm fails.

Note: The algorithm's theoretical analysis could be simplified and the failure rate improved if step (4) of Fig. 1 is replaced by: "If ω is composite then goto 1; else $q \leftarrow \omega$". The quality of the generated primes will also become theoretically uniform because NextPrime favors primes p_i whose distance from the previous prime p_{i-1} is large. This modification will, however, come at the cost of more computation time. The same note is applicable to Algorithm 3 as well.

τ	0	1	2	3	4
$\|\bar{n}_h\|$	503	502	501	500	499
success rate	85.66%	97.96%	99.96%	100%	100%

Fig. 1. Success rates of Algorithm 2 for $N = 1024, H = 512$ and 10^4 experiments.

Algorithm 2. Folklore method

Input: $N, H \leq N/2, n_h < 2^H$
Output: $n = n_h 2^{N-H} + n_\ell$, such that $0 < n_\ell < 2^{N-H}$
1 Generate a random prime p, such that $2^{N-H-1} < p < 2^{N-H} - 1$;
2 $\eta \leftarrow n_h 2^{N-H}$;
3 $\omega \leftarrow \left\lceil \frac{\eta}{p} \right\rceil$;
4 $q \leftarrow \text{NextPrime}(\omega)$;
5 $n \leftarrow pq$;
6 **return** n

Algorithm 3. Barrett-friendly modulus generator

Input: $L = 2N = 4U$
Output: n, an RSA modulus such that $2^{N-1} < n < 2^{N-1} + (0.7U + 2)(2^U - 1)$
   whose associated κ is such that $2^{N+1} - 2^{U+1}(1 + 0.7U) < \kappa < 2^{N+1}$
1 Generate a random integer r such that $2^{U-1} < r < 2^U - 1$;
2 $\eta \leftarrow 2^{N-1} + r$;
3 Generate a random prime p such that $2^{U-1} < p < 2^U - 1$;
4 $\omega \leftarrow \left\lceil \frac{\eta}{p} \right\rceil$;
5 $q \leftarrow \text{NextPrime}(\omega)$;
6 $n \leftarrow pq$;
7 **return** n

4   Barrett-Friendly Moduli

We note that both multiplications in Algorithm 1 are multiplications by <u>constants</u>. Namely by n and κ. It is known (*e.g.* [2]) that multiplications by constants can be performed faster than multiplications by arbitrary integers. Our goal is to generate a composite n whose leading bits do not need to be multiplied and whose associated κ also features a most significant part that does not need to be multiplied. As for the least significant parts of n and κ, these are constants and can hence *independently* benefit of speedup techniques such as [2]. The algorithm is given for the very common setting $L = D = 2N$. For convenience we introduce a bitlength unit U such that $L = 2N = 4U$.

Example 1. Let $N = 100$ and $L = 200$:

$r = \text{1ace38e78e29f}$ $\eta = \text{8000000000001ace38e78e29f}$
$p = \text{322a28626f0a7}$ $\omega = \text{28d356763fe4a}$
$q = \text{51a6acec7fcd5}$ $n = \text{80000000000a8c93071ac14d9}$
                                          $\kappa = \text{1fffffffffffd5cdb3e394fe440}$

Lemma 2. *If* $0 < x < 2^{P/2-1}$, *then* $\left\lfloor \frac{2^{2P}}{2^{P-1}+x} \right\rfloor = 2^{P+1} - 4x$.

Proof. Observe that:

$$\frac{2^{2P}}{2^{P-1}+x} - (2^{P+1} - 4x) = \frac{4x^2}{2^{P-1}+x}. \tag{2}$$

Furthermore,

$$\frac{4x^2}{2^{P-1}+x} < 1 \Leftrightarrow 4x^2 - x < 2^{P-1}$$

This is a polynomial of degree 2, that has one positive and one negative root. We assumed $x > 0$, therefore we only need to consider the positive root x_{max}:

$$x_{max} = \frac{1}{8}\left(1 + \sqrt{1 + 2^{P+4}}\right) > 2^{P/2-1}$$

Therefore, if $x < 2^{P/2-1}$, then the fraction in Eq. 2 is smaller than one. As a consequence, we have

$$\left\lfloor \frac{2^{2P}}{2^{P-1}+x} - (2^{P+1} - 4x)\right\rfloor = \left\lfloor \frac{2^{2P}}{2^{P-1}+x}\right\rfloor - (2^{P+1} - 4x) = 0,$$

as $2^{P+1} - 4x$ is an integer. □

Lemma 3. (Bounding n, ω and κ in Algorithm 3) *Consider the parameters used in Algorithm 3 and let $m = q - \omega$. Then, $n < 2^{N-1} + (2 + m)(2^U - 1)$, $2^{N+1} - 2^{U+1}(1 + m) < \kappa < 2^{N+1}$ and $\omega < 2^U + 2$.*

Proof. By definition:

$$\omega = \left\lceil \frac{\eta}{p}\right\rceil, \text{ thus } \exists \alpha < p \text{ such that } \omega = \frac{\eta}{p} + \frac{\alpha}{p}.$$

Substituting the value of η, we get:

$$\omega = \frac{2^{N-1}+r}{p} + \frac{\alpha}{p} \Rightarrow q = \omega + m = \frac{2^{N-1}}{p} + \frac{r}{p} + \frac{\alpha}{p} + m.$$

Thus:

$$n = pq = 2^{N-1} + r + \alpha + mp$$

$$\Downarrow$$

$$n < 2^{N-1}+r+(1+m)p < 2^{N-1}+2^U-1+(1+m)(2^U-1) < 2^{N-1}+(2+m)(2^U-1).$$

We observe that

$$2^{N-1}+r+\alpha+mp \leq 2^{N-1}+r+mp \Rightarrow \frac{1}{2^{N-1}+r+\alpha+mp} \geq \frac{1}{2^{N-1}+r+mp}.$$

Bounding κ we obtain:

$$\kappa = \left\lfloor \frac{2^L}{n}\right\rfloor > \frac{2^L}{n} - 1 \geq \frac{2^L}{2^{N-1}+r+mp} - 1,$$

Now observe that $r + mp < 2^{N-1}$, therefore we can write

$$\frac{2^L}{2^{N-1}+r+mp} = \frac{2^{2N}}{2^{N-1}+r+mp} = 2^{N+1}\frac{1}{1+2^{1-N}(r+mp)} = 2^{N+1}\sum_{\ell=0}^{\infty}(-2)^{\ell(1-N)}(r+mp)^{\ell}$$

This series is convergent, alternating, and the term is strictly decreasing, therefore its sum is bounded below (resp. above) by the partial sum of odd (resp. even) degree S_ℓ. As a consequence,

$$\kappa > S_1 - 1 = 2^{N+1}\left(1 - 2^{1-N}(r+pm)\right) - 1 = 2^{N+1} - 4(r+pm) - 1 > 2^{N+1} - 2^{U+1}(1+m).$$

We observe that

$$2^{N-1}+r+\alpha+mp > 2^{N-1} \Rightarrow \frac{1}{2^{N-1}+r+\alpha+mp} < \frac{1}{2^{N-1}}.$$

Thus:

$$\kappa \leq \frac{2^L}{n} = \frac{2^L}{2^{N-1}+r+\alpha+mp} < \frac{2^L}{2^{N-1}} < 2^{N+1}.$$

Upper bounding ω we get:

$$\omega < \frac{\eta}{p}+1 = \frac{2^{N-1}+r}{p}+1 < \frac{2^{N-1}+2^{U-1}}{2^{U-1}}+1 = 2^{N-1-U+1}+1+1 < 2^U+2.$$

Note that the most significant bit of p must be set to 1, i.e. $2^{U-1} < p < 2^U - 1$. □

It follows directly from Lemma 3 that:

$$q = \text{NextPrime}[\omega] \leq \text{NextPrime}[2^U + 2] = \text{NextPrime}[2^U + 1].$$

Let n_h denote the predetermined portion of n, i.e. $n_h = 2^{U-1}$. Applying the Prime Number Theorem, we obtain $m \simeq \ln(2^U + 1) \simeq 0.7U$. Put differently, the $\log_2(m + 2) \simeq \log_2(0.7U + 2) < \log_2 U$ least significant bits of n_h are likely to get polluted. We hence rectify the size of n_h to $U - \tau - \log_2 U$ where $\tau \in \mathbb{N}$ is a parameter allowing to reduce the failure probability of Algorithm 3 at the cost of further shortening n_h. For the sake of clarity, we do not integrate these fine-tunings in the description of Algorithm 3 but consider that n_h is composed of a "real" prescribed pattern $\bar{n}_h$ of size $U - \tau - \lceil\log_2 U\rceil$ bits right-padded with $\tau + \lceil\log_2 U\rceil$ zero bits. Various success rates for $N = 1024, U = 512$ are given in Fig. 2. Based on those we recommend to set $\tau = 0$ or $\tau = 1$ and re-launch the generation process if the algorithm fails.

It is easy to see that multiplication by both n and κ is not costly at all. To be more specific, n and κ satisfy the inequalities:

$$2^{N-1} < n < 2^{N-1} + (0.7U + 2)(2^U - 1) \text{ and } 2^{N+1} - 2^{U+1}(1+0.7U) < \kappa < 2^{N+1}.$$

As a result, this can double the speed of Barrett reduction[2].

---

[2] A few more complexity bits can be grabbed if the variant described in the note at the end of Sect. 3 is used.

τ	0	1	2	3	4
$\|\bar{n}_h\|$	503	502	501	500	499
success rate	85.16%	97.51%	99.91%	100%	100%

Fig. 2. Success rates of Algorithm 3 for $N = 1024, U = 512$ and 10^4 experiments.

Algorithm 4. DSA prime generation

Input: Key lengths P and $Q \leq P$.
Output: Parameters (p, q).

1 Choose a Q−bit prime q;

2 Choose a P−bit prime modulus p such that $p - 1$ is a multiple of q;
3 **return** (p, q)

---

5 Extensions

The parameter generation phase of DL cryptosystems requires the generation of two primes (*e.g.* p and q). Computations modulo these two primes represent important steps within the algorithms. Thus, a modular reduction speedup is necessary. It is thus desirable that both p and q to contain significantly long patterns (*i.e.* many successive 1 s or 0s). We will now propose a Barrett-friendly parameter generation approach to do so. For the sake of clarity, we choose a particular algorithm to describe our method: the Digital Signature Algorithm (DSA).

5.1 Barrett-Friendly DSA Parameters Generation

DSA's parameter generation is presented in Algorithm 4. For the complete description of the DSA, we refer the reader to [14].

We suggest a modified DSA prime generation process leveraging the idea of Sect. 4. The procedure is described in Algorithm 5.

Lemma 4. (Structure of κ_q) *Let κ_q be the κ associated to q. With the notations of Algorithm 5, we have $\kappa_q = 2^{Q+1} - 4\omega$, assuming that $\omega < 2^{\frac{Q}{2}-1}$.*

Proof. Let $z = \frac{p-1}{q}$ and $\omega = q - 2^{Q-1}$. We observe that $\|z\| = P - Q$ and $q = 2^{Q-1}|\omega$. By definition, $\kappa_q = \left\lfloor \frac{2^{L_q}}{q} \right\rfloor$, where $L_q = 2Q$. As we assumed $\omega < 2^{\frac{Q}{2}-1}$, using Lemma 2 we have:

$$\kappa_q = \left\lfloor \frac{2^{L_q}}{q} \right\rfloor = \left\lfloor \frac{2^{2Q}}{2^{Q-1} + \omega} \right\rfloor = 2^{Q+1} - 4\omega.$$

$\square$

Algorithm 5. Barrett-friendly DSA prime generation

Input: Key lengths P and $Q \leq P$.
Output: Parameters (p, q).

1 Generate a Q–bit prime as follows:
2 $q \leftarrow$ NextPrime(2^{Q-1}) ;
3 Construct a P–bit prime modulus p such that $p - 1$ is a multiple of q in the
   following way:
4 $p \leftarrow 4$;
5 $i \leftarrow 1$;
6 $F \leftarrow 2^{P-Q-1}$;
7 **while** p is composite **do**
8      $\quad$ $p \leftarrow 2q(F + i) + 1$;
9      $\quad$ $i + +$;
10 **end while**
11 **return** (p, q)

The key consequence of Lemma 4 is that κ_q consists of a long pattern concatenated to a short different sequence, with a predetermined portion that is the complement of $q_h = 2^{Q-\Omega}$. The computation of κ_q is easy.

Let $L_p = 2P$. By definition, $\kappa_p = \left\lfloor \frac{2^{L_p}}{p} \right\rfloor$.

Lemma 5. *Let* $m(n) = \frac{1}{8}\left(n + \sqrt{n^2 + 2^{P+3}n}\right)$. *Let* x *be a positive integer such that* $0 < x < 2^{P-1}$ *and* $m(n) \leq x < m(n+1)$. *Then,*

$$\left\lfloor \frac{2^{2P}}{2^{P-1} + x} \right\rfloor = 2^{P+1} - 4x + n \quad and \quad 0 \leq n < 2^P.$$

Proof. The proof consists of writing the fraction as a geometric series:

$$\kappa = \left\lfloor \frac{2^{2P}}{2^{P-1} + x} \right\rfloor = \left\lfloor 2^{P+1} \sum_{n=0}^{\infty} (-x)^n 2^{n(1-P)} \right\rfloor$$

$$= \left\lfloor 2^{P+1}\left(1 - 2^{1-P}x + 2^{2-2P}x^2 - 2^{3-3P}x^3 + \ldots\right)\right\rfloor$$

$$= \left\lfloor 2^{P+1} - 4x + 2^{3-P}x^2 - 2^{4-2P}x^3 + \ldots\right\rfloor$$

Now, $2^{P+1} - 4x$ is always a positive integer, it can therefore be safely taken out of the floor function. None of the remaining terms of the sum is an integer. We have:

$$\kappa = 2^{P+1} - 4x + \left\lfloor \sum_{n=2}^{\infty} (-x)^n 2^{n(1-P)} \right\rfloor.$$

The rightmost term is essentially a sum of shifted versions of powers of x. If x is small, then this contribution quickly vanishes. We now provide an exact value for this sum, by rewriting:

$$\kappa = 2^{P+1} - 4x + \left\lfloor 2^{2-P}x^2 \frac{2^{P-1}}{2^{P-1}+x} \right\rfloor$$

$$= 2^{P+1} - 4x + \left\lfloor \frac{4x^2}{2^{P-1}+x} \right\rfloor.$$

For any positive integer n, we have:

$$\frac{4x^2}{2^{P-1}+x} = n \Leftrightarrow x = \frac{1}{8}\left(n + \sqrt{n^2 + 2^{P+3}n}\right).$$

We assumed $x > 0$, thus we only need to consider the positive root. The leftmost fraction is a strictly increasing function of x as its derivative is >0. Therefore, the rightmost formula strictly increases with n.

Let $m(n) = \frac{1}{8}\left(n + \sqrt{n^2 + 2^{P+3}n}\right)$ and assume that $m(n) \le x < m(n+1)$. Then, we have:

$$n \le \frac{4x^2}{2^{P-1}+x} < n+1$$

Therefore:

$$\left\lfloor \frac{4x^2}{2^{P-1}+x} \right\rfloor = n.$$

Finally, $x < 2^{P-1}$ implies an upper bound on the value of n, which must therefore be smaller than 2^P.

An illustrative example for $P = 1024$ and $Q = 160$ is given next.

Example 2.

$$\omega = 299$$

$$i_p = 1$$

$$L_q = 2 \cdot 160$$

$$q = 2^{159} + 299$$

$$\kappa_q = 2^{163} - 4 \cdot 299$$

$$L_p = 2 \cdot 1024 = 2^{11}$$

$$p = (2^{864} + 2)q + 1 = (2^{864} + 2)(2^{159} + 299) + 1$$

$$x = 2^{60} + 299 \cdot 2^{864} + 2 \cdot 299 + 1$$

$$\kappa_p = 2^{71} \sum_{k=0}^{5} 2^{159k}(-299)^{6-k} - 2^{162} + 2387$$

Thus, multiplication by p, q, κ_p and κ_q is easy.

References

1. Barrett, P.: Implementing the Rivest Shamir and Adleman public key encryption algorithm on a standard digital signal processor. In: Odlyzko, A.M. (ed.) CRYPTO 1986. LNCS, vol. 263, pp. 311–323. Springer, Heidelberg (1987)
2. Bernstein, R.: Multiplication by integer constants. Softw. Pract. Exp. 16(7), 641–652 (1986)
3. Bosselaers, A., Govaerts, R., Vandewalle, J.: Comparison of three modular reduction functions. In: Stinson, D.R. (ed.) CRYPTO 1993. LNCS, vol. 773, pp. 175–186. Springer, Heidelberg (1994)
4. Brickell, E.F.: A Fast Modular Multiplication Algorithm with Applications to TwoKey Cryptography. Crypto 1982, pp. 51–60. Springer, New York (1983)
5. Douguet, M., Dupaquis, V.: Modular reduction using a special form of the modulus. U.S. Patent Application 12/033,512, filed February 19, Atmel Corporation (2008)
6. Joye, M.: RSA moduli with a predetermined portion: techniques and applications. In: Chen, L., Mu, Y., Susilo, W. (eds.) ISPEC 2008. LNCS, vol. 4991, pp. 116–130. Springer, Heidelberg (2008)
7. Knežević, M., Batina, L., Verbauwhede, I.: Modular reduction without precomputational phase. In: Proceedings of the IEEE International Symposium on Circuits and Systems (ISCAS), pp. 1389–1392. IEEE (2009)
8. Knobloch, H.-J.: A smart card implementation of the Fiat-Shamir identification scheme. In: Günther, C.G. (ed.) EUROCRYPT 1988. LNCS, vol. 330, pp. 87–95. Springer, Heidelberg (1988)
9. Knuth, D.E.: The Art of Computer Programming. Seminumerical Algorithms, vol. 2, 2nd edn. Addison Wesley, Reading (1981)
10. Lenstra, A.K.: Generating RSA moduli with a predetermined portion. In: Ohta, K., Pei, D. (eds.) ASIACRYPT 1998. LNCS, vol. 1514, pp. 1–10. Springer, Heidelberg (1998)
11. Meister, G.: On an implementation of the Mohan-Adiga algorithm. In: Damgård, I.B. (ed.) EUROCRYPT 1990. LNCS, vol. 473, pp. 496–500. Springer, Heidelberg (1991)
12. Montgomery, P.L.: Modular multiplication without trial division. Math. Comput. 44(170), 519–521 (1985)
13. National Institute of Standards and Technology (NIST): Digital Signature Standard. FIPS PUB 186-2 (2013)
14. National Institute of Standards and Technology (NIST): Digital Signature Standard. FIPS PUB 186-4 (2013)
15. Rivest, R.L., Shamir, A., Adleman, L.M.: A method for obtaining digital signatures and public-key cryptosystems. Commun. Assoc. Comput. Mach. 21(2), 120–126 (1978)
16. Shparlinski, I.E.: On RSA moduli with prescribed bit patterns. Des. Codes Cryptogr. 39(1), 113–122 (2006)
17. Vanstone, S.A., Zuccherato, R.J.: Short RSA keys and their generation. J. Cryptol. 8(2), 101–114 (1995)

Treachery and Perfidy

Failure is Also an Option

Antoine Amarilli[1], Marc Beunardeau[2], Rémi Géraud[2], and David Naccache[2(✉)]

[1] Institut Mines-Télécom, Télécom ParisTech, CNRS LTCI,
46 rue Barrault, 75634 Paris Cedex 13, France
antoine.amarilli@telecom-paristech.fr
[2] École normale supérieure, Département d'informatique,
45 rue d'Ulm, 75230 Paris Cedex 05, France
{marc.beunardeau,remi.geraud,david.naccache}@ens.fr

Abstract. The Nijmeegse Vierdaagse (http://www.4daagse.nl/en/) is the world's most famous walking event. The walk is known to be challenging and each year about 10 % of the participants drop out. In 2016 the Vierdaagse will celebrate its centennial anniversary. In the walker community there is a frenzy about participating in the centennial walk. Initially, the rules governing participation were the following: A walker who succeeds the n-th walk is admitted to walk at year $(n + 1)$. Walkers who fail a walk enter a lottery. If they win the lottery, they are also granted tickets to the walk. Finally, walkers who fail two successive draws are admitted to the walk following the second lottery failure. In 2013, while computing our chances to be admitted to the centennial walk, we noticed a rather counterintuitive fact: By purposely failing the 97-th walk, walkers can actually... increase their chances to attend the centennial walk.

We notified this inconsistency to the organizers. We never got an answer but the rules were subsequently changed.

1 Introduction

The Nijmeegse Vierdaagse is the world's most famous walking event. The walk is known to be challenging and each year about 10 % of the participants drop out. In 2016 the Vierdaagse will celebrate its centennial anniversary.

In the walker community there is a frenzy about participating in the centennial walk. Initially, the rules governing participation were the following:

Let $\mathcal{P}$ be a participant.

- **Rule 1:** If $\mathcal{P}$ finishes the walk of year n then $\mathcal{P}$ is admitted to the walk on year $n + 1$.
- **Rule 2:** If $\mathcal{P}$ fails the walk of year n then $\mathcal{P}$ enters a lottery:
  - If $\mathcal{P}$ wins the lottery then $\mathcal{P}$ is admitted to walk of year $n + 1$.
  - If $\mathcal{P}$ fails the lottery then $\mathcal{P}$ is excluded from the walk of year $n + 1$.
- **Rule 3:** If $\mathcal{P}$ fails the two successive lotteries of years n and $n + 1$ then $\mathcal{P}$ is admitted to walk at year $n + 2$.

© Springer-Verlag Berlin Heidelberg 2016
P.Y.A. Ryan et al. (Eds.): Kahn Festschrift, LNCS 9100, pp. 161–165, 2016.
DOI: 10.1007/978-3-662-49301-4_11

Rule 3 is meant to avoid a situation where, by sheer bad luck, a person will never be given a chance to attend the Vierdaagse.

On the eve of the 97-th walk we wished to estimate our odds to reach the centennial walk. While doing so, we noticed a rather counter-intuitive fact: By purposely failing the 97-th walk, walkers can actually... increase their chances to attend the centennial walk.

Interestingly, this strategy does not depend on one's walking skills nor on the chances to succeed the lottery.

2   Failing, to Succeed...

2.1   The Underlying Markov Chain

The rules define a Markov chain having two terminal states: being admitted to the centennial walk, and not being admitted. Let W, $\mathcal{W}$, L, $\mathcal{L}$ denote the following events:

- W: $\mathcal{P}$ walked and succeeded
- $\mathcal{W}$: $\mathcal{P}$ walked and failed
- L: $\mathcal{P}$ participated in lottery and won
- $\mathcal{L}$: $\mathcal{P}$ participated in lottery and failed

We distinguish two categories of scenarios: those leading to the centennial walk, and those that do not. Let the probability to succeed a walk be $w = \Pr[W]$ and let the probability to be selected during a draw be $\ell = \Pr[L]$. Naturally $\Pr[\mathcal{W}] = 1 - w$ and $\Pr[\mathcal{L}] = 1 - \ell$.

The transition graph is described in Table 1 and Fig. 1.

2.2   The Optimal Strategy

If we sum the probabilities of the events leading to the centennial walk we get that the probability A to arrive to the centennial walk is:

$$A = 1 - 2\ell + 3\ell^2 - \ell^3 - w + 4\ell w - 4\ell^2 w + \ell^3 w + \ell w^2 - 2\ell^2 w^2$$
$$+ \ell^3 w^2 + w^3 - 3\ell w^3 + 3\ell^2 w^3 - \ell^3 w^3$$

The honest reader would usually stop reading here. A cryptographer seeking for algorithmic loopholes would notice that there is a further option: Purposely fail the 97-th walk!

What would happen then? The Markov chain is simplified as in Table 2 and Fig. 2.

If we sum the probability of events leading to the centennial walk we get that the new probability to arrive to the centennial walk is:

$$B = 1 - 2\ell + 3\ell^2 - \ell^3 + \ell w - \ell^2 w + \ell w^2 - 2\ell^2 w^2 + \ell^3 w^2.$$

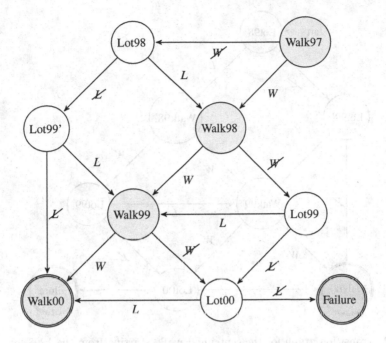

Fig. 1. Transition graph for the centennial walk, starting from the 1997 walk.

Table 1. Transition graph to the centennial walk.

97-th	98-th	99-th	100-th	centennial?
~~W~~	~~L~~	~~L~~		Yes
~~W~~	~~L~~	L ~~W~~	~~L~~	No
~~W~~	~~L~~	L ~~W~~	L	Yes
~~W~~	~~L~~	L W		Yes
~~W~~	L ~~W~~	~~L~~	~~L~~	No
~~W~~	L ~~W~~	~~L~~	L	Yes
~~W~~	L ~~W~~	L ~~W~~	~~L~~	No
~~W~~	L ~~W~~	L ~~W~~	L	Yes
~~W~~	L ~~W~~	L W		Yes
~~W~~	L W	~~W~~	~~L~~	No
~~W~~	L W	~~W~~	L	Yes
~~W~~	L W	W		Yes
W	~~W~~	~~L~~	~~L~~	No
W	~~W~~	~~L~~	L	Yes
W	~~W~~	L ~~W~~	~~L~~	No
W	~~W~~	L ~~W~~	L	Yes
W	~~W~~	L W		Yes
W	W	~~W~~	~~L~~	No
W	W	~~W~~	L	Yes
W	W	W		Yes

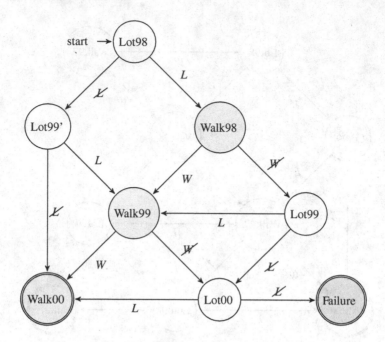

Fig. 2. Transition graph for the centennial walk, starting from the 1998 lottery.

Table 2. Simplified transition graph after failing the 97th walk.

98-th	99-th	100-th	centennial?
$\not L$	$\not L$		Yes
$\not L$	$L \not W$	$\not L$	No
$\not L$	$L \not W$	L	Yes
$\not L$	$L W$		Yes
$L \not W$	$\not L$	$\not L$	No
$L \not W$	$\not L$	L	Yes
$L \not W$	$L \not W$	$\not L$	No
$L \not W$	$L \not W$	L	Yes
$L \not W$	$L W$		Yes
$L W$	$\not W$	$\not L$	No
$L W$	$\not W$	L	Yes
$L W$	W		Yes

Let us determine the values of ℓ, w for which $B > A$. It turns out that:

$$B > A \implies (\ell - 1)^3 w(w^2 - 1) > 0$$

Since $w \geq 0$ is a positive probability this is equivalent to:

$$(\ell - 1)^3(w^2 - 1) > 0 \implies (\ell - 1)(w^2 - 1) > 0$$

And because ℓ and w are probabilities (which are smaller than 1), this inequality is... always satisfied!

Hence, to optimize the chances to get the centennial ticket, the best thing to do is... purposely fail the 97-th walk! and this independently of one's walking skills (i.e., it is valid for all w)!

3   Aftermath

We notified this inconsistency to the organizers. We never got an answer but the rules were subsequently changed. As we write these lines[1]:

> "... Walkers who have successfully completed the Four Days Marches at least four times between 2010 and 2015 will be guaranteed a starting ticket for the 100-th edition ..."

The main problem is Rule 3. This rule, meant to protect walkers from a strike of bad luck, opens a loophole to the centennial walk. Despite the modifications made to the rules, this loophole still exists: The most successful path, for a weak walker, is through the lotteries. Indeed, lotteries provide a guaranteed win at some probability which is completely independent from the walker's abilities.

Note that even if walking skills and lottery probabilities vary in time, it still pays to fail on purpose. Denoting by ℓ_i the probability to win the lottery at year i and by ω_i the probability to finish the walk of year i. We get an updated inequality for $B > A$:

$$(\ell_{100} - 1)(\ell_{98} - 1)(\ell_{99} - 1)\omega_{97}(\omega_{98}\omega_{99} - 1) > 0$$

Which is, again, always true for all ℓ_i, ω_i values. This also implies that failing on purpose is useful even when we take into account the option of purposedly failing later walks, which amounts to setting $\omega_i = 0$ for some values of $i > 97$.

Is there a simple way to both reward strong walkers while not penalizing bad luck? We make the following suggestion: Let the lottery probability p_i for a walker $\mathcal{P}$ depend on their number of successful walks k, and the number of years since their last selection a, in a way that grows lexicographically:

$$(k, a) \mapsto 1 - \frac{1}{k+1} + \frac{1}{(k+1)(k+2)}\left(1 - \frac{1}{a+1}\right)$$

Of course, the probability must be adjusted depending on the desired number of participants to select to a walk; the principle is just that the probability of a walker to succeed the lottery should depend lexicographically on k and a. This should intuitively guarantee that losing on purpose is never a better idea than walking, because walking gives a better chance of winning a later lottery.

This solution might not be perfect, however. For one thing, good walkers have better chances to be selected in a lottery; as a quick fix, instead of k we could use $N - k$, i.e. count the number of *failed* walks. Such a function acts as an incentive not to deliberately fail: The outcomes are better if one finishes the walk rather than relying on the lottery.

---

[1] http://www.4daagse.nl/en/home.html?id=273.

How to (Carefully) Breach a Service Contract?

Céline Chevalier, Damien Gaumont,
David Naccache[⊠], and Rodrigo Portella Do Canto

Paris Center for Law and Economics (CRED),
Sorbonne Universités – Université Paris II, 12 Place du Panthéon,
75231 Paris Cedex 05, France
{celine.chevalier,damien.gaumont,
david.naccache,rodrigo.portella.canto}@u-paris2.fr

Abstract. Consider a firm S providing support to clients A and B.

The contract $S \leftrightarrow A$ stipulates that S must continuously serve A and answer its calls immediately. While servicing A, S incurs two costs: personnel fees (salaries) that A refunds on a per-call-time basis and technical fees that are not refunded.

The contract $S \leftrightarrow B$ is a pay-per-call agreement where S gets paid an amount proportional to B's incoming call's duration. We consider that the flow of incoming B calls is unlimited and regular.

S wishes to use his workforce for both tasks, switching from A to B if necessary. As $S \leftrightarrow B$ generates new benefits and $S \leftrightarrow A$ is the fulfilling of a contracted obligation, S would like to devote as little resources as necessary to support A and divert as much workforce as possible to serve B. Hence, S's goal is to minimize his availability to serve A without incurring too high penalties.

This paper models A as a naïve player. This captures A's *needs* but not A's *game-theoretic interests* – which thorough investigation remains an open question.

1 Introduction

Consider a firm that provides a service to locked-in customers (*e.g.* state-run postal services). Given that clients are locked-in by contract or by law there is no client-loss (churn) risk. However, unhappy clients may sue the supplier if contract breaches are repeated or if quality of service degrades too much.

To imagine a concrete example, consider a firm S doing client-support for clients A and B.

The contract $S \leftrightarrow A$ stipulates that S must serve A's clients 24 h/day and answer incoming calls immediately. While servicing A, S incurs two costs: personnel fees (salaries) that A refunds on a per-call-time basis and technical fees that are not refunded. We use this split-cost model to capture the traditional combination of associating a "lump sum" and "premium rate call fees"[1] in the same commercial contract.

---

[1] *i.e.* 1–900 call.

© Springer-Verlag Berlin Heidelberg 2016
P.Y.A. Ryan et al. (Eds.): Kahn Festschrift, LNCS 9100, pp. 166–173, 2016.
DOI: 10.1007/978-3-662-49301-4_12

The contract $S \leftrightarrow B$ is a pay-per-call agreement meaning that whenever S answers an incoming call by one of B's clients, S gets paid an amount proportional to the incoming call's duration. We consider that the flow of incoming B calls is unlimited and regular (*i.e.* "all you can eat").

S wishes to use his agent for both tasks, switching from A to B if necessary. As $S \leftrightarrow B$ generates new benefits and $S \leftrightarrow A$ is the fulfilling of a contracted obligation, S would like to devote as little resources as necessary to support A and divert as much agent-time as possible to serve B. Hence, S's goal is to minimize the availability of the agent's awaiting of incoming A-calls over the day.

An agent can start treating a call for B to generate pay-per-call revenues. However, it takes a certain amount of time for the agent to finish a current B-case and switch to take an incoming A-call. Such delays necessarily breach the contract $S \leftrightarrow A$. This can be a source of annoyance for customers and possibly result in a lawsuit by A. S's goal is therefore to find a strategy that minimizes availability for A without creating too much annoyance to A's customers.

2 The Model

To capture a variety of practical cases we use the following model:

- $x(t)$ is the number of incoming A calls per hour during a day. The function $x(t)$ can be obtained by performing statistics on previously processed calls.
- γ is the agent's cost per hour. We assume that while working for B the agent covers exactly his salary costs[2].
- Answering an incoming A call consume one (normalized) unit of cost of technical fees.
- The total agent time t spent by S for servicing A is measured and A refunds S by the amount γt (*e.g.* via a 1–900 call). However, technical fee costs are not refunded to S by A.
- α is the penalty incurred by an incoming A call while the agent works for B. If the agent is in standby for A calls, no penalty is incurred since in this case the incoming call can be immediately processed by the agent. α is a monetized measure of A's sensitivity to the delay due to the agent's switch-back. A large α means that A's waiting time must be reduced to a minimum.

We consider a daily sequence of calls that follows a distribution given by $x(t)$. We denote by E the total cost consumed by the agent and by N the number of incurred penalties over a day. We define the total penalty function:

$$P = E + N \cdot \alpha \tag{1}$$

The total penalty P is therefore the sum of the consumed cost plus the total customer annoyance penalty, over a day. Note that to properly add-up, α's unit must be a monetary value (same unit as E).

---

[2] The model can be easily generalized to cases where working for B generates a positive margin.

Note that if we take $\alpha = 0$ (no customer annoyance penalty), then only the agent's cost must be minimized. In this case, the best strategy is simply to ask the agent to immediately start serving incoming $\mathcal{B}$-calls as soon as he finishes answering an $\mathcal{A}$-call.

On the other hand, for large α the cost E in Eq. (1) becomes negligible compared to the customer annoyance penalty $N \cdot \alpha$; in this case only the number of customer penalties N must be minimized. The best strategy is then to keep the agent always awaiting incoming $\mathcal{A}$-calls, i.e. never ask the agent to service incoming $\mathcal{B}$-calls.

Define $f(N)$ as the probability to get sued for breach of contract $\mathcal{S} \leftrightarrow \mathcal{A}$ before N incidents occur. f increases monotonously with N. It is hence desirable to reduce N as much as possible but... not at the cost of a too high revenue loss.

For "medium" values of customer sensitivity α, our goal is therefore to find a strategy that minimizes the total penalty function P as determined by Eq. (1). More precisely, given as input $x(t), \gamma, \alpha$, our goal is to determine when the agent should service $\mathcal{B}$ and when the agent should better switch back to await incoming $\mathcal{A}$-calls.

It remains to precise how α can be reasonably estimated. The most evident way to do so is to consider that a successful lawsuit for contract breach will cost ℓ dollars[3] to $\mathcal{S}$. Let $0 \leq \rho \leq 1$ reflect $\mathcal{S}$'s willingness to take risks ($\rho = 0$ means that $\mathcal{S}$ is very reluctant to take legal risks while $\rho = 1$ means that $\mathcal{S}$ takes extreme legal risks).

Let $f(n-1) \leq \rho \leq f(n)$ we set $\alpha \triangleq \ell/n$. As a sanity-check we see that if $\mathcal{S}$ has an extremely strong aversion to courts, his n will be equal to 1 resulting in $\alpha = \ell$. At the other extreme, if $\mathcal{S}$ doesn't care to get sued then $n = \infty$ and $\alpha = 0$.

3   Optimizing Income While Avoiding Lawyers

We now derive an optimal strategy to comply with Eq. (1).

We consider an observed increase ΔP in the total penalty function during a short period of time ΔT.

According to the previous model, this comprises the cost of the agent during ΔT, and possibly a penalty if an incoming $\mathcal{A}$ call occurred when the agent was serving a $\mathcal{B}$ client. We distinguish four possible cases during the period ΔT:

1. **Committing a victimless crime:** The agent serviced $\mathcal{B}$ and no $\mathcal{A}$-call occurred.
   $\mathcal{B}$ covered the agent's salary costs.
   ▶ In this case no cost is consumed and no penalty is incurred, so $\Delta P = 0$.
2. **Passively abiding by law:** The agent was in $\mathcal{A}$-standby and no $\mathcal{A}$-call occurred.
   S covered the agent's salary costs.
   ▶ By definition the cost consumed by the agent during ΔT is $\gamma \cdot \Delta T$; therefore the penalty function is increased by $\Delta P = \gamma \cdot \Delta T$.

---

[3] ℓ represents the legal fees, image negative impact and compensations paid to $\mathcal{A}$.

3. **Blazing offence:** The agent was servicing $\mathcal{B}$ and an $\mathcal{A}$-call occurred.
   $\mathcal{B}$ and $\mathcal{A}$ covered the agent's salary costs.
   ▶ The cost consumed by the agent during this configuration is equal to 1 (technical fees). Moreover a penalty α applies since the agent was unable to service $\mathcal{A}$ immediately. Therefore the total penalty function is increased by $\Delta P = 1 + \alpha$.
4. **Actively abiding by law:** The agent was in $\mathcal{A}$-standby and an $\mathcal{A}$-call occurred.
   $\mathcal{A}$ covered the agent's salary costs.
   ▶ No penalty is incurred and the total penalty function is only increased by $\Delta P = 1$, the technical fee cost required for treating the incoming $\mathcal{A}$-call.

We now determine the average increase of P during the time period ΔT. During ΔT the probability p to witness an incoming $\mathcal{A}$-call is approximated[4] by:

$$p = x(t) \cdot \Delta T$$

where $x(t)$ is the number of incoming $\mathcal{A}$-calls per hour (Table 1).

Table 1. Increase ΔP of the penalty function in a short time period ΔT.

	S was servicing $\mathcal{B}$	S was not servicing $\mathcal{B}$
$\mathcal{A}$ called	$1 + \alpha$	1
$\mathcal{A}$ did not call	0	$\gamma \cdot \Delta T$

Therefore, when the agent is working for $\mathcal{B}$, with probability p there is an incoming $\mathcal{A}$-call and the penalty function is increased by $1 + \alpha$, whereas with probability $1 - p$ the penalty function remains the same. The variation $\Delta P_{\mathcal{B}}$ of the penalty function while working for $\mathcal{B}$ is therefore:

$$\Delta P_{\mathcal{B}} = p \cdot (1 + \alpha) + (1 - p) \cdot 0 = (1 + \alpha) \cdot x(t) \cdot \Delta T \tag{2}$$

Similarly, when the agent is working for $\mathcal{A}$ (or waiting incoming calls from $\mathcal{A}$) we obtain the following average variation $\Delta P_{\mathcal{A}}$ of the penalty function:

$$\Delta P_{\mathcal{A}} = p \cdot 1 + (1 - p) \cdot \gamma \cdot \Delta T = x(t) \cdot \Delta T + (1 - x(t) \cdot \Delta T) \cdot \gamma \cdot \Delta T$$

Neglecting the terms in ΔT^2, we get:

---

[4] Assume, for instance, that $x(t) = 10$ calls/hour and consider a one second time interval $\Delta T = 1/3600$ h. The probability to witness a call during ΔT is indeed $10\Delta T = 1/360$. During each one second time interval the probability to witness a call is $1/360$ and over 3600 s we indeed get an average of 10 calls. Hence, p is indeed the probability to witness a call between time t and $t + \Delta T$ when ΔT is very small.

$$\Delta P_{\mathcal{A}} \simeq (x(t) + \gamma) \cdot \Delta T \qquad (3)$$

From Eqs. (2) and (3) we obtain:

$$\Delta P_{\mathcal{B}} \leq \Delta P_{\mathcal{A}} \Leftrightarrow (1 + \alpha) \cdot x(t) \leq x(t) + \gamma$$

which gives our main result:

$$\boxed{\Delta P_{\mathcal{B}} \leq \Delta P_{\mathcal{A}} \Leftrightarrow \alpha \cdot x(t) \leq \gamma}$$

We can therefore distinguish two cases:

1. If $\alpha \cdot x(t) \leq \gamma$, then $\Delta P_{\mathcal{B}} \leq \Delta P_{\mathcal{A}}$. The penalty function is minimized by having the agent service $\mathcal{B}$.
2. If $\alpha \cdot x(t) > \gamma$, then $\Delta P_{\mathcal{B}} > \Delta P_{\mathcal{A}}$. Here it is more advantageous to switch the agent into an $\mathcal{A}$-availability mode (even in the absence of an incoming $\mathcal{A}$-call).

Finally, we can define an incoming $\mathcal{A}$-call frequency threshold $x_0 \triangleq \frac{\gamma}{\alpha}$ (Fig. 1).

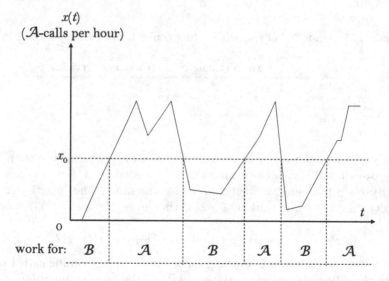

Fig. 1. Example of an $\mathcal{A}$-call function $x(t)$ with a threshold x_0. When $x(t) \geq x_0$, it is more advantageous to keep servicing $\mathcal{A}$. Otherwise the agent should better service $\mathcal{B}$.

As illustrated in Fig. 3, when $x(t) \leq x_0$, it is more advantageous to service $\mathcal{B}$, and when $x(t) > x_0$, it is more advantageous to keep working for $\mathcal{A}$. We note that this strategy does not depend on the cost of a call E_t; here we have assumed that $E_t = 1$, but the strategy would be the same for any value of E_t; this is because cost is spent whenever an $\mathcal{A}$-call occurs, no matter if the agent was working for $\mathcal{B}$ or in $\mathcal{A}$-mode.

Finally, we note that this strategy is clearly optimal since at any time t we are minimizing the increase in the penalty function.

4   The General Case

Assume that the technical fee cost is u (instead of 1), that the 1–900 rates applied to $\mathcal{A}$ and $\mathcal{B}$ (respectively $r_\mathcal{A}$ and $r_\mathcal{B}$) are potentially nonidentical and differ from γ (Table 2).

Table 2. Increase ΔP of the penalty function in a short time period ΔT. $(r_\mathcal{A} + r_\mathcal{B})/2$ represents the average rate due to the alternation of $\mathcal{A}$ and $\mathcal{B}$ during the call.

	$\mathcal{S}$ was servicing $\mathcal{B}$	$\mathcal{S}$ was not servicing $\mathcal{B}$
$\mathcal{A}$ called	$u + \alpha + (\gamma - (r_\mathcal{A} + r_\mathcal{B})/2) \cdot \Delta T$	$u + (\gamma - r_\mathcal{A}) \cdot \Delta T$
$\mathcal{A}$ did not call	$(\gamma - r_\mathcal{B}) \cdot \Delta T$	$\gamma \cdot \Delta T$

An analysis, similar to that of the previous section yields:

$$\Delta P_\mathcal{B} \leq \Delta P_\mathcal{A} \Leftrightarrow -2r_\mathcal{B} + 2\alpha x(t) + r_\mathcal{A} x(t)\Delta T + r_\mathcal{B} x(t)\Delta T < 0$$

That is (neglecting the terms with ΔT):

$$\Delta P_\mathcal{B} \leq \Delta P_\mathcal{A} \Leftrightarrow \alpha \cdot x(t) < r_\mathcal{B}$$

As expected u vanished and when $r_\mathcal{B} = \gamma$ this yields x_0.

5   Probabilistic Strategies

In this section we analyze an alternative strategy for $\mathcal{S}$. Here, $\mathcal{S}$ generates a function $0 \leq v(t) \leq 1$ and tosses a biased coin (probability $v(t)$ for tail and $1 - v(t)$ for head) during each interval ΔT. If the coin falls on a head $\mathcal{S}$ will make himself available for $\mathcal{A}$ otherwise he will make himself available to $\mathcal{B}$.

For such a strategy we need:

$$v(t) \cdot p \cdot (1 + \alpha) < (1 - v(t)) \cdot (p \cdot 1 + (1 - p) \cdot \gamma \cdot \Delta T)$$

Substituting p by $x(t)\Delta T$:

$$v(t) \cdot x(t)\Delta T \cdot (1 + \alpha) < (1 - v(t)) \cdot (x(t)\Delta T \cdot 1 + (1 - x(t)\Delta T) \cdot \gamma \cdot \Delta T)$$

Expanding, neglecting the terms in ΔT^2 and dividing by ΔT we get:

$$v(t) \cdot x(t) + \alpha \cdot v(t) \cdot x(t) < \gamma - \gamma \cdot v(t) + x(t) - v(t) \cdot x(t) \Rightarrow v(t) \cong \frac{\gamma + x(t)}{\gamma + (2 + \alpha)x(t)}$$

In other words, we get a "mirror" coin-toss function $v(t)$ that attempts to correct the variation of $x(t)$ by increasing or decreasing the coin-toss probability to keep the penalty as low as possible. This is well illustrated in the following graphics where we plotted two $x(t)$ functions (in blue) and their corresponding $v(t)$ (in purple). We see that a burst in $x(t)$ is immediately compensated by a descent of $v(t)$ and vice versa (Fig. 2).

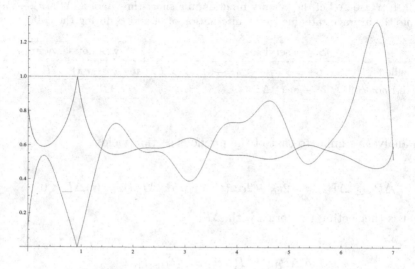

Fig. 2. Example of $v(t)$ (purple) for an example function $x(t)$ (blue) (Color figure online).

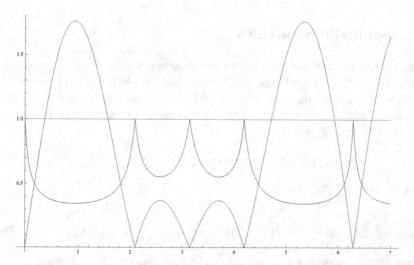

Fig. 3. Example of $v(t)$ (purple) for $x(t) = |\sin(x) + \sin(2x)|$ (blue) (Color figure online).

6   The Open Question: Find the Equilibrium

Throughout this paper $\mathcal{A}$ was assumed to adopt an automatic and "natural" behavior. Namely, $\mathcal{A}$ calls whenever he needs to be serviced and refunds $\mathcal{S}$'s personnel's salaries *prorata temporis*. This model captures $\mathcal{A}$'s *needs* but not $\mathcal{A}$'s *game-theoretic interests*. Indeed, $\mathcal{A}$ could adopt nontrivial behaviors meant to prevent $\mathcal{S}$ from implementing the strategies described in this paper. For instance, $\mathcal{A}$ could prevent $\mathcal{S}$ from estimating the function $x(t)$ by making purposeless calls. These however has a cost for $\mathcal{A}$ and it is unclear under which circumstances such a strategy would pay-off. Note that even in a setting where $x(t)$ is known to $\mathcal{S}$, $\mathcal{A}$ could attempt to corner $\mathcal{S}$ using purposeless calls.

We encourage interested readers to investigate this question.

Acknowledgment. We thank Jean-Sébastien Coron for his contribution to this work.

Information Security

SpoofKiller: *You Can Teach People How to Pay, but Not How to Pay Attention*

Markus Jakobsson[1](✉) and Hossein Siadati[2]

[1] ZapFraud Inc, Portola Valley, CA, USA
`markus@zapfraud-inc.com`
[2] NYU Tandon School of Engineering, New York, USA
`hossein@nyu.edu`

Abstract. We describe a novel approach to reduce the impact of spoofing by a subtle change in the login process. At the heart of our contribution is the understanding that current anti-spoof technologies fail largely as a result of the difficulties to communicate *security* and *risk* to typical users. Accordingly, our solution is *oblivious* to whether the user was tricked by a fraudster or not. We achieve that by modifying the user login process, and letting the browser or operating system cause different results of user login requests, based on whether the site is trusted or not. Experimental results indicate that our new approach, which we dub "SpoofKiller", will address approximately 80% of spoofing attempts.

1 Introduction

As people interact with each other, they observe cues that indicate the identity of the party they interact with. This is a form of authentication that is implicitly taking place. It is not limited to human-to-human interaction, but people also implicitly form opinions about the identity and validity of websites, as they observe these. Given human inaccuracy, this is a very vulnerable form of authentication, and one that makes *spoofing* possible.

Just as fraudsters may attempt to impersonate a trusted person to an intended victim, they may also *spoof* emails, websites and apps. This is a common technique used by phishers. Phishers use webpage spoofing to dupe Internet users into believing that they are visiting trusted websites, and giving out their passwords (or other credentials) to these sites.

At the risk of stating the obvious, phishers are only successful if (a) they manage to trick their intended victims, *and* (b) the resulting actions of these victims are beneficial to the fraudsters. Both conditions are necessary.

Typical security measures aim to mitigate the threat of spoofing by addressing the first condition, i.e., by avoiding that intended victims are tricked. This is done by conveying security and risk to users – e.g., using locks and conveying recognizable URLs to represent security, and by issuing warnings and requiring unusual user action to represent risk. This general approach is not very effective, as it relies on users paying close attention to subtle cues and to not act out of habit. The simple but somewhat ironic beauty of the approach we introduce is

© Springer-Verlag Berlin Heidelberg 2016
P.Y.A. Ryan et al. (Eds.): Kahn Festschrift, LNCS 9100, pp. 177–194, 2016.
DOI: 10.1007/978-3-662-49301-4_13

that it turns reflexive user behavior from being a danger (as it is today) to being a distinct *advantage*. When users are habituated to the methods we promote, the very same reactions that currently make these users fail to notice and act on indications of risk are harnessed and made to protect them. The approach we take to achieve this goal relies on undermining the *second* condition for success for phishers, namely that *the resulting actions of victims are beneficial to the fraudsters.*

We modify the user login behavior to include an action that generates an interrupt (i.e., power button press). Normally, this means "terminate" or "turn the screen off and terminate" (depending on the phone operating system), but the meaning is changed to mean "go ahead" for whitelisted sites. We make this action mandatory for whitelisted sites. As a result, as a user visits a spoofed site – believing she is at a legitimate site – acts just as she does on legitimate sites. On spoofed sites, this causes the termination of the browser, and therefore also of the offending website. (It is worth mentioning that while malware with root access can spoof the pressing of the power button, a spoofed webpage *cannot*; nor can a malicious app without root access.)

The new functionality can easily be achieved by modifying browsers, as demonstrated in a proof-of-concept implementation we have made by modifying the open-source browser Zirco. In our modified version, which runs on Android devices, the meaning of the power button is changed in the context of whitelisted sites. It could either simply be made to mean "go ahead, enter your password now" as in our implementation, or "we have autofilled your user name; now enter your password", to provide a user incentive for make up for the extra button press. However, the meaning of the power button is not changed for other sites. Therefore, if a user presses the power button on a spoof site – not necessarily because she thinks it is a secure site, but simply habitually performing her normal login actions – then the browser session will end and the user be brought back to the home screen, because the interrupt handler did not find the URL on the whitelist.

A technique of potential independent value is one that we developed to force users to comply with the new login procedure, all while respecting legacy sites not to have to be aware of our needs and actions. The approach we take is simply to let the browser inject javascript in the DOM of the visited site (thereby making it appear that this javascript code was part of the website); where the injected javascript code searches for tags indicative of password fields, and rewrite the website source code to signal the whereabouts of such fields to the browser. If a user attempts to enter text in any such field without first having pressed the power button, the browser will give the user tactile feedback and an alert explaining the need to press the power button on trusted sites. This, in fact, can be the only teaching process by which user behavior is changed.

At first sight, this may seem to mean that a phishing site could modify the HTML so make sure that there would be no tag to trigger the detection of the password field. However, this is a misunderstanding, as the detection of the password field is merely a tool to train the user to press power, by recurrent conditioning as the user visits legitimate sites. *Legitimate sites* will not attempt to circumvent the detection of the password field. The abortion of phishing sites does not depend to any extent on the code of the webpages; it is simply a consequence of the user's actions.

Outline. We begin with a brief overview of related work (Sect. 2), after which we describe the psychological principles that our solution is based on (Sect. 3). In Sect. 4, we describe an implementation of SpoofKiller, followed in Sect. 5 by an experimental evaluation of it.

2   Related Work

The problem of web spoofing was first given attention by Felten, Balfanz, Dean and Wallach [5], years before it was embraced by phishers as a tool of deceit. While credential theft aided by social engineering took place on AOL as early as the mid-nineties, it was not until 2001 that phishing of the type we are used to today started to appear, first targeting e-gold account holders [10] and then gradually becoming a threat against regular banking. Around 2005, phishing was commonly recognized as a significant problem.

Spoofing is a complex socio-technical problem, and researchers have long studied what typical users pay attention to, and *fail* paying attention to [4,11,14–16,26,28]. They have also studied the more general question of what makes people assign trust [17,18,21,24,25]. Much of this research, sadly, supports what can be understood simply from observing the rising trend of online fraud: *Typical users are not good at making proper online trust decisions.*

To attempt to improve how trust decisions are made, substantial efforts have been made to better convey statements of security to users [1,3,9,12,20,29] and more generally, to educate users about the need to pay attention to security indicators [19,23]. While we are not against such efforts, we think of them as last resorts – approaches to take in the absence of automated protection mechanisms.

In line with this view is a body of work aimed at protecting the user *without* any attempt at messaging [6,8,22]. We believe that in order for the system to be reliable, it *should not* depend on the user making proper security decisions. That is the view on which the proposed solution is based.

3   Understanding Conditioning

In learning theory, two major classes of learning processes have been identified: *classical conditioning* and *operant conditioning*. In his famous classical conditioning experiment, Pavlov described how dogs learn to associate the ring of a bell (which is referred to as the *conditioned stimulus*) to food (the so-called *unconditioned stimulus*) [13]. While classical conditioning relates to performing actions *in response to* a potential reward or punishment, operant conditioning relates to performing actions intended to *cause or avoid* the reward or punishment. More specifically, operant conditioning identifies how an individual learns that a operant or action may have specific consequences (see, e.g., [7]). As a result of operant conditioning, the individual modifies her behavior to increase the chances of the desired outcome.

Operant conditioning could be used to describe the process by which users learn how to interact with computer systems. For example, a user may learn that a click on an X-icon (operant or action) in a window results in the abortion of the associated application (consequence). Similarly, users of Android devices have learnt that pressing the power button terminates an application and locks the phone.

When a user aims to reach a goal for the first few times, she performs a collection of actions until the desirable outcome is caused. As the desired consequence occurs (e.g., the user succeeds in locking the phone), the relation to the operant/action (e.g., to press the power button) is reinforced – we say that she *learnt*.

Similarly, in the context of login, users have learnt to enable username and password entries by a click or tap in order to enter their credentials. This is *both* a matter of classical conditioning, where the opportunity to log in is communicated by the display of the login page; and of operant conditioning, where the user knows that by clicking or tapping on the fields, she will be rewarded by the access to her account.

SpoofKiller habituates users to pressing the power button to log in to legitimate sites, using a combination of rewards and punishments. In the context of whitelisted webpages, the *reward* is access to the associated account, while the *punishment* for not pressing the power button consists of tactile feedback and an alert. At the same time, the desirable login action (i.e., the pressing of the power button) is interpreted by the device as a request to terminate the session outside the context of a whitelisted website. Therefore, as soon as users have learnt the new login procedure (pressing the power button to log in), they are protected against spoof sites, which will be terminated by this action.

This leaves two important cases to be considered. First of all, it is evident that good sites that are not whitelisted would potentially suffer the same fate as spoof sites – the termination of the user's session as a result of the user's intention to log in. Apart from requesting to get whitelisted, this problem can be addressed by the operators of such sites by replacing the conditioned stimulus (the login page) with an alert that makes the user aware of the procedural exception.

A second important question to consider is how fraudsters may react to the threat of having their sessions terminated. One general approach is to display an exception alert similar to that shown by legitimate entities without a certificate. While this may trick some users to proceed, it will at least raise their awareness of the login session being a special case; institutional messaging by whitelisted sites could attempt to minimize this risk by reinforcing that they will *never* ask the user to avoid the power button. Another adversarial strategy is to make the user experience as similar as possible to the real experience (which is typically the path taken by today's spoofers), and hope that the targeted user is not yet conditioned to pressing power, or will somehow fail to do this anyway.

4 App Implementation

Typical Android devices are equipped with an array of sensors – such as the touch screen; means for voice input; GPS; and an accelerometer. The events are delivered from the underlying device drivers to the OS. The OS forwards the events to active applications, or (for events such as location events or incoming calls) broadcasts them as a new *Intent*. Intents are delivered to all subscribed apps – even those that were not active at the time of the event. As a result of the broadcast of an Intent, a subscribing application may be activated. (Apps subscribe to Intents by setting up a BroadcastReceiver and its associated intent filters in the manifest of the Android application.) There are two exceptions to this rule. First, the *home button* press is just delivered to the *Launcher* (an application responsible to manage the home screen); second, the *power button* press is not delivered to *any* third party application.

For SpoofKiller to be triggered by the power button, one *either* needs to modify the Android OS to deliver the event to our augmented browser (which would result in complications for us, as it would limit the experiment to users with dev phones), *or* one needs to trigger SpoofKiller using something that is a *consequence* of the power button being pressed – such as the *screen off* event. We did the latter.

As it is shown in the code below, we registered for the broadcast event of Screen Off. The onReceive method is called when the Power Press is occurred. As a result, we have an event which is not catchable – or possible to generate – by a web page, and which is used to trigger SpoofKiller to check the whitelist.

```
BroadcastReceiver screenoff =
    new BroadcastReceiver() {

    public static final String Screenoff =
    "android.intent.action.SCREEN_OFF";
    //Indicate what to do
    //when the power is pressed
    @Override
    public void onReceive(
    Context context,Intent intent) {
      //Enable password field
    }};

    //Indicate the type of
    //event interested to receive
    IntentFilter offfilter =
      new IntentFilter (Intent.ACTION_SCREEN_OFF);

    //Application registers
    //to receive screen off event
    registerReceiver(screenoff, offfilter);
}
```

Most Android-based browsers use the WebView class, which is incorporated in Android WebKit package. This class is given URL's as input and loads and displays the content of associated web-pages. In addition to performing standard functionality associated with web browsing, such as running Javascript code and rendering HTML and CSS, WebView allows a web page to call a method of the browser. This functionality, as shown in the code below, allows browser manufacturers to incorporate SpoofKiller in their browsers in a straightforward manner.

```
class JavaScriptInterface {

    @SuppressWarnings("unused")
    public boolean enableSpoofKiller() {
        //set up page to handle Power Press
        //If the page is not in whitelist,
        //this call causes page abortion
    }
}
.
.
.
mWebView.addJavascriptInterface(
    new JavaScriptInterface(),
    "spoofkillerhandler");
```

In the code above, the browser provides a JavaScript interface named spoofkillerhandler, which enables JavaScript code in the webpage to communicate with SpoofKiller. This lets a webpage announce that it wants the support of SpoofKiller on a particular page. (Not all pages on a legitimate website needs the support, but just those that ask for credentials).

We also incorporated other functionality, such as a method to give tactile feedback when a user tries to enter his password – without first having pressed power. This has to be triggered by JavaScript in the webpage. To support legacy webpages, we have used a technique we call "on the Air Manipulation of Page" (AMP), which enables browsers to modify the contents of the webpage by injecting scripting code that determines whether the webpage should request SpoofKiller support. This is done simply by injecting a string of JavaScript as a URL to each webpage that is loaded. This is done by the browser, a trick that permits access to the document object model (DOM) of the current webpage in spite of the fact that the JavaScript code was not *really* served by the domain associated with the webpage in question.

In our implementation of ZircoSecure – our proof-of-concept browser supporting SpoofKiller – we used the AMP technique to inject JavaScript code in a page loaded in the browser in order to let this injected routine identify fields of importance (using tags) and communicate to the browser when any such field is accessed by the user. This is to accommodate legacy websites while at the same time making sure that whitelisted pages are modified to help the browser identify fields that the user is not allowed to access without first pressing the power button. This, in other words, is what enables the user conditioning described in Sect. 3.

The AMP technique makes it possible to deploy SpoofKiller locally, without infrastructure changes or modifications of legacy pages. Browser manufacturers – or those writing plugins for browsers – simply need to incorporate *spoofkiller-Handler* and the JavaScript injection code into their browsers.

The current implementation of SpoofKiller suffers from the screen blackout, since the operating system performs that task as a direct result of detecting an interrupt caused by the power button being pressed. In order to make the SpoofKiller work smoothly and without this undesirable effect, there is a need for a modification of the Android OS. This is a straightforward modification. Using the OTA (over the air update) technology for Android, is possible to incorporate this with any new release of the Android OS.

5   Experimental Evaluation

While convinced that SpoofKiller would work in *theory*, based on known observations on human conditioning, we also need to find heuristic support to back this belief, and to estimate the steepness of the typical learning curve as people start to use SpoofKiller. More specifically, we need to answer the following questions:

(1) Is it practically feasible for users to change a frequently practiced habit, namely the manner in which they log in?
(2) How long does it typically take for users to acquire a *new* login behavior, provided initial instructions and appropriate reinforcement?

These two questions relate directly to the practicability and likely user acceptance of the new approach. In particular, if the new behavior is commonly embraced and quickly becomes habitual, then this reduces the size of the population that is susceptive to abuse and reduces the risk of corruption for those who have adopted the new behavior. A core question to be answered is then:

(3) *What percentage of users would be protected against typical phishing attacks after an initial period of learning?*

To find answers to these questions, we designed and carried out an experiment, which we will describe next.

5.1   Experiment Design

We recruited subjects to download and run an experiment app, either from a webpage of ours or from Google's Android marketplace. During setup, we asked subjects to select a username and password – ostensibly so that only *the subject* would have access to his or her environment. Then, subjects were asked to participate in a number of sessions over time, each session having the following two parts:

(1) Perform a login, wherein the username was autofilled, and where the subject had to enter the password; but where he or she had to press the power button before doing so. Unbeknownst to the user, all actions and the time at which they were performed were logged. We will refer to this part as the *authentication phase.*

(2) Type three words – chosen at random from a large set of words – as fast as possible. After performing this task, the user would be told how long it took; what his or her average time to date was; and what her ranking based on speed was. This part of the experiment was only there to take the attention away from the first part. (To add to the impression that the timing to typing was what the experiment was about, we named the experiment app *Speed Test.*)

In the authentication phase, the user was given tactile and textual feedback if she attempted to enter her password without first having pressed the power button. The textual feedback was (in blinking font) *"Notice: For security reasons, you always must press the power button before entering your password in our test."* This constituted the main tool of user conditioning.

The experiment had three different *treatments*, all of them providing slightly different versions of what was shown to the user during the authentication phase. We refer to the three treatments as Instruction, Empty and Bad: The I treatment contained the instruction *"Notice: For security reasons, you always must press the power button before entering your password in our test"*, as shown in Fig. 1. The E treatment was identical to the I treatment, except that it did *not* contain this instruction. Finally, the B treatment, had a "bad" instruction, prompting the user *"Notice: Do not press power. Enter the password you use to log in to [user's email address]."* That last treatment was introduced to determine whether subjects pay attention to instructions after having learnt what to do; and if so, whether they were willing to follow an instruction that has the semblance of being abusive.

To be eligible for the participation incentive, subjects had to participate for 21 days out of a month. Many subjects participated in more than one session per day – probably because we emphasized the competitive aspects of the experiment, and many tried hard to improve their speed during the phase where they typed three words. If a subject participated in more than one session per day, all sessions of that day proceeding the first session were chosen as treatment E.

We ran two versions of the experiment, which we may refer to as the *instruction heavy* and the *instruction light* version. In the instruction heavy version, the

Fig. 1. The figure shows the Instruction treatment in our experiment, wherein the user is told "Notice: For security reasons, you always must press the power button before entering your password in our test". In the Empty treatment, that instruction is absent, whereas in the Bad treatment the instruction given to the user is instead "Notice: Do not press power. Enter the password you use to log in to [user's email address]".

I treatment was the most common, while in the instruction light version, it was only used for a small number of days in the beginning. The aim of using these two experiments was to determine whether the conditioning that we expected to take place was a result of pre-action messaging (i.e., the instruction); post-action reinforcement (whether success or the tactile/textual feedback); or a combination of the two.

More specifically, in the instruction heavy version, the treatment shown to a user was always I, except on days 9 and 18 on which treatment E was used, and on day 21, on which treatment B was used. In contrast, in the instruction light version, I was only shown on days 1–5, after which treatment E was used until day 21, at which treatment B was used.

5.2   Subject Recruiting

Before starting to recruit subjects, we attempted to estimate the number of subjects we would need, for a desired confidence of 95%. Since the population of the smart phone users is large, we used Cochrans' formula. Based on this, we established that we needed to recruit 385 subjects, given $z = 1.96$ (i.e., confidence level 95%), $e = 0.05$ (the precision level), $p = 0.5$ and $q = 0.5$ (the maximum variability). We assumed maximum variability at first since we did not know to what extent different users behave differently. As we analyzed the results, it become evident that users behave similarly to each other.

The drop-off rates in the unsupervised experiments are different based on the assigned task and the reward which is given to the participants. Based on

Table 1. Ages of subjects in the experiment versions.

Age range	Heavy%	Light%	Combined%
18–25	28.1	36.8	33.5
26–32	29.5	34.6	32.7
33–45	28.1	21.9	24.3
46+	14.4	6.6	9.5

our experience with structurally similar experiments in the past, we assumed an approximate 50% drop-off rate, suggesting the need to recruit close to 800 participants.

Recruitment of such a large number of participants was challenging, given the fact that users had to be over 18 years of age (to comply with guidelines outlined in the Belmont report); have an Android Phone; be willing to install an application; and to participate for 21 days during the course of a month. Moreover, in order to avoid bias, we avoided recruiting anybody who knew what the experiment was about, which excluded some of the otherwise most passionate potential participants.

(a) **Instruction Heavy Version:** We recruited subjects by requesting participation from our LinkedIn contacts; our Google+ contacts; and our Facebook contacts. Moreover, we recruited participants among colleagues at PayPal and Google; and from members of HCI research groups. Subjects were incentivized by the chance of winning a raffle for an iPad2, with extra raffle tickets given to people who helped recruit subjects. Out of 198 subjects who registered, 15 entered as a result of a referral. A total of 77 of the 198 registered users completed their participation; 6 of those were due to referrals. All of these users participated in the instruction heavy version of the experiment, which was intended as the only version of the experiment until the disappointing numbers prompted us to recruit another batch of users – at which time we also decided to tweak the experiment to see whether the amount of instructions would matter much.

(b) **Instruction Light Version:** In the second round of the experiment, which corresponded to the instruction light version, we recruited workers from Amazon Mechanical Turk to participate[1] and gave them the option of a $5 bonus or the chance to win an iPad/Android pad. Among the 307 who registered, 231 completed the study; more than 90% selected the cash bonus.

(c) **Demographics:** Tables 1 and 2 show the breakdown in terms of age and gender among the subjects in our two experiment versions (instruction heavy

---

[1] It is against the terms of service of Amazon to ask a user to install a piece of software. While we used the payment methods associated with Amazon Mechanical Turk to pay participants, we did not use their services to *recruit* participants, and so, did not break the terms of service. These users had *voluntarily* provided contact information in previous interactions, and were contacted in this manner to ask whether they would like to participate.

Table 2. Subjects' gender in experiment versions.

Age range	% Heavy	% Light	% Combined
Female	47.8	24.5	39.0
Male	52.2	75.5	61.0

Table 3. Password use on handsets.

Use	% of subjects
Daily	30
Weekly	26
Rarely	33
Never	11

vs light.) This is very similar to the demographic of the Android phone owners [2,27]. Table 3 shows the experience with entering passwords on handsets of the subjects.

5.3 Observation of Actions

The experiment app recorded all the user actions as the user ran our app, including page taps, keyboard presses, and hard-key presses (volume, home, back, menu, and power press) – along with the time at which each such action was performed. It stored the recorded data in a local database on user' handset, and then transmitted it to a back-end server for analysis. (The data was submitted asynchronously, to make it possible for test takers to take the test when they are offline, and to avoid the data lost in the case of exceptional conditions.)

From the collected data, we could determine the time it took for subjects to press the power button, after starting the authentication phase, and the number and type of actions – if any – that she performed before pressing power.

5.4 Findings

Using the data collected in the experiment, we used statistical analysis techniques to answer the questions and validate the hypotheses outlined at the beginning of Sect. 5.

(d) **Feasibility and Learning Curve:** The cumulative performance, shown in Fig. 2, is a measure of the how quickly subjects adopt to the new behavior. It shows the percentage of subjects performing the correct action – pressing the power button before attempting to log in – as a function of the number of days of participation in the experiment. It shows the performance of subjects in both experiment versions – instruction heavy and instruction light.

The learning curve shown in Fig. 2 is Sigmoid-like for both experiment versions, and the cumulative performance exhibits a dramatic increase during the

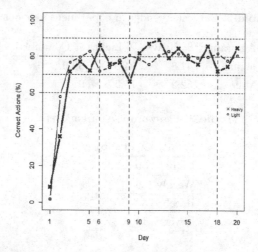

Fig. 2. The figure shows the cumulative distribution of the acquisition of the safe habit (to press power before entering a password), as a function of days of exposure to the new procedure. We see a dip on days 9 and 18 in the heavy version, and one on day 6 for the light version; these all coincides with a sudden $\underline{E}$ treatment after a number of $\underline{I}$ treatments.

first few days of participation; we refer to these days as the *acquisition period*, during which user tries different actions (like keyboard press, screen touch), and finally is conditioned to performing the correct operant. We can see that the proportion of correct actions is 80% ±5% (with $n = 305, \chi^2 = 0.0461$) for both versions, once the users have acquired the new habit (starting at day 10). We refer to the period starting at that point in time as the *protected period*. A reverse regression model suggests that the cumulative percentage of correct actions is: $88.415 - 76.986/t$, where t denotes the number of days of participation. This suggests a cumulative performance of 87.5% after 84 days, with a significance level of 99%.

In the instruction heavy version ($n = 73$), we used the $\underline{E}$ treatment (in which no instruction is provided) on days 9 and 18 in order to determine what portions of subjects have internalized the pressing of the power button by then. Our results show that 52% of the subjects had internalized the secure behavior by day 9, and 72% by day 18. In the light version ($n = 246$), treatment $\underline{E}$ is used from day 6 to day 20. As it could be seen in Fig. 2, the performance is hovering around 80% during this time, with a mean of 80% ±1.1%.

The speed with which a user "forgets" an acquired habit is referred to as the *extinction rate*. During the *protected period* (days 10 to 20), the average extinction rate for subjects of the heavy version is 4.70 ($n = 86$), meaning that users make one mistake after 4.70 days on average, and then reacquire the habit again. During the same period, subjects in the light version have an average extinction rate of 5.07 ($n = 246$). See Fig. 3 for a distribution of this aspect of the users behavior. We argue that the instruction light approach is preferable

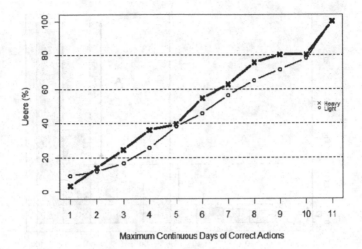

Fig. 3. The figure shows the cumulative distribution of the extinction as a function of maximum number of days of continuously correct behavior.

to the instruction heavy approach due to the similar user performance and its cleaner user interface.

We do not believe that the differences in behavior between the instruction heavy and light versions are due to a bias in the choice of subjects – in particular since the instruction light subjects were faster learners, while – coming from Mechanical Turk – are believed to be less likely to care as much as colleagues and friends & family would.

(e) **Protection and Prediction.:** We want to establish the extent to which practice makes perfect in the context of SpoofKiller – or put another way, how the probability of performing a login action that is "spoof killing" depends on the number of days of exposure.

It is evident that the effects of conditioning are most notable during the first few days of exposure, given the rather rapid learning process (see Fig. 2 above.)

It is also very clear that not all users are equally protected, as can be seen in Fig. 4. Therein we show the results of performing hierarchical clustering on the experimental data based on the subjects' performance during the period we refer to as the "protected period". Three meaningful clusters are detected; we refer to these as the "A students", the "B students" and the "C students", the names indicating the extent to which subjects in these clusters learnt the new login procedure. Having made this distinction, it is interesting to see the adoption behavior of the subjects, partitioned into these three classes (See Fig. 5). The partition of users into different risk classes, as above, suggests the potential need for additional security measures for users who are identified as being more risk prone – what we refer to as "C students". These are easily detected based on their behavior.

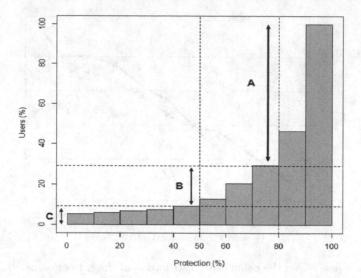

Fig. 4. Clustering of users based on their performance during days 10 to 20. We informally refer to the high performers as "A students", the intermediate performers as "B students", and the low performers as "C students".

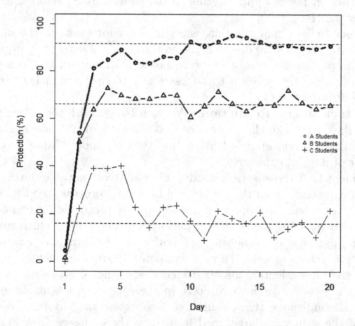

Fig. 5. The performance of subjects as a function of time, where the subjects are partitioned into the classes "A students" (70% of all subjects, 92% average performance), "B students" (20% of the subjects, 66% average performance) and "C students" (10% of the subjects, 14% average performance).

One difficulty facing "C students" is that they do not maintain the desirable behavior when the instruction is removed. This can be seen from Fig. 5, wherein we see that the performance drops for these subjects after the instruction is removed in the instruction light version on day 6. C Students have a very high extinction rate (mean = 0.47 days), which means that they have not internalized the desired habit. In comparison,"B students" have an extinction rate of 1.72 days, while "A students" 6.60 days on average. In general, there is a strong correlation (cor = 0.7) between user's performance and the extinction rate.

(f) **Fraud Protection:** On the last day of the experiment, we used treatment <u>B</u>ad, in which users were asked not to press the power button, and to enter their email password instead of the password used in the experiment. (We did not record what password was entered, but only whether the same password was entered as during the previous session; this was to avoid stealing anybody's email password.)

Table 4. User behavior in <u>B</u>ad treatment (%)

Instruction	Correct	Delayed	Oblivious	Tricked
Heavy	22%	4%	48%	26%
Light	27%	4%	57%	12%
Combined	27%	4%	55%	15%

The <u>B</u> treatment was used to mimic a fraud case. As Table 4 shows, roughly 30% of the users pressed the power button – most of them as rapidly as during "normal" days (the "correct" reaction), and about 4% after a slight delay. The rest of the users did not press the power button. Approximately 55% of the users – independently of whether they pressed the power button or not – entered the same password as previously during the experiment, apparently oblivious to the request to enter something else, or unwilling to do so. 15% entered something else – supposedly the password to their email account.

Table 5. Behavior of classes of users in <u>B</u>ad treatment

Class	Correct	Delayed	Oblivious	Tricked
A Student	29%	3%	55%	11%
B Student	21%	3%	50%	25%
C Student	3%	14%	60%	21%

Table 5 shows that A students are better protected in comparison to others, in contexts involving deceit.

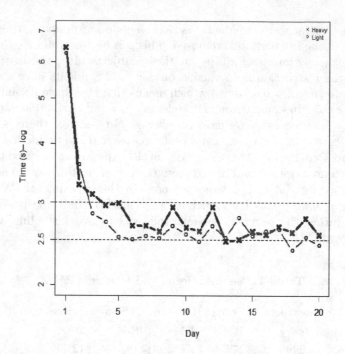

Fig. 6. The graph shows the average time for subjects from page rendering to the subject pressing the power button. This is shown as a function of the day of participation. We only show the time for users who perform the correct action. The average reaction time in the protected period (day 10 onwards) for the heavy version is 2.62 s, and 2.56 s for the light version. In comparison, the user reaction time for similar-style pages but where the user does not need to press the power button is 2.5 s – the average time for this corresponds to the dotted line. The time associated with pressing the power button is therefore less than half a second.

6   User Reactions

After a few days of participation, the added action – to have to press the power button – added less than half a second to the time the login took; see Fig. 6.

The reaction time is also a factor of age; younger subjects have shorter reaction time, in comparison to older subjects. For example, users between 18–25 took on average 3 s, while users in the 26–31 age interval took 3.5 s, and 33–45 took 3.67 s.

As subjects completed their participation in their experiment, we asked them what they thought about having to press the power button before logging in with a password. Out of the 227 subjects, 127 subjects (56%) selected the response "I got used to it quickly" while 24 subjects (11%) selected the opposite response "I would have a hard time getting used to that", leaving 76 subjects (33%) having expressed neither opinion.

References

1. Chou, N., Ledesma, R., Teraguchi, Y., Boneh, D., Mitchell, J.C.: Client-side defense against web-based identity theft (2004)
2. Daniel, P.: Android users demographics, 19 November 2010. http://www.phonearena.com/news/Android-users-demographics_id14786/
3. Dhamija, R., Tygar, J.D.: The battle against phishing: dynamic security skins. In: Proceedings of the 2005 Symposium on Usable Privacy and Security, SOUPS 2005. ACM, New York, pp. 77–88 (2005)
4. Dhamija, R., Tygar, J.D., Hearst, M.: Why phishing works. In: Proceedings of the SIGCHI Conference on Human Factors Incomputing Systems, CHI 2006. ACM, New York, pp. 581–590 (2006)
5. Felten, E.W., Balfanz, D., Dean, D., Wallach, D.S.: Web spoofing: an internet con game. Technical report 540-96, Department of Computer Science, Princeton University, February 1997. http://www.cs.princeton.edu/sip/pub/spoofing.pdf
6. Fette, I., Sadeh, N., Tomasic, A.: Learning to detect phishing emails. In: Proceedings of the 16th International Conference on World Wide Web, WWW 2007. ACM, New York, pp. 649–656 (2007)
7. Fulcher, E.: Cognitive psychology (2003). http://www.eamonfulcher.com/CogPsych/page5.htm
8. Garera, S., Provos, N., Chew, M., Rubin, A.D.: A framework for detection and measurement of phishing attacks. In: Proceedings of the 2007 ACM Workshop on Recurring Malcode, WORM 2007. ACM, New York, pp. 1–8 (2007)
9. Garfinkel, S.L., Miller, R.C.: Johnny 2: a user test of key continuity management with s/mime and outlook express. In: Proceedings of the 2005 Symposium on Usable Privacy and Security, SOUPS 2005. ACM, New York, pp. 13–24 (2005)
10. Goldberg, I.: e-gold stomps on phishing?, July 2004. http://www.financialcryptography.com/mt/archives/000190.html
11. Herzberg, A.: Why Johnny can't surf (safely)? attacks and defenses for web users. Comput. Secur. 28(1–2), 63–71 (2009)
12. Herzberg, A., Gbara, A.: Security and identification indicators for browsers against spoofing and phishing attacks. Cryptology ePrint Archive, Report 2004/155 (2004)
13. Ivan Petrovich Pavlov, G.V.A.: Conditioned reflexes : an investigation of the physiological activity of the cerebral cortex. Dover Publications, September 2003
14. Jackson, C., Simon, D.R., Tan, D.S., Barth, A.: An evaluation of extended validation and picture-in-picture phishing attacks. In: Dietrich, S., Dhamija, R. (eds.) FC 2007 and USEC 2007. LNCS, vol. 4886, pp. 281–293. Springer, Heidelberg (2007)
15. Jagatic, T.N., Johnson, N.A., Jakobsson, M., Menczer, F.: Social phishing. Commun. ACM 50(10), 94–100 (2007)
16. Jakobsson, M., Ratkiewicz, J.: Designing ethical phishing experiments: a study of (ROT13) rOnl query features. In: WWW 2006: Proceedings of the 15th International Conference on World Wide Web. ACM, New York, pp. 513–522 (2006)
17. Jakobsson, M., Tsow, A., Shah, A., Blevis, E., Lim, Y.: What instills trust? a qualitative study of phishing. In: Dietrich, S., Dhamija, R. (eds.) FC 2007 and USEC 2007. LNCS, vol. 4886, pp. 356–361. Springer, Heidelberg (2007)
18. Kirlappos, I., Sasse, M.A.: Security education against phishing: a modest proposal for a major re-think. IEEE Secur. Priv. 10(2), 24–32 (2011)
19. Kumaraguru, P., Rhee, Y., Sheng, S., Hasan, S., Acquisti, A., Cranor, L.F., Hong, J.: Getting users to pay attention to anti-phishing education: evaluationof retention and transfer. In: Proceedings of the Anti-phishing Working Groups 2nd Annual eCrime Researchers Summit, eCrime 2007. ACM, New York, pp. 70–81 (2007)

20. McCune, J.M., Perrig, A., Reiter, M.K.: Seeing is believing; using camera phones for human verifiable authentication. Int. J. Secur. Netw. **4**, 43–56 (2009)
21. Riegelsberger, J., Sasse, M.A., McCarthy, J.D.: The mechanics of trust: a framework for research and design. Int. J. Hum.-Comput. Stud. **62**, 381–422 (2005)
22. Ross, B., Jackson, C., Miyake, N., Boneh, D., Mitchell, J.C.: Stronger password authentication using browser extensions. In: Proceedings of the 14th Conference on USENIX Security Symposium. USENIX Association, Berkeley, vol. 14, p. 2 (2005)
23. Srikwan, S., Jakobsson, M.: Using cartoons to teach Internet security. Cryptologia **32**(2), 137–154 (2008)
24. Stajano, F., Wilson, P.: Understanding scam victims: seven principles for systems security. Commun. ACM **54**, 70–75 (2011)
25. Wash, R.: Folk models of home computer security. In: Proceedings of the Sixth Symposium on Usable Privacy and Security, SOUPS 2010. ACM, New York, pp. 11:1–11:16 (2010)
26. Whalen, T., Inkpen, K.M.: Gathering evidence: use of visual security cues in web browsers. In: Proceedings of Graphics Interface 2005, GI 2005, School of Computer Science, University of Waterloo. Canadian Human-Computer Communications Society, Waterloo, Ontario, Canada, pp. 137–144 (2005)
27. Woolston, L.: Mobclix index: android marketplace, 17 November 2010. http://blog.mobclix.com/2010/11/17/mobclix-index-android-marketplace/
28. Wu, M., Miller, R.C., Garfinkel, S.L.: Do security toolbars actually prevent phishing attacks? In: Proceedings of the SIGCHI Conference on Human Factors Incomputing Systems, CHI 2006. ACM, New York, pp. 601–610 (2006)
29. Wu, M., Miller, R.C., Little, G.: Web wallet: preventing phishing attacks by revealing user intentions. In: Proceedings of the Second Symposium on Usable Privacy and Security, SOUPS 2006. ACM, New York, pp. 102–113 (2006)

Cyber-Physical Systems Security

Dieter Gollmann[✉] and Marina Krotofil

Security in Distributed Applications,
Hamburg University of Technology, Hamburg, Germany
{diego,Marina.Krotofil}@tuhh.de

Abstract. We argue that cyber-physical systems cannot be protected just by protecting their IT infrastructure and that the CIA approach to security is insufficient. Rather, the IT components should be treated as a control system, inputs to that control system should be checked for veracity, and control algorithms should be designed in a way that they can handle a certain amount of adversarial actions.

Keywords: Cyber-physical systems security · Integrity · Plausibility veracity · Safety · Hard real time

1 Introduction

Cyber-physical systems were mapped as a research area in a series of NFS workshops starting from 2006. Lee's position paper at the inaugurating event already observed that in this field *timing precision and security issues loom large* [13]. Cyber-physical systems, by their very nature, cause effects in the physical world. In some cases, e.g. aircrafts, chemical plants, nuclear facilities, medical devices, or critical infrastructures in general, malfunction of a system can have disastrous physical consequences. On one hand, this is an issue that had to be dealt with already before physical systems were connected to cyberspace. Well-designed systems would have been deployed with appropriate safety measures in place. Conceivably, those measures can restrain cyber-physical attacks once they have transited from cyberspace into the physical domain. On the other hand, those countermeasures were designed under certain assumptions, e.g. physical security protecting access to premises or independence of component failures. Conceivably, those assumptions get invalidated once modern IT systems get integrated with existing physical plants.

Integrating modern IT systems with existing physical systems exposes those installations to new security threats. Some of these threats are well-known in IT security and countermeasures have been studied at length. Those threats are new only because of a new application area. Other threats may indeed be specific to cyber-physical systems. This paper aims at making a distinction between "old" attacks in new settings, and new attacks intrinsic to cyber-physical systems that would establish cyber-physical security as an object of study in its own rights.

We will start with a brief introduction to cyber-physical systems and some general remarks on security. We will then explore the limitations of traditional

© Springer-Verlag Berlin Heidelberg 2016
P.Y.A. Ryan et al. (Eds.): Kahn Festschrift, LNCS 9100, pp. 195–204, 2016.
DOI: 10.1007/978-3-662-49301-4_14

security measures before trying to identify the new challenges in cyber-physical systems from a technical as well as from a conceptual angle.

1.1 Cyber-Physical Systems

Cyber-physical systems consist of IT systems "embedded" in applications in the physical world. They combine sensors, actuators, control units, operator consoles, and communication networks. Some of these systems are critical because they are part of an infrastructure critical for society. Critical infrastructure protection has been a high profile topic for a decade at least. The design of cyber-physical systems has been characterized in [5] as follows (our emphasis):

> Although the 20th-century science and technology has provided us with effective methods and tools for designing both computational and physical systems, the design of cyberphysical systems is much more than the union of those two fields. Traditionally, information scientists have had only a hazy notion of the requirements imposed by the physical environment attached to their computers. Similarly, mechanical, civil, and chemical engineers have viewed computers strictly as devices executing algorithms and ignored the physical properties of the embedded computing platforms. To the extent that we have designed cyber-physical systems, we have done so in an ad hoc, one-off manner that is not repeatable.
>
> A new science of cyber-physical system design will allow us to create new machines with complex dynamics and high reliability; it will allow us to be able to apply the principles of cyber-physical systems to new industries and applications in a reliable and economically efficient way. *Progress requires nothing less than the reintegration of physical and information sciences*—the construction of a new science and technology foundation for CPS that is simultaneously physical and computational.

The fundamental challenge then is to bring (IT) security experts and experts from the physical domains to the same table and make them understand how the other side thinks.

1.2 Security

Industry had faced security challenges long before the advent of IT, notably *espionage* and *sabotage*. Evocative phrases such as *putting a spanner into the works* or *bringing to a grinding halt* bear witness to acts of sabotage and their effects in a mechanical world. Blaming the internet for all ills of the world would thus not do justice to the facts.

This brings us to a first observation on security. There is, by design or accident, a not so commendable habit of favoring publicity over factual precision when reporting on security incidents. Take, for example, the following incident in the energy sector in 2012 that was reported both under the heading of espionage[1]

A company whose software and services are used to remotely administer and monitor large sections of the energy industry began warning customers last week that it is investigating a sophisticated hacker attack spanning its operations in the United States, Canada and Spain. Experts say digital fingerprints left behind by attackers point to a Chinese hacking group tied to repeated cyber-espionage campaigns against key Western interests.

and sabotage[2]

Criminals can now study the documents for vulnerabilities in the systems, and potentially devise attacks to sabotage nations' electricity distribution networks.

It is of course true that espionage might be a step on the way to sabotage. However, focusing on the most visible damage might actually be misleading and obscure the fact that a big bang may be less effective in terms of sabotage than long lasting but more difficult to detect low-level damage. Langner's reports on Stuxnet have elaborated on this aspect, see e.g. [12].

2   Communications Security in Cyber-Physical Systems

The current orthodoxies in information security are strongly influenced by communications security. The CIA triad confidentiality – integrity – availability can be traced back to the ISO/OSI Security Framework[3]. The CIA triad is also the basis of the ubiquitous claim that a core difference between "traditional" security, whatever that may be, and cyber-physical systems security is the importance of availability. While traditionally confidentiality is supposedly most important and availability least, in cyber-physical systems security the order is reversed. The latter also happens to be true for commercial IT security, a dominant influence in security practice and research for the past 25 years at least. What is true is that cyber-physical systems often have to meet hard real time requirements, a topic rarely studied in security research. This can, for example, lead to a readjustment of priorities in vulnerability scoring schemes [9]. The distinction is thus much more about hard versus soft real time than about availability versus confidentiality (as those terms are understood in IT security.)

Security measures following the above orthodoxy focus on cyber-threats to the IT core, like attacks targeting network traffic, like attacks infecting nodes with malware, like attacks by unauthorized users. The cyber part of a cyber-physical system is viewed as an infrastructure and defenses protecting this

---

[1] https://krebsonsecurity.com/2012/09/chinese-hackers-blamed-for-intrusion-at-energy-industry-giant-telvent/, retrieved February 2015.

[2] http://www.theregister.co.uk/2012/09/28/telvent_hack/.

[3] The earliest source in the authors' possession is a draft for ISO 7498/2 from 1985.

infrastructure are considered. Indeed, traditional IT security is infrastructure security geared towards networks or operating systems. This section will examine its potential contributions and limitations when applied in cyber-physical systems.

2.1 Confidentiality

Communications protocols developed for industrial control systems had been developed without including cryptographic protections. To communications security specialists this is a glaring deficiency. However, as long as these protocols were deployed in protected internal networks only there may have been no strong case for communications security. The situation changed when those protocols were used over public networks, but whether confidentiality needs to be considered remains an open question. In safety-critical applications, encryption might actually get in the way of reacting to emergencies.

2.2 Integrity

Three challenges arise when designing cryptographic integrity protection in the above context. First, message formats and field sizes may be fixed. Long term solutions may remove these restrictions. In the short and medium term, cryptographic solutions have to be found that provide adequate security under the given limitations, e.g. relating to the length of message authentication codes.

Secondly, there is the question of how to react to verification failures. Again, in safety critical situations the standard IETF advice that messages MUST be discarded if integrity verification fails may be counterproductive.

Third, communications security provides the "wrong" integrity guarantee. Digital signatures and message authentication codes protect messages in transit. They do not guarantee that the data transmitted are factually correct. Database security has a definition of integrity (*external consistency* [4]) that covers the latter aspect. Section 3.1 will explore this issue further.

2.3 Availability

Industrial control systems often use architectures where sensor readings update dedicated registers in a controller. Delaying or disrupting the communication between sensor and controller thus does not imply that no value is available at the controller, but that the register remains stuck at a stale value. A study of denial of service attacks inducing such *stuck-at faults* has been conducted in [10].

2.4 Fingerprinting

Remote *fingerprinting* of networked devices, be it browsers, operating systems, or for that matter, DNS servers [2], is a familiar technique in network security. Shodan[4] extended this approach to the Internet of Things. For IT security

---

[4] https://www.shodan.io/, accessed February 2015.

experts it is thus no surprise that devices connected to the internet can be found and analyzed by outsiders. From a security perspective, this is a case of applying known methods to new applications.

2.5 Network Separation

Splitting a network into subnets protected by perimeter defenses is another familiar network security technique that can be gainfully employed in cyber-physical systems. Raising alarms when behavior out of the normal is being observed would be a standard method in safety-critical applications. Whether intrusion detection has something substantially novel to contribute has yet to be seen.

2.6 End System Security

The transition from sensors taking analog measurements to smart instruments incorporating reconfigurable software components changes the situation in opposing ways. Remote calibration and remote maintenance promise efficiency gains, but remote reconfigurability can open the gate for new attacks. E.g., around 1990 virus writers developed *stealth* techniques that would compress and store an infected file, and intercept memory reads and return the "correct" file when anti-virus software was scanning the file system [8]. A similar technique was used by Stuxnet, impairing the *situational awareness* of the operators [11].

As a net effect, *risk analysis* becomes more complicated. Efficiency gains that are probably quantified more easily have to be set against security costs that are much more difficult to quantify. There may be a general lesson. IT raises efficiency only as long as security is not taken into consideration.

3 Cyber-Physical System Security

The threats considered so far are in essence generic IT security threats. Defenses are generic IT security defenses: firewalls, intrusion detection systems, authentication, access control, code signing, cryptographic mechanisms, proper security and risk management, etc. Educating industry sectors currently introducing IT in their processes about IT specific dangers is, of course, commendable, but this is a matter of education much more than a matter of research.

We are still missing the close integration between the cyber part and the physical part of cyber-physical systems that is meant to differentiate cyber-physical systems from embedded systems. Defenses end at the interfaces between the physical world and the IT infrastructure.

There are, for example, no defenses against attacks manipulating inputs before they are passed to the IT infrastructure. A secure infrastructure will pass wrong data securely to their destination; this is not good for security. Infrastructure does not know about the meaning of data.

An attacker may manipulate inputs in the physical domain before they are fed to the IT infrastructure. This can be done by manipulation of sensors, by manipulation of the environment around sensors, or by providing misleading user input. The attack goal is to get the system into a state desired by the attacker or make the system perform actions desired by the attacker. Attacks use existing controls to influence system behavior by manipulating inputs (physical domain) or by corrupting nodes in the system (cyber domain). Langner wrote on Stuxnet:

> Manipulations of a controller have less to do with the confidentiality, integrity, and availability of information and more to do with the performance and output of a physical production process [11].

We thus propose to treat the IT core as a control system, not as an infrastructure. We are concerned whether the data processed in the system fairly reflect reality. This leads to new security requirements, *veracity*, or *plausibility* of data. If necessary, the control system might be enhanced by adding further sensors. As a security strategy one has to look for aspects of the physical world that are related but cannot be easily manipulated simultaneously.

3.1 Veracity

Assertions are statements about an aspect relevant in a given application domain. They may, rightly or wrongly, be attributed to some source; authentication verifies the claimed origin of an assertion. Assertions may be factually true. We thus define *veracity* as the property that an assertion truthfully reflects the aspect it makes a statement about [6]. Here, we are following Borselius who had proposed a similar definition for mobile agent systems [3]:

> Veracity. The concept that an agent will not knowingly communicate false information.

Veracity is not guaranteed by the familiar IT infrastructure security services. Authentication does not verify the veracity of assertions. Veracity refers to aspects outside the IT infrastructure. The adversary is not an entity launching an attack on the infrastructure but an entity making false assertions; data are already false when fed to the infrastructure.

One could then try to protect the sensors making the observations reported in assertions. Such *trusted* sensors must be tamper-resistant. Their environment must be tamper resistant; it must not be possible to deceive sensors by interfering with their observations. This approach may work in scenarios where there is a sufficient degree of physical security. In general, trust is a brittle security assumption. As noted by Robert Morris sr., *if it is trusted it can hurt you.*

3.2 Plausibility

It may not always be feasible to ascertain veracity. The next best option is *plausibility*.

Plausibility. An assertion is plausible if it does not deviate too far from other assertions it is related to or from values estimated by some model.

A security analysis now has to consider the possibility of false rejects and false accepts.

Plausibility can be established by *consistency checks* (sanity checks). Consistency checks may compare an assertion with related assertions or with a prediction made by a (local) model of the application. Consistency check may be performed on facts reported in assertions made by several *witnesses*. This approach relies on the assumption that the adversary is unable to corrupt a sufficient number of witnesses. This brings us closer to research on reliability where solutions are designed on the basis that some but not all inputs are corrupted.

Plausibility checks rely on models of the physical world that capture the expected behavior of the application. E.g., let two sensors observe the same quantity; their readings should be the same within the bounds of measurement errors. We might model physical relationships between different quantities to check the consistency of a collection of observations. We might also use models to check consistency between predicted and observed behavior. Such solutions have been reported for systems assigning synthetic network coordinates, suitably called Veracity [15], for WLAN positioning systems [17], and for GPS [16].

3.3 Witnesses

Sensors act as *witnesses*. Schemes relying on witnesses can be undermined by witnesses making false statements. Schemes can be designed so that they can handle a certain proportion of colluding witnesses (see Fig. 1). Security proofs will then be based on assumptions that only a limited number of witnesses is compromised. Witness selection influences how easy it is to form powerful collusions. For this reason, Veracity [15] selects witnesses deterministically based on hash chains. When statistical independence is assumed, this assumption must match reality.

Security analysis is performed in threat models where not all system components are trusted. This points to Byzantine fault tolerance where only the number of colluding parties is limited but not the strategies they may use. Efficiency of security mechanisms may improve when suitable independence assumptions can be made. Provably secure systems may be broken by violating some assumption of the security proof. Independence assumptions are attractive targets.

3.4 Physics and Security

Physical relationships between the variables in an industrial process, e.g. between volume, pressure, and temperature in a vessel, can be viewed as information flows from a modeling perspective. This would not be quite new for IT security experts. *Covert timing channels* intentionally leaking sensitive information and timing-based *side channels* that inadvertently leak sensitive information are based on the fact that computations take time, i.e. on an aspect from the physical world.

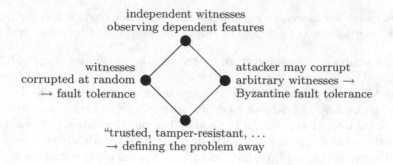

independent witnesses
observing dependent features

witnesses   attacker may corrupt
corrupted at random   arbitrary witnesses →
→ fault tolerance   Byzantine fault tolerance

"trusted, tamper-resistant, . . .
→ defining the problem away

Fig. 1. Assumptions on witnesses.

A further aspect is the integrity of physical components. Cyber-physical attacks may destroy or impair physical components, maybe because this is the ultimate goal of the attack or because it is a necessary step towards that goal. Physical modifications can rarely be undone. In contrast, changes to IT components could possibly be reversed after an attack making a forensic analysis of the attack considerably more difficult.

Critical cyber-physical systems will be designed in a way that they can be controlled by their operators. Sensors (and actuators) will be placed in a way that supports the operators' task. An attacker wanting to take over control may find that the measurements needed to control the attack are not readily available. An operator of a system under attack may find that the attacker is inducing physical behavior that had not been anticipated during design and cannot be observed by the sensors available. So-called water hammers may serve as example [14].

4   Betriebsblindheit

This German word describes a state of mind where someone knows a given process – and its normal failures – so well that it becomes impossible to imagine how things may go wrong differently. For security, such a blinkered view can be debilitating. The problem can apply equally to IT security experts and to application experts. For the case of IT security, we refer to a quote Butler Lampson and Roger Needham liked to attribute to each other:

Whoever thinks his problem can be solved using cryptography, doesn't understand his problem and doesn't understand cryptography [1, Chap. 21].

Industrial control system folklore knows about *salty cookie* scenarios. The incident giving the name is touched upon in [7]. Engineers asked to attack a cookie factory all came up with variations of putting too much salt in the cookies so they would become uneatable. In reality, the factory was damaged (accidentally) when simultaneously too much product was created while the emergency flushing system was disabled. The pipes got clogged and had to be replaced after attempts to clear them by water pressure and by chemical means had failed.

Our last example relates to business processes and refers to an incident[5] that occurred during the privatization of British Rail in 1996. London travelcards were valid on British Rail and London Transport lines (buses, underground). Revenue was shared according to estimated journey patterns. E.g., London Transport's share of revenue was 22 % for tickets sold at Fenchurch Street (no underground) but 48 % for tickets sold at Upminster (underground). Managers of the Fenchurch Street to Tilbury line had travelcards printed at Fenchurch Street but sold from their ticket offices in Upminster to increase the profitability of their operations.

London Transport was well aware of numerous methods used by staff and passengers to dodge fares. The practice described above was, however, not detected by London Transport (the victim) but by internal audit at British Rail noting a steep increase in ticket sales at Fenchurch Street. The management buyout of the Fenchurch Street to Tilbury line was stopped at the last moment.

5 Conclusion

Cyber-physical systems security is looking at applications with observations and effects in the physical world that rely on services provided by an IT infrastructure. Securing the IT infrastructure protects against an adversary who can manipulate data as it is processed in the infrastructure. Securing the IT infrastructure does not protect against an adversary feeding misleading data to the infrastructure, possibly by manipulating sensors. Traditional CIA security is neither necessary nor sufficient.

We therefore propose to treat the cyber part of a cyber-physical system as a control system instead and focus on the interfaces between physical space and cyberspace. To this effect, the veracity of inputs has to be established, maybe individually by relying on tamper-resistant trusted sensors and by controlling their environment, which may only be feasible in restricted circumstances, or collectively by suitable plausibility checks based on models of underlying physical (and chemical) relationships.

The integrity of the programmable devices used in the control infrastructure has to be protected. Attestation of the software configurations of these devices, e.g. by Trusted Platform Modules, may be an option. The privacy concerns often associated with the deployment of TPMs do not directly apply. Linkability of the readings from a given sensor may be a feature rather than a problem. Obfuscation may impede the attacker but also the operator.

The final challenge relates to the people performing the security analysis. They need expertise both in cyber security and in safety and have to be willing to look over the fence. Even more difficultly, they have to appreciate their limitations in their own domain. In security the past is a poor predictor of the future and familiar solutions may miss the point. To work on cyber-physical systems

---

[5] http://www.independent.co.uk/news/rail-fraud-aimed-to-help-success-of-selloff-1317413.html.

security, one has to combine the devious mind of the security expert with the technical expertise of the control engineer.

References

1. Anderson, R.: Security engineering. John Wiley & Sons, Hoboken (2008)
2. Arends, R., Koch, P.: DNS for fun and profit. In: 12. DFN-CERT Workshop, 2005 (2005). https://www.dfn-cert.de/dokumente/workshop/2005/dfncert-ws2005-f7paper.pdf. Accessed February 2015
3. Borselius, N.: Mobile agent security. Electron. Commun. Eng. J. **14**(5), 211–218 (2002)
4. Clark, D.R., Wilson, D.R.: A comparison of commercial and military computer security policies. In: Proceedings of the IEEE Symposium on Security and Privacy, pp. 184–194 (1987)
5. CPS Steering Group. Cyber-physical systems executive summary (2008). http://iccps.acm.org/2013/_doc/CPS-Executive-Summary.pdf. Accessed February 2015
6. Gollmann, D.: Veracity, plausibility, and reputation. In: Askoxylakis, I., Pöhls, H.C., Posegga, J. (eds.) WISTP 2012. LNCS, vol. 7322, pp. 20–28. Springer, Heidelberg (2012)
7. Howard, S., Lorenzin, L.: Utilize open standards to protect control systems networks. RTC Magazine, pp. 28–31, February 2010
8. Hruska, J.: Computer viruses. In: Grover, D. (ed.) The Protection of Computer Software - Its Technology and Applications, 2nd edn, pp. 183–219. Cambridge University Press, Cambridge (1992)
9. Khalili, A., Sami, A., Azimi, M., Moshtari, S., Salehi, Z., Ghiasi, M., Safavi, A.: Employing secure coding practices into industrial applications: a case study. Empirical Software Engineering, pp. 1–13, December 2014
10. Krotofil, M., Cárdenas, A.A., Manning, B., Jason Larsen, C.P.S.: Driving cyber-physical systems to unsafe operating conditions by timing DoS attacks on sensor signals. In Proceedings of the 30th Annual Computer Security Applications Conference, ACSAC 2014, pp. 146–155. ACM, New York (2014)
11. Langner, R.: Stuxnet: dissecting a cyberwarfare weapon. IEEE Secur. Priv. **3**(9), 49–51 (2011)
12. Langner, R.: To kill a centrifuge. Technical report, Langner Communications (2013)
13. Lee, E.A.: Cyber-physical systems - are computing foundations adequate? NSF Workshop on Cyber-Physical Systems (2006)
14. Leishear, R.A.: Fluid Mechanics. Dynamic Stresses, and Piping Design. ASME, Water Hammer (2013)
15. Sherr, M., Blaze, M., Loo, B.T.: Veracity: Practical secure network coordinates via vote-based agreements. In: USENIX Annual Technical Conference (USENIX-ATC). USENIX, June 2009
16. Tippenhauer, N.O., Pöpper, C., Rasmussen, K.B., Capkun, S.: On the requirements for successful GPS spoofing attacks. In: Proceedings of the 18th ACM Conference on Computer and Communications Security, pp. 75–86. ACM (2011)
17. Tippenhauer, N.O., Rasmussen, K.B., Pöpper, C., Čapkun, S.: Attacks on public WLAN-based positioning systems. In: Proceedings of the 7th International Conference on Mobile Systems, Applications, and Services, pp. 29–40. ACM (2009)

Practical Techniques Building on Encryption for Protecting and Managing Data in the Cloud

Sabrina De Capitani di Vimercati, Sara Foresti,
Giovanni Livraga, and Pierangela Samarati[⊠]

Università degli Studi di Milano, 26013 Crema, Italy
{sabrina.decapitani,sara.foresti,giovanni.livraga,
pierangela.samarati}@unimi.it

Abstract. Companies as well as individual users are adopting cloud solutions at an over-increasing rate for storing data and making them accessible to others. While migrating data to the cloud brings undeniable benefits in terms of data availability, scalability, and reliability, data protection is still one of the biggest concerns faced by data owners. Guaranteeing data protection means ensuring confidentiality and integrity of data and computations over them, and ensuring data availability to legitimate users. In this chapter, we survey some approaches for protecting data in the cloud that apply basic cryptographic techniques, possibly complementing them with additional controls, to the aim of producing efficient and effective solutions that can be used in practice.

1 Introduction

The rapid advancements in Information and Communication Technologies (ICTs) have encouraged the development and use of storage services based on public clouds (e.g., Microsoft Azure and Amazon S3). Users as well as companies have been therefore moving their data to the cloud, thus enjoying several benefits such as data and service availability, scalability, and reliability at a relatively low cost. Although there is no doubt that the use of cloud services brings several benefits, the storage and management of data by external cloud providers introduce new security and privacy risks that can slow down or affect the widespread acceptance of the cloud (e.g., [29,47,49,65]). A major issue concerns the fact that moving data to the cloud, data owners lose control over them and the cloud environment, being not under the direct control of the data owners, may not be fully trusted. This implies the need to protect confidentiality and provide integrity guarantees for data stored or processed in the cloud, as well as for accesses to such data. In the recent years, the research and development communities have dedicated attention to these problems, designing novel techniques to ensure proper data protection in the cloud. Guaranteeing data protection in the cloud requires ensuring their *confidentiality*, *integrity*, and *availability* [36,48,63]. Confidentiality means that data should be accessible and known only to parties authorized for that. Guaranteeing confidentiality requires then to protect: the data externally stored; the identity and/or personal information of the users

© Springer-Verlag Berlin Heidelberg 2016
P.Y.A. Ryan et al. (Eds.): Kahn Festschrift, LNCS 9100, pp. 205–239, 2016.
DOI: 10.1007/978-3-662-49301-4_15

accessing the data; and the actions that users perform over the data. Integrity means that data should be protected against unauthorized or improper modifications. Guaranteeing integrity requires ensuring the authenticity of: the subjects interacting in the cloud; the data stored and maintained at cloud providers; the response returned from queries and computations. Availability means that data should be available upon user requests and that cloud providers should satisfy requirements expressed in the Service Level Agreements (SLAs) established between data owners/users and the cloud providers. Guaranteeing availability requires then providing data owners and users with the required services and enabling them to assess the satisfaction of the SLAs.

Cryptography is one of the key techniques that can be adopted to address such confidentiality, integrity, and availability problems and to increase the confidence of cloud service users. Cryptography has evolved from ancient science, mainly dedicated to the design of secret writing codes, to the scientific discipline of modern cryptography that provides techniques for addressing a wide range of security issues. While in the past cryptographic techniques were principally used to protect communications (*data in transit*), today they are also used to protect *data at rest* and *data at use* (e.g., [5,11,44]). Data at rest are recorded on a storage device (e.g., a hard drive) and can remain valuable for very long periods of time. Data at use are processed by applications to respond to queries or to make computations. In this chapter, we discuss some security problems related to the protection of data at rest and data at use in cloud environments. We analyze the relevance of cryptographic techniques to address these problems, also when they are combined with other solutions to improve protection guarantees and/or to limit the computational overhead, thus making such techniques applicable in practice. Figure 1 illustrates the reference scenario: a data owner outsources her data collection to a cloud provider, and different users access these data through their clients. This scenario is characterized by the following key security challenges, which will be covered in the remainder of this chapter.

- *Storage security:* data stored in the cloud should be: protected from unauthorized accesses, even by the storing provider (confidentiality), accessible by authorized users (availability), and correct (integrity).
- *Selective access:* data stored in the cloud should be selectively accessible by users as demanded by the access control policy defined by the data owner.
- *Fine-grained access:* encrypted outsourced data should be used for fine-grained retrieval and query execution.
- *Query confidentiality:* the target of accesses to data should be kept private.
- *Query integrity:* the results of queries and computations should be correct, complete, and fresh.

Note that cryptographic techniques have an important role in protecting data in transit also in cloud environments, where data are often transferred from one cloud provider to another one or within components of the cloud system. In these cases, classical solutions can be applied (e.g., virtual private networks and secure socket layers) and therefore we do not further elaborate on them.

The remainder of this chapter is organized as follows. Section 2 describes solutions for the secure storage of data in the cloud. Section 3 presents some

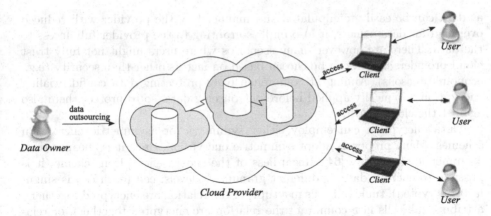

Fig. 1. Reference scenario

approaches enforcing selective access on encrypted data stored in the cloud. Section 4 illustrates approaches that enable the fine-grained access to encrypted outsourced data. Section 5 presents solutions for query privacy, focusing on techniques that protect the accesses to data. Section 6 discusses possible approaches to verify the integrity of query results. Finally, Sect. 7 gives our conclusions.

2   Protection of Data in Storage

When data are stored and managed by an external cloud provider, their confidentiality, integrity, and availability become of paramount importance. In this section, we illustrate the role of cryptographic techniques to ensure such properties. For simplicity, in the discussion we assume that outsourced data are organized in a relational database. We note however that all the approaches illustrated can be easily adapted to other data models.

2.1   Data Confidentiality

When a data collection is outsourced to a cloud provider, its owner loses control over the data themselves, which should therefore be properly protected. The problem of protecting data when outsourcing them to external providers has been under the attention of the research community since the introduction of the Database-As-a-Service (DAS) paradigm [64]. Different approaches have been proposed to protect data confidentiality, typically relying on data encryption [64] to make data unintelligible to subjects who do not know the encryption keys.

Currently, there are two different approaches for dealing with encryption on the data outsourced to cloud providers: *(1)* encryption is managed by the provider itself, which therefore encrypts the data with a key it knows; *(2)* data are encrypted before sending them to the cloud provider, which does not know the encryption key. While the first approach allows for enhanced functionality as data can be easily manipulated and managed by the provider with reduced overhead for data owners, it also implies granting to the provider full access to the data. There are however many scenarios where users might not fully trust cloud providers, which can be chosen based on factors other than security (e.g., economic reasons). Aiming at comprehensively protecting data confidentiality, encryption is typically applied before outsourcing data, so to protect them also against the cloud provider.

Data encryption can employ either symmetric or asymmetric encryption schemes. Many proposals adopt symmetric encryption, since it is cheaper than asymmetric encryption [64]. Regardless of the chosen encryption scheme, it is possible to encrypt data at different granularity levels: cell (each cell is singularly encrypted), tuple (all cells in a tuple of the relation are encrypted together), attribute (all cells in a column of the relation are encrypted together), or relation (the entire relation is encrypted as a single chunk). While the granularity at which encryption operates does not affect the confidentiality of the data, the majority of the existing approaches adopt tuple level encryption as it better supports query evaluation at the cloud provider (see Sect. 4). In fact, relation-level and attribute-level encryption require to communicate to the client issuing the query the entire relation or the subset of attributes involved in the query without the possibility of filtering at the provider side the encrypted tuples that are not of interest. On the other hand, cell-level encryption would require an excessive workload for data owners and clients in encrypting/decrypting data. Tuple-level encryption represents therefore a good tradeoff between encrypt/decrypt workload for clients and data owners, and query execution efficiency [64].

Adopting tuple level encryption, relation r, defined over relation schema $R(a_1,\ldots,a_n)$, is represented at the cloud provider as an encrypted relation r^k defined over schema $R^k(\underline{\texttt{tid}}, \texttt{enc})$, with $\texttt{tid}$ the primary key added to the encrypted relation and $\texttt{enc}$ the encrypted tuple. Each tuple t in r_is represented as an encrypted tuple t^k in r^k where $t^k[\texttt{tid}]$ is a random identifier and $t^k[\texttt{enc}]=E_k(t)$ is the encrypted tuple content, with E a symmetric encryption function with key k. Figure 2(a) illustrates relation MEDICALDATA, storing medical information about eight patients of a hospital, and Fig. 2(b) illustrates the corresponding encrypted relation.

The use of encryption to protect data confidentiality is based on the underlying assumption that all data are equally sensitive and therefore encryption is a price to be paid to protect them. However, this assumption can be an overkill in scenarios where data are not sensitive per se but what is sensitive is their association (e.g., the lists of patients' names and of their diseases in Fig. 2(a) might not be sensitive, but the association of each patient's name with her disease should be protected). In these scenarios, encryption can be combined with data fragmentation to protect sensitive associations among attribute values [9,11]. Fragmentation consists in vertically partitioning the set of attributes in relation R in different (vertical) fragments, so that attributes forming a sensitive association are split among different fragments, and sensitive attributes are possibly obfuscated (e.g., sensitive attributes are encrypted or not released).

MEDICALDATA

	SSN	Name	ZIP	Job	Disease
t_1	123456789	Alice	94110	nurse	asthma
t_2	234567891	Bob	94112	farmer	asthma
t_3	345678912	Carl	94118	teacher	gastritis
t_4	456789123	David	94110	teacher	chest pain
t_5	567891234	Eric	94112	surgeon	gastritis
t_6	678912345	Fred	94117	secretary	asthma
t_7	789123456	Greg	94115	manager	chest pain
t_8	891234567	Hal	94110	secretary	asthma

(a)

MEDICALDATA^k

tid	enc
1	a%g6
2	1p(y
3	Hu8$
4	lR=+
5	kqW
6	nTy&
7	6_R&u
8	fp*r;

(b)

Fig. 2. An example of a relation (a) and corresponding encrypted version (b)

Different solutions have been proposed to define a correct fragmentation that minimizes query evaluation costs (e.g., [10,11,18]).

2.2 Data Integrity and Availability

Data integrity and availability are two critical elements that should be guaranteed when data are stored at an external cloud provider. Data integrity means that neither the cloud provider nor unauthorized parties can improperly tamper with data in storage without being detected. Like for confidentiality, also techniques that provide data integrity can operate at different granularity levels: cell, attribute, tuple, or relation level. Verifying integrity at the relation or at the attribute level, however, would require to access the entire relation (or column, respectively) for each integrity check. On the other hand, integrity verification at the cell level would require a considerable overhead for the client. To find a good tradeoff between integrity guarantees and the additional overhead for the client, the majority of the existing proposals operate at the tuple level. In the following, we illustrate some of the most well-known (encryption-based) techniques for ensuring data integrity and availability.

Digital and Aggregate Signatures. Data integrity can be ensured through *digital signatures* (e.g., [44]). Each data owner has its own pair ⟨*private_key,public_key*⟩ of private and public keys. Each tuple is first signed with the private key of its owner. The signature is then concatenated to the actual tuple, and this concatenated chunk is encrypted and sent to the cloud provider for storage. Unauthorized modifications to a tuple can be immediately detected by checking the signature associated with it. This basic approach, while effective, has the disadvantage that the cost associated with integrity verification linearly grows with the number of accessed tuples.

To limit this burden, multiple digital signatures (related to multiple tuples) can be combined in a single signature by adopting *condensed RSA, BGLS*, or batch *DSA signature aggregation* [55]. Condensed RSA is an extension of the traditional RSA encryption scheme that permits to combine signatures generated by the same signer (i.e., signatures associated with tuples of the same owner). BGLS [6] is an encryption scheme based on bilinear mappings that supports the aggregation of signatures even when they have been generated by different signers (i.e., when the signatures have been generated by different owners). Batch DSA is an extension of traditional DSA signature schema that permits to combine the signature of different tuples, which can be verified together. The verification of a batch DSA signature aggregation is based on the multiplicative homomorphic property of these signatures. The signature verification processes for condensed RSA and BGLS schemas are more efficient than the verification process of batch DSA. However, both condensed RSA and BGLS are *mutable*, meaning that the knowledge of multiple aggregated signatures allows their composition, thus obtaining a valid signature that may correspond to the aggregate signature of an arbitrary set of tuples. This might represent a threat to the integrity guarantees of the cloud data collection.

POR-PDP. Encryption is also at the basis of Proof Of Retrievability (POR [50]) and Provable Data Possession (PDP [4]) proposals, which aim at ensuring data integrity and availability. These techniques allow a *verifier* (e.g., a requesting client or the data owner) to obtain a proof that the storage cloud provider is correctly maintaining a resource of interest (ensuring its integrity) and can therefore correctly return it (ensuring its availability). The main difference between POR and PDP is the mechanism used to obtain the proof. POR is based on the insertion in the data collection (before outsourcing) of ad-hoc random *sentinels* generated by the data owner, which are made indistinguishable from real data through a layer of encryption. In the verification step, the verifier challenges the provider by requesting some sentinel values. If the data collection has been tampered with by the provider or unauthorized parties, then these values will be incorrect with non-negligible probability, hence signaling that both data integrity and availability have been compromised. This basic technique has been extended along several directions to generate compact proofs to be returned to the data owner (or to an arbitrary verifier) [68]. PDP is based on ad-hoc *homomorphic verifiable tags*. The owner pre-computes a set of tags associated with the data items in her collection, combines the tags and the collection, and stores them at the cloud provider. In the verification step, the client challenges the provider against a randomly selected data item. The provider then generates a proof of possession for the required data item, using both the requested data and the corresponding tags, that the client can easily verify. It is interesting to note that, since tags enjoy the homomorphic property, tags computed for multiple data items can be combined into a single value [4]. We note that POR, whose security is based on the impossibility for the cloud provider to recognize sentinels, can only be employed to guarantee the integrity of encrypted data collections. On the contrary, PDP is more flexible and can be adopted with both encrypted and plaintext datasets.

Auditing. The aforementioned approaches require the client to check itself the integrity of a resource of interest. Aiming at reducing the burden at the client side, in some scenarios it might be desirable to delegate the verification process to a third party, trusted for enforcing integrity checks and to access the data content. The solution in [74] relies on the presence of a trusted auditor in charge of evaluating the integrity of a data collection stored at a cloud provider. Specific techniques (e.g., homomorphic linear authenticators and random masking) can be used if the auditor is not trusted to access the outsourced data collection [74]. Another solution relying on public auditing has been proposed in [86], and aims at increasing the performances of the auditing process.

3 Selective Access to Data

Data owners outsourcing their data to the cloud may wish to selectively make them visible/accessible to other users. Such a feature requires the support of access control correctly enforcing authorizations defined by the data owners (e.g., [16,24,30,37]). In a cloud scenario, neither the data owners (for performance reasons), nor the cloud providers (for security reasons) can however enforce such authorizations. A promising direction for solving this problem consists in making the outsourced data *self-enforce* the access restrictions [14,20,21]. In this section, we present two families of approaches specifically designed to enforce access control over outsourced data: selective encryption (Sect. 3.1) and attribute-based encryption (Sect. 3.2).

3.1 Selective Encryption

Selective encryption consists in using different keys to encrypt different tuples, and in selectively distributing those keys to authorized users so that each user can decrypt all and only the tuples she is authorized to access.

Basic Technique. The authorization policy, regulating which user in the set U of users of the system can read which tuple of relation r, can be represented as an *access matrix* M with a row for each user $u \in U$, and a column for each tuple $t \in r$, where: $M[u,t]=1$ iff u can access t; $M[u,t]=0$ otherwise. The jth column of an access matrix represents the access control list $acl(t_j)$ of tuple t_j, for each $j = 1, \ldots, |r|$ (i.e., the set of users who can access it). Figure 3 illustrates an example of access matrix regulating access to the tuples in relation MEDICALDATA in Fig. 2(a) by users A, B, C, and D. According to the access matrix, $acl(t_1)=AC$.

Enforcing an access control policy with encryption requires to establish keys for encrypting resources and keys to be distributed to users. Equivalence among an *encryption policy* and an access control policy demands that every user should able to decrypt all and only the tuples she is entitled to access according to the access control policy.

There are different ways in which an access control policy can be translated into an equivalent encryption policy. However, this translation should take into account two main desiderata [21]: *(i)* each user must manage only one key; and *(ii)* each tuple must be encrypted with only one key (i.e., no tuple is replicated). These two desiderata are needed to reduce the overhead at user side caused

	t_1	t_2	t_3	t_4	t_5	t_6	t_7	t_8
A	1	0	1	0	1	0	1	0
B	0	1	0	1	1	1	0	0
C	1	0	0	0	0	0	1	0
D	0	1	1	0	0	0	1	1

Fig. 3. An example of access matrix for the relation in Fig. 2

by key management, and the consistency problems typically caused by data replication. To obey these two constraints, selective encryption approaches rely on *key derivation techniques*, which permit to compute an encryption key k_j starting from the knowledge of another key k_i, and of a piece of publicly available information. These techniques are based on the definition of a *key derivation hierarchy* that can be graphically represented as a directed graph with a vertex v_i for each key k_i in the system, and an edge (v_i, v_j) from key k_i to key k_j iff k_j can be directly derived from k_i. Key derivation can be recursively applied, meaning that a generic key k_j can be computed starting from another key k_i if there is a path, of arbitrary length, from vertex v_i to vertex v_j in the key derivation hierarchy. Depending on the kind of the key derivation hierarchy, different key derivation techniques can be applied, as illustrated in the following.

- *Chain of vertices* (e.g., [66]): the key k_j associated with vertex v_j is computed by applying a one-way function to key k_i associated with the predecessor vertex v_i of v_j in the chain. No public information is needed to derive keys.
- *Tree hierarchy* (e.g., [67]): the key k_j associated with vertex v_j is computed by applying a one-way function to key k_i of the direct ancestor of v_j, and a public label l_j associated with k_j. Public labels are necessary to guarantee that different children of the same node in the tree have different keys.
- *DAG hierarchy* (e.g., [2]): vertices in the hierarchy can have more than one direct ancestor, and each edge in the hierarchy is associated with a public *token* [3]. Given two keys k_i and k_j associated with vertices v_i and v_j such that (v_i, v_j) is an edge in the DAG, and the public label l_j of k_j, token $t_{i,j}$ permits to compute k_j from k_i and l_j. Token $t_{i,j}$ is computed as $t_{i,j} = k_j \oplus f(k_i, l_j)$, where $\oplus$ is the bitwise XOR operator, and f is a deterministic cryptographic function. By means of $t_{i,j}$, all users who know, or can derive, key k_i can also derive key k_j.

A key derivation hierarchy can be defined according to any of the above-mentioned models. In the following, we consider the most general case of a DAG, with token-based key derivation [21].

Enforcement of Read Privileges. A straightforward approach to define a key derivation hierarchy to enforce an access control policy consists in inserting a vertex in the hierarchy for each subset of users in U, and in exploiting the set containment relationship $\subseteq$ among these subsets to connect vertices. Given a pair of vertices v_i and v_j, there is a path from v_i to v_j iff the set of users represented

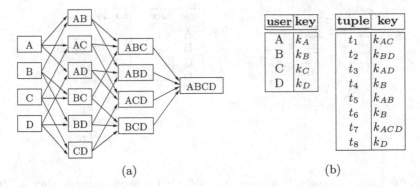

user	key
A	k_A
B	k_B
C	k_C
D	k_D

tuple	key
t_1	k_{AC}
t_2	k_{BD}
t_3	k_{AD}
t_4	k_B
t_5	k_{AB}
t_6	k_B
t_7	k_{ACD}
t_8	k_D

(a)   (b)

Fig. 4. An example of encryption policy equivalent to the access control policy in Fig. 3: key derivation hierarchy (a) and user and tuple keys (b)

by v_i is a subset of that represented by v_j. For instance, Fig. 4(a) illustrates the key derivation hierarchy induced by the set $U=\{A,B,C,D\}$ of users and the set containment relationship over it. In the figure, vertices are labeled with the set of users they represent. The encryption policy induced by such a hierarchy is equivalent to (and thus, correctly enforces) the authorization policy iff: *(i)* each user u_i is provided with the key associated with the vertex representing her; and *(ii)* each tuple t_j is encrypted with the key of the vertex representing $acl(t_j)$. These encryption and key distribution strategies guarantee that each tuple can be decrypted by all and only the users in its access control list. Moreover, each user has to manage one key only, and each tuple is encrypted with one key only. With reference to the key derivation hierarchy in Fig. 4(a) and the access control policy in Figs. 3, 4(b) illustrates the keys assigned to users and those used to encrypt the tuples in relation MEDICALDATA in Fig. 2. Note that the encryption policy in Fig. 4 is equivalent to the authorization policy in Fig. 3 as each user can derive, from her own key, the keys of the vertices representing sets of users including her, and hence can decrypt the tuples she is authorized to read. For instance, user C can derive the keys used to encrypt tuples t_1 and t_7.

While correctly enforcing the given authorization policy, the encryption policy illustrated above defines more keys and tokens than necessary. Managing a large set of tokens reduces the efficiency of the derivation process and, ultimately, increases the response time to users. In fact, tokens are stored in a publicly available catalog, maintained at the provider side: when a user u wants to access a tuple t, she needs to perform a search across the catalog to retrieve a chain of tokens that, starting from her own key, ends in the one used to encrypt t. The total number of tokens is therefore a critical factor for the efficiency of access to remotely stored data. The problem of minimizing the number of tokens in the key derivation hierarchy while still guaranteeing equivalence between the authorization and the encryption policies is NP-hard as it can be reduced to the set cover problem [21]. In [21], the authors present a heuristic approach to reduce the number of tokens that is based on the following two observations:

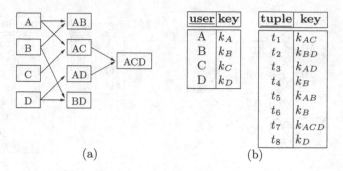

(a)   (b)

Fig. 5. An example of encryption policy equivalent to the access control policy in Fig. 3 with reduced number of tokens: key derivation hierarchy (a) and user and tuple keys (b)

- the vertices necessary to enforce an authorization policy are those vertices, called *material*, that represent singleton sets of users (whose keys are communicated to users) and the access control lists of the tuples in r (whose keys are used for encryption);
- when two or more vertices have more than two common direct ancestors, the insertion of a vertex representing the set of users in these ancestors reduces the total number of tokens.

Given an authorization policy, the heuristics first identifies the material vertices and, for each vertex v, finds a set of material vertices that form a *non-redundant set covering* for v (i.e., the smallest set V of vertices such that, for each user u represented by v, there is at least a vertex v_i in V such that u appears in v_i), which become direct ancestors of v. For each set $\{v_1, \ldots, v_m\}$ of vertices that have $n > 2$ common ancestors $v'_1, \ldots, v'_n$, the algorithm inserts an intermediate vertex v representing all the users in $v'_1, \ldots, v'_n$, connects each v'_i, $i = 1, \ldots, n$, with v, and v with each v_j, $j = 1, \ldots, m$. In this way, the encryption policy includes $n + m$, instead of $n \cdot m$ tokens in the catalog [21]. Figure 5 illustrates an encryption policy equivalent to the authorization policy in Fig. 3 with a reduced number of tokens. Comparing the key derivation hierarchy in Fig. 5(a) with the one in Fig. 4(a) it is easy to see the reduction in the number of tokens needed to correctly enforce the access control policy.

Enforcement of Write Privileges. The approach in [21] assumes outsourced data to be read-only, meaning that only the data owner can update the content of her tuples while other parties can only be granted read privileges over them. This assumption is not aligned with current trends in technology (e.g., collaborative scenarios), where the data owner might want to selectively grant to other users also write privileges over her resources. The proposal in [17] adopts selective encryption to manage also write authorizations. The basic idea is to associate each tuple with an encrypted *write tag* (i.e., a random value chosen independently from the tuple content), and to allow the update of a tuple t only to users who know the plaintext value of the write tag of t. Access to write tags is regulated through selective encryption: the write tag of tuple t is encrypted with a key derivable only by the users authorized to write t (i.e., the users specified within its write access control list) and the provider. The provider will accept a write request on a tuple only if the requesting user proves to know the corresponding write tag. To this aim, the key derivation hierarchy is extended with the keys used to encrypt write tags and with key $k_{\mathcal{P}}$, specifically assigned to the provider $\mathcal{P}$ to enable write tags verification.

The keys used to encrypt write tags are defined in such a way that: *(i)* authorized users can compute them applying a *secure hash function* to a key they already know (or can derive via a sequence of tokens); and *(ii)* the provider can directly derive them from key $k_{\mathcal{P}}$ through a token specifically added to the key derivation hierarchy. Note that keys used to encrypt write tags cannot be used to derive other keys in the hierarchy, because the provider is not trusted to access the plaintext content of the tuples in the outsourced relation. For instance, consider the encryption policy in Fig. 5 and suppose that the write privilege over tuple t_1 is granted to user A, over t_2 to B and D , over t_3 and t_8 to D, over t_4, t_5, and t_6 to B, and over t_7 to C. Figure 6 illustrates the key derivation hierarchy extended with the key $k_{\mathcal{P}}$ of the provider and the keys necessary to encrypt write tags. In the figure, the additional vertices are in gray, and both additional vertices and edges are dotted. Figure 6(b) reports the keys assigned to users and to the provider, and the keys used to encrypt the tuples in relation MEDICALDATA and their write tags.

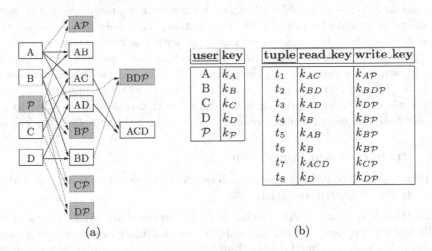

(a)   (b)

Fig. 6. Encryption policy in Fig. 5 extended to enforce write privileges: key derivation hierarchy (a) and user and tuple keys (b)

Updates to the Authorization Policy. Since the equivalence between the authorization and encryption policies must be always guaranteed to ensure proper enforcement of authorizations, any change in the access control policy should be enforced by updating the encryption policy. In fact, the keys used to encrypt each tuple t and its write tag depend on the set of users who can read and write it, respectively. To enforce updates to read privileges, it is then necessary to re-encrypt the tuple involved in a policy update with a different key that only the users in its new access control list know or can derive. The overhead for the data owner in executing re-encryption operations is reduced in [21] by introducing the *over-encryption* approach to partially delegate to the provider the management of grant and revoke of read privileges, thus greatly reducing the overhead at the data owner side. Over-encryption adopts two different layers of encryption: the *Base Encryption Layer* (BEL) and the *Surface Encryption Layer* (SEL), each of which is characterized by its own encryption policy (i.e., set of keys, key derivation hierarchy, and key distribution). Each tuple t is protected with two different layers of encryption, and then a user can access t only if she knows both the keys used to encrypt t at BEL and SEL. At initialization time, the encryption policies at BEL and SEL coincide (more precisely, they are both equivalent to the initial authorization policy). In case of policy updates, BEL is updated by only inserting tokens (to allow for new key derivations) in the public catalog. Re-encryption is instead performed at the SEL by the cloud provider.

While effective for updates to the read authorization policy, the over-encryption approach cannot be adopted in case of updates to write privileges. In fact, users are not oblivious, and adding a layer of encryption to a write tag would not prevent a user, whose write privilege on a tuple has been revoked, from exploiting their previous knowledge of the tag of the tuple to perform unauthorized updates. Indeed, to *grant* user u write access to tuple t, the write tag of t can be simply re-encrypted with a key known to the provider and the users authorized to update its content. On the contrary, to *revoke* from user u write access to tuple t, it is necessary to associate with t a fresh write tag, with a new plaintext value independent from the previous one, and to encrypt it with a key known to the provider and the users in the new write access control list of the tuple [17]. Note that, since the provider knows the write tag of each tuple to correctly enforce write privileges, the data owner can delegate to the storing provider both the generation and re-encryption of the write tag of her tuples [17].

3.2   Attribute-Based Encryption

Another approach to enforce selective access in cloud scenarios is represented by *Attribute-Based Encryption* (ABE [43]).

Basic Technique and Authorization Enforcement. ABE is based on public-key encryption schemes, and enforces access restrictions according to an authorization policy defined on attributes associated with tuples or with users. Based on how attributes and policies are associated with data and users, it is possible to implement ABE as either *Ciphertext-Policy ABE* (CP-ABE [77]) or *Key-Policy ABE* (KP-ABE [43]). In the following, we briefly describe these two approaches.

CP-ABE associates each user u with a set of descriptive attributes and a private key, generated on the basis of these attributes. The attributes associated with u describe her characteristics considered relevant for access control

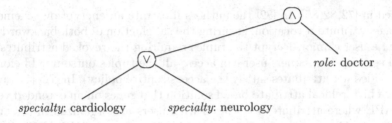

Fig. 7. Access structure associated with tuple t_7 of relation MEDICALDATA in Fig. 2 with CP-ABE

enforcement (e.g., her role and department in a company). Each tuple t in a relation r is instead associated with an *access structure* modeling the authorization policy regulating accesses to t. Graphically, an access structure is a tree whose leaves represent basic conditions over attributes, and whose internal nodes represent logic gates (i.e., conjunctions and disjunctions). For instance, suppose that the access to tuple t_7 in relation MEDICALDATA in Fig. 2 should be granted only to doctors specialized in cardiology or neurology. Figure 7 illustrates the access structure associated with tuple t_7, representing the Boolean formula (*role*='doctor') ∧ (*specialty*='cardiology' ∨ *specialty*='neurology'). The key generation technique adopted by CP-ABE is specifically designed to guarantee that the key k of user u can decrypt tuple t iff the set of attributes used when generating k satisfies the access control policy represented by the access structure considered when encrypting t.

KP-ABE associates each user u with an access structure and each tuple with a set of attributes describing its characteristics. The key associated with each user is then generated on the basis of her access structure, while the key used to encrypt each tuple depends on its attributes. The key generation technique adopted by KP-ABE is specifically designed to guarantee that each user u can decrypt a tuple t iff the attributes associated with t satisfy the access structure associated with user u.

The support of write privileges is provided by the adoption of Attribute-Based Signature (ABS) techniques. The proposal in [35] combines CP-ABE and ABS techniques to enforce read and write access privileges, respectively. This approach, although effective, has the disadvantage of requiring the presence of a trusted party for correct policy enforcement. A similar approach, based on the combined use of ABE and ABS for supporting both read and write privileges, is illustrated in [62]. This solution has the advantage over the approach in [35] of being applicable also to distributed scenarios.

Updates to the Authorization Policy. Although CP-ABE effectively and efficiently enforces access control policies, one of its main drawbacks is related to the management of attribute revocation. When a user loses one of her attributes, she should not be able to access tuples that require the revoked attribute for the access. Attribute revocation is however hard to enforce without causing expensive re-keying and/or re-encryption operations. Solutions to this problem are presented in [72,82,85]. In [82] the authors illustrate an encryption scheme able to manage attribute revocation, ensuring the satisfaction of both backward security (i.e., a user cannot decrypt the tuples requiring the revoked attributes) and forward security (i.e., a new user can access all the tuples outsourced before her join, provided her attributes satisfy the access control policy). In [72] the authors propose a hierarchical attribute-based solution that relies on an extended version of CP-ABE where attributes associated with users are organized in a recursive set structure. Aiming at enforcing updates in the context of KP-ABE, the solution in [85] proposes to couple ABE with proxy re-encryption, in such a way to delegate to the storage provider most of the re-encryption operations necessary to enforce attribute revocation. To reduce the overhead inevitably caused by the adoption of asymmetric encryption, this approach also proposes to adopt KP-ABE to protect the symmetric keys used to encrypt tuple contents. By doing so, only authorized users can retrieve the key physically used to protect the content of the tuples.

4   Fine-Grained Access to Data

Encryption represents an effective means to protect data confidentiality in the cloud. However, cloud providers cannot directly evaluate users' queries on the data they store, as they do not know the encryption keys and therefore cannot access data content. It is also infeasible to require the client to download the encrypted data collection and locally evaluate the queries, as this would nullify the benefits of delegating data storage to cloud providers. Current solutions addressing this issue are based on the definition of *indexes* that enable (partial) query evaluation at the provider side without the need to decrypt data [64], or on specific encryption schemas that support the execution of operations (Fig. 8) or SQL queries [60] directly over encrypted data. In the remainder of this section, we describe these two solutions in more details.

Encryption	Operations	Security	Cost
Randomized	anything	no leakage	practical
Deterministic	$=$	leaks duplicates	practical
OPE	$\geq$	leaks order	practical
Pallier	$+$	no leakage	expensive
El Gamal	$\times$	no leakage	expensive
Fully homomorphic	everything	no leakage	impractical

Fig. 8. Characteristics of some encryption functions

4.1   Indexes for Query Execution

Indexes are metadata whose values depend on the plaintext values of the attributes in the original relation on which they are defined. Indexes are

MEDICALDATA

	SSN	Name	ZIP	Job	Disease
t_1	123456789	Alice	94110	nurse	asthma
t_2	234567891	Bob	94112	farmer	asthma
t_3	345678912	Carl	94118	teacher	gastritis
t_4	456789123	David	94110	teacher	chest pain
t_5	567891234	Eric	94112	surgeon	gastritis
t_6	678912345	Fred	94117	secretary	asthma
t_7	789123456	Greg	94115	manager	chest pain
t_8	891234567	Hal	94110	secretary	asthma

(a)

MEDICALDATA^k

tid	enc	I_Z	I_J	I_D
1	a%g6	α	η	κ
2	1p(y	β	ζ	κ
3	Hu8\$	γ	θ	λ
4	lR=+	α	θ	λ
5	kqW	β	θ	λ
6	nTy&	δ	η	κ
7	6_R&u	ϵ	ζ	λ
8	fp*r;	α	η	κ

(b)

Fig. 9. Plaintext relation MEDICALDATA (a) and corresponding encrypted and indexed relation (b)

represented in the encrypted relation as additional attributes. Given a relation r, defined over schema $R(a_1, \ldots, a_n)$, the corresponding encrypted and indexed relation r^k is defined over schema $R^k(\underline{\text{tid}}, \text{enc}, I_{i_1}, \ldots, I_{i_j})$, where I_{i_l}, $l = 1, \ldots, j$, is the index defined over attribute a_{i_l} in R. Note that not all the attributes in R need to have a corresponding index in R^k, but only those that are expected to be involved in queries. For instance, Fig. 9(b) represents the encrypted version of relation MEDICALDATA in Fig. 2(b), reported also in Fig. 9(a) for the reader's convenience, where attributes ZIP, Job, and Disease have been associated with indexes I_Z, I_J, and I_D, respectively. Index values are denoted with Greek letters.

The introduction of indexes allows the cloud provider to (partially) evaluate a query q submitted by the client. The query evaluation process in presence of indexes operates as follows.

- *Step 1.* The user formulates a query q that is sent to the client. Note that, since encryption must be transparent for final users (which could be unaware of the fact that the relation is stored in encrypted form at the cloud provider), q is formulated over the plaintext relation.
- *Step 2.* Upon receiving q, the client generates two queries: q_p, operating on the encrypted relation at the provider using indexes; and q_c, operating on the result of q_p at the client. Query q_p is then communicated to the cloud provider.
- *Step 3.* Upon receiving q_p, the cloud provider executes it on the encrypted relation. The result is then sent to the client.
- *Step 4.* The client decrypts the result obtained from the provider, and evaluates q_c on the resulting relation to possibly remove *spurious tuples* (i.e., tuples that satisfy the condition on the index but not the original condition specified by the user) and returns the query result to the user.

Figure 10 illustrates the query evaluation process. Clearly, the translation of query q into queries q_p and q_c depends on the kind of indexes involved in the query. We now illustrate some of the most well-known indexing techniques, classified according to the conditions they support.

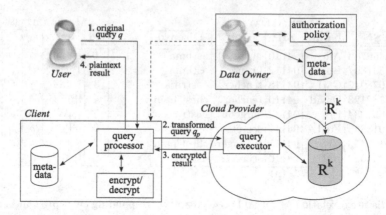

Fig. 10. Query evaluation process

Equality Conditions (e.g., [15,46]). Equality conditions are conditions of the form $a = v$, with a an attribute and v a value in the domain of a, and are supported by three classes of indexes: *encryption-based* [15], *bucket-based* [46], and *hash-based* [15] indexes.

The encryption-based index for a tuple t over attribute a is computed as $E_k(t[a])$, where E_k is a symmetric encryption function and k the encryption key. An equality condition of the form $a=v$ is then translated as $I=E_k(v)$. For instance, suppose that index I_Z in Fig. 9(b) is an encryption-based index of attribute ZIP. Equality condition ZIP = '94110' on relation MEDICALDATA is then translated into I_Z='α' operating on indexed relation MEDICALDATA^k.

The definition of a bucket-based index over attribute a requires instead to partition the domain of a into non-overlapping subsets of contiguous values, and to associate each partition with a label. Given a tuple t in the outsourced relation r, the value of the index associated with attribute a is the label of the partition containing value $t[a]$. An equality condition of the form $a=v$ is therefore translated as $I=l$, where l is the label of the partition including v. For instance, suppose that index I_J in Fig. 9(b) is a bucket-based index where ζ, η, and θ are the labels of partitions $\{farmer, manager\}$, $\{nurse, secretary\}$, and $\{surgeon, teacher\}$, respectively. Equality condition Job = '*farmer*' on relation MEDICALDATA is then translated as I_J = 'ζ' operating on indexed relation MEDICALDATA^k.

The definition of a hash-based index over attribute a is based on the adoption of a deterministic hash function h that generates collisions. Given a tuple t in r, the value of the index associated with attribute a is computed as $h(t[a])$. An equality condition of the form $a=v$ is therefore translated as $I=h(v)$. For instance, suppose that index I_D in Fig. 9(b) is a hash-based index computed using function h such that $h(asthma)=\kappa$ and $h(gastritis)=h(chest\ pain)=\lambda$. Equality condition Disease = '*gastritis*' on relation MEDICALDATA is then translated as I_D = 'λ' operating on indexed relation MEDICALDATA^k.

Note that, differently from encryption-based indexes, both bucket-based and hash-based indexes map different plaintext values to the same index value. Therefore, the result computed by the provider from the evaluation of an equality condition can include spurious tuples that the client must filter out to obtain the final query result.

Range Conditions (e.g., [1,15,75]). Range conditions are conditions of the form a IN $[v_1, v_2]$, with a an attribute and $[v_1, v_2]$ a range in the domain of a. Bucket-based indexes can support range queries, provided that labels are defined so to preserve the ordering among attribute values. This solution would however leak the order of attribute values to the provider. An alternative solution specifically designed to support equality and range conditions is based on the definition of a $B+$-tree index over the indexed attribute [15]. The $B+$-tree index is built over the plaintext values of the attribute, and is represented at the provider as an encrypted relation with two attributes: id, containing the node identifier, and content, containing the encrypted node content. Pointers to children are represented through node identifiers.

Fig. 11 illustrates an example of a $B+$-tree built over attribute Name of relation MEDICALDATA in Fig. 2(a). To retrieve the tuples satisfying a range condition, the client iteratively queries the encrypted relation representing the $B+$-

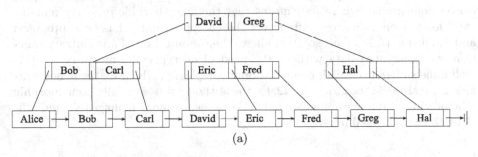

(a)

id_node	node
1	2, David, 3, Greg, 4
2	5, Bob, 6, Carl, 7
3	8, Eric, 9, Fred, 10
4	11, Hal, 11
5	Alice, 6, t_1
6	Bob, 7, t_2
7	Carl, 8, t_3
8	David, 9, t_4
9	Eric, 10, t_5
10	Fred, 11, t_6
11	Greg, 12, t_7
12	Hal, NIL, t_8

(b)

id	content
1	8/*5sym,p
2	mw39wio[
3	gtem945/*c
4	21!p8dq59
5	8dq59wq*d'
6	ue63/)w
7	=wco21!ps
8	oieb5(p8*
9	gte3/)8*
10	rfoi7/(
11	=o54'?c
12	Fer3!-r

(c)

Fig. 11. An example of $B+$tree index (a), its relational representation (b), and the corresponding encrypted relation (c)

tree at the provider. The client will then perform a sequence of queries to retrieve at each level, starting from the root, the node along the path to the leaf of interest. For instance, with reference to the example in Fig. 11, to retrieve patients whose name is between E and G, the client accesses tuples 1, 3, 9, and 10, in the order, in the encrypted relation.

An alternative technique for supporting range conditions relies on *Order Preserving Encryption Schemas* (OPES [1]) or on *Order Preserving Encryption with Splitting and Scaling* schemas (OPESS [75]). OPES is an encryption technique that takes as input a target distribution of index values, and applies an order preserving transformation guaranteeing that the index values follow the target distribution. OPESS guarantees instead that the produced index values follow a flat frequency distribution. This is obtained by mapping the same plaintext value to multiple index values. Since index values preserve ordering, range conditions can be directly evaluated by the provider over indexes.

Aggregate Operators (e.g., [38,45]). To compute aggregate functions (such as SUM and AVG), it is necessary to use indexes that support arithmetic operations, which are defined adopting homomorphic encryption [61], a particular encryption scheme that permits the evaluation of basic arithmetic operations (i.e., $+$, $-$, $\times$). These indexes can therefore be used by the provider to evaluate aggregate functions, as well as equality and range conditions [45]. A *fully* homomorphic encryption scheme (where *fully* means that the homomorphic property remains valid for any operation computed over the encrypted data) has been proposed and studied in [7,38]. This solution allows the computation of an arbitrary function over encrypted data without the need of decryption. Unfortunately, this technique suffers from high computational complexity, which makes it not suitable for real-world scenarios. In [12,13] the authors propose a fully homomorphic scheme enforceable with smaller public keys, hence more manageable and efficient than traditional ones.

4.2   CryptDB

CryptDB [60] supports query execution at the cloud provider directly over encrypted data, without the need of indexes associated with the outsourced relation. To this aim, CryptDB adopts for each attribute different kinds of encryption (i.e., random, deterministic, order-preserving, homomorphic, join, order-preserving join, and word search [60]), which are dynamically adjusted depending on the queries that need to be executed. Each cell in the outsourced relation is then wrapped in multiple encryption layers, forming an onion structure, in such a way that the same attribute value is encrypted multiple times to obtain the value stored at the provider. Note that the encryption layers are the same for all the cells in the same column, but they may vary from an attribute to another (depending on the kinds of queries to be supported). Figure 12 illustrates an example of the onion encryption structure wrapped around a plaintext data item. The outermost level features the strongest encryption (i.e., *random*

Fig. 12. An example of encryption layers adopted by CryptDB [60]

encryption, a probabilistic scheme where two equal values can be mapped to different ciphertexts with non-negligible probability [60]), while the innermost level represents plaintext data. Proceeding through the innermost level, the adopted encryption scheme provides weaker security guarantees but supports more computations over the encrypted data.

CryptDB proposes to dynamically regulate the usage of encryption, possibly removing some of the encryption layers, depending on the operations in the query to be evaluated. The adjustments in the encryption layers is dynamic, that is, it depends on the specific query being evaluated. For instance, if the provider needs to perform a GROUP BY on attribute a, then it should be able to determine which values of a are equal to each other, but without discovering the plaintext values of a. Since random encryption does not support such a functionality, it is removed, leaving data encrypted with a deterministic scheme. As this latter scheme supports grouping operations, it is then not necessary to further peel it out. Note that once a layer of encryption is removed from an attribute, it cannot be restored as data have been exposed to the provider.

Query execution with CryptDB assumes a trusted proxy intercepting all communications between users and the cloud provider. The proxy stores a secret master key k, the database schema, and the current encryption layers of each attribute in the relation. The query evaluation process operates as follows.

– *Step 1.* The user formulates a query q that is sent to the proxy, which rewrites it into an equivalent query $\hat{q}$ operating over the encrypted version of the attributes involved. The proxy then, with its own key k, encrypts all constant values in q adopting the encryption scheme that best suits the operation to be computed.
– *Step 2.* The proxy checks if the provider should be given keys to remove some of the encryption layers before executing the query $\hat{q}$, and if so, issues an UPDATE query that removes specific layers of encryption for the attributes of interest. The proxy forwards $\hat{q}$ to the cloud provider, which executes it.
– *Step 3.* The provider returns the encrypted result of $\hat{q}$ to the proxy.
– *Step 4.* The proxy decrypts the received result of $\hat{q}$ and sends it to the user.

Figure 13 illustrates the query evaluation process in CryptDB.

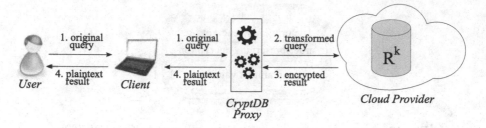

Fig. 13. Query processing in CryptDB

5 Protecting Query Confidentiality

When a user submits a query to a cloud provider, her privacy (and also the privacy of accessed data) can be put at risk due to the knowledge of the query itself [25,31,79]. For instance, knowing that a user submitted a query to an out-sourced medical database looking for the symptoms of liver cancer can implicitly reveal that either her or a person close to her suffers from such a disease. Also, it might be possible to analyze the data accesses performed by users to infer the (private) content of the outsourced data collection. For instance, by monitoring patterns of frequently accessed tuples, an observer can draw inferences on their values if she knows how frequently the values in the considered data domain are accessed. To counteract these privacy risks, query confidentiality must be prop-erly protected. Protecting query confidentiality requires ensuring both *access* and *pattern* confidentiality, which consist in protecting the target of an access and the fact that two accesses aim at the same target, respectively.

Traditionally, access and pattern confidentiality have been addressed through Private Information Retrieval (PIR) techniques. These approaches however do not protect the confidentiality of accessed data and are characterized by high computational costs (e.g., [8,56]). Several solutions have been proposed to pro-tect data and access confidentiality (e.g., [39,59,69,73]), but they fall short in protecting pattern confidentiality. In the remainder of this section, we illustrate recent techniques that protect data, access, and pattern confidentiality. The basic idea behind such solutions is to break the otherwise static association between disk blocks and the information they store, by adopting *dynamically allocated data structures* [52,83].

Oblivious RAM (ORAM). The *Oblivious RAM* (ORAM) [40] data structure is at the basis of several approaches that aim at protecting access and pattern confidentiality in encrypted data collections. With ORAM, the encrypted data are organized as a set of n encrypted blocks, stored in a pyramid-shaped data structure. Each level l of the ORAM structure stores 4^l blocks and is associated with a Bloom filter and a hash table to determine whether a given block is stored at level l and, if this is the case, to identify the block where it is stored [79]. During the search process, the ORAM structure is visited level by level from the top of the pyramid. At each level, one element is extracted (the target of the access or a random element, if the target does not belong to the visited level) and placed in a cache. Note that the visit does not terminate when the target block is found to not reveal any information to the cloud provider. When the cache is full, it is merged with the first level of the ORAM and all elements are then shuffled (i.e., allocated to a different physical block on the provider's disk) to destroy any correspondence between old and new data items. Analogously, when the first (i-th in general) level is full, it is merged with the second ($i+1$-th, in general) one and their elements are shuffled.

While ORAM effectively guarantees access and pattern confidentiality, the re-organization of the lower levels of the pyramid is highly expensive. Access requests submitted during the reordering of lower levels of the database might therefore suffer from a high response time. To mitigate such cost, the proposal in [34] limits the shuffling operation to the blocks that store accessed tuples. Most ORAM solutions rely on the presence of a secure coprocessor operating at the provider side. This assumption however may not be viable in many real world scenarios. Alternative solutions for reducing access times are based on the idea of minimizing the number of interactions between the client and the provider [41,78], or support concurrent accesses [42,80].

Path-ORAM is a recent enhancement of the traditional ORAM structure, which reduces the overhead due to the re-organization of lower layers in the ORAM structure [70,71]. Path-ORAM proposes to organize data in a tree, whose nodes are buckets storing a fixed number of blocks that can contain either dummy or real tuples. Each block is mapped to a random leaf, and stored either at the client side (in a local cache called *stash*), or in one of the buckets along the path to the leaf with which it is associated. Read operations download from the provider and store in the stash all the buckets along the path from the root to the leaf to which the tuple of interest is mapped. The mapping of the target tuple is then changed randomly, choosing a new leaf in the tree. The accessed path is then written back, possibly inserting into the written block some of the tuples in the local stash. A tuple can be inserted into a block if such a block is along the path to the leaf to which it is mapped and it is not full. In the insertion of a tuple into a block, Path-ORAM privileges blocks close to the leaf to which the tuple is mapped.

Shuffle Index. An efficient technique recently proposed to protect both access and pattern confidentiality is based on the definition of a *shuffle index* [25]. The shuffle index is a privacy-preserving indexing technique used for organizing data in storage and for efficiently executing users' queries. It can be seen at three abstraction levels: abstract, logical, and physical. At the *abstract level*, the shuffle index is an *unchained B+-tree* with fan-out F, built over a candidate key K of the indexed relation. Each internal node in the tree has $q \geq \lceil F/2 \rceil$ children (except for the root node, where $1 \leq q \leq F$), and stores $q-1$ ordered key values $val_1 \leq \ldots \leq val_{q-1}$. The i-th child of a node represents the root of the subtree storing all the values between val_i and val_{i+1}. The leaves store the actual tuples together with their key values. Unlike traditional $B+$-tree structures, leaves are

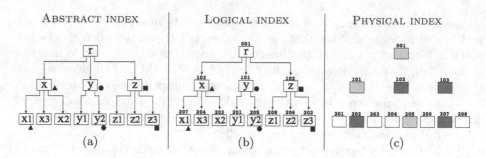

Fig. 14. An example of abstract (a), logical (b), and physical (c) shuffle index Legend: ■ target, • node in cache, ▲ cover; blocks read and written: dark gray filling, blocks written: light gray filling

not connected in a chain (to hide the relative value order). Figure 14(a) illustrates an example of unchained $B+$-tree with fan-out 3.

At the *logical level*, each abstract node n is represented by a pair $\langle id, n \rangle$ where *id* is the *logical identifier* associated with the node and n is its content. Pointers to children of internal nodes of the abstract data structure are represented through node identifiers. Figure 14(b) illustrates an example of logical representation of the abstract index in Fig. 14(a). Note that the order of logical identifiers does not necessarily reflect the value-order relationship between the node contents. For readability, in the figure logical identifier are reported on the top of each node, and their first digit corresponds to the level of the node in the tree. Finally, at the *physical level*, each logical node $\langle id, n \rangle$ is concatenated with a random salt, to destroy plaintext distinguishability, and then encrypted in CBC mode, using a symmetric encryption algorithm. The logical identifier of the node easily translates into the physical address where the block representing the encrypted node is stored at the provider. Figure 14(c) illustrates an example of physical representation of the logical index in Fig. 14(b), which corresponds to the view of the cloud provider.

Protection of access and pattern confidentiality is provided by the combined adoption of the following three protection techniques.

– *Cover searches.* Cover searches are *fake* searches, not recognizable as such by the provider, executed in conjunction with the actual search for the target value. For each level of the shuffle index (but the root level) the client downloads *num_cover*+1 blocks: one for the node along the path to the target, and *num_cover* for the nodes along the paths to the covers. Hence, from the provider point of view, each of the *num_cover*+1 accessed leaf blocks has the same probability of storing the target. Cover searches must guarantee both *indistinguishability* with respect to target searches (i.e., the provider should not be able to determine whether an accessed block is a cover or the target) and *block diversity* (i.e., paths to covers and to the target must be disjoint, except for the root).

- *Cached searches.* Cached searches make repeated accesses to a node content *indistinguishable* from non-repeated accesses. The cache is a layered structure, with a layer for each level in the shuffle index. It is maintained plaintext at the client side and stores the nodes along the paths to the targets of the *num_cache* most recent accesses to the shuffle index. Each layer of the cache is managed according to the Least Recently Used (LRU) policy: in this way, the parent of each cached node (and hence the path connecting it to the root of the tree) is also in cache. Whenever the target of an access is in cache, an additional cover is used during the access, to guarantee that *num_cover*+1 blocks are downloaded for each level of the tree (but the root level). The adoption of a local cache prevents short-time intersection attacks, which could be exploited by the provider to identify repeated accesses when subsequent searches download non-disjoint sets of blocks.
- *Shuffling.* Shuffling breaks the relationship between a block and the content of the node it stores. In this way, accesses to the same physical block may not correspond to accesses to the same node content. Shuffling consists in *moving* the content of accessed (either as target or as covers) and cached nodes to different blocks. Shuffling then assigns a different block to each accessed node, choosing among the downloaded blocks. To prevent the provider from inferring information about shuffling, every time a node is moved to a different block, it is re-encrypted using a different random salt. The parent of a shuffled node is updated to preserve the consistency of the structure.

The search process, operating at the client side, visits the $B+$-tree of the shuffle index level-by-level, from the root to the leaves. Each access combines the three protection techniques illustrated above, and the search process is guaranteed to protect both access and pattern confidentiality [25]. As an example of access to the shuffle index in Fig. 14, consider a search for $z3$, and suppose that the adopted cover is $x1$, and that the cache contains the path to value $y2$. Since the client has the root r in cache, it first downloads from the provider the blocks at level 1 along the paths to $x1$ (block 103 storing value x) and to $z3$ (block 102 storing value z). It then decrypts and shuffles the accessed and cached nodes at level 1 allocating, for example, x to block 102, y to 101, and z to 103. As a consequence of the shuffling, the client updates the root node, encrypts its content and writes it back at the provider. It then updates the cache at level 1 inserting node z. The client then downloads and decrypts the blocks at level 2 along the path to $z3$ and $x1$ (202 and 207, respectively). It decrypts these blocks retrieving the target of the search, and shuffles their content along with node $y2$ (205) in the cache. The client updates the content of nodes x, y, and z according to the shuffling, re-encrypts them and writes them back to the provider. Analogously, it encrypts and writes at the provider blocks 202, 205, and 207. Also, it inserts node $z3$ in the cache. Figure 14(c) illustrates the cloud provider's view over the access in terms of blocks read and/or written. It is easy to note that the provider can detect neither which among the accessed leaves is the target of the access, nor how the block contents have been shuffled [25].

The original shuffle index proposal has been extended to support concurrent accesses to the data, accesses to attributes different from the key (e.g., [27]), and to operate in a distributed system (e.g., [26,28]).

6 Protecting Query Integrity

Another important issue that needs to be considered when storing and processing data in the cloud is the ability of users to verify the correct behavior of cloud providers. This implies providing users with techniques that allow them to check the *correctness*, *completeness*, and *freshness* of query results. Correctness means that the result has been performed on the original data and the computation performed correctly. Completeness means that no tuple is missing from the query result. Freshness means that the query result has been computed on the most up-to-date version of the data. Two classes of techniques have been proposed to provide such guarantees: *deterministic* techniques (Sect. 6.1) and *probabilistic* techniques (Sect. 6.2).

6.1 Deterministic Approaches

Deterministic approaches are typically based on the adoption of *authenticated data structures* such as signature chaining, Merkle hash trees, and skip lists (e.g., [32,51,54,57,58,84]). These solutions build an authenticated data structure on the outsourced dataset and return, for each query q, a *verification object* VO extracted from the structure that can be used for verification. If VO is consistent with the data structure, this guarantees that the query result is correct and complete. Since they are defined over the whole data collection, authenticated data structures also provide integrity of data in storage, as unauthorized modifications can be immediately detected when checking the integrity of query results.

Signature Chaining. Signature chaining has been originally proposed to verify the integrity of the result of *range* queries [57] operating on an attribute a of the outsourced relation r, defined over domain D, and characterized by a total order relationship. These techniques adopt a one-way hash function h, and require to order the tuples in r according to the values of attribute a. The signature associated with each tuple t_i is computed by signing the string resulting from the concatenation of $h(t_{i-1})$ with $h(t_i)$, with t_{i-1} the tuple preceding t_i in the order. Given a range query q operating on a, incompleteness of the result can be immediately detected by checking the signature associated with the tuples in the query result. For instance, suppose that tuple t_i has been omitted in the computation of the query result. While checking the signature of the tuples, the client would discover that the computed signature of t_{i+1} (i.e., $h(t_{i-1})||h(t_{i+1})$) is different from the one stored with t_{i+1}, which is $h(t_i)||h(t_{i+1})$.

Since signature chaining guarantees completeness of query results only with respect to the attribute on which the signature chain has been defined, a signature chain should be defined for each attribute that may be involved in a range query. The main limitation of this approach is related to the size of the signature associated with each tuple, which increases linearly with the number of signature chains.

Merkle Hash Trees. Integrity of query computations can be provided also by using a Merkle hash tree built over the outsourced relation [54]. Given a relation r, a Merkle hash tree is a binary tree that stores in each leaf the result of a one-way hash function h over a tuple of r, and in each internal node the hash of the concatenation of its children. The tuples in the leaves of the tree are ordered according to the values of an attribute a. The root of the Merkle hash tree is signed by the data owner and communicated to authorized users. Figure 15 illustrates an example of a Merkle hash tree defined over attribute Name of relation MEDICALDATA in Fig. 2(a). Given a range query to be evaluated over attribute a, the result returned to the requesting client includes also a verification object VO with the values of the nodes needed by the client to compute the value of the root. To verify the correctness and completeness of the query result, the client computes the value of the root using the VO and the tuples in the query result. It then checks if the computed value is the same as the root initially received from the data owner [32]. The computation of VO depends on the type of query to be evaluated. For instance, in case of a selection query that returns a specific tuple, the VO contains the values of all the nodes being sibling of those in the path from the root to the leaf corresponding to the returned tuple. With reference to relation MEDICALDATA in Fig. 2 and the Merkle hash tree in Fig. 15, consider a query returning the patient with name *Fred*. The query returns tuple t_6 and its VO contains the gray nodes in the figure.

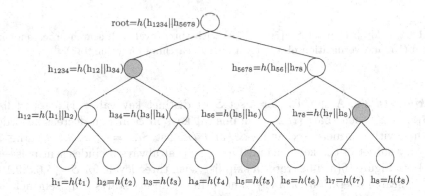

Fig. 15. A Merkle hash tree over attribute Name of relation MEDICALDATA in Fig. 2

The original technique illustrated in [32] has been extended to improve the efficiency of the verification processes (e.g., [51,58]), and to support integrity verification of join results [84].

Skip Lists. Another authenticated structure that can be used to verify the integrity of queries searching for a key value in a set of elements is represented

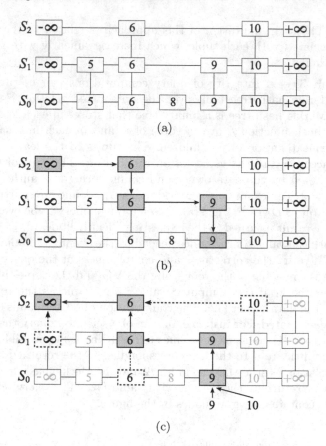

Fig. 16. A skip list for set $\mathcal{S}$={5,6,8,9,10} with three levels (a), search process for key value 9 (b), and verification object for a query searching for value 9 (c)

by *skip lists* [33]. A skip list for a set $\mathcal{S}$ of distinct key values is a set of lists $S_0, S_1, \ldots, S_k$ such that: *(i)* S_0 contains all keys in $\mathcal{S}$ in non-decreasing order, together with sentinels $-\infty$ and $+\infty$; and *(ii)* list $S_i, i = 1, \ldots, k$, contains an arbitrary subset of the keys included in S_{i-1} that always includes sentinels $-\infty$ and $+\infty$. Figure 16(a) illustrates a skip list with three levels for $\mathcal{S}$={5,6,8,9,10}.

The search operation for a key value v in a skip list starts from sentinel $-\infty$ in the top list (i.e., S_k) and operates through operations *hop forward*, moving right along the current list until the visited key value v_i is the largest value lower than or equal to v, and *drop down*, moving down a list (i.e., from S_j to S_{j-1}). The search iteratively hops forward and drops down until it reaches the bottom list S_0. For instance, with reference to the skip list in Fig. 16(a), (b) illustrates a search for value 9, where accessed nodes are denoted in gray.

Skip lists can be efficiently used to verify the integrity of queries searching for a value v in $\mathcal{S}$. To this aim, the skip list defined for $\mathcal{S}$ is authenticated adopting a *commutative* and *collision-resistant* hash function (i.e., a hash function such that $h(x,y)=h(y,x)$). Each node in the skip list is associated with a label, computed through the commutative and collision-resistant hash function, that depends on the elements on its right and below it. For the nodes in the bottom list S_0, the label $f(v, S_0)$ of node v is computed as the hash of its value v and: the value of the node w on its right, if w also belongs to S_1 (i.e., $f(v, S_0) = h(v, w)$); the label $f(w, S_0)$ of the node w on its right (i.e., $f(v, S_0) = h(v, f(w, S_0))$), otherwise. For instance, with reference to Fig. 16(a), $f(9, S_0) = h(9, 10)$ while $f(6, S_0) = h(6, f(8, S_0))$. For the nodes in S_i, $i > 0$, the label $f(v, S_i)$ of node v is: the same as the label of v at S_{i-1}, if the node w on its right also belongs to S_{i+1} (i.e., $f(v, S_i) = f(v, S_{i-1})$); the hash of the labels of the node below v and on of the node w on the right of v (i.e., $f(v, S_i) = h(f(v, S_{i-1}), f(w, S_i))$), otherwise. For instance, with reference to S_1 in Fig. 16(a), $f(5, S_1) = f(5, S_0)$ while $f(6, S_1) = h(f(9, S_1), f(6, S_0))$. The label of the starting node s of the skip list (i.e., the first sentinel node in the top list) is signed by the data owner and sent to all the authorized users.

If a query searching for element v returns a positive answer (i.e., $v \in S$), the integrity verification process checks the existence of the value itself. Otherwise, it verifies the existence of two elements v' and v'', consecutive in list S_0, such that $v' < v < v''$. To this aim, the client receives a verification object that includes the label of the nodes on the right and below the nodes forming the path to v, which are necessary and sufficient to the client for computing the label of the received nodes. For instance, consider the skip list in Fig. 16(a) and suppose to search key value 9. Figure 16(c) highlights the visited nodes (gray nodes) and the node included in the verification object (dashed nodes). The verification object then corresponds to the list $\langle 9,\ 10,\ f(6, S_0),\ f(-\infty, S_1),\ f(10, S_2)\rangle$. The client verifies the answer by hashing the values in the verification object and comparing the result with the label $f(s)$ of the starting node s of the skip list.

A modification to S due to insertion/deletion of a value v translates to an update, efficiently performed in $O(\log(|S|))$, of the associated skip list for inserting/deleting v.

6.2   Probabilistic Approaches

All the techniques described in Sect. 6.1 can assess the integrity of query results only for the attribute(s) over which the authenticated structures have been built. While ensuring integrity with full confidence, no guarantee is provided for queries operating over other attributes. *Probabilistic* approaches are not limited to operate on specific subsets of attributes, but ensure integrity with a certain degree of confidence. Current probabilistic approaches are based on the insertion of *fake tuples* in the outsourced relation, on the *controlled replication* of a subset of tuples, or on a combination of these two techniques.

Fake Tuples [53,81]. Fake tuples are inserted in the relation before storing it at the cloud provider, and are built in such way to appear indistinguishable, to the eyes of the cloud provider, from original tuples. The insertion of fake tuples is driven by the data owner according to a deterministic function f operating over the domains of the attributes in the relation. Users authorized to check query integrity know this function. Given the result of a query q returned to the requesting client, the client checks whether all the expected fake tuples belong to the query result. Absence of one or more expected fake tuples satisfying the query signals incompleteness of the query result. As proved in [81], even a limited number of fake tuples ensures high probabilistic guarantee of completeness.

Controlled Replication [76]. An alternative probabilistic approach to verify the completeness of selection queries consists in replicating all tuples in the relation to be outsourced that satisfy a *replication condition* C_r. The original tuples in the outsourced relation are then encrypted with a key k_1, and the tuples satisfying the replication condition are duplicated and encrypted with a different key k_2. The relation stored at the provider then includes two copies of each tuple satisfying C_r, one encrypted with k_1 (i.e., $E_{k_1}(t)$), and one encrypted with k_2 (i.e., $E_{k_2}(t)$). Given a query q formulated by the user over the original relation, the client transforms it into two queries q_1 and q_2 equivalent to q. One of these queries operates on the original data collection (i.e., on tuples encrypted with k_1), while the other operates on replicated tuples only (i.e., on tuples encrypted with k_2). To verify the completeness of the query result, the client checks the presence of two copies of each tuple in the query result that satisfy the replication condition C_r. The presence of one copy only of these tuples signals the incompleteness of the query result.

Combining Fake Tuples and Controlled replication [19,22,23]. These proposals permit to assess the integrity of join queries in a scenario where two trusted storage providers S_l and S_r store the base relations L and R to be joined, and a non fully trusted computational provider C_p is in charge of evaluation the join. To verify the correctness and completeness of the join result, the client collaborates with the storage providers, asking them to insert *markers* and *twins* in their relations before being sent to the computational provider. Markers are fake tuples, not recognizable as such by the computational provider, dynamically inserted into the operand relations by the storage providers. To ensure the presence of markers in the result of the join operation, the same set of markers is inserted into both L and R. The client then coordinates the number of markers and their values of the join attribute. Twins are copies of the original tuples that satisfy a twinning condition C_{twin} defined by the client and communicated to both the storage providers. The twinning condition regulates the percentage of twins to be inserted in the operand relations (and hence also in the join result). To be applicable to both L and R, the twinning condition operates on the join attribute (which is the only attribute common to the two operand relations). Note that the values of the join attribute for markers and twins are chosen outside the domain of the original join attribute values, to prevent the insertion of spurious tuples in the result computed by the computational provider. To protect the confidentiality of the data and to prevent the computational provider from identifying markers and twins, the operand relations are *encrypted* (with a key chosen by the client) before sending them to the computational provider.

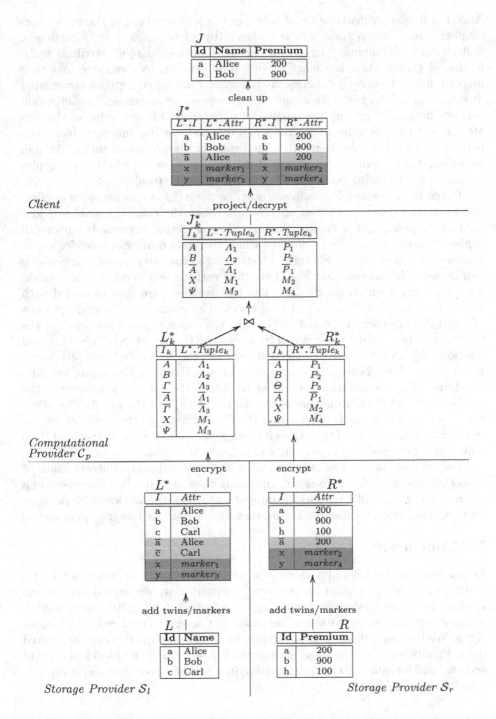

Fig. 17. An example of query evaluation process with twins (light gray) on 'a' and 'c' and two markers (dark grey)

Also, the frequency distribution of values of the join attribute of the tuples participating in a one-to-many join is flattened by adopting *salts* and/or *buckets*. Salts consist in combining different occurrences of the same join attribute value in the relationon the side "many" with a different salt, to guarantee that they map to different encrypted values. At the same time salted replicas are created at side "one" of the join so to create the corresponding matching. Bucketization consists instead in making the number of occurrences of each value of the join attribute at the side many of the join equal by also inserting dummy tuples when necessary. The client checks whether the tuples in the join result satisfy the join condition, the presence of the expected markers, and verifies whether the tuples satisfying the twinning condition are duplicated in the result.

Twins and markers offer complementary controls [22]: twins are twice as effective as markers, but loose their effectiveness when the computational provider omits a large fraction of tuples; markers allow detecting extreme behavior (all tuples omitted) and provide effective when the computational provider omits a large fraction of tuples. Figure 17 illustrates the computation of a one-to-one join between L(Id,Name) and R(Id,Premium) with the adoption of twins, markers, and encryption on-the-fly [22]. The two relations are first extended with twins (light gray) and markers (dark gray). The resulting extended relations (L^* and R^*) are then encrypted and sent to the computational provider (in the figure, encrypted values are denoted by uppercase Greek letters). The encrypted relations L_k^* and R_k^* have two attributes: I_k, the encrypted join attribute; $L^*.Tuple_k$ and $R^*.Tuple_k$, the encryption of all attributes (including the join attribute). The computational provider computes the natural join between the received encrypted relations and sends the result (J_k^*) to the client. The client projects over attributes $L^*.Tuple_k$ and $R^*.Tuple_k$, decrypts the result of projection (obtaining relation J^*), verifies its completeness and correctness, and if no omission is detected, removes twins and markers to obtain the join result (J).

The solution in [22] has been extended in [19] to support arbitrary kinds of joins (i.e., one-to-one, one-to-many, and many-to-many) and join sequences in a distributed and parallel platform (MapReduce). Also, the work in [23] presents some optimizations for limiting the overhead to be paid for integrity guarantees.

7   Conclusions

In this chapter, we have illustrated some encryption-based approaches for protecting and managing data in the cloud. In particular, we have discussed the application of encryption for protecting confidentiality, integrity, and availability of externally stored data, and for enforcing access control restrictions over them. We have also illustrated techniques for evaluating queries over encrypted data. Finally, we have discussed approaches for protecting the confidentiality of accesses and for guaranteeing the integrity, in terms of correctness and completeness, of query results.

Acknowledgements. This work was supported in part by: the EC within the 7FP under grant agreement 312797 (ABC4EU) and within the H2020 program under grant agreement 644579 (ESCUDO-CLOUD), and the Italian Ministry of Research within PRIN project "GenData 2020" (2010RTFWBH).

References

1. Agrawal, R., Kierman, J., Srikant, R., Xu, Y.: Order preserving encryption for numeric data. In: Proceeding of SIGMOD 2004, Paris (2004)
2. Akl, S., Taylor, P.: Cryptographic solution to a problem of access control in a hierarchy. ACM Trans. Comput. Syst. 1(3), 239–248 (1983)
3. Atallah, M., Blanton, M., Fazio, N., Frikken, K.: Dynamic and efficient key management for access hierarchies. ACM TISSEC 12(3), 18:1–18:43 (2009)
4. Ateniese, G., Burns, R., Curtmola, R., Herring, J., Kissner, L., Peterson, Z., Song, D.: Provable data possession at untrusted stores. In: Proceeding of CCS 2007 (2007)
5. Barni, M., Bianchi, T., Catalano, D., Raimondo, M.D., Labati, R.D., Failla, P., Fiore, D., Lazzeretti, R., Piuri, V., Scotti, F., Piva, A.: A privacy-compliant fingerprint recognition system based on homomorphic encryption and fingercode templates. In: Proceeding of BTAS 2010, Washington, D.C (2010)
6. Boneh, D., Gentry, C., Lynn, B., Shacham, H.: Aggregate and verifiably encrypted signatures from bilinear maps. In: Proceeding of EUROCRYpPT 2003, Warsaw, May 2003
7. Brakerski, Z., Vaikuntanathan, V.: Efficient fully homomorphic encryption from (standard) LWE. SIAM J. Comput. 43(2), 831–871 (2014)
8. Cachin, C., Micali, S., Stadler, M.: Computationally private information retrieval with polylogarithmic communication. In: Proceeding of EUROCRYpPT 1999. Prague, May 1999
9. Ciriani, V., De Capitani di Vimercati, S., Foresti, S., Jajodia, S., Paraboschi, S., Samarati, P.: Fragmentation and encryption to enforce privacy in data storage. In: Biskup, J., López, J. (eds.) ESORICS 2007. LNCS, vol. 4734, pp. 171–186. Springer, Heidelberg (2007)
10. Ciriani, V., De Capitani di Vimercati, S., Foresti, S., Jajodia, S., Paraboschi, S., Samarati, P.: Keep a few: outsourcing data while maintaining confidentiality. In: Backes, M., Ning, P. (eds.) ESORICS 2009. LNCS, vol. 5789, pp. 440–455. Springer, Heidelberg (2009)
11. Ciriani, V., De Capitani di Vimercati, S., Foresti, S., Jajodia, S., Paraboschi, S., Samarati, P.: Combining fragmentation and encryption to protect privacy in data storage. ACM TISSEC 13(3), 22:1–22:3 (2010)
12. Coron, J.-S., Mandal, A., Naccache, D., Tibouchi, M.: Fully homomorphic encryption over the integers with shorter public keys. In: Rogaway, P. (ed.) CRYPTO 2011. LNCS, vol. 6841, pp. 487–504. Springer, Heidelberg (2011)
13. Coron, J.S., Naccache, D., Tibouchi, M.: Public key compression and modulus switching for fully homomorphic encryption over the integers. In: Proceeding of EUROCRYPT 2012, Cambridge, April 2012
14. Damiani, E., De Capitani di Vimercati, S., Foresti, S., Jajodia, S., Paraboschi, S., Samarati, P.: Selective data encryption in outsourced dynamic environments. In: Proceeding of VODCA 2006, Bertinoro, September 2006
15. Damiani, E., De Capitani di Vimercati, S., Jajodia, S., Paraboschi, S., Samarati, P.: Balancing confidentiality and efficiency in untrusted relational DBMSs. In: Proceeding of ACM CCS 2003, Washington, DC, October 2003

16. Damiani, E., De Capitani di Vimercati, S., Samarati, P.: New paradigms for access control in open environments. In: Proceeding of ISSPPI 2005, Athens, December 2005

17. De Capitani di Vimercati, S., Foresti, S., Jajodia, S., Livraga, G., Paraboschi, S., Samarati, P.: Enforcing dynamic write privileges in data outsourcing. Computers & Security, November 2013

18. De Capitani di Vimercati, S., Foresti, S., Jajodia, S., Livraga, G., Paraboschi, S., Samarati, P.: Fragmentation in presence of data dependencies. IEEE TDSC **11**(6), 510–523 (2014)

19. De Capitani di Vimercati, S., Foresti, S., Jajodia, S., Livraga, G., Paraboschi, S., Samarati, P.: Integrity for distributed queries. In: Proceeding of CNS 2014, San Francisco, October 2014

20. De Capitani di Vimercati, S., Foresti, S., Jajodia, S., Paraboschi, S., Pelosi, G., Samarati, P.: Preserving confidentiality of security policies in data outsourcing. In: Proceeding of WPES 2008, Alexandria, October 2008

21. De Capitani di Vimercati, S., Foresti, S., Jajodia, S., Paraboschi, S., Samarati, P.: Encryption policies for regulating access to outsourced data. ACM TODS **35**(2), 12:1–12:46 (2010)

22. De Capitani di Vimercati, S., Foresti, S., Jajodia, S., Paraboschi, S., Samarati, P.: Integrity for join queries in the cloud. IEEE TCC **1**(2), 187–200 (2013)

23. De Capitani di Vimercati, S., Foresti, S., Jajodia, S., Paraboschi, S., Samarati, P.: Optimizing integrity checks for join queries in the cloud. In: Atluri, V., Pernul, G. (eds.) DBSec 2014. LNCS, vol. 8566, pp. 33–48. Springer, Heidelberg (2014)

24. De Capitani di Vimercati, S., Foresti, S., Jajodia, S., Samarati, P.: Access control policies and languages in open environments. In: Yu, T., Jajodia, S. (eds.) Secure Data Management in Decentralized Systems, pp. 21–58. Springer, New York (2007)

25. De Capitani di Vimercati, S., Foresti, S., Paraboschi, S., Pelosi, G., Samarati, P.: Efficient and private access to outsourced data. In: Proceeding of ICDCS 2011, Minneapolis, June 2011

26. De Capitani di Vimercati, S., Foresti, S., Paraboschi, S., Pelosi, G., Samarati, P.: Distributed shuffling for preserving access confidentiality. In: Crampton, J., Jajodia, S., Mayes, K. (eds.) ESORICS 2013. LNCS, vol. 8134, pp. 628–645. Springer, Heidelberg (2013)

27. De Capitani di Vimercati, S., Foresti, S., Paraboschi, S., Pelosi, G., Samarati, P.: Supporting concurrency and multiple indexes in private access to outsourced data. JCS **21**(3), 425–461 (2013)

28. De Capitani di Vimercati, S., Foresti, S., Paraboschi, S., Pelosi, G., Samarati, P.: Protecting access confidentiality with data distribution and swapping. In: Proceeding of BDCloud 2014, Sydney, December 2014

29. De Capitani di Vimercati, S., Foresti, S., Samarati, P.: Managing and accessing data in the cloud: privacy risks and approaches. In: Proceeding of CRiSIS 2012, Cork, October 2012

30. De Capitani di Vimercati, S., Samarati, P., Jajodia, S.: Policies, models, and languages for access control. In: Bhalla, S. (ed.) DNIS 2005. LNCS, vol. 3433, pp. 225–237. Springer, Heidelberg (2005)

31. Delerue Arriaga, A., Tang, Q., Ryan, P.: Trapdoor privacy in asymmetric searchable encryption schemes. In: Proceeding of AFRICACRYPT 2014, Marrakesh, May 2014

32. Devanbu, P., Gertz, M., Martel, C., Stubblebine, S.: Authentic third-party data publication. In: Proceeding of DBSec 2000, Schoorl, August 2000

33. Di Battista, G., Palazzi, B.: Authenticated relational tables and authenticated skip lists. In: Proceding of DBSec 2007, Redondo Beach, July 2007
34. Ding, X., Yang, Y., Deng, R.: Database access pattern protection without full-shuffles. IEEE Trans. Inf. Forensics Secur. 6(1), 189–201 (2011)
35. Zhao, F., Nishide, T., Sakurai, K.: Realizing fine-grained and flexible access control to outsourced data with attribute-based cryptosystems. In: Bao, F., Weng, J. (eds.) ISPEC 2011. LNCS, vol. 6672, pp. 83–97. Springer, Heidelberg (2011)
36. Foresti, S.: Preserving Privacy in Data Outsourcing. Springer, New York (2011)
37. Gamassi, M., Piuri, V., Sana, D., Scotti, F.: Robust fingerprint detection for access control. In: Proceeding of RoboCare Workshop 2005, Rome, May 2005
38. Gentry, C.: Fully homomorphic encryption using ideal lattices. In: Proceeding of STOC 2009, Bethesda, May 2009
39. Goh, E.J.: Secure indexes. Technical report. 2003/216, Cryptology ePrint Archive (2003)
40. Goldreich, O., Ostrovsky, R.: Software protection and simulation on oblivious RAMs. J. ACM 43(3), 431–473 (1996)
41. Goodrich, M., Mitzenmacher, M., Ohrimenko, O., Tamassia, R.: Practical oblivious storage. In: Proceeding of CODASPY 2012, San Antonio, February 2012
42. Goodrich, M., Mitzenmacher, M., Ohrimenko, O., Tamassia, R.: Privacy-preserving group data access via stateless oblivious RAM simulation. In: Proceeding of SODA 2012, Kyoto, January 2012
43. Goyal, V., Pandey, O., Sahai, A., Waters, B.: Attribute-based encryption for fine-grained access control of encrypted data. In: Proceeding of ACM CCS, Alexandria (2006)
44. Hacigümüs, H., Iyer, B., Mehrotra, S.: Ensuring integrity of encrypted databases in database as a service model. In: Proceeding of DBSec 2003, Estes Park, August 2003
45. Hacıgümüş, H., Iyer, B., Mehrotra, S.: Efficient execution of aggregation queries over encrypted relational databases. In: Lee, Y.J., Li, J., Whang, K.-Y., Lee, D. (eds.) DASFAA 2004. LNCS, vol. 2973, pp. 125–136. Springer, Heidelberg (2004)
46. Hacigümüs, H., Iyer, B., Mehrotra, S., Li, C.: Executing SQL over encrypted data in the database-service-provider model. In: Proceeding of SIGMOD 2002, Madison, June 2002
47. Jhawar, R., Piuri, V., Samarati, P.: Supporting security requirements for resource management in cloud computing. In: Proceeding of CSE 2012, Paphos, December 2012
48. Jhawar, R., Piuri, V., Santambrogio, M.: A comprehensive conceptual system-level approach to fault tolerance in cloud computing. In: Proceeding of SysCon 2012, Vancouver, March 2012
49. Jhawar, R., Piuri, V., Santambrogio, M.: Fault tolerance management in cloud computing: a system-level perspective. IEEE Syst. J. 7(2), 288–297 (2013)
50. Juels, A., Kaliski Jr., B.S.: PORs: proofs of retrievability for large files. In: Proc. of ACM CCS, Alexandria (2007)
51. Li, F., Hadjieleftheriou, M., Kollios, G., Reyzin, L.: Dynamic authenticated index structures for outsourced databases. In: Proceeding of SIGMOD 2006, Chicago, June 2006
52. Lin, P., Candan, K.: Hiding traversal of tree structured data from untrusted data stores. In: Proceeding of WOSIS 2004, Porto, April 2004
53. Liu, R., Wang, H.: Integrity verification of outsourced XML databases. In: Proceeding of CSE 2009, Vancouver, August 2009

54. Merkle, R.C.: A certified digital signature. In: Brassard, G. (ed.) CRYPTO 1989. LNCS, vol. 435, pp. 218–238. Springer, Heidelberg (1990)
55. Mykletun, E., Narasimha, M., Tsudik, G.: Authentication and integrity in outsourced databases. ACM TOS **2**(2), 107–138 (2006)
56. Ostrovsky, R., Skeith III., W.E.: A survey of single-database private information retrieval: techniques and applications. In: Proceeding of PKC 2007, Beijing, April 2007
57. Pang, H., Jain, A., Ramamritham, K., Tan, K.: Verifying completeness of relational query results in data publishing. In: Proceeding of SIGMOD 2005, Baltimore, June 2005
58. Pang, H., Tan, K.: Authenticating query results in edge computing. In: Proceeding of ICDE 2004, Boston, April 2004
59. Pang, H., Zhang, J., Mouratidis, K.: Enhancing access privacy of range retrievals over $B+$-trees. IEEE TKDE **25**(7), 1533–1547 (2013)
60. Popa, R., Redfield, C., Zeldovich, N., Balakrishnan, H.: CryptDB: Protecting confidentiality with encrypted query processing. In: Proceeding of SOSP 2011, Cascais, October 2011
61. Rivest, R., Adleman, L., Dertouzos, M.: On data banks and privacy homomorphisms. In: DeMillo, R., Lipton, R., Jones, A. (eds.) Foundation of Secure Computations. Academic Press (1978)
62. Ruj, S., Stojmenovic, M., Nayak, A.: Privacy preserving access control with authentication for securing data in clouds. In: Proceeding of CCGrid 2012, Ottawa, May 2012
63. Samarati, P.: Data security and privacy in the cloud. In: Huang, X., Zhou, J. (eds.) ISPEC 2014. LNCS, vol. 8434, pp. 28–41. Springer, Heidelberg (2014)
64. Samarati, P., De Capitani di Vimercati, S.: Data protection in outsourcing scenarios: Issues and directions. In: Proceeding of ASIACCS 2010, Beijing, April 2010
65. Samarati, P., De Capitani di Vimercati, S.: Cloud security: Issues and concerns. In: Murugesan, S., Bojanova, I. (eds.) Encyclopedia on Cloud Computing. Wiley (2015)
66. Sandhu, R.: On some cryptographic solutions for access control in a tree hierarchy. In: Proceeding of the 1987 Fall Joint Computer Conference on Exploring Technology: Today and Tomorrow, Dallas, October 1987
67. Sandhu, R.: Cryptographic implementation of a tree hierarchy for access control. Inf. Process. Lett. **27**(2), 95–98 (1988)
68. Shacham, H., Waters, B.: Compact proofs of retrievability. In: Proceeding of ASIACRYPT 2008, Melbourne, December 2008
69. Song, D., Wagner, D., Perrig, A.: Practical techniques for searches on encrypted data. In: Proceeding of IEEE S&P 2000, Berkeley, May 2000
70. Stefanov, E., van Dijk, M., Shi, E., Fletcher, C., Ren, L., Yu, X., Devadas, S.: Path ORAM: an extremely simple oblivious RAM protocol. In: Proceeding of ACM CCS 2013, Berlin, November 2013
71. Stefanov, E., Shi, E.: ObliviStore: high performance oblivious cloud storage. In: Proceeding of IEEE S&P 2013, Berkeley, May 2013
72. Wan, Z., Liu, J., Deng, R.H.: HASBE: a hierarchical attribute-based solution for flexible and scalable access control in cloud computing. IEEE Trans. Inf. Forensics Secur. **7**(2), 743–754 (2012)
73. Wang, C., Cao, N., Ren, K., Lou, W.: Enabling secure and efficient ranked keyword search over outsourced cloud data. IEEE Trans. Parallel Distrib. Syst. **23**(8), 1467–1479 (2012)

74. Wang, C., Chow, S.S., Wang, Q., Ren, K., Lou, W.: Privacy-preserving public auditing for secure cloud storage. IEEE Trans. Comput. **62**(2), 362–375 (2013)
75. Wang, H., Lakshmanan, L.: Efficient secure query evaluation over encrypted XML databases. In: Proceeding of VLDB 2006, Seoul, September 2006
76. Wang, H., Yin, J., Perng, C., Yu, P.: Dual encryption for query integrity assurance. In: Proceeding of CIKM 2008, Napa Valley, October 2008
77. Waters, B.: Ciphertext-policy attribute-based encryption: an expressive, efficient, and provably secure realization. In: Proceeding of PKC 2011, Taormina, March 2011
78. Williams, P., Sion, R.: Single round access privacy on outsourced storage. In: Proceeding of ACM CCS 2012, Raleigh, October 2012
79. Williams, P., Sion, R., Carbunar, B.: Building castles out of mud: practical access pattern privacy and correctness on untrusted storage. In: Proceeding of ACM CCS 2008, Alexandria, October 2008
80. Williams, P., Sion, R., Tomescu, A.: PrivateFS: A parallel oblivious file system. In: Proceeding of ACM CCS 2012, Raleigh, October 2012
81. Xie, M., Wang, H., Yin, J., Meng, X.: Integrity auditing of outsourced data. In: Proceeding of VLDB 2007, Vienna, September 2007
82. Yang, K., Jia, X., Ren, K.: Attribute-based fine-grained access control with efficient revocation in cloud storage systems. In: Proceeding of ASIACCS 2013, Hangzhou, May 2013
83. Yang, K., Zhang, J., Zhang, W., Qiao, D.: A light-weight solution to preservation of access pattern privacy in un-trusted clouds. In: Atluri, V., Diaz, C. (eds.) ESORICS 2011. LNCS, vol. 6879, pp. 528–547. Springer, Heidelberg (2011)
84. Yang, Y., Papadias, D., Papadopoulos, S., Kalnis, P.: Authenticated join processing in outsourced databases. In: Proceeding of SIGMOD, Providence (2009)
85. Yu, S., Wang, C., Ren, K., Lou, W.: Achieving secure, scalable, and fine-grained data access control in cloud computing. In: Proceeding of INFOCOM 2010, San Diego, March 2010
86. Zhu, Y., Ahn, G.J., Hu, H., Yau, S., An, H., Hu, C.J.: Dynamic audit services for outsourced storages in clouds. IEEE Trans. Serv. Comput. **6**(2), 227–238 (2013)

Cryptanalysis

Cryptography as an Attack Technology: Proving the RSA/Factoring Kleptographic Attack

Adam Young[1] and Moti Yung[2]([✉])

[1] Cryptovirology Labs, New York, USA
ayoung235@gmail.com
[2] Department of Computer Science, Columbia University, New York, USA
moti@cs.columbia.edu

Abstract. Since 1996 we have dedicated research effort on discovering new threats to the computing infrastructure that are the result of combining malicious software (malware) technology with modern cryptography. To the best of our knowledge, this was the first attempt to employ cryptographic methodologies not for defense (e.g., to hide messages, protect their integrity, or even to generate polymorphic malware for hiding it, etc.), but for attack. Our focus was on using cryptography specifically as an attack technology (e.g., we introduced secure data kidnapping attacks now referred to as ransomware). At some point during our investigation we ended up asking ourselves the following question: what if the malware (i.e., Trojan horse) resides within a cryptographic system itself (replacing existing cryptographic logic)? This led us to realize that in certain scenarios of black-box cryptography there are attacks that employ cryptography itself against cryptographic systems. Examples of black-box cryptography include when the code is inaccessible to scrutiny, say, due to software obfuscation, due to tamper-resistant housing, or when no one cares enough to scrutinize the code as has happened to many open source programs. The attack involves replacing the algorithm in a way that black-box access to the program does not reveal the attack. We showed that when the attack utilizes cryptography such that the trapdoor is in the hands of the attacker but not in the program itself then the attack possesses unique asymmetric properties. For example, it grants the attacker exclusive access to private information where the exclusive access privilege holds even when the Trojan is reverse-engineered. This asymmetric Trojan is much stronger than the more naive symmetric Trojan where the reverse-engineer recovers the power of the attacker from the code. We called the art of designing this set of attacks "kleptography." In more recent years, there have been allegations that kleptographic attacks have been mounted for real against the American public. Here, we present a demonstration of the power of kleptography by illustrating a carefully designed attack against the RSA key generation algorithm and we prove the security of the attack.

Keywords: RSA · Rabin · Integer factorization · Public key cryptography · SETUP · Kleptography · Random oracle · Security threats · Attacks · Malicious cryptography

© Springer-Verlag Berlin Heidelberg 2016
P.Y.A. Ryan et al. (Eds.): Kahn Festschrift, LNCS 9100, pp. 243–255, 2016.
DOI: 10.1007/978-3-662-49301-4_16

1   Introduction

In this work we discuss what we call kleptographic attacks which are attacks on black-box cryptography. One might assume that this applies only to tamper-proof devices. However, it is seldom the case that code (even when made available) is sufficiently scrutinized. For example, Nguyen in Eurocrypt 2004 analyzed an open source digital signature scheme. He demonstrated a very significant implementation error whereby obtaining a single signature allows one to recover the signing private key [3]. Many other problems with open source cryptographic code have been found over the years.

We present a definition of an attack based on embedding the attacker's public key inside the public-key cryptosystem of a victim. This will grant the attacker an exclusive advantage that enables the subversion of the victim's cryptosystem. This type of attack employs cryptography against the implementation of a cryptosystem and we call this kleptography.

We demonstrate a kleptographic attack on the RSA key generation algorithm and survey how to prove that the attack works. Originally we presented kleptography in Crypto '96 [8]. The presentation here follows our presentation in [11]. In [9,10] we presented kleptographic attacks on discrete-log based cryptosystems. Therein we presented and used what we called the *discrete-log kleptogram*. The alleged kleptographic attack in the Dual Elliptic Curve Deterministic Random Bit Generator seems to have followed this methodology by using a discrete-log kleptogram.

What is interesting is that: (1) the attacker employs modern cryptographic tools in these attacks, and (2) the attacks work due to tools developed in what some call the "provable security" sub-field of modern cryptographic research. From the perspective of research methodologies, what we try to encourage by our example is for cryptographers and other security professionals to dedicate time to research new attack scenarios and possibilities beyond the obvious methodologies. We have dedicated time to research the feasibility of attacks that we call "malicious cryptography" (see [6]). Our discovery of kleptography grew out of our overall effort to explore the intersection of strong cryptography with the theory of malware.

2   SETUP Attacks

A number of backdoor attacks against RSA [5] key generation (and Rabin [4]) have been presented that exploit secretly embedded trapdoors [7–9]. Also, attacks have been presented that emphasize speed [1]. This latter attack is intended to work even when Lenstra's composite generation method is used [2] whereas the former three will not. However, all of these backdoor attacks fail when half of the bits of the composite are chosen pseudorandomly using a seed [8] (this drives the need for improved public key standards, and forms a major motivation for the present work). It should be noted that [1] does not constitute a SETUP attack since it assumes that a secret key remains hidden even after reverse-engineering.

We adapt the notion of a strong SETUP [9] to two games. For clarity this definition is tailored after RSA key generation (as opposed to being more general). The threat model involves three parties: the designer, the eavesdropper, and the inquirer.

The designer is a malicious attacker and builds the SETUP attack into some subset of all of the black-box key generation devices that are deployed. The goal of the designer is to learn the RSA private key of a user who generates a key pair using a device contained in this subset when the designer only has access to the RSA public keys. Before the games start, the eavesdropper and inquirer are given access to the SETUP algorithm in its entirety.[1] However, in the games they play they are not given access to the internals of the particular devices that are used (they cannot reverse-engineer them).

Assumptions. The eavesdropper and inquirer are assumed to be probabilistic poly-time algorithms. It is assumed that the RSA key generation algorithm is deployed in tamper-proof black-box devices. It is traditional to supply an RSA key generation algorithm with 1^k where k is the security parameter. This tells the generator what security parameter is to be used and assures that running times can be derived based on the size of the input. For simplicity we assume that the generator takes no input and that the security parameter is fixed. It is straightforward to relax this assumption.

Let D be a device that contains the SETUP attack.

Game 1. The inquirer is given oracle access to two devices A and B. So, the inquirer obtains RSA key pairs from the devices. With 50 % probability A has a SETUP attack in it. A has a SETUP attack in it iff B does not. The inquirer wins if he determines whether or not A has the SETUP attack in it with probability significantly greater than $1/2$.

Property 1. (indistinguishability) The inquirer fails Game 2 with overwhelming probability.

Game 2. The eavesdropper may query D but is only given the public keys that result, not the corresponding private keys. He wins if he can learn one of the corresponding private keys.

Property 2. (confidentiality) The eavesdropper fails Game 1 with overwhelming probability.

Property 3. (completeness) Let (y, x) be a public/private key generated using D. With overwhelming probability the designer computes x on input y.

In a SETUP attack, the designer uses his or her own private key in conjunction with y to recover x. In practice the designer may learn y by obtaining it from a Certificate Authority.

Property 4. (uniformity) The SETUP attack is the same in every black-box cryptographic device.

---

[1] e.g., found in practice via the costly process of reverse-engineering one of the devices.

When property 4 holds it need not be the case that each device have a unique identifier ID. This is important in a binary distribution in which all of the instances of the "device" will necessarily be identical. In hardware implementations it would simplify the manufacturing process.

Definition 1. *If a backdoor RSA key generation algorithm satisfies properties 1, 2, 3, and 4 then it is a* **strong SETUP**.

3 SETUP Attack Against RSA Key Generation

The notion of a SETUP attack was presented at Crypto '96 [8] and was later improved slightly [9]. To illustrate the notion of a SETUP attack, a particular attack on RSA key generation was presented. The SETUP attack on RSA keys from Crypto '96 generates the primes p and q from a skewed distribution. This skewed distribution was later corrected while allowing e to remain fixed[2] [7]. A backdoor attack on RSA was also presented by Crépeau and Slakmon [1]. They showed that if the device is free to choose the RSA exponent e (which is often not the case in practice), the primes p and q of a given size can be generated uniformly at random in the attack. Crépeau and Slakmon also give an attack similar to PAP in which e is fixed. Crépeau and Slakmon [1] noted the skewed distribution in the original SETUP attack as well.

3.1 Notation and Building Blocks

Let $L(x/P)$ denote the Legendre symbol of x with respect to the prime P. Also, let $J(x/N)$ denote the Jacobi symbol of x with respect to the odd integer N.

The attack on RSA key generation makes use of the probabilistic bias removal method (PBRM). This algorithm is given below [9].

$PBRM(R, S, x)$:
input: R and S with $S > R > \frac{S}{2}$ and x contained in $\{0, 1, 2, ..., R-1\}$
output: e contained in $\{-1, 1\}$ and x' contained in $\{0, 1, 2, ..., S-1\}$
1. set $e = 1$ and set $x' = 0$
2. choose a bit b randomly
3. if $x < S - R$ and $b = 1$ then set $x' = x$
4. if $x < S - R$ and $b = 0$ then set $x' = S - 1 - x$
5. if $x \geq S - R$ and $b = 1$ then set $x' = x$
6. if $x \geq S - R$ and $b = 0$ then set $e = -1$
7. output e and x' and halt

Recall that a random oracle $R(\cdot)$ takes as input a bit string that is finite in length and returns an infinitely long bit string. Let $H(s, i, v)$ denote a function that invokes the oracle and returns the v bits of $R(s)$ that start at the ith bit position, where $i \geq 0$. For example, if $R(110101) = 01001011110101...$ then,

---

[2] For example, with $e = 2^{16} + 1$ as in many fielded cryptosystems.

$$H(110101, 0, 3) = 010$$

and

$$H(110101, 1, 4) = 1001$$

and so on.

The following is a subroutine that is assumed to be available.

RandomBitString1():
input: none
output: random $W/2$-bit string
1. generate a random $W/2$-bit string str
2. output str and halt

Finally, the algorithm below is regarded as the "honest" key generation algorithm.

GenPrivatePrimes1():
input: none
output: $W/2$-bit primes p and q such that $p \neq q$ and $|pq| = W$
1. for $j = 0$ to ∞ do:
2. $p = RandomBitString1()$ /* at this point p is a random string */
3.   if $p \geq 2^{W/2-1} + 1$ and p is prime then break
4. for $j = 0$ to ∞ do:
5. $q = RandomBitString1()$
6.   if $q \geq 2^{W/2-1} + 1$ and q is prime then break
7. if $|pq| < W$ or $p = q$ then goto step 1
8. if $p > q$ then interchange the values p and q
9. set $S = (p, q)$
10. output S, zeroize all values in memory, and halt

3.2   The SETUP Attack

When an honest algorithm *GenPrivatePrimes1* is implemented in the device, the device may be regarded as an honest cryptosystem C. The advanced attack on composite key generation is specified by *GenPrivatePrimes2* that is given below. This algorithm is the infected version of *GenPrivatePrimes1* and when implemented in a device it effectively serves as the device C' in a SETUP attack.

The algorithm *GenPrivatePrimes2* contains the attacker's public key N where $|N| = W/2$ bits, and $N = PQ$ with P and Q being distinct primes. The primes P and Q are kept private by the attacker. The attacker's public key is half the size of p times q, where p and q are the primes that are computed by the algorithm.

In hardware implementations each device contains a unique $W/2$-bit identifier ID. The IDs for the devices are chosen randomly, subject to the constraint that they all be unique. In binary distributions the value ID can be fixed. Thus, it will be the same in each copy of the key generation binary. In this case the security argument applies to all invocations of all copies of the binary as a whole.

The variable i is stored in non-volatile memory and is a counter for the number of compromised keys that the device created. It starts at $i = 0$. The variable j is not stored in non-volatile memory. The attack makes use of the four constants (e_0, e_1, e_2, e_3) that must be computed by the attacker and placed within the device. These quantities can be chosen randomly, for instance. They must adhere to the requirements listed in Table 1.

It may appear at first glance that the backdoor attack below is needlessly complicated. However, the reason for the added complexity becomes clear when the indistinguishability and confidentiality properties are proven. This algorithm effectively leaks a Rabin ciphertext in the upper order bits of pq and uses the Rabin plaintext to derive the prime p using a random oracle.

Table 1. Constants used in key generation attack

Constant	Properties
e_0	$e_0 \in \mathbb{Z}_N^*$ and $L(e_0/P) = +1$ and $L(e_0/Q) = +1$
e_1	$e_2 \in \mathbb{Z}_N^*$ and $L(e_2/P) = -1$ and $L(e_2/Q) = +1$
e_2	$e_1 \in \mathbb{Z}_N^*$ and $L(e_1/P) = -1$ and $L(e_1/Q) = -1$
e_3	$e_3 \in \mathbb{Z}_N^*$ and $L(e_3/P) = +1$ and $L(e_3/Q) = -1$

Note that due to the use of the probabilistic bias removal method, this algorithm is not going to have the same expected running time as the honest algorithm *GenPrivatePrimes1()*. The ultimate goal in the attack is to make it produce outputs that are indistinguishable from the outputs of an honest implementation. It is easiest to utilize the Las Vegas key generation algorithm in which the only possible type of output is (p, q) (i.e., "failure" is not an allowable output).

The value Θ is a constant that is used in the attack to place a limit on the number of keys that are attacked. It is a restriction that simplifies the algorithm that the attacker uses to recover the private keys of other users.

GenPrivatePrimes2():
input: none
output: $W/2$-bit primes p and q such that $p \neq q$ and $|pq| = W$
1. if $i > \Theta$ then output *GenPrivatePrimes1()* and halt
2. update i in non-volatile memory to be $i = i + 1$
3. let I be the $|\Theta|$-bit representation of i
4. for $j = 0$ to ∞ do:
5.   choose x randomly from $\{0, 1, 2, ..., N - 1\}$
6.   set $c_0 = x$
7.   if $gcd(x, N) = 1$ then

8.   choose bit b randomly and choose u randomly from $\mathbb{Z}_N^*$

9.   if $J(x/N) = +1$ then set $c_0 = e_0^b e_2^{1-b} u^2 \bmod N$

10.   if $J(x/N) = -1$ then set $c_0 = e_1^b e_3^{1-b} u^2 \bmod N$

11.   compute $(e, c_1) = PBRM(N, 2^{W/2}, c_0)$

12.   if $e = -1$ then continue

13.   if $u > -u \bmod N$ then set $u = -u \bmod N$ /* for faster decr. */

14.   let T_0 be the $W/2$-bit representation of u

15.   for $k = 0$ to ∞ do:

16.   compute $p = H(T_0||ID||I||j, \frac{kW}{2}, \frac{W}{2})$

17.   if $p \geq 2^{W/2-1} + 1$ and p is prime then break

18.   if $p < 2^{W/2-1} + 1$ or if p is not prime then continue

19. $c_2 = RandomBitString1()$

20.   compute $n' = (c_1 \; || \; c_2)$

21.   solve for the quotient q and the remainder r in $n' = pq + r$

22.   if q is not a $W/2$-bit integer or if $q < 2^{W/2-1} + 1$ then continue

23.   if q is not prime then continue

24.   if $|pq| < W$ or if $p = q$ then continue

25.   if $p > q$ then interchange the values p and q

26.   set $S = (p, q)$ and break

27. output S, zeroize everything in memory except i, and halt

It is assumed that the user, or the device that contains this algorithm, will multiply p by q to obtain the public key $n = pq$. Making n publicly available is perilous since with overwhelming probability p can easily be recovered by the attacker. Note that c_1 will be displayed verbatim in the upper order bits of $n = n' - r = pq$ unless the subtraction of r from n' causes a borrow bit to be taken from the $W/2$ most significant bits of n'. The attacker can always add this bit back in to recover c_1.

Suppose that the attacker, who is either the malicious manufacturer or the hacker that installed the Trojan horse, obtains the public key $n = pq$. The attacker is in a position to recover p using the factors (P, Q) of the Rabin public key N. The factoring algorithm attempts to compute the two smallest ambivalent roots of a perfect square modulo N. Let t be a quadratic residue modulo N. Recall that a_0 and a_1 are ambivalent square roots of t modulo N if $a_0^2 \equiv a_1^2 \equiv t \bmod N$, $a_0 \neq a_1$, and $a_0 \neq -a_1 \bmod N$. The values a_0 and a_1 are the two smallest ambivalent roots if they are ambivalent, $a_0 < -a_0 \bmod N$, and $a_1 < -a_1 \bmod N$. The Rabin decryption algorithm can be used to compute the two smallest ambivalent roots of a perfect square t, that is, the two smallest ambivalent roots of a Rabin ciphertext.

For each possible combination of ID, i, j, and k the attacker computes the algorithm $FactorTheComposite$ given below. Since the key generation device can only be invoked a reasonable number of times, and since there is a reasonable number of compromised devices in existence, this recovery process is tractable.

$FactorTheComposite(n, P, Q, ID, i, j, k)$:
input: positive integers i, j, k with $1 \leq i \leq \Theta$

distinct primes P and Q
n which is the product of distinct primes p and q
Also, $|n|$ must be even and $|p| = |q| = |PQ| = |ID| = |n|/2$
output: *failure* or a non-trivial factor of n
1. compute $N = PQ$
2. let I be the Θ-bit representation of i
3. $W = |n|$
4. set U_0 equal to the $W/2$ most significant bits of n
5. compute $U_1 = U_0 + 1$
6. if $U_0 \geq N$ then set $U_0 = 2^{W/2} - 1 - U_0$ /* undo the PBRM */
7. if $U_1 \geq N$ then set $U_1 = 2^{W/2} - 1 - U_1$ /* undo the PBRM */
8. for $z = 0$ to 1 do:
9.   if U_z is contained in $\mathbb{Z}_N^*$ then
10.   for $\ell = 0$ to 3 do: /* try to find a square root */
11.   compute $W_\ell = U_z {e_\ell}^{-1} \bmod N$
12.   if $L(W_\ell/P) = +1$ and $L(W_\ell/Q) = +1$ then
13.   let a_0, a_1 be the two smallest ambivalent roots of W_ℓ
14.   let A_0 be the $W/2$-bit representation of a_0
15.   let A_1 be the $W/2$-bit representation of a_1
16.   for $b = 0$ to 1 do:
17.   compute $p_b = H(A_b||ID||I||j, \frac{kW}{2}, \frac{W}{2})$
18.   if p_0 is a non-trivial divisor of n then
19.   output p_0 and halt
20.   if p_1 is a non-trivial divisor of n then
21.   output p_1 and halt
22. output *failure* and halt

The quantity $U_0 + 1$ is computed since a borrow bit may have been taken from the lowest order bit of c_1 when the public key $n = n' - r$ is computed.

4   Security of the Attack

Here we argue the success of the attack and how it holds unique properties.

The attack is indistinguishable to all polynomially bounded adversaries.[3] Let C denote an honest device that implements the algorithm $GenPrivatePrimes1()$ and let C' denote a dishonest device that implements $GenPrivatePrimes2()$. A key observation is that the primes p and q that are output by the dishonest device are chosen from the same set and same probability distribution as the primes p and q that are output by the honest device. So, it can be shown that p and q in the dishonest device C' are chosen from the same set and from the same probability distribution as p and q in the honest device C.[4]

---

[3] Polynomial in $W/2$, the security parameter of the attacker's Rabin modulus N.

[4] The key to this being true is that n' is a random W-bit string and so it can have a leading zero. So, $|pq|$ can be less than W bits, the same as in the operation in the honest device before p and q are output.

In a nutshell confidentiality is proven by showing that if an efficient algorithm exists that violates the confidentiality property then either $W/2$-bit composites PQ can be factored or W-bit composites pq can be factored. This reduction is not a randomized reduction, yet it goes a long way to show the security of this attack.

The proof of confidentiality is by contradiction. Suppose for the sake of contradiction that a computationally bounded algorithm A exists that violates the confidentiality property. For a randomly chosen input, algorithm A will return a non-trivial factor of n with non-negligible probability. The adversary could thus use algorithm A to break the confidentiality of the system. Algorithm A factors n when it *feels* so inclined, but must do so a non-negligible portion of the time.

It is important to first set the stage for the proof. The adversary that we are dealing with is trying to break a public key pq where p and q were computed by the cryptotrojan. Hence, pq was created using a call to the random oracle R. It is conceivable that an algorithm A that breaks the confidentiality will make oracle calls as well to break pq. Perhaps A will even make some of the *same* oracle calls as the cryptotrojan. However, in the proof we cannot assume this. All we can assume is that A makes at most a polynomial[5] number of calls to the oracle and we are free to "trap" each one of these calls and take the arguments.

Consider the following algorithm $SolveFactoring(N, n)$ that uses A as an oracle to solve the factoring problem.

$SolveFactoring(N, n)$:
input: N which is the product of distinct primes P and Q
      n which is the product of distinct primes p and q
      Also, $|n|$ must be even and $|p| = |q| = |N| = |n|/2$
output: *failure*, or a non-trivial factor of N or n
1. compute $W = 2|N|$
2. for $k = 0$ to 3 do:
3.   do:
4.   choose e_k randomly from $\mathbb{Z}_N^*$
5.   while $J(e_k/N) \neq (-1)^k$
6. choose ID to be a random $W/2$-bit string
7. choose i randomly from $\{1, 2, ..., \Theta\}$
8. choose bit b_0 randomly
9. if $b_0 = 0$ then
10.   compute $p = A(n, ID, i, N, e_0, e_1, e_2, e_3)$
11.   if $p < 2$ or $p \geq n$ then output *failure* and halt
12.   if $n \bmod p = 0$ then output p and halt /* factor found */
13.   output *failure* and halt
14. output $CaptureOracleArgument(ID, i, N, e_0, e_1, e_2, e_3)$ and halt

---

[5] Polynomial in $W/2$.

$CaptureOracleArgument(ID, i, N, e_0, e_1, e_2, e_3)$:
1. compute $W = 2|N|$
2. let I be the Θ-bit representation of i
3. for $j = 0$ to ∞ do: /* try to find an input that A expects */
4.   choose x randomly from $\{0, 1, 2, ..., N-1\}$
5.   set $c_0 = x$
6.   if $gcd(x, N) = 1$ then
7.   choose bit b_1 randomly and choose u_1 randomly from $\mathbb{Z}_N^*$
8.   if $J(x/N) = +1$ then set $c_0 = e_0^{b_1} e_2^{1-b_1} u_1^2 \bmod N$
9.   if $J(x/N) = -1$ then set $c_0 = e_1^{b_1} e_3^{1-b_1} u_1^2 \bmod N$
10.   compute $(e, c_1) = PBRM(N, 2^{W/2}, c_0)$
11.   if $e = -1$ then continue
12.   if $u_1 > -u_1 \bmod N$ then set $u_1 = -u_1 \bmod N$
13.   let T_0 be the $W/2$-bit representation of u_1
14.   for $k = 0$ to ∞ do:
15.   compute $p = H(T_0 || ID || I || j, \frac{kW}{2}, \frac{W}{2})$
16.   if $p \geq 2^{W/2-1} + 1$ and p is prime then break
17.   if $p < 2^{W/2-1} + 1$ or if p is not prime then continue
18. $c_2 = RandomBitString1()$
19.   compute $n' = (c_1 || c_2)$
20.   solve for the quotient q and the remainder r in $n' = pq + r$
21.   if q is not a $W/2$-bit integer or if $q < 2^{W/2-1} + 1$ then continue
22.   if q is not prime then continue
23.   if $|pq| < W$ or if $p = q$ then continue
24. simulate $A(pq, ID, i, N, e_0, e_1, e_2, e_3)$, watch calls to R, and
        store the $W/2$-most significant bits of each call in list ω
25. remove all elements from ω that are not contained in $\mathbb{Z}_N^*$
26. let L be the number of elements in ω
27. if $L = 0$ then output $failure$ and halt
28. choose α randomly from $\{0, 1, 2, ..., L-1\}$
29. let β be the αth element in ω
30. if $\beta \equiv \pm u_1 \bmod N$ then output $failure$ and halt
31. if $\beta^2 \bmod N \neq u_1^2 \bmod N$ then output $failure$ and halt
32. compute $P = gcd(u_1 + \beta, N)$
33. if $N \bmod P = 0$ then output P and halt
34. compute $P = gcd(u_1 - \beta, N)$
35. output P and halt

Note that with non-negligible probability A will not balk due to the choice of ID and i. Also, with non-negligible probability e_0, e_1, e_2, and e_3 will conform to the requirements in the cryptotrojan attack. So, when $b_0 = 0$ these four arguments to A will conform to what A expects with non-negligible probability. Now consider the call to A when $b_0 = 1$. Observe that the value pq is chosen from the same set and probability distribution as in the cryptotrojan attack. So, when $b_0 = 1$ the arguments to A will conform to what A expects with non-negligible probability. It may be assumed that A balks whenever e_0, e_1, e_2, and e_3 are not appropriately chosen without ruining the efficiency of *SolveFactoring*. So, for the remainder of the proof we will assume that these four values are as defined in the cryptotrojan attack.

Let u_2 be the square root of $u_1^2 \bmod n$ such that $u_2 \neq u_1$ and $u_2 < -u_2 \bmod n$. Also, let T_1 and T_2 be u_1 and u_2 padded with leading zeros as necessary such that $|T_1| = |T_2| = W/2$ bits, respectively. Denote by E the event that in a given invocation algorithm A calls the random oracle R at least once with either T_1 or T_2 as the $W/2$ most significant bits. Clearly only one of the two following possibilities hold:

1. Event E occurs with negligible probability.
2. Event E occurs with non-negligible probability.

Consider case (1). Algorithm A can detect that n was not generated by the cryptotrojan by appropriately supplying T_1 or T_2 to the random oracle. Once verified, A can balk and not output a factor of n. But in case (1) this can only occur at most a negligible fraction of the time since changing even a single bit in the value supplied to the oracle elicits an independently random response. By assumption, A returns a non-trivial factor of n a non-negligible fraction of the time. Since the difference between a non-negligible number and negligible number is a non-negligible number it follows that A factors n without relying on the random oracle. So, in case (1) the call to A in which $b_0 = 0$ will lead to a non-trivial factor of n with non-negligible probability.

Now consider case (2). Since E occurs with non-negligible probability it follows that A may in fact be computing non-trivial factors of composites n by making oracle calls and constructing the factors in a straightforward fashion. However, whether or not this is the case is immaterial. Since A makes at most a polynomial number of calls[6] to R the value for L cannot be too large. Since with non-negligible probability A passes either T_1 or T_2 as the $W/2$ most significant bits to R and since L cannot be too large it follows that β and u_1 will be ambivalent roots with non-negligible probability. Algorithm A has no way of knowing which of the two smallest ambivalent roots *SolveFactoring* chose in constructing the upper order bits of pq. Algorithm A, which may be quite uncooperative, can do no better than guess at which one it was, and it could in fact have been either. Hence, *SolveFactoring* returns a non-trivial factor of N with non-negligible probability in this case.

It has been shown that in either case, the existence of A contradicts the factoring assumption. So, the original assumption that adversary A exists is wrong. This proves that the attack satisfies Property 2 of a SETUP attack.

Immediately following the test for $p = q$ in C and in C' it is possible to check that $gcd(e, (p-1)(q-1)) = 1$ and restart the entire algorithm if this does not hold. This handles the generation of RSA primes by taking into account the public RSA exponent e. This preserves the indistinguishability of the output of C' with respect to C.

---

[6] Polynomial in W.

5 Conclusion

Attacks on cryptosystems can occur from many different angles: a specification may be incorrect which requires provable security as a minimum requirement— preferably based on a complexity theoretic assumption and if not than on some idealization (e.g., assuming a random oracle like the idealization of unstructured one-way hash functions). However, implementations can have problems of their own. Here a deliberate attack by someone who constructs the cryptosystem (e.g., a vendor) has been demonstrated. This attack is not unique to the RSA cryptosystem and is but one of many possible attacks. However, it serves to demonstrate the overall approach. At a minimum, the message that we try to convey is that the scrutiny of code and implementations is crucial to the overall security of the cryptographic infrastructure. And even when practitioners scrutinize designs and implementations it is crucial to be aware that trust is needed in each and every instance of an implementation, trust that may not be efficiently testable given black-box access (as our attack has demonstrated). A kleptographic attack can be carried out at other stages of life of an algorithm, e.g., by those who draft standards. So, it is important to take into account the immense trust given to those that specify algorithms and choose their constants, trust that should not be given lightly, and that should perhaps not be renewed once lost. In general, kleptography demonstrates how hard it is to have "trust" in a system, since backdoors can only be detected by directly scrutinizing the algorithms, code, and in fact all layers of an implementation. The feasibility of such extensive and intense scrutiny is beyond the scope of this work.

References

1. Crépeau, C., Slakmon, A.: Simple backdoors for RSA key generation. In: Joye, M. (ed.) CT-RSA 2003. LNCS, vol. 2612, pp. 403–416. Springer, Heidelberg (2003)
2. Lenstra, Arjen K.: Generating RSA moduli with a predetermined portion. In: Ohta, Kazuo, Pei, Dingyi (eds.) ASIACRYPT 1998. LNCS, vol. 1514, pp. 1–10. Springer, Heidelberg (1998)
3. Nguyên, P.Q.: Can we trust cryptographic software? cryptographic flaws in gnu privacy guard v1.2.3. In: Cachin, C., Camenisch, J.L. (eds.) EUROCRYPT 2004. LNCS, vol. 3027, pp. 555–570. Springer, Heidelberg (2004)
4. Rabin, M.: Digitalized signatures and public-key functions as intractable as factorization, TR-212, MIT Laboratory for Computer Science, January 1979
5. Rivest, R., Shamir, A., Adleman, L.: A method for obtaining digital signatures and public-key cryptosystems. Commun. ACM 21(2), 120–126 (1978)
6. Young, A., Yung, M.: Malicious Cryptography: Exposing Cryptovirology. Wiley Publishing Inc, Indianapolis (2004)
7. Young, A.: Kleptography: using cryptography against cryptography. Ph.D. thesis, Columbia University (2002)
8. Young, Adam, Yung, Moti: The dark side of "black-box" cryptography, or: should we trust capstone? In: Koblitz, Neal (ed.) CRYPTO 1996. LNCS, vol. 1109, pp. 89–103. Springer, Heidelberg (1996)

9. Young, A., Yung, M.: Kleptography: using cryptography against cryptography. In: Fumy, W. (ed.) EUROCRYPT 1997. LNCS, vol. 1233, pp. 62–74. Springer, Heidelberg (1997)
10. Young, A., Yung, M.: The prevalence of kleptographic attacks on discrete-log based cryptosystems. In: Kaliski Jr., B.S. (ed.) CRYPTO 1997. LNCS, vol. 1294, pp. 264–276. Springer, Heidelberg (1997)
11. Young, A., Yung, M.: Malicious cryptography: kleptographic aspects. In: Menezes, A. (ed.) CT-RSA 2005. LNCS, vol. 3376, pp. 7–18. Springer, Heidelberg (2005)

Dual EC: A Standardized Back Door

Daniel J. Bernstein[1,2](✉), Tanja Lange[1], and Ruben Niederhagen[1]

[1] Department of Mathematics and Computer Science,
Technische Universiteit Eindhoven, P.O. Box 513,
5600 MB Eindhoven, The Netherlands
tanja@hyperelliptic.org,ruben@polycephaly.org
[2] Department of Computer Science,
University of Illinois at Chicago, Chicago, IL 60607–7045, USA
djb@cr.yp.to

Abstract. Dual EC is an algorithm to compute pseudorandom numbers starting from some random input. Dual EC was standardized by NIST, ANSI, and ISO among other algorithms to generate pseudorandom numbers. For a long time this algorithm was considered suspicious – the entity designing the algorithm could have easily chosen the parameters in such a way that it can predict all outputs – and on top of that it is much slower than the alternatives and the numbers it provides are more biased, i.e., not random.

The Snowden revelations, and in particular reports on Project Bullrun and the SIGINT Enabling Project, have indicated that Dual EC was part of a systematic effort by NSA to subvert standards.

This paper traces the history of Dual EC including some suspicious changes to the standard, explains how the back door works in real-life applications, and explores the standardization and patent ecosystem in which the standardized back door stayed under the radar.

Keywords: Random-number generation · Back doors · NSA · ANSI · NIST · ISO · RSA · Certicom · Undead RNGs

1 Introduction

The story of the Dual EC standard is one of the most interesting ones in modern cryptography.

Dual EC is a pseudorandom number generator. Soon after its publication it was criticized by experts for its poor design. It is thousands of times slower

This work was supported by the European Commission through the ICT program under contract INFSO-ICT-284833 (PUFFIN), by the Netherlands Organisation for Scientific Research (NWO) under grant 639.073.005, and by the U.S. National Science Foundation under grants 1018836 and 1314919. "Any opinions, findings, and conclusions or recommendations expressed in this material are those of the author(s) and do not necessarily reflect the views of the National Science Foundation." Permanent ID of this document: **d3ueae12e7c4i2s3b7a0cek0d2o3o5r4e2d**. Date: 2015.08.01.

© Springer-Verlag Berlin Heidelberg 2016
P.Y.A. Ryan et al. (Eds.): Kahn Festschrift, LNCS 9100, pp. 256–281, 2016.
DOI: 10.1007/978-3-662-49301-4_17

than alternatives; the numbers that it produces as output are biased, flunking the most basic requirement for a pseudorandom number generator; and, most importantly, it is mathematically guaranteed to have a skeleton key that makes the output entirely predictable to anyone in possession of the key. An honest designer would not have kept the key, but a pseudorandom number generator should not have a skeleton key in the first place.

Bruce Schneier wrote a damning article [34] about Dual EC in Wired Magazine. By the end of 2007, in the view of the public cryptographic community, Dual EC was dead and gone.

1.1   The Awakening

On 5 September 2013, the New York Times [31], ProPublica [19], and The Guardian [2] reported on the "SIGINT Enabling Project". The New York Times wrote:

> Cryptographers have long suspected that the agency planted vulnerabilities in a standard adopted in 2006 by the National Institute of Standards and Technology and later by the International Organization for Standardization, which has 163 countries as members.
>   Classified N.S.A. memos appear to confirm that the fatal weakness, discovered by two Microsoft cryptographers in 2007, was engineered by the agency. The N.S.A. wrote the standard and aggressively pushed it on the international group, privately calling the effort "a challenge in finesse."

The surprise for the public cryptographic community was not so much this confirmation of what had already been suspected, but rather that NSA's backdooring of Dual EC was part of an organized approach to weakening cryptographic standards. Not mentioned in the reports was the biggest surprise, namely that Dual EC was not dead at all: NIST's list of "DRBG validations" [21] showed that Dual EC was provided in dozens of commercial cryptographic software libraries. Dual EC was even the *default* pseudorandom number generator in RSA Security's BSAFE library.

How could an algorithm so thoroughly criticized in public by the experts be flourishing in fielded implementations? A partial explanation surfaced in December 2013, when Reuters [20] reported that NSA paid RSA "$10 million in a deal that set [Dual EC] as the preferred, or default, method for number generation in the BSafe software."

1.2   Contents

This article covers the history of Dual EC to the extent that it is known to the public, including some information that had not previously been brought to light. This article also explains technical aspects of how the back door works and how it can be exploited in practical applications.

Section 2 introduces the ecosystem that brings random numbers to cryptographic users. Section 3 tells the story of how Dual EC was standardized, including NSA's control over NIST and ANSI, and ANSI's control over ISO. Section 4 tells the story of how Dual EC escaped modifications that would have destroyed the back door. Section 5 explains the mathematical details of the back door, including a March 2007 modification to the NIST standard that improved Dual EC's exploitability. Section 6 explains how to exploit the back door inside TLS. Section 7 describes "Extended Random", a TLS extension whose overt purpose lacks justification and whose covert effect is to further improve the exploitability of Dual EC. Section 8 describes Certicom's patents on Dual EC exploitation and Dual EC escrow avoidance.

We thank Jeff Larson for interesting discussions and for providing us with the public comments used in Sect. 3. We thank Bart Preneel for providing us with the change history for ISO used in Sect. 3.3. We thank another expert who chose to remain anonymous for support in the investigation and interpretation of Certicom's United States patent application.

We also relied on a repository of public documents OCRed and posted by Matt Green [11] as a result of two FOIA requests, one from Matthew Stoller and United States Representative Alan Grayson, the other from Andrew Crocker and Nate Cardozo from the Electronic Frontier Foundation. NIST subsequently posted higher-quality color copies of these documents [26], although without OCR.

Our website https://projectbullrun.org/dual-ec/ contains more detail regarding several aspects of Dual EC and its history and a collection of links to related documents.

2   Where Do Random Numbers Come From?

Random numbers are the most basic building block of cryptographic protocols. Some random numbers are secrets, used as keys that must never be guessed; security relies on these numbers not being predictable. Other random numbers are public "nonces", numbers that must be used just once by the sender and receiver and never used again.

Random-number generation normally starts with a limited amount of physical randomness harvested from unpredictable elements of the computer. This physical randomness is then cleaned from possible biases, resulting in an even smaller amount of "true randomness", which is then stretched into many random numbers using a cryptographic algorithm called a "pseudorandom number generator" (PRNG). Such an algorithm is "deterministic", meaning that anybody who knows the initial true randomness can predict all future outputs—but this true randomness is always kept secret. The most important design goal for a PRNG is that outputs should not be predictable from any *other* outputs. This implies that it should be impossible to learn anything about the internal state of the algorithm based on the outputs.

A cryptographic algorithm is simply a sequence of instructions. Dedicated users who need to protect high-value information in a world full of compromised computers occasionally follow cryptographic instructions using pencil and paper and dice, but normal users rely on their computers to run cryptographic software. This software comes from developers who have collected implementations of various cryptographic algorithms into "cryptographic software libraries", such as the open-source OpenSSL library, RSA Security's BSAFE library, and Microsoft's SChannel library. Each of these libraries includes PRNGs, and uses the random numbers from those PRNGs to support advanced cryptographic operations such as Transport Layer Security (TLS), the security mechanism that defends HTTPS web pages against espionage and sabotage.

Where do software developers obtain the cryptographic algorithms that they decide to implement? The ultimate answer is cryptographic algorithm designers. Many designers have published cryptographic algorithms, and in particular PRNGs, allowing them to be freely used by software developers. However, there are also public evaluations showing that some of these designs are unsafe: the resulting random numbers are biased (think of loaded dice that roll 6 more often than 1), or have other detectable output patterns, or allow someone to figure out the true randomness that was used as input. Sometimes software developers quietly design their own PRNGs, but these PRNGs are usually shown to be unsafe as soon as they are exposed to public scrutiny.

Software developers can, in principle, read the entire public literature on designs and evaluations of PRNGs, and select safe PRNGs that have survived careful evaluation. However, this is time-consuming, so most software developers instead rely on standardization organizations to issue standards specifying trusted PRNGs. Noteworthy PRNG standards have been issued by the National Institute of Standards and Technology (NIST), part of the United States Department of Commerce; the American National Standards Institute (ANSI), a non-profit organization; and the International Organization for Standardization (ISO), a non-governmental organization whose members consist of ANSI and the national standards institutes of 163 other countries.

To summarize, there is a large ecosystem of people and organizations involved in designing, evaluating, standardizing, selecting, implementing, and deploying PRNGs. Available documents and news stories strongly suggest that Dual EC was part of a deliberate, coordinated, multi-pronged attack on this ecosystem: designing a PRNG that secretly contains a back door; publishing evaluations claiming that the PRNG is more secure than the alternatives; influencing standards to include the PRNG; further influencing standards to make the PRNG easier to exploit; and paying software developers to implement the PRNG, at least as an option but preferably as default.

3   Standardizing Dual EC

Dual EC is known as a NIST standard for the simple reason that NIST standards are freely available online. Dual EC was also standardized by ANSI and by ISO, and those standards are published in the sense that anyone can buy copies of the standards, but the costs are high enough to interfere with public evaluation.

As NIST cryptographer John Kelsey put it in 2014 [18, p. 15], "public review" for ANSI standards was "not very public".

Dual EC was publicly presented at a NIST workshop on random number generation in July 2004. NIST posted the workshop slides [23] and has kept the slides online since then. NIST also received special permission from ANSI to post a June 2004 draft of ANSI standard X9.82 "Random Number Generation" before the workshop, but NIST took the draft down after the workshop.

Several NSA employees participated actively in the workshop, but they did not present Dual EC. Instead Dual EC was described as part of a presentation "Number Theoretic DRBGs" [16] by Don Johnson from Entrust. Dual EC was obviously a very slow PRNG, but Johnson's presentation claimed that this was justified because Dual EC provided "**increased assurance**" (boldface and underline in original) compared to other PRNGs. Dual EC appeared in full detail in the June 2004 ANSI X9.82 draft.

NIST developed its own Special Publication (SP) 800–90 in parallel with ANSI X9.82, with essentially the same text. NIST published a draft of SP 800–90 on 16 December 2005, asking for comments by 1 February 2006, six and a half weeks later. The draft specified 4 PRNGs; one of those PRNGs was Dual EC.

3.1 Ignoring Biases

Kristian Gjøsteen from the Norwegian University of Sciences and Technology sent NIST a paper [10] in March 2006 objecting to Dual EC as being "flawed". Johnson's slides, after presenting schematics for Dual EC, had discussed biases in the resulting bit strings and made recommendations of how to deal with these biases; but Gjøsteen's paper showed that the bit strings were even more strongly biased.

"While the practical impact of these results are modest, it is hard to see how these flaws would be acceptable in a pseudo-random bit generator based on symmetric cryptographic primitives," Gjøsteen wrote. "They should not be accepted in a generator based on number-theoretic assumptions."

Gjøsteen's attack was improved in a May 2006 paper [35] by Berry Schoenmakers and Andrey Sidorenko from Technische Universiteit Eindhoven. "Our experimental results and also empirical argument show that [Dual EC] is *insecure*," Schoenmakers and Sidorenko wrote.

The most obvious way to stop the attacks would have been to modify Dual EC to output far fewer bits per step, but Schoenmakers and Sidorenko emphasized that this would not make Dual EC "provably secure" and that there would still be "no reasons to use this generator". In retrospect it is easy to see that this modification would also have closed the back door in Dual EC; but at that time the existence of a back door had not yet been publicly announced.

NIST's retrospective April 2014 online compilation of public 800–90 comments [25] does not include either of these papers. Obviously NIST had received Gjøsteen's paper after its 1 February 2006 deadline for comments. On the other hand, it turns out that NIST did not take this deadline seriously: NIST considered and acted upon comments that it received from Matt Campagna at Pitney Bowes on 3 February 2006, and comments that it received from Johnson on 31 March 2006, also not included in the online compilation.[1] NIST was continuing to actively edit SP 800–90 into May 2006; see [11].

NIST standardized SP 800–90 in June 2006. Despite the objections from Gjøsteen, Schoenmakers, and Sidorenko, this final version of SP 800–90 included Dual EC, with its full bias.

3.2 Hiding Behind NIST

None of the NIST workshop documents listed any author or designer of Dual EC. The authors listed for SP 800–90 were both from NIST: Elaine Barker and John Kelsey. As far as we know, none of the documents published at the time pointed to NSA as the source of Dual EC.

However, NIST's private response to Campagna sheds interesting light on the authorship of Dual EC.[2] Campagna had sent email to Kelsey, cc'ing Barker. Barker wrote back to Campagna as follows:

Elaine Barker <elaine.barker@nist.gov>	To Matthew.Campagna@pb.com, John Kelsey <john.kelsey@nist.gov>
02/03/2006 09:17	cc
	Subject Re: some DRBG Items

Matt: John isn't the person to ask about the Dual_EC_DRBG. I've forwarded your email to Debby Wallner and Bob Karkoska at NSA.

Elaine

This appears to confirm public statements from Kelsey in December 2013 [17] and May 2014 [18] referring to "designers of Dual EC DRBG at NSA" and saying that "NSA provided Dual EC DRBG".

Further confirmation that Kelsey was not the designer of Dual EC appears in one of Kelsey's internal drafts [22] of ANSI X9.82 Sect. 9.12, "Choosing a DRBG algorithm". The notes signed "JMK" (brackets in original) show that Kelsey did not even feel competent to comment on Dual EC's security, and that he was relying critically on advice from NSA. See [22, p. 9]:

X.3 DRBGs Based on Hard Problems
[[Okay, so here's the limit of my competence. Can Don or Dan or one of the NSA guys with some number theory/algebraic geometry background please look this over? Thanks! --JMK]]

See also a bit later in the document [22, p. 10]:

---

[1] These extra documents were obtained by journalist Jeff Larson in January 2014. We are indebted to Larson for allowing us to present this new information here.

[2] As above, we are indebted to Larson for tracking down this information.

X.3.1 Dual_EC_DRBG

The DUAL_EC_DRBG relies for its security on the difficulty of the elliptic curve discrete log problem--given (P,xP), determine x. Widely used signature and key agreement schemes are based on this problem, as well. A very conservative system design which had few performance requirements on its random number generator mechanism might thus choose the DUAL_EC_DRBG as its DRBG. This would ensure that the security of the whole application or system relied very cleanly on the difficulty of this one problem.

[[I'm really blowing smoke here. Would someone with some actual understanding of these attacks please save me from diving off a cliff right here? --JMK]]

3.3   Taking Control of ISO

By summer 2003, ISO/IEC Joint Technical Committee 1 Subcommittee 27 was far into its own multi-year process of standardizing random-number generators, not including Dual EC. Its internal 2003 draft received more than 150 comments, but most of those comments were minor corrections and clarifications such as changing "Any secure hash" to "Any secure hash function". The draft was approved by 19 of the 24 countries that voted, including half of the countries that had sent in comments.

The United States comment [14] was strikingly different, the only comment objecting to the "whole document":

> The U.S. National Body has reviewed ISO/IEC 2 CD 18031, N3578. We feel that this document is lacking sufficient depth in many areas and simply is not developed enough to be an ISO standard which encompasses both Non-deterministic and Deterministic Random Bit Generation. We do feel that ANSI X9.82 Random Bit Generation standardization work is much further developed and should be used as the basis for this ISO standard.
>
> To make ISO/IEC 18031 consistent with X9.82 would require extensive commenting and revisions. To better progress this standard, the U.S. has instead developed a contribution for ISO that is consistent with ANSI X9.82, but written in ISO format. Furthermore, we believe this contribution will also be complementary to ISO/IEC 19790.
>
> We provide this contribution as an attachment, and propose that ISO further develop this contribution as their standard.
>
> Additionally, the U.S. recognizes that ANSI X9.82 is not an approved standard and still requires further work. As ANSI X9.82 develops, the U.S. will contribute these changes to ISO.

The attachment, 153 pages, was an early version of ANSI X9.82, including a full description of Dual EC (using the same points P and Q that were later standardized by NIST for the curves P-256, P-384, and P-521; see Sect. 4 for discussion of the importance of P and Q).

ISO did what the United States told it to do. After two years it released standard ISO 18031:2005, including Dual EC. This rather blunt takeover of the ISO standard is, presumably, what NSA internally referred to as a "challenge in finesse".

4   Minding the P's and Q's

Every summer hundreds of cryptographers gather in Santa Barbara for the annual Crypto conference. The highlight of the conference is the three-hour "rump session" on the evening of the second day, featuring a series of short talks on very recent results.

Dan Shumow and Niels Ferguson, cryptographic researchers at Microsoft, announced at the Crypto rump session in August 2007 that there was a "possibility of a back door" in Dual EC. The name Dual EC refers to two "elliptic curve points" P and Q used inside the algorithm; what Shumow and Ferguson explained [36] was a way for whoever had generated the points P and Q to start from one random number produced by Dual EC and predict all subsequent random numbers. Recall that some PRNG outputs are made public, while others are secret; releasing just one public output would allow the attacker to predict all subsequent secret outputs, obviously a security disaster.

"Break the random-number generator, and most of the time you break the entire security system. Which is why you should worry about a new random-number standard that includes an algorithm that is slow, badly designed and just might contain a backdoor for the National Security Agency," Bruce Schneier wrote in a November 2007 article [34] for Wired Magazine. "My recommendation, if you're in need of a random-number generator, is not to use Dual_EC_DRBG under any circumstances."

However, NIST did not withdraw Dual EC from its standard. NIST sent Schneier a letter [3] saying "We have no evidence that anyone has, or will ever have, the 'secret numbers' for the back door ... For this reason, we are not withdrawing the algorithm at this time."

4.1   Behind the Scenes

Kelsey had already been asking questions about P and Q as early as October 2004, as shown by the following email exchange [15] between Kelsey and Johnson, made public in 2014:

```
Subject: [Fwd: RE: Minding our Ps and Qs in Dual_EC]
Date:    Wednesday, October 27, 2004 at 12:09:25 PM Eastern Daylight Time
From:    John Kelsey
To:      larry.basham@nist.gov

--------------------------- Original Message ---------------------------
Subject: RE: Minding our Ps and Qs in Dual_EC
From:    ''Don Johnson'' <DJohnson@cygnacom.com>
Date:    Wed, October 27, 2004 11:42 am
```

```
To:       ''John Kelsey'' <john.kelsey@nist.gov>

John,

P=G.
Q is (in essence) the public key for some random private key.

It could also be generated like a(nother) canonical G, but NSA kyboshed
this idea, and I was not allowed to publicly discuss it, just in case you
may think of going there.                                    .


Don B. Johnson

-----Original Message-----
From: John Kelsey [mailto:john.kelsey@nist.gov]
Sent: Wednesday, October 27, 2004 11:17 AM
To: Don Johnson
Subject: Minding our Ps and Qs in Dual_EC

Do you know where Q comes from in Dual_EC_DRBG?

Thanks,

-John
```

The "random private key" mentioned in Johnson's message is the simplest way that the Dual EC authors could have generated Q. However, from the perspective of the Shumow–Ferguson attack, this private key is exactly the secret information needed to unlock the back door in Dual EC.

The alternative mentioned in Johnson's message, generating Q "like a(nother) canonical G", would have made it much more difficult for the Dual EC authors to know this "random private key". It is hard to imagine any legitimate reasons for NSA to have told Johnson not to talk about this idea. "I didn't catch why this was significant then," Kelsey wrote in 2014.

According to Kelsey [18, p. 24], Ferguson reported the Shumow–Ferguson attack to ANSI in 2005. Two other participants in the ANSI discussions, Dan Brown and Scott Vanstone from Certicom, had discovered the same attack before 21 January 2005 (see Sect. 8), but apparently did not report it to ANSI.

NSA's response, according to Kelsey, was that NSA had "generated (P, Q) in a secure, classified way"; that NSA wanted to allow existing devices using this P and Q "to get FIPS validated" (i.e., certified by a testing laboratory to meet NIST standards); and that it "would be reasonable to allow other users to generate their own (P, Q)".

NIST could easily have generated a new Q "like another canonical G", and recommended this Q as a replacement for NSA's Q, which as noted above would have made Dual EC exploitation much more difficult. NIST could nevertheless have allowed NSA's Q as a non-recommended option, answering NSA's request for FIPS validation. NIST could also have entirely eliminated this problematic PRNG from the standard, ignoring NSA's request.

Instead NIST added an appendix to its draft of SP 800–90 explaining how users *could* generate their own P and Q, but ("to avoid using potentially weak points") specifically recommending *against* doing this. Furthermore, another paragraph in SP 800–90 prohibits FIPS validation for any users doing this: see [27, p. 84] ("One of the following NIST approved curves with associated points shall be used in applications requiring certification under FIPS 140-2") and the detailed testing instructions [24, p. 19] ("CAVS Dual_EC_DRBG tests use only the NIST Approved curves and associated points").[3] The rule forcing the pre-described points for FIPS validation was already in the June 2004 draft of ANSI X9.82 and was not modified when a section on using alternative points was added.

SP 800–90 did not discuss the origin of P and Q, and did not explain the power available to whoever had generated P and Q. In hindsight it is quite amazing how blindly NIST trusted NSA.

4.2 NSA's Public Story

Richard George, who was Technical Director of the Information Assurance Directorate at NSA from 2003 until his retirement in 2011, made the following claims regarding Dual EC in a talk [9] at the Infiltrate conference in May 2014: "We were gonna use the Dual Elliptic Curve randomizer. And I said, if you can put this in your standard, nobody else is gonna use it, because it looks ugly, it's really slow. It makes no sense for anybody to go there. But I'll be able to use it. And so they stuck it in, and I said by the way, you know these parameters that we have here, as long as they're in there so we can use them, you can let anybody else put any parameters in that they want."

As far as we know, there have been no public comments from NSA regarding the prohibition on FIPS validation of alternative P and Q; NSA instructing Johnson not to talk about generating a new Q; NSA paying RSA Security to implement and use Dual EC; and NSA internally advertising its PRNG standardization as part of a systematic effort to weaken cryptographic standards.

5   How the Dual EC Back Door Works

This section digs into mathematical details: how PRNGs work in general; how Dual EC works; and how the back door works.

SP 800–90 allows users to refresh the internal state of PRNGs with some additional input. This complicates the definition of Dual EC. There are actually two slightly different versions of Dual EC in two releases of SP 800–90: the June 2006 version [27], now called Dual EC 2006, and an updated March 2007 version, now called Dual EC 2007. Additional input breaks the back door in Dual EC 2006 in many cases, often preventing the attacker from predicting the

---

[3] CAVS stands for NIST's Cryptographic Algorithm Validation System. "Cryptographic algorithm validation is a prerequisite to the Cryptographic Module Validation Program (CMVP)." See http://csrc.nist.gov/groups/STM/cavp/.

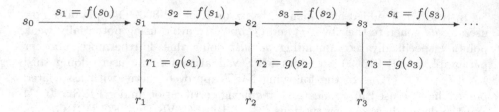

Fig. 1. General schematic of a state-based PRNG with functions f and g.

Dual EC output. Fortunately for the attacker, Dual EC 2007 repairs the back door, allowing the back door to be used in all cases, even when additional input is provided.

5.1   PRNG Structure: State Updates and Output Functions

Figure 1 shows a general schematic of a PRNG. The PRNG maintains an internal state s_i; the initial state s_0 is initialized from an entropy source. Each time some random output is requested from the PRNG, the internal state is updated from s_{i-1} to s_i using a function f such that $s_i = f(s_{i-1})$. After the internal state is updated, the PRNG derives a certain number of random bits using another update function g by computing $r_i = g(s_i)$ and returning some bits of r_i. If more bits are requested than available from r_i, the PRNG updates the state again by computing $s_{i+1} = f(s_i)$. Then $r_{i+1} = g(s_{i+1})$ is computed, and some bits from r_{i+1} are appended to the previously generated bits. This process is repeated until the requested number of bits have been generated.

For this process to be secure, it is crucial that the internal state is not learned by an attacker. An attacker who knows some internal state s_i is able to compute all following states $s_{i+1}, s_{i+2}, \ldots$ and to reproduce all output bits by computing $r_i, r_{i+1}, r_{i+2}, \ldots$. Therefore, the function g must be a one-way function; otherwise an attacker who learns some random output is able to compute the internal state of the PRNG. If the function g has a back door that allows an attacker to compute the internal state of the PRNG, then the complete PRNG is insecure.

5.2   Basic Dual EC Algorithm

Dual EC follows the general PRNG scheme described above. Dual EC specifies two points P and Q on the standard NIST P-256 elliptic curve. The internal state of Dual EC is a 256-bit integer s. The function f for updating the internal state is defined as $f(s) = x(sP)$, computing the sth multiple of P and returning the x-coordinate of the resulting point. The function g for deriving some random output is defined as $g(s) = x(sQ)$.

Both functions f and g are cryptographically secure one-way functions. It is computationally hard to compute s given sP and P, i.e., to solve the elliptic-curve discrete-logarithm problem (ECDLP).

$s_1 = x(s_0 P)$ $s_2 = x(s_1 P)$ $s_3 = x(s_2 P)$

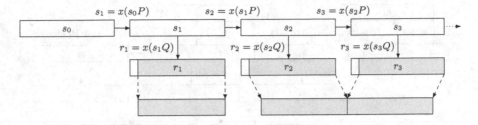

Fig. 2. Basic Dual EC algorithm using points P and Q on an elliptic curve.

Figure 2 illustrates the Dual EC algorithm. Given an initial state s_0, the PRNG updates the internal state by computing $s_1 = x(s_0 P)$ when some random bits are requested. Then $r_1 = x(s_0 Q)$ is computed and the most significant 16 bits of r_1 are discarded. Finally up to 30 random bytes are returned. If more than 30 bytes are required, the process is performed repeatedly, each time dropping the most significant 16 bits of r. The output bits are concatenated and finally returned.

Dual EC also allows larger variants using the P-384 and P-521 curves. The state sizes are 384 and 521 bits respectively. The outputs are correspondingly larger: 46 bytes (368 bits) and 63 bytes (504 bits).

5.3 Basic Dual EC Back Door

The Shumow–Ferguson attack works as follows. Assume that the attacker knows a scalar d such that $P = dQ$, and sees the random output r_1 (e.g., when r_1 is used as a public nonce). Now he can recompute a y-coordinate corresponding to the x-coordinate r_1 using the curve equation and obtains $R = (r_1, y_{r_1}) = s_1 Q$ for some s_1 unknown to the attacker. Finally, he computes $d \cdot R = d \cdot s_1 Q = s_1 dQ = s_1 P$ and learns the internal state s_2 as the x-coordinate $x(dR) = x(s_1 P)$. Now, the attacker can reproduce all the following Dual EC output of the victim. Thus, the knowledge of the scalar factor d with $P = dQ$ provides a back door for the attacker to the internal state of Dual EC.

As described above, the most significant 16 bits of r_i are discarded. However, the attacker is able to recover the missing bits easily: the attacker requires at most 2^{16} attempts in order to find the missing bits.

5.4 Dual EC 2006

As mentioned earlier, NIST allows users to enter additional input into Dual EC. The additional input string may be, e.g., the current system time, some counter value, some high-entropy randomness, or simply 0 if no refresh is desired.

When random output is requested from Dual EC 2006, the hash of some additional input string "adin" is xor'ed into the state before the basic state update is performed. For example, in Fig. 3, 30 bytes are requested when the state is s_0, 60 bytes are requested when the state is s_1, and further bytes are requested when the state is s_3, so hashes of additional inputs are xor'ed into s_0, s_1, and s_3.

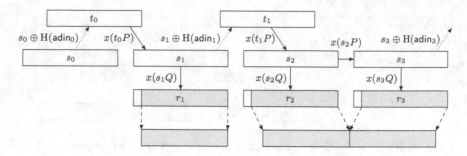

Fig. 3. Dual EC 2006 with additional input. Compare Fig. 2.

5.5   The Partially Broken Dual EC Back Door

If additional input is used in Dual EC 2006, and the attacker sees random output of at most 30 bytes, then the back door does not work any more. Assume the attacker observes r_1. Since s_1 has been modified with some additional input string and since there is no more known relation between r_1 and s_2, the attacker can no longer apply his back-door computation. Even if the attacker can guess $adin_1$, he is not able to recover the internal state from r_1.

The back door still works in case the attacker observes some random output that is longer than 30 bytes. For example, if the attacker observes combined output from r_2 and r_3, he can simply compute $R_2 = (r_2, y_{r_2})$ and obtain the internal state $s_3 = x(dR_2) = x(ds_2Q) = x(s_2P)$. In order to compute the following output values, the attacker needs to correctly guess the following additional input strings.

The ability of an implementation of Dual EC to refresh the internal state using an additional input string breaks the back door for the attacker in many practical cases where the amount of randomness observed by the attacker is smaller than or equal to 30 bytes.

5.6   Dual EC 2007: The Repaired Back Door

Dual EC 2007 demands an additional update step of the internal state at the end of each invocation. That means that after the requested number of random bits have been generated, the internal state is updated one more time by computing $s_{i+1} = x(s_iP)$. Figure 4 illustrates the modified algorithm.

Because of this additional state update, the attacker is able to apply his back-door computation. Given the random output r_1, the attacker computes $R_1 = (r_1, y_{r_1})$ and obtains the internal state $s_2 = x(dR_1) = x(ds_1Q) = x(s_1P)$. However, in order to compute the following random output, the attacker still has to guess any additional input strings (if the specific implementation of Dual EC used by the victim is making use of additional input).

5.7   Forward Secrecy

The official reason for the change from Dual EC 2006 to Dual EC 2007 was to provide "backtracking resistance".

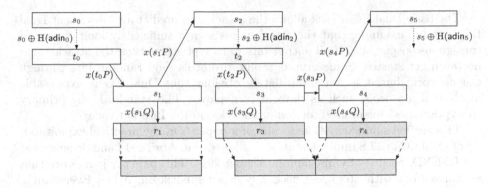

Fig. 4. Dual EC 2007 with additional input. Note the additional state update compared to Fig. 3.

"Backtracking" does not mean working backwards from random outputs to earlier random outputs, which would be a serious security problem. It means working backwards from *the internal state* to earlier random numbers. For example, if f in Fig. 1 is not one-way, the attacker can backtrack to all previous internal states and compute all previous random numbers.

Of course, PRNGs are designed to preserve the secrecy of the internal state. The idea of "backtracking resistance", also called "forward secrecy", is to reduce the damage in the extreme situation of an attacker somehow *stealing* the internal state: the attacker will be able to predict all future random numbers but will not be able to compute earlier random numbers.

The function f in Dual EC has always been one-way. The only issue with "backtracking resistance" in Dual EC 2006 with additional input is that an attacker who sees the current state s_1 can compute the *current* random number r_1. This issue disappears as soon as the next additional input is provided, allowing s_1 to be replaced with s_2; i.e., the current random number is protected against theft as soon as a new random number is generated.

The obvious way to fix theft of the current random number is to *first* output this number, *then* immediately absorb additional input, *then* apply the function f to update the state. This provides full "backtracking resistance"; it is also simpler and more efficient than Dual EC 2007. However, from the attacker's perspective, Dual EC 2007 is much more satisfactory because it fixes the back door.

6 Exploiting the Back Door in Dual EC Implementations

> *Their eyes open wide when I talk about how hard it is to really get the information they assume they just get to attack this thing. ... I've challenged any of them to actually generate their own parameters and show me that in real life they can recover that. No one has done it yet.*
> —Richard George, May 2014 [9]

The basic Dual EC attack allows the attacker to predict all subsequent Dual EC outputs, *assuming* that the attacker has seen a sufficiently long stretch of contiguous output bits. If all output bits were kept secret then the attack could not even get started. Some cryptographic protocols send random bits through the network, but it is not immediately obvious that Dual EC is exploitable inside real protocols, such as the widely deployed TLS standard, the primary encryption mechanism used for communication in the Internet today.

This section summarizes the results of a paper "On the practical exploitability of Dual EC in TLS implementations" [8] posted in April 2014 and presented at the USENIX Security Symposium in August 2014. This paper is joint work that we carried out with Stephen Checkoway, Matt Fredrikson, Adam Everspaugh, Matt Green, Tom Ristenpart, Jake Maskiewicz, and Hovav Shacham.

The paper shows that the basic Dual EC attack ignores critical limitations and variations in the amount of the PRNG output actually exposed in TLS, additional inputs to the PRNG, PRNG reseeding, alignment of PRNG outputs, and outright bugs in Dual EC implementations. The levels of Dual EC exploitability vary between RSA Security's BSAFE, Microsoft's SChannel, and OpenSSL.

However, in all analyzed situations where Dual EC was actually used in TLS, the Dual EC back door turned out to be exploitable by anyone who knows the secret d. TLS transmits enough random data in plain text during the TLS handshake, while it uses other random data to generate secret keys; the paper showed how to recover those secret keys.

6.1 How Targets Vary

The paper investigated four TLS libraries offering Dual EC: OpenSSL-FIPS (a FIPS-validated version of OpenSSL), Microsoft's SChannel, and two versions of RSA Security's BSAFE, namely BSAFE-Java and BSAFE-C.

The key to the back door, i.e., the factor d such that $P = dQ$, is not publicly known, so the paper replaced (P, Q) in each library with a new (P, Q) using a known key. Replacing the points in SChannel, BSAFE-Java, and BSAFE-C required some reverse engineering. Replacing the points in OpenSSL-FIPS was relatively easy because OpenSSL is open-source.

OpenSSL-FIPS turned out to have a severe Dual EC bug, despite FIPS validation: the self-test of the library consistently failed when OpenSSL-FIPS was configured to use Dual EC. It is therefore reasonable to guess that nobody ever used Dual EC with OpenSSL. On the other hand, there is an obvious fix for the bug, producing a modified library "OpenSSL-fixed" studied in the paper; users of OpenSSL-FIPS might have silently fixed this bug without reporting it. The other libraries had functional Dual EC implementations, and Dual EC was the default PRNG for both BSAFE-Java and BSAFE-C.

OpenSSL-fixed was the only library that used an additional input string for each request for random output, thus increasing the cost of the basic attack by the need to guess the adin; the other three libraries did not use any adin. BSAFE-Java, BSAFE-C, and OpenSSL-fixed implemented Dual EC 2007, with the additional update step at the end of each invocation. It appears that SChannel tried to implement Dual EC 2007 but accidentally implemented something equivalent to Dual EC 2006 instead: SChannel computes the additional state update but discards the result and continues with the previous state. This does not hurt Dual EC exploitability since SChannel does not use adin. One other difference between the Dual EC implementations is that BSAFE-C buffered unused random bytes for consecutive invocations, reducing the computational cost of Dual EC.

Beyond the differences in the Dual EC implementations, the implementations of TLS varied in how they used random output from Dual EC. By default each library generated a different number of random values, used random values in a different order in the TLS handshake, and used a different cipher suite. The paper used each library as a TLS server, and investigated an ephemeral cipher suite.

In a typical example of a TLS handshake with an ephemeral key exchange, the server generates random numbers for the *session ID*, the *server random*, the ephemeral secret a, and (depending on the cipher suite) the *signature nonce*. Both server random and session ID are sent in plaintext over the wire and therefore can be used as entry points for the attack. If the cipher suite uses "ECDHE", an ephemeral elliptic-curve Diffie–Hellman key exchange, the ephemeral secret is used to compute aP; if the cipher suite uses "DHE", an ephemeral Diffie–Hellman key exchange (without elliptic curves), the ephemeral secret is used to compute g^a (for some integer g). The nonce is used to compute a signature. The value from the key exchange and the signature (if available) are sent over the wire as well and can be used to verify that the correct Dual EC internal state has been found. Finally, client and server compute their secret encryption key from the exchanged data; the attacker is able to recompute the same key once he has found the internal state and obtained the server's ephemeral secret.

6.2   Attack Cost

Table 1 shows an overview of the worst-case runtimes for the attack. The attacker has to spend a different computational effort for each case, reflecting differences in the implementations of Dual EC and TLS.

The attack on BSAFE-C is the cheapest. For a TLS connection using DHE, the server draws in consecutive order 32 bytes for the session ID, 28 bytes for the server random, and 20 bytes for the ephemeral secret. The internal buffering of random bytes reduces the number of bits that need to be guessed to only 16, because the consecutively drawn random values "session ID" and "server random" can simply be concatenated to obtain 30 bytes of a single invocation output. Therefore, at most 2^{16} bit combinations need to be checked. A small 16-CPU research cluster was able to recover the internal state and break the connection within 0.04 min.

Attacking the BSAFE-Java version is more expensive. Here, the TLS implementation (using an ECDHE cipher suite) does not obtain the session ID from a call to Dual EC; the first value drawn from the PRNG is 28 bytes of the server

Table 1. Experimental timings for recovering the internal state of Dual EC from a TLS handshake for several implementations on a four-node, quad-socket AMD Opteron 6276 (Bulldozer) computing cluster

Attack	Total Worst Case Runtime (min)
BSAFE-C v1.1	0.04
BSAFE-Java v1.1	63.96
SChannel I	62.97
SChannel II	182.64
OpenSSL-fixed I	0.02
OpenSSL-fixed II	83.32
OpenSSL-fixed III	$2^k \cdot 83.32$

random. This is followed by a call for 32 random bytes for the secret DH key and finally an ECDSA nonce. Thus, using the 28 bytes of the server random, 32 bits need to be guessed to recover the 32-byte internal state, resulting in 2^{32} possible combinations. The research cluster used at most 64 min for the attack.

SChannel requests random data for an ECDHE cipher suite in a different order. The TLS implementation first requests 32 bytes for the session ID, but does not make all of these available to the attacker: it reduces the top four bytes modulo 20000 before transmission. It then requests 40 bytes for the secret ephemeral key; 28 bytes for the server random; and, finally, 32 bytes for the secret ECDSA nonce.

For SChannel, there are two cases. "SChannel I" means that a sequence of TLS handshakes is available to the attacker, so he can use the server random from a previous TLS handshake in order to compute the internal state. In this case, the attacker needs to guess the missing 32 bits from the 28-byte server random. This requires up to 2^{32} operations. The research cluster used less than 63 min.

"SChannel II" means that only data from a single TLS handshake is available to the attacker in order to compute the internal state. In this computationally more complex case, the back door computation must use the session ID as entry point for computing the ephemeral key. This requires about 2^{18} guesses to recover the original value before the modulo operation; each guess, in turn, requires checking 2^{16} possibilities since the most significant 16 bits were discarded. Testing a possibility means recomputing the ECDHE public key. In total, this case requires up to 2^{34} recomputations. The research cluster used a bit more than three hours.

OpenSSL-fixed requests first 32 bytes for the session ID, then 28 bytes for the server random, and finally 32 bytes for the ephemeral key. The randomness for the session ID is obtained in two 30-byte pieces, so it is particularly easy to recompute the internal state. Only the first 16 "discarded" bits need to be guessed; the correct state can quickly be verified by comparing the corresponding 16 bytes of the second piece with the last two bytes of the session ID.

Recall, however, that OpenSSL uses an additional input string in each request for random data, to refresh the randomness of the internal state. This adin is a concatenation of the current system time in seconds, the current system time in microseconds, a monotonically increased 32-bit counter, and the process ID. The current system time in seconds is known to the attacker since it is contained in the TLS handshake. However, the remaining data of the adin needs to be guessed.

Table 1 shows three cases. "OpenSSL-fixed I" assumes that the entire adin is known to the attacker; thus he only needs to guess the 16 missing bits for the session ID and is able to recompute the state and follow all internal state updates. The cluster used 0.02 min to recompute the state on 16 CPUs in parallel.

"OpenSSL-fixed II" assumes that the attacker knows the counter (because he may be attacking the very first TLS handshake when the counter is 0) and the process ID (because it may be determined depending on the order in which systems services are started during boot time). Then the attacker only needs to recompute the current microsecond in which the adin was computed; this requires at most 1,000,000 guesses. The research cluster recomputed the internal state within 84 min.

Finally, if counter and/or process ID are not known, a multiple of the time for OpenSSL II is required. "OpenSSL III" in the table includes a factor 2^k, giving an idea about the required time in case k bits of unknown adin need to be guessed.

The attacks are easy to parallelize and scale well on a large number of CPUs. Thus, an attacker who can afford a large CPU cluster is able to compute the internal state in a much shorter time than the 16-CPU research cluster used in the experiment. About 1,000 CPUs are sufficient to finish most of the attacks (all except SChannel II and OpenSSL-fixed III) within 1 min. A computing cluster of the size of the Tianhe-2 supercomputer with 70,000 CPUs computes most of the attacks in under one second.

6.3 Attack Scenarios

An attack on a TLS connection does not need to be done "online", while the communication between the client and the server is ongoing. It is possible to use the back door to retroactively break into a recorded TLS connection at any time. The attack on TLS connections works as well when the client instead of the server is targeted.

If the server is targeted, the recovered internal state can be used not only to compute the encryption keys of the targeted connection but also of all future connections to the server by any client (see the discussion of SChannel I). If a signature scheme based on the digital signature algorithm (DSA, designed by NSA) is used for server authentication, the knowledge of just one signature nonce enables the attacker to compute the server's secret identity key and thus to impersonate the server.

7 Extended Random

The basic Dual EC attack requires the attacker to see at least a block of 30 Dual EC output bytes (and, of course, to know the back door for the Dual EC parameters). As shown in the previous section, implementations of TLS often make only 28 consecutive bytes public. This increases the cost of using the back door from about 2^{15} to about 2^{31}.

A single 2^{31} computation is not a problem, but if the same attack is carried out many times, say 2^t times, then the attack costs are increased from 2^{15+t} to 2^{31+t}. This is a serious issue when t is large. Even worse, if Dual EC is used with P-384 or P-521 instead of P-256, then there is a critical gap between the standard 224 bits revealed by TLS and the 368 or 504 bits in a Dual EC output block, and the attack becomes infeasible.

There are four proposals of TLS extensions that increase the amount of PRNG output visible to an attacker: "Opaque PRF" [32] from 2006, "Extended Random" [33] from 2008, "Additional PRF Inputs" [13] from 2009, and "Additional Random" [12] from 2010. None of these extensions were standardized, but BSAFE implements Extended Random as an option, and a 2012 summary of TLS monitoring [1] reveals that occasionally, about once in every 77000 connections, clients actively requested Extended Random.

7.1   How Extended Random Affects Dual EC Exploitation

A client that supports "Extended Random" sends more random data in its initial "client random" in its TLS handshake: instead of 224 bits it sends a string of random bits at least "twice as long as the security level", i.e., ≥ 256 bits. If the server also supports "Extended Random" then the server responds with its own "server random" of the same length that the client chose.

Extended Random reduces the Dual EC attack cost from 2^{31} to 2^{15}, since the attacker no longer needs to guess 16 extra missing bits. Extended Random also simplifies the attack, because it includes more than one block of output: the attacker easily and efficiently confirms guesses for internal Dual EC states by comparing the potential next output to the next bits of the extended randomness. A 512-bit Extended Random also makes attacks feasible against, e.g., the P-521 variant of Dual EC.

To summarize: From the perspective of a Dual EC attacker, there are obvious benefits to Extended Random.

7.2   The Official Reason for Extended Random

Extended Random was proposed in an Internet-Draft by Eric Rescorla (RTFM, Inc.) and Margaret Salter (NSA) in April 2008. The latest version, draft 02, is from 2 March 2009:

```
Network Working Group                              E. Rescorla
Internet-Draft                                      RTFM, Inc.
Intended status:  Informational                      M. Salter
Expires:  September 3, 2009         National Security Agency
                                                 March 02, 2009
```

Section 6 of the document acknowledges a funding source: "This work was supported by the US Department of Defense."

The Internet-Draft states the following rationale for extended randomness:

> The United States Department of Defense has requested a TLS mode
> which allows the use of longer public randomness values for use with
> high security level cipher suites like those specified in Suite B
> [I-D.rescorla-tls-suiteb]. The rationale for this as stated by DoD
> is that the public randomness for each side should be at least twice
> as long as the security level for cryptographic parity, which makes
> the 224 bits of randomness provided by the current TLS random values
> insufficient.

"Cryptographic parity" is not a common phrase among cryptographers. It is not defined in the document, and its intended meaning is highly unclear. Furthermore, there is no known attack strategy that comes even close to exploiting the 224 bits of randomness used in TLS.

TLS encrypts data using a "master secret" computed from the server's 224-bit random value, the client's 224-bit random value, and a "pre-master secret". The pre-master secret is the foundation of TLS security: in ECC cipher suites it is obtained from a DH key exchange between client and server, and in RSA cipher suites it is chosen by the client and encrypted to the RSA key of the server. The pre-master key is already at least twice as large as the security level. Even if the client constantly reuses the same pre-master secret and random value, the server has negligible chance of ever repeating its 224-bit random value with a properly functioning RNG: a server generating an incredible 10000000000000000000 random 224-bit values has chance below 0.0000000000000000000000000000001 of seeing the same value twice.

The Internet-Draft contains no further explanation to support its allegation of 224 bits being insufficient. As far as we know, NSA has not attempted to defend this allegation in other venues. Meanwhile, to the extent that Extended Random is supported, it has an undisputed impact on the exploitability of Dual EC.

8   Certicom Patents

The Canadian company Certicom (now part of Blackberry) has patents in multiple countries on

- Dual EC exploitation: the use of Dual EC for key escrow (i.e., for a deliberate back door) and
- Dual EC escrow avoidance: modifying Dual EC to avoid key escrow.

The patent filing history also shows that

- Certicom knew the Dual EC back door by January 2005;

- NSA was informed of the Dual EC back door by April 2005 (even if they did not know it earlier); and
- the patent application, including examples of Dual EC exploitation, was publicly available in July 2006, just a month after SP 800–90 was standardized.

This section cites several documents related to the patent applications and patents. We have a web page [5] with more details and cached copies of the documents.

A short summary of the general patenting process is that a party seeking to protect its intellectual property files a patent application with a national patent office. Often the initial application is a so-called "provisional" application, meaning that the details or the claims are not fully worked out; this gives an official time stamp on the possible invention. Often patent applications are submitted for more than one country using the "Patent Cooperation Treaty" (PCT) to start with the national filing. Certicom submitted the patent in the US and also filed for patents in Canada, Europe, and Japan.

8.1   Publicity and the Avoidance Thereof

In early 2005, Certicom began trying to patent both Dual EC exploitation and Dual EC escrow avoidance. The patent application lists Daniel R. L. Brown and Scott A. Vanstone as "inventors".

Certicom never drew public attention to these patenting efforts, or to the possibility of a back door in Dual EC. Their actions went generally unnoticed until 28 December 2013, when Certicom's patent application was announced by Lange in a presentation [4] with Bernstein and Heninger at the 30th Chaos Communication Congress, crediting a tweet [28] by "nymble" earlier in the month.

"At some point, I clued into the possibility of a backdoor, and, among other things, tried to make sure the possibility was at least publicly known, at first quietly: with a patent, and with a comment within my March 2006 eprint," Brown wrote in email [6] to the CFRG mailing list a few days after the presentation. "Later, others raised much more publicity, which seemed sufficient to me. I had expected such publicity to cause the proposers, X9F1 and NIST to withdraw the default P&Q from the standard."

8.2   The Provisional Patent Application

The provisional patent application does not claim to have invented Dual EC per se, and does not clarify who invented Dual EC. It cites ANSI X9.82 [29, p. 2, paragraph 0003]:

The American National Standards Institute (ANSI) has set up an Accredited Standards Committee (ASC) X9 for the financial services industry, which is preparing a [sic] American National Standard (ANS) X9.82 for cryptographic random number generation (RNG). One of the RNG methods in the draft of X9.82, called Dual_EC_DRBG, uses elliptic curve cryptography (ECC) for its security. Dual_EC_DRBG will hereinafter be referred to as elliptic curve random number generation (ECRNG).

The provisional patent application describes the Dual EC back door [29, p. 4, paragraphs 0010–0013]:

> The applicant has recognised that anybody who knows an integer d such that $Q = dP$ ... can compute U from R as $U = eR$. ... The truncation function means that the truncated bits of R would have to be guessed. ... The updated state is $u = z(U)$, so it can be determined from the correct value of R. Therefore knowledge of r and e allows one to determine the next state to within a number of possibilities somewhere between 2^6 and 2^{19}. This uncertainty will invariably be eliminated once another output is observed, whether directly or indirectly through a one-way function. ... It has therefore been identified by the applicant that this method potentially possesses a trapdoor, whereby standardizers or implementers of the algorithm may possess a piece of information with which they can use a single output and an instantiation of the RNG to determine all future states and output of the RNG, thereby completely compromising its security.

The provisional patent application also describes ideas of how to make random numbers available to "trusted law enforcement agents" or other "escrow administrators". For example [29, p. 9, paragraph 0039]:

> In order for the escrow key to function with full effectiveness, the escrow administrator ... needs direct access to an ECRNG output value r that was generated before the ECRNG output value ... which is to be recovered. It is not sufficient to have indirect access to r via a one-way function or an encryption algorithm. ... A more seamless method may be applied for cryptographic applications. For example, in the SSL and TLS protocols, which are used for securing web (HTTP) traffic, a client and server perform a handshake in which their first actions are to exchange random values sent in the clear.

The provisional patent application also describes various ways to avoid the back door, such as [29, p. 7, paragraphs 0028 and 0031] choosing P and Q as hashes of random seeds in a way similar to ANSI X9.62 (the idea that NSA told Johnson not to talk about; see Sect. 4.1):

> An arbitrary string is selected ... the hash is then converted to a field element ... regarded as the x-coordinate of Q ... To effectively prevent the existence of escrow keys, a verifiable Q should be accompanied with either a verifiable P or a pre-established P.

It is clear that Brown and Vanstone were aware of the Dual EC back door, and ways to exploit it, by January 2005 when the provisional patent application was filed. Technically, the applications were filed by Certicom, but both Brown and Vanstone signed a "Declaration and Power of Attorney For Patent Application" document in April 2006 [30, pp. 39–41] declaring that they were the "inventors" and had reviewed the 23 January 2006 patent application, which includes a priority claim to the January 2005 provisional. Furthermore, the 23 January 2006 patent application contains all of the quotes given above, except that instead of "verifiable" it used the phrase "verifiably random".

8.3   Secrecy-Order Review

The United States Patent and Trademark Office (USPTO) forwards patent applications to "appropriate agencies" [37] to decide whether to impose secrecy orders on those applications:

> [Applications] are screened upon receipt in the USPTO for subject matter that, if disclosed, might impact the national security. Such applications are referred to the appropriate agencies for consideration of restrictions on disclosure of the subject matter as provided for in 35 U.S.C. 181.
>
> If a defense agency concludes that disclosure of the invention would be detrimental to the national security, a secrecy order is recommended to the Commissioner for Patents. The Commissioner then issues a Secrecy Order and withholds the publication of the application or the grant of a patent for such period as the national interest requires.

The USPTO referred Certicom's provisional patent application to the Department of Defense (DoD) for review. Eventually, on 2 February 2006, DoD returned a "Department of Defense: Access acknowledgment/Secrecy order recommendation for patent application" form [29, p. 19] recommending against a secrecy order.

According to the USPTO, the referral letter was mailed on 7 April 2005, and the response was entered into PAIR on 27 February 2006. The response itself states that the referral was on 7 March 2005 and that the response was forwarded on 7 February 2006.

The patent application was referred to DoD on 13 March 2006. The Navy responded "No comments" on 15 March 2006. NSA recommended against a secrecy order on 16 April 2007; see [30, p. 48].

8.4   International Patent Applications

Certicom filed its patent application internationally under the PCT in 2006. The international publication number is WO2006/076804. This filing alone does not lead to national patents: the applicant needs to request examination in the designated countries (and pay the applicable fees). Searching for WO2006076804 on http://patentscope.wipo.int shows applications filed in Canada, Europe, and Japan.

The PCT stipulates (with certain exceptions) that international patent applications are published 18 months after the priority date. WIPO, the World Intellectual Property Organization, published the patent application on 27 July 2006 in full length online [7]. This means that a clear explanation of the back door and its (ab-)use was publicly available as of July 2006.

8.5 Resulting Patents

Certicom received a European patent on 4 July 2012, and subsequently received patents in the United States, Japan, and Canada. The United States patent covers only escrow avoidance; the same seems to hold for the Canadian and Japanese patents. However, the European patent reaches farther than the United States patent: it covers both Dual EC exploitation and Dual EC escrow avoidance. The claims on escrow use are more refined than in the original patent application where they accounted for only one claim. The European patent lapsed in many countries because Certicom did not pay maintenance fees in those countries, but Certicom paid its January 2015 fees for France, Germany, the Netherlands, and Great Britain.

References

1. Amann, B., Vallentin, M., Hall, S., Sommer, R.:Revisiting SSL: A large-scale study of the Internet's mosttrusted protocol (2012). http://www.icsi.berkeley.edu/pubs/techreports/ICSI_TR-12-015.pdf
2. Ball, J., Borger, J., Greenwald, G.: Revealed: how US and UK spy agencies defeat internet privacy andsecurity. The Guardian, 5 September 2013. http://www.theguardian.com/world/2013/sep/05/nsa-gchq-encryption-codes-security
3. Barker, E.: Letter to Bruce Schneier (2007). https://github.com/matthewdgreen/nistfoia/blob/master/6.4.2014%20production/109%20-%20Nov%2028%2020d07%20Letter%20to%20Bruce%20from%20Barker%20-%20Wired%d20Commentary%20.pdf
4. Bernstein, D., Heninger, N., Lange, T.: The year in crypto, 2013. In: Presentation at 30th Chaos Communication Congress. https://hyperelliptic.org/tanja/vortraege/talk-30C3.pdf
5. Bernstein, D.J., Lange, T., Niederhagen, R.: Certicom's patent applications regarding Dual EC key escrow (2014). https://projectbullrun.org/dual-ec/patent.html
6. Brown, D.R.L.: Re: Dual_EC_DRBG (2014). http://permalink.gmane.org/gmane.ietf.irtf.cfrg/2300
7. Brown, D.R.L., Vanstone, S.A.: Elliptic curve random number generation. Patent application published by WIPO (2006). http://tinyurl.com/oowkk36
8. Checkoway, S., Niederhagen, R., Everspaugh, A., Green, M., Lange, T., Ristenpart, T., Bernstein, D.J., Maskiewicz, J., Shacham, H., Fredrikson, M.: On the practical exploitability of Dual EC in TLS implementations. In: 23rd USENIX Security Symposium (USENIX Security 14), pp. 319–335. USENIX Association, August 2014. https://projectbullrun.org/dual-ec/documents/dualectls-20140606.pdf
9. George, R.: Life at both ends of the barrel: an NSA targeting retrospective, keynote talk at Infiltrateconference (2014). http://vimeo.com/97891042

10. Gjøsteen, K.: Comments on Dual-EC-DRBG/NIST SP 800-90, draft December 2005, 2006. http://www.math.ntnu.no/~kristiag/drafts/dual-ec-drbg-comments.pdf

11. Green, M.D.: Results of a recent FOIA for NIST documents related to the designof Dual EC DRBG (2015). https://github.com/matthewdgreen/nistfoia

12. Hoffman, P.: Additional random extension to TLS, Internet-Draft version 01, February 2010. http://tools.ietf.org/html/draft-hoffman-tls-additional-random-ext-01

13. Hoffman, P., Solinas, J.: Additional PRF inputs for TLS, Internet-Draft version 01, October 2009. http://tools.ietf.org/html/draft-solinas-tls-additional-prf-input-01

14. Joint Technical Committee ISO/IEC JTC 1, Informationtechnology, Subcommittee SC 27, IT Security techniques. US national body comments on ISO/IEC 2nd CD 18031. Attachment 10 to SC27 N3685(2003). https://projectbullrun.org/dual-ec/documents/us-comment-to-iso.pdf

15. Johnson, D.: Minding our Ps and Qs in Dual_EC (2004). http://csrc.nist.gov/groups/ST/crypto-review/documents/Email_Oct

16. Johnson, D.: Number theoretic DRBGs (2004). http://csrc.nist.gov/groups/ST/toolkit/documents/rng/NumberTheoreticDRBG.pdf

17. Kelsey, J.: 800-90 and Dual EC DRBG (2013). http://csrc.nist.gov/groups/SMA/ispab/documents/minutes/2013-12/nist_cryptography_800-90.pdf

18. Kelsey, J.: Dual EC in X9.82 and SP 800-90 (2014). http://csrc.nist.gov/groups/ST/crypto-review/documents/dualec_in_X982_and_sp800-90.pdf

19. Larson, J., Perlroth, N., Shane, S.: Revealed: The NSA's secret campaign to crack, undermine Internetsecurity. *ProPublica*, September 2013. https://www.propublica.org/article/the-nsas-secret-campaign-to-crack-undermine-internet-encryption

20. Menn, J.: Exclusive: Secret contract tied NSA and security industry pioneer. Reuters, December 2013. http://www.reuters.com/article/2013/12/20/us-usa-security-rsa-idUSBRE9BJ1C220131220

21. National Institute for Standards and Technology. DRBG validation list. http://csrc.nist.gov/groups/STM/cavp/documents/drbg/drbgval.html

22. National Institute for Standards and Technology. Internal draft of X9.82 section 9.12, 2004? https://github.com/matthewdgreen/nistfoia/blob/master/6.4.2014 %20production/011%20-%209.12%20Choosing%20a%20DRBG%20Algorithm.pdf, received through FOIA

23. National Institute for Standards and Technology. RNG workshop and standards development (2004). http://csrc.nist.gov/groups/ST/toolkit/random_number.html#RNG%20WSD

24. National Institute for Standards and Technology. The NIST SP 800-90A Deterministic Random Bit Generator ValidationSystem (DRBGVS); current version from 2013, first version from 2009, 2013. http://csrc.nist.gov/groups/STM/cavp/documents/drbg/DRBGVS.pdf

25. National Institute for Standards and Technology. Compilation of public comments on 2005 draft of SP 800-90 (2014). http://csrc.nist.gov/groups/ST/toolkit/documents/CommentsSP800-90_2006.pdf

26. National Institute for Standards and Technology. NIST FOIA material released to COV: X9.82 and NIST SP800-90 process, 10 June, 2014. http://csrc.nist.gov/groups/ST/crypto-review/review_materials.html

27. National Institute of Standards and Technology. Special Publication 800-90: Recommendation for random numbergeneration using deterministic random bit generators, 2012. First version June 2006, second version March 2007. http://csrc.nist.gov/publications/PubsSPs.html#800-90A

28. nymble. Interesting patent on use of ECC random number generator for 'escrow'. Designed as backdoor in 2005. Twitter post on 3 December, 2013. https://twitter.com/nymble/status/408023522284285952
29. Patent Application Information Retrieval (PAIR). Image file wrapper for provisional application 60644982 (2005). https://projectbullrun.org/dual-ec/documents/60644982.pdf
30. Patent Application Information Retrieval (PAIR). Image file wrapper for patent application 11336814 (2006). https://projectbullrun.org/dual-ec/documents/11336814.pdf
31. Perlroth, N., Larson, J., Shane, S.: N.S.A. able to foil basic safeguards of privacy on web. International New York Times, September 2013. http://www.nytimes.com/2013/09/06/us/nsa-foils-much-internet-encryption.html
32. Rescorla, E., Salter, M.: Opaque PRF inputs for TLS. Internet-Draft version 00, December 2006. http://tools.ietf.org/html/draft-rescorla-tls-opaque-prf-input-00
33. Rescorla, E., Salter, M.: Extended random values for TLS, Internet-Draft version 02, March 2009. http://tools.ietf.org/html/draft-rescorla-tls-extended-random-02
34. Schneier, B.: Did NSA put a secret backdoor in new encryption standard? (2007). http://archive.wired.com/politics/security/commentary/securitymatters/2007/11/securitymatters_1115
35. Schoenmakers, B., Sidorenko, A.: Cryptanalysis of the Dual Elliptic Curve pseudo random generator. Cryptology ePrint Archive, Report 2006/190 (2006). https://eprint.iacr.org/2006/190
36. Shumow, D., Ferguson, N.: On the possibility of a back door in the NIST SP800-90 Dual EcPrng.CRYPTO 2007 Rump Session, August 2007. http://rump2007.cr.yp.to/15-shumow.pdf
37. United States Patent and Trademark Office.Review of applications for national security and property rightsissues. Manual of Patent Examining Procedure, Section 115 (2013). http://www.uspto.gov/web/offices/pac/mpep/s115.html

An Improved Differential Attack on Full GOST

Nicolas T. Courtois[✉]

University College London, Gower Street, London, UK
n.courtois@cs.ucl.ac.uk

Abstract. GOST 28147-89 is a well-known block cipher. Its large key size of 256 bits and incredibly low implementation cost make it a plausible alternative for AES-256 and triple DES. Until 2010 "despite considerable cryptanalytic efforts spent in the past 20 years", GOST was not broken see [30]. Accordingly, in 2010 GOST was submitted to ISO 18033 to become a worldwide industrial encryption standard.

In paper we focus on the question of how far one can go in a dedicated Depth-First-Search approach with several stages of progressive guessing and filtering with successive distinguishers. We want to design and optimized guess-then-truncated differential attack on full 32-bit GOST and make as efficient as we can. The main result of this paper is a single-key attack against full 32-round 256-bit GOST with time complexity of 2^{179} which is substantially faster than any other known single key attack on GOST.

Keywords: Block ciphers · GOST · Differential cryptanalysis · Truncated differentials · Guess-then-determine · Gaussian distribution · Distinguisher attacks

1 Introduction

GOST 28147-89 is a well-known block cipher and a government standard of the Russian Federation. A 256-bit block cipher which can claim to be a serious alternative for AES-256 and triple DES, given its very low implementation cost [30]. Until 2010 there was no attack on GOST, cf. [30].

Then in 2011 it was discovered that GOST can be broken and is insecure on more than one account. There is a substantial variety of recent attacks on GOST [3–6, 11, 12, 16, 17, 19, 23, 24]. In particular there is a large variety of self-similarity and black-box reduction attacks [3, 9, 11, 16, 17, 19, 24]. There have also been quite a few papers about advanced differential attacks on GOST [4–6, 8, 13, 15, 29, 31–33]. In contrast to other recent works on this topic we do not focus on the complex question of how such attacks can be discovered, cf. [7, 14, 29], or how reliable some heuristic results are [4–6, 8, 15, 33] especially given the fact that GOST is not a Markov cipher [14, 25, 29] or how to optimize them in general for one given set of S-boxes cf. [7, 13, 29] or for major alternative sets of S-boxes cf. [8, 13, 29, 31, 32]. We don't look at multiple key attacks [9, 11, 16, 17, 24] or at more advanced "combination"

© Springer-Verlag Berlin Heidelberg 2016
P.Y.A. Ryan et al. (Eds.): Kahn Festschrift, LNCS 9100, pp. 282–303, 2016.
DOI: 10.1007/978-3-662-49301-4_18

attacks which combine the complexity reduction approach based on high-level self-similarity of [3,11,16] with advanced differential properties with 2, 3 and 4 points, [16,17].

This paper is about developing a complex advanced differential attack on GOST block cipher which involves several steps with progressive guessing of well-chosen key bits, and several statistical distinguisher steps.

1.1 GOST and Differential Cryptanalysis

Differential cryptanalysis (DC) is based on tracking of changes in the differences between two messages as they pass through the consecutive rounds of encryption. It is one of the oldest classical attacks on modern block ciphers [2,18], we refer to cf. [8] for a short historical survey. Differential attacks are very well known. Yet researchers have until recently failed to accurately evaluate the strength of GOST against DC. GOST was quite frequently claimed very secure against such attacks. In late 1990s Schneier writes that: "against differential and linear cryptanalysis, GOST is probably stronger than DES", cf. [34]. Later in 2000 Russian researchers claimed that breaking GOST with five or more rounds is "very hard" and claim that as few as 7 rounds out of 32 are sufficient to protect GOST against DC [20]. Needless to say later research have not confirmed at all such very optimistic claims [14,15,25,26]. GOST appears to be quite secure in the very basic historical Biham-Shamir formulation of DC with single differences on the full state [2,20,33]. A more powerful family of attacks are "truncated differential" attacks by Knudsen [27] which have been applied to GOST as early as in 2000 by Seki and Kaneko [33] with some success. In 2011 Courtois and Misztal have found new differential sets for GOST [6] which are substantially better than previously known. The possibilities offered by such attacks remain poorly understood in the research community. For example in the a recent survey paper specifically about advanced differential cryptanalysis and specifically on block ciphers with small blocks in Sect. 1.1. page 3 of [1] we read: *Truncated differentials, [...] in some cases allow to push differential attacks one or two rounds further*. This paper and our other recent research on GOST [4–6,8,13–15] shows that we can gain not two but much closer to 20 rounds (!) compared to what we would expected to achieve with single differentials [20,21,33].

In this paper we work on essentially one single highly optimized attack, the best we could find. It is a balancing act between the time complexity of different consecutive steps of a complex attack. An intermediate goal is to construct distinguishers on say 20 rounds of GOST: this question has been studied in [7,8,13–15,29]. This paper is about how to transform one such distinguisher into an efficient attack on the full 32-round GOST cipher.

This paper is organized as follows: In Section we explain the high-level structure of GOST and explain the role played by GOST key scheduling. We explain the principle of splitting GOST into three sections of for example 6+20+6 rounds. Then in Sect. 3 we study the question of constructing a distinguisher for 20 rounds of GOST which is a central question in this paper. This is further extended into a sequence on of "concentric" distinguishers for decreasing supersets of 20 rounds cf. Sect. 4. In Sect. 5 we study the propagation inside GOST in order to be able to construct well chosen subsets of key bits to be guessed at various stages of our attack. Thus finally in Sect. 6 we describe a full advanced differential attack on 32 rounds of GOST which works in 5 stages in which well-chosen assumptions on the key and data (plaintext) bits are progressively refined with early rejection.

2   GOST and Key Schedule

GOST is a block cipher with a simple Feistel structure, 64-bit block size, 256-bit keys and 32 rounds. Each round contains a key addition modulo 2^{32}, a set of 8 bijective S-boxes on 4 bits, and a simple circular rotation by 11 positions. Each round of GOST looks exactly the same except for the key k used:

$$(L, R) \mapsto (R, L \oplus f_k(R))$$

GOST has 32 rounds such as the one described in Fig. 1 below. The ⊞ denotes the addition modulo 2^{32}. On our picture below the ⊞ denotes the addition modulo 2^{32}. We number the inputs of the S-box Si for $i = 1, 2, \ldots, 8$ by integers from $4i + 1$ to $4i + 4$ out of 1..32 and its outputs are numbered according to their final positions after the rotation by 11 positions: for example the inputs of S6 are $20, 21, 22, 23$ and the outputs are $32, 1, 2, 3$. At the left margin in Fig. 1 we also show S-box numbers in the next round, to see which bits are successfully determined in our attacks on GOST, cf. later Fig. 7 page 11.

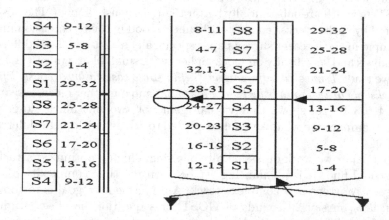

Fig. 1. One round of GOST and connections in the following round

The key structural property of GOST which makes it suitable for cryptanalytic attacks of the specific kind and specific form, is that the last 8 rounds are identical to the fist 8 rounds run in the opposite direction (however this symmetry does not follow for more inner rounds).

rounds	1	8	9	16
keys	$k_0 k_1 k_2 k_3 k_4 k_5 k_6 k_7$		$k_0 k_1 k_2 k_3 k_4 k_5 k_6 k_7$	
rounds	17	24	25	32
keys	$k_0 k_1 k_2 k_3 k_4 k_5 k_6 k_7$		$k_7 k_6 k_5 k_4 k_3 k_2 k_1 k_0$	

Fig. 2. Key schedule in GOST

This property has a big impact on security of GOST: 32 bits of the whole key, a fairly small proportion, are used in one round, and for every 32 bits guessed we can remove two full outer rounds, instead of 1 round for a similar cipher without a weak key scheduling. Thus for example if we guess 192 key bits, we can remove 12 full rounds of GOST cf. [4]. In this paper we exploit this symmetry even further: we will look at differential which are a member of a certain set of differentials which is totally symmetric for the first 8 rounds and the last 8 rounds. Our key guesses will be far more precise than guessing keys for full rounds and specially adapted to this highly symmetric situation.

Given one round in Fig. 1 and key scheduling in Fig. 2 we have a complete description of GOST. In this paper we will only study the most popular set of GOST S-boxes a.k.a. the "GostR3411_94_TestParamSet" which was published by Schneier in 1994 and which claimed to be used by the Central Bank of the Russian Federation [34]. This is exactly what most researchers call just "the GOST cipher" (without any additional mention) in the cryptographic literature. This choice of S-boxes greatly affects all the differential probabilities we use in this paper, we refer to [7,8,13,29,29,31,32] for the study of similar attacks for other S-boxes.

2.1 Preliminary Remarks

In our later attack which will be described in Sects. 4, 5 and 6 we are going to split GOST into three pieces with 6+20+6 rounds. Early advanced differential attacks were based on a for up to 20 rounds of GOST [4,5] and mandated guessing complete 32-bit keys for several outer rounds in order to fully reconstruct these internal differentials. This approach is refined in [7,13,14,29] and in this paper. We will guess only some well-chosen key bits which will be used to filter P/C (Plaintext,Ciphertext) pairs used later in the attack. As in [4] the attack runs through many stages with great many filtering/guessing steps, where at each step we reduce the number of cases to consider (the plaintext space, some key bits already guessed and pre-computed relations between all these) and only after this reduction of number of cases we make additional guesses. Large parts of this whole process can be viewed as an adaptive Depth-First-Search (DFS) attack on a tree of possibilities which is constructed adaptively depending on the assumptions currently considered as valid. This type of process is very widely used in cryptanalysis.

There is a substantial difficulty in differential attacks where the key size is much larger than the block size as in GOST: there are false positives, differentials which do not propagate but occur naturally, by accident. The key point is that for a very long time the false positives are not eliminated in a differential attack on GOST. We are just dealing with assumptions on internal difference bits in GOST, their consequences and relations between these assumptions but for many steps none of the steps of the attack is able to see if the inner 20 rounds are 20 rounds of GOST, more rounds of GOST, or maybe just some other permutation. This can only be seen at a much later stage of the attack.

Before we get there we need to study a number of preliminary technical questions.

2.2 Sets of Differentials, Aggregated and Truncated Differentials

Truncated differential attacks [27] have been studied since 1994. Some attacks on GOST are proposed in 2000 by Seki and Kaneko [33] and since 2011 better and stronger differential properties have been found, cf. [4,6]. We consider differences with respect to the popular bitwise XOR operation. Following previous work on this topic [4,5] we define *an aggregated differential A, B* as the transition where any non-zero difference $a \in A$ will produce an arbitrary non-zero difference $b \in B$ with a certain probability.

In particular we consider the case when A is a set of all possible non-zero differentials contained within a certain mask. This also is a special case of "Truncated Differentials" [27] which are defined as fixing the difference not on all but a subset of data bits. However we need to be careful and explicitly exclude all-zero differentials from this set. For example for

$$\Delta = 0x80700700$$

we obtain a set of all differences on 32 bits with between 1 and 7 active bits (but not 0) and where the active bits are contained within the mask 0x80700700. Similarly, the set denoted by (Δ, Δ) is a set of difference on 64 bits with up to 14 active bits, where any non-zero difference is allowed, including also differences where the difference is zero in one half, but not the all-zero difference on both halves. We have $|A| = 2^{14} - 1$: there are exactly $2^{14} - 1$ single 64-bit differences in this set of differentials A.

For example the following fact was established in [4–6]:

Fact 2.3. *The aggregated differential (Δ, Δ) with uniform sampling of all differences it allows, produces an element of the same aggregated differential set (Δ, Δ) after 4 rounds of GOST with probability about $2^{-13.6}$ on average over all possible keys, where $\Delta = 0x80700700$ has 7 active bits.*
For 6 rounds the probability is $2^{-18.7}$ on average over all possible keys.
For 8 rounds the probability is $2^{-25.0}$ on average over all possible keys.

Remark: Recent research shows that the size of 14 bits is close to optimum, i.e. set with a different size are less likely to be as good, see [15]

Now we look at a one particular differential set, which we have noticed, arrives with a particularly large probability:

Fact 2.4. *The set* $(\Delta, \Delta) = (0x80700700, 0x80700700)$ *produces a differential of the form* $(0x00000700, 0x80780000)$ *with probability of* $2^{-22.19}$ *for 7 rounds of GOST.*

This was obtained by a computer simulation. We have $|A| = 2^{14} - 1$ and $|B| = 2^8 - 1$. This *an aggregated differential* A, B contains $(2^{14} - 1)(2^8 - 1)$ single differential characteristics.

Truncated differential attacks on GOST are facilitated by a strong internal structure inside GOST where GOST splits very neatly into two loosely connected parts, cf. Fig. 3 and Sect. 4 of [7] and different interesting truncated differential attacks can be classified in relation to this structure [7, 13, 14].

For example some of the best known attacks cf. Fact 2.3 which are also exploited in this paper are said to be of type 3+3 S-boxes in each of the loosely connected parts. These 3 S-boxes and their connections are shown in Fig. 3 below.

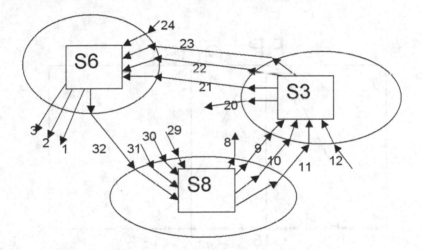

Fig. 3. Connections between S-boxes exploited in Fact 2.3.

3   Our Main Distinguisher for 20 Rounds

Our goal is to design an attack on the full 32-round GOST. As in [4, 5] we guess some key bits and use a distinguisher, however our new distinguisher is symmetric and the attack will have more stages. The key question is how a differential attack on GOST can cope with false positives. There are differentials which occur due to propagation of small Hamming weight differentials for 20 rounds of GOST, and other which occur "by accident" for an arbitrary permutation on 64 bis. Not only for a Random Permutation (RP) but also almost always, with overwhelming probability $1 - \varepsilon$ for ANY permutation such as several rounds of GOST block cipher. We need to quantify precisely the interaction between these two sets, which is essential in we want to reliably distinguish between 20 rounds of GOST and some other permutation.

Fact 3.1. *We look at the combination of a non-zero input difference of type* $(0x80780000, 0x00000700)$ *and a non-zero output difference of type* $(0x00000700, 0x80780000)$ *for 20 rounds of GOST.*

For a typical permutation on 64-bits we expect that there are 2^{15} pairs P_i, P_j with such differences. The distribution of this number can be approximated by a Gaussian with a standard deviation of $2^{7.5}$.

For 20 rounds of GOST and for a given random GOST key, there exists two disjoint sets of $2^{15} + 2^{13.9}$ such pairs P_i, P_j. These are two entirely disjoint sets of pairs, which can be distinguished by the fact that $2^{13.9}$ pairs will have the difference $0x80700700, 0x80700700$ after 6 rounds from the beginning AND 6 rounds from the end, and none of the 2^{15} will have such internal differences.

The distribution of the sum can be approximated by a Gaussian with an average of about $2^{15} + 2^{13.9}$ and the standard deviation of $2^{7.8}$.

We are at $2^{6.1} \times$ the standard deviation.

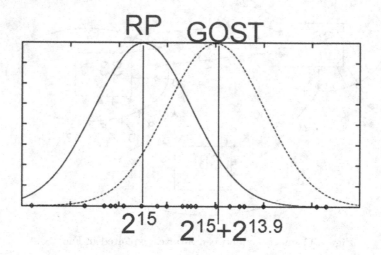

Fig. 4. Signal vs. Noise differential distinguisher for 20 rounds of GOST

Justification: For any permutation, we observe that every single combination of an input differential on 64 bits, and on an output differential on 64 bits, is expected to occur about 0.5 times on average. Indeed we have 2^{127} pairs and about 2^{128} possible sets of two differentials. Now we have $(2^8 - 1)(2^8 - 1)$ possibilities of type $(0x80780000, 0x00000700) \rightarrow$ (after some permutation OR 20 inner rounds of GOST) $\rightarrow (0x00000700, 0x80780000)$. Overall we expect to obtain $0.5 \cdot 2^{8+8} = 2^{15}$ pairs P_i, P_j for a given GOST key, with any of these $2^8 - 2^3 + 1$ differences (Fig. 4).

For the actual 20 rounds of GOST the situation is more complex. We need to distinguish between pairs which occur "by accident" and those which occur due to "propagation". We are going to develop a precise argument showing that both sets are entirely disjoint and their numbers can be added. In order to do this we are going to give a precise meaning to the word "propagation" in this precise 20 rounds case: we say that the differential "propagates" if it goes through two additional differences in the middle as follows:

$$0x80780000 \quad 0x00000700$$
$$(7 \text{ Rounds})$$
$$0x80700700 \quad 0x80700700$$
$$(6 \text{ Rounds})$$
$$0x80700700 \quad 0x80700700$$
$$(7 \text{ Rounds})$$
$$0x00000700 \quad 0x80780000$$

Fig. 5. "Propagation" for 20 rounds with specific middle differentials

Following Fact 2.3 and given $2^{64+14-1}$ pairs with the initial difference, we have $2^{77-18.7} = 2^{58.3}$ pairs for the middle 6 rounds.

Then following Fact 2.4 the propagation in the next 7 rounds occurs with probability $2^{-22.2}$ on average over GOST keys. Since this is a permutation, the same propagation can be applied backwards in the preceding 7 rounds. Overall, we expect that $2^{58.3-44.4} = 2^{13.9}$ pairs survive.

Now we are going to show that typically, none of these $2^{13.9}$ pairs P_i, P_j is a member of the set of 2^{15} established beforehand. This can be established as follows: for any of the 2^{15} cases which occur naturally at random, we have a non-zero input differential $(0x80780000, 0x00000700)$. Then a computer simulation shows that a differential of type $(0x80700700, 0x80700700)$ CAN occur at 7 rounds from the beginning (as in Fig. 5 which is 6+7 rounds from the beginning in GOST) but only with probability of $2^{-16.2}$. Similarly it can also occur 7 rounds from the end, but only with probability of $2^{-16.2}$. Overall we expect that only about $2^{15-16.2-16.2} = 2^{-17}$ pairs P_i, P_j on average will have the "propagation" characteristics according to Fig. 5. Therefore the two sets are entirely disjoint with a very high probability.

To summarize, we expect to get always a mix of $2^{15} + 2^{13.9}$ cases, which are unlikely to have an intersection, just subject to the standard deviation for each set. Because we are dealing with a sum of a very large number of almost totally independent events, and exactly in the same way as in [4,5], and due to the Central Limit Theorem these numbers are expected to follow a Gaussian distribution and the standard deviation is expected to be equal exactly to the square root of their expected average number which will be about $2^{15.55}$ for 20 rounds and about $2^{15.0}$ for other permutations.

4 Concentric Distinguishers

We have constructed one very good distinguisher for 20 rounds of GOST. Now the question is as follows. In the similar way as in [5] we want to avoid the necessity to examine all possibilities for the key in the first 6 rounds, and just apply the distinguisher. We want to progressively reduce the key size and the data space on the way, and for this to build a sequence of **concentric distinguishers** for 22, 24 and more rounds which allow early rejection of many cases, so that we are going to examine 20 rounds of GOST with some assumptions on the key and some subset of data much less frequently. This is expected to lead to really efficient attacks on full 32-round of GOST. One very simple example of such attack was already described in [5]. In this paper we are going to study much more complex distinguishers.

4.1   Extending with Additional Weakly Constrained Rounds

We start with our distinguisher property of Fact 3.1. This property is going to be extended with a "weakly constrained" differential propagation which occurs with quite a high probability for 6 more rounds on each side.

We also need a model to account for what is going to happen when our assumptions are wrong. Therefore we are going to compare what happens with GOST split as 6+20+6 rounds to a situation which involves a random permutation (RP) as follows. We look at combination of 6 rounds of GOST, some permutation, and 6 rounds of GOST with the same keys in the backwards direction, as in GOST. This is illustrated in Fig. 6 which accounts for both sort of situations. It can represent the full 32-round GOST with 20 rounds in the middle, and it could also be a situation which we wrongly assumed to be the full 32-round GOST and the middle permutation is not exactly a random permutation however it is not at all what we assumed in our attack and we can expect that it might behave as a random permutation for the properties we study.

This leads to the following property which is the core property in our later attack on full 32-round GOST.

Definition 4.2 (Alpha Property). *We say that a pair of encryptions for the full 32-round GOST (or for a combination of 6 rounds of GOST, some permutation, and 6 rounds of GOST with reversed keys) has the Alpha Property if the following whole configuration of sets of differentials simultaneously holds:*

We note that this property is perfectly symmetric (encryption/decryption).

4.3   Alpha Property: GOST vs. Random Permutation

In a similar way as before, a key problem in our distinguisher is that unhappily the Alpha property can occur also "by accident", not at all for the reasons we expect. This question needs to be formulated more precisely, as this property is about differentials also inside GOST, and therefore we cannot just compare GOST to a random permutation. The right question which we need to ask is as follows: in our composition of 6 rounds of GOST, some permutation and then the same 6 rounds in the decryption mode, can we have a fully consistent situation with all the differences which we have in the property Alpha on the outer 2×6 rounds, similar as in Fig. 6.

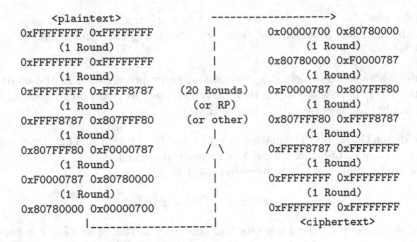

Fig. 6. The Alpha property

We have the following result:

Fact 4.4. *For the full 32-round GOST and on average over the GOST keys, there exists $2^{13.0} + 2^{11.9}$ distinct pairs of plaintexts $P_i \neq P_j$ which have the Alpha property.*

If we replace the inner 20 rounds by a random permutation or with GOST with more rounds, we expect only about $2^{13.0}$ distinct pairs with a standard deviation of $2^{6.5}$.

Justification: We apply Fact 3.1 and obtain $2^{15} + 2^{13.9}$ pairs for the inner 20 rounds with two disjoint sets as explained before. Then it is easy to verify, by a computer simulation, that this provokes the 6 difference sets in the following 6 rounds, simultaneously, with probability as large as $2^{-0.98}$, which is due to slow diffusion in GOST. The same applies in the first 6 rounds. Overall we obtain about $2^{13.9-2.0} \approx 2^{11.9}$ pairs with propagation, and a disjoint set (because subsets of disjoint sets from Fact 3.1) with $2^{15-2.0} \approx 2^{13.0}$ pairs which occur by accident.

Again, because we are dealing with a sum of many almost totally independent events, as in [4,5] and due to the Central Limit Theorem [35], the standard deviation is expected to be exactly the square root of $2^{13.0}$.

5   Guess Then Determine Attacks on GOST

In this section we explain how to compute output bits for a certain round of GOST with incomplete knowledge of all the key bits on which this bit depends in this and previous rounds. We have the following basic fact (cf. [7,12]):

Fact 5.1. *The input on 4 bits of any particular S-box in GOST can be computed as: $a = x + k + c \bmod 16$ where k are the 4 key bits at this S-box, c is a single* *carry bit with $c = 1 \Leftrightarrow x' + k' + c' \geq 16$ where x' and k' are the data and the key at the previous S-box, and c' is the previous carry bit. This is illustrated in Fig. 7 below.*

In our attack we exploit the weakness of carry propagation in the addition modulo 2^{32}. It is possible to see that carry bits such as c can be guessed with a surprisingly high accuracy. We observe that:

1. We define $Wr(i)$ by the equation $Wr(i) - 1 = (i-1) \bmod 8$. This corresponds to the number of S-box within 1..8 with wrap-around.
2. The input of each S-box Si in round $r + 1$ is

$$a = x + k + c \bmod 16$$

and depends on (i) the 4 key bits k at the entry of this Si and (ii) x obtained from the outputs of two S-boxes in round r with numbers $Wr(i - 2)$ and $Wr(i - 3)$ XORred with the appropriate bits after round $r - 2$ (this part does not change in round $r - 1$), and (iii) one carry bit c.
3. The carry bit c is such that

$$c = 1 \Leftrightarrow x' + k' + c' \geq 16$$

where x' and k' are the data and the key at the previous S-box, and c' is the previous carry bit.
4. The previous carry bit influences the result with low probability which will be quantified below.

From here we easily obtain that:

Fact 5.2. *Let $i > 1$ (with S1 there is no carry entering as in Fig. 7.*
We assume that the attacker knows the whole 64-bit output of round $r - 2$, the input of one S-box Si at round $r + 1$, and the key k at the same Si in round $r + 1$, and the state of $Wr(i - 2)$ and $Wr(i - 3)$ in round r.
Let k' be the unknown key at S-box i-1 in round $r + 1$ (cf. Fig. 7).
Then we have the following results:

1. *Let d, e be respectively the most significant bits of k' and x'. The bit d is obtained from 1 lower bit from $Wr(i - 3)$ XORred with the appropriate state from round $r - 2$, which is bit 20 on our example at Fig. 7,*
   If $d = e = 1$, we have $c = 1$ with probability 1 and we can compute a.
   If $d = e = 0$, we have $c = 0$ with probability 1 and we can compute a.
   If $d + e = 1$, we have $c = 0$ or $c = 1$ which are more or less equally likely. Here we get exactly two possibilities for a.
   On average we obtain $2 \times 1/4 \times 1 + 1/2 \times 2 = 1.5 = 2^{0.6}$ possibilities for a.
   These possibilities for a are computed using only 5 bits of the key and the state of only 2 S-boxes in the previous round.

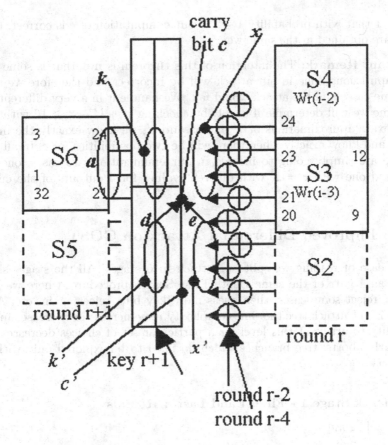

Fig. 7. Computation of the input of one S-box with a carry bit

2. *If the attacker knows the whole 4-bit x' he can compute $k'+x'$ with an interval of incertitude of 8 instead of 16 previously. Thus only with probability 1/4 there will be two answers. Thus on average we obtain $1/4 \times 2 + 3/4 \times 1 = 1.25 = 2^{0.3}$ possibilities for a.*
3. *The same happens if the attacker knows the whole 4-bit k' but not x'.*
4. *If the attacker knows k' AND the whole state of $Wr(i-4)$ in round r, he can compute c correctly with probability of roughly about $1 - 2^{-4}$.*

Justification: The first result is straightforward and we will derive the second result. Each of these probabilities can be established by checking all the possible cases. The top bit b of x' is known due to $Wr(i-3)$, therefore the expected value of x' is about $x' \approx 8*b+4$, and the whole k' is known. It is easy to see that the expected approximation error (computed as average over 8×8 cases) is $|x'-8*b+4| = 1.31$. We decide that $c = 1 \Leftrightarrow 8*b+4+k'+c' \geq 16$. This will be accurate unless $x'+k'+c' < 16$ AND $8*b+4+k'+c' \geq 16$ or the vice versa with the difference between these two numbers being on average 1.31. Each of these 2 cases occurs with probability of very roughly about $1.3/16 \approx 2^{-4}$. Overall we expect that with probability $1 - 2^{-3}$ our computation of c is correct. Other results are obtained in the same way.

Important Remark: The intention of this theorem is **not** that is some cases the computations done in our attack will be incorrect and therefore we might miss some cases and the attack would fail. We handle it in a very different way. Each time we will determine if $c = 1$, by checking $x' + k' + c' \geq 16$ with more or less exact approximations of x' and k' and c', we know exactly the margin of error and know exactly when there will be two possibilities for c. In all these cases we are simply going to include in our enumeration two cases, one with $c = 0$ and one with $c = 1$, with different values for 4 outputs of the current S-box.

6   An Improved Differential Attack on GOST

For the ease of reading we split our attack in 5 stages. All the stages should be seen as a part of the same Depth First Search procedure, where we guess key bits, reject some cases, then guess more key bits, reject again, etc. As we advance in the attack tree the time complexity may increase or decrease, and the probability to arrive at this level for a particular set of choices decreases with many early aborts: tree branches which do need to be explored only with low probability.

6.1   Attack Stage 1 - First 4 and Last 4 Rounds

We proceed as follows:

1. We are given 2^{64} KP which are assumed to be stored in a database.
2. We have the Alpha property cf. Fig. 6 which holds for $2^{13} + 2^{11.9}$ distinct pairs i, j of encryptions for the full 32=6+20+6 rounds, cf. Fact 4.4.
3. First we are going to reduce the total number of pairs from 2^{127} to a lower number, by a birthday-like approach which avoids the enumeration of all possible pairs.
4. Given an assumption on a certain number of key bits, we define as **inactive bit** a bit where P_i and P_j collide (the difference is 0) at a certain bit location inside the cipher, **if** our assumption about the key is correct.
5. Our attack will have many steps in which we are going progressively guess some key bits, then reduce the space of pairs considered due to our differentials, which reduce the number of pairs under attack and make it feasible to guess additional key bits at a later stage.
6. We want to write constraints which describe the following events which occur in the first 3 then 4 and the last 3,4 rounds in our property Alpha, cf. Fig. 8.
   - The output after the addition of the output of S7 and S1 after round 2 gives 8 inactive bits at 0 which are 3–6,11–14. This is implied by the set $0xFFFF8787$ which our Alpha property imposes after round 2.

- The output after the addition of the output of S4,S5,S6,S7 after round 3 gives 15 inactive difference bits at 0 which are 24–31,1–7 (excluding bit 32). This is implied by the set $0x807FFF80$ which occurs after round 3.

7. We consider and try to guess the following key bits: all key bits at rounds 1,2,3 and 20 key bits for S-boxes S12345 in round 4.

8. We observe that for any guess of these $96 + 20 = 116$ key bits, we get 8+15+13=36 cancelations after rounds 1–4 as explained above, and 36 more cancelations on exactly the same S-boxes with the same keys after round 29 going backwards.

   This can be seen as a collision on 36+36=72 bits, computed as a function of type $f_k(P_i)$ where k represents 116 bits of the key and i is one of the 2^{64} KP cases.

9. For each 116 possible guesses for our selected key bits we compute 2^{64} possible strings on 72 bits for each P_i. Only a proportion of one out of 2^8 values on 72 bits are taken. For any given case i the probability that there is another j for which the 72 bits collide is 2^{-8}.

10. Then we can enumerate in time of maybe $4 \cdot 2^{64}$ CPU clocks some $2^{64-8} = 2^{56}$ possible i or j with $2^{56}/2 = 2^{55}$ distinct pairs i, j which collide on these 72 bits.

    Another way of looking at this is as follows: there are (we do NOT ever enumerate all of them) about 2^{127} pairs P_i, P_j and there are about 2^{127} differences $f_k(P_i) - f_k(P_j)$ on 72 bits. Some $2^{127-72} = 2^{55}$ of these differences will have all the 72 bits at 0.

11. These 2^{55} pairs per key assumption can be enumerated efficiently. A simplified method is as follows: We make a hash table where at address being a hash of $f_k(P_i)$ on 72 bits, and we store i as well. Each time the value is already taken we output a collision. We will output a list of 2^{55} pairs P_i, P_j. Memory required is roughly about 2^{70} bytes.

12. The total time spent in these steps of the attack should not exceed 2^{116+64} times the cost of computing roughly speaking 1 round of GOST.

    It is not needed to do as much work as computing 2^{116} times 4 first rounds of GOST and 4 last rounds of GOST. Basically the cost of computing the first 3+ and the last 3+ rounds of GOST can be neglected. More precisely it will be amortized in 2^{20} sub-cases of the 2^{96} cases, in which we just need to evaluate 4 S-boxes in round 3 and 4 S-boxes in round 30, which is roughly feasible to do in most an equivalent of 1 round of GOST.

    Therefore we estimate that we need only about $2^{116+64} \cdot 8$ CPU clocks, which could be seen as an equivalent of roughly about 2^{174} GOST encryptions.

To summarize, we can thus in total overall time equivalent to about 2^{174} GOST encryptions and with memory of about 2^{70} bytes, enumerate $2^{171} = 2^{116+55}$ cases of type k_{116}, i, j. We get on average 2^{55} possible pairs i, j for each key assumption on 116 bits.

In Fig. 9 we summarize all the current and further steps of our attack.

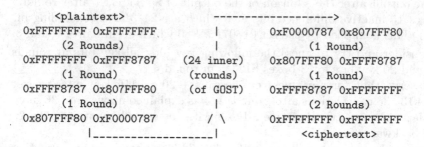

```
    <plaintext>                 ------------------->
OxFFFFFFFF OxFFFFFFFF         |      0xF0000787 0x807FFF80
    (2 Rounds)                |          (1 Round)
OxFFFFFFFF OxFFFF8787     (24 inner)     0x807FFF80 OxFFFF8787
    (1 Round)            (rounds)            (1 Round)
OxFFFF8787 0x807FFF80    (of GOST)     OxFFFF8787 OxFFFFFFFF
    (1 Round)                |             (2 Rounds)
0x807FFF80 0xF0000787       / \      OxFFFFFFFF OxFFFFFFFF
    |_____|              <ciphertext>
```

Fig. 8. First 4 and last 4 rounds in the Alpha property of Fig. 6

guess key at S-boxes	correct	difference	new bits to cancel after outputs of	after round	new inactive bits (60 in total)		enumerate cases	per key	key bits assum.	time GOST encrypt.
								2^{127}		
all bits in R12	2^{-64}	FFFF8787	S7,S1	2,31	8	4-7, 12-15		birthday		
S3*4567R3	2^{-20}	807FFF80	S456³7	3,30	15	24-31,1-7		attack		
S812R3 S12345R4	2^{-32}	F0000787	S2345¹	4,29	13	16-28	2^{55+116}	2^{55}	116	2^{174}
								2^{171}		
S6R4 S78R5	2^{-12}	80780000	S8	5,28	4	8-11	$2^{171+12-4-4}$	2^{47}	128	2^{179}
S7R4 S1R5	2^{-8}	80780000	S1	5,28	4	12-15	$2^{175+8-4-4}$	2^{39}	136	2^{174}
S8R4 S2R5	2^{-8}	80780000	S2	5,28	4	16-19	$2^{175+8-4-4}$	2^{31}	144	2^{174}
								2^{175}		
S3R5 S4¹5R6	2^{-9}	00000700	S5³	6,27	3	29,30,31	$2^{175+9+1.2-3-3}$	$2^{26.2}$	153	2^{176}
S4R5 S6R6	2^{-8}	00000700	S6	6,27	4	32,1-3	$2^{179.2+8-4-4}$	$2^{18.2}$	161	$2^{178.2}$
$2^{18.2}+2^{11.5}$	is	chosen	at	2^{24}		standard	deviations	*2^{-24}	to survive	
except for the	right	161 bits	we	have		to remain	$2^{179.2-24}$	or 2^{-6}	per key only	
S56R5 S781R6 S23R7	2^{-28}	00000700 80000000	S8¹ S3	6,27 7,26	1+ 4	8 20-23	$2^{155.2+28-5-5}$	$2^{8.2*}$	189	2^{175}
$2^{8.2}+2^{10}$	is	chosen	at	2^{59}		standard	deviations	-	certitude	
								total	2^{179}	

Fig. 9. Summary of major steps in our attack on GOST

6.2   Attack Stage 2 - Working on Rounds 5 and 28

Now we are going to work on additional key assumptions with the objective to decrease the number of pairs per key from 2^{55} to a much lower number so that we will be able later at Stage 4 apply the distinguisher given by Fact 4.4.

1. Now we look at the difference $0x80780000$ obtained after round 5, where outputs of S-boxes S8, S1 and S2 are 'newly' inactive which is a cancelation on 12 bits after round 5, cf. earlier Figs. 6 or 10.
   First we will work on S8, then on S1, then on S2.

2. First we guess additional 4+4 key bits. The situation is the same as in Fig. 7 with boxes S78 at round 5 depending mostly on boxes S456 in round 4.

   We guess 4 bits at S-box S6 in round 4, needed only to compute the bit 31 entering S8 at round 5, and the 4 key bits at S8 in round 5, and an approximation on the 4-key bits at S7 in round 5, which together with outputs of S4 and 1 bit from S5 in round 4, can be used to compute the carry entering S-box S8 at round 5 with probability of about $1 - 2^{-4}$ (cf. Fact 5.2).

3. More over and quite importantly we do **not** allow any errors in our computations. In rare cases where there is an ambiguity about the carry, because for example we have 15 and the carry added from S6 in round 5 could matter, we simply check both cases. This leads to a negligible increase in the total number of cases checked from about 2^{171+12} to about $(1+2^{-4})2^{171+12}$, see Fact 5.2.3. For simplicity we ignore these additional numbers which are negligible compared to other numbers in this attack.

   Later during the attack, when the key at $S6$ and early S-boxes becomes known, these additional cases will be eliminated instantly. In fact we can also leave these additional cases, everything we do later in our attack can tolerate a small proportion of additional incorrect cases.

4. With these 12 new key bits, we can enumerate 2^{171+12} cases k_{116+12}, i, j. In each cases with probability 2^{-4} the 4 bits XORed to the output of S-box S8 become inactive at round 4, and with probability 2^{-4} they also become inactive at round 29.

5. Accordingly in time of about 2^{177} computations of 2/32 full GOST, which is about 2^{179} GOST computations, (assuming one takes 2^9 CPU clocks). We reject most cases except $2^{171+12-4-4} = 2^{175}$ cases k_{128}, i, j.

6. This, is 2^{47} cases per key.

7. Now we guess 8 more key bits. These are 4 bits at S-box S7 in round 4 which output 3 is needed to compute the input of S1 in round 5 (there is no carry entering S1). We also guess 4 key bits at S1 in round 5.

8. Now we have an enumeration of 2^{175+8} cases k_{136}, i, j, where we now have 136 key bits. In this list with probability 2^{-4} the 4 bits XORed to the output of S-box S1 become inactive at round 4, and with probability 2^{-4} they also become inactive at round 29.

9. Accordingly in time of about 2^{175+8} computations of 2/32 full GOST, which is about 2^{174} GOST computations, we have an enumeration $2^{175+8-4-4} = 2^{175}$ cases k_{136}, i, j.

10. Now we guess 8 more key bits. These are 4 bits at S-box S8 in round 4 which outputs are 8–11 and which are needed to compute the input of S-box S2 in round 5 (the carry entering S2 is already known for S1 in round 5 above). We also guess 4 key bits at S2 in round 5.

11. Thus we consider the enumeration of 2^{175+8} cases k_{144}, i, j, where we now have 144 key bits. In this list with probability 2^{-4} the 4 bits XORed to the output of S-box S2 become inactive at round 4, and with probability 2^{-4} they also become inactive at round 29.

Accordingly in time of about 2^{175+8} computations of 2/32 full GOST, which is about 2^{174} GOST computations, we enumerate about $2^{175+8-4-4} = 2^{175}$ cases k_{144}, i, j. We are left with 2^{31} pairs i, j on average for each key assumption on 144 bits which will be the cases which we will check in later steps of our attack.

For the right key assumption we will also obtain the $2^{11.9}$ cases which have the property Alpha for the correct GOST key

6.3 Attack Stage 3

We will continue the process of guessing additional key bits and decreasing the number of cases per key assumption.

```
        <plaintext>                 -------------------->
    0xFFFFFFFF 0xFFFFFFFF       |      0x00000700 0x80780000
        (2 Rounds)             |          (2 Rounds)
    0xFFFFFFFF 0xFFFF8787    (20 Rounds)  0xF0000787 0x807FFF80
        (1 Round)             (or RP)        (1 Round)
    0xFFFF8787 0x807FFF80    (or other)   0x807FFF80 0xFFFF8787
        (1 Round)             |            (1 Round)
    0x807FFF80 0xF0000787      / \        0xFFFF8787 0xFFFFFFFF
        (2 Rounds)             |          (2 Rounds)
    0x80780000 0x00000700      |      0xFFFFFFFF 0xFFFFFFFF
        |-------------------|           <ciphertext>
```

Fig. 10. First 6 and last 6 rounds in the Alpha property of Fig. 6

1. At this stage, in each case, we know all key bits in rounds 1,4 and key bits S-boxes S1278 in round 5, for a total of 144 key bits.
2. Now in round 6 we have the difference 0xF0000787 which becomes 0x00000700 , cf. Fig. 10. The S-box outputs which are going to become inactive are: 3 outputs of S5 with numbers 29,30,31, the whole of S6 with numbers 32,1-3, and one lower bit of S8 with number 8.
3. We will first work on S5, then on S6, and later on S8.
4. First we guess 9 key bits: for S3 at round 5, and for S5 at round 6 and just one most significant bit for S4 at round 6. We have 3 inactive bits 29-31. Following Fact 5.2. this allows to determine exactly the carry bit c with probability 1/2, and the attacker knows in which case it is (when $d = e$, cf. Fact 5.2.1.), and otherwise we have two cases to include (when $d \neq e$, cf. Fact 5.2.1.).

   Overall on average we have $(1 + 2)/2 \approx 2^{0.6}$ more cases to check and we compute the output of S5 at round 6 about $2^{175+9+0.6} = 2^{177}$ times.
5. In addition we also need to compute the output of S5 at round 27 in each of these cases. In the same way sometimes this generates 1 or 2 cases to check, and overall we get another factor of $2^{0.6}$.

6. Accordingly in time of about $2^{175+9+0.6+0.6}$ computations of 2/32 full GOST, which is about $2^{176.2}$ GOST computations, we obtain a list of $2^{175+9+1.2-3-3} = 2^{179.2}$ cases k_{153}, i, j. This is $2^{26.2}$ cases per key.

7. Then we guess 8 more key bits: for S4 at round 5, and for S6 at round 6. We have 4 inactive bits 32,1–3.

8. Accordingly in time of about $2^{179.2+8}$ computations of 2/32 full GOST, which is about $2^{178.2}$ GOST computations, we obtain a list of $2^{179.2+8-4-4} = 2^{179.2}$ cases k_{161}, i, j.

9. This is only $2^{18.2}$ cases per key on 161 bits which is within reach of our distinguisher attacks.

10. The total time spent in all the above steps is about $2^{178.5}$ GOST computations, and probably only half of this number on average is needed.

6.4   Attack Stage 4

Now we are going to be able to see if 161 key bits are right or wrong.

We recall Fact 4.4. For the full 32-round GOST and on average over the GOST keys, there exists two disjoint sets with $2^{13} + 2^{11.9}$ distinct pairs of plaintexts $\Gamma_i \neq \Gamma_j$ which have the Alpha property.

We have $2^{18.2}$ cases per key, which for the right key on 161 bits contains these correct $2^{13} + 2^{11.9}$ cases. All these cases come from the fact that we have independently in the first 6 and the last 6 rounds, checked if certain set of twice 55 differences are at 0, which gives 2^{17} pairs surviving. We have also produced an overhead of some $2^{1.2}$ additional cases which result from incertitude due to further unknown key bits which gives $2^{18.2}$ pairs total.

As before, It is clear that these $2^{18.2}$ pairs obtained in the specific case of the right 161-bit key, occur at random due to the random intersection between cases which may occur at the beginning of GOST, and at the end of GOST, without correlation between these events.

It is easy to see that $2^{18.2}$ such pairs on average, with an expected standard deviation of about $2^{9.1}$, are still going to occur if we explicitly exclude about $2^{64+14-1} \ll 2^{127}$ cases where a difference of type $(0x80700700, 0x80700700)$ occurs after 6+7 rounds AND at 6+7 rounds from the end, which as explained for Fact 3.1 occurs with very low probability of about $2^{-32.4}$ and in fact less, because in our case it is not yet certain that the difference is as expected after round 7.

However because the $2^{11.9}$ cases do ALL have differences of type $(0x80700700, 0x80700700)$ after 6+7 rounds AND at 6+7 rounds from the end, the two sets are disjoint. To summarize we obtain the following result:

Fact 6.5. *After Stage 3 of our attack, if the 161 bits are wrong, most of the time (this will be quantified below) we get about $2^{18.2}$ cases per key.*

We assume that the attacker will decide that the key on 161 bits is correct if he sees at least $2^{18.2} + 2^{11.5}$ cases for this key. Otherwise he will reject it.

The correct 161-bits key will be accepted with probability of 95 %.

Incorrect 161 bits will be accepted with probability of about 2^{-39}.

Justification: A correct 161 bits should give about $2^{18.2} + 2^{11.9}$ cases with standard deviation of $2^{9.1}$ and will be rejected only if we are below $2^{18.2} + 2^{11.5}$ cases which is on one side of and outside of $(2^{11.9-11.5})/2^{9.1} = 2$ standard deviations. By applying the Gauss error function [35] we see that a correct key will be accepted with probability of about 95 %.

If the 161 bits are wrong, we are outside of and on one side of, $2^{11.5-9.1} = 2^{2.4}$ standard deviations. Here the Gauss error function [35] gives a probability only about 2^{-24}.

6.6   Attack Stage 5

We need to do some additional guessing and filtering. Up till now, with total time of up to about $2^{178.5}$ GOST computations, we are able to enumerate $2^{179.2-24} = 2^{155.2}$ cases k_{161}, i, j. Our 161 bits of the key are all the bits for the first 4 rounds, and 24 bits at round 5 for S781234, and 9 bits at round 6 for S5,S6 and one bit at S4.

1. We guess the remaining 8 bits to complete round 5 with boxes S56. Then we guess the key at boxes S7181 at round 6 and at S213 in round 7. This is a total of 28 bits. For simplicity we guess all these bits (a more refined approach is NOT needed because the total time spent in this step is small).
2. The output after S8 in round 6 needs to cancel on 1 bit which is number 8, and the output of S3 in round 7 needs to cancel on 4 bits which are 20-23. This is implied by the sets 0x00000700 and 0x80000000 in the Alpha property obtained after round 6 and 7.
3. Accordingly in time of about $2^{155.2+28}$ computations of 2/32 full GOST, which is about 2^{175} GOST computations, we reject most cases except some $2^{155.2+28-5-5} = 2^{173.2}$ cases k_{189}, i, j.

   This seems to be about 2^{-16} per key on average, which comes from the fact that only some 161-bit sub-keys are present in the keys on 189 bits. However if we look only at 2^{165} keys on 189 bits which are actually present, we have $2^{8.2}$ cases per key.
4. We assume that the attacker will reject all cases where the count is less than $2^{8.2} + 2^{10}$.
5. Then it is easy to see that if the key is correct, it will be accepted with probability very close to 1.
6. If the key is wrong, we observe that $2^{8.2} + 2^{10}$ is outside $2^{5.9}$ standard deviations. Here the Gauss error function [35] gives a figure much smaller than 2^{-256}.

Summary: Thus given 2^{64} KP and in an average time of about 2^{179} GOST computations, we are able to determine with certitude 189 bits of GOST key. The remaining 66 bits can then be found by brute force. The attack was designed to work for 95 % of GOST keys.

Applicability: Current attack was optimized for just one set of GOST S-boxes. The space of possible variants ot this attack is very large It is very much premature to claim [32] that it would not work for a certain well-designed set of S-boxes

[31,32]. On the contrary. Similar results exist for any set of S-boxes [8,13,29]. We conjecture that for any set of bijective S-boxes in GOST (the worst case) there is a differential attack substantially faster than brute force and very similar to the one presented in this paper.

7 Conclusion

GOST 28147-89 is a well-known block cipher and a Russian government standard. In his 1994 book [34] Schneier has written that "against differential and linear cryptanalysis, GOST is probably stronger than DES". In 2000 Russian researchers claimed that as few as 7 rounds out of 32 are sufficient to protect GOST against differential cryptanalysis, see [20,21]. In the same year Japanese researchers [33] show that more powerful differential attacks exist, exploiting sets of differentials [33] which allow to break about 13 rounds of GOST out of 32. Many new attacks on GOST have been proposed since 2011 [3–6,11,12,16,17,19,23] including new combined attacks which also exploit multiple differentials. In 2011 Courtois and Misztal have found new differential sets for GOST [6] most of which can also be seen as "truncated" differential attacks [27]. If one exploits the key scheduling one can break full GOST faster than brute force [4]. This attack was further improved in [5] to achieve about 2^{224}. In a recent paper about advanced differential cryptanalysis, we read: *Truncated differentials, [...] in some cases allow to push differential attacks one or two rounds further.* In this paper we gain not 1 or 2 but much closer to 20 rounds, compared to previous more basic differential attacks [20,21,33].

The main result of this paper is a multi-stage advanced differential attack on full 32-round GOST. Given 2^{64} KP we can recover the full 256-bit key for GOST within only about 2^{179} GOST computations on average for a success probability of 95 %. The memory is about 2^{70} bytes. This is the fastest **single-key** attack on GOST found so far. The best previous single-key attack on GOST was 2^{192} of [19] which could be improved to 2^{191} in [16]. Our 2^{179} is an inexact result assuming independence of certain events. At this moment the attack was optimized only for one set of S-boxes.

In practice ciphers are NOT used with single keys. Faster and more realistic attacks exist when we are dealing with **multiple keys generated at random**, cf. [11,16,17,24]. Numerous such attacks use very similar truncated differential properties as in this paper or more advanced properties with 3 or 4 points cf. [16,17]. Many such attacks also require only 2^{32} of data per key instead of 2^{64} in this paper, cf. [16,17]. One such attack allows to recover a full GOST key at a total cost as low as 2^{101} GOST computations total, cf. [16,17].

References

1. Albrecht, M., Leander, G.: An All-In-One Approach to Differential Cryptanalysis for Small Block Ciphers. eprint.iacr.org/2012/401/
2. Biham, E., Shamir, A.: Differential cryptanalysis of the full 16-round DES. In: Brickell, E.F. (ed.) CRYPTO 1992. LNCS, vol. 740, pp. 487–496. Springer, Heidelberg (1993)
3. Courtois, N.: Security evaluation of GOST 28147–89 in view of international standardisation. Cryptologia **36**(1), 2–13 (2012)
4. Courtois, N.T., Misztal, M.: First differential attack on full 32-round GOST. In: Qing, S., Susilo, W., Wang, G., Liu, D. (eds.) ICICS 2011. LNCS, vol. 7043, pp. 216–227. Springer, Heidelberg (2011)
5. Courtois, N., Misztal, M.: Differential Cryptanalysis of GOST, 14 June 2011. http://eprint.iacr.org/2011/312
6. Courtois, N., Misztal, M.: Aggregated differentials and cryptanalysis of PP-1 and GOST. Periodica Mathematica Hungarica **65**(2), 177–192 (2012). CECC 2011, 11th Central European Conference on Cryptology
7. Courtois, N.: An Improved Differential Attack on Full GOST, March 2012. http://eprint.iacr.org/2012/138. Accessed 17 December 2015
8. Courtois, N.T., Mourouzis, T., Misztal, M., Quisquater, J.-J., Song, G.: Can GOST be made secure against differential cryptanalysis? Cryptologia **39**(2), 145–156 (2015)
9. Courtois, N.: Cryptanalysis of two GOST variants with 128-bit keys. Cryptologia **38**(4), 348–361 (2014). http://www.tandfonline.com/doi/full/10.1080/01611194.2014.915706
10. Courtois, N., Gawinecki, J.A., Song, G.: Contradiction immunity and guess-then-determine attacks on GOST. Tatra Mountains Math. Publ. **53**(3), 65–79 (2012)
11. Courtois, N.T.: Cryptanalysis of GOST in the multiple key scenario. Tatra Mountains Mathematical Publications **57**(4), 45–63 (2013). Post-proceedings of CECC 2013. http://www.sav.sk/journals/uploads/0124133006Courto.pdf
12. Courtois, N.T.: Low-complexity key recovery attacks on GOST block cipher. Cryptologia **37**(1), 1–10 (2013)
13. Courtois, N.T., Mourouzis, T.: Enhanced truncated differential cryptanalysis of GOST. In: SECRYPT 2013, Reykjavik, July 2013 (2013). http://www.nicolascourtois.com/papers/sec13.pdf
14. Courtois, N.T., Mourouzis, T.: Propagation of truncated differentials in GOST. In: Proceedings of SECURWARE 2013 (2013). http://www.thinkmind.org/download.php?articleid=securware_2013_7_20_30119
15. Courtois, N., Mourouzis, T., Grocholewska-Czurylo, A., Quisquater, J.-J.: On optimal size in truncated differential attacks. In: Post-proceeding of CECC 2014 Conference. Stud. Scient. Math, Hungarica (2015)
16. Courtois, N.: Algebraic Complexity Reduction and Cryptanalysis of GOST, Preprint, 2010–2014. http://eprint.iacr.org/2011/626
17. Courtois, N.: On multiple symmetric fixed points in GOST. Cryptologia **39**(4), 322–334 (2015). http://www.tandfonline.com/doi/full/10.1080/01611194.2014.988362
18. Coppersmith, D.: The development of DES, Invited Talk, Crypto'2000, vol. 8 (2000)
19. Dinur, I., Dunkelman, O., Shamir, A.: Improved attacks on full GOST. In: Canteaut, A. (ed.) FSE 2012. LNCS, vol. 7549, pp. 9–28. Springer, Heidelberg (2012)

20. Shorin, V.V., Jelezniakov, V.V., Gabidulin, E.M.: Linear and Differential Cryptanalysis of Russian GOST, submitted Elsevier preprint, 4 April 2001
21. Shorin, V.V., Jelezniakov, V.V., Gabidulin, E.M.: Security of algorithm GOST 28147–89 (in Russian). In: Abstracts XLIII MIPT Science Conference, 8–9 December 2000 (2000)
22. Zabotin, I.A., Glazkov, G.P., Isaeva, V.B.: Cryptographic Protection for Information Processing Systems. Government Standard of the USSR, GOST 28147–89, Government Committee of the USSR for Standards (1989)
23. Isobe, T.: A single-key attack on the full GOST block cipher. In: Joux, A. (ed.) FSE 2011. LNCS, vol. 6733, pp. 290–305. Springer, Heidelberg (2011)
24. Kara, O., Karakoç, F.: Fixed points of special type and cryptanalysis of full GOST. In: Pieprzyk, J., Sadeghi, A.-R., Manulis, M. (eds.) CANS 2012. LNCS, vol. 7712, pp. 86–97. Springer, Heidelberg (2012)
25. Kovalchuk, L.V.: Generalized Markov ciphers: evaluation of practical security against differential cryptanalysis. In: Proceedings of the 5th All-Russian Science Conference "Mathematics and Safety of Information Technologies" (MaBIT 2006), MGU, Moscow, 25–27 October 2006, pp. 595–599 (2006). (in Russian)
26. Alekseychuk, A.N., Kovalchuk, L.V.: Towards a Theory of Security Evaluation for GOST-like Ciphers against Differential and Linear Cryptanalysis. Preprint 9 September 2011. http://eprint.iacr.org/2011/489
27. Knudsen, L.R.: Truncated and higher order differentials. In: Preneel, B. (ed.) FSE 1994. LNCS, vol. 1008, pp. 196–211. Springer, Heidelberg (1995)
28. Leander, G., Poschmann, A.: On the classification of 4 bit S-boxes. In: Carlet, C., Sunar, B. (eds.) WAIFI 2007. LNCS, vol. 4547, pp. 159–176. Springer, Heidelberg (2007)
29. Mourozis, T.: Optimizations in Algebraic and Differential Cryptanalysis, Ph.D. thesis, under superivsion of Dr. Nicolas T. Courtois, University College London, January 2015. http://discovery.ucl.ac.uk/1462141/2/PhD_Thesis_Theodosis_Mourouzis.pdf
30. Poschmann, A., Ling, S., Wang, H.: 256 Bit standardized crypto for 650 GE – GOST revisited. In: Mangard, S., Standaert, F.-X. (eds.) CHES 2010. LNCS, vol. 6225, pp. 219–233. Springer, Heidelberg (2010)
31. Rudskoy, V., Chmora, A.: Working draft for ISO/IEC 1st WD of Amd1/18033-3: Russian Block Cipher GOST, ISO/IEC JTC 1/SC 27 N9423, MD5=feb236fe6d3a79a02ad666edfe7039aa, 14 January 2011
32. Rudskoy, V., Dmukh, A.: Algebraic and differential cryptanalysis of GOST: fact or fiction. In: CTCryppt 2012, Workshop on Current Trends in Cryptology, Nizhny Novgorod, 2 July 2012 (2012). An extended abstract is available at: https://www.tc26.ru/invite/spisokdoc/CTCrypt_rudskoy.pdf slides are available at: https://www.tc26.ru/documentaryslides/CTCrypt_rudskoy_slides_final.pdf
33. Seki, H., Kaneko, T.: Differential cryptanalysis of reduced rounds of GOST. In: Stinson, D.R., Tavares, S. (eds.) SAC 2000. LNCS, vol. 2012, pp. 315–323. Springer, Heidelberg (2001)
34. Schneier, B.: Section 14.1 GOST, in Applied Cryptography, 2nd edition. John Wiley and Sons (1996). ISBN 0-471-11709-9
35. Standard Deviation - wikipedia article, 13 June 2011. http://en.wikipedia.org/wiki/Standard_deviation

Cryptographic Hash Functions
and Expander Graphs: The End of the Story?

Christophe Petit[1,2] and Jean-Jacques Quisquater[1,2(✉)]

[1] Information Security Group, University College London, London, UK
christophe.petit@ucl.ac.uk
[2] Crypto Group, Université Catholique de Louvain, Louvain-la-Neuve, Belgium
jjq@uclouvain.be

Abstract. Cayley hash functions are a family of cryptographic hash functions constructed from the Cayley graphs of non-Abelian finite groups. Their security relies on the hardness of mathematical problems related to long-standing conjectures in graph and group theory. We recall the Cayley hash design and known results on the underlying problems. We then describe related open problems, including the cryptanalysis of relevant parameters as well as new applications to cryptography and outside, assuming either that the problem is "hard" or easy.

1 Cryptographic Hash Functions from Expander Graphs

Cryptology is the science and art of guaranteeing secure communications in the presence of adversaries. To design and analyze complex protocols, cryptographers combine simpler cryptographic primitives such as encryption schemes, digital signatures, block ciphers and hash functions. These elementary primitives may themselves be constructed from notoriously "hard" number-theoretic mathematical problems like the integer factorization and the discrete logarithm problems. A cryptographer's security "proof" will typically show that the protocol cannot be broken without solving one of these upposedly "hard" problems. The actual "hardness" of the problems can then be investigated separately by mathematicians and cryptanalysts.

1.1 Cryptographic Hash Functions

Hash functions are a very important primitive in many cryptographic protocols, including message authentication codes, digital signatures, password storage applications or pseudorandom number generation. A cryptographic hash function $H : \{0,1\}^* \rightarrow \{0,1\}^n$ takes arbitrary-length *message* inputs and it returns short, fixed-length *hash values*. A hash function is usually required to at least satisfy the following three properties:

- **Collision resistance:** it must be hard to compute $m, m' \in \{0,1\}^*$, $m' \neq m$, such that $H(m) = H(m')$.

© Springer-Verlag Berlin Heidelberg 2016
P.Y.A. Ryan et al. (Eds.): Kahn Festschrift, LNCS 9100, pp. 304–311, 2016.
DOI: 10.1007/978-3-662-49301-4_19

- **Second preimage resistance:** given $m \in \{0,1\}^*$, it must be hard to compute $m' \in \{0,1\}^*$, $m' \neq m$, such that $H(m) = H(m')$.
- **Preimage resistance:** given $h \in \{0,1\}^n$, it must be hard to compute $m \in \{0,1\}^*$ such that $h = H(m)$.

Hash funtions may also be required to satisfy much stronger security properties such as "behaving like a random function". To satisfy these properties, classical hash functions like MD5 or SHA follow a heuristic design consisting in cutting the messages into smaller pieces, mixing the pieces together with some non-linear transformations, and then iterating the whole process until the output is "random enough". In particular, the security of these hash functions must be studied independently of any "neat" mathematical problem. Collision-resistant hash functions can also be built from the integer factorization or the discrete logarithm problems [8,12], but the resulting constructions are by far too inefficient in practice.

1.2   Cayley Hash Functions

Let G be a finite (non Abelian) group, and let $S = \{g_0, g_1, \ldots, g_{k-1}\}$ be a generator set for this group. The *Cayley graph* associated to (G, S) is the directed graph (V, E) such that any vertex $v \in V$ corresponds to one group element and there is an edge from v_1 to v_2 if and only if $v_2 = v_1 g$ for some $g \in S$. The *Cayley hash function* associated to (G, S) is defined as follows: the message m is first mapped onto $m_1 m_2 \ldots m_N \in \{0, \ldots, k-1\}^*$ according to some deterministic procedure, then the group element

$$h := \prod_{i=1}^{N} g_{m_i}$$

is computed, and h is finally mapped onto some bitstring. We remark that computing this product step by step corresponds to making a walk in the corresponding Cayley graph. The initial and final mapping have usually no impact on security, so we simply ignore them in the remaining of this paper. In particular, we slightly change the definition of a hash function such that it can take messages from $\{0, \ldots, k-1\}^*$ and return a hash value in G.

The first hash function following this design was proposed by Zémor in 1991 [37]. His choice of parameters was quickly invalidated by Tillich and himself [34], so they suggested new parameters with the group $SL(2, \mathbb{F}_{2^n})$. The design was rediscovered ten years later by Charles, Goren and Lauter [7], this time with parameters taken from Lubotzky-Philips-Sarnak's Ramanujan graphs [22]. We point out that all the parameters used in these particular instances were very "special": the first two sets of parameters were chosen for efficiency reasons, and the last one to ensure that the hash values were distributed as uniformly as possible.

Cayley hash functions have a number of interesting properties compared to other hash functions. Their computation can be easily parallelized for a better efficiency, and even the non-parallelized version is competitive with classical hash functions for some parameters [9]. The near-uniformity of the output distribution can be linked with the *expansion* properties of the corresponding Cayley graphs [7,16]. Last but not least, the main security properties of Cayley hash functions trivially rely on some "neat" mathematical problems.

1.3 Rubik's for Cryptographers

For any G and S as before, we define the three following problems:

- **Balance problem:** find $m_i, m_i' \in \{0, \ldots, k-1\}$ such that $\prod_{i=1}^{\ell} g_{m_i} = \prod_{i=1}^{\ell'} g_{m_i'}$ and ℓ, ℓ' "small".
- **Representation problem:** find $m_i \in \{0, \ldots, k-1\}$, such that $\prod_{i=1}^{\ell} g_{m_i} = 1$ and ℓ "small".
- **Factorization problem:** given an element $h \in G$, find $m_i \in \{0, \ldots, k-1\}$ such that $\prod_{i=1}^{\ell} g_{m_i} = h$ and ℓ "small".

Clearly, the collision resistance of a Cayley hash function is equivalent to the hardness of the corresponding balance problem; its preimage resistance is equivalent to the hardness of the factorization problem; and the function cannot be second preimage resistant if the representation problem is not hard. Among the three problems, the factorization problem is the hardest one. The balance problem can be trivially solved if some generators in S commute, hence the restriction to non-Abelian groups. Interestingly, the factorization problem in non-Abelian groups can also be seen as a generalization of the well-known Rubik's cube [28].

Although not classical in cryptography, the above problems are related to long-standing open problems in graph and group theory. In particular in the late eighties, Babai conjectured that there exists a constant $c > 0$ such that the diameter of any Cayley graph of any finite simple non-Abelian group G is bounded by $\log^c |G|$ [2,15]. For an appropriate definition of "small", the factorization problem essentially requires a *constructive* proof of Babai's conjecture. Replacing "small" by "minimal", it becomes equivalent to the NP-hard well-known *word problem* [11,17].

1.4 Cryptanalysis Results

Babai's conjecture has recently attracted a lot of attention after a breakthrough result of Helfgott for the group $SL(2, p)$ (p prime) [15]. It is now proved for any generator set of any group of Lie type with a bounded rank [6,29]. For permutation groups, a slightly weaker quasipolynomial bound on the diameter has been recently obtained for all generator sets [14]. Most of these results are combinatoric and non constructive in nature. Constructive proofs are known for *almost all* generator sets of permutation groups [3], so these groups should be avoided in the Cayley hash construction. When the group order is particularly smooth, the factorization problem can often be solved with subgroup attacks [10,

28, 32] so groups that possess a rich subgroup structure should also be avoided in teh construction.

In all other groups, the factorization problem can only be solved efficiently for a few generator sets, particularly chosen to make it easier [1,4,18,19,21,30]. On the other hand, all the particular parameters suggested for Cayley hash functions have now been broken [13,25,27,33,35]. We stress, however, that all these parameters were very "special": in all cases the parameters were either very "small" to optimize the efficiency [33,37], or very "symmetric" to optimize the output distribution of the function [7,26]. The cryptanalysis attacks exploited these particularities and are currently defeated with slight modifications of the generators.

2 The End of the Story ?

At first sight, the cryptanalysis of the four Cayley hash instances may cast some doubts on the design, but these doubts are unjustified or at least premature. After all, even well-established cryptographic schemes such as RSA can be easily broken for some "small" parameters [36]. In fact, the actual hardness of the factorization problem in non-Abelian groups is still a widely open problem today, despite many years of research by both the mathematics and cryptography communities. Any progress in that direction would lead to interesting constructive or destructive applications in cryptography, as well as other applications outside cryptography.

2.1 Open Problem: Finding Good Parameters for the Cayley Hash Construction

Cryptographic hash functions should be both secure and efficient to compute. The parameters chosen by Zémor [37] and Tillich and Zémor [34] led to a computation cost of only a few field additions per message bit, but these parameters turned out to be insecure. On the other hand, generic generator sets in the same groups seem secure today, but require a few field multiplications per message bits, which is by far less efficient. Slight modifications of previously broken functions have been proposed in [25,28,33] to counter existing attacks. Their actual security is still an open problem today.

2.2 Open Problem: Break All Relevant Parameters

More generally, the security of Cayley hash functions is still a widely open problem for most groups and generator sets.

Due to the particularly efficient arithmetic over binary fields, it is interesting to start with the group $SL(2, 2^n)$ used in the Tillich-Zémor hash function. The study of the factorization problem for generic generator sets has been initiated in [24]. In that paper it is shown through various heuristic reductions that it is enough to focus on generator sets with two matrices $A, B \in SL(2, 2^n)$ such that

– $A := \begin{pmatrix} \lambda & 0 \\ 0 & \lambda^{-1} \end{pmatrix}$ is diagonal and $B := \begin{pmatrix} w+1 & w \\ w & w+1 \end{pmatrix}$ is orthogonal, for $\lambda \in \mathbb{F}_{2^n}^*$ and $w \in \mathbb{F}_{2^n}$.
– $A := \begin{pmatrix} t_A & 1 \\ 1 & 0 \end{pmatrix}$ and $B := \begin{pmatrix} t_B & 1 \\ 1 & 0 \end{pmatrix}$ where $t_A, t_B \in \mathbb{F}_{2^n}$.

Indeed, any algorithm solving the factorization problem in $SL(2, 2^n)$ for a significant subset of these parameters would also lead to a heuristic algorithm solving the factorization problem for any generator set of $SL(2, 2^n)$. Note that we obtain parameters equivalent to the (already broken) Tillich-Zémor parameters if $t_A = t_B + 1$, but the security of the above parameters is still an open problem in general [24, 28].

After the factorization problem is solved for $SL(2, 2^n)$, the next most interesting groups for the construction (and the cryptanalysis) will be other special linear groups over finite fields $SL(m, K)$. The group $SL(2, K)$ is naturally embedded into $SL(m, K)$. Independently of the work on $SL(2, 2^n)$, it will be interesting to relate the security of $SL(m, K)$ to the security of $SL(2, K)$. Such a reduction is another interesting open problem.

2.3 Open Problem: (Constructive) Proof of Babai's Conjecture

Solving the factorization problem may appear harder than proving Babai's conjecture at first sight since non constructive proofs are useless for the cryptanalysis. However, a Cayley hash function will already be considered as broken with a heuristic attack working with a "good enough" probability, whereas a proof of Babai's conjecture shall eliminate all heuristic assumptions and be valid for all parameters. Proving Babai's conjecture in all generality is of course a big open problem. Replacing or adapting known partial non-constructive proofs is another interesting open problem.

2.4 Open Problem: Further Cryptographic Applications

As discussed in the introduction, many cryptographic protocols ultimately rely on the actual hardness of some mathematical problems. The factorization problem in non-Abelian groups may very well be "hard enough" for cryptography when using generic parameters. In that case, it would be interesting to look for further cryptographic applications of the problem.

Abelian finite groups are ubiquituous in cryptography, but non-Abelian groups have not had the same success, in particular for public key cryptography [31]. While some computational problems in non-Abelian groups are seemingy hard in general, embedding a trapdoor (necessary for public key cryptography) has always required to specialize these problems to new, much weaker instances. It is an interesting open problem today to build a secure public key encryption scheme from the factorization problem in a non-Abelian group, or more generally from any computational problem in a non-Abelian group.

2.5 Open Problem: New Applications of Factorization Algorithms in Non-Abelian Groups

While the factorization problem in non-Abelian groups has interesting cryptographic applications when it is "hard", easy instances might also find interesting applications outside cryptography. Cayley graphs tend to be good *expanders graphs* [5,20], and expander graphs have a tremendous number of applications in building optimal networks, error correcting codes or derandomized algorithms, as well as in number theory and group theory [16,23]. We now have good algorithms solving the factorization problem for some particular instances. It will be interesting to find new applications of these algorithms, in particular to improve some of the various applications of expander graphs.

3 Conclusion

The appealing properties of Cayley hash functions justify an extensive study of their security. Although particular instances were broken in the past, the generic underlying problems can still be considered as potential cryptographic "hard" problems, in particular due to their connection to an old-standing conjecture of Babai. We described several open problems related to the cryptanalysis of these functions and to new applications of the underlying problems.

Acknowledgements. Part of this work was done while Christophe Petit was visiting the Computer Science Department at University College London and the Number Theory Group at the University of Oxford, under an FRS-FNRS Research Collaborator grant at Universit catholique de Louvain. He is grateful to Jens Groth (UCL) and Alan Lauder (Oxford) for the fruitful work he could do there. The research leading to these results has also received funding from the European Research Council under the European Union's Seventh Framework Programme (FP/2007-2013) / ERC Grant Agreement n. 307937 and the Engineering and Physical Sciences Research Council grant EP/J009520/1.

References

1. Babai, L., Kantor, W.M., Lubotzky, A.: Small-diameter Cayley graphs for finite simple groups. European J. Combin. **10**, 507–552 (1989)
2. Babai, L., Seress, Á.: On the diameter of permutation groups. European J. Combin. **13**(4), 231–243 (1992)
3. Babai, L., Hayes, T.P.: Near-independence of permutations and an almost sure polynomial bound on the diameter of the symmetric group. In: SODA, pp. 1057–1066. SIAM (2005)
4. Babai, L., Hetyei, G., Kantor, W.M., Lubotzky, A., Seress, Á.: On the diameter of finite groups. In: FOCS, vol. II, pp. 857–865. IEEE (1990)
5. Bourgain, J., Gamburd, A.: Uniform expansion bounds for cayley graphs of $sl_2(\mathbb{F}_p)$. Ann. Math. **167**(2), 625–642 (2008)
6. Breuillard, E., Green, B., Tao, T.,Approximate subgroups of linear groups. arXiv: 1005.1881v1, May 2010

7. Charles, D.X., Lauter, K.E., Goren, E.Z.: Cryptographic hash functions from expander graphs. J. Cryptology **22**(1), 93–113 (2009)
8. Damgård, I.B.: Collision free hash functions and public key signature schemes. In: Price, W.L., Chaum, D. (eds.) EUROCRYPT 1987. LNCS, vol. 304, pp. 203–216. Springer, Heidelberg (1988)
9. de Meulenaer, G., Petit, C., Quisquater, J.-J.: Hardware implementations of a variant of the Zmor-Tillich hash function: can a provably secure hash function be very efficient ? Cryptology ePrint Archive, Report /229 (2009). http://eprint.iacr.org/
10. Dinai, O.: Poly-log diameter bounds for some families of finite groups. Proc. Amer. Math. Soc. **134**, 3137–3142 (2006)
11. Even, S., Goldreich, O.: The minimum-length generator sequence problem is NP-hard. J. Algorithms **2**(3), 311–313 (1981)
12. Goldwasser, S., Micali, S., Rivest, R.L.: A "paradoxical" solution to the signature problem (extended abstract). In: FOCS, pp. 441–448. IEEE (1984)
13. Grassl, M., Ilic, I., Magliveras, S.S., Steinwandt, R.: Cryptanalysis of the Tillich-Zémor hash function. J. Cryptology **24**(1), 148–156 (2011)
14. Helfgott, H., Seress, A.: On the diameter of permutation groups (2011). http://arxiv.org/abs/1109.3550
15. Helfgott, H.A.: Growth, generation in $SL_2(Z, pZ)$. Ann. Math. **167**(2), 601–623 (2008)
16. Hoory, S., Linial, N., Wigderson, A.: Expander graphs and their applications. Bull. Amer. Math. Soc. **43**, 439–561 (2006)
17. Jerrum, M.R.: The complexity of finding minimum-length generator sequences. Theor. Comput. Sci. **36**(2–3), 265–289 (1985)
18. Kantor, W.M.: Some large trivalent graphs having small diameters. Discrete Appl. Math. **37**(38), 353–357 (1992)
19. Kassabov, M., Riley, T.R.: Diameters of Cayley graphs of Chevalley groups. Eur. J. Comb. **28**(3), 791–800 (2007)
20. Landau, Z., Russell, A.: Random cayley graphs are expanders: a simple proof of the alon-roichman theorem. Electr. J. Comb. **11**(1) (2004)
21. Larsen, M.: Navigating the Cayley graph of $SL_2(\mathbb{F}_p)$. Int. Math. Res. Not. IMRN **27**, 1465–1471 (2003)
22. Lubotzky, A., Phillips, R., Sarnak, P.: Ramanujan graphs. Combinatorica **8**, 261–277 (1988)
23. Lubotzky, A.: Expander graphs in pure and applied mathematics. Bull. Amer. Math. Soc. **49**, 113–162 (2012)
24. Petit, C.: Towards factoring in $SL(2, \mathbb{F}_{2^n})$. Design, Codes and Cryptography, September 2012. doi:10.1007/s10623-012-9743-x
25. Petit, C., Lauter, K., Quisquater, J.-J.: Full cryptanalysis of LPS and Morgenstern hash functions. In: Ostrovsky, R., De Prisco, R., Visconti, I. (eds.) SCN 2008. LNCS, vol. 5229, pp. 263–277. Springer, Heidelberg (2008)
26. Petit, C., Lauter, K.E., Quisquater, J.-J.: Cayley hashes: a class of efficient graph-based hash functions (2007). http://perso.uclouvain.be/christophe.petit/index.html
27. Petit, C., Quisquater, J.-J.: Preimages for the Tillich-Zémor hash function. In: Biryukov, A., Gong, G., Stinson, D.R. (eds.) SAC 2010. LNCS, vol. 6544, pp. 282–301. Springer, Heidelberg (2011)
28. Petit, C., Quisquater, J.-J.: Rubik's for cryptographers. Not. Am. Math. Soc. **60**, 733–739 (2013)

29. Pyber, L., Szab, E.: Growth in finite simple groups of Lie type. arXiv: 1001.4556v1, January 2010
30. Riley, T.R.: Navigating in the Cayley graphs of $SL_N(\mathbb{Z})$ and $SL_N(\mathbb{F}_p)$. Geom. Dedicata **113**(1), 215–229 (2005)
31. Mullan, C., Blackburn, S.R., Cid, C.: Group theory in cryptography (2010). http://arxiv.org/abs/0906.5545
32. Steinwandt, R., Grassl, M., Geiselmann, W., Beth, T.: Weaknesses in the $SL_2(\mathbb{F}_{2^n})$ hashing scheme. In: Bellare, M. (ed.) CRYPTO 2000. LNCS, vol. 1880, pp. 287–299. Springer, Heidelberg (2000)
33. Tillich, J.-P., Zémor, G.: Group-theoretic hash functions. In: Cohen, G., Lobstein, A., Zémor, G., Litsyn, S.N. (eds.) Algebraic Coding 1993. LNCS, vol. 781, pp. 90–110. Springer, London (1994)
34. Tillich, J.-P., Zémor, G.: Hashing with SL_2. In: Desmedt, Y.G. (ed.) CRYPTO 1994. LNCS, vol. 839, pp. 40–49. Springer, Heidelberg (1994)
35. Tillich, J.-P., Zémor, G.: Collisions for the LPS expander graph hash function. In: Smart, N.P. (ed.) EUROCRYPT 2008. LNCS, vol. 4965, pp. 254–269. Springer, Heidelberg (2008)
36. Wiener, M.J.: Cryptanalysis of short RSA secret exponents. IEEE Trans. Inf. Theory **36**(3), 553–558 (1990)
37. Zémor, G.: Hash functions and graphs with large Girths. In: Davies, D.W. (ed.) EUROCRYPT 1991. LNCS, vol. 547, pp. 508–511. Springer, Heidelberg (1991)

Side-Channel Attacks

Polynomial Evaluation
and Side Channel Analysis

Claude Carlet[1]([✉]) and Emmanuel Prouff[2,3]

[1] Department of Mathematics, LAGA, UMR 7539, CNRS, University of Paris XIII
and University of Paris VIII, Saint-Denis, France
`claude.carlet@univ-paris8.fr`
[2] ANSSI, Saint-Denis, France
`emmanuel.prouff@ssi.gouv.fr`
[3] POLSYS, UMR 7606, LIP6, Sorbonne Universities,
UPMC University Paris VI, Saint-Denis, France

Abstract. Side Channel Analysis (SCA) is a class of attacks that
exploits leakage of information from a cryptographic implementation
during execution. To thwart it, masking is a common countermeasure.
The principle is to randomly split every sensitive intermediate variable
occurring in the computation into several shares and the number of
shares, called the *masking order*, plays the role of a security parameter. The main issue while applying masking to protect a block cipher
implementation is to specify an efficient scheme to secure the s-box computations. Several masking schemes, applicable for arbitrary orders, have
been recently introduced. Most of them follow a similar approach originally introduced in the paper of Carlet *et al.* published at FSE 2012; the
s-box to protect is viewed as a polynomial and strategies are investigated
which minimize the number of field multiplications which are not squarings. This paper aims at presenting all these works in a comprehensive
way. The methods are discussed, their differences and similarities are
identified and the remaining open problems are listed.

1 Introduction

Side-channel analysis is a class of cryptanalytic attacks that exploit the physical
environment of a cryptosystem to recover some *leakage* about its secrets. It
is often more efficient than a cryptanalysis mounted in the so-called *black-box
model* where no leakage occurs. In particular, *continuous side-channel attacks* in
which the adversary gets information at each invocation of the cryptosystem are
especially threatening. Common attacks as those exploiting the running-time,
the power consumption or the electromagnetic radiations of a cryptographic
computation fall into this class.

Many implementations of block ciphers have been practically broken by continuous side-channel analysis — see for instance [8,39,41,44] — and securing
them has been a longstanding issue for the embedded systems industry. A sound
approach is to use *secret sharing* [5,59], often called *masking* in the context of

© Springer-Verlag Berlin Heidelberg 2016
P.Y.A. Ryan et al. (Eds.): Kahn Festschrift, LNCS 9100, pp. 315–341, 2016.
DOI: 10.1007/978-3-662-49301-4_20

side-channel attacks. This approach consists in splitting each sensitive variable Z of the implementation (*i.e.* each variable depending on the secret key, or better for the attacker, on a small part of it, and of public data such as the plaintext) into $d + 1$ shares $M_0, \ldots, M_d$, where d is called the *masking order*, such that Z can be recovered from these shares but no information can be recovered from less than $d + 1$ shares. It has been shown that the complexity of mounting a successful side-channel attack against a masked implementation increases exponentially with the masking order [11,23,49]. Starting from this observation, the design of efficient *masking schemes* for different ciphers has become a foreground issue. When specified *at higher order d*, such a scheme aims at specifying how to update the sharing of the internal state throughout the processing while ensuring that (1) the final sharing corresponds to the expected ciphertext, and (2) the dth-order security property is satisfied. The latter property, which is equivalent to the *probing security* model introduced in [34], states that every tuple of d or less intermediate variables is independent of the secret parameter of the algorithm. When satisfied, it guarantees that no attack of order lower than or equal to d is possible.

Most block cipher structures (*e.g.* AES or DES) are iterative, meaning that they apply several times a same transformation, called *round*, to an internal state initially filled with the plaintext. The round itself is composed of a key addition, one or several linear transformation(s) and one or several non-linear transformation(s) called s-box(es). Key addition and linear transformations are easily handled as linearity enables to process each share independently. The main difficulty in designing masking schemes for block ciphers hence lies in masking the s-box(es).

During the last decade, several attempts have been done to define higher-order schemes working for any order d. The proposals [1,2,16,21,29,58] either did unrealistic assumptions on the adversary capabilities or have been broken in subsequent papers [19,20,48,50,51]. Actually, there currently exist four masking schemes which have not been broken, and even benefit from formal security proofs:

- The first method is due to Genelle *et al.* [27] and consists in mixing additive and multiplicative sharings. This scheme is primarily dedicated to the AES sbox and seems difficult to generalize efficiently to other s-boxes (not affinely equivalent to a power function).
- The second masking scheme is due to Prouff and Roche [52] and it relies on solutions developed in secure *multi-party computation* [3]. It is much less efficient than the other schemes (see *e.g.* [31]) but, contrary to them, remains secure even in presence of hardware glitches [40].
- The third approach has been recently proposed by Coron in [17]. The core idea is to represent the s-box by several look-up tables which are regenerated from fresh random masks and the s-box truth table, each time a new s-box processing must be done. It extends the *table re-computation technique* introduced in the original paper by Kocher *et al.* [39]. The security of Coron's scheme against higher-order SCA is formally proven under the assumption

that the variable shares M_i leak independently. Its asymptotic timing complexity is quadratic in the number of shares and can be applied to any s-box. However, the RAM memory consumption to secure (at order d) an s-box with input (resp. output) dimension n (resp. m) is $m(d + 1)2^n$ bits, which can quickly exceed the memory capacity of the hosted device (e.g. a smart card).

– Only the following fourth approach is then practical, when d is greater than or equal to 3 and when the s-box to secure is not a power function and has input/output dimensions close to 8. This approach, proposed in [9], generalizes the study conducted in [54] for power functions (the latter work is itself inspired by techniques proposed for Boolean circuits by Ishai, Sahai and Wagner in [34]). The core idea is to split the s-box processing into a short sequence of field multiplications and $\mathbb{F}_2$-linear operations, and then to secure these operations independently. The complexity of the masking schemes for the multiplication and for an $\mathbb{F}_2$-linear operation[1] is $O(d^2)$ and $O(d)$ respectively. Moreover, for dimensions n greater than 6, the constant terms in these complexities are (usually) significantly greater for the multiplication than for the $\mathbb{F}_2$-linear operations. Based on this observation, the authors of [9] propose to look for operations sequences (aka s-box representations) that minimize the number of field multiplications which are not $\mathbb{F}_2$-linear[2] (this kind of multiplication shall be called *non-linear* in this paper). This led them to introduce the notion of *s-box masking complexity*, which corresponds to the minimal number of non-linear multiplications needed to evaluate the s-box. This complexity is evaluated for any power function defined in $\mathbb{F}_{2^n}$ with $n \leq 10$ (in particular, the complexity of $x \in \mathbb{F}_{2^8} \mapsto x^{254}$, which is the non-linear part of the AES s-box, is shown to be equal to 4). Tight upper bounds on the masking complexity are also given for any random s-box. The analysis in [9] has been further improved by Roy and Vivek in [56], where it is in particular shown that the masking complexity of the DES s-boxes is lower bounded by 3. The authors of [56] also present a polynomial evaluation method that requires 7 non-linear multiplications (instead of 10 in [9]). Another improvement of [9] has been proposed in [14], where it is shown that it is possible to improve the processing of the non-linear multiplications which have the particular form $x \times \mathcal{L}(x)$ with $\mathcal{L}$ being $\mathbb{F}_2$-linear. Recently, Coron, Roy and Vivek proposed an heuristic method which may be viewed as an extension of the ideas developed in [18,56]. For all the tested s-boxes it is at least as efficient as the previous methods and it often requires less non-linear multiplications (e.g. 4 for the DES s-boxes). Eventually, in [10], Carlet, Prouff, Rivain and Roche continued the generalization of [9] by proposing to split the evaluation of any s-box into a short sequence of evaluations of polynomial functions with upper bound

---

[1] A function f is $\mathbb{F}_2$-linear if it satisfies $f(x \oplus y) = f(x) \oplus f(y)$ for any pair (x, y) of elements in its domain. This property must not be confused with $\mathbb{F}_{2^m}$-linearity of a function, where m divides n and is larger than 1, which is defined such that $f(ax \oplus by) = af(x) \oplus bf(y)$, for every $a, b \in \mathbb{F}_{2^m}$. An $\mathbb{F}_{2^m}$-linear function is $\mathbb{F}_2$-linear but the converse is false in general.

[2] A multiplication over a field of characteristic 2 is $\mathbb{F}_2$-linear if it corresponds to a Frobenius automorphism, *i.e.* to a series of squarings.

algebraic degree. It is for instance shown that the processing of any s-box of dimension $n = 8$ can be split into 11 evaluations of quadratic functions, or into 4 evaluations of cubic functions. For the latter evaluations of low degree polynomials, the authors propose several methods, among which an adaptation of CRV which is more efficient than the original one when the degree is low.

The purpose of this paper is to give an overview of the results presented in the sequence of works [9,14,15,30,56] and we also prove that the masking scheme introduced in [14] for functions in the form $x \times \mathcal{L}(x)$ can be extended to any function of algebraic degree 2. Since the work [10] was published several months after the writing of this paper, it is not fully detailed here, except in Sect. 3.4 where some results are discussed.

2 Securing Elementary Operations over Finite Fields

Except the masking schemes by Genelle *et al.* [27] and by Coron [17] (which cannot be applied to any s-box for the first one, or has a too important RAM memory complexity for the second one), the state-of-the-art masking schemes [9,15,30,52,56] all follow the same principle: the sbox evaluation is split into a sequence of so-called *elementary operations* which are independently protected thanks to dedicated masking schemes. The set of elementary operations contains the field additions and multiplications and, for reasons that will be exposed in this section and in Subsect. 3.4, it also includes all quadratic transformations (whose polynomial representations include exponents which are the sums of at most two powers of 2) and possibly cubic transformations. In the following, we recall the secure masking schemes which have been introduced in the literature to process elementary operations. When defined with respect to an operation (aka transformation) f, such a scheme takes at input a $(d+1)^{\text{th}}$-order sharing of f's input(s) and returns a $(d+1)^{\text{th}}$-order sharing of its output, while ensuring that any d-tuple of intermediate results during the processing is independent of the unshared input.

2.1 Securing Multiplications in Finite Fields

Let us first start the section with a few basics on finite field multiplications.

Basics on Multiplication Processing. Different time/memory trade-offs exist in the literature for implementing multiplications. For hardware implementations and large dimensions n, several works have been published among which the Omura-Massey method [46], the Sunar-Koc method [61,64], the Karatsuba algorithm [35], etc. For software implementations in small dimensions (*e.g.* $n \leqslant 10$), the number of pertinent possibilities is reduced. We recall them in the following and we give their time/memory complexities (time complexities are given in terms of number of cycles). For illustration, we also give a pseudo-code. We moreover assume that the multiplication in $\mathbb{F}_{2^n}$ corresponds to some irreducible polynomial $p(X)$ of degree n over $\mathbb{F}_2$ (*i.e.* we use the representation $\mathbb{F}_{2^n} \simeq \mathbb{F}_2[X]/(p(X))$ or $\mathbb{F}_{2^n} \simeq \{\alpha^i; i \in [0; n-2]\} \cup \{0\}$ where α is a primitive element, root of $p(X)$).

- The most efficient multiplication method in terms of timing, and the most costly in terms of memory, is based on a complete tabulation of the processing(s). The calculation of $c = a \times b$ in $\mathbb{F}_{2^n}$ is done by reading the content of a table $multFn$ in ROM containing all the pre-computed results. The size of the table is $n2^{2n}$ bits and the timing of the operation is constant, around 5 cycles depending on the device architecture.

$$c = multFn[a, b]$$

- The most efficient in terms of memory, and the most costly in terms of timing, is the direct processing of the multiplication in $\mathbb{F}_{2^n}$. The memory consumption is reduced to 0 but the timing complexity is $O(n^{\log_3(2)})$ with important constants. The latter complexity is achieved thanks to Karatsuba's method. The core idea of this method is that the product $(a_h Y + a_l) \times (b_h Y + b_l)$, where a_h, a_l, b_h, b_l live in some ring R, say of characteristic 2, can be computed with 3 multiplications and 4 additions in R, thanks to the following processing decomposition called 2-*segment Karatsuba's method*:

$$(a_h Y + a_l) \times (b_h Y + b_l) = c_h Y^2 + c_{hl} Y + c_l,$$

where $c_h \doteq a_h \times b_h$, $c_l \doteq a_l \times b_l$ and $c_{hl} \doteq (a_h + a_l) \times (b_h + b_l) - c_h - c_l$. With the formula above, two elements a and b of $\mathbb{F}_{2^n}$ (viewed as polynomials over $\mathbb{F}_2$) can be rewritten and multiplied using the formula:

$$(a_h X^m + a_l) \times (b_h X^m + b_l) = c_h X^{2m} + c_{hl} X^m + c_l, \qquad (1)$$

where a_h, a_l, b_h, b_l, c_{hl}, c_h and c_l are polynomials of degree lower than or equal to $m = \lceil \frac{n}{2} \rceil$. The polynomials c_i are computed by applying the Karatsuba method to the polynomials a_i and b_i as single coefficients and adding coefficients of common powers of X together. Formula (1) is afterwards repeated recursively, either until getting multiplications in $\mathbb{F}_2$ only or until getting low-cost multiplications (*e.g.* because they are tabulated). We will call r-Karatsuba (or $K_{n,r}$ for short), a multiplication processing where Karatsuba's method is applied r times recursively. Eventually, the reduction by the polynomial $p(X)$ can be interleaved to get the field multiplication.

- The *log-alog* method is a compromise between the two previous methods. Its memory complexity is $n2^{n+1}$ bits and its timing complexity is constant with respect to n. It assumes that the functions $log : x \in \mathbb{F}_{2^n} \mapsto i = \log_\alpha(x)$ and $alog : i \mapsto x = \alpha^i$ have been tabulated in ROM. The processing of $a \times b$ then simply consists in processing:

$$c = alog[(log[a] + log[b]) \bmod 2^n - 1].$$

It may be observed that this addition modulo $2^n - 1$ can be processed on n-bit architecture by simply adding $log[a]$ to $log[b]$ (modulo 2^n) and by adding to the result the carry which has possibly been raised (if $log[a] + log[b] \geq 2^n$).

- Another compromise is obtained thanks to the so-called *Tower Fields* approach (see *e.g.* [33,57]). It can be applied when n is even (*i.e.* $n = 2m$ with $m \in \mathbb{N}$) and first consists in representing $\mathbb{F}_{2^n}$ has a degree-2 extension of $\mathbb{F}_{2^m}$, allowing to perform the computations in $\mathbb{F}_{2^m} \simeq \mathbb{F}_2[X]/(p'(X))$ instead of $\mathbb{F}_{2^n}$. Concretely, the elements of $\mathbb{F}_{2^n}$ are viewed as elements of $\mathbb{F}_{2^m}[X]/(p''(X))$, where $p''(X)$ is a degree-2 polynomial irreducible over $\mathbb{F}_{2^m}$. The field isomorphism mapping an element $a \in (\mathbb{F}_2[X]/p(X))$ into the pair $(a_h, a_l) \in (\mathbb{F}_{2^m}[X]/p''(X))$ is denoted by L. Assuming that the polynomial $p''(X)$ takes the form $X^2 + X + \beta$ (which is always possible thanks to a scaling on X and normalization of the polynomial), the multiplication $a \times b$ is then executed by the following sequence of operations:

$$
\begin{aligned}
(a_h, a_l) &\leftarrow L(a) \\
(b_h, b_l) &\leftarrow L(b) \\
c_l &\leftarrow a_h \times b_h \times \beta + a_l \times b_l \\
c_h &\leftarrow (a_h + a_l) \times (b_h + b_l) - a_l \times b_l \\
c &\leftarrow L^{-1}(c_h, c_l)
\end{aligned}
$$

Actually, the technique can be applied to decompose the multiplications in any subfield $\mathbb{F}_{2^m}$ such that 2^r divides n and $m = \frac{n}{2^r}$. We will call r-Tower (or $\text{Tow}_{n,r}$ for short), a multiplication processing where the Tower Fields approach is applied downto $\mathbb{F}_{2^m}$. It may be observed that this multiplication method combines the specificity of Tower fields and Karatsuba's method (one could also use Toom-Cook's multiplication [13,62] instead but it is only advantageous for high dimensions which is out of scope here). In the following, we assume that β is chosen such that the cost of the multiplication by β is negligible.

We sum-up hereafter the complexities of the listed multiplication methods in terms of memory consumption (ROM in bits), elementary field additions (ADD) and calls to look-up tables (LUT). For Karatsuba and Tower Fields approaches, we give the complexities depending on whether the multiplications in the final subfield are performed with the log-alog method or is tabulated in ROM. Moreover, for simplicity reasons, complexities are given in the case where n is a power of 2.

We give hereafter some examples of costs (in cycles) of the elementary operations listed in Table 1 when performed on 8051 and AVR chip micro-controllers. For simplicity, we assume that the operations are performed whose bit-length is below that of the processor architecture:

- Addition: 1 cycle (for 8051 and AVR).
- Multiplication: 25 cycles (8051), 36 cycles (AVR).
- LUT call: 1–4 cycle(s) (8051), 3–7 cycles (AVR).

State-of-the art methods proposed to secure a finite field multiplication between two elements a and b are general and apply similarly for all the multiplication techniques previously recalled. The choice of the latter technique will

Table 1. Complexities of multiplication methods

Method	ROM (in bits)	ADD	LUT
Global look-up table (LUT_n)	$n \times 2^{2n}$	0	1
Log-alog method (LAL_n)	$3n \times 2^n$	2	3
r-Karatsuba ($\mathrm{K}_{n,r}$) + $\mathrm{LUT}_{\frac{n}{2^r}}$	$\frac{n}{2^r} \times 2^{\frac{2n}{2^r}}$	$2 \times (3^r - 1)$	$3 \times \frac{3^r - 1}{2}$
r-Karatsuba ($\mathrm{K}_{n,r}$) + $\mathrm{LAL}_{\frac{n}{2^r}}$	$3\frac{n}{2^r} \times 2^{\frac{n}{2^r}}$	$5 \times (3^r - 1)$	$9 \times \frac{3^r - 1}{2}$
r-Tower ($\mathrm{Tow}_{n,r}$) + $\mathrm{LUT}_{\frac{n}{2^r}}$	$\frac{n}{2^r} \times 2^{\frac{2n}{2^r}} + 2n \times 2^n$	$2 \times (3^r - 1)$	$3 \times (3^r - 1)$
r-Tower ($\mathrm{Tow}_{n,r}$) + $\mathrm{LAL}_{\frac{n}{2^r}}$	$3\frac{n}{2^r} \times 2^{\frac{2n}{2^r}} + 2n \times 2^n$	$6 \times (3^r - 1)$	$5 \times (3^r - 1)$

however impact the practical cost of the scheme (in terms of both memory and cycles count). This explains why a security designer will often favour one of these techniques according to some pre-defined timing/memory trade-off chosen with respect to the context (application, device, cost of the random values generation, etc.). For instance, if the ROM memory is not a constrained resource (and/or if the dimension n is small, *e.g.* lower than 5), then the field multiplication can be tabulated and all the operations $\times$ in the hereafter schemes will simply consist in a LUT call (which costs around 4 cycles). At the opposite, when the ROM memory is a constrained resource (and/or the dimension n is between 5 and 8), then the multiplications can be performed thanks to the log-alog method (in this case each of them will cost around 25 – or 35 – cycles).

Masking Schemes for Finite Multiplications (Additive Sharing). When the inputs a and b are additively shared into $(a_0, a_1, \cdots, a_d)$ and $(b_0, b_1, \cdots, b_d)$ respectively, a straightforward solution consists in applying the following scheme:

Algorithm 1. Higher-Order Masking Scheme for the Multiplication (Additive Sharing)

Input : a $(d+1)^{\mathrm{th}}$-order sharing $(a_0, a_1, \cdots, a_d)$ and $(b_0, b_1, \cdots, b_d)$ of a and b in $\mathbb{F}_{2^n}$
Output: a $(d+1)^{\mathrm{th}}$-order sharing $(c_0, c_1, \cdots, c_d)$ of $c = a \times b$

1   Randomly generate $(d+1)^2$ elements $r_{ij} \in \mathbb{F}_{2^n}$ such that $\sum_{i \in [0..d]} r_{ij} = 0$ for every $j \leqslant d$
2   **for** $i = 0$ to d **do**
3      $c_i = 0$
4   **for** $j = 0$ to d **do**
         /* Construct $c_i = \sum_j a_i \times b_j + \sum_j r_{ij}$ */
5         $c_i \leftarrow c_i + a_i \times b_j + r_{ij}$

6   **return** $(c_0, c_1, \cdots, c_d)$

Algorithm 1 has been proved to be d^{th}-order secure in [25]. In [34], the authors show that the number of random values r_{ij} can be reduced to $d(d-1)/2$ with no impact on the security. Initially, the scheme was presented over $\mathbb{F}_2$ and it was generalized to any finite field in [54]. The improved scheme, recalled hereafter, involves $2d(d+1)$ additions and $(d+1)^2$ multiplications in $\mathbb{F}_{2^n}$.

Algorithm 2. Improved Higher-Order Masking Scheme for the Multiplication (Additive Sharing)

> **Input** : a $(d+1)^{\text{th}}$-order sharing $(a_0, a_1, \cdots, a_d)$ and $(b_0, b_1, \cdots, b_d)$ of a and b in $\mathbb{F}_{2^n}$
> **Output:** a $(d+1)^{\text{th}}$-order sharing $(c_0, c_1, \cdots, c_d)$ of $c = a \times b$

1 Randomly generate $d(d+1)/2$ elements $r_{ij} \in \mathbb{F}_{2^n}$ indexed such that $0 \leqslant i < j \leqslant d$
2 **for** $i = 0$ **to** d **do**
3 $\quad$ **for** $j = i+1$ **to** d **do**
4 $\quad\quad \lfloor \; r_{j,i} \leftarrow (r_{i,j} + a_i \times b_j) + a_j \times b_i$

5 **for** $i = 0$ **to** d **do**
6 $\quad c_i \leftarrow a_i \times b_i$
7 $\quad$ **for** $j = 0$ **to** $d, j \neq i$ **do**
8 $\quad\quad \lfloor \; c_i \leftarrow c_i + r_{i,j}$

9 **return** $(c_0, c_1, \ldots, c_d)$

Masking Schemes for Finite Multiplications (Polynomial Sharing).

When polynomial masking/sharing [59] is used, an alternative to Algorithm 2 exists which has been proposed by Ben-Or *et al.* in [4]. The complexity of the latter algorithm in terms of additions and multiplications is $O(d^3)$ and its application is more complex than Algorithm 2 (see [45]). As explained in [52], it however stays secure even in presence of glitches [42] and, compared to additive sharing, it offers better resistance against unbounded adversaries (namely adversaries who can get noisy observations on all the shares of a). Before recalling Ben-Or's *et al.* algorithm, let us give some basics about Shamir's polynomial sharing.

In [59] Shamir has introduced a simple and elegant way to split a secret $a \in \mathbb{F}_{2^n}$ into a well chosen number ℓ of shares such that no tuple of shares with cardinality at most d depends on a, where d is some positive integer smaller than ℓ. Shamir's protocol consists in generating a degree-d polynomial with coefficients randomly generated in $\mathbb{F}_{2^n}$, except the constant term which is always fixed to a. In other terms, Shamir proposes to associate a with a polynomial $P_a(X)$ defined such that $P_a(X) = a + \sum_{i=1}^{d} u_i X^i$, where the u_i denote random coefficients. Then, $\ell > d$ distinct non-zero elements $\alpha_0, \ldots, \alpha_{\ell-1}$ are publicly chosen in $\mathbb{F}_{2^n}$ and the polynomial $P_a(X)$ is evaluated in the α_i to construct a so-called (ℓ, d)-*sharing* $(a_0, a_1, \cdots, a_{\ell-1})$ of a such that $a_i = P_a(\alpha_i)$ for every $i \in [0..\ell-1]$. To re-construct a from its sharing, polynomial interpolation is first applied to re-construct $P_a(X)$ from its ℓ evaluations a_i. Then, the polynomial is evaluated in 0. Those two steps indeed lead to the recovery of a since, by construction, we have $a = P_a(0)$. Actually, using Lagrange's interpolation formula, the two steps can be combined in a single one thanks to the following equation:

$$a = \sum_{i=0}^{\ell-1} a_i \cdot \beta_i, \tag{2}$$

where the constants β_i are defined as follows:

$$\beta_i := \prod_{k=0, k \neq i}^{\ell-1} \frac{\alpha_k}{\alpha_i + \alpha_k}.$$

Remark 1. The β_i can be precomputed once for all and can hence be considered as public values. They can moreover be also considered as the evaluation in 0 of the polynomials:

$$\beta_i(x) := \prod_{k=0, k\neq i}^{\ell-1} \frac{x + \alpha_k}{\alpha_i + \alpha_k}.$$

To securely process the multiplications of two values a and b represented by polynomial sharings, Ben-Or *et al.* have introduced a protocol in the context of the Multy-Party Computation Theory [4]. For this protocol to work, the number of shares n per variable must be at least $2d + 1$ and for $\ell = 2d + 1$, it is proved that it satisfies a security property encompassing the dth-order SCA security. We give hereafter the adaptation of [4] in the SCA context as proposed in [52,55][3].

Algorithm 3. Higher-Order Masking Scheme for the Multiplication (Polynomial Sharing)

Input : two integers ℓ and d such that $\ell \geq 2d+1$, the (ℓ, d)-sharings $(a_i)_i = (P_a(\alpha_i))_i$ and
$(b_i)_i = (P_b(\alpha_i))_i$ of a and b respectively.
Output: the (ℓ, d)-sharing $(P_c(\alpha_i))_i$ of $c = a \cdot b$.
Public : the ℓ distinct points α_i, the interpolation values $(\beta_0, \cdots, \beta_{\ell-1})$

1 **for** $i = 0$ **to** $\ell - 1$ **do**
2 $\quad\lfloor$ $w_i \leftarrow P_a(\alpha_i) \cdot P_b(\alpha_i)$

   /* Compute a sharing $(Q_i(\alpha_j))_{j\leq d}$ of w_i with $Q_i(X) = w_i + \sum_{j=1}^d a_j \cdot X^j$ */
3 **for** $i = 0$ **to** $\ell - 1$ **do**
4 $\quad\mid$ **for** $j = 1$ **to** d **do**
5 $\quad\mid\quad\lfloor$ $a_j \leftarrow \mathrm{rand}(\mathbb{F}_{2^n})$
6 $\quad\mid$ **for** $j = 0$ **to** $\ell - 1$ **do**
7 $\quad\mid\quad\lfloor$ $Q_i(\alpha_j) \leftarrow w_i + \sum_{k=1}^d a_k \cdot \alpha_j^k$

   /* Compute the share $c_i = P_c(\alpha_i)$ for $c = a \cdot b$ */
8 **for** $i = 0$ **to** $\ell - 1$ **do**
9 $\quad\lfloor$ $c_i \leftarrow \sum_{j=0}^{\ell-1} Q_j(\alpha_i) \cdot \beta_j$

10 **return** $(c_i)_i$

The completeness of Algorithm 3 is discussed in [4]. Its dth-order SCA security can be straightforwardly deduced from the proof given by Ben-Or *et al.* in [4] in the secure multi-party computation context. Eventually, for $\ell = 2d+1$ (which is the parameter choice which optimizes the security/efficiency overhead), the complexity of Algorithm 3 in terms of additions and multiplications is $\mathcal{O}(d^3)$. In [20], it is reduced to $O(d^2 \log d)$, essentially by computing polynomial evaluations with a Discrete Fourier Transform as proposed in [65] instead of a naive evaluation[4]. In [32], Grosso and Standaert apply a classical technique from multi-party computation, called *packet secret sharing* and introduced by Franklin and Yung [26], which essentially consists in sharing several secrets with the same polynomial. This technique is of interest when several multiplications, say t, between

---

[3] The protocol is an improved version of the protocol originally proposed by Ben-Or *et al.* [4], due to Gennaro *et al.* in [28].

[4] Such improvement was already known in the context of multi-party computation [22].

secrets must be secured. In such a case, the achieved complexity is $O((t + d)^3)$ instead of $O(td^3)$, which implies a complexity improvement if d is greater than $t(t^{\frac{1}{3}} - 1)^{-1}$.

Masking Schemes for Finite Multiplications (Sharing by Linear Codes). As initially observed by Massey [43], there is an equivalence between the existence of linear sharing schemes and the existence of linear codes with certain parameters. Indeed, the set $\{(a, a_0, a_1, \cdots, a_{\ell-1}) \in \mathbb{F}_{2^n}^{\ell+1}\}$ defined by the linear sharings of the elements $a \in \mathbb{F}_{2^n}$ into $(a_0, \cdots, a_{\ell-1}) \in \mathbb{F}_{2^n}^{\ell}$ is a subspace of $\mathbb{F}_{2^n}^{\ell+1}$ (aka a linear code). Reciprocally, from any linear $[\ell+1, k, d]$-code[5] C with $d \geq 2$ and such that the corresponding dual code $C^\perp$ has a distance $d^\perp$ satisfying $d^\perp \geqslant 2$, one can define a linear ℓ-sharing over $\mathbb{F}_{2^n}$. If G denotes the generator matrix of C, with first column equal to the transpose of $10 \ldots 0$, e. g. in *systematic* form (*i.e.* $G = [I_k \mid M]$ where I_k is the k-dimensional identity matrix over $\mathbb{F}_{2^n}$), then the sharing $(a_0, a_1, \cdots, a_{\ell-1})$ of a is built from a $(k-1)$-tuple of random values $(r_0, r_1, \cdots, r_{k-2})$ such that $(a, a_0, a_1, \cdots, a_{\ell-1}) = (a, r_0, \cdots, r_{k-2}) \times G$. The reconstruction of a from its sharing $(a_0, \cdots, a_{\ell-1})$ is obtained by processing the scalar product between the latter vector and a so-called *reconstruction vector* $(\beta_i)_i$ given by (2). It can moreover be proved that the sharing defined in such a way defeats any side channel attack of order lower than or equal to $d^\perp - 2$ [12]. The thesis of Renner [53] is dedicated to this subject: for all the studied linear sharings (deduced from linear codes) the proposed multiplication schemes have complexity $O(d^3)$. In the particular case of Shamir's polynomial sharing, new methods are however proposed that enable to decrease the constant terms in this complexity and to get interesting practical timing complexity improvements (compared to the methods proposed in [4, 28]).

2.2   Securing Affine Transformations

For $\mathbb{F}_2$-affine transformations, defining a higher-order masking scheme is straightforward. If $(a_0, \cdots, a_d) \in \mathbb{F}_{2^n}^{d+1}$ denotes the *additive sharing* of an intermediate variable $a \in \mathbb{F}_{2^n}$ (*i.e.* the a_i are randomly generated such that $a = \sum_{i \in [0..d]} a_i$) and $\mathcal{A}$ denotes the affine transformation to securely apply on a, then the following simple scheme may be involved. It essentially applies the affine transformation $\mathcal{A}$ to each share of a:

---

[5] Where $\ell + 1$ corresponds to the code length and where k (resp. d) denotes its dimension (resp. minimum distance).

Algorithm 4. Higher-Order Masking Scheme for Affine Transformation (Additive Sharing)

Input : a $(d+1)^{\text{th}}$-order sharing $(a_0, a_1, \cdots, a_d)$ of a, an affine transformation $\mathcal{A}$
Output: a $(d+1)^{\text{th}}$-order sharing $(c_0, c_1, \cdots, c_d)$ of $c = \mathcal{A}(a)$

1 **for** $i = 0$ **to** d **do**
2     $c_i \leftarrow \mathcal{A}(a_i)$
3 **if** d *is odd* **then**
4     $c_0 \leftarrow c_0 + \mathcal{A}(0)$
5 **return** $(c_0, c_1, \cdots, c_d)$

The same scheme can be straightforwardly extended to any group law and any function $\mathcal{A}$ which is affine for the latter law (see *e.g.* [25]). It can moreover be extended when the sharing is no longer additive with respect to the group law but is more generally based on a linear code [53]. For instance, if the linear code corresponds to Shamir's polynomial sharing (in this case the code is a Reed-Solomon one), then the a_i (resp. the c_i) correspond to the evaluation in $d + 1$ public points α_i of a random degree-d polynomial $P_a(X)$ (resp. $[P_a \circ \mathcal{A}](X)$) with constant term a (resp. c). Namely, the input shares are defined such that $a_i = P_a(\alpha_i)$ and, by construction, the output shares satisfy $c_i = [P_a \circ \mathcal{A}](\alpha_i)$ (see for instance [52]).

2.3 Securing Quadratic Transformations

In [14], Coron *et al.* have recently shown that multiplications of the form $a \times \mathcal{L}(a)$, with $\mathcal{L}$ being $\mathbb{F}_2$-linear, can be securely evaluated more efficiently than standard multiplications when n is small enough to allow for the tabulation of univariate transformation in $\mathbb{F}_{2^n}$ (*i.e.* when $n \leqslant 10$ for nowadays devices). This scheme is recalled hereafter where the operation $a \mapsto a \times \mathcal{L}(a)$ is denoted by $\mathcal{Q}(a)$.

Algorithm 5. Higher-Order Masking Scheme for Multiplication in the form $a \times \mathcal{L}(a)$ (Additive Sharing)

Input : the $(d+1)^{\text{th}}$-order sharing $(a_0, a_1, \cdots, a_d)$ of a in $\mathbb{F}_{2^n}$
Output: a $(d+1)^{\text{th}}$-order sharing $(c_0, c_1, \cdots, c_d)$ of $c = a \times \mathcal{L}(a)$

1 Randomly generate $d(d+1)^2/2$ elements $r_{ij} \in \mathbb{F}_{2^n}$ indexed such that $0 \leqslant i < j \leqslant d$
2 Randomly generate $d(d+1)^2/2$ elements $r'_{ij} \in \mathbb{F}_{2^n}$ indexed such that $0 \leqslant i < j \leqslant d$
3 **for** $i = 0$ **to** d **do**
4   **for** $j = i+1$ **to** d **do**
5        $r_{j,i} \leftarrow r_{i,j} + \mathcal{Q}(a_i + r'_{i,j}) + \mathcal{Q}(a_j + r'_{i,j}) + \mathcal{Q}((a_i + r'_{i,j}) + a_j) + \mathcal{Q}(r'_{i,j})$
6 **for** $i = 0$ **to** d **do**
7     $c_i \leftarrow \mathcal{Q}(a_i)$
8   **for** $j = 0$ **to** d, $j \neq i$ **do**
9        $c_i \leftarrow c_i + r_{i,j}$
10 **return** $(c_0, c_1, \ldots, c_d)$

Algorithm 5 can actually be extended to any quadratic function (instead of only the quadratic functions $a \in \mathbb{F}_{2^n} \mapsto a \times \mathcal{L}(a)$). Let $\mathcal{Q}$ be any quadratic function from $\mathbb{F}_{2^n}$ to $\mathbb{F}_{2^n}$. The bivariate function $\varphi^{(2)}(a_0, a_1) = \mathcal{Q}(a_0 + a_1) + \mathcal{Q}(a_0) + \mathcal{Q}(a_1) + \mathcal{Q}(0)$ is bilinear (this is a necessary and sufficient condition for

h to be quadratic), symmetric and null when a_0, a_1 are linearly dependent over $\mathbb{F}_2$ (that is, when $a_0 = 0$ or $a_1 = 0$ or $a_0 = a_1$). The equality $\mathcal{Q}(a_0 + a_1) = \varphi^{(2)}(a_0, a_1) + \mathcal{Q}(a_0) + \mathcal{Q}(a_1) + \mathcal{Q}(0)$ can be iterated: it can be easily proven by induction on $d \geq 1$ that for every $(a_0, a_1, \ldots, a_d) \in \mathbb{F}_{2^n}{}^{d+1}$, we have;

$$\mathcal{Q}\left(\sum_{i=0}^{d} a_i\right) = \sum_{0 \leq i < j \leq d} \varphi^{(2)}(a_i, a_j) + \sum_{i=0}^{d} \mathcal{Q}(a_i) + (d \, [\mathrm{mod}\ 2]) \, \mathcal{Q}(0). \tag{3}$$

Note that this formula, which has been extended from the quadratic case to any algebraic degree s in [10] (see Sect. 3.4, is also valid for $d = 0$. Moreover, for every $a_i, a_j, r'_{i,j}$ in $\mathbb{F}_{2^n}$ we have

$$\varphi^{(2)}(a_i, a_j) = \mathcal{Q}(a_i + a_j + r'_{i,j}) + \mathcal{Q}(a_i + r'_{i,j}) + \mathcal{Q}(a_j + r'_{i,j}) + \mathcal{Q}(r'_{i,j}), \tag{4}$$

since $\varphi^{(2)}(a_i, a_j) + \mathcal{Q}(a_i + a_j + r'_{i,j}) + \mathcal{Q}(a_i + r'_{i,j}) + \mathcal{Q}(a_j + r'_{i,j}) + \mathcal{Q}(r'_{i,j}) = \varphi^{(2)}(a_i, a_j) + \varphi^{(2)}(a_i, r'_{i,j}) + \varphi^{(2)}(a_i, a_j + r'_{i,j})$ is null ($\varphi^{(2)}$ being bilinear). Hence, the same calculations as above can be made by injecting $r'_{i,j}$ into each processing of $\varphi^{(2)}(a_i, a_j)$ and we have then:

$$\mathcal{Q}\left(\sum_{i=0}^{d} a_i\right) = \sum_{0 \leq i < j \leq d} \mathcal{Q}(a_i + a_j + r'_{i,j}) + \mathcal{Q}(a_i + r'_{i,j}) + \mathcal{Q}(a_j + r'_{i,j}) + \mathcal{Q}(r'_{i,j})$$

$$+ \sum_{i=0}^{d} \mathcal{Q}(a_i) + (d \, [\mathrm{mod}\ 2]) \, \mathcal{Q}(0). \tag{5}$$

From (5) we deduce that a quadratic function $\mathcal{Q}$ can be securely evaluated for any d by processing the following sequence of operations:

Algorithm 6. Higher-Order Masking Scheme for Quadratic Vectorial Function

---

Input : a $(d + 1)^{\mathrm{th}}$-order sharing $(a_0, a_1, \cdots, a_d)$ of a in $\mathbb{F}_2^n$
Output: a $(d + 1)^{\mathrm{th}}$-order sharing $(c_0, c_1, \cdots, c_d)$ of $c = \mathcal{Q}(a)$

1 Randomly generate $d(d + 1)/2$ elements $r_{ij} \in \mathbb{F}_{2^n}$ indexed such that $0 \leqslant i < j \leqslant d$
2 Randomly generate $d(d + 1)/2$ elements $r'_{ij} \in \mathbb{F}_{2^n}$ indexed such that $0 \leqslant i < j \leqslant d$
3 **for** $i = 0$ **to** d **do**
4   **for** $j = i + 1$ **to** d **do**
        /* process $r_{j,i} = \varphi_h^{(2)}(a_i, a_j) + r_{i,j}$ */
5          $r_{j,i} \leftarrow r_{i,j} + \mathcal{Q}(a_i + r'_{i,j}) + \mathcal{Q}(a_j + r'_{i,j}) + \mathcal{Q}((a_i + r'_{i,j}) + a_j) + \mathcal{Q}(r'_{i,j})$

6 **for** $i = 0$ **to** d **do**
7      $c_i \leftarrow \mathcal{Q}(a_i)$
8   **for** $j = 0$ **to** d, $j \neq i$ **do**
9          $c_i \leftarrow c_i + r_{i,j}$

10 $c_0 \leftarrow c_0 + (d \bmod 2)\mathcal{Q}(0)$
11 **return** $(c_0, c_1, \ldots, c_d)$

Except the addition of the constant term at Step 7, Algorithm 6 is exactly the same as Algorithm 5. It involves $5d(d+1)$ additions and $2d(d+1)$ calls to the transformation $\mathcal{Q}$. In order to satisfy the dth-order security, the sequence of operations at Step 5 must be done from left to right.

2.4   Conclusion About Elementary Masking Schemes

We sum-up hereafter the complexities of Algorithms[6] 2, 3, 4 and 6:

Scheme	Additions	Multilpications	LUT calls
Scheme for multiplications (Algorithm 2)	$2d(d+1)$	$(d+1)^2$	0
Scheme for multiplications (Algorithm 3)	$4d^3+8d^2+3d$	$4d^3+4d^2+5d+2$	0
Scheme for affine transformations	0	0	$d+1$
Scheme for quadratic transformations	$5d(d+1)$	0	$(2d+1)(d+1)$

In [30], Grosso et al. experimentally validated for $n=8$ the advantage of using Algorithm 5 instead of Algorithm 2 to securely process multiplications in the form $a \times \mathcal{L}(a)$. For $d \in \{1,2,3\}$, they indeed implemented both approaches in C and in Assembly on ATMEGA644p. We recall their results hereafter (Table 2):

Table 2. Costs comparison (in cycles) between Algorithms 2 and 5 over $\mathbb{F}_{2^n}$ [8].

Operation	C $d=1$	C $d=2$	C $d=3$	[Assembly] $d=1$
Algorithm 2	146	430	802	136
Algorithm 5	61	152	344	54

3   Securing Polynomial Evaluation

3.1   On the Notion of Masking Complexity

The core idea of the secure polynomial evaluations proposed in the literature is to split the processing into a sequence of field multiplications and $\mathbb{F}_2$-linear operations, and then to secure both operations independently thanks to the methods recalled in previous section. Taking into account that the complexity of masking schemes for $\mathbb{F}_2$-linear operations is linear in d, whereas that for multiplications is at least quadratic, the proposed techniques try to minimize the number of field multiplications which are not $\mathbb{F}_2$-linear[7] (this kind of multiplication shall be

---

[6] The improvement of Algorithm 3 proposed in [53] involves d^3+9d^2+5d additions and d^3+8d^2+9d+2 multiplications, which leads to an improvement when $d \geqslant 3$ (see [53]).

[7] Recall that a multiplication over a field of characteristic 2 corresponding to a Frobenius automorphism, i.e. to a series of squarings, is $\mathbb{F}_2$-linear.

called *non-linear* in this paper). This strategy led the authors of [9] to introduce the notion of *polynomial masking complexity*, which corresponds to the minimal number of non-linear multiplications needed to evaluate a given polynomial (aka s-box). Computing this masking complexity for any given function is today a challenge. Following a brute force approach, the authors of [9] exhibited the masking complexity for all monomials in $\mathbb{F}_{2^n}$ with $n \leq 8$. Since the complexity is the same for all powers in the same cyclotomic class, results are grouped by classes. We recall the following table from [9]:

Determining the masking complexity of a monomial $x^\alpha \in \mathbb{F}_{2^n}[x]$ amounts to find the shortest 2-*addition chain* for α, with the supplementary assumption that multiplications by 2 are for free. The notion of q-addition chain has been introduced in [37] and studied *e.g.* in [63]. The general problem (without the assumption that multiplications by q are for free) is known to be a NP-hard problem. In [56], the authors argue that the notion of *cyclotomic class addition chain* (CC-addition chain for short) is more accurate to refer to the processing of x^α from cyclotomic class elements. A CC-addition chain for a non-zero element $\alpha \in \mathbb{Z}/(2^n - 1)\mathbb{Z}$ is a collection of cyclotomic classes $(C_{a_i})_{0 \leq i \leq r}$ such that $a_0 = 1$ and $a_r = \alpha$, and for every $i \in [1..r]$ there exist $(j, k) \in [0..r]^2$, $\beta_j \in C_{a_j}$ and $\beta_k \in C_{a_k}$ such that $\beta_i \equiv \beta_j + \beta_k \bmod 2^n - 1$. The value r is called the size of the CC-addition chain. The masking complexity of x^α corresponds to the shortest CC-addition chain of α.

In some contexts, it may be pertinent to evaluate a monomial defined over $\mathbb{F}_{2^n}$ thanks to operations defined over subfields $\mathbb{F}_{2^{n/2^r}}$ of $\mathbb{F}_{2^n}$ (*e.g.* applying the Tower Fields approach recalled in Sect. 2.1). This strategy increases the overall number of multiplications. However, operating in $\mathbb{F}_{2^{n/2^r}}$ instead of $\mathbb{F}_{2^n}$ may have a significant practical impact on the processing cost (in terms of CPU cycles number). For instance, according to Table 1, the number of cycles required to process multiplications in $\mathbb{F}_{2^4}$ with $\mathrm{LUT}_{n=4}$ is 4 (in 8051) if 256 bytes of ROM are available. Since the multiplication in $\mathbb{F}_{2^8}$ cannot be tabulated (it would require 256^2 bytes of ROM), the best timing/memory trade-off is achieved with $\mathrm{LAL}_{n=8}$ method and leads to a cost of around 25 cycles in 8051 architecture. Eventually, we get a multiplication over $\mathbb{F}_{2^4}$ which is around 6 times faster than a multiplication over $\mathbb{F}_{2^8}$. Hence exchanging the latter operation by 6 or less multiplications in $\mathbb{F}_{2^4}$ leads to a practical efficiency gain. This strategy has been followed by Kim *et al.* in [36] for the evaluation of the monomial x^{254} in $\mathbb{F}_{2^8}$ (which is affinely equivalent to the AES sbox) and led to a practical improvement compared to the approach in [18].

3.2   Masking Complexity of Polynomials

When the polynomial representation is not reduced to a single monomial, the notions of CC-addition chain can be straightforwardly extended. Actually, the notion of polynomial chain is given in [37, Sect. 4.6.4] and the shortest size of such a chain (when only non-linear multiplications are counted) exactly corresponds to the masking complexity.

Table 3. Cyclotomic classes for $n \in \{4, 6, 8\}$ w.r.t. the masking complexity k

k	Cyclotomic classes C_α of elements α in $\mathbb{Z}/(2^n - 1)\mathbb{Z}$ for $n \in \{4, 6, 8\}$
	$n = 4$
0	$C_0 = \{0\}$, $C_1 = \{1, 2, 4, 8\}$
1	$C_3 = \{3, 6, 12, 9\}$, $C_5 = \{5, 10\}$
2	$C_7 = \{7, 14, 13, 11\}$
	$n = 6$
0	$C_0 = \{0\}$, $C_1 = \{1, 2, 4, 8, 16, 32\}$
1	$C_3 = \{3, 6, 12, 24, 48, 33\}$, $C_5 = \{5, 10, 20, 40, 17, 34\}$ $C_9 = \{9, 18, 36\}$
2	$C_7 = \{7, 14, 28, 56, 49, 35\}$, $C_{11} = \{11, 22, 44, 25, 50, 37\}$ $C_{13} = \{13, 26, 52, 41, 19, 38\}$, $C_{15} = \{15, 30, 29, 27, 23\}$ $C_{21} = \{21, 42\}$, $C_{27} = \{27, 54, 45\}$
3	$C_{23} = \{23, 46, 29, 58, 53, 43\}$, $C_{31} = \{31, 62, 61, 59, 55, 47\}$
	$n = 8$
0	$C_0 = \{0\}$, $C_1 = \{1, 2, 4, 8, 16, 32, 64, 128\}$
1	$C_3 = \{3, 6, 12, 24, 48, 96, 192, 129\}$, $C_5 = \{5, 10, 20, 40, 80, 160, 65, 130\}$, $C_9 = \{9, 18, 36, 72, 144, 33, 66, 132\}$, $C_{17} = \{17, 34, 68, 136\}$
2	$C_7 = \{7, 14, 28, 56, 112, 224, 193, 131\}$ $C_{11} = \{11, 22, 44, 88, 176, 97, 194, 133\}$, $C_{13} = \{13, 26, 52, 104, 208, 161, 67, 134\}$ $C_{15} = \{15, 30, 60, 120, 240, 225, 195, 135\}$, $C_{19} = \{19, 38, 76, 152, 49, 98, 196, 137\}$ $C_{21} = \{21, 42, 84, 168, 81, 162, 69, 138\}$, $C_{25} = \{25, 50, 100, 200, 145, 35, 70, 140\}$ $C_{27} = \{27, 54, 108, 216, 177, 99, 198, 141\}$, $C_{37} = \{37, 74, 148, 41, 82, 164, 73, 146\}$ $C_{45} = \{45, 90, 180, 105, 210, 165, 75, 150\}$, $C_{51} = \{51, 102, 204, 153\}$, $C_{85} = \{85, 170\}$
3	$C_{23} = \{23, 46, 92, 184, 113, 226, 197, 139\}$ $C_{29} = \{29, 58, 116, 232, 209, 163, 71, 142\}$, $C_{31} = \{31, 62, 124, 248, 241, 227, 199, 143\}$ $C_{39} = \{39, 78, 156, 57, 114, 228, 201, 147\}$, $C_{43} = \{43, 86, 172, 89, 178, 101, 202, 149\}$ $C_{47} = \{47, 94, 188, 121, 242, 229, 203, 151\}$ $C_{53} = \{53, 106, 212, 169, 83, 166, 77, 154\}$ $C_{55} = \{55, 110, 220, 185, 115, 230, 205, 155\}$ $C_{59} = \{59, 118, 236, 217, 179, 103, 206, 157\}$ $C_{61} = \{61, 122, 244, 233, 211, 167, 79, 158\}$ $C_{63} = \{63, 126, 252, 249, 243, 231, 207, 159\}$ $C_{87} = \{87, 174, 93, 186, 117, 234, 213, 171\}$, $C_{91} = \{91, 182, 109, 218, 181, 107, 214, 173\}$ $C_{95} = \{95, 190, 125, 250, 245, 235, 215, 175\}$ $C_{111} = \{111, 222, 189, 123, 246, 237, 219, 183\}$ $C_{119} = \{119, 238, 221, 187\}$
4	$C_{127} = \{127, 254, 253, 251, 247, 239, 223, 191\}$

For $n \leq 8$, Table 3 can of course be used to deduce an upper-bound of the masking complexity of any polynomial defined over $\mathbb{F}_{2^n}$, by summing the masking complexities of its monomials. However, as we will see hereafter, the achieved bounds are far from being tight since the evaluation of a polynomial can be performed more efficiently than simply evaluating each of its monomials separately. Actually, the authors of [9] present two polynomial evaluation methods which aim at minimizing the number of required non-linear multiplications. They have been afterwards improved in [56] and recently in [15]. We recall these works afterwards.

In [9], the authors propose two solutions to securely evaluate a polynomial $P(x) \in \mathbb{F}_{2^n}[x]$.

The *cyclotomic method* consists in rewriting $P(x)$ in the form:

$$P(x) = u_0 + \sum_{i=1}^{q} L_i(x^{\alpha_i}) + u_{2^n-1} x^{2^n-1}, \tag{6}$$

where q is a positive integer and $(L_i)_{i \leqslant q}$ is a family of linearized polynomials[8]. Since the transformations $x \in \mathbb{F}_{2^n} \mapsto x^{2^j}$ are $\mathbb{F}_2$-linear, their masking complexity is null. This implies that the masking complexity of $\sum_{i=1}^{q} L_i(x^{\alpha_i})$ equals the number of non-linear multiplications required to evaluate all the monomials x^{α_i}. It is shown in [9], that the latter number is bounded above by the number of cyclotomic classes in $\mathbb{F}_{2^n}$ minus 2, which led to the following proposition:

Proposition 1. [9] *Let n be a positive integer. For every* $P(x) \in \mathbb{F}_{2^n}[x]$*, the masking complexity of $P(x)$, denoted $\mathcal{MC}(P)$, satisfies:*

$$\mathcal{MC}(P) \leqslant \sum_{\delta | (2^n-1)} \frac{\varphi(\delta)}{\mu(\delta)} - 1,$$

where $\mu(\delta)$ denotes the multiplicative order of 2 modulo δ and $\varphi(\cdot)$ denotes the Euler totient function.

Remark 2. The proposition is a direct implication of the fact that the number of cyclotomic classes in $\mathbb{F}_{2^n}$ is $\sum_{\delta | (2^n-1)} \frac{\varphi(\delta)}{\mu(\delta)}$, which is bounded below by $(2^n-1)/n$.

Remark 3. It is proved in [56] that the masking complexity is invariant w.r.t. field representation.

Proposition 1 has been afterwards completed in [56] with the following result giving a lower bound on the masking complexity.

Proposition 2. [56] *Let n be a positive integer. For every polynomial $P(x) = \sum_{i=0}^{2^n-1} u_i x^i$ in $\mathbb{F}_{2^n}[x]$, the masking complexity of $P(x)$ satisfies:*

$$\max_{\substack{0 < i < 2^n-1 \\ u_i \neq 0}} m_n(i) \leqslant \mathcal{MC}(P),$$

---

[8] *i.e.* a linear combination of monomials in the form x^{2^j} with $j < n$.

where, for every $i \in [1..2^n - 2]$, $m_n(i)$ *denotes the size of the shortest* cyclotomic-class addition chain.

Remark 4. It may be observed that the masking complexity of the monomial x^i exactly corresponds to $m_n(i)$ [9,56]. The authors of [56] recall that the $m_n(i)$ is itself bounded above by $\lceil \log_2(\text{HW}(i)) \rceil$. They moreover show that techniques proposed by Brauer in [7] may be applied to prove that $m_n(i)$ is bounded below by $\frac{\log_2(i)}{\log_2 \log_2(i)} \times (1 + O(1))$ when i (and thus n) tends towards infinity.

Thanks to Proposition 2, Roy and Vivek argue that the masking complexity of the DES s-boxes is lower bounded by 3, whereas the s-box of AES is bounded below by 4 (actually the bound is tight with the representation introduced in [54]). Proposition 2 has been further improved by Coron, Roy and Vivek in [15] where the following new lower bound has been exhibited by adapting a technique initially introduced by Paterson and Stockmeyer [47].

Proposition 3. *For every positive integer* n, *there exists a polynomial* $P(x) \in \mathbb{F}_{2^n}[x]$ *with masking complexity satisfying:*

$$\sqrt{\frac{2^n}{n}} - 2 \leqslant \mathcal{MC}(P). \tag{7}$$

For the polynomials $P(x) = \sum_{i=0}^{2^n - 1} u_i x^i$ whose masking complexity is bounded above by $\sqrt{\frac{2^n}{n}} - 2$, Proposition 3 improves the lower-bound $\max_{i, u_i \neq} \lceil \log_2(\text{HW}(i)) \rceil$ given in Proposition 2 when n is greater than or equal to 9.

The *Knuth-Eve method* proposed in [9] is actually a direct application of Knuth-Eve algorithm [24,38] which is based on a recursive use of the following lemma.

Lemma 1. *Let* n *and* t *be two positive integers and let* $P(x)$ *be a polynomial of degree* t *over* $\mathbb{F}_{2^n}[x]$. *There exist two polynomials* $P_1(x)$ *and* $P_2(x)$ *of degrees bounded above by* $\lfloor t/2 \rfloor$ *over* $\mathbb{F}_{2^n}[x]$ *such that:*

$$P(x) = P_1(x^2) \oplus P_2(x^2)x. \tag{8}$$

Applying Lemma 1 to the polynomial $P(x)$ gives $P(x) = P_1(x^2) + P_2(x^2)x$, where $P_1(x)$ and $P_2(x)$ are two polynomials of degrees bounded above by $2^{n-1} - 1$. The authors of [9] deduce that $P(x)$ can be computed after computation of all monomials $(x^{2j})_{j \leq 2^{n-1} - 1}$ with a single multiplication by x. Then, applying Lemma 1 again to the polynomials $P_1(x)$ and $P_2(x)$ both of degree bounded above by $2^{n-1} - 1$ leads to two new pairs of polynomials $(P_{11}(x), P_{12}(x))$ and $(P_{21}(x), P_{22}(x))$ such that $P_1(x^2) = P_{11}(x^4) + P_{12}(x^4)x^2$ and $P_2(x^2) = P_{21}(x^4) + P_{22}(x^4)x^2$. The degree of the new polynomials is bounded above by $2^{n-2} - 1$. Eventually, applying Lemma 1 recursively r times gives an evaluation of $P(x)$

involving evaluations in x^{2^r} of polynomials of degree bounded above by $2^{n-r} - 1$ plus $2^r - 1 = \sum_{i=0}^{r-1} 2^i$ multiplications by powers of x in the form x^{2^i} with $i \leq 2^{r-1}$. This observation leads to the following proposition.

Proposition 4. *Let n be a positive integer. For every $P(x) \in \mathbb{F}_{2^n}[x]$, the masking complexity of $P(x)$ satisfies:*

$$\mathcal{MC}(P) \leqslant \min_{0 \leq r \leq n} (2^{n-r-1} + 2^r) - 2 = \begin{cases} \frac{3}{2} 2^{n/2} - 2 & \text{if } n \text{ is even} \\ 2^{(n+1)/2} - 2 & \text{if } n \text{ is odd} \end{cases}. \tag{9}$$

Roy-Vivek's method has been introduced in [56]. It follows an approach very close to that of Paterson and Stockmeyer in [47] and it essentially consists in expressing $P(x)$ as a function of several lower degree polynomials, each of degree at most k for some fixed k. In its most simple version, the method assumes that the degree of $P(x)$ equals $k(2t - 1)$ and it starts by dividing $P(x)$ by x^{kt}. The remainder $R_0(x)$ has degree at most $kt - 1$, whereas the quotient $Q_0(x)$ has degree $k(t - 1)$. Adding the term $x^{k(t-1)}$ to $R_0(x)$ and dividing the sum by $Q_0(x)$ leads to $R_0(x) - x^{k(t-1)} = C_0(x) \times Q_0(x) + S_0(x)$ where $C_0(x)$ and $S_0(x)$ have degree at most k and $k(t - 1) - 1$ respectively. We then get:

$$P(x) = (x^{kt} + C_0(x)) \times Q_0(x) + x^{k(t-1)} + S_0(x).$$

The method is then applied recursively to the polynomials $Q_0(x)$ and $x^{k(t-1)} + S_0(x)$ (both of degree $k(t - 1)$). Namely, they are both divided by $x^{\frac{kt}{2}}$ leading to:

$$Q_0(x) = (x^{\frac{kt}{2}} + C_1(x)) \times Q_1(X) + x^{k(\frac{t}{2}-1)} + S_1(x)$$

and

$$x^{k(t-1)} + S_0(x) = (x^{\frac{kt}{2}} + C_2(x)) \times Q_2(x) + x^{k(\frac{t}{2}-1)} + S_2(x),$$

where, for $i \in \{1,2\}$, the polynomials $C_i(x)$ have degree at most k, the polynomials $Q_i(x)$ have degree $k(\frac{t}{2} - 1)$ and the polynomials $S_i(x)$ have degree strictly lower than $k(\frac{t}{2}-1)$). Repeating the procedure $\lceil \log_2(t) \rceil$ times eventually splits $P(x)$ as a combination of polynomials of degree upper bounded by k and of monomials in the cyclotomic class of x^k. For a polynomial $P(x)$ representing an s-box from $\mathbb{F}_{2^n}$ to $\mathbb{F}_{2^m}$, the number of non-linear multiplications needed with Roy-Vivek's method is around $k \times (2^m - 1)$ (assuming that the polynomial representation is dense). It involves around $(k + 1) \times (2^m - 1)$ additions and $k/2 + \log_k \deg(P)$ squarings.

Roy-Vivek's method enables to process the DES s-boxes with 7 non-linear multiplications which is smaller than the numbers 10 and 11 respectively needed with the cyclotomic and Knuth-Eve's methods. Actually, for CAMELIA, CLEFIA, PRESENT and SERPENT s-boxes, Roy-Vivek's method is at least as efficient as the latter methods, and often performs more efficiently.

Coron-Roy-Vivek's method has been recently proposed in [15] and may be viewed as an extension of [56]. It first consists in building an union $\mathcal{C}$ of some cyclotomic classes C_i of elements in $\mathbb{Z}/(2^n - 1)\mathbb{Z}$. The number of non-linear multiplications required to build C is denoted by μ. The set of monomials x^j with j in C spans a subspace of $\mathbb{F}_{2^n}[x]$ which is denoted by $\mathcal{P}$. The second step of Coron's method consists in finding a t-variate polynomial $R \in \mathbb{F}_{2^n}[x_1, \cdots, x_t]$ such that:

$$P(x) = R(P_1(x), \cdots, P_t(x)), \tag{10}$$

and $\mathcal{MC}(R) + \mu$ is as small as possible. To ease the search of the polynomial R, Coron suggests to limit the search to some polynomials and to apply the following heuristic approach:

1. build the union set C such that all the powers of P's monomials are in $C + C$.
2. Choose/fix a set of r polynomials $P_1(x)$, ..., $P_r(x)$ in $\mathcal{P}$ and search $r + 1$ polynomials $P_{r+1}(x)$, ..., $P_{2r+1}(x)$ such that:

$$P(x) = \sum_{i=1}^{r} P_i(x) \times P_{r+i}(x) + P_{2r+1}(x). \tag{11}$$

To find the $r + 1$ polynomials $P_{r+i}(x)$, with $i \in [1..r + 1]$, Coron suggests to solve the linear system of $n2^n$ Boolean equations implied by the evaluation of Eq. (11) in every $x \in \mathbb{F}_{2^n}$. Let ℓ denote the size of C. The number of unknown values in the system is bounded above by $\min(r, \ell) \times \ell + \ell$. Hence, the condition $2^n \leqslant \ell \times (1 + \min(r, \ell))$ ensures that the method outputs at least one solution.

In [15], it is pointed out that the method is heuristic and that there is currently no proof that it leads to a solution. In practice however, it is observed that the method always leads to a solution in the cases considered by the author. Its complexity (in terms of the number of non-linear multiplications) in those cases is $O(\sqrt{2^n/n})$, which is asymptotically better than the complexity of Knuth-Eve's method that equals $O(\sqrt{2^n})$ (due to Inequality (9)). Moreover, a comparison of Coron's complexity with Inequality (7) shows that it is asymptotically optimal.

The method is applied for the first DES s-box and leads to an evaluation with only 4 non-linear multiplications, implying that the masking complexity of this sbox is at most 4 (and at least 3 due to Proposition 2). The method is also applied to the sboxes of CLEFIA [60], PRESENT [6] leading to a complexity of 10 and 2 respectively (which improves all previous methods).

3.3   The Extended Masking Complexity

As recalled in previous section, the secure processing of monomials in the form x^{1+2^s} (which corresponds to Algorithm 5) is more efficient than that of any other power functions which are not in the cyclotomic class of x. Based on this observation, the authors of [30] followed an approach close to [9] in order to exhibit a new processing of power functions where calculi of the form $x \mapsto x \times x^{2^s}$ are no longer considered as nonlinear multiplications but as a third type of operations. Namely, for every power function $x \mapsto x^\alpha$, [30] presents new operations' sequences which first minimize the number of non-linear multiplications (which are neither $\mathbb{F}_2$-affine nor in the form $x \mapsto x \times x^{2^s}$) (referred as Type II operation), and then minimize the number of processings in the form $x \mapsto x \times x^{2^s}$ (referred as Type III operation). As observed by the authors themselves, this amounts to output, for each exponent α, the shortest cyclotomic class addition chain with the supplementary constraint that multiplications by 2^s, for any integer s, or additions in the form $v + 2^s v$ are for free. The length corresponding to this type of addition chain is referred to as *extended length* in [30]. It is defined as a pair (k_1, k_2) where k_1 refers to the number of Type III operations and k_2 refers to the number of Type II operations. The results obtained in [30] are recalled in Table 4.

Remark 5. Costs given in Table 4 have been obtained by first minimizing the global number of Type-II and Type-III operations, and then by minimizing the number of Type-III multiplications. It can be noticed that other minimization strategies could be applied. For instance, if the goal is to minimize the number of Type-III multiplications, then it can be checked that x^{254} can be evaluated without such operation: first process x^{63}, then $(x + x^{63})^3 = x^{189} + x^{127} + x^{65} + x^3$, end eventually process x^{189}, x^{65} and x^3, and subtract them to $(x + x^{63})^3$ to get $x^{254} = (x^{127})^2$ (which gives a processing without Type-III operations and 9 Type-II operations).

For the exponentiation $x \mapsto x^{254}$ (the non-linear part of the AES S-box), the extended addition chain is $(1, 2, 5, 25, 125, 127, 254)$ whose extended length is $1 + 3$. This sequence requires only 1 operation of Type II (to get x^{127}), 2 linear operations (aka Type I operations) (to get and x^2 and x^{254}) and 3 operations of Type II (to get x^5, x^{25} and x^{125})). It may moreover be observed that the sequence involves the same operation $y \mapsto y^{1+2^2}$ each time, which reduces the memory required to implement the solution (Tables 5 and 6).

The interest of using extended addition chains instead of addition chains has been experimentally validated by Grosso *et al.* [30] for the particular case of the exponentiation $x \mapsto x^{254}$ over $\mathbb{F}_{2^n}$ [8] and the first DES sbox. We recall their implementation results hereafter[9]:

3.4   Some Recent Progresses Made While This Paper Was Reviewed

The present paper was written in November 2014. The publication process makes it published approximately one year later. Meanwhile, important advances have been made, that we wish to briefly present. In [10], it has been introduced a new method for masking s-boxes, which decomposes them by means of functions of low algebraic degree, and masks each such low degree function. The decomposition step starts by deriving a family of generators: $\begin{cases} G_1(x) = F_1(x) \\ G_i(x) = F_i(G_{i-1}(x)) \end{cases}$ where the F_i are random polynomials of algebraic degree s, that is, whose exponents

---

[9] Implementations have been done in C and compiled for ATMEGA644p microcontroller thanks to the compiler avr_gcc with optimisation flag -o2.

Table 4. Cyclotomic classes for $n \in \{4, 6, 8\}$ w.r.t. the masking complexity k

(k_1, k_2)	Cyclotomic classes C_α of elements α in $\mathbb{Z}/(2^n - 1)\mathbb{Z}$ for $n \in \{4, 6, 8\}$
	$n = 4$
$(0,0)$	$C_0 = \{0\}, C_1 = \{1, 2, 4, 8\}$
$(0,1)$	$C_3 = \{3, 6, 12, 9\}, C_5 = \{5, 10\}$
$(1,1)$	$C_7 = \{7, 14, 13, 11\}$
	$n = 6$
$(0,0)$	$C_0 = \{0\}, C_1 = \{1, 2, 4, 8, 16, 32\}$
$(0,1)$	$C_3 = \{3, 6, 12, 24, 48, 33\}, C_5 = \{5, 10, 20, 40, 17, 34\}, C_9 = \{9, 18, 36\}$
$(0,2)$	$C_{11} = \{11, 22, 44, 25, 50, 37\}, C_{15} = \{15, 30, 60, 57, 51, 39\} \; C_{27} = \{27, 54, 45\}$
$(1,1)$	$C_7 = \{7, 14, 28, 56, 49, 35\} \; C_{13} = \{13, 26, 52, 41, 19, 38\}$
	$C_{21} = \{21, 42\} \; C_{31} = \{31, 62, 61, 59, 55, 47, \}$
$(1,2)$	$C_{23} = \{23, 46, 29, 58, 53, 43\}$
	$n = 8$
$(0,0)$	$C_0 = \{0\}, C_1 = \{1, 2, 4, 8, 16, 32, 64, 128\}$
$(0,1)$	$C_3 = \{3, 6, 12, 24, 48, 96, 192, 129\}, C_5 = \{5, 10, 20, 40, 80, 160, 65, 130\}$
	$C_9 = \{9, 18, 36, 72, 144, 33, 66, 132\}, C_{17} = \{17, 34, 68, 136\}$
$(0,2)$	$C_{15} = \{15, 30, 60, 120, 240, 225, 195, 135\}$
	$C_{21} = \{21, 42, 84, 168, 81, 162, 69, 138\}$
	$C_{25} = \{25, 50, 100, 200, 145, 35, 70, 140\}$
	$C_{27} = \{27, 54, 108, 216, 177, 99, 198, 141\}$
	$C_{45} = \{45, 90, 180, 105, 210, 165, 75, 150\}$
	$C_{51} = \{51, 102, 204, 153\}, C_{85} = \{85, 170\}$
$(0,3)$	$C_{63} = \{63, 126, 252, 249, 243, 231, 207, 159\}$
	$C_{95} = \{95, 190, 125, 250, 245, 235, 215, 175\}$
	$C_{111} = \{111, 222, 189, 123, 246, 237, 219, 183\}$
$(0,4)$	$C_{39} = \{39, 78, 156, 57, 114, 228, 201, 147\}$
	$C_{55} = \{55, 110, 220, 185, 115, 230, 205, 155\}$
	$C_{87} = \{87, 174, 93, 186, 117, 234, 213, 171\}$
$(1,1)$	$C_7 = \{7, 14, 28, 56, 112, 224, 193, 131\}$
	$C_{11} = \{11, 22, 44, 88, 176, 97, 194, 133\}$
	$C_{13} = \{13, 26, 52, 104, 208, 161, 67, 134\}$
	$C_{19} = \{19, 38, 76, 152, 49, 98, 196, 137\}$
	$C_{37} = \{37, 74, 148, 41, 82, 164, 73, 146\}$
$(1,2)$	$C_{23} = \{23, 46, 92, 184, 113, 226, 197, 139\}$
	$C_{29} = \{29, 58, 116, 232, 209, 163, 71, 142\}$
	$C_{31} = \{31, 62, 124, 248, 241, 227, 199, 143\}$
	$C_{43} = \{43, 86, 172, 89, 178, 101, 202, 149\}$
	$C_{47} = \{47, 94, 188, 121, 242, 229, 203, 151\}$
	$C_{53} = \{53, 106, 212, 169, 83, 166, 77, 154\}$
	$C_{59} = \{59, 118, 236, 217, 179, 103, 206, 157\}$
	$C_{61} = \{61, 122, 244, 233, 211, 167, 79, 158\}$
	$C_{91} = \{91, 182, 109, 218, 181, 107, 214, 173\}$
	$C_{119} = \{119, 238, 221, 187\}$
$(1,3)$	$C_{127} = \{127, 254, 253, 251, 247, 239, 223, 191\}$

Table 5. Secure AES S-box for ATMEGA644p.

Solution	[C] $d = 1$	[C] $d = 2$	[C] $d = 3$
Addition-chain method [55]	753	1999	3702
Extended addition-chain method [30]	488	1227	2319

Table 6. Secure DES S-box for ATMEGA644p.

Solution	C $d = 1$	C $d = 2$	C $d = 3$
Cyclotomic method [9]	2001	4646	8182
Cyclotomic method with Type-III operation [30]	1623	3574	7413

are the sums of at most s powers of 2. Then it randomly generates t polynomials $Q_i = \sum_{j=1}^{r} L_j \circ G_j$, where the L_j are linearized polynomials. Eventually, it searches for t polynomials P_i of algebraic degree s and for $r + 1$ linearized polynomials L_i such that:

$$P(x) = \sum_{i=1}^{t} P_i(Q_i(x)) + \sum_{i=1}^{r} L_i(G_i(x)) + L_0(x).$$

As in the CRV method, the search of polynomials P_i and L_i amounts to solve a system of linear equations over $\mathbb{F}_{2^n}$.

For masking a function F of algebraic degree at most s, the method uses that for such function, the mapping

$$\varphi_F^{(s)}(a_1, a_2, \ldots, a_s) = \sum_{I \subseteq \{1,\ldots,s\}} F\left(\sum_{i \in I} a_i\right)$$

is multilinear (this is characteristic of functions of algebraic degree at most s). Then, it is proved that, for every $d \geq s$:

$$F\left(\sum_{i=1}^{d} a_i\right) = \sum_{1 \leq i_1 < \cdots < i_s \leq d} \varphi_F^{(s)}(a_{i_1}, \ldots, a_{i_s}) + \sum_{j=0}^{s-1} \eta_{d,s}(j) \sum_{\substack{I \subseteq \{1,\ldots,d\} \\ |I|=j}} F\left(\sum_{i \in I} a_i\right),$$

where $\eta_{d,s}(j) = \binom{d-j-1}{s-j-1} \bmod 2$ for every $j \leq s - 1$, and this allows proving that:

$$F\left(\sum_{i=1}^{d} a_i\right) = \sum_{j=0}^{s} \mu_{d,s}(j) \sum_{\substack{I \subseteq \{1,\ldots,d\} \\ |I|=j}} F\left(\sum_{i \in I} a_i\right),$$

where $\mu_{d,s}(j) = \binom{d-j-1}{s-j} \mod 2$ for every $j \leq s$.
This reduces the complexity of the d-masking of a degree s function to several s-maskings.

4   Conclusion and Perspectives

In this paper we have recalled the main techniques proposed in the literature to evaluate functions over finite fields while defeating higher-order side channel attacks. All of them start by splitting the evaluation into a sequence of elementary operations which are afterwards independently protected with bespoke schemes that operate on shared values and output a sharing of the result. A section has been dedicated to the presentation and analysis of these schemes. Essentially, they allow for the secure processing of any field multiplication or quadratic function (or more general low degree function). Their construction differs depending on the underlying data sharing (e.g. additive, polynomial or, more generally, based on a linear code). When additive sharing is used, the complexity of the secure processing of affine transformations is linear in the security order d and it is quadratic for the secure processing of multiplications or quadratic functions. If data are represented by polynomial (aka Shamir's) sharing, the complexity of the scheme for affine functions stays linear in d but the complexity of the scheme dedicated to the multiplication becomes cubic. As argued in [32,52], polynomial sharing (and the dedicated schemes) may however be preferred to additive sharing since it provides better resistance against unbounded side-channel attacks[10]. For practical values of d (e.g. $d \leqslant 10$), the timing complexity of the recalled schemes in terms of CPU cycles strongly depends on the cost of the underlying field multiplication. The latter one itself depends on the field dimension n and the memory constraints. We recalled different multiplication implementation strategies which offer various timing/memory trade-offs. The choice among them depends on the context constraints.

Since the complexity of the schemes dedicated to the secure processing of multiplications is quadratic, several polynomial evaluation strategies published in the literature essentially try to split the evaluation into a sequence of elementary operations including a minimal number of multiplications. We recalled these strategies which are: the Cyclotomic method [9], the Knuth-Eve method [38] and the Coron-Roy-Vivek's method [15]. This approach has raised the need to introduce a new notion, called masking complexity of a polynomial, which corresponds to the minimum number of non-linear multiplications required to evaluate the polynomial on any field element. Computing this complexity for any polynomial seems to be a difficult problem but we recalled several results published in [9,15,56] which enable to have lower and upper bounds. Among the three evaluation methods presented in the three latter papers, the one by Coron et al. seems to be the most efficient one in general, i.e. when d and n are not

---

[10] These attacks assume that the adversary is not limited to the observation of d intermediate results during the evaluation but can observe any family of intermediate results.

too small and the polynomial has no particular structure (but the very recent Carlet-Prouff-Rivain-Roche CPRR method further improves the efficiency). It involves only $O(\sqrt{2^n/n})$ non-linear multiplications which can be proved to be asymptotically optimal. Despite its qualities, Coron *et al.* 's method is heuristic, as well as the more recent CPRR method, and no formal rules today exist to parametrize the main steps (the construction of the union of cyclotomic classes and the choice of the fixed polynomials). Dealing with this issue seems to be an interesting open avenue for further research. Moreover, several ways could be investigated to improve Coron-Roy-Vivek's approach. For instance, it can be studied whether the cost of the building of the classes of cyclotomic classes (which is the first step of the method) could not be reduced.

References

1. Akkar, M.-L., Goubin, L.: A generic protection against high-order differential power analysis. In: Johansson, T. (ed.) FSE 2003. LNCS, vol. 2887, pp. 192–205. Springer, Heidelberg (2003)
2. Balasch, J., Faust, S., Gierlichs, B., Verbauwhede, I.: Theory and practice of a leakage resilient masking scheme. In: Wang, X., Sako, K. (eds.) ASIACRYPT 2012. LNCS, vol. 7658, pp. 758–775. Springer, Heidelberg (2012)
3. Bellare, M., Goldwasser, S., Micciancio, D.: "Pseudo-random" number generation within cryptographic algorithms: the DSS case. In: Kaliski Jr., B.S. (ed.) CRYPTO 1997. LNCS, vol. 1294, pp. 277–291. Springer, Heidelberg (1997)
4. Ben-Or, M., Goldwasser, S., Wigderson, A.: Completeness theorems for noncryptographic fault-tolerant distributed computation. In: STOC 1988: Proceedings of the Twentieth Annual ACM Symposium on Theory of Computing, pp. 1–10. ACM, New York (1988)
5. Blakely, G.: Safeguarding cryptographic keys. In: National Computer Conference, vol. 48, pp. 313–317. AFIPS Press, New York, June 1979
6. Bogdanov, A., Knudsen, L.R., Leander, G., Paar, C., Poschmann, A., Robshaw, M.J.B., Seurin, Y., Vikkelsoe, C.: PRESENT: an ultra-lightweight block cipher. In: Paillier and Verbauwhede [48], pp. 450–466
7. Brauer, A.: On addtion chains. Bull. Amer. MAth. Soc. **45**, 736–739 (1939)
8. Brier, E., Clavier, C., Olivier, F.: Correlation power analysis with a leakage model. In: Joye, M., Quisquater, J.-J. (eds.) CHES 2004. LNCS, vol. 3156, pp. 16–29. Springer, Heidelberg (2004)
9. Carlet, C., Goubin, L., Prouff, E., Quisquater, M., Rivain, M.: Higher-order masking schemes for s-boxes. In: Canteaut, A. (ed.) FSE 2012. LNCS, vol. 7549, pp. 366–384. Springer, Heidelberg (2012)
10. Carlet, C., Prouff, E., Rivain, M., Roche, T.: Algebraic decomposition for probing security. In: Gennaro, R., Robshaw, M. (eds.) CRYPTO 2015. LNCS, pp. 742–763. Springer, Heidelberg (2015)
11. Chari, S., Jutla, C.S., Rao, J.R., Rohatgi, P.: Towards sound approaches to counteract power-analysis attacks. In: Wiener, M. (ed.) CRYPTO 1999. LNCS, vol. 1666, p. 398. Springer, Heidelberg (1999)
12. Chen, H., Cramer, R., Goldwasser, S., de Haan, R., Vaikuntanathan, V.: Secure computation from random error correcting codes. In: Naor, M. (ed.) EUROCRYPT 2007. LNCS, vol. 4515, pp. 291–310. Springer, Heidelberg (2007)

13. Cook, S.A.: On the minimum computation time of functions. Ph.D. thesis, Harvard University, Cambridge, MA, USA (1966). http://cr.yp.to/bib/entries.html#1966/cook

14. Coron, J.-S., Prouff, E., Rivain, M., Roche, T.: Higher-order side channel security and mask refreshing. In: Moriai, S. (ed.) FSE 2013. LNCS, vol. 8424, pp. 410–424. Springer, Heidelberg (2014)

15. Coron, J.-S., Roy, A., Vivek, S.: Fast evaluation of polynomials over binary finite fields and application to side-channel countermeasures. In: Batina, L., Robshaw, M. (eds.) CHES 2014. LNCS, vol. 8731, pp. 170–187. Springer, Heidelberg (2014)

16. Coron, J.-S.: A new DPA countermeasure based on permutation tables. In: Ostrovsky, R., De Prisco, R., Visconti, I. (eds.) SCN 2008. LNCS, vol. 5229, pp. 278–292. Springer, Heidelberg (2008)

17. Coron, J.-S.: Higher order masking of look-up tables. In: Nguyen, P.Q., Oswald, E. (eds.) EUROCRYPT 2014. LNCS, vol. 8441, pp. 441–458. Springer, Heidelberg (2014)

18. Coron, J.-S., Giraud, C., Prouff, E., Renner, S., Rivain, M., Vadnala, P.K.: Conversion of security proofs from one leakage model to another: a new issue. In: Schindler, W., Huss, S.A. (eds.) COSADE 2012. LNCS, vol. 7275, pp. 69–81. Springer, Heidelberg (2012)

19. Yoo, H.S., Kim, C.K., Ha, J.C., Moon, S.-J., Park, I.H.: Side channel cryptanalysis on SEED. In: Lim, C.H., Yung, M. (eds.) WISA 2004. LNCS, vol. 3325, pp. 411–424. Springer, Heidelberg (2005)

20. Coron, J.-S., Prouff, E., Roche, T.: On the use of shamir's secret sharing against side-channel analysis. In: Mangard, S. (ed.) CARDIS 2012. LNCS, vol. 7771, pp. 77–90. Springer, Heidelberg (2013)

21. Courtois, N.T., Goubin, L.: An algebraic masking method to protect AES against power attacks. In: Won, D.H., Kim, S. (eds.) ICISC 2005. LNCS, vol. 3935, pp. 199–209. Springer, Heidelberg (2006)

22. Damgård, I., Ishai, Y., Krøigaard, M., Nielsen, J.B., Smith, A.: Scalable multiparty computation with nearly optimal work and resilience. In: Wagner, D. (ed.) CRYPTO 2008. LNCS, vol. 5157, pp. 241–261. Springer, Heidelberg (2008)

23. Duc, A., Dziembowski, S., Faust, S.: Unifying leakage models: from probing attacks to noisy leakage. In: Nguyen, P.Q., Oswald, E. (eds.) EUROCRYPT 2014. LNCS, vol. 8441, pp. 423–440. Springer, Heidelberg (2014)

24. Eve, J.: The evaluation of polynomials. Comm. ACM 6(1), 17–21 (1964)

25. Faust, S., Rabin, T., Reyzin, L., Tromer, E., Vaikuntanathan, V.: Protecting circuits from leakage: the computationally-bounded and noisy cases. In: Gilbert, H. (ed.) EUROCRYPT 2010. LNCS, vol. 6110, pp. 135–156. Springer, Heidelberg (2010)

26. Franklin, M.K., Yung, M.: Communication complexity of secure computation (extended abstract). In: Kosaraju, S.R., Fellows, M., Wigderson, A., Ellis, J.A. (eds.) STOC, pp. 699–710. ACM, New York (1992)

27. Genelle, L., Prouff, E., Quisquater, M.: Thwarting higher-order side channel analysis with additive and multiplicative maskings. In: Preneel, B., Takagi, T. (eds.) CHES 2011. LNCS, vol. 6917, pp. 240–255. Springer, Heidelberg (2011)

28. Gennaro, R., Rabin, M.O., Rabin, T.: Simplified vss and fact-track multiparty computations with applications to threshold cryptography. In: PODC, pp. 101–111 (1998)

29. Goubin, L., Martinelli, A.: Protecting AES with shamir's secret sharing scheme. In: Preneel, B., Takagi, T. (eds.) CHES 2011. LNCS, vol. 6917, pp. 79–94. Springer, Heidelberg (2011)

30. Grosso, V., Prouff, E., Standaert, F.-X.: Efficient masked s-boxes processing – a step forward –. In: Pointcheval, D., Vergnaud, D. (eds.) AFRICACRYPT. LNCS, vol. 8469, pp. 251–266. Springer, Heidelberg (2014)
31. Grosso, V., Standaert, F.-X., Faust, S.: Masking vs. multiparty computation: how large is the gap for AES? In: Bertoni, G., Coron, J.-S. (eds.) CHES 2013. LNCS, vol. 8086, pp. 400–416. Springer, Heidelberg (2013)
32. Grosso, V., Standaert, F.-X., Faust, S.: Masking vs. multiparty computation: how large is the gap for aes? J. Cryptographic Eng. 4(1), 47–57 (2014)
33. Gueron, S., Parzanchevsky, O., Zuk, O.: Masked inversion in $GF(2^n)$ usingmixed field representations and its efficient implementation for AES. In: Nedjah, N., Mourelle, L.M. (eds.) Embedded Cryptographic Hardware: Methodologies and Architectures, pp. 213–228. Nova Science Publishers, New York (2004)
34. Ishai, Y., Sahai, A., Wagner, D.: Private circuits: securing hardware against probing attacks. In: Boneh, D. (ed.) CRYPTO 2003. LNCS, vol. 2729, pp. 463–481. Springer, Heidelberg (2003)
35. Karatsuba, A., Ofman, Y.: Multiplication of many-digital numbers by automatic computers. Transl. Acad. J. Phys. Dokl. 7, 595–596 (1963). Proceedings of the USSR Academy of Sciences, 145, pp. 293–294 (1962)
36. Kim, H.S., Hong, S., Lim, J.: A fast and provably secure higher-order masking of AES S-Box. In: Preneel, B., Takagi, T. (eds.) CHES 2011. LNCS, vol. 6917, pp. 95–107. Springer, Heidelberg (2011)
37. Knuth, D.: The Art of Computer Programming, vol. 2, 3rd edn. Addison Wesley, USA (1988)
38. Knuth, D.E.: Evaluation of polynomials by computers. Comm. ACM 5(12), 137–138 (1962)
39. Kocher, P.C., Jaffe, J., Jun, B.: Differential power analysis. In: Wiener, M. (ed.) CRYPTO 1999. LNCS, vol. 1666, p. 388. Springer, Heidelberg (1999)
40. Mangard, S., Popp, T., Gammel, B.M.: Side-channel leakage of masked CMOS gates. In: Menezes, A. (ed.) CT-RSA 2005. LNCS, vol. 3376, pp. 351–365. Springer, Heidelberg (2005)
41. Mangard, S., Pramstaller, N., Oswald, E.: Successfully attacking masked AES hardware implementations. In: Rao, J.R., Sunar, B. (eds.) CHES 2005. LNCS, vol. 3659, pp. 157–171. Springer, Heidelberg (2005)
42. Mangard, S., Schramm, K.: Pinpointing the side-channel leakage of masked AES hardware implementations. In: Goubin, L., Matsui, M. (eds.) CHES 2006. LNCS, vol. 4249, pp. 76–90. Springer, Heidelberg (2006)
43. Massey, J.: Minimal codewords and secret sharings. In: Sixth Joint Sweedish-Russian Workshop on Information Theory, pp. 246–249 (1993)
44. Messerges, T.S.: Using second-order power analysis to attack DPA resistant software. In: Paar, C., Koç, Ç.K. (eds.) CHES 2000. LNCS, vol. 1965, pp. 238–251. Springer, Heidelberg (2000)
45. Moradi, A., Mischke, O.: How far should theory be from practice? In: Prouff, E., Schaumont, P. (eds.) CHES 2012. LNCS, vol. 7428, pp. 92–106. Springer, Heidelberg (2012)
46. Omura, J., Massey, J.: Computational method and apparatus for finite fieldarithmetic. Technical report, Omnet Associates. Patent Number 4,587,627, May 1986
47. Paterson, M., Stockmeyer, L.J.: On the number of nonscalar multiplications necessary to evaluate polynomials. SIAM J. Comput. 2(1), 60–66 (1973)
48. Prouff, E., McEvoy, R.: First-order side-channel attacks on the permutation tables countermeasure. In: Clavier, C., Gaj, K. (eds.) CHES 2009. LNCS, vol. 5747, pp. 81–96. Springer, Heidelberg (2009)

49. Prouff, E., Rivain, M.: Masking against side-channel attacks: a formal security proof. In: Johansson, T., Nguyen, P.Q. (eds.) EUROCRYPT 2013. LNCS, vol. 7881, pp. 142–159. Springer, Heidelberg (2013)

50. Prouff, E., Rivain, M., Roche, T.: On the practical security of a leakage resilient masking scheme. In: Benaloh, J. (ed.) CT-RSA 2014. LNCS, vol. 8366, pp. 169–182. Springer, Heidelberg (2014)

51. Prouff, E., Roche, T.: Attack on a higher-order masking of the aes based on homographic functions. In: Gong, G., Gupta, K.C. (eds.) INDOCRYPT 2010. LNCS, vol. 6498, pp. 262–281. Springer, Heidelberg (2010)

52. Prouff, E., Roche, T.: Higher-order glitches free implementation of the AES using secure multi-party computation protocols. In: Preneel, B., Takagi, T. (eds.) CHES 2011. LNCS, vol. 6917, pp. 63–78. Springer, Heidelberg (2011)

53. Renner, S.: Protection des Algorithmes Cryptographiques Embarqués. Ph.D. thesis, University of Bordeaux (2014). http://www.math.u-bordeaux1.fr/~srenner/Thesis_Soline_Renner.pdf

54. Rivain, M., Prouff, E.: Provably Secure higher-order masking of AES. In: Mangard, S., Standaert, F.-X. (eds.) CHES 2010. LNCS, vol. 6225, pp. 413–427. Springer, Heidelberg (2010)

55. Roche, T., Prouff, E.: Higher-order glitch free implementation of the AES using secure multi-party computation protocols - extended version. J. Cryptographic Eng. 2(2), 111–127 (2012)

56. Coron, J.-S., Kizhvatov, I., Roy, A., Vivek, S.: Analysis and improvement of the generic higher-order masking scheme of FSE 2012. In: Bertoni, G., Coron, J.-S. (eds.) CHES 2013. LNCS, vol. 8086, pp. 417–434. Springer, Heidelberg (2013)

57. Rudra, A., Dubey, P.K., Jutla, C.S., Kumar, V., Rao, J.R., Rohatgi, P.: Efficient rijndael encryption implementation with composite field arithmetic. In: Koç, Ç.K., Naccache, D., Paar, C. (eds.) CHES 2001. LNCS, vol. 2162, pp. 171–184. Springer, Heidelberg (2001)

58. Schramm, K., Paar, C.: Higher order masking of the AES. In: Pointcheval, D. (ed.) CT-RSA 2006. LNCS, vol. 3860, pp. 208–225. Springer, Heidelberg (2006)

59. Shamir, A.: How to share a secret. Commun. ACM 22(11), 612–613 (1979)

60. Shirai, T., Shibutani, K., Akishita, T., Moriai, S., Iwata, T.: The 128-bit blockcipher CLEFIA (Extended Abstract). In: Biryukov, A. (ed.) FSE 2007. LNCS, vol. 4593, pp. 181–195. Springer, Heidelberg (2007)

61. Sunar, B., Koç, C.K.: An efficient optimal normal basis type II multiplier. IEEE Trans. Comput. 50(1), 83–87 (2001)

62. Toom, A.L.: The complexity of a scheme of functional elements realizing the multiplication of integers. Sov. Math. Dokl., 3, 714–716 (1963). http://www.de.ufpe.br/toom/articles/engmat/MULT-E.PDF

63. von zur Gathen, J.: Efficient and optimal exponentiation in finite fields. Comput. Complex. 1, 360–394 (1991)

64. von zur Gathen, J., Shokrollahi, M.A., Shokrollahi, J.: Efficient multiplication using type 2 optimal normal bases. In: Carlet, C., Sunar, B. (eds.) WAIFI 2007. LNCS, vol. 4547, pp. 55–68. Springer, Heidelberg (2007)

65. Wang, Y., Zhu, X.: A fast algorithm for the Fourier transform over finite fields and its VLSI implementation. IEEE J. Sel. Areas Commun. 6(3), 572–577 (1988)

Photonic Power Firewalls

Jean-Max Dutertre[1], Amir-Pasha Mirbaha[1],
David Naccache[2][(✉)], and Assia Tria[3]

[1] École nationale supérieure des Mines de Saint-Étienne Centre Microélectronique de
Provence - Georges Charpak Département Systèmes et Architectures Sécurisés (SAS),
880 Avenue de Mimet, 13541 Gardanne, France
{dutertre,mirbaha}@emse.fr
[2] École normale supérieure Département d'informatique Équipe de cryptographie,
45 Rue d'Ulm, 75230 Paris Cedex 05, France
david.naccache@ens.fr
[3] CEA Tech PACA Laboratoire Systèmes et Architectures Sécurisés (LSAS),
880 Avenue de Mimet, 13541 Gardanne, France
assia.tria@cea.fr

Abstract. This paper describes a new countermeasure against side-channel power attacks. We show that a conventional chipcard can be powered using an organic electroluminescent diode (OLED) facing a photovoltaic cell. By doing so, the card's power consumption becomes constant and equal to the OLED's power consumption. Despite size, energy conversion and heat dissipation issues, we believe that this countermeasure nicely suits several high security applications. Because photonic power firewalls guarantee physical isolation, we recommend photonic firewalls for applications where energy and form factor considerations are not as important as security (*e.g.* diplomatic encryption devices).

1 Introduction

In addition to its usual complexity postulates, cryptography silently assumes that secrets can be physically protected in tamper-proof locations. All cryptographic operations are physical processes where data elements must be represented by physical quantities in physical structures. These physical quantities must be stored, sensed, and combined by the elementary devices (gates) of any technology out of which we build tamper-resistant machinery. At any given point in the evolution of technology, the smallest logic devices must have a definite physical extent, require a certain minimum time to perform their function, and dissipate a minimal switching energy when transiting from one state to another. Power attacks exploit correlations between secret parameters and power consumption [6,7,9]. The design and the analysis of power attack countermeasures has grown during the past decades into a scientific research field by its own right.

This paper describes a new power side-channel countermeasure called *photonic power firewalls*. A photonic power firewall makes the target's consumption independent from its electrical activity by physically cutting the leakage channel.

© Springer-Verlag Berlin Heidelberg 2016
P.Y.A. Ryan et al. (Eds.): Kahn Festschrift, LNCS 9100, pp. 342–354, 2016.
DOI: 10.1007/978-3-662-49301-4_21

Our experiments show that a typical smart card can be optically powered using an organic electroluminescent diode (OLED) panel and a photovoltaic cell. By doing so, the card's power consumption becomes constant and equal to the OLED's power consumption. Despite size, energy conversion and heat dissipation issues, we believe that this countermeasure nicely suits several high security applications, such as diplomatic encryption machines or mission-critical Hardware Security Modules (HSMs).

2 Photonic Power Delivery

Photonic power delivery is a recent form of energy transport to remote electronic circuits. Electricity, converted to photonic power is delivered over optical fibers to distant devices, and transduced back to electrical energy upon arrival to destination. This energy transportation method has several advantages over electrical wires [16]. In particular, copper and coaxial cables are often subject to electromagnetic interferences, radio frequency (RF) heating, ground loops and lightning damage. Optical fibers are interference-free and immune to such exposures. Photonic power delivery eliminates electrocution risks[1] and is more environmentally friendly than electrical cables.

This work avoids power attacks by adopting the most radical solution: cut all electrical contacts between the power supply and the target, and power the circuit by a photonic source.

2.1 Light Emitting Diodes (LEDs)

A light-emitting diode (LED) is a semiconductor that emits light when it is forward-biased. When a LED is switched on, electrons recombine with holes and release energy as photons.

A LED's light wavelength can be either visible or invisible (*e.g.* ultraviolet and infrared). Wavelength is determined by the semiconductor material's energy gap and corresponds to the photons' energy level [1].

LEDs have many advantages over traditional light sources. The most frequently quoted advantages are: better luminous efficiency, longer lifetime, improved robustness, smaller size, faster switching, greater durability and reliability. LEDs are currently considered as a good source for general lighting and are the subject of intensive research.

2.2 Organic Light Emitting Diodes (OLEDs)

An OLED, is a LED with organic electroluminescent layers. The OLED's electroluminescent layer is composed of a film of organic compounds. The film is sandwiched between an anode and a cathode, and deposited on a substrate. The substrate can be flexible (polymer plastic) or rigid (*e.g.* made of metal or glass).

---

[1] Note that Lasers may, however, severely damage sight.

When voltage is applied to the electrodes, holes from the anode and electrons from the cathode create charges in the organic layers. Thus, the organic emissive layer emits photons [3,8].

OLEDs are routinely used as smartphone displays. OLEDs can be thinner and lighter than LCD panels and achieve higher contrast ratios, but have a shorter lifetime. Current consumer electronics research focuses on the use of OLEDs for screens and as light sources for general lighting. Many OLED-based products are currently commercialized [11].

2.3   Photovoltaic Cells

A photovoltaic cell is an electronic component composed of semiconductor layers. The cell converts the energy of light into electricity by exploiting the photovoltaic effect. When light hits a photovoltaic cell, the cell's semiconductor absorbs photons. The photons' impacts generate electron-hole pairs (and heat). These electrons flow through the semiconductor. Due to the semiconductive nature of the photovoltaic cell, electrons can only move in a single direction. Hence, they create an electrical field between the two poles of the cell. This difference of potential corresponds to the electrical current's direction. The produced electricity is collected as a direct current between the two poles of the cell [15].

Contemporary photovoltaic cell technology has an efficiency of about 20%. New materials and new cell architecture sometimes even achieve an efficiency of about 40% [4]. The most efficient photovoltaic cells are often used for satellite or military purposes and are not available on the general semiconductor market.

3   Building a Photonic Power Firewall

Our idea consists of using an OLED panel as a light emitter and a photovoltaic cell as a power supply for the smart card's microcontroller. Our hope is that without any change in the card reader, it will be possible to power and operate the card.

To implement the photonic power firewall, we evaluated several technologies. For the light emitter, we looked for something as small as a smart card with good energy. We tested many single and array LEDs, some OLED displays for mobile phones, and finally set our choice on the Osram Orbeos CDW-031 OLED [12]. The CDW-031 is a thin panel shown on the left side of Fig. 1. The OLED layer, without its protective glass, has a thickness of several hundred nanometers. Some of the CDW-031's technical characteristics are given in Table 1. We also evaluated some LED arrays.

Many photovoltaic cell models are available on the market. However, given our restrictions on output power and size, very few choices left for LED arrays and OLED surfaces with the required efficiency. We tested the models listed in Table 2 because of their high power output values. For two models with small dimensions, we associated several cells to cover the LED arrays or the OLED's surface.

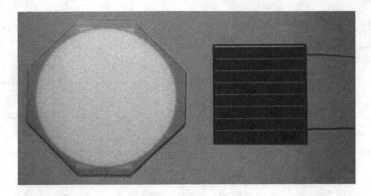

Fig. 1. An Osram Orbeos OLED panel and a Sanyo Amorton AM-8801 photovoltaic cell.

Table 1. Osram Orbeos CDW-031 OLED panel technical information [12].

Parameters	Value	Unit
Diameter of light output area	79	mm
Forward voltage (maximum value)	4.5	V
Power consumption (maximum value)	0.71	W
Luminance (for a forward current of 186 mA)	1000	cd/m^2
Luminous efficacy (typical value)	23	lm/W

To find the most efficient photovoltaic cell, we tested the output of different cells when illuminated with LED arrays and OLED panels. Since energy output results obtained with the OLED proved much superior to the LEDs, we decided to use the OLED in all following experiments.

We measured the photovoltaic cells' output for five different OLED power input levels. We boosted the OLED to its maximum authorized power and used this level for a first measurement. Then, we increased input levels by factors ranging from 2 to 8.5. To obtain more precise results, we applied 9 different resistors ranging from 470 Ω to 1 MΩ to the cells' output for each light input level. Table 2 shows the maximum output power and the applied resistance for each photovoltaic cell. Finally, we chose the Sanyo Amorton AM-8801 cell [13] (right side of Fig. 1) because it turned out to be the most efficient of all tested cells.

Boosting the OLED panel during the test always increased output, but efficiency did not improve beyond the third power level shown in Fig. 2. In fact, it even decreased quickly. Figure 2 shows the AM-8801's output and efficiency curves using a 1 kΩ resistor.

We started by connecting directly the card's V_{cc} contact to the photovoltaic cell's output. The current supplied by the cell was sufficient to successfully reset cards whose supply voltage varied between 3 V to 5 V. Nonetheless, the cell's output was insufficiently stable to perform a complete EMV transaction.

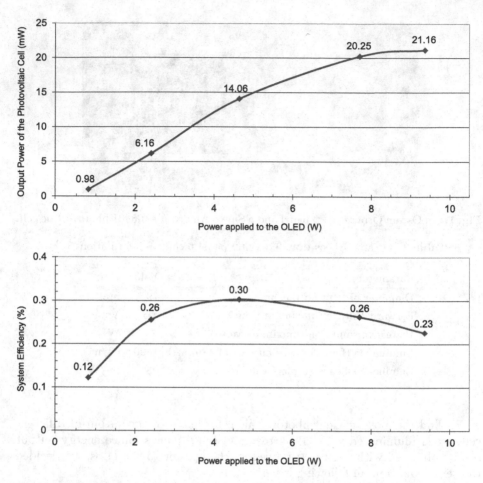

Fig. 2. System output and efficiency measured by using the Sanyo Amorton AM-8801 photovoltaic cell and by boosting the Osram Orbeos OLED panel beyond its authorized power limits.

According to the ISO/IEC 7816-3 standard [5] and to the EMV specifications [2], cards should stop operating if their V_{cc} varies beyond ±10 % of its nominal value. So, we used an Infineon TLE 4264 as a 5 V low drop fixed voltage regulator to maintain voltage stability. This regulator needs two capacitors at entry and exit to stabilize voltage at 5 V . A 100 µF electrolytic input capacitor and a 10 µF electrolytic output capacitor were used to test different cards. Figure 3 shows a schematic of the initial power source.

We can consider the set containing the OLED panel, the photovoltaic cell, the voltage regulator, the two capacitors and the card's chip as the *protected system* that must hide power consumption variations from the external world. We built a card adapter by soldering the protected system's elements and a smart card connector onto a Krystal Universal Card, shown in Fig. 4.

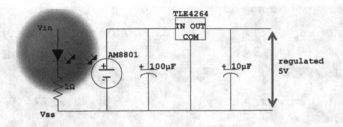

Fig. 3. Initial (insecure) power source.

We tried this setting with different smart cards. We could successfully reset (receive a correct ATR = Answer To Reset) four different cards using the above initial power source. The best results were obtained using two recent EMV cards: one supplied by GyD Iberica's 05/09 16953410 and Sagem Orga's 04/10 103043-1.

We boosted the OLED panel's input power to approximately 3.5 times the maximum authorized power to reset these cards. This power level is also about 7.6 times higher than the maximum standard value for class A cards (*i.e.* 5 V cards) [5]. ISO/IEC 7816-3 permits a current up to 60 mA. However, as the older cards have higher power consumption, they could not be reset by the limited energy output of our photovoltaic cell. For these cards, we boosted the OLED panel to about 16 times its maximum authorized power. Table 3 shows these results.

To perform our tests, we used a Smartware UltraSmart X-CORE T series card reader. Reset commands were sent by the SMarT-I (Secured Multi-characterisation Test Interface) program to the reader. SMarT-I is a GUI (Graphical User Interface) developed under LabVIEW. SMarT-I can send commands to smart cards and save their response signals.

Figure 7 shows that after applying our countermeasure, the power consumption signal measured at the reader's V_{cc} contact became entirely flat and did not show any variations.

The minimum value of the input capacitor is a function of the photovoltaic cell's output power and the card's power consumption. For the GyD Iberica card, the input capacitor's value can be decreased to 50 μF to successfully respond to a single reset command. However, when a second reset command was sent immediately, the voltage regulator could not maintain the regulated voltage at 5 V and the card went mute. Tests reveal that to continuously send commands, the input capacitor's value must be at least 70 μF (Fig. 5).

More experiments showed that the OLED's input power can be reduced by using higher input capacitor values. For instance, by using two 100 μF capacitors instead of only one with the Gemalto 04/03 46156 card only needs an OLED input power of 3.29 mW (instead of the initial value of 4.13 mW) (Fig. 6).

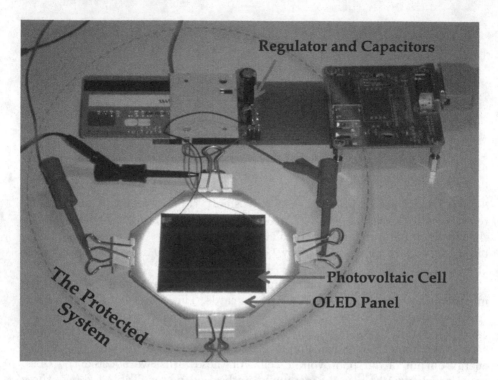

Fig. 4. The protected system.

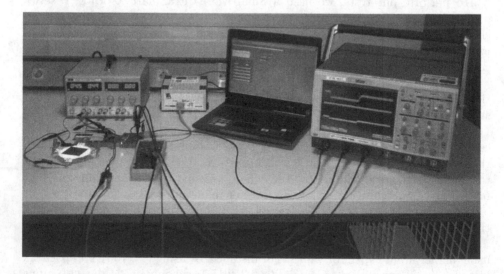

Fig. 5. The test bench.

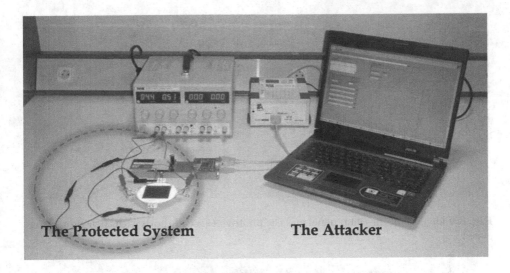

Fig. 6. The protected system and the attacker.

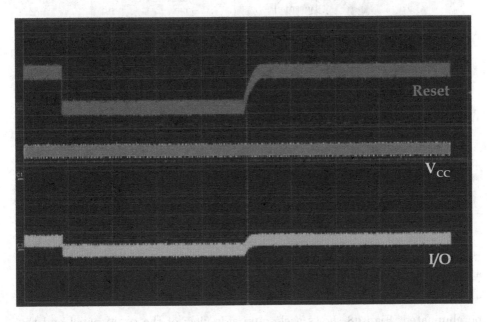

Fig. 7. Reset, power consumption and I/O signals observed on the card contacts at the reset moment (Scales: 5 V /div, 5 ms/div, 500MS/s).

Given that the OLED-cell sandwich is a few hundred microns thick (without their protective glass), the sandwich can be integrated into a PC card form factor. In this case, the energy accumulated in the glass and wasted will also

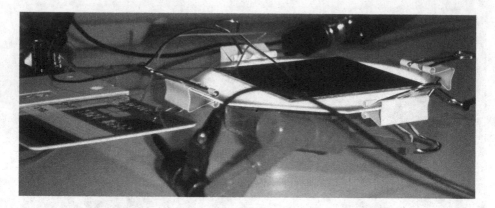

Fig. 8. Side view of the OLED panel and the photovoltaic cell (both with their protecting glass).

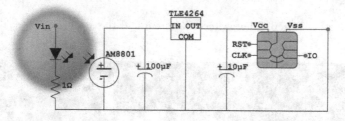

= to the smart card reader

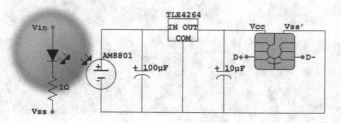

Fig. 9. Electronic schematic of the countermeasure and the card contacts, before and after applying the new secure solution.

be eliminated. Figure 8 shows a close-up side-view of the OLED panel and the photovoltaic cell with their protective glasses and a smart card.

Despite the flat power consumption curve, because we connect all ground connections together, power attacks on the card's I/O and ground contact still remain possible [14]. By connecting a resistor between the card's V_{ss} and the reader's V_{ss}, an attacker may still collect information about the card's power consumption. We did not manage to successfully conduct such an attack but this does not preclude its existence.

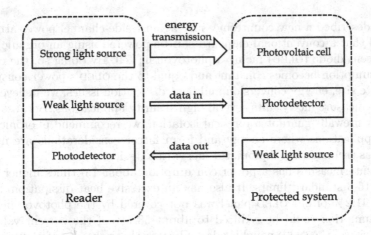

Fig. 10. A fully optical Photonic Power Firewall.

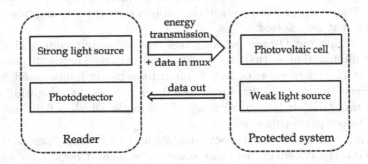

Fig. 11. A fully optical Photonic Power Firewall with data in transmission over power.

To overcome this problem, we separate the two ground lines. As shown in Fig. 9, we considered a twisted pair connection between the I/O and the clock contacts of the card and the reader. The principle resembles the implementation of two data lines, namely D+ and D-, in an Universal Serial Bus (USB) that establishes a direct data transfer connection between two components without a common ground line.

This work raises the interesting question of *all-optical* (data and power) as shown in Figs. 10 and 11. Amongst the numerous implementation options, a particularly interesting one seems to be the replacement of the photodetector by a QR-code reader and the replacement of the light source by a QR-code display.

4   Conclusion

This work described a new countermeasure against side-channel power attacks. We showed that a conventional chipcard can be powered using an organic electroluminescent diode (OLED) facing a photovoltaic cell. By doing so, the card's power consumption becomes constant and equal to the OLED's power consumption. Despite size, energy conversion and heat dissipation issues, we believe that this countermeasure nicely suits several high security applications. Because photonic power firewalls guarantee physical isolation, we recommend photonic firewalls for applications where energy and form factor considerations are not as important as security (e.g. diplomatic encryption devices).

Our countermeasure has a power consumption about 7.6 times higher than ISO/IEC 7816-3 standard limits. It also has an excessive heat dissipation. Since more than 41.2 % of our OLED panel was not covered by the photovoltaic cell, power consumption could be reduced to about 58.7 % of the current value as long as the size of the OLED panel is adapted correctly to the size of photovoltaic cell.

In addition, by boosting our OLED panel above its authorized power, the system output increases but the system efficiency decreases after a short period. So, by finding a more efficient panel, the problem of over consumption and heat dissipation may be resolved.

It seems that our Osram Orbeos panel was the only commercialized OLED panel for illumination at the time of our experiments. The OLED panels came onto the market after our experiments often have better luminous efficacy. The most efficient OLED device developed to date is the new NEC Lighting OLED in size of 2 mm×2 mm. It has an efficiency of 156 lm/W which is 6.8 times greater than our tested panel [10].

Boosting our OLED panel above its authorized power, increased output increases but the system efficiency decreases after a short period. So, by finding a more efficient panel, the over consumption problem and heat dissipation may be resolved.

For commercial use of our countermeasure in smart cards, some other technical criteria should be taken in account. It is especially important that the ISO/IEC 7816-3 specifications for the authorized values of other electrical parameters in a smart card and also the card's response time restrictions be considered in the design.

Our photonic power firewall has no specific impact on electromagnetic attacks (EMA). Theoretically, wires might act as antennae and conduct a negligible EMA residue. Nonetheless, in summary, our solution is a countermeasure close to perfect against power attacks because it can completely hide power consumption variations. Because photonic power firewalls offer such a physically guaranteed leakage isolation, we recommend their adoption for highly sensitive applications such as diplomatic encryption devices or HSMs.

References

1. Bourget, C.M.: An introduction to light-emitting diodes. HortScience **43**(7), 1944–1946 (2008)
2. emvco. emv Integrated Circuit Card Specification for Payment Systems, Book 1: Application Independent ICC to Terminal Interface Requirements - Version 4.2. (2008)
3. Geffroy, B., Le Roy, P., Prat, C.: Organic Light-Emitting Diode (OLED) technology: materials, devices and display technologies. Polym. Int. **55**(6), 572–582 (2006)
4. Green, M.A., Emery, K., Hishikawa, Y., Warta, W., Dunlop, E.D.: Solar cell efficiency tables (version 45). Prog. Photovoltaics Res. Appl. **23**(1), 1–9 (2015)
5. International Organization for Standardization (ISO) / International Electrotechnical Commission (IEC). ISO/IEC 7816-3: Information Technology - Identification Cards - Integrated Circuit(s) Cards with Contacts - Part 3: Electronic Signals and Transmission Protocols (2006)
6. Kocher, P.C., Jaffe, J., Jun, B.: Differential power analysis. In: Wiener, M. (ed.) CRYPTO 1999. LNCS, vol. 1666, pp. 388–397. Springer, Heidelberg (1999)
7. Kocher, P., Jaffe, J., Jun, B., Rohatgi, P.: Introduction to differential power analysis. J. Cryptographic Eng. **1**(1), 5–27 (2011)
8. Kunić, S., Šego, Z.: OLED technology and displays. In: Proceedings of ELMAR 2012, pp. 31–35. IEEE (2012)
9. Mangard, S., Oswald, E., Popp, T.: Power Analysis Attacks: Revealing the Secrets of Smart Cards. Springer, US (2007)
10. Mertens, R.: The OLED Handbook: A Guide to OLED Technology, Industry and Market. Ron Mertens (2015)
11. National Research Council. Assessment of Advanced Solid State Lighting. The National Academies Press (2013)
12. Osram Opto Semiconductors. Orbeos for OLED Lighting - Preliminary Data (2009). http://tinyurl.com/orbeos-031
13. Sanyo. Sanyo Amorphous Solar Cell - Amorton - am-8801 (2008). http://tinyurl.com/amorton-8801
14. Schmidt, J.-M., Plos, T., Kirschbaum, M., Hutter, M., Medwed, M., Herbst, C.: Side-channel leakage across borders. In: Gollmann, D., Lanet, J.-L., Iguchi-Cartigny, J. (eds.) CARDIS 2010. LNCS, vol. 6035, pp. 36–48. Springer, Heidelberg (2010)
15. Sze, S.M., Ng, K.K.: Physics of Semiconductor Devices. John Wiley & Sons, Hoboken (2006)
16. Werthen, J.-G., Cohen, M.: The power of light: photonic power innovations in medical energy and wireless applications. Photonics Spectra **40**(5), 68–70 (2006)

Appendix

Table 2. Maximum of photovoltaic cells' power output when exposed to an Osram Orbeos OLED panel light, boosted to 8.25 W.

Manufacturer	Model	Effective area for each cell (mm×mm)	Number of serially cells	Output power (mW)	Applied resistance (Ω)
Sanyo	Amorton AM-1437	27.8 × 8.4	14	11.80	100 k
Sanyo	Amorton AM-8801	54.3 × 53.0	1	21.16	1 k
Solarex	MSX-005F	95.8 × 57.0	1	5.17	1.5 k
Solems	07/048/016	48.0 × 16.0	6	9.19	100 k
Taizhou Lead Strong	LS60 × 60-4M150	50.0 × 50.0	1	8.17	470

Table 3. Powering attempts for different smart cards using the photovoltaic cell's energy.

Card Type	Manufacturer	Reference No	V_{in} on OLED (V)	Power on OLED (W)	Supplied V_{cc} by the protected system (V)	ATR
EMV chipcard	Gemalto	04/03 46156	4.35	4.13	5.042	✓
EMV chipcard	GyD Iberica	05/09 16953410	4.08	2.51	5.042	✓
EMV chipcard	Oberthur	05/07 45785	5.95	12.19	1.930	
EMV chipcard	Oberthur	01/08 47576	5.75	11.78	5.042	
EMV chipcard	Oberthur	06/08 49064	5.95	12.19	2.113	
EMV chipcard	Sagem Orga	04/10 103043-1	4.09	2.74	5.042	✓
French health card	Sagem DS	07/2007	4.78	5.83	5.042	✓

A Heuristic Approach to Assist Side Channel Analysis of the Data Encryption Standard

Christophe Clavier[1]([envelope]) and Djamal Rebaine[2]

[1] XLIM-CNRS, Université de Limoges, Limoges, France
christophe.clavier@unilim.fr
[2] Département d'informatique et de mathématique,
Université du Québec à Chicoutimi, Chicoutimi, Canada
djamal_rebaine@uqac.ca

Abstract. This paper describes the method adopted by the winning attack proposal to the first edition of the DPA contest. Two original ideas allowed to efficiently recover the secret key of a hardware implementation of the DES function. The first one was to consider full 56-bit guesses on the whole key (instead of only 6, 8, or even 12 or 16 bits that are usually used) to optimally exploit the side-channel leakage. We used a maximum likelihood based distinguisher fitted to the hardware characteristics of the leakage (32-bit register Hamming distance model). The second original idea was to design a smart sampling of the key space in order to find the correct key without requiring to exhaust a substantial proportion of the 2^{56} keys. We adopted a hill climbing heuristic approach using a likelihood based objective function, combined with a clever candidate update function that takes into account the main specificities of the DES key schedule.

Keywords: DPA contest · DES algorithm · Correlation power analysis · Hamming distance leakage model · Maximum likelihood distinguisher · Meta-heuristic · Hill climbing

1 Introduction

Tamper-resistant devices – e.g. smart cards – play an important role in cryptographic applications as they allow secret cryptographic keys to be securely stored in memory so that they cannot be accessed from outside the device. It is expected that only applications inside the card with the appropriate permissions for that memory area can access those keys. However, a powerful set of attacks, introduced by Kocher et al. [6] and later formalized by Messerges et al. [7], makes it possible to infer information about the key from a side-channel leakage such as the power consumption of the chip while it performs cryptographic computations. Indeed, a chip consumes a varying amount of power as it executes an algorithm. By making observations one can attempt to deduce information about what is occurring, namely which instructions are executed or which data

© Springer-Verlag Berlin Heidelberg 2016
P.Y.A. Ryan et al. (Eds.): Kahn Festschrift, LNCS 9100, pp. 355–373, 2016.
DOI: 10.1007/978-3-662-49301-4_22

are manipulated. So, with some knowledge of the algorithm and hardware characteristics, keys can be extracted during normal processing by monitoring and analyzing the power consumption of the device.

In 2008, an international scientific challenge, the so-called *DPA contest*, has been organized to compare and improve side-channel analysis techniques such as the Differential Power Analysis (DPA) initially proposed by Kocher et al., or other related methods among which the Correlation Power Analysis (CPA) introduced by Brier et al. [2], or other ones. In this paper we describe the winning attack proposal to this first edition of the DPA contest. Two original ideas allowed to efficiently recover the secret key of a hardware implementation of the DES function[1]. The first one was to consider full 56-bit guesses on the whole key – while only 6, 8, or even 12 or 16-bit partial guesses are usually used – in order to optimally exploit the side-channel leakage. We used a maximum likelihood based distinguisher – originaly introduced by Bevan et al. [3] – fitted to the hardware characteristics of the leakage (32-bit register Hamming distance model). The second original idea was to design a smart sampling of the key space in order to find the correct key without requiring to exhaust a substantial proportion of the 2^{56} keys. We adopted a hill climbing heuristic approach using a likelihood based objective function, combined with a clever candidate update function that takes into account the main specificities of the DES key schedule.

This paper is organized as follows. Section 2 presents an overview of the DPA contest. We provide in Sect. 3 the necessary background on the DES algorithm in order to understand the details of our attack. Section 4 describes our method in detail, including the characterization of the device (leakage model inference), the definition of our maximum likelihood distinguisher, and the presentation of the hill climbing heuristic together with our original key space sampling strategy. We present in Sect. 5 three different variants of our method submitted to the DPA contest and discuss the experimental results we conducted. Finally, Sect. 6 summarizes our concluding remarks.

2   The First Edition of the DPA Contest

In August 2008, the electronic and communication department of the french Télécom ParisTech university launched the first edition of an international scientific challenge, the *DPA contest*[2]. Its name comes from "Differential Power Analysis", the emblematic side-channel attack introduced by Kocher et al. [6]. The goal of this open contest is to improve existing side-channel analysis techniques – not necessarily strictly speaking DPA – or design new ones that can efficiently recover the cryptographic key used while encrypting arbitrary plaintexts

---

[1] The Data Encryption Standard (DES) has been the most commonly used block cipher function from 1977 when it has been standardized [8] to 2001 when it has been replaced by the Advanced Encryption Standard (AES). While it is now obsolete in its original version, it is worth noticing that it is still widely used as 3-DES notably for banking transactions.

[2] See the web page of the DPA contest: www.dpacontest.org.

(usually considered as randomly generated) with a hardware implementation of the DES algorithm [8].

Before this DPA contest, side-channel attacks that were published were mounted internally by their designers in their own laboratories. They acquired the power measurements themselves with their own equipment and evaluated the attacks on their own implementation of some cryptographic algorithm, and possibly used different protocols and metrics. No need to say that it was difficult to compare them to each other. In this context the DPA contest comes as an initiative to become an international benchmark reference for side-channel attacks. It is the first opportunity offered to the community to compare the different attacks in an objective manner for both of the following reasons:

1. All attacks proposed by the participants are evaluated using the same set of measurements formerly acquired by the organizing team on a reference hardware implementation of a DES co-processor [4]. This set comprises 81 089 power traces of 20 003 samples, where trace T_i measures the electrical activity of the DES device while it is encrypting a random plaintext block M_i to compute the ciphertext block $C_i = \mathrm{DES}_K(M_i)$. All the 81 089 pairs (M_i, C_i) where made public to capture the known plaintext attack scenario. All encryptions used the same key K which is the target of the attack. Figure 1 gives an illustrative example of a power trace measured during the encryption process. The portion of the trace between clock cycles 0 and 16 corresponds to the execution of the 16 rounds of the DES algorithm.

2. The rules are the same for all the participants. In particular, the metric to evaluate the merit of a proposed method is precisely defined. As usual, for side-channel analysis evaluation, this metric is the number of traces required to successfully retrieve the key. Due to the influence of measuring noises, the success of an attack for a given number of traces is probabilistic and depends on the subset of traces that has been selected from the whole set for this attack. Obviously, the more traces are used, the larger the probability that the attack is successful. However, there is no precise limit on the number of traces under which the attack always fails or above which it always succeeds. We define an attack run as follows. One starts with an empty set of traces $S_0 = \varnothing$, and for incremental values n of the number of traces, the attack is performed using the set S_n defined by adding to S_{n-1} an extra trace picked at random from the large available pool. The score of the attack run is defined by the organizers as the smallest value n^* for which the attack successfully recovers the key for all $n \in \{n^* - 99, \ldots, n^* - 1, n^*\}$. The score of a proposed side-channel analysis method is then defined as the average score of this attack on a sufficiently large (typically 100) number of runs performed with random subsets of traces.

It is worth mentioning that the cryptographic key K itself was known from the participants of the contest. At first glance, it may be strange to provide an attacker with the value of the key that he is supposed to recover. However, this information was considered useful in order for the participants to evaluate the quality of their method by knowing whether they have found the correct solution.

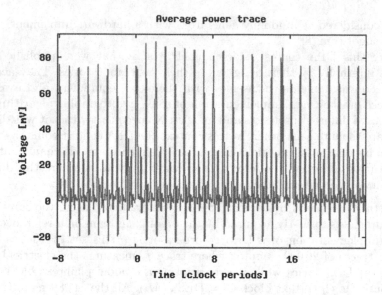

Fig. 1. Example of an hardware DES execution power trace used in the DPA contest.

Note that knowing the key, a participant can perform a preliminary white-box characterization of the device leakage that can be helpful for designing an attack. While the organizers of the contest deliberately accept the possibility to conduct such prior characterization, it should be kept in mind that an attacker does not necessarily have a known-key device at hand in a real-life scenario. Taking advantage of the precise information issued from this phase can thus mitigate the realistic aspects of the designed attack.

3   Description of the Data Encryption Standard

The Data Encryption Standard (DES) is a well-known encryption algorithm adopted by the National Bureau Standard in 1977 [8]. This algorithm, based on a Feistel structure, encrypts a 64-bit block of plaintext M with a 56-bit[3] key K to produce a 64-bit block of ciphertext C. For $r = 1, \ldots, 16$, a round function is iterated 16 times on a couple of 32-bit left and right halves (L_{r-1}, R_{r-1}) to produce the round output (L_r, R_r), which is itself the input of the next round.

---

[3] From an application point of view, the key is actually handled as an 8-byte array so that bits of the key are numbered from 1 to 64 (k_1 to k_8 for the first byte, up to k_{57} to k_{64} for the last one). From a cryptographic point of view, all 8 least significant bits (whose indices are multiples of eight) are unused so that the cryptographic key is actually made of the 56 following bits: $\{k_1, \ldots, k_7\} \cup \{k_9, \ldots, k_{15}\} \cup \ldots \cup \{k_{57}, \ldots, k_{63}\}$.

The round function, depicted on Fig. 2, is defined as follows:

$$\begin{cases} L_r & \leftarrow R_{r-1} \\ R_r & \leftarrow L_{r-1} \oplus f(K_r, R_{r-1}) \end{cases}$$

where $\oplus$ denotes the bitwise addition modulo 2, also known as the XOR (eXclusive OR) operation, and f is a function that takes the 32-bit right half R_{r-1} as an input and a round key K_r as a parameter. Note that the 64 bits of M are first shuffled by a 64 to 64-bit initial permutation IP whose output is split into two halves L_0 and R_0. Similarly the bits of the last round output (L_{16}, R_{16}) are also permuted by a 64 to 64-bit final permutation FP (which is equal to IP^{-1}) to produce the ciphertext.

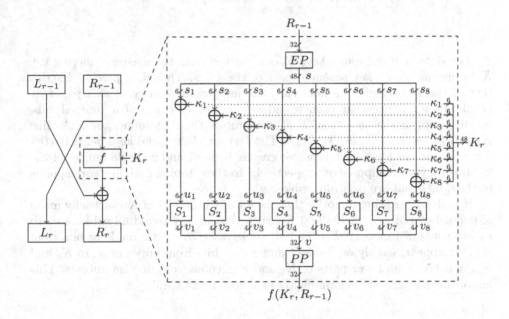

Fig. 2. The DES round function.

The function f itself is made of several steps. First, the 32-bit input is expanded (by duplicating some input bits) to a 48-bit intermediate value $s = (s_1, \ldots, s_8)$ by a 32 to 48-bit permutation EP. Then the 48-bit input $u = (u_1, \ldots, u_8)$ of the S-Box layer is computed as $u = s \oplus K_r$, that is by XOR-ing for $j = 1, \ldots, 8$ each 6-bit part s_j of s with each 6-bit so-called subkey κ_j of $K_r = (\kappa_1, \ldots, \kappa_8)$ to produce the respective 6-bit parts $u_j = s_j \oplus \kappa_j$ of u. The S-Box substitution layer, which forms the only non linear part of the DES round, is then applied by independently substituting 4-bit values $v_j = S_j(u_j)$ to each input u_j. Finally the 32 bits of the S-Boxes output $v = (v_1, \ldots, v_8)$ are permuted by transformation PP to produce $f(K_r, R_{r-1})$, which is then XOR-ed with L_{r-1}.

Table 1. Indices of key bits for subkeys of K_1

K_1						
κ_1	10	51	34	60	49	17
κ_2	33	57	2	9	19	42
κ_3	3	35	26	25	44	58
κ_4	59	1	36	27	18	41
κ_5	22	28	39	54	37	4
κ_6	47	30	5	53	23	29
κ_7	61	21	38	63	15	20
κ_8	45	14	13	62	55	31

Table 2. Indices of key bits for subkeys of K_{16}

K_{16}						
κ_1	18	59	42	3	57	25
κ_2	41	36	10	17	27	50
κ_3	11	43	34	33	52	1
κ_4	2	9	44	35	26	49
κ_5	30	5	47	62	45	12
κ_6	55	38	13	61	31	37
κ_7	6	29	46	4	23	28
κ_8	53	22	21	7	63	39

The sixteen 48-bit round keys K_r are derived from the master ciphering key K by means of the key schedule part of the DES. Though a precise description of the key schedule is not really needed for the clarity of this paper, it is relevant to notice that each round key is simply made of a shuffled subset of 48 out of the 56 bits of K. For example, the first round key looks like $K_1 = (k_{10}, k_{51}, k_{34}, \ldots, k_{62}, k_{55}, k_{31})$. The first and last round keys being particularly important for our analysis, we give in Tables 1 and 2 the 48 indices of the key bits they are composed of, respectively. In these tables, each line corresponds to the 6 bits that are part of a subkey κ_j.

It is also interesting to notice that the set of the 56 bits of K is actually made of two subsets of 28 bits K_A and K_B such that at any round all subkeys κ_1 to κ_4 are made of bits from K_A, and all subkeys κ_5 to κ_8 are made of bits from K_B.[4] It appears clearly on Tables 1 and 2 that bits from upper parts of K_1 and K_{16} and bits from lower parts of K_1 and K_{16} come from disjoint subsets. This important property will be implicitly exploited in Sect. 4.3.

4   Description of the Attack

Let us recall that the primary goal of a heuristic algorithm is to deliver as good solution as possible for all instances of the considered problem. Usually this approach starts with an initial solution. At each iteration, it moves from one solution to another according to some predefined strategy in the so-called search space, which represents the collection of all possible solutions for a given problem. The ways the search space is examined and moving from one solution to another, the quality of the objective function and some other parameters

---

[4] $K_A = \{k_1, k_2, k_3, k_9, k_{10}, k_{11}, k_{17}, k_{18}, k_{19}, k_{25}, k_{26}, k_{27}, k_{33}, k_{34}, k_{35}, k_{36}, k_{41}, k_{42}, k_{43}, k_{44}, k_{49}, k_{50}, k_{51}, k_{52}, k_{57}, k_{58}, k_{59}, k_{60}\}$,
$K_B = \{k_4, k_5, k_6, k_7, k_{12}, k_{13}, k_{14}, k_{15}, k_{20}, k_{21}, k_{22}, k_{23}, k_{28}, k_{29}, k_{30}, k_{31}, k_{37}, k_{38}, k_{39}, k_{45}, k_{46}, k_{47}, k_{53}, k_{54}, k_{55}, k_{61}, k_{62}, k_{63}\}$.

determine the specificity and the efficiency of a heuristic. In this section, we consider the so-called hill climbing approach.

The hill climbing method can be roughly summarized as an iterative search procedure that, starting from an initial solution, progressively improves it by applying a series of local modifications. At each iteration of the algorithm, the search moves to an improved solution that differs slightly from the current one. The search terminates when no more improvement is possible. For more details, see e.g. [1,5].

In order to proceed with the description of this algorithm, we need to define the objective function that we designed and the neighborhood of a given solution for the problem we are considering as presented in Sects. 4.2 and 4.3, respectively. Let us first present some preliminaries in Sect. 4.1.

4.1 Prior Characterization of the Device

In order to optimally exploit the side-channel leakage of a device (for example its power consumption), an attacker should preferably have characterized the properties of this leakage and its relationship with the functioning of the program, in particular with the manipulated intermediate data.

The current consumption is usually modeled by either the Hamming weight or the Hamming distance, defined as follows:

Definition 1 (Hamming Weight). *The Hamming weight of a given n-bit integer a is the number of bits that are equal to 1 in its binary representation* $(a_{n-1}, \ldots, a_0)$. *We have:*

$$\mathrm{HW}(a) = \sum_{i=0}^{n-1} a_i.$$

Definition 2 (Hamming Distance). *The Hamming distance between two given n-bit integers $a = (a_{n-1}, \ldots, a_0)$ and $b = (b_{n-1}, \ldots, b_0)$ is the number of bit positions where the two bit values of a and b differ. If $\oplus$ denotes the XOR operation, then we have:*

$$\mathrm{HD}(a, b) = \sum_{i=0}^{n-1} (a_i \oplus b_i).$$

The current consumed when manipulating a data is related to the energy required to write the bits of this data on a bus or in the memory register holding this data. The Hamming weight model assumes that the consumption depends only on the value which is currently written on the bus or in the register, with 1 bits consuming more than 0 bits. Thus, the more bits are equal to 1 the more is the consumption, which obviously leads to a power consumption which linearly depends on the Hamming weight of the data.

On the other hand, one may consider that the energy required to write a bit depends on whether or not this bit value induces a bit flip with the bit value previously stored at this location. Considering that the amount of energy to flip a bit is greater than that to let it unchanged, we easily derive the Hamming distance model where the power consumption linearly depends on the Hamming distance (the number of bit flips) between the written data and the data that was previously stored at this location.

On hardware implementations of a block cipher function, a complete round is typically executed in only one clock cycle, at the end of which the output of the round function replaces in a register the value of the round input. This memory writing is an important source of power leakage which is usually well described by the Hamming distance model.

In the particular case of the hardware DES considered in the DPA contest, we have performed a prior characterization of the device that confirmed the relevance of the Hamming distance model. At the end of the clock cycle computing the round r, the output half R_r that has been computed replaces the former value R_{r-1} in a 32-bit register. At that instant of time, this writing produces a power consumption which linearly depends on the Hamming distance between the previous value stored in the register ($R_{r-1} = L_r$) and the current one (R_r) that erases the former. The power consumption at time t, $W(t)$, is expressed as follows:

$$W(t) = \alpha(t) \times \mathrm{HD}(L_r, R_r) + \beta(t) + \omega(t), \tag{1}$$

where $\alpha(t)$ denotes a fixed scalar gain between HD and W, $\beta(t)$ encloses offsets and data independent components, whereas $\omega(t)$ represents a centered Gaussian noise.

We performed this characterization by computing for each round r the Correlation Power Analysis [2] (CPA) trace between the measured power consumption and the Hamming distance between L_r and R_r. This correlation trace is defined at each instant t by the value of the Pearson's correlation coefficient $\rho_{W,HD}(t)$ defined as follows:

$$\rho_{W,HD}(t) = \frac{\mathrm{Cov}(W(t), HD)}{\sqrt{\mathrm{Var}(W(t))}\,\sqrt{\mathrm{Var}(HD)}}.$$

This coefficient measures the linear dependency between the set of 81 089 Hamming distances $\mathrm{HD}(L_r, R_r)_i$ computed from the values of M_i and K of each execution, and the set of corresponding power consumptions at time t. Figure 3 shows the CPA traces related to the Hamming distance between L_1 and R_1, and between L_{15} and R_{15}. One can clearly see two relevant peaks occurring at two time instants of interest $t_1 = 5\,743$ and $t_{16} = 15\,745$ which correspond respectively to the end of computation of rounds 1 and 16. Their respective correlation levels of $+0.795$ and $+0.849$ clearly indicate that the model defined by Eq. (1) is quite accurate.

Let us note that given the knowledge of the secret key, not only one can produce the CPA traces of Fig. 3, but one can also infer – by linear regression – estimations of the coefficients α and β of the consumption function at any time t, and especially at the two time instants of interest t_1 and t_{16} corresponding to the maximum correlation levels. For instance, based on the whole set of traces,

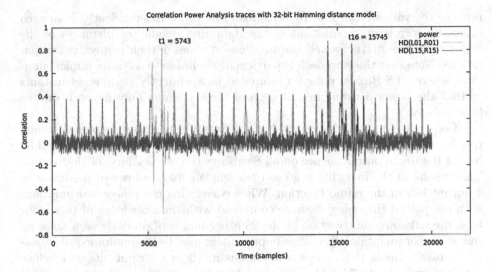

Fig. 3. Correlation peaks with $\mathrm{HD}(L_1, R_1)$ and $\mathrm{HD}(L_{15}, R_{15})$

we found estimations of the coefficients α_1, β_1, α_{16} and β_{16} resulting in the two following good models for the power consumption at these instants of interest.

$$W(t_1) = W_1 = \alpha_1 \times \mathrm{HD}(L_1, R_1) + \beta_1 + \omega_1 \tag{2}$$
$$= 9.51 \; 10^{-4} \times \mathrm{HD}(L_1, R_1) + 7.19 \; 10^{-2} + \omega_1 \tag{3}$$

$$W(t_{16}) = W_{16} = \alpha_{16} \times \mathrm{HD}(L_{15}, R_{15}) + \beta_{16} + \omega_{16} \tag{4}$$
$$= 1.34 \; 10^{-3} \times \mathrm{HD}(L_{15}, R_{15}) + 5.40 \; 10^{-2} + \omega_{16} \tag{5}$$

As discussed at the end of Sect. 2, in a real-life scenario an attacker may not be able to perform such prior characterization which allows to infer the instants of interest, the variables involved in the consumption model, and the values of parameters α_i and β_i. However let us note that the instants of interest are located when the power consumption itself is maximal at the end of rounds 1 and 16. This is a classic behavior which make them easily guessable without the knowledge of the key. Furthermore, the model as a linear function of the Hamming distances between to successive contents of the R register is somewhat classic and can be assumed without any secret knowledge. Finally, knowing beforehand the precise parameter values is not strictly required since they may well be derived on-the-fly from the exploited measures as demonstrated in Sect. 5.

4.2   The Maximum Likelihood Criterion

The classic approach to recover a DES secret key by side-channel analysis like DPA or CPA makes use of a divide-and-conquer strategy where the key is recovered piece by piece. More precisely, on a software implementation, it is usual to retrieve the values of all first round subkeys κ_1 to κ_8 independently from each other, by correlating predictions of the Hamming weight (or distance) of the S-Box outputs with the power consumptions at times of their respective computations. Note that this approach is particularly suitable to software implementations where all S-Box outputs are computed independently at different instants so that the power consumption at each of these instants only depends on one 6-bit subkey.

If one tries to apply this method in the case of a hardware implementation, then the major problem is the dependency of the power consumption on all 32 bits of the round output, hence on all 8 subkeys (i.e. 48 key bits) of that round. This results in the fact that a guess on a single subkey allows to predict only 4 output bits of the round function. When correlating the power consumptions with the partial Hamming distance computed with the knowledge of these four bits, the unknown contribution of the 28 other bits acts similarly as a noise on the power consumption. A possible improvement may be to simultaneously guess two subkeys. Doing that, one can predict as much as 8 output bits and reduce the unknown part to 24 bits. The signal to noise ratio thus reduces from 28/4 = 7 to 24/8 = 3 so that one can expect better results at the cost of four 12-bit exhaustive searches instead of eight 6-bit ones. Going further in this direction would result in guessing all 8 subkeys of a round at a time. This would allow to correctly predict the whole 32-bit distance between the first round (or last round) input and output, but tackling with 2^{48} guesses and computing as many correlations is unfortunately considered almost impossible in practice.

Despite this difficulty we chose to face the challenge of predicting the full Hamming distance that is related to the power consumption. More precisely, we even chose to predict Hamming distances $\mathrm{HD}(L_1, R_1)$ and $\mathrm{HD}(L_{16}, R_{16})$ involved in both first and last round computations. This means that we have to guess not only 48 bits belonging to either K_1 or K_{16} but actually all 56 key bits in order to make a guess on both K_1 and K_{16}. Instead of considering all possible keys, which is unfeasible, we use a supervised random search heuristic, described in Sect. 4.3, that allows to efficiently sample the key space so that more and more promising key candidates are successively considered until eventually hitting the correct one. Obviously, in order to define what is a *promising* key we must introduce a quantitative criterion that can be seen as a figure of merit (a kind of score) of a key candidate.

Given the two leakage models expressed by Eqs. (2) and (4), and for any key candidate described as a couple (K_1, K_{16}), one can compute predictions of the power consumption at times t_1 and t_{16} from any plaintext/ciphertext pair (M, C):

$$\widetilde{W_1} = \alpha_1 \times \mathrm{HD}(L_1, R_1) + \beta_1,$$
$$\widetilde{W_{16}} = \alpha_{16} \times \mathrm{HD}(L_{15}, R_{15}) + \beta_{16}.$$

Indeed, $HD(L_1, R_1)$ can be computed from K_1 since L_0 and $L_1 = R_0$ are directly derived from M, and $R_1 = L_0 \oplus f(K_1, R_0)$. Similarly, $HD(L_{15}, R_{15})$ can be computed from K_{16} since R_{16} and $R_{15} = L_{16}$ are directly derived from C, and $L_{15} = R_{16} \oplus f(K_{16}, R_{15})$.

The estimation errors $\omega_1 = W_1 - \widetilde{W_1}$ and $\omega_{16} = W_{16} - \widetilde{W_{16}}$ are modeled as realizations of a centered Gaussian noise. Assuming that ω_1 and ω_{16} random variables have similar standard deviations[5], one can derive that $\omega_1^2 + \omega_{16}^2$ is equal – up to a negative multiplicative constant factor – to the posterior likelihood of the key, given the observed power consumptions W_1 and W_{16}.

Definition 3 (Score of a key candidate). *For a given set of traces $T_{\mathcal{I}} = \{T_i : i \in \mathcal{I}\}$, and for a key candidate K – possibly represented as (K_1, K_{16}) – we define the score $\sigma(K)$ of this candidate as the sum of both quadratic estimation errors ω_1^2 and ω_{16}^2 over all considered executions:*

$$\sigma(K) = \sum_{i \in \mathcal{I}} \omega_{1,i}^2 + \sum_{i \in \mathcal{I}} \omega_{16,i}^2.$$

The score of a key candidate is inversely proportionally related to its posterior likelihood given the observed power consumptions.

4.3   Sampling the Key Space by Hill Climbing

Being able to assign a likelihood to any given key candidate does not lead, by itself, to an efficient way to find the correct key. While this may not be true if the set of the considered traces is too small, we naturally expect that the correct key is the one with the maximum likelihood, that is with the minimum score. The idea behind this assumption is that if a key candidate is incorrect then the predicted Hamming distances $HD(L_1, R_1)$ and $HD(L_{15}, R_{15})$ are also incorrect, and thus the residues (estimation errors) produced by incorrectly estimating these Hamming distances must be counter-balanced, for each execution, by higher noise realizations in order to lead to a likelihood similar to that of the correct key. The probability of such compensation effect being exponentially decreasing with the number of observations, the goal is to find key candidates with as low scores as possible. Doing so implies that we are able to minimize the differences between predicted and actual values of both Hamming distances $HD(L_1, R_1)$ and $HD(L_{15}, R_{15})$.

Notice that the relationship between a key candidate and its score is neither linear nor a monotonous function of the number of correctly guessed key bits. Actually a relevant notion in order to minimize the difference between predicted and actual values of $HD(L_1, R_1)$ is rather the number of correctly predicted first round subkeys. Indeed, the expected number of bits of the predicted round output $f(K, R_0)$ that match their actual values is 4 for each S-Box output whose

---

[5] This can be expected since the electrical activity when computing each round is not supposed to depend on the round number.

subkey is correctly guessed plus (a value quite closed to) 2 on average per S-Box whose subkey is not correctly guessed. For instance, suppose that a given candidate K_1 matches the correct values of K_1 only on subkeys κ_1 and κ_6. Then the expected number of correct bits in the prediction of $f(K, R_0)$ – and so in the prediction of $L_1 \oplus R_1$ – is $2 \times 4 + 6 \times 2 = 20$ bits. Consequently, the more first round subkeys that are correctly guessed, the more first round output bits that are correctly predicted on average, and so the less residue that needs to be compensated for by the noise. To be even more precise, when changing only one bit in a K_1 candidate there may be three possible effects:

1. the active bit belongs to a correctly guessed subkey; in that case this S-Box output is no more correctly predicted and the expected number of correctly predicted bits in the round output decreases by 2,
2. the active bit belongs to an incorrectly guessed subkey and flipping this bit makes the value of the subkey it belongs to become correct; then one more S-Box output is systematically correctly predicted and the expected number of correctly predicted bits in the round output increases by 2,
3. in all other cases an incorrect subkey guess is changed into a still incorrect value, and the expected number of correctly predicted bits in the round output is unchanged (note that this is true whether or not the active bit flipped from an incorrect value to a correct one).

We understand that minimizing the residue related to the estimation of the power consumption at the end of the first round is achieved by correctly guessing more and more K_1 subkeys rather than more and more K_1 individual bits.

All this reasoning about guessing K_1 similarly holds about the guessing of K_{16}. However things become more intricate when one considers what happens on both round keys simultaneously. This is due to the fact that K_1 and K_{16} share as much as 40 bits. For example, assume that a bit flip in K_1 allows to correctly guess one more K_1 subkey (this is the second case detailed above). If this particular bit also belongs to K_{16}, then a change occurs to the value of the K_{16} subkey this bit belongs to. Depending on the ciphertexts values and on the actual noise realizations of the set of exploited traces, it may happen – particularly when the number of traces is small – that this bit flip results in an increase of the total quadratic estimation error ($\sum_{i \in \mathcal{I}} \omega_{16,i}^2$) on the K_{16} side. In this case the positive effect of this bit flip on the K_1 side may not be enough to surpass the negative effect on the other side, and the correct value of the K_1 subkey may not be retained. Besides these 40 key bits belonging to both round keys, which may make difficult to simultaneously maximize the number of correctly guessed subkeys, we must also mention the case of the 16 other key bits which belong to one round key and not to the other. It is possible to freely modify the value of these bits to try to increase the number of correctly guessed subkeys on one side without risking to deteriorate the situation on the other side.

With all these considerations in mind we are now in a position to describe the process that allows to progressively find better and better key candidates. This process follows the hill climbing heuristic approach, and works as follows. Starting from an initial random candidate $K^{(0)}$, we generate a sequence $(K^{(0)}, K^{(1)}, K^{(2)}, \ldots)$ of keys with the property that each key in the sequence is better than the previous one, that is $\sigma(K^{(i)}) < \sigma(K^{(i-1)})$. Once it becomes not possible to find a key better than the current one the process stops on the current key candidate that we denote by $K^{(\mathrm{end})}$. To describe how the process jumps from key $K^{(i-1)}$ to key $K^{(i)}$ we must introduce the following notations:

Notation 1. *For any S-Box number $1 \leq s \leq 4$, we denote by $\mathcal{N}_1(K, s)$ the set of all neighboring keys derived from K by changing in all possible ways the 6 key bits implied in S-Box number s in the first round (e.g. bits $k_{10}, k_{51}, k_{34}, k_{60}, k_{49}, k_{17}$ if $s = 1$) as well as the 4 bits not belonging to K_1 and implied in one of the first four S-Box in the last round (i.e. bits $k_{11}, k_{43}, k_{50}, k_{52}$).*

Notation 2. *For any S-Box number $5 \leq s \leq 8$, we denote by $\mathcal{N}_1(K, s)$ the set of all neighboring keys derived from K by changing in all possible ways the 6 key bits implied in S-Box number s in the first round (e.g. bits $k_{22}, k_{28}, k_{39}, k_{54}, k_{37}, k_4$ if $s = 5$) as well as the 4 bits not belonging to K_1 and implied in one of the last four S-Box in the last round (i.e. bits k_6, k_7, k_{12}, k_{46}).*

Notation 3. *For any S-Box number $1 \leq s \leq 4$, we denote by $\mathcal{N}_{16}(K, s)$ the set of all keys neighboring derived from K by changing in all possible ways the 6 key bits implied in S-Box number s in the last round as well as the 4 bits not belonging to K_{16} and implied in one of the first four S-Box in the first round.*

Notation 4. *For any S-Box number $5 \leq s \leq 8$, we denote by $\mathcal{N}_{16}(K, s)$ the set of all neighboring keys derived from K by changing in all possible ways the 6 key bits implied in S-Box number s in the last round as well as the 4 bits not belonging to K_{16} and implied in one of the last four S-Box in the first round.*

Let us also denote by $\mathcal{N}(K)$ the set of all keys belonging to either $\mathcal{N}_1$ or $\mathcal{N}_{16}$ sets:

$$\mathcal{N}(K) = \bigcup_{s=1}^{8} \mathcal{N}_1(K, s) \cup \bigcup_{s=1}^{8} \mathcal{N}_{16}(K, s)$$

Notation 5. *For any key K', we denote by $\mathcal{N}_1'(K')$ the set of all neighboring keys derived from K' by changing in all possible ways the 8 key bits that do not belong to K_1' (i.e. bits $k_{11}, k_{43}, k_{50}, k_{52}, k_6, k_7, k_{12}, k_{46}$).*

Notation 6. *For any key K', we denote by $\mathcal{N}_{16}'(K')$ the set of all neighboring keys derived from K' by changing in all possible ways the 8 key bits that do not belong to K_{16}' (i.e. bits $k_{19}, k_{51}, k_{58}, k_{60}, k_{14}, k_{15}, k_{20}, k_{54}$).*

Here also we denote by $\mathcal{N}'(K')$ the set of all keys belonging to either $\mathcal{N}_1'(K')$ or $\mathcal{N}_{16}'(K')$ set:

$$\mathcal{N}'(K') = \mathcal{N}_1'(K') \cup \mathcal{N}_{16}'(K')$$

The transformation of a key $K^{(i-1)}$ into a key $K^{(i)}$ is defined in a two-step way via an intermediate key K' as follows: K' is defined as the best key belonging to $\mathcal{N}(K^{(i-1)})$, while $K^{(i)}$ is defined as the best key belonging to $\mathcal{N}'(K')$.[6]

Observe that the process of generating a sequence of $K^{(i)}$ from an initial candidate $K^{(0)}$ up to a terminal key $K^{(\text{end})}$ is deterministic. The value of $K^{(\text{end})}$ only depends on $K^{(0)}$, and all possible sequences do not necessarily converge to the same $K^{(\text{end})}$. One calls *basin of attraction* of a given $K^{(\text{end})}$ the set of all initial keys $K^{(0)}$ that would lead to this particular terminal key. We expect that when the number of exploited traces increases the number of basins of attraction (i.e. the number of possible terminal keys) decreases in favor of the size of the basin of attraction of the correct key[7]. For this reason, when the number of traces is small, the initial point often belongs to the basin of attraction of an incorrect key (i.e. the correct key is not recovered). In order to increase the probability of success of our attack with a small number of traces, we consider in parallel several sequences $(K^{(0)}, K^{(1)}, K^{(2)}, \ldots, K^{(\text{end})})$ starting from as many randomly chosen starting points $K^{(0)}$, and define the output of our attack as being the best ending key of all these sequences. The number of considered sequences should be reasonably small – about one hundred or less in our experiments – in order not to increase too much the total attack time. We allowed to consider fewer parallel sequences when the number of exploited traces increases since the probability of ending to the correct key – which is related to the size of its basin of attraction – also increases in this case.

In order to clarify the ideas presented in this section we give in Appendix the sketches of the procedures that:

- computes the score of a key based on a given set of traces (Algorithm 1),
- suggests the best key found in the process of generating several sequences $(K^{(0)}, K^{(1)}, K^{(2)}, \ldots, K^{(\text{end})})$ of key candidates (Algorithm 2),
- evaluates the score of a run of attacks with an increasing set of traces and a decreasing number of generated sequences (Algorithm 3).

5   Variants of the Method and Experimental Results

The maximum likelihood criterion that defines the objective function, together with the hill climbing heuristic with a dedicated candidate updating strategy for an efficient key space sampling, are presented in detail in Sect. 4. This method

---

[6] The number of key candidates considered to find K' in the neighborhood of $K^{(i-1)}$ is equal to $2.8.2^6.2^4 = 2^{14}$. The number of key candidates considered to find $K^{(i)}$ in the neighborhood of K' is equal to $2.2^8 = 2^9$. In both cases, the computation of the local exhaustive search is not expensive.

[7] Practical experiments whose results are described in Sect. 5 seem to confirm this behavior.

was applied in the first DPA contest. Actually, we have submitted three[8] variants of our method. We now describe these variants, that we name A, B and C[9], which share exactly the same key space sampling and hill climbing strategies. Our three variants only differ on two points: (i) the number of instants of interest, and the consumption functions that define the leakage model at those instants, (ii) the way the different parameters of the consumption functions are estimated.

Method A. For this method we use three instants of interest: $t_1 = 5\,743$ and $t_{16} = 15\,745$, already introduced in Sect. 4, that correspond to the end of rounds 1 and 16, as well as a third instant $t_{15} = 14\,491$ which corresponds to the end of round 15. By prior characterization we noticed that at time t_1 (resp. t_{16}) the power consumption is not only linearly correlated with $\mathrm{HD}(L_1, R_1)$ (resp. $\mathrm{HD}(L_{15}, R_{15})$) but also – though with a lower correlation level – with $\mathrm{HD}(L_0, R_0)$ (resp. $\mathrm{HD}(L_{16}, R_{16})$). In addition, we noticed that the power consumption at time t_{15} is strongly linearly correlated with $\mathrm{HD}(L_{15}, R_{15})$. Thus we adopted two bivariate leakage models at t_1 and t_{16} and a univariate model at t_{15}:

$$W(t_1) = \alpha_1 \times \mathrm{HD}(L_1, R_1) + \beta_1 \times \mathrm{HD}(L_0, R_0) + \gamma_1 + \omega_1,$$
$$W(t_{15}) = \alpha_{15} \times \mathrm{HD}(L_{15}, R_{15}) + \beta_{15} + \omega_{15},$$
$$W(t_{16}) = \alpha_{16} \times \mathrm{HD}(L_{15}, R_{15}) + \beta_{16} \times \mathrm{HD}(L_{16}, R_{16}) + \gamma_{16} + \omega_{16}.$$

Note that the values of coefficients α_i, β_i and γ_i that we used have been derived during the characterization phase by (multi-)linear regression on the whole set of traces. Moreover, with three instants of interest, we have straightforwardly adapted the definition of the score of a key candidate as being the integrated sum of quadratic residues at all three time instants:
$\sigma(K) = \sum_{i \in \mathcal{I}} (\omega_{1,i}^2 + \omega_{15,i}^2 + \omega_{16,i}^2).$

Method B. The difference between this method and method A is twofold. First, we do not use the power consumption at time t_{15} but only at times t_1 and t_{16}. The leakage models we use are thus the following:

$$W(t_1) = \alpha_1 \times \mathrm{HD}(L_1, R_1) + \beta_1 \times \mathrm{HD}(L_0, R_0) + \gamma_1 + \omega_1,$$
$$W(t_{16}) = \alpha_{16} \times \mathrm{HD}(L_{15}, R_{15}) + \beta_{16} \times \mathrm{HD}(L_{16}, R_{16}) + \gamma_{16} + \omega_{16}.$$

The second difference with method A is that we do not rely on the previously obtained precise estimations of the coefficients. This is important since deriving these values during the characterization phase requires the knowledge of the secret key (or more generally another similar device with a known key),

---

[8] We only consider our submissions to the so-called *Representative Order* category which has been declared the official category by the organizers of the contest. Contrarily to the *Fixed Order* category, in the official representative order category participants cannot choose in advance the set of traces used in the attack.

[9] These three variants A, B and C correspond to submitted program files named "dpa_contest.representative.1.c", "dpa_contest.representative.4.c" and "dpa_contest. representative.3.c", respectively.

which may be considered as a not realistic attack scenario. Instead, we chose to compute estimations of the coefficients on-the-fly based on the currently available observations. Obviously, such estimation of the parameter values is expected to be less accurate than with prior characterization, particularly when exploiting a reduced set of traces. Nevertheless, we believe that this way of deriving the model parameters makes this attack more applicable than that of method A.

Method C. This variant is quite similar to method B. The only difference is that we consider univariate models at times t_1 and t_{16} instead of bivariate ones. The leakage model of method C is thus exactly the same as the one considered in Sect. 4:

$$W(t_1) = \alpha_1 \times \mathrm{HD}(L_1, R_1) + \beta_1 + \omega_1,$$
$$W(t_{16}) = \alpha_{16} \times \mathrm{HD}(L_{15}, R_{15}) + \beta_{16} + \omega_{16}.$$

Here also we estimate parameters α_1, β_1, α_{16} and β_{16} on-the-fly.

Table 3 presents the experimental results produced by the three variants. They have been derived from 100 runs for each variant. A run consists in selecting a random set of $n = 30$ traces, and then iteratively applying the attack on this set and adding an extra random trace to the set. The run terminates with $n = n^\star$ traces as soon as the attack is successful[10] with $n^\star$ traces as well as with all 99 previous numbers of traces $n \in \{n^\star - 99, \ldots, n^\star - 1\}$. Note that, unlike the convention adopted in the DPA contest website, we considered more appropriate to use the value $n^\star - 99$ (instead of $n^\star$) as the number of traces required to correctly recover the key for each run.

Table 3. Experimental results over 100 runs for all three variants

Variant	Leakage model	Parameters estimation	Number of traces ($n^\star - 99$)		
			Min	Average	Max
A	Bivariate at t_1	Fixed	30	42.42	94
	Univariate at t_{15}				
	Bivariate at t_{16}				
B	Bivariate at t_1	On-the-fly	30	46.06	82
	Bivariate at t_{16}				
C	Univariate at t_1	On-the-fly	35	53.42	97
	Univariate at t_{16}				

---

[10] Here "successful" means that the best terminating key $K^{(\mathrm{end})}$ (the one with the smallest score among all considered sequences) matches the correct key.

From these results, we observe that for each campaign of 100 runs there always occurred at least one run for which the number of traces needed to recover the key was the initial size of the set of traces[11]. This means that if we had chosen to initialize the set with less traces, we may probably have ended with a slightly better average figure.

A second and interesting observation is that "on-the-fly" variants B and C are only slightly less efficient than variant A, which uses priorly determined parameter values.

Finally, all three variants we proposed were ranked as the three best proposals of the DPA contest. The next three best proposals require 77.62, 125 and 131.78 traces on average, respectively.

6   Conclusion

We have presented the best proposed attack in the first DPA contest. The reason why it succeeds in finding the DES key with as few as less than fifty traces on average is that the leakage signal is exploited as optimally as possible. This is achieved by combining two features: (i) the maximum likelihood distinguisher combined with a relevant leakage model based on the specifics of the underlying hardware and, (ii) the choice of making guesses on the full 56-bit key in order to be able to predict the whole data that influences the power consumption. This latter point was quite challenging due to the computational barrier of the full key exhaustive search. Fortunately, we have managed to solve this issue through an original – in the field of cryptography and security – usage of a heuristic method – the hill climbing strategy in our case – that made it possible to efficiently sample the key space and reach the correct solution by considering a negligible proportion of all keys. We circumvented some difficulties in the progression of the sequences of solutions by analyzing and defining the rule to change from one key to the next one in a way that is relevant with respect to the specificities of the key schedule.

We believe that in our case study using a heuristic approach has been of great help. For further research, it would be of interest to tackle the resolution of security related problems with other metaheuristic approaches, such as simulated annealing, tabu search or evolutionary methods, along with the study of their efficiency.

---

[11] The initial set had 30 traces for the runs of methods A and B, and 35 traces for the runs of method C.

References

1. Boussaïd, I., Lepagnot, J., Siarry, P.: A survey on optimization metaheuristics. Inf. Sci. **237**, 82–117 (2013)
2. Brier, E., Clavier, C., Olivier, F.: Correlation power analysis with a leakage model. In: Joye, M., Quisquater, J.-J. (eds.) CHES 2004. LNCS, vol. 3156, pp. 16–29. Springer, Heidelberg (2004)
3. Bévan, R., Knudsen, E.W.: Ways to enhance differential power analysis. In: Lee, P.J., Lim, C.H. (eds.) ICISC 2002. LNCS, vol. 2587, pp. 327–342. Springer, Heidelberg (2003)
4. Guilley, S., Hoogvorst, P., Pacalet, R.: A fast pipelined multi-mode DES architecture operating in IP representation. Integr. VLSI J. **40**(4), 479–489 (2007)
5. Hertz, A., Widmer, M.: Guidelines for the use of meta-heuristics in combinatorial optimization. Eur. J. Oper. Res. **151**, 247–252 (2003)
6. Kocher, P.C., Jaffe, J., Jun, B.: Differential power analysis. In: Wiener, M. (ed.) CRYPTO 1999. LNCS, vol. 1666, pp. 388–397. Springer, Heidelberg (1999)
7. Messerges, T.S., Dabbish, E.A., Sloan, R.H.: Investigations of power analysis attacks on smartcards. In: USENIX Workshop on Smartcard Technology, pp. 151–162 (1999)
8. National Bureau of Standards. Data Encryption Standard. Federal Information Processing Standard #46 (1977)

A Pseudo-code of the Method

Algorithm 1. Score of a key candidate

Input: a set $T_{\mathcal{I}} = \{T_i : i \in \mathcal{I}\}$ of traces and corresponding sets of plaintexts $(M_{\mathcal{I}})$ and ciphertexts $(C_{\mathcal{I}})$,

a key candidate K,

a predictive linear model $\widetilde{W_1}(x) = \alpha_1 \times x + \beta_1$ for the power consumption at the end of round 1 (time instant t_1) as a function of $x = \mathrm{HD}(L_1, R_1)$,

a predictive linear model $\widetilde{W_{16}}(x) = \alpha_{16} \times x + \beta_{16}$ for the power consumption at the end of round 16 (time instant t_{16}) as a function of $x = \mathrm{HD}(L_{15}, R_{15})$.

Output: a maximum likelihood related figure of merit of the candidate K.

1: $\sigma \leftarrow 0$
2: **for** $i \in \mathcal{I}$ **do**
3:     $(L_0, R_0) \leftarrow \mathrm{IP}(M_i)$
4:     $(L_1, R_1) \leftarrow (R_0, L_0 \oplus f(K_1, R_0))$ [K_1: first round key derived from K]
5:     $\omega_1 \leftarrow W_1 - \widetilde{W_1}(\mathrm{HD}(L_1, R_1))$ [W_1: sample from T_i at time t_1]
6:     $(L_{16}, R_{16}) \leftarrow \mathrm{FP}^{-1}(C_i)$
7:     $(L_{15}, R_{15}) \leftarrow (R_{16} \oplus f(K_{16}, L_{16}), L_{16})$ [K_{16}: last round key derived from K]
8:     $\omega_{16} \leftarrow W_{16} - \widetilde{W_{16}}(\mathrm{HD}(L_{15}, R_{15}))$ [W_{16}: sample from T_i at time t_{16}]
9:     $\sigma \leftarrow \sigma + \omega_1^2 + \omega_{16}^2$
10: **return** σ

Algorithm 2. Key suggested by an attack

Input: a set $\mathcal{I} \subset \{0,\ldots,81\,088\}$ of indexes of DES executions,
   U a number of key candidates sequences.
Output: a key K suggested by the attack on power traces $T_\mathcal{I}$.

1: **for** $u = 1$ **to** U **do**
2:    $stop[u] \leftarrow$ **false**
3:    $K_{\mathrm{best}}[u] \leftarrow$ a random key
4:    $\sigma_{\mathrm{best}}[u] \leftarrow$ score of the key $K_{\mathrm{best}}[u]$ on the set $\mathcal{I}$ [c.f. Algorithm 1]

5: **while** $stop[u] =$ **false** for some $u \in \{1,\ldots,U\}$ **do**
6:    **for each** u such that $stop[u] =$ **false do**
7:       $K_{\mathrm{base}}[u] \leftarrow K_{\mathrm{best}}[u]$; $\sigma_{\mathrm{base}}[u] \leftarrow \sigma_{\mathrm{best}}[u]$
8:       $K[u] \leftarrow K_{\mathrm{base}}[u]$; $\sigma[u] \leftarrow \sigma_{\mathrm{base}}[u]$
9:       **for** $s = 1$ **to** 8 **do**
10:          **for each** $K \in \mathcal{N}_1(K_{\mathrm{base}}[u], s) \cup \mathcal{N}_{16}(K_{\mathrm{base}}[u], s)$ **do**
11:             **if** $score(K) < \sigma[u]$ **then**
12:                $K[u] \leftarrow K$; $\sigma[u] \leftarrow score(K)$
13:       $K_{\mathrm{base}}[u] \leftarrow K[u]$; $\sigma_{\mathrm{base}}[u] \leftarrow \sigma[u]$
14:       **for each** $K \in \mathcal{N}_1'(K_{\mathrm{base}}[u]) \cup \mathcal{N}_{16}'(K_{\mathrm{base}}[u])$ **do**
15:          **if** $score(K) < \sigma[u]$ **then**
16:             $K[u] \leftarrow K$; $\sigma[u] \leftarrow score(K)$
17:       **if** $\sigma[u] < \sigma_{\mathrm{best}}[u]$ **then**
18:          $K_{\mathrm{best}}[u] \leftarrow K[u]$; $\sigma_{\mathrm{best}}[u] \leftarrow \sigma[u]$
19:       **else**
20:          $stop[u] \leftarrow$ **true**
21: $u_{\mathrm{best}} \leftarrow \arg\max \sigma_{\mathrm{best}}[u]$
22: **return** $K_{\mathrm{best}}[u_{\mathrm{best}}]$

Algorithm 3. Score of a run of attacks

Input: the correct key K^*,
   two parameters a and τ controlling the decrease of the number of sequences.
Output: the score of a run of attacks.

1: $\mathcal{I} \leftarrow$ a set of 30 indexes randomly chosen from $\{0,\ldots,81\,088\}$
2: $n \leftarrow 30$; $success \leftarrow 0$
3: **while true do**
4:    $U \leftarrow \max(a\,e^{-n/\tau}, 5)$ [U exponentially decreases with n]
5:    $K \leftarrow$ the key recovered from an attack on $\mathcal{I}$ with U sequences [c.f. Algorithm 2]
6:    **if** $K = K^*$ **then**
7:       $success \leftarrow success + 1$
8:       **if** $success = 100$ **then**
9:          $n^* \leftarrow n$
10:          **return** $n^* - 99$
11:    **else**
12:       $success \leftarrow 0$
13:    $\mathcal{I} \leftarrow \mathcal{I} \cup$ a randomly chosen index not belonging to $\mathcal{I}$
14:    $n \leftarrow n + 1$

Improving the Big Mac Attack on Elliptic Curve Cryptography

Jean-Luc Danger[1,2], Sylvain Guilley[1,2],
Philippe Hoogvorst[2], Cédric Murdica[1,2(✉)], and David Naccache[3]

[1] Secure-IC S.A.S., 80 Avenue des Buttes de Coësmes, 35700 Rennes, France
{jean-luc.danger,sylvain.guilley,cedric.murdica}@secure-ic.com
[2] Département COMELEC, Institut TELECOM, TELECOM ParisTech,
CNRS LTCI, Paris, France
{jean-luc.danger,sylvain.guilley,philippe.hoogvorst,
cedric.murdica}@telecom-paristech.fr
[3] Département d'informatique, École Normale Supérieure,
45, rue d'Ulm, 75230 Paris Cedex 05, France
david.naccache@ens.fr

Abstract. At CHES 2001, Walter introduced the Big Mac attack against an implementation of RSA. It is an horizontal collision attack, based on the detection of common operands in two multiplications. The attack is very powerful since one single power trace of an exponentiation permits to recover all bits of the secret exponent. Moreover, the attack works with unknown or blinded input. The technique was later studied and improved by Clavier *et alii* and presented at INDOCRYPT 2012. At SAC 2013, Bauer *et alii* presented the first attack based on the Big Mac principle on implementations based on elliptic curves with simulation results.

In this work, we improve the attack presented by Bauer *et alii* to considerably increase the success rate. Instead of comparing only two multiplications, the targeted implementation permits to compare many multiplications. We give experiment results with traces taken from a real target to prove the soundness of our attack. In fact, the experimental results show that the original Big Mac technique given by Walter was better that the technique given by Clavier *et alii*. With our experiments on a real target, we show that the theoretical improvements are not necessarily the more suitable methods depending on the targeted implementations.

Keywords: Elliptic Curve Cryptography · Side-channel attack · Big Mac attack · Side-channel atomicity

1 Introduction

RSA and Elliptic Curve Cryptography (ECC) are vulnerable to side-channel attacks. Walter introduced at CHES 2001 the Big Mac attack on RSA [16].

P.Y.A. Ryan et al. (Eds.): Kahn Festschrift, LNCS 9100, pp. 374–386, 2016.
DOI: 10.1007/978-3-662-49301-4_23

It consists in comparing the power trace of two multiplications, and detect if they share a common operand. The Big Mac attack as presented in [16] is not applicable on ECC because the manipulated integers are too small. The size of the integers is an important factor for the success of the attack [1,5,16]. The Big Mac was then improved at INDOCRYPT 2012 for RSA implementations in [5]. Finally, in their publication at SAC 2013, Bauer et al. were able to perform an improved Big Mac attack on ECC [2]. They target a particular implementation on ECC. The implementation uses a side-channel countermeasure called *Side-Channel Atomicity* [9,11]. In [2], the authors noticed a vulnerability in the Side-Channel Atomicity. If an attacker is able to detect if two different multiplications share a common operand, she can recover the scalar. They illustrated the soundness of their attack with simulation results.

In this paper, we extend the work of [2]. If the Side-Channel Atomicity is used, the attacker is able to compare many multiplications (precisely fourteen pairs) instead of only two. Moreover, we present experimental results on a real target. With our experimentation, it turns out that the method presented in the first place by Walter [16] works better (*in practice*) than the improved ones (*from a theoretical standpoint*) presented in [2,16].

The rest of the paper is organized as follows. In Sect. 2, we give the backgrounds on ECC. In Sect. 2.3, we recall on the Side-Channel Atomicity countermeasure, which brings protection on ECC against the Simple Power Analysis. Section 3 describes the Big Mac attack of Walter [16] and the improved ones of [2,5]. Our attack is presented in Sect. 4. Finally, we conclude in Sect. 6.

2   Elliptic Curve Cryptography

An elliptic curve over a finite prime field $\mathbb{F}_p$ of characteristic $p > 3$ can be described by its reduced Weierstraß form:

$$E: y^2 = x^3 + ax + b \ . \tag{1}$$

We denote by $E(\mathbb{F}_p)$ the set of points $(x, y) \in \mathbb{F}_p^2$ satisfying Eq. (1), plus the point at infinity $\mathcal{O}$.

$E(\mathbb{F}_p)$ is an additive abelian group defined by the following addition law. Let $P = (x_1, y_1) \neq \mathcal{O}$ and $Q = (x_2, y_2) \notin \{\mathcal{O}, -P\}$ be two points on $E(\mathbb{F}_p)$. Point addition $R = (x_3, y_3) = P + Q$ is defined by the formula:

$$
\begin{aligned}
x_3 &= \lambda^2 - x_1 - x_2 \\
y_3 &= \lambda(x_1 - x_3) - y_1
\end{aligned}
\quad \text{where } \lambda =
\begin{cases}
\frac{y_1 - y_2}{x_1 - x_2} & \text{if } P \neq Q, \\
\frac{3x_1^2 + a}{2y_1} & \text{if } P = Q.
\end{cases}
$$

The inverse of point P is defined as $-P = (x_1, -y_1)$.

ECC relies on the difficulty of the elliptic curve discrete logarithm problem (ECDLP, compute k given P and $Q = [k]P$) or on the hardness of related problems such as ECDH or ECDDH, which can be solved if ECDLP can be.

2.1 Jacobian Projective Arithmetic

To avoid costly divisions when using the formulæ previously described, projective or Jacobian are preferably used.

The equation of an elliptic curve in the Jacobian projective coordinates system in the reduced Weierstraß form is:

$$E^{\mathcal{J}} : Y^2 = X^3 + aXZ^4 + bZ^6 \ .$$

The projective point (X, Y, Z) corresponds to the affine point $(X/Z^2, Y/Z^3)$ and there is an equivalence relation between the points: the point (X, Y, Z) is equivalent to any point $(r^2 X, r^3 Y, rZ)$ with $r \in \mathbb{F}_p^*$. The point at infinity is defined as $\mathcal{O} = (1, 1, 0)$ in Jacobian coordinates.

We give addition (ECADD) and doubling (ECDBL) formulas in the Jacobian projective coordinates system. Let $P_1 = (X_1, Y_1, Z_1)$ and $P_2 = (X_2, Y_2, Z_2)$ two points of $E^{\mathcal{J}}(\mathbb{K})$.

- **ECDBL.** $P_3 = (X_3, Y_3, Z_3) = 2P_1$ is computed as:
  $X_3 = T, \ Y_3 = -8Y_1^4 + M(S - T), \ Z_3 = 2Y_1 Z_1,$
  $S = 4X_1 Y_1^2, \ M = 3X_1^2 + aZ_1^4, \ T = -2S + M^2$
- **ECADD.** $P_3 = (X_3, Y_3, Z_3) = P_1 + P_2$ is computed as:
  $X_3 = -H^3 - 2U_1 H^2 + R^2, \ Y_3 = -S_1 H^3 + R(U_1 H^2 - X_3), \ Z_3 = Z_1 Z_2 H,$
  $U_1 = X_1 Z_2^2, \ U_2 = X_2 Z_1^2, \ S_1 = Y_1 Z_2^3, \ S_2 = Y_2 Z_1^3, \ H = U_2 - U_1, \ R = S_2 - S_1$

For speeding up the doubling, Cohen et al. introduced the modified Jacobian coordinates [7]. A point P is represented by the coordinates (X, Y, Z, W) where X, Y, Z are the Jacobian coordinates of P and $W = aZ^4$. The doubling of the point $P_1 = (X_1, Y_1, Z_1, W_1)$ is given below.

- **modECDBL.** $P_3 = (X_3, Y_3, Z_3, W_3) = 2P_1$ is computed as:
  $X_3 = A^2 - 2C, \ Y_3 = A(C - X_3) - D, \ Z_3 = 2Y_1 Z_1, \ W_3 = 2DW_1$
  $A = 3X_1^2 + W_1, \ B = 2Y_1^2, \ C = 2BX_1, \ D = 2B^2$

Remark 1. We summarize in this remark the conventional use of indices for field variables names in ECC operations. The inputs of **ECDBL** and **ECADD**, namely variables X, Y, Z in Jacobian coordinates (X, Y, Z, W in modified Jacobian coordinates), have indices 1 and 2. Of course, for **ECDBL**, indices 2 are not used. Index 3 is reserved for the **ECDBL**, **ECADD** and modECDBL outputs.

The indices used in the other (temporary) variables simply serve to uniquify them.

2.2 Elliptic Curve Scalar Multiplication

In ECC applications, one has to compute scalar multiplications (ECSMs), *i.e.* compute $[k]P$, given P and an integer k. Several methods exist to perform such a computation. This study focuses on the *Right-to-Left binary NAF mixed coordinates multiplication* [12]. Indeed, the countermeasure that we target was presented on this ECSM.

Algorithm 1. Right-to-Left binary NAF multiplication using mixed coordinates [11]

Input: $k, P = (X, Y, Z)$
Output: $[k]P$
  $(X_1, Y_1, Z_1) \leftarrow \mathcal{O}$
  $(T_1, T_2, T_3, T_4) \leftarrow (X, Y, Z, aZ^4)$
  while $k \geq 1$ **do**
    if $k_0 = 1$ **then**
      $u \leftarrow 2 - (k \bmod 4)$
      $k \leftarrow k - u$
      if $u = 1$ **then**
        $(X_1, Y_1, Z_1) \leftarrow \text{ECADD}((X_1, Y_1, Z_1), (T_1, T_2, T_3))$
      else
        $(X_1, Y_1, Z_1) \leftarrow \text{ECADD}((X_1, Y_1, Z_1), (T_1, -T_2, T_3))$
      end if
    end if
    $k \leftarrow k/2$
    $(T_1, T_2, T_3, T_4) \leftarrow \text{modECDBL}(T_1, T_2, T_3, T_4)$
  end while
  $(X_1, Y_1, Z_1) \leftarrow \text{ECADD}((X_1, Y_1, Z_1), (T_1, T_2, T_3))$
  return (X_1, Y_1, Z_1)

2.3 Side-Channel Atomicity

Naive ECSM, such as the Right-to-Left binary NAF mixed coordinates multiplication (Algorithm 1), is vulnerable to the Simple Power Analysis [8]. Indeed, the field operations involved for a doubling or an addition are quite different. Using the power trace of the ECSM, an attacker can detect which operation (doubling or addition of points) is performed and therefore deduce the scalar with a single trace.

Chevallier-Mames, Ciet and Joye introduced the concept of *side-channel atomicity* [9]. The formulæ to perform a doubling and an addition are rewritten into sequences of identical *atomic patterns*.

It was later improved by Giraud and Verneuil for ECADD and modECDBL for the Right-to-Left binary NAF mixed coordinates multiplication [11]. Figure 1 describes the computation of $\text{ECADD}((X_2, Y_2, Z_2), (X_1, Y_1, Z_1))$ and $\text{modECDBL}(X_1, Y_1, Z_1, W_1)$ (see [11] for the details). Each column represents an atomic pattern. The addition is written with two patterns while the doubling is written with only one.

This implementation is not vulnerable to SPA anymore since the attacker cannot distinguish between the operations performed simply by regarding the power consumption trace during the execution of the scalar multiplication.

	ECADD - part 1 ($\mathcal{A}1$)	ECADD - part 2 ($\mathcal{A}2$)	modECDBL ($\mathcal{D}$)
1.	$T_1 \leftarrow Z_2^2$	$T_1 \leftarrow T_6^2$	$T_1 \leftarrow X_1^2$
2.	$\star$	$\star$	$T_2 \leftarrow Y_1 + Y_1$
3.	$T_2 \leftarrow Y_1 \times Z_2$	$T_4 \leftarrow T_5 \times T_1$	$Z_3 \leftarrow T_2 \times Z_1$
4.	$\star$	$\star$	$T_4 \leftarrow T_1 + T_1$
5.	$T_5 \leftarrow Y_2 \times Z_1$	$T_5 \leftarrow T_1 \times T_6$	$T_3 \leftarrow T_2 \times Y_1$
6.	$\star$	$\star$	$T_6 \leftarrow T_3 + T_3$
7.	$T_3 \leftarrow T_1 \times T_2$	$T_1 \leftarrow Z_1 \times T_6$	$T_2 \leftarrow T_6 \times T_3$
8.	$\star$	$\star$	$T_1 \leftarrow T_4 + T_1$
9.	$\star$	$\star$	$T_1 \leftarrow T_1 + W_1$
10.	$T_4 \leftarrow Z_1^2$	$T_6 \leftarrow T_2^2$	$T_3 \leftarrow T_1^2$
11.	$T_5 \leftarrow T_5 \times T_4$	$Z_3 \leftarrow T_1 \times Z_2$	$T_4 \leftarrow T_6 \times X_1$
12.	$\star$	$T_1 \leftarrow T_4 + T_4$	$T_5 \leftarrow W_1 + W_1$
13.	$T_2 \leftarrow T_2 - T_3$	$T_6 \leftarrow T_6 - T_1$	$T_3 \leftarrow T_3 - T_4$
14.	$T_5 \leftarrow T_1 \times X_1$	$T_1 \leftarrow T_5 \times T_3$	$W_3 \leftarrow T_2 \times T_5$
15.	$\star$	$X_3 \leftarrow T_6 - T_5$	$X_3 \leftarrow T_3 - T_4$
16.	$\star$	$T_4 \leftarrow T_4 - X_3$	$T_6 \leftarrow T_4 - X_3$
17.	$T_6 \leftarrow X_2 \times T_4$	$T_3 \leftarrow T_4 \times T_2$	$T_4 \leftarrow T_6 \times T_1$
18.	$T_6 \leftarrow T_6 - T_5$	$Y_3 \leftarrow T_3 - T_1$	$Y_3 \leftarrow T_4 - T_2$

Fig. 1. ECADD and modECDBL operations written with the same atomic pattern ($\star$ represents a dummy operation)

3   Big Mac Attack

3.1   Big Mac Attack on RSA

We present in this section the Big Mac Attack introduced by Walter against RSA implementations [16].

Long Integer Multiplication. We give in Algorithm 2 the classical field multiplication. w is the word size (w is generally equal to $8, 16, 32$ or 64 in common architectures).

Modular multiplication is performed either with the classical modular multiplication followed by a reduction, like the Montgomery [14] or the Barrett reduction [3], or with an interleaved modular multiplication. The important feature for the attack is the word-wise multiplication.

Goal of the attack. Denote T_1, T_2 the traces during the computation of respectively two multiplications $A \times B$, $C \times D$, with $A \neq C$. The attacker tries to assert if $B = D$ given T_1 and T_2.

Averaging. We suppose that the device leaks the Hamming Weight (denoted **HW**) of the manipulated values.

The power consumption during the computation of $a_i \times b_j$ (line 5 of Algorithm 2) can be expressed with $\mathbf{HW}(b_j)$, and other activities of the device (including $\mathbf{HW}(a_i)$, $\mathbf{HW}(a_i \times b_j)$) and the noise.

Algorithm 2. Long Integer Multiplication

Input: $A = (a_{m-1}, \ldots, a_0)_{2^w}, B = (b_{m-1}, \ldots, b_0)_{2^w}$
Output: $C = (c_{2m-1}, \ldots, c_0)_{2^w} = A \times B$
1: $C \leftarrow 0$
2: **for** $i = 0$ **to** $m - 1$ **do**
3:      $u \leftarrow 0$
4:      **for** $j = 0$ **to** $m - 1$ **do**
5:          $(u, v)_{2^w} \leftarrow a_i \times b_j$
6:          $(u, v)_{2^w} \leftarrow (u, v)_{2^w} + c_{i+j} + u$
7:          $c_{i+j} \leftarrow v$
8:      **end for**
9:      $c_{i+m} \leftarrow u$
10: **end for**
11: **return** S

$$s_{i,j} = \mathbf{HW}(b_j) + r_{i,j} . \tag{2}$$

with $r_{i,j}$ corresponds to other activities and the noise. The sample points of the trace T_1, in which each $b_j, j \in [0, m[$ is manipulated, are averaged into one single value s_j.

$$s_j = \sum_0^{m-1} s_{i,j} \tag{3}$$

$$= \mathbf{HW}(b_j) + r_j \tag{4}$$

with r_j having a much smaller value compared with each $r_{i,j}$. The computation of s_0 is illustrated in Fig. 2.

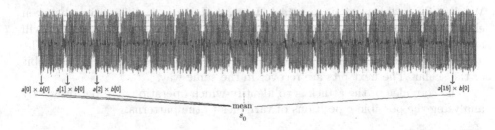

Fig. 2. Illustration of the computation of s_0 with a modular multiplication of integers of four words (256-bit integers in a 64-bit architecture)

Euclidean Distance. Denote $S_1 = s_0 || \ldots || s_{m-1}$ the concatenation of the s_j. The same is done with T_2 to obtain S_2.

If $B = D$, the Euclidean distance between S_1 and S_2 is small. In the case of $B \neq D$, the distance is high.

Big Mac CoCo. Instead of using a Euclidean Distance, the authors of [5] suggest to use the Pearson correlation instead of the Euclidean Distance. This refined attack is called *Big Mac CoCo* (CoCo for collision-correlation) in [5].

Comparison between Big Mac and Big Mac CoCo. They give simulation results to compare the Euclidean Distance with the Pearson correlation. The Big Mac CoCo gives much better results than the original Big Mac of Walter.

3.2 Big Mac Attack on ECC

The classical Big Mac of Walter is considered not applicable on ECC because the number of words is large compared to ECC[1].

However, Bauer et al. give simulation results of the Big Mac CoCo on elliptic curves size [2]. They target the Side-Channel Atomicity. Indeed, they notice that there are common operands regarding the side-channel atomicity formulæ. For instance, to distinguish an addition from a doubling, they suggest to compare the first multiplication (line 1) and the second multiplication (line 3) of Fig. 1. If it is a doubling, the two multiplications share a common operand. They give the success rate on simulation results using a correlation which was high enough even for a 32 architecture.

We experimentally tried both the Big Mac and the Big Mac CoCo on real measurements on a 64 bits architecture and we failed. In the next section, we present a significant improvement of the attack of [2]. We also present experimental results of our attack.

4 Improving the Big Mac Attack on the Side-Channel Atomicity

We describe in this section our attack. Instead of trying to differentiate between elliptic curves operations (addition or doubling) and only two patterns, we will analyses a sequence of several patterns depending of a bit of the scalar. The attack is recursive. For a better clarity, we will see how to recover the first bit of the scalar. The next bits are recover in the same way.

The core idea of the attack is to identify which operations are performed by analysing the possible repetitions of variables in the patterns.

4.1 Possibilities of the Atomic Patterns

For the first iteration of Algorithm 1, the possible operations of the three first atomic patterns are:

---

[1] For a 128 bits security, ECC must use 256-bit integers length, while RSA must use 3072-bit integers.

1. $\mathcal{A}1; \mathcal{A}2; \mathcal{D}$. In this case, $k_0 \neq 0$.
2. $\mathcal{D}; \mathcal{A}1; \mathcal{A}2$. In this case, $k_0 = 0$.
3. $\mathcal{D}; \mathcal{D}; \mathcal{A}1$. In this case, $k_0 = 0$.
4. $\mathcal{D}; \mathcal{D}; \mathcal{D}$. In this case, $k_0 = 0$.

More precisely, the four cases are for the three first bits of k equal to $1xx$, $01x$, 001 and 000 respectively, where x represents any value (0 or 1). We want to assert if the first three patterns correspond to $\mathcal{A}1; \mathcal{A}2; \mathcal{D}$ ($k_0 \neq 0$).

4.2   Same Values in the Different Patterns

With Fig. 1 and the different possibilities of the three first patterns, we label the operations with a common operand *only* if the operations are $\mathcal{A}1; \mathcal{A}2; \mathcal{D}$; we neglect the multiplications sharing a common operand if they possibly occur in another sequence of patterns.

The common operands are illustrated in Fig. 3. They are denoted with boxes with the same index. For example, the square at line 1 of the 1st pattern and the multiplication at line 3 of the 1st pattern share a common operand (Z_2) only if the sequence is $\mathcal{A}1; \mathcal{A}2; \mathcal{D}$. Note that the multiplication at line 17 of the 1st pattern and the multiplication at line 11 of the 3rd pattern share a common operand (X_2 and X_1) only if $\mathcal{A}1; \mathcal{A}2; \mathcal{D}$ is performed. The same holds for Z_2 in $\mathcal{A}1; \mathcal{A}2$ and Z_1 in $\mathcal{D}$. Indeed, the point (X_2, Y_2, Z_2) of $\mathcal{A}1; \mathcal{A}2$ and the point (X_1, Y_1, Z_1) of $\mathcal{D}$ both correspond to the point R or $-R$ in Algorithm 1.

The total number of pairs of multiplications or squares sharing a common operand is sixteen in the sequence $\mathcal{A}1; \mathcal{A}2; \mathcal{D}$.

4.3   Assembling the Pieces of the Puzzle

We want to apply the method of the Big Mac attack to detect if the three first patterns indeed correspond to $\mathcal{A}1; \mathcal{A}2; \mathcal{D}$. The low number of words is compensated by the large number of modular multiplications we compare. We can compare sixteen pairs (see Fig. 3) instead of one, thanks to the atomicity countermeasure.

First, we split the trace of the three first patterns; we separate the field operations. We denote $s(\cdot)$ the method for constructing S_1 or S_2 as previously described for the Big Mac attack.

We then construct two sets U_1, U_2 as follows. U_1, U_2 are first set empty. We perform $s(\cdot)$ for the power traces of the multiplications that might share a common operand. One element of each pair is put in U_1, the other is put in U_2. The construction of U_1, U_2 is illustrated in Fig. 4 for the first three pairs possibly sharing the same operand Z_2.

The Euclidean distance between U_1 and U_2 is low if each pair share a common operand. In this case the three patterns observed are actually $\mathcal{A}1; \mathcal{A}2; \mathcal{D}$, and the attacker concludes that $k_0 \neq 0$. She then iterates the method with the next three patterns to target the digit k_1. The Euclidean distance between U_1 and U_2 is high if no multiplication among all multiplications shares a common operand.

	ECADD - part 1 ($\mathcal{A}1$)	ECADD - part 2 ($\mathcal{A}2$)	modECDBL ($\mathcal{D}$)
1.	$T_1 \leftarrow \boxed{Z_2}_{1,2,14}^2$	$T_1 \leftarrow \boxed{T_6}_{9,10}^2$	$T_1 \leftarrow \boxed{X_1}_{12}^2$
2.	$\star$	$\star$	$T_2 \leftarrow Y_1 + Y_1$
3.	$T_2 \leftarrow Y_1 \times \boxed{Z_2}_{1,3,15}$	$T_4 \leftarrow T_5 \times T_1$	$Z_3 \leftarrow T_2 \times \boxed{Z_1}_{14,15,16}$
4.	$\star$	$\star$	$T_4 \leftarrow T_1 + T_1$
5.	$T_5 \leftarrow Y_2 \times \boxed{Z_1}_{4,5}$	$T_5 \leftarrow T_1 \times \boxed{T_6}_{9,11}$	$T_3 \leftarrow T_2 \times Y_1$
6.	$\star$	$\star$	$T_6 \leftarrow T_3 + T_3$
7.	$T_3 \leftarrow \boxed{T_1}_7 \times T_2$	$T_1 \leftarrow \boxed{Z_1}_{5,6} \times \boxed{T_6}_{10,11}$	$T_2 \leftarrow T_6 \times T_3$
8.	$\star$	$\star$	$T_1 \leftarrow T_4 + T_1$
9.	$\star$	$\star$	$T_1 \leftarrow T_1 + W_1$
10.	$T_4 \leftarrow \boxed{Z_1}_{4,6}^2$	$T_6 \leftarrow T_2^2$	$T_3 \leftarrow T_1^2$
11.	$T_5 \leftarrow T_5 \times \boxed{T_4}_8$	$Z_3 \leftarrow T_1 \times \boxed{Z_2}_{2,3,16}$	$T_4 \leftarrow T_6 \times \boxed{X_1}_{13}$
12.	$\star$	$T_1 \leftarrow T_4 + T_4$	$T_5 \leftarrow W_1 + W_1$
13.	$T_2 \leftarrow T_2 - T_3$	$T_6 \leftarrow T_6 - T_1$	$T_3 \leftarrow T_3 - T_4$
14.	$T_5 \leftarrow \boxed{T_1}_7 \times X_1$	$T_1 \leftarrow T_5 \times T_3$	$W_3 \leftarrow T_2 \times T_5$
15.	$\star$	$X_3 \leftarrow T_6 - T_5$	$X_3 \leftarrow T_3 - T_4$
16.	$\star$	$T_4 \leftarrow T_4 - X_3$	$T_6 \leftarrow T_4 - X_3$
17.	$T_6 \leftarrow \boxed{X_2}_{12,13} \times \boxed{T_4}_8$	$T_3 \leftarrow T_4 \times T_2$	$T_4 \leftarrow T_6 \times T_1$
18.	$T_6 \leftarrow T_6 - T_5$	$Y_3 \leftarrow T_3 - T_1$	$Y_3 \leftarrow T_4 - T_2$

Fig. 3. Common operands in the atomic patterns

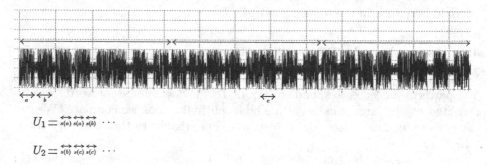

Fig. 4. Assembling the pieces of the puzzle of three atomic patterns

In this case, the three patterns observed are not $\mathcal{A}1; \mathcal{A}2; \mathcal{D}$, and the attacker concludes that $k_0 = 0$. She starts again with the two last patterns of the three, added together with the fourth pattern of the ECSM to target k_1.

4.4   Experimental Results

We implemented a modular multiplication on a 64-bit architecture in the Side-channel Attack Standard Evaluation Board SASEBO-GII [15]. We mounted the attack with 384-bit integers (six words of 64 bits).

Characterization. The first step of the attack is the characterisation of the arithmetic module. We constructed U_1, U_2 as previously described with fourteen pairs of multiplications sharing a common operand[2] 1000 times. The average Euclidean distance was 2.165. The same was done with fourteen pairs of multiplication with random operands. The average Euclidean distance was 3.198. We established that a distance lower than the mean 2.682 correspond to $\mathcal{A}1; \mathcal{A}2; \mathcal{D}$.

Attack on real operations. We then assembled the pieces of the puzzle as previously described with a trace of $\mathcal{A}1; \mathcal{A}2; \mathcal{D}$ 100 times. Only three distances were higher than 2.682. We conclude that the attacker can detect $\mathcal{A}1; \mathcal{A}2; \mathcal{D}$ with a success of 97 %. The same was done with $\mathcal{D}; \mathcal{D}; \mathcal{A}1$ 100 times. Only four distances were lower than 2.682. We conclude that the attacker wrongly detects a patterns triplet as $\mathcal{A}1; \mathcal{A}2; \mathcal{D}$ with probability 4 %.

We performed the experiment with 256-bit integers (four words) as well. We obtained a probability of 96 % to correctly detect $\mathcal{A}1; \mathcal{A}2; \mathcal{D}$, and a probability of 16 % that $\mathcal{D}; \mathcal{D}; \mathcal{A}1$ was detected as $\mathcal{A}1; \mathcal{A}2; \mathcal{D}$, which is still acceptable to perform the attack.

We believe that the success probability is higher on a 32-bit architecture because of the larger number of words.

Big Mac CoCo. We also tried using the Pearson correlation as in [2,5]. Surprisingly, the coefficient was high (around 0.9) each time, even if the guess was incorrect (i.e. even if there are no common operand for all multiplications).

The reason is that there are similarities in long integer multiplications even if the values are different such as the variation of the word numbers manipulated. Our experiment shows that in certain cases, the Euclidean Distance is better than the correlation.

5 Countermeasures

In this section, we discuss on the classical countermeasures on ECC that thwart or not our attack.

5.1 Ineffective Countermeasures

Scalar Randomization [8, Sect. 5.1]. If k is the scalar and $P \in E$ the base point, Coron suggests to randomize the scalar as $k' = k + r\#E$ with $\#E$ the number of points in the curve and r a random integer. This prevents from the Differential Power Analysis [8]. When applying our attack, the attacker recovers k' and trivially recovers the original previous secret $k = k' \mod \#E$.

Scalar Splitting [10, Sect. 4.2]. Clavier and Joye proposed a method to randomize the scalar. Instead of computing $[k]P$, one can compute $Q = [k - r]P +$

---

[2] We use fourteen pairs instead of sixteen as shown in Fig. 3 because we avoid the pairs where the possibly same operand is not in the same side: boxes 5 and 13.

$[r]P$ with a random r. If the two scalar multiplications are performed successively, the attack presented in this paper can trivially be applied for both ECSMs and recover the initial scalar k. On the other hand, if the two ECSMs are performed in parallel, it is quite more difficult. Indeed, when attacking the scalar of one ECSM, the power consumption or the electromagnetic radiation coming from the second ECSM is necessarily considered as noise. To conclude, the attack can still be applied in theory but the success rate should be decreased considerably.

Point Binding [8, Sect. 5.2]. The countermeasure, by Coron, consists in computing $Q = [k](P + R)$ instead of $[k]P$, with R a pseudo-random point. The chip returns $Q - [k]R$. Our attack does not need the knowledge of the base point and therefore the countermeasure is ineffective. We focus on possible collisions of values that will happen even if the base point is randomized this way.

Random Projective Coordinates [8, Sect. 5.3]. A point $P = (X, Y, Z)$ in Jacobian coordinates is equivalent to any point $(r^2 X, r^3 Y, rZ)$, with $r \in \mathbb{F}_p^*$. Coron suggests to randomize the base point at the beginning of the ECSM by choosing a random nonzero r. The previous analysis on the point blinding stands here.

Random Curve Isomorphism [13]. Elliptic curves $E \colon y^2 = x^3 + ax + b$ and $E' \colon y^2 = x^3 + a'x + b'$ are isomorphic if and only if there exists $u \in \mathbb{F}_p^*$ such that $u^4 a' = a$ and $u^6 b' = b$. The isomorphism φ is defined as:

$$\varphi \colon E \xrightarrow{\sim} E', \begin{cases} \mathcal{O} \to \mathcal{O} \\ (x, y) \to (u^{-2}x, u^{-3}y) \end{cases}$$

The countermeasure, introduced by Joye and Tymen, consists in computing the ECSM on a random curve E' instead of E. The previous analysis on the point blinding stands here.

5.2   Effective Countermeasures

Multiplication with Random Permutation [1,6]. Clavier, Feix, Gagnerot, Rousselet and Verneuil introduced the Multiplication with Random Permutation countermeasure [6]. It consists in randomizing the order of the manipulation of the words during a long multiplication. For example, in Algorithm 2, it consists in randomizing the order of both loops (lines 2 and 4) with two random permutations in $[0, m[$ (m being the word number of the manipulated integers). The construction of $s_0, 0 \le j < m$ is no longer possible for the Big Mac attack. Another method for randomizing the loops was proposed in [1].

No Same Values Algorithm. We suggest to implement elliptic curves without the possible repetitions of values depending on the scalar. The side-channel atomicity brings too much multiplications that we can compare. That makes our attack possible and practicable.

Other countermeasures exist to prevent the Simple Power Analysis aside the Side-Channel Atomicity. Regularizing the ECSM, *i.e.* perform the same elliptic curve operations at each iteration of the ECSM prevents the Simple Power Analysis without bringing many multiplications that possibly share common operands.

6 Conclusion

A practical horizontal attack on ECC is presented against the Side-Channel Atomicity countermeasure, based on the Big Mac principle [16]. It is an extension of the attack presented in [2]. The difference is that we compare many multiplications instead of only one. The Side-Channel Atomicity permits to compare many multiplications.

This attack is powerful since it permits to recover the entire scalar with a single trace. The secret scalar can thus be recovered with a single execution of the ECSM and we can target protocol such as ECDSA where the scalar is randomly chosen for each new signature. Also, scalar randomization techniques are ineffective.

Moreover, the base point does not matter for the attack. Therefore, countermeasures which consist in randomizing the inputs are ineffective.

To prove the soundness of our attack, we give experimental results. We emphasis in the fact that the correlation used as a distinguisher is not the optimal solution in our case (in fact we failed) as presented in [2,5]. The Euclidean Distance, as presented in the original Big Mac attack [16].

We target a particular countermeasure which has the particularity to bring multiple possible common operands during the elliptic curve operations (addition and doubling). However, we believe that the method might be adapted on other implementations, where many modular multiplications can be compare. This is not the case for classical implementations of ECC (with classical addition and doubling formulæ) but might be the case for other specific implementations.

References

1. Bauer, A., Jaulmes, É., Prouff, E., Wild, J.: Horizontal and vertical side-channel attacks against secure RSA implementations. In: Dawson, E. (ed.) CT-RSA 2013. LNCS, vol. 7779, pp. 1–17. Springer, Heidelberg (2013)
2. Bauer, A., Jaulmes, É., Prouff, E., Wild, J.: Horizontal Collision Correlation Attack on Elliptic Curves. In: SAC 2013 (2013, to appear)
3. Barrett, P.: Implementing the rivest shamir and adleman public key encryption algorithm on a standard digital signal processor. In: Odlyzko, A.M. (ed.) CRYPTO 1986. LNCS, vol. 263, pp. 311–323. Springer, Heidelberg (1987)
4. Ciet, M., Joye, M.: (Virtually) free randomization techniques for elliptic curve cryptography. In: Qing, S., Gollmann, D., Zhou, J. (eds.) ICICS 2003. LNCS, vol. 2836, pp. 348–359. Springer, Heidelberg (2003)
5. Clavier, C., Feix, B., Gagnerot, G., Giraud, C., Roussellet, M., Verneuil, V.: ROSETTA for single trace analysis. In: Galbraith, S., Nandi, M. (eds.) INDOCRYPT 2012. LNCS, vol. 7668, pp. 140–155. Springer, Heidelberg (2012)
6. Clavier, C., Feix, B., Gagnerot, G., Roussellet, M., Verneuil, V.: Horizontal correlation analysis on exponentiation. In: Soriano, M., Qing, S., López, J. (eds.) ICICS 2010. LNCS, vol. 6476, pp. 46–61. Springer, Heidelberg (2010)

7. Cohen, H., Miyaji, A., Ono, T.: Efficient elliptic curve exponentiation using mixed coordinates. In: Ohta, K., Pei, D. (eds.) ASIACRYPT 1998. LNCS, vol. 1514, pp. 51–65. Springer, Heidelberg (1998)

8. Coron, J.-S.: Resistance against differential power analysis for elliptic curve cryptosystems. In: Koç, Ç.K., Paar, C. (eds.) CHES 1999. LNCS, vol. 1717, pp. 292–302. Springer, Heidelberg (1999)

9. Chevallier-Mames, B., Ciet, M., Joye, M.: Low-cost solutions for preventing simple side-channel analysis: side-channel atomicity. J. IEEE Trans. Comput. **53**(6), 460–468 (2004)

10. Clavier, C., Joye, M.: Universal exponentiation algorithm. In: Koç, Ç.K., Naccache, D., Paar, C. (eds.) CHES 2001. LNCS, vol. 2162, p. 300. Springer, Heidelberg (2001)

11. Giraud, C., Verneuil, V.: Atomicity improvement for elliptic curve scalar multiplication. In: Gollmann, D., Lanet, J.-L., Iguchi-Cartigny, J. (eds.) CARDIS 2010. LNCS, vol. 6035, pp. 80–101. Springer, Heidelberg (2010)

12. Joye, M.: Fast point multiplication on elliptic curves without precomputation. In: Gathen, J., Imaña, J.L., Koç, Ç.K. (eds.) WAIFI 2008. LNCS, vol. 5130, pp. 36–46. Springer, Heidelberg (2008)

13. Joye, M., Tymen, C.: Protections against Differential Analysis for Elliptic Curve Cryptography. In: Koç, Ç.K., Naccache, D., Paar, C. (eds.) CHES 2001. LNCS, vol. 2162, pp. 377–390. Springer, Heidelberg (2001)

14. Montgomery, P.L.: Modular multiplication without trial division. J. Math. Comput. **44**(170), 519–521 (1985)

15. Side-channel Attack Standard Evaluation Board (SASEBO). http://www.rcis.aist.go.jp/special/SASEBO/

16. Walter, C.D.: Sliding windows succumbs to Big Mac attack. In: Koç, Ç.K., Naccache, D., Paar, C. (eds.) CHES 2001. LNCS, vol. 2162, p. 286. Springer, Heidelberg (2001)

Randomness

Randomness Testing: Result Interpretation and Speed

Marek Sýs and Vashek Matyáš[(⊠)]

Masaryk University, Brno, Czech Republic
{syso,matyas}@fi.muni.cz

Abstract. In cryptography, randomness is typically tested using a battery of tests consisting of many tests of randomness – each focusing on a different feature. Probability that data produced by a good generator would pass all the tests in a battery can get quite small for a large number of used tests. Therefore, results of many tests should be interpreted with a particular focus on this issue. We argue for the Šidák correction – this is a statistical method that can be used for evaluating multiple but independent tests. We analyzed the accuracy of the Šidák correction since tests of randomness are usually correlated, and we undertook this analysis for the NIST Statistical Test Suite. Results show that correlation of tests of randomness has got only a marginal influence on the accuracy of the Šidák correction. We also provide a speed-optimized version of NIST STS that achieved test results more than 30-times faster than the original NIST codes.

Keywords: Berlekamp-Massey algorithm · Efficient implementation · NIST STS · Randomness statistical testing

1 Introduction

Randomness plays a very important role in cryptography because the security of many cryptosystems relies on the quality of random data they work with. Well-designed cryptographic primitives (block ciphers, stream ciphers, hash functions, etc.) should produce data where, without knowledge of the algorithm/key, one cannot distinguish these data from a truly random data stream. In fact, primitives should represent a good random number generator (RNG), producing data with no recognizable patterns. Empirical tests of randomness are often used to assess whether primitives produce random data. There are many empirical tests of randomness, each testing randomness according to different characteristics of bits or blocks.

While an empirical randomness test result has a clear interpretation, the interpretation of the results of multiple tests is problematic. Firstly, with an increasing number of tests, even a good RNG is more likely to fail some tests. Secondly, the tests are sometimes mutually dependent (correlated). In this article, we focus on a correct interpretation of tests implemented in the NIST Statistical Test Suite (NIST STS), an important testing suite for randomness analysis

© Springer-Verlag Berlin Heidelberg 2016
P.Y.A. Ryan et al. (Eds.): Kahn Festschrift, LNCS 9100, pp. 389–395, 2016.
DOI: 10.1007/978-3-662-49301-4_24

that is often used for formal certifications or approvals. We also provide a speed-optimized version of NIST STS, which achieved test results even more than 30-times faster.

2 Test Suites

Empirical tests are usually grouped into testing suites (also called batteries) to provide a more comprehensive randomness analysis. There are three commonly used testing suites for randomness analysis: NIST Statistical Test Suite [1] (NIST STS), Dieharder [2] and TestU01 [3]. Each test suite implements several tests of randomness, but tests are often performed in more variants, examining more properties of the same type. In fact, each test suite implements many tests: NIST STS – 188 (default settings), Diehard – 24, TestU01 – 106.

2.1 Hypothesis Testing

In hypothesis testing, a given hypothesis called a null hypothesis (e.g., data are generated by a good RNG) is evaluated using a specific statistical test (e.g., Frequency test). The statistical test is defined by a relevant statistic (e.g., statistic of bits) to determine the acceptance or rejection of the null hypothesis. A statistic is a function of the data and compresses analyzed data into a single value (e.g., $s_{obs} = |\#0's - \#1's|/\sqrt{n}$, where n is number of bits in the data) reflecting the property of data relevant to the tested null hypothesis. A test statistic is usually transformed into a p-value, which can be simply interpreted. The p-value represents the probability that for the true hypothesis, we would get a more extreme test statistic (e.g., $s > s_{obs}$) than we obtained. In fact, the p-value indicates how extreme our data are or how often we can see worse results for the true hypothesis. A small p-value (e.g., 0.01) means that data are too extreme because we will get comparable or worse results with a small probability (1 %) for the true hypothesis (e.g., data are random). To evaluate a test, the p-value is compared with the significance level α that is chosen by a tester (for cryptography, α is usually set to $\alpha = 0.01$). If the p-value is smaller/bigger than α, the hypothesis is rejected/accepted. We can commit two types of errors Type I and Type II in the hypothesis testing. A Type I error occurs when the true hypothesis is rejected although the hypothesis is true (e.g., sequence was produced by a good RNG). The probability of a Type I error is equal to the significance level α. A Type II error represents the probability of accepting the false hypothesis (e.g., defective RNG).

2.2 Testing Methodology

All test suites are usually used to assess the quality of the RNG in two common scenarios. In both scenarios, the goal of the testing process is to compute a p-value for each particular empirical test of randomness. In the first scenario, a RNG generates a single sequence. The tests of a battery are applied to this sequence, producing a set of p-values (one for each test). In the second scenario, multiple sequences are generated and tested. Therefore, one set of p-values is computed by each particular test. The evaluation of randomness, based on a single p-value, is simple and straightforward. On the other hand, there are many ways to evaluate randomness according to a set of p-values computed by a test, all based on the expected uniformity of p-values. A common way is to test the uniformity of p-values for each particular test. The uniformity of p-values computed by an empirical test (first-level test) forms another hypothesis, which can be tested using a statistical test (second-level test), producing another p-value. Test suites use various statistical second level tests (e.g., Kolmogorov-Smirnov, χ^2, Cramer-Mises), each analyzing the uniformity of p-values from different points of view. Test suites usually produce two p-values for each empirical test: one p-value computed by the empirical test itself and another p-value obtained using some uniformity test applied to the set of p-values computed by the empirical test.

3   Interpretation of Results

Randomness is evaluated in the same way for both p-values. The p-value (first or second level) is compared with the predefined significance level α. If the p value is too small (smaller than α), the null hypothesis is rejected and the RNG is considered as bad, producing non-random sequences. Randomness is a probabilistic property, and therefore NIST recommends that "additional numerical experiments should be conducted on different samples of the generator to determine whether the phenomenon was a statistical anomaly or a clear evidence of non-randomness" [1]. The interpretation of the results of the test suite is not trivial. The probability that a good RNG fails a test is non-zero (α), which means that a good RNG rarely passes a whole battery. The interpretation of multiple tests should be performed with a focus on this issue. Bonferroni and more accurate Šidák corrections are the most frequently used procedures for evaluating multiple tests solving this problem.

3.1   Issues

The main problem of the randomness testing is the interpretation of multiple p-values computed by different tests. The issue is that even sequences produced by a good RNG may fail ($p - value < \alpha$) a test, with the probability α. As the number of tests increases, the probability that the RNG passes all tests decreases geometrically. Therefore, we often need to generate and test additional samples according to the recommendation of NIST. The probability that even the sequence produced by a good RNG passes all tests of the test suite is small (15 % for NIST STS, 78 % for Diehard, 34 % for TestU01, for $\alpha = 0.01$). These probabilities of the Type I error are significantly different from the expected $\alpha = 1$ % and need to be "corrected". The Šidák correction is a statistical method that can be used for evaluating multiple but independent tests. Empirical tests are usually correlated and dependent and therefore the Šidák testing procedure should be adjusted accordingly.

4   Šidák Correction

In the hypothesis testing, a hypothesis (randomness of data) is rejected when the p-value computed by a statistical test is smaller than α. For a single test, α represents the probability of a Type I error. The probability is set by the tester to a small value he can tolerate. For k tests and corresponding p-values $p_1, \cdots, p_k$, data can be considered random if they pass $(p_i > \alpha)$ all used empirical tests. For many tests, it is likely that even random data fail $(p_i < \alpha)$ at least one test. This means that the probability of a Type I error (data produced by a good RNG are considered non-random) is significantly bigger than α such a large value is no longer tolerable. Therefore, the set of p-values $p_1, \cdots, p_k$ should be evaluated in a different way (not just comparing each p-value with α). The Šidák correction is proposed to compute one resulting p-value for all tests. The Šidák procedure processes a set of p-values $p_1, \cdots, p_k$ computed by k tests into a "joined" p-value. The resulting p-value is computed simply as $P_{Sidak} = (1 - P_{min})^k$, where P_{min} denotes the smallest of the p-values $p_1, \cdots, p_k$. In fact, P_{Sidak} represents p-value for all k tests. Therefore – in order to evaluate multiple tests – it suffices to compare single p-value P_{Sidak} with the significance level α. The procedure guarantees a Type I error rate of α for independent tests, i.e., tests whose p-values are not correlated.

4.1   Šidák Correction and NIST STS

The Šidák correction gives accurate results for independent tests, i.e., the probability that a sequence generated by a good RNG fails the Šidák procedure $(P_{Sidak} < \alpha)$ is equal to the probability of the Type I error (α). Some tests implemented in batteries are strongly correlated, e.g., it was shown in [4] that if a random sequence fails the Cumulative sum test, then the probability that it also fails the Frequency test is 70 %. This probability is significantly different from the expected $\alpha = 1\%$ therefore, such a strong dependency clearly affects the accuracy of the Šidák procedure for these two tests. We tested random data produced by a physical source of randomness [5] to measure how the dependency of all NIST STS tests affects the accuracy of the Šidák procedure. We focused on the difference between the probability of a Type I error $Pr(P_{Sidak} < \alpha)$ and significance level α. We tested 100 GB of data using a new optimized implementation of NIST STS [6] corresponding to 819 200 binary sequences, each consisting of a million bits. We measured the accuracy of the Šidák procedure for all NIST STS tests with their default settings. We analyzed the accuracy of the Šidák procedure in the context of both scenarios for randomness testing – empirical and uniformity tests.

4.2   Šidák Correction and Empirical Tests

NIST STS examines the randomness of data using 188 empirical tests, but not all tests are applicable for certain sequences. Random Excursion and Random Excursion Variant are two tests of the NIST STS that are applicable only if some requirements are fulfilled. Both tests are applicable/non-applicable at the same time. Moreover, the tests consist of several tests of the same type (Random Excursion – 8, Random Excursion Variant – 18) thus, a sequence can by tested by 188 or 162 tests. We analyzed the ratio of the probability that a sequence generated by a good RNG fails the Šidák correction procedure $Pr(P_{Sidak} < x)$ to the expected value given by significance level x. The following graph shows values of $ratio = Pr(P_{Sidak} < x)/x$ computed for different x, with a step of 0.001 (Fig. 1).

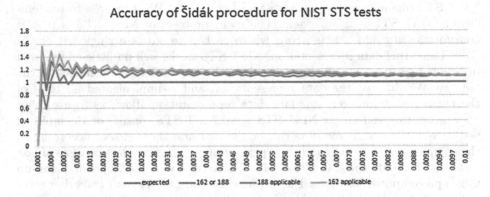

Accuracy of Šidák procedure for NIST STS tests

Fig. 1. Ratio of the probability that a sequence generated by a good RNG fails the Šidák correction procedure $Pr(P_{Sidak} < x)$ to the expected value given by significance level x for the various levels of significance x (Color figure online).

The red line represents values of the ratio computed from all 819 200 sequences. Using the Šidák procedure with $k = 188$ or $k = 162$, the p-values were processed according to the applicability/non-applicability of the tests Random Excursion and Random Excursion Variant. We also measured the accuracy of the Šidák procedure for 505 557 sequences, where all 188 tests were applicable – blue values. The gray values were computed from the remaining 313 643 sequences, where the Random Excursion tests were not applicable ($k = 162$). The graph shows that the value of ratio is stable and is close to the expected value of 1 for $x > 0.001$. This means that the accuracy of the Šidák procedure is almost not affected by the dependency of the NIST STS tests. More precisely, the ratio oscillates around the value of 1.1 and $Pr(P_{Sidak} < x) = 1.1x$. Therefore, if $P_{Sidak} < \alpha/1.1$, the data can be considered as non-random for a significance level $\alpha > 0.001$.

We also measured the accuracy of the Šidák procedure for the uniformity tests used in the second common scenario used for randomness testing. We analyzed the accuracy of the Šidák procedure in the context of two uniformity tests – the Kolmogorov-Smirnov (KS) test and χ^2 test. The results show that the Šidák correction is an accurate procedure for evaluating the uniformity of p-values computed by tests for $\alpha > 0.001$. Moreover, the results also show that the KS test is a more appropriate test of uniformity than the χ^2 test. The reason is that the probability of Type I error for KS is constant (1.5) for different $\alpha > 0.001$, but for the χ^2 test, the probability oscillates at approximately 2 with a big amplitude.

5   Speed Improvements NIST STS

To assess the quality of a generator, a large amount of data has to be tested by a battery. It takes almost 50 min to analyze the randomness of 1 GB using NIST STS (default setting) on a standard computer. With regards to test efficiency, NIST STS is troublesome. The main problem of NIST STS is that it transforms data into a byte array, where each byte stores a single bit of the data. Using this data representation, NIST STS works well on little-endian and big-endian systems, but the cost of universality is the bad performance of the battery. We changed the data representation and re-implemented all tests of the battery [6]. Moreover, standard data representation allows us to use other approaches to speed up the NIST STS tests. NIST STS consists of 15 empirical test of randomness. These tests can be divided into three classes according to the complexity of the tests and their performance. The first class consists of fast tests that compute the statistics of bits. These tests were sped up using look-up tables precomputed for bytes. The second class consists of slower tests that compute statistics of m-bit blocks (m is typically small – 8 or 9). These tests were sped up by our function, which is able to compute a histogram of m-bit blocks for 100 MB within a second. The third class consists of complex and very slow tests. We modified tests in this class in such a way that word-word operations instead of original bit-bit operations can be used. This optimization sped up the well-known Berlekamp-Massey algorithm in the Linear complexity test by 64x. The optimization is available at [7].

6   Conclusions

We analyzed the accuracy of the Šidák procedure for evaluating multiple empirical tests of randomness. We tested the Šidák procedure with the NIST STS battery and its default settings for two standard scenarios (single sequence, multiple sequences) used in randomness testing. Experiments show that the dependency of all tests has only a marginal influence on the accuracy of the Šidák procedure and that this approach can be used to evaluate the results of NIST STS for the significance level $\alpha > 0.001$. We also provided a significantly (30x) faster implementation of NIST STS.

References

1. Rukhin, A., Soto, J., Nechvatal, J., Smid, M., Barker, E., Leigh, S., Levenson, M., Vangel, M., Banks, D., Heckert, A., Dray, J., Vo, S.: A statistical test suite for the validation of random number generators and pseudo random number generators for cryptographic applications, Version STS-2.1. In: NIST Special Publication 800–22rev1a. http://csrc.nist.gov/publications/nistpubs/800-22-rev1a/SP800-22rev1a.pdf
2. Brown, R.G.: Dieharder: A random number test suite, Version 3.31.1 (2004)
3. L'Ecuyer, P., Simard, R.: TestU01: A C library for empirical testing of random number generators. ACM Trans. Math. Softw. **33**(4), Article 22 (2007)
4. Doganaksoy, A., Ege, B., Mus, K.: Extended results for independence and sensitivity of NIST randomness tests. In: (3rd) Information Security and Cryptography Conference, Turkey (2008)
5. Nano-Optics groups at the Department of Physics of Humboldt University and PicoQuant GmbH: QRNG Service. https://qrng.physik.hu-berlin.de
6. Sýs, M., Říha, Z.: Faster randomness testing with the nist statistical test suite. In: Chakraborty, R.S., Matyas, V., Schaumont, P. (eds.) SPACE 2014. LNCS, vol. 8804, pp. 272–284. Springer, Heidelberg (2014)
7. Sýs, M., Říha, Z.: Optimised implementation of NIST STS (2014). https://github.com/sysox/NIST-STS-optimised

A Fully-Digital Chaos-Based Random Bit Generator

Marco Bucci[✉] and Raimondo Luzzi[✉]

Infineon Technologies AG, Graz, Austria
{marco.bucci,raimondo.luzzi}@infineon.com

Abstract. In this paper, the design of a fully-digital chaos-based random bit generator (RBG) is reported. The proposed generator exploits a chaotic system whose map is implemented in the time domain where the state variables of the system are represented by the phase of digital ring oscillators. This results in an extremely robust and efficient entropy source which can be implemented as a digital standard-cell thus overcoming the main drawbacks of chaotic RBGs. An implementation in a $40\,nm$ CMOS technology shows a final throughput after post-processing of $12.5\,\mathrm{Mbit/s}$ at $50\,\mathrm{MHz}$ with a worst case current consumption below $40\,\mu A$.

The entropy rate of the source can be determined a priori and, in our implementation, it results to be >1.43 bits over 4 bits generated by the source in one clock cycle. After a 16 times compression in a 32-bit linear feedback shift register (LFSR), the final data has full-entropy. A method for a direct evaluation of the entropy after post-processing is provided which can cancel the pseudo-randomness introduced by the LFSR.

Keywords: Random bit source · Random numbers · Entropy · Chaos · Security

1 Introduction

Random numbers are extensively used in many cryptographic operations. Public/private key pairs for asymmetric algorithms are generated from a random bit stream; a random bit generator (RBG) is also needed for key generation in symmetric algorithms, for generating challenges in authentication protocols, and for creating padding bytes and blinding values.

For random numbers used in cryptography, a uniform statistic is not sufficient and their unpredictability is the main requirement: a potential attacker must not be able to carry out any useful prediction about the generator's output even if its design is known. As a consequence, the focus is on the verification of a minimum entropy requirement and statistical tests are significant only if the statistical model of the random source under evaluation is known [1,2].

A true RBG must be necessarily based on some kind of non-deterministic phenomena that could act as the source of the system randomness. Electronic noises and time jitter are usually the only stochastic phenomena that are suitable for the integration in embedded systems as chip-card controllers. Three different classes of noise sources can be distinguished:

© Springer-Verlag Berlin Heidelberg 2016
P.Y.A. Ryan et al. (Eds.): Kahn Festschrift, LNCS 9100, pp. 396–414, 2016.
DOI: 10.1007/978-3-662-49301-4_25

1. *Sources without a well known noise model:* an estimation a priori of the entropy is not possible. A possible approach in this case consists of comparing the output of the source with the output produced in case no noise would be available (deterministic model of the source). This approach has been introduced in [5,6] where the noise source consists of two digital ring oscillators which are reset after the generation of each bit in order to obtain a straightforward deterministic model which allows an on-line entropy estimation to control a variable compression post-processing algorithm. The post-processor itself is reset (at least during evaluation) before compressing a new random word thus allowing a direct entropy evaluation on the final data. The obtained entropy estimation is very conservative since the reset operation (of both noise source and post-processor) destroys the internal entropy of the system which has not been extracted yet. As a consequence, the efficiency of the source in terms of energy per bit of entropy is reduced.

2. *Source with a well known noise model:* RBGs based on the direct amplification of thermal noise [3,4] or on a noisy oscillator [7] belong to this category. The availability of a noise model allows to estimate the entropy rate of the source. Of course, the method proposed in [6] can still be used to verify on-line the correct behavior of the source. Even if this seems to be a clean approach from the theoretical point of view, this type of sources have a complex implementation and can be quite weak with respect to parameter and environmental variations, external disturbances and invasive attacks.

3. *Chaotic sources:* the entropy rate can be determined a priori without needing a noise model. Actually, an explicit noise source is not even necessary. This is a well known result in the chaos theory and it is expressed by the definition of the Kolmogorov-Sinai entropy and the link between this one and the Shannon entropy (Sect. 8, [8]). Examples of chaos-based RBGs are reported in [9–12].

It is worth noting that a chaotic source is efficient and robust at the same time. Any perturbation (noise on the state variables or system parameter variations) is amplified exponentially according to the Lyapunov exponent. This can easily results in a RBG which is much more efficient, in terms of energy per bit, than a pseudo random number generator where expensive cryptographic functions must be used. As a result, chaos-based RBGs are particularly suitable for power constrained applications like RFIDs or contact-less supplied chip-cards. In addition, if the system is correctly implemented, external perturbations can influence the source but cannot control it. In other terms, the system remains chaotic as long as the external perturbation is not properly chosen as a function of the internal state of the system. In practice, this is not possible without having the ability to completely manipulate the circuit.

   The main drawback of chaotic noise sources is usually the weakness of their implementation. If a chaotic system is implemented as an analog circuit, where the state variables are either voltages or currents, it could be sensitive to process and environmental variations which can force the system to leave the chaotic behavior (e.g. causing a saturation of the state). In this work, we address this issue by using the phase of ring oscillators as state variable thus allowing a fully-digital implementation of the chaos-based RBG which is as robust as any other digital circuit.

After a short introduction on the well known Bernoulli map and its generalization (Sects. 2 and 3), the proposed noise source is reported in Sect. 4. The optimal entropy extractor (i.e. the extractor which allows to collect the complete entropy of the system) for the proposed source is discussed in Sect. 5. Finally, implementation details of the noise source, digital post-processing and results of the entropy evaluation on the raw and post-processed data are shown in Sects. 6, 7 and 8 respectively.

2   The Bernoulli Map

The Bernoulli map (Fig. 1), also known as dyadic transformation or bit shift map, is a well known 1-dimensional time discrete chaotic system which is able to generate a perfect binary random sequence, i.e. a sequence of symbols independent and identically distributed (i.i.d.). It is an interesting example in order to understand how a chaotic system can generate entropy and how it can be extracted.

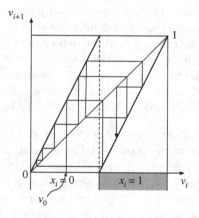

Fig. 1. Bernoulli map

Formally, the system is described by the following 1-dimensional map:

$$v_{i+1} = \mathrm{mod}\,(2 \cdot v_i, 1) \qquad (1)$$

which defines how the value of the state variable at the $(i+1)$-th iteration v_{i+1} is calculated from the current value v_i.

It is easy to verify that the symbol sequence

$$x_i = \lfloor 2 \cdot v_i \rfloor \qquad (2)$$

generated from a certain initial state $v_0 \in [0,1)$, is the binary representation of v_0,

$$v_0 = \sum_{i=0}^{\infty} x_i \cdot 2^{-(i+1)} \tag{3}$$

Therefore, the Bernoulli map can be considered as a deterministic transformation that sequentially extracts the infinite entropy in a physical quantity represented by the real number v_0. Actually, it is possible to show that the symbol sequence x_i, after a short initial transient, is i.i.d: it is known that, for any distribution of the initial state v_0, the distribution of the state variable v_i converges exponentially fast to a uniform invariant distribution [8]. On the other hand, if v_i is uniformly distributed then $P\{0 \le v_i < .5\} = P\{.5 \le v_i < 1\} = 1/2$ and, being $P\{x_i = 0\} = P\{0 \le v_i < .5\}$ and $P\{x_i = 1\} = P\{.5 \le v_i < 1\}$, it follows $P\{x_i = 0\} = P\{x_i = 1\} = 1/2$, i.e. the binary symbols x_i are also uniformly distributed.

Similarly, it can be verified that, due to the uniform distribution of v_i, the symbols x_i are also independent, i.e. $P\{x_{i+1} = \bar{x} \mid x_i - 0\} - P\{x_{i+1} = \bar{x} \mid x_i = 1\}$. For instance, from the Bayes theorem, it follows:

$$P\{x_{i+1} = 0 \mid x_i = 1\} = \frac{P\{x_{i+1} = 0, x_i = 1\}}{P\{x_i = 1\}} = \frac{P\{.5 \le v_i < .75\}}{P\{.5 \le v_i < 1\}} = \frac{1/4}{1/2} = 1/2 \tag{4}$$

3   Generalized Sawtooth Map

The Bernoulli map can be easily generalized by considering the following map and symbol sequence:

$$v_{i+1} = \mathrm{mod}\,(k \cdot v_i, 1) \tag{5}$$

$$x_i = \lfloor |k| \cdot v_i \rfloor \tag{6}$$

which, for $k = 2$, coincide with the Bernoulli map case. It is worth observing that if k is integer, the distribution of v_i still converges to the uniform distribution. In effect, this property derives from the stretching (by the multiplication factor k) and folding (by the modulus operation) of the state v_i in k perfectly overlapped segments. Therefore, if k is integer, the chaotic system described by (5) and (6) generates i.i.d. symbols on an alphabet with $|k|$ symbols and its entropy rate is $\log_2 |k|$.

For $k \notin \mathbb{Z}$, the invariant (i.e. stationary) distribution of the system is not uniform and, as a consequence, the symbols x_i are not i.i.d. any more. However, it could be verified experimentally that the entropy rate of the system is still $\log_2 |k|$. It is worth observing that this is not in contradiction with the fact that the entropy of the sequence x_i is not maximal (since its symbols are not i.i.d.). In effect, in this case the cardinality of the alphabet is $\lceil |k| \rceil > |k|$ and the bit rate of the system (i.e. $\log_2 \lceil |k| \rceil$) is greater than its entropy rate ($\log_2 |k|$) and, of course, the sequence cannot have maximum entropy.

Actually, the entropy rate of the system (5), (6) is well known from the chaos theory and the results can be extended to any 1-dimensional map $v_{i+1} = G(v_i)$ with $\left| \dot{G}(v_i) \right| = |k|$, i.e. to any piecewise linear map with constant absolute slope. It is known that the characteristic Lyapunov exponent of the considered dynamic system, which provides a measure of the degree of its instability, is equal to [8]:

$$\lambda = \ln(|k|) \tag{7}$$

It has been also proved that, in the uni-dimensional case, the Lyapunov exponent is equal to the Kolmogorov-Sinai entropy of the system which is the supremum of the entropy rate of the sequence x_i with respect to all possible partition functions $x_i = C(v_i)$:

$$h_{KS} = \sup_A \{h(A)\} = \lambda \tag{8}$$

where

$$h(A) = \lim_{N \to \infty} \frac{H_N(A)}{N} \tag{9}$$

and A is a partition of the phase space Ω defined by $C(v_i)$.
Two points should be remarked:

1. the entropy extracted from the system is equal to its intrinsic entropy ($\log_2 |k|$) only if the output symbols are generated with a proper partition function (*generating partition*) of the state variable;
2. as already observed above, if $k \notin \mathbb{Z}$, the output entropy rate cannot be maximum since the bit rate of the output (i.e. $\log_2 \lceil |k| \rceil$) is greater than its maximum entropy rate $\log_2 |k|$.

The problem of defining a generating partition is discussed in Sect. 5 while the second point is addressed by using a compression function which concentrating the source entropy allows to approach the limit of 1 entropy bit per bit (Sect. 7).

4   The Proposed Noise Source

The noise source we propose in this work is based on a chaotic map similar to the map (5) considered in Sect. 3. It is interesting noting that, since the entropy rate is a logarithmic function of only one parameter (k), the mechanism is efficient and robust (large variations of k result in small variations of the entropy rate). Actually, it is not even necessary for $|k|$ to remain constant with respect to v_i or to the process and/or environmental variations. In practice, it is sufficient to control the minimum value of $|k|$. In other terms, the linearity of $G(v_i)$ is a useful abstraction but the results are still valid if the derivative of the map does not vary significantly. In the general case, for a 1-dimension discrete time chaotic system, the Lyapunov exponent is defined as [8]:

$$\lambda = \lim_{N \to \infty} \frac{1}{N} \sum_{i=1}^{N} \ln \left| \dot{G}(v_i) \right|$$

where $\dot{G}(v_i)$ is the derivative of the map in the point v_i.

On the other hand, even if formally the map (5) seems to be straightforward, its implementation with an analog circuit, where v_i is either a voltage or a current, results to be rather complex due to the modulus function which implicitly requires one or more comparison and a conditional subtraction. Indeed, from the implementation point of view, (5) should be written, for $k > 0$, as:

$$v_{i+1} = \begin{cases} k \cdot v_i & k \cdot v_i < p_1 \\ k \cdot v_i - q_1 & p_1 \leq k \cdot v_i < p_2 \\ k \cdot v_i - q_2 & p_2 \leq k \cdot v_i < p_3 \\ \vdots & \vdots \end{cases}$$

where, in the ideal case, it holds $p_j = q_j = j \in \{1, 2, \ldots\}$. Even if an extremely precise implementation is not necessary, the thresholds p_j and the quantities q_j have to satisfy some constraints otherwise the system can stuck or saturate at a fixed value loosing its chaotic behavior. Moreover, in practice, the implementation of a voltage or current comparison is always an issue since it is vulnerable to external disturbances (e.g. through the power supply) which can force its outcome. This is clearly not acceptable for a RBG.

The solution we adopted consists in implementing the map in the time domain where the modulus operation represents the phase evolution of an oscillator and, therefore, its implementation is straightforward and intrinsically robust. According to this approach, the chaotic noise source we propose in this work is described by the following continuous-time equations:

$$u(t) = \mathrm{mod}(t, 1) \tag{10}$$

$$\dot{v}(t) = \begin{cases} slope_{slow} & \text{if } mode = slow \\ slope_{fast} & \text{if } mode = fast \end{cases} \tag{11}$$

$$\lim_{\Delta t \to 0} v(t + \Delta t) = \mathrm{mod}(v(t) + \dot{v}(t) \cdot \Delta t, 1) \tag{12}$$

$$mode \leftarrow \begin{cases} slow & \text{when } u = 0 \\ fast & \text{when } v = 0 \end{cases} \tag{13}$$

Substantially, the system consists of two oscillators: the first one (reference oscillator), whose normalized phase is represented by the state variable u, is the time reference of the system and its period is assumed to be 1. The second oscillator (controlled oscillator), whose normalized phase is represented by the state variable v, has two possible working modes (*fast* or *slow*), as described in (13). The variable v is also limited on the normalized interval $[0, 1)$, as in (12).

According to (13), the controlled oscillator is forced in *slow* mode at the end/beginning of a period of the reference oscillator ($u = 0$), while it is forced back in *fast* mode at the end/beginning of its own period ($v = 0$). The time evolution of the state variables is shown in Fig. 2.

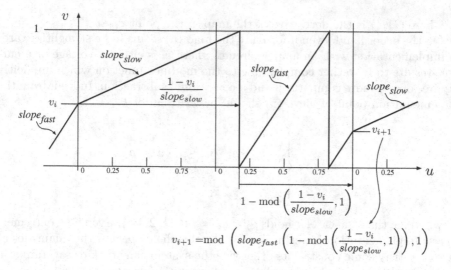

Fig. 2. Evolution of the oscillator phases

The system can be easily analyzed as a time-discrete system described by the evolution of the single variable v (or u) at each iteration of the system. For this purpose, an iteration can be assumed as the period between two $fast \to slow$ transitions (if the variable u is used, the opposite transition must be assumed to define an iteration). From Fig. 2, with simple geometric calculations, it follows:

$$v_{i+1} = \text{mod}\left(slope_{fast}\left(1 - \text{mod}\left(\frac{1 - v_i}{slope_{slow}}, 1 \right) \right), 1 \right) \qquad (14)$$

which represents the uni-dimensional map $G(v_i)$ of the proposed chaotic system.

Equation (14) is still a piecewise linear function whose derivative is constant and given by $k = slope_{fast}/slope_{slow}$. Therefore, if $|k| > 1$, the system is chaotic and can generate entropy at a rate of $\log_2 |k|$. It can be observed that, for $slope_{slow} = 1$, the (14) is equivalent to (5) and, for $slope_{slow} = 1$ and $slope_{fast} = 2$, it gives the Bernoulli map (1), as shown in Fig. 3.

Figure 4 shows how an initial distance $\triangle v_i$ between two trajectories is amplified by a factor $k = slope_{fast}/slope_{slow}$ at each iterations. This is equivalent to state that the Lyapunov exponent of the system is $\ln |k|$. It is important noting that, even if the system depends on two parameters ($slope_{fast}$ and $slope_{slow}$), the entropy rate depends only on their ratio k.

As shown in Fig. 5, the map (14) can assume three different shapes depending on the system parameters. In particular, if $slope_{slow} > 1$ (Fig. 5(a)), the inner modulus operation plays no role and the discontinuities are due to the outer modulus. Conversely, if $slope_{fast} < 1$ (Fig. 5(c)), the outer modulus can be simplified and the discontinuities are determined by the inner one. In the intermediate cases, $slope_{fast} > 1$ and $slope_{slow} < 1$ (Fig. 5(b)), both modulus

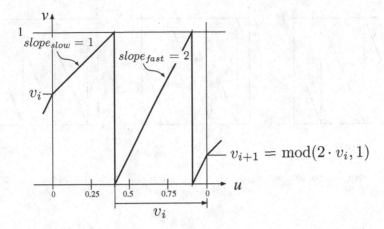

Fig. 3. Timing diagram for $slope_{slow} = 1$ and $slope_{fast} = 2$, which results in the implementation of the Bernoulli map

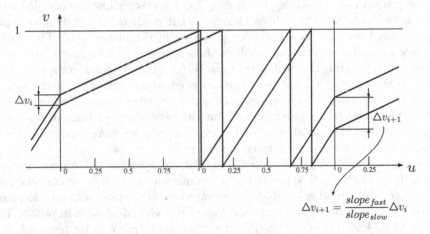

Fig. 4. Evolution of two trajectories with a initial distance Δv_i

operations cause discontinuities in the map. It can be observed that, in Fig. 5(c), the dynamic of the system is reduced since it holds:

$$0 \leq v_{i+1} < \min\left(1, slope_{fast}\right) \tag{15}$$

5   Entropy Extractor

By observing the maps in Fig. 5, it follows that in our case, a simple definition of the output sequence x_i as in (6) does not allow to extract the complete entropy of the system. In general, the entropy of x_i would depend on $slope_{fast}$

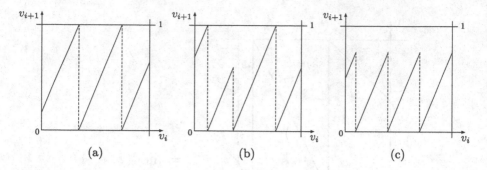

Fig. 5. Chaotic maps for: $slope_{slow} > 1$ (a); $slope_{fast} > 1$ and $slope_{slow} < 1$ (b); $slope_{fast} < 1$ (c)

and $slope_{slow}$ and not only on their ratio, thus resulting to be lower than the expected maximum $\log_2 |k|$.

The problem of extracting the entropy from a system like the one described above is well known in the chaos theory and it consists in the definition of a proper embedded space, i.e. a proper partition of the phase state. The output sequence x_i is the sequence of symbols that represent the regions of the state that are visited during the evolution of the system. In particular, for a *generating partition*, the entropy rate of the sequence is equal to that of the system or, in other terms, the output sequence extracts the complete entropy of the system. A partition is a generating partition if, from the generated symbols, it is possible to come back to the initial state of the system with an increasing precision as the length of the observed sequence increases [8].

In our case, it is easy to be convinced that a generating partition consists of the partition of the state space in the segments where the uni-dimensional map (14) is invertible. In other words, the generated sequence represents the sequence of invertible segments of the map that have been visited at each iteration. This implies that, knowing the sequence, the state evolution can be reversed. It is also intuitive to observe that if the effect of an initial perturbation explodes exponentially as the system evolves, the error in the determination of the current state implodes exponentially if the system evolution is reversed. This is exactly the definition of a generating partition.

According to observations above, the symbols x_i can be conveniently defined as:

$$x_i = x_{i,0}, x_{i,1} \tag{16}$$

where $x_{i,0}$ and $x_{i,1}$ are suitable transformations of the quantities

$$\hat{x}_{i,0} = \left\lfloor slope_{fast} \left(1 - \mathrm{mod} \left(\tfrac{1-v_i}{slope_{slow}}, 1 \right) \right) \right\rfloor \tag{17}$$

$$\hat{x}_{i,1} = \left\lfloor \tfrac{1-v_i}{slope_{slow}} \right\rfloor$$

It can be easily verified that the quantity $\hat{x}_{i,0}, \hat{x}_{i,1}$ takes a different value for each invertible segment in (14) and, therefore, the partition of the state space v defined in (17) is actually a generating partition. Of course, the same propriety holds for any reversible transformation of (17) (any reversible transformation of a sequence does not affect its entropy). In particular, taking into account of (15), it can be proven that

$$\tilde{x}_{i,0} = \text{mod}\left(1 + \left\lfloor slope_{fast}\left(1 - \text{mod}\left(\frac{1-v_i}{slope_{slow}}, 1\right)\right)\right\rfloor, M\right) \tag{18}$$

$$\tilde{x}_{i,1} = \text{mod}\left(1 + \left\lfloor \frac{1-v_i}{slope_{slow}}\right\rfloor, M\right)$$

is a reversible transformation of (17), if $M > \lceil slope_{fast}/slope_{slow}\rceil = \lceil k\rceil$.

Actually, (18) has a precise physical meaning since $\tilde{x}_{i,0}$ and $\tilde{x}_{i,1}$ represent the number of cycles modulus M performed during one system iteration by the controlled and reference oscillator respectively. With reference to Fig. 6, it can be observed that, for $slope_{fast} < 1$, the controlled oscillator runs for only one cycle per iteration, as also shown in the first equation in (18). Similarly, for $slope_{slow} > 1$, the reference oscillator performs only one cycle per iteration (second equation in (18)). In practice, depending on the relative frequencies of the two oscillators, the entropy is extracted by $\tilde{x}_{i,0}$, or $\tilde{x}_{i,1}$ or by both counters. It is worth noting that M fixes the number of possible symbols and, therefore, it must be chosen large enough to contain the whole entropy generated by the system in each iteration.

In practice, the implementation of (18) could be unnecessary complex due to the reset of the counters $\tilde{x}_{i,0}$ and $\tilde{x}_{i,1}$ at each iteration. Of course, such resets do not affect the entropy of the sequence and can be omitted. Formally, it corresponds to a further transformation:

$$x_{i,0} = \text{mod}\left(\sum_{j=0}^{i} \tilde{x}_{j,0}, M\right) \tag{19}$$

$$x_{i,1} = \text{mod}\left(\sum_{j=0}^{i} \tilde{x}_{j,1}, M\right)$$

which is still reversible being

$$\tilde{x}_{i,0} = \text{mod}\left(x_{i,0} - x_{i-1,0}, M\right) \tag{20}$$

$$\tilde{x}_{i,1} = \text{mod}\left(x_{i,1} - x_{i-1,1}, M\right).$$

Ultimately, as shown in Sect. 6, the (19) can be easily implemented in practice.

6   Implementation Details

The chaotic system represented by (14) and (19) can be implemented in an efficient and robust way. A possible realization of the noise source (14) is depicted

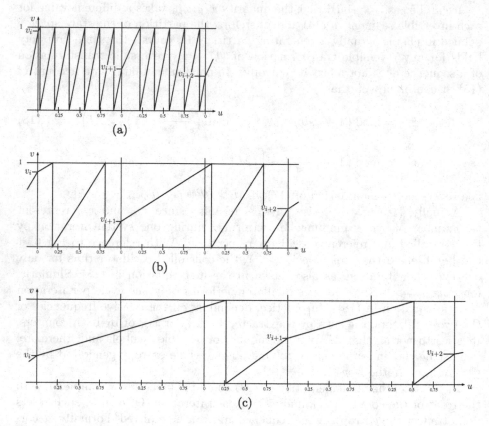

Fig. 6. Time evolution for: $slope_{slow} > 1$ (a); $slope_{fast} > 1$ and $slope_{slow} < 1$ (b); $slope_{fast} < 1$ (c)

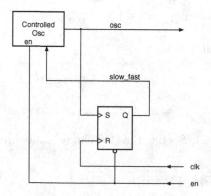

Fig. 7. Chaotic noise source implementation

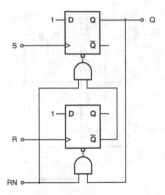

Fig. 8. Edge-triggered set/reset flip-flop implementation

in Fig. 7, where the reference oscillator is the system clock (*clk*) and the switching *fast/slow* is controlled by an edge-triggered set/reset flip-flop (Fig. 8).

Different implementations for the controlled oscillators are possible. A particularly interesting solution consists of using a ring oscillators (Fig. 9) with inverters (Fig. 10) whose strength can be changed by means of a digital control signal (*slow_fast*). This allows a fully-digital implementation for the proposed noise source where the inverters and, ultimately, the whole oscillator can be lay-outed as a custom standard-cell and hidden in the semi-custom area of a security controller with obvious advantages in terms of protection against reverse engineering and invasive attacks (probing and forcing).

It is also worth noting that the main system parameter k depends on the ratio of the propagation speed of a digital signal in an inverter chain when the inverters are strong or weak respectively (f_{fast} and f_{slow}). This means that the ratio cannot change significantly. On the other side, if a variation in the propagation delay were so large to produce a non negligible variation of the entropy rate, it would also prevent any synchronous digital device to operate. Therefore, the noise source is not weaker than any other digital functions with respect to process and environmental variations (power supply, temperature, etc.).

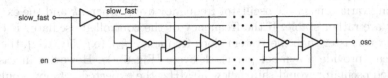

Fig. 9. Controlled oscillator implementation

An alternative implementation of the controlled oscillator based on analog components is shown in Fig. 11 where $R_4 = 2R_3$, $R_2 = R_1\frac{k+1}{k-1}$ and $C_1 = \frac{1}{f_{slow}R_1(k+1)}$. The first inverter works has an integrator while the second

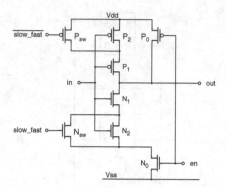

Fig. 10. Two-strength inverter: if *slow_fast* = 1 (fast mode), the weak transistors N_2 and P_2 are short-circuited and the inverter (N_1, P_1) is strong. Vice versa, if *slow_fast* = 0, the transistors N_2, P_2 are connected in series to N_1, P_1, thus making the inverter weaker.

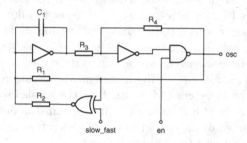

Fig. 11. An alternative implementation of the controlled oscillator using analog components

one and the NAND gate implement a Schmitt trigger. The oscillation period is either $2R_{slow}C_1$ (for *slow_fast* = 0) or $2R_{fast}C_1$ (for *slow_fast* = 1), where $R_{slow} = \frac{R_1 \cdot R_2}{R_2 - R_1}$ and $R_{fast} = \frac{R_1 \cdot R_2}{R_1 + R_2}$.

The controlled oscillator of Fig. 9 has been implemented in a 40 nm CMOS process and the results of a back-annotated Spice simulation over corners (process, temperature and power supply) are reported in Table 1: in spite of the strong variations of the oscillator frequency over corners, k and the expected entropy are rather stable. If the frequency of the controlled oscillator is chosen to be always faster than the system clock frequency f_{clk} (e.g. 50 MHz), the noise source can provide a symbol per clock cycle (Fig. 6(a)). However, in case the controlled oscillator would shift below 50 MHz, the expected entropy would still be guaranteed, with a reduced data-rate. The area of the custom standard-cell implementing the oscillator is $73\,\mu m^2$.

The complete entropy source including the entropy extractor described by (19) is shown in Fig. 12: two counters count the number of cycles performed during an iteration (between two transitions *fast* → *slow* or *slow* → *fast*) by

Table 1. Simulation outcome of the controlled oscillator of Fig. 9

Parameter	Min	Nom	Max
$f_{fast} = slope_{fast} \times f_{clk}$	177 MHz	342 MHz	578 MHz
$f_{slow} = slope_{slow} \times f_{clk}$	62.9 MHz	120 MHz	214 MHz
k	2.81	2.85	2.70
$\log_2 k$	1.49	1.51	1.43
$I\bar{D}D$	8.04 μA	18.3 μA	39.7 μA

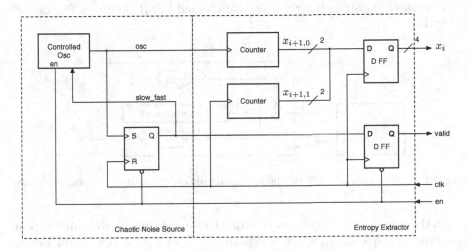

Fig. 12. Entropy source

both oscillators. Since $\log_2 k \le 2$, two bit counters are sufficient to contain the complete entropy generated at each iteration ($M = 2^2$).

A strobe signal to sample the counter output (*valid*) is derived by sampling the *slow_fast* signal with the system clock *clk*: therefore, *valid* = 1 at the end of an iteration, on the *fast → slow* transition.

7   Post-processing

As shown in Sect. 6, the noise source provides at least 1.43 bits of entropy on 4 bits ($2 \times \log_2 M$). In order to obtain a full entropy bit sequence, a post-processing with a compression function is necessary. The adopted post-processing is quite simple and, as discussed in Sect. 8, has the important feature of making possible the estimation of the output entropy. On the other side, due to the extreme efficiency and robustness of the source, a more complex post-processing would not be convenient. Indeed, data quality is achieved by means of a large compression factor and, in case an higher data rate were requested, more current could be invested in the source oscillator or more sources could be used in parallel.

The proposed RBG is depicted in Fig. 13: a 32-bit linear feedback shift register (LFSR) is used where, at each clock cycle, if *valid* = 1, the 4 raw bits x_i from the source are processed in parallel and one bit is extracted. This is functionally equivalent to a conventional (i.e. with a single bit input) LFSR which operates with a 4 times faster clock and delivers one bit every 4. In other terms, at each clock step, the output is the ×4 decimation of the output that would be delivered by the corresponding conventional LFSR fed by the same 4 bit input. For the implementation of the 4-bit parallel LFSR, it is sufficient to consider the state transition matrix A of the equivalent serial LFSR. The matrix $\hat{A} = A^4$ gives the state transition matrix of the parallelized LFSR (feedback function F^4 in Fig. 13).

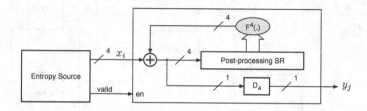

Fig. 13. Architecture of the RBG including details on the post-processing structure

On the output, an additional decimation factor 4 is applied to obtain the post-processed bit sequence y_j, which is expected to have full entropy. From Table 1, it follows that, for system clock frequencies below about 60 MHz (Fig. 6(a)), the *valid* signal is always asserted and therefore the proposed RBG can provide one bit every 4 clock cycles which means a throughput of 12.5 Mbit/s at 50 MHz.

8   Entropy Evaluation

In order to confirm the expected entropy rate derived from the theory, a direct evaluation of the entropy rate has been performed in simulation. From the definition of entropy rate or source information rate of a strongly stationary stochastic process:

$$h(X) = \lim_{n \to \infty} h\left(X_n \,|\, X_{n-1}, X_{n-2}, \ldots, X_1\right) \tag{21}$$

where X_n is the n-th member of the process and $h\left(X \,|\, Y\right)$ is the conditional entropy. For a binary entropy source, the entropy rate is the entropy of the n-th symbol knowing the previous $n-1$ symbols and it can be calculated as:

$$h(X) = \lim_{n \to \infty} - \left[\sum_{x_{n-1}, x_{n-2}, \ldots, x_1 \in X_{n-1}, X_{n-2}, \ldots, X_1} p(x_{n-1}, x_{n-2}, \ldots, x_1) \right. \tag{22}$$
$$\left. \sum_{x_n \in X_n} p(x_n \,|\, x_{n-1}, x_{n-2}, \ldots, x_1) \log_2 p(x_n \,|\, x_{n-1}, x_{n-2}, \ldots, x_1) \right]$$

where $p(x_{n-1}, x_{n-2}, \ldots, x_1)$ is the probability of a $n-1$ symbol sequence and $p(x_n \,|\, x_{n-1}, x_{n-2}, \ldots, x_1)$ is the conditional probability of the n-th symbol with respect to the previous $n-1$. Both probabilities have been estimated over a sequence of 10^8 symbols generated with a numerical model of the source implementing the map (14) and the entropy extractor (19) . In a numerical simulation, the state variables have a finite precision (about 10^{-15} for the IEEE 754 double precision floating point numbers) and, therefore, it is necessary to introduce a small pseudo-random noise to emulate the infinite precision of the real case. On the other hand, in a real implementation, each iteration and each parameter of the system is affected by noise. For the simulation, the (14) is modified as:

$$v_{i+1} = \text{mod}\left(slope_{fast}(1 + \eta_i)\left(1 - \text{mod}\left(\frac{1 - v_i}{slope_{slow}(1 + \eta_i)}, 1\right)\right), 1\right) \quad (23)$$

where η_i is a Gaussian pseudo-random process with standard deviation 10^{-12}.

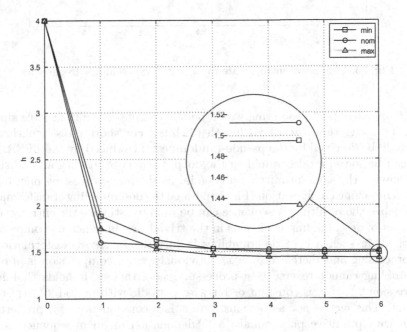

Fig. 14. Estimated entropy rate of the noise source

A plot of entropy rate is shown in Fig. 14 for $n = 0, 1, \ldots, 6$ and for the values of $slope_{slow}$ and $slope_{fast}$ in Table 1: the estimate converges quickly to the theoretical values of $\log_2 k$ in Table 1.

A sweep over the oscillator frequencies, keeping k constant is depicted in Fig. 15: the entropy rate converge always to the expected value $\log_2 k$, thus confirming that the entropy extractor is able to extract the complete entropy in all the three cases in Fig. 6.

The direct measurement of the entropy rate is feasible only for a process with a limited memory (n small), as it is the case of a chaotic system. Evaluating

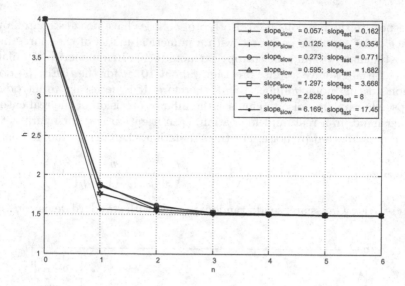

Fig. 15. Estimated entropy rate for $k = 2^{1.5}$ vs. oscillator frequencies

the entropy after post-processing would not be computationally feasible since n should be larger than the LFSR length (32 bits). For shorter test lengths, the test would be deceived by the pseudo-randomness introduced by the LFSR. The issue can be solved by descrambling the output sequence y_j with an additional LFSR having the same primitive polynomial as the post-processing one, but in self-synchronizing configuration (Fig. 16). Since the descrambling transformation is reversible, the resulting z_j sequence can be used to estimate the entropy of y_j. The effect of descrambling is obvious in the trivial case in which no compression is applied: in such a case descrambling is just the inverse transformation of post-processing and therefore $z_j = x_i$. Obviously, when compression is applied, descrambling cannot reverse post-processing, nevertheless, it holds that for a compression 2^N, if x_i is constant or bit-wise periodic with period 2^N, z_j is also constant. This fact is not as obvious, but it is a consequence of a property of LFSRs with primitive polynomials: a 2^N decimation of an m-sequence is just a shift of the same sequence. For a generic input sequence x_i, it can be seen experimentally that the descrambling LFSR is still able to remove the pseudo-randomness introduced by the post-processing LFSR.

As an example, the entropy rate estimation before and after the descrambling for a 12-bit LFSR and a compression factor 4 of a noise source with 0.25 entropy bit per bit is shown in Fig. 17: the estimate of the sequence z_j is the 12 step shifted version of the estimate done directly on y_j.

A test performed over 10^{10} bits of the descrambled sequence with test memory length 22, when a 32-bit LFSR is used, shows a maximal entropy rate (within the estimator error). It is worth observing that the descrambling can be performed off-line in software.

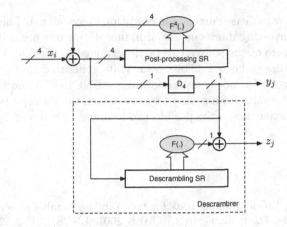

Fig. 16. Descrambler

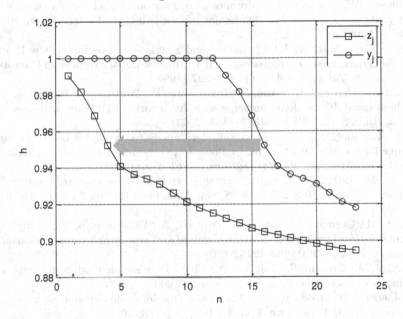

Fig. 17. Example of an estimated entropy rate before and after descrambling for a 12-bit LFSR

9   Conclusions

A novel fully-digital chaos-based RBG suitable to be used in security devices has been introduced. The proposed generator exploits a chaotic system whose map is implemented in the time domain where the state variables of the system are represented by the phase of digital ring oscillators. An implementation in a $40\,nm$ CMOS technology shows a final throughput after post-processing of $12.5\,\mathrm{Mbit/s}$

at 50 MHz with a worst case current consumption below 40 μA. The design can be easily scaled by investing more current, if higher data-rates are needed.

The entropy rate of the source can be determined a priori and, in our implementation, it results to be > 1.43 bits over 4 bits generated by the source in one clock cycle. After a 16 times compression in a 32-bit LFSR, the final data have full-entropy, as it results from a direct evaluation of the entropy performed on a descrambled sequence where the pseudo randomness introduced by the LFSR is removed.

References

1. Schindler, W.: Efficient online tests for true random number generators. In: Koç, Ç.K., Naccache, D., Paar, C. (eds.) CHES 2001. LNCS, vol. 2162, pp. 103–117. Springer, Heidelberg (2001)
2. Killmann, W., Schindler, W.: A proposal for: Functionality classes for random number generators, version 2.0, Bundesamt fur Sicherheit in der Informationstechnik (BSI), Bonn (2011)
3. Petrie, C.S., Connelly, J.A.: Modeling and simulation of oscillator-based random number generators. In: Proceedings of IEEE International Symposium Circuits and Systems, ISCAS 1996, vol. 4, pp. 324–327 (1996)
4. Bucci, M., Germani, L., Luzzi, R., Tommasino, P., Trifiletti, A., Varanonuovo, M.: A high-speed IC random-number source for smart-card microcontrollers. IEEE Trans. Circ. Syst. I 50(11), 1373–1380 (2003)
5. Bock, H., Bucci, M., Luzzi, R.: An offset-compensated oscillator-based random bit source for security applications. In: Joye, M., Quisquater, J.-J. (eds.) CHES 2004. LNCS, vol. 3156, pp. 268–281. Springer, Heidelberg (2004)
6. Bucci, M., Luzzi, R.: Design of testable random bit generators. In: Rao, J.R., Sunar, B. (eds.) CHES 2005. LNCS, vol. 3659, pp. 147–156. Springer, Heidelberg (2005)
7. Bucci, M., Germani, L., Luzzi, R., Trifiletti, A., Varanonuovo, M.: A high-speed oscillator-based truly random number source for cryptographic applications. IEEE Trans. Comput. 52(4), 403–409 (2003)
8. Cencini, M., Cecconi, F., Vulpiani, A.: Chaos from simple models to complex systems, World Scientific Publishing Company (2009)
9. Stojanovski, T., Kocarev, L.: Chaos-based random number generators - part I: Analysis. IEEE Trans. Circ. Syst. I 48(3), 281–288 (2001)
10. Stojanovski, T., Pihl, J., Kocarev, L.: Chaos-based random number generators - part II: Practical realization. IEEE Trans. Circ. Syst. I 48(3), 382–385 (2001)
11. Callegari, S., Rovatti, R., Setti, G.: Embeddable ADC-based true random number generator for cryptographic applications exploiting nonlinear signal processing and chaos. IEEE Trans. Sig. Process. 53, 793–805 (2005)
12. Demirkol, A.S., Ozoguz, S., Tavas, V., Kilinc, S.: A CMOS realization of double-scroll chaotic circuit and its application to random number generation. In: Proceedings IEEE International Symposium on Circuits and Systems (ISCAS), pp. 2374–2377 (2008)

Embedded System Security

Secure Application Execution in Mobile Devices

Mehari G. Msgna[1](✉), Houda Ferradi[2],
Raja Naeem Akram[1], and Konstantinos Markantonakis[1]

[1] Information Security Group, Smart Card Centre,
Royal Holloway, University of London, Egham, UK
{mehari.msgna.2011,r.n.akram,k.markantonakis}@rhul.ac.uk
[2] Ecole normale supérieure, Paris, France
houda.ferradi@ens.fr

Abstract. Smart phones have rapidly become hand-held mobile devices capable of sustaining multiple applications. Some of these applications allow access to services including healthcare, financial, online social networks and are becoming common in the smart phone environment. From a security and privacy point of view, this seismic shift is creating new challenges, as the smart phone environment is becoming a suitable platform for security- and privacy-sensitive applications. The need for a strong security architecture for this environment is becoming paramount, especially from the point of view of Secure Application Execution (SAE). In this chapter, we explore SAE for applications on smart phone platforms, to ensure application execution is as expected by the application provider. Most of the proposed SAE proposals are based on having a secure and trusted embedded chip on the smart phone. Examples include the GlobalPlatform Trusted Execution Environment, M-Shield and Mobile Trusted Module. These additional hardware components, referred to as secure and trusted devices, provide a secure environment in which the applications can execute security-critical code and/or store data. These secure and trusted devices can become the target of malicious entities; therefore, they require a strong framework that will validate and guarantee the secure application execution. This chapter discusses how we can provide an assurance that applications executing on such devices are secure by validating the secure and trusted hardware.

Keywords: Smart phone · Apple iOS · Android · Mobile trusted manager · Globalplatform trusted execution environment · Secure application execution

1 Introduction

Mobile phones have changed the way we communicate and stay in touch with friends and family. This revolution, including ubiquitous voice communication and Short Messaging Services (SMS), was pivotal in the early adoption of mobile devices. However, smart phones went a step further and enabled consumers to carry a powerful computing device in their pocket. This has changed the way

© Springer-Verlag Berlin Heidelberg 2016
P.Y.A. Ryan et al. (Eds.): Kahn Festschrift, LNCS 9100, pp. 417–438, 2016.
DOI: 10.1007/978-3-662-49301-4_26

we interact with computer technology. With ubiquitous access to the internet and a range of services being designed for the smart phone platform, they have not only inherited the security and privacy issues of traditional computer- and internet-based technology, but also amplified them due to the convergence of services like healthcare, banking, and Online Social Networking (OSN) applications. Therefore, with ever-increasing adoption of smart phones and their role as an integral part of daily life, the challenge is to build such devices in a manner that provides a trusted and secure environment for all sensitive applications. There have been many different proposals on how such an environment can be built, including different architectures such as software protection (including compile time and link time code hardening), application management, and hardware protection (e.g. ARM TrustZone, GlobalPlatform Trusted Execution Environment, Trusted Platform Module, and Secure Elements). In this chapter, we discuss most of the listed examples in order to highlight issues related to Secure Application Execution (SAE) on smart phone platforms. Most of these proposals rely on:

1. Pre-installation secure coding and analysis
2. Post-installation secure application management and analysis
3. Trusted hardware to provide software validation
4. Executing a portion of the activity (usually the most sensitive part of the application code and associated data) on secure and trusted hardware.

A crucial issue regarding the secure execution of sensitive applications on smart phone platforms is: how can we trust the execution environment? Most of the proposals for SAE are based, one way or another, on secure hardware that will provide some level of security, trust and possibly privacy, giving an assurance that the application in execution (at runtime) on such hardware will be secure. This means that the application code executing on the trusted hardware will run without interference from attackers and that each line of code executes as intended by the application developer (or application provider). For a secure and trusted hardware that will not enable a malicious entity to interfere with the execution of an application, we require a runtime protection mechanism. In this chapter, we will discuss such a mechanism, explain its operation and show how it can achieve secure runtime monitoring of sensitive applications on trusted hardware.

1.1 Structure of the Chapter

In Sect. 2, we discuss the smart phone ecosystem and briefly describe the two major smart phone platforms Apple iOS and Google Android. This leads us to a discussion of the SAE frameworks including code hardening, application management and device attestation in Sect. 3. We then discuss proposals for trusted execution environments that are usually based on secure hardware in Sect. 4. In Sect. 5, we address the issue of ensuring that the trusted execution environment will provide a secure and trusted application execution. This section also describes application runtime protection deployed in a trusted execution environment. Finally, in Sect. 6 we provide concluding remarks on SAE for smart phone platforms along with suggestions for future work.

2   Smart Phone Ecosystems

We will first describe the two major smart phone platforms currently in use: Apple's iOS and Google's Android. The subsequent sections introduce the security-related provisions present on these two platforms.

2.1   Apple's iOS Ecosystem

This section briefly outlines Apple's security ecosystem. This security ecosystem is meant to prevent insecure or malicious applications from being installed on handsets in the field.

2.1.1   Secure Boot Chain

The secure boot is the process by which Apple ensures that only signed and trusted software is loaded into iOS devices. Amongst other desirable features, this ensures that the lowest levels of software are not tampered with, and allows iOS to run only on validated Apple devices. The secure boot chain encompasses the bootloaders, kernel, kernel extensions, and baseband firmware with each component verifying the next. If any boot process component cannot be loaded or verified correctly, then the boot sequence (also called *boot-up*) is stopped. Each component that is part of the boot process must be signed by Apple. The boot chain sequence is as follows:

1. The **Boot ROM** is considered to be an implicitly trusted code embedded within the A5 processor during chip manufacturing. The Boot ROM code contains the public key of Apple's Root CA, which is used upon iDevice power-up. This public key allows verification that the Low-Level Bootloader has been signed by Apple before allowing it to load.
2. The **bootloaders** are a piece of software executed whenever the hardware is powered up. There are two bootloader components: the *Low-Level Bootloader (LLB)* and *iBoot*. The LLB is the lowest-level code on an Apple device that can be updated. The LLB runs several firmware setup routines. The bootloaders attempt to verify the iOS Kernel's signature; if this verification fails the device enters into Recovery Mode (visible to the user as a "connect to iTunes" mode).
3. The **iOS Kernel** includes an XNU kernel, system modules, services and applications. When the LLB and the iBoot finish their tasks, iBoot verifies and runs the next kernel stage of the iOS. The iOS Kernel is the ultimate authority for allowing the secure boot.

This process was designed by Apple to ensure the integrity of the booting process. Each step is checked cryptographically: this means that each OS component, including the bootloaders, kernel, kernel extensions, and baseband firmware must be signed with a trusted certified key, in order to assemble into a *chain of trust*.

2.1.2   Hardware Encryption Features

The cryptographic operations that we have just described require modular exponentiations and hashings of long data streams (executable code). These tasks are resource-consuming and require efficient hardware processing. iOS provides access to a specific API that, besides allowing the system to access such computational resources, also allows developers to add custom cryptographic operations to their applications. Such hardware acceleration features:

1. An AES [34] engine implemented on the "DreamFactory Mobile Application" (DMA) path between the flash storage and the main system memory.
2. An SHA-1 [34] API allowing high-speed hashing for integrity check purposes.
3. iOS devices have two fuse-protected (non-erasable) device keys burnt into the processor during manufacturing. These keys, which are only accessible by the AES crypto-engine, are:
   a. The **User ID (UID) key**: a 256-bit AES key unique to each device. The UID key is used to bind data to a given device.
   b. The **Group ID (GID) key**: a 256-bit AES key common to all processors using Apple A5 chips. the GID key is used if required by Apple to install and restore software [37].

2.1.3   Data Security

To secure the data stored in flash memory, Apple has constructed a data protection mechanism in conjunction with the hardware-based encryption. The data protection mechanism allows the interaction of the device with incoming phone calls, which are treated as incoming events from identified sources (called IDs) and includes a remote wipe function, passcodes, and data protection, which are briefly described as follows:

1. The **Remote wipe feature** allows the device owner to sanitise the device if it is stolen or if too many passcode attempts fail. Remote wiping can be initiated *via* MDM (Mobile Device Management), Exchange, or iCloud.
2. The **Passcode** serves two purposes: it protects the device's accessibility by locking it and provides entry to the encryption/decryption keys stored on board. This ensures that certain sensitive files can be decrypted only upon successful passcode presentation by the user.
3. In addition to the above features, Apple devices have also methods for collecting and distilling entropy for creating new encryption keys on the fly. As attested by many Apple patent applications, methods range from collecting application data to the monitoring of device movements and hashing them into random information.

4. The **Key chain data protection** uses a hardware encryption accelerator, shipped with all 3GS or newer iPhone devices. The accelerator can encrypt selected sensitive data fields that many apps need to handle (*e.g.* passwords, credentials and keys). Data stored in the keychain is logically zoned to prevent applications from accessing confidential information belonging to other applications. An application developer can therefore easily manage his application's data by simply declaring it as private to his application.

2.1.4 Sandboxing

The kernel of iOS is the XNU kernel [38]. XNU is the OS kernel initially developed for the Mac OS X operating system and subsequently released as free open source software. The security model for iOS is therefore very similar to that of the Mac OS, where code is secured using signatures, sandboxing and entitlement checking. Sandboxing is a software environment where codes are isolated from each other, and where an applications access to resources is controlled by the OS. Each application has access to its own files, preferences, and network resources. The camera, GPS and other system resources on the device are accessible through an interface of abstract classes [36].

2.1.5 Application Code Signing (Vetting)

To guarantee the integrity of data stored in the mobile device, code signing (or vetting) is a process allowing the application developer to certify that an application was created by them. Once an application is signed, the system can detect any changes (be these accidental or malicious) in the signed code. Apple signs all components in the boot process (*e.g.* the bootloaders, kernel, kernel extensions, and baseband firmware). Signatures are required for all programs running on the device regardless of whether these are Apple codes or third-party applications (*e.g.* Safari). Thereby iOS avoids loading unsigned codes or applications that may be malicious.

2.2 The Android Ecosystem

Because Linux is at the heart of Android [39], most Linux security concepts also apply to Android.

2.2.1 Sandboxing

Android inherits a permission model from the Linux kernel that provides data isolation based on UIDs and GIDs. Therefore, each user has an assigned UID and one or more GIDs. To enforce data confidentiality, Android uses two concepts that permit users to access only files that they own:

1. The **Discretionary Access Control** (DAC) concept is a Linux mechanism allowing only the device owner to access her own files [42]

2. The **Mandatory Access Control** (MAC) is an OS protection mechanism that constrains the ability to access or perform certain operations on specific objects or targets. Generally, the MAC is used to control access by applications to system resources [42].

To differentiate one user from another or one user group from another, each application within a Linux system is given a UID and a GID. Each file's access rules are specified for three sets of subjects: user, group and everyone. Each subject set has valid or invalid permissions to read, write and execute a file. To restrict file access to owners only, the Android kernel sandbox uses UIDs and GIDs to enforce DAC.

2.2.2   Applications Permissions

By default an Android application has no specific permissions to access mobile resources. This means that the application cannot do anything that would adversely impact [41]. However, application developers can add permissions to their applications using tags in the `AndroidManifest.xml` file. These tags allow developers to describe the functionality and the requirements of a target Android application and thereby adapt security to increase functionality. For example, an application that needs to monitor incoming SMS messages would specify:

```
uses-permission android:name="android.permission.RECEIVE_SMS"
```

2.2.3   Application Code Signing

Android requires that all apps be digitally signed by the application providers signature key before they can be installed [40]. This functionality is used to:

- Identify the code's author,
- Detect if the application has changed, and
- Establish trust between applications

However, applications signed using the same digital signature can grant each other permission to access signature-based APIs. Such applications can also run in the same process if they share user IDs, allowing access to each other's code and data.

3   Secure Application Execution (SAE)

In this section, we briefly discuss existing secure application frameworks for smart phone or embedded platforms.

3.1   Code Hardening

A program code is a group of executable processor instructions designed to achieve a desired output. During program execution each instruction performs a certain operation. These instructions can be individually targeted by an attacker to force the processor into generating a faulty output. An example of such an attack is a fault injection attack, where the attacker uses equipment such as laser perturbations and clock manipulators to induce a fault [16]. This type of attack can be prevented by manipulating the code in such a way that either (a) makes it impossible for the attacker to locate and target these instructions, or (b) enables the code to detect induced faults during execution of the program. This code protection process is known as *code hardening*. Yet another code hardening technique is *obfuscation*. Obfuscation is defined in the Oxford Dictionary as *"making something obscure, unclear and unintelligible"* [22]. In a software development context, obfuscation is the deliberate act of creating a source and/or machine code that is difficult for other programmers to understand and manipulate. Program developers may deliberately obfuscate code to conceal its purpose or logic in order to prevent tampering. Because the attacker does not know exactly what each instruction does, it becomes harder to inject faults into specific software functions. A further common method for avoiding faults is *redundancy*. Redundancy in this context involves duplicating critical code parts. The main principle behind this technique is that induced faults are detected by executing the duplicate codes and checking whether execution results match or not. If both codes generate identical results, then the execution is considered fault-free; otherwise, execution is terminated. The redundant code may be inserted either into the source code or into the machine code. In the case of source-level injection, source code has to pass through a tool, called a source-to-source rewriter, which essentially inserts redundancy by duplicating selected statements. Source-to-source rewriters, however, suffer from major drawbacks. Firstly, modern compilers are equipped with code optimisation tools. One such tool is the Common Subexpression Elimination (CSE) tool [15], which removes redundant expressions/statements. During compilation the CSE searches for identical expressions and removes them. One of the great advantages of CSE is that it reduces the program size and speed by removing duplicated codes, but this risks undoing the security protection provided by redundant code execution. To ensure that sufficient redundancy survives the CSE and remains in the generated code, the source-to-source rewriter inserts either; (i) Non-optimised and non-analysed code by disabling the CSE or (ii) a code that is complex enough to withstand the compiler optimisation and analysis process. Secondly, source-to-source rewriters are very dependent on the language and the compiler being used. Hence, they need to be redeveloped (ported) for every programming language. In other words, neither the protection nor the minimal performance overhead can be ported between compilers and languages. As a result of these drawbacks, it still remains a challenge to guarantee the presence of only the necessary degree of redundancy with acceptable performance overheads. It can be very difficult or in some cases impossible to have redundant source code statements that (i) will survive compiler optimisation, and (ii) will not limit the compiler's existing analysis and optimisation scope. To avoid source-to-source rewriter problems, in certain cases redundancy is inserted into the binary code of the program.

Such tools are known as link-time rewriters. These rewriters do not suffer from the drawbacks of source-to-source code rewriters. However, they do suffer from a lack of high-level semantic information such as symbol and type information. This lack of information limits the precision and scope of protection provided by binary code rewriters. The best example of a binary rewriter is Diablo [21].

3.2 Device Attestation

Device attestation is a technique allowing a verifying entity V to check that the hardware, the firmware and/or the software of a proving entity P are genuine. V is called the *verifier* (or the challenger or the authenticator) whereas P is called the *prover* (or the attestator). In this section, we will distinguish two common device attestation method variants. The distinction between the two methods, called *remote attestation* and *local attestation*, is based on V's location and on V's access to P.

3.2.1 Remote Attestation

This concept was first promoted by the Trusted Computing Group (TCG) and implemented in the Trusted Platform Module (TPM) specifications [9]. In most modern telecommunication services remote attestation is widely used for authentication and is referred to as Direct Anonymous Attestation (DAA) [11]. DAA is a method by which one P can prove to another V that a given secret statement is true without revealing any information about P's secret apart from the fact that the statement is indeed true. This attestation is the means by which trusted software proves to remote parties that it is trustworthy, thereby confirming that a remote server is communicating with authentic software rather than malware. For instance, a remote bank server could use DAA to ensure that the banking application in a particular OS has not been changed. At present, there are several ways to provide a Secure Element (SE) to allow the storage of a root-of-trust for mobile devices. The best known implementations are FreeScale's i.MX53 and Texas Instruments M-Shield. There are three SE categories:

- Embedded SEs, generally used to provide security for Near Field Communication (NFC);
- Embedded hardware SEs,
- and Removable hardware SEs implemented in form-factors such as smartcards and secure SD cards.

In case of a security breach, simply replacing the SE could potentially bring the overall security back to its desired level, the most popular SEs are tamper-resistant smartcards. In this section we will only consider tamper-resistant security chips implementing remote attestation available on trusted hardware modules such as TPMs.

Remote attestation is a technique allowing P to attest to V that Ps hardware, firmware and software are genuine. Remote attestation allows a remote entity V to reach a level of trust concerning the integrity of a second remote entity $\mathbb{P}$. Because $\mathbb{P}$ and $\mathbb{V}$ are at a distance from each other, cryptographic keys must be used to convince $\mathbb{P}$ and $\mathbb{V}$ that information is being exchanged between them and not between one of the parties and an opponent. The remote authentication process breaks down into two steps. The first step, called *"integrity measurement"* involves the measurement of different system parameters by $\mathbb{P}$. $\mathbb{P}$ might collect information such as BIOS, OS and kernel execution times, system memory consumption, installed software, user access patterns, version numbers, stack level usage, and data hash imprints. This information μ can be monitored under nominal conditions or under randomly chosen working conditions. μ can be a system response to a challenge sent by $\mathbb{V}$ (e.g. compress file X using the built-in compression function Y and measure the stack user imprint during the compression process), jointly chosen with $\mathbb{P}$, or can result from the processing and monitoring of user-generated activity. After this data collection phase, $\mathbb{P}$ and $\mathbb{V}$ execute a *remote attestation protocol*. This protocol is a public-key cryptographic interaction secure against man-in-the-middle attacks, by which the $\mathbb{P}$ and $\mathbb{V}$ check each other's knowledge of respective secret keys and create a session key allowing $\mathbb{P}$ to safely transmit μ to $\mathbb{V}$. The value of μ allows $\mathbb{V}$ to ascertain that $\mathbb{P}$ is malware-free. When $\mathbb{V}$ is convinced that μ matches good values (either known or re-computed), $\mathbb{V}$ issues a digital signature. The detailed description of remote attestation protocols falls beyond the goal of this introductory discussion, but is briefly summarised as follows. Both parties use public-key key exchange, public-key encryption and signatures to create a secure channel through which μ will later transit. To prevent malware from emulating $\mathbb{P}$'s behavior, secret operations and measurement data storage do not take place in $\mathbb{P}$'s open hardware region but in $\mathbb{P}$'s TPM referred as $\mathbb{P}_{TMP}$ whose public-keys are certified by some certification authority A. A specific register bench of $\mathbb{P}_{TMP}$, called the Platforms Configuration Register (PCR), is devoted to measurement data storage.

Schematically, an application App running on $\mathbb{P}$ starts by generating public/private encryption and signature key-pairs and submits these keys to $\mathbb{P}_{TMP}$ to be certified. $\mathbb{P}_{TMP}$ hashes App, signs its digest and gets an Attestation Identity Key (AIK) (see Sect. 4.6) that $\mathbb{P}_{TMP}$ returns to App. Then, App uses $\mathbb{P}$'s communication stack to send the AIK and $\mathbb{P}_{TMP}$'s certificates to $\mathbb{V}$, which checks that $\mathbb{P}$ is indeed known to $\mathbb{V}$ (*i.e.* present in the database of devices with which $\mathbb{V}$ is entitled to communicate) and that all aforementioned signatures and certificates are correct. If this succeeds, $\mathbb{P}$ and $\mathbb{V}$ establish a secure channel and start communicating measurement information. In general, the attestation protocol described above is usually run twice, with $\mathbb{P}$ and $\mathbb{V}$ switching roles. For added security, the code of $\mathbb{V}$ that validates the measurements is not published but is provided as a *cloud-based security-service* that does not expose (to potential attackers) the models that reflect $\mathbb{P}$'s structure [43]. Cloud-based verifiers also have the advantage of allowing a complete (memory and time consuming) virtual emulation of relatively complex $\mathbb{P}$'s so as to infer their expected measurements quickly and accurately.

3.2.2 Local Attestation

Without strict control over the boot process of an operating system, unauthorised software can be introduced via the boot sequence or the BIOS and attack the platform in devastating ways [44–46]. In comparison to remote attestation, which is done by a remote $\mathbb{V}$, in local attestation, the verification is a sort of security self-test, allowing a platform $\mathbb{P} + \mathbb{V}$ to protect itself from infection. This is achieved using a variety of techniques ranging from code hash values to real-time hardware watchdogs. Because it is impossible to enforce security if the boot process is compromised, local attestation tries to carefully ascertain that that the boot process does not feature any anomalous warning signs. This is done in two steps: **Authenticated Boot:** Upon power-up the system is executed and measured to infer μ. Then the PCRs are initialized with μ using a specific PCR extension function that updates (extends) the PCR value using the formula:

$$\mathrm{PCR}_{i+1} \leftarrow \mathrm{SHA1}(\mathrm{PCR}_i | \mu_{i+1})$$

where the vertical bar | stands for data concatenation. Upon reboot, the system will re-perform all the measurements $\mu_1, \ldots, \mu_\ell$ (where ℓ is the number of PCR extensions done so far, and ascertain that at least the previously measured features remain unaltered. **Secure Boot:** The previous accumulation idea can also be applied to the "measurements" μ_i consisting of the digital signatures of the various software components present in the platform. These signatures are recorded in the TPM upon software installation. Here the accumulation process is not a simple hash but a signature accumulation and screening process [47–49] allowing accumulation of ℓ individual RSA signatures $s_1, \ldots, s_\ell$ into one "global" RSA signature s checked together:

$$s = \prod_{i=1}^{\ell} s_i \mod n$$

Note that when program k is uninstalled, s must be corrected by updating it as follows $s \leftarrow s \times s_k^{-1} \mod n$. The above assumes that the code implementing the signature verification is itself secure. To that end, a small part of $\mathbb{P}$'s code is saved in an inerasable (immutable) ROM space called the *boot-ROM*. The boot-ROM measures the OS loader's components and, upon successful measurement, hands over execution to the OS loader. The OS loader will measure the OS and again, hand over execution to the OS and its drivers, which, ultimately, will measure the applications installed in the platform. All these measurements are done by verifying a tree of digital signatures where the ancestor is the measuring code and where the offspring are measured codes. When the process ends, the entire platform has been attested and is considered as having reached an *approved configuration*.

4   Trusted Execution Environment

In this section we briefly introduce some of the proposals for a secure and trusted application execution and data storage.

4.1   Mobile Trusted Module (MTM)

The growth of mobile computing platforms has encouraged the Trusted Computing Group (TCG) to propose the Mobile Trusted Module (MTM). In this section, we briefly discuss the MTM architecture and its operations along with how this differs from the TPM. In Sect. 4.6, we will discuss the proposed TPM MOBILE whose origins lie in the TPM v1.2. The ecosystems of mobile computing platforms (e.g. mobile phones, tablets, and PDAs) are fundamentally different from traditional computing platforms. Therefore, the architecture of the MTM has some features from the TPM specification, but it introduces new features to support its target environment. The main changes introduced in the MTM that make it different from the TPM specification are:

1. The MTM is required not only to perform integrity measurements during the device boot up sequence, but also to enforce a security policy that prevents the system from initiating securely if it does not meet the trusted (approved) state transition.
2. The MTM does not have to be in the hardware; it is considered as a functionality, which can be implemented by device manufacturers as an add-on to their existing architectures.
3. The MTM specification supports parallel installations of MTMs associated with different stakeholders.

The MTM specification [6] is dynamic and scalable to support the existence of multiple MTMs interlocked with each other, as shown in Fig. 1. The MTM refers to them as engines, where each of these engines is under the control of a stakeholder. Stakeholders may include the device manufacturer (Device Engine), the mobile network operator (Cellular Engine), the application provider (Application Engine), and the user (User Engine); as illustrated in Fig. 1. Each engine is an abstraction of trusted services associated with a single stakeholder. Therefore, on a mobile platform there can be a single hardware that supports the MTM functionality and is accessed by different engines. Each mobile platform abstract engine supports:

1. Provision to implement trusted and non-trusted services (normal services) associated with a stakeholder.
2. Self-test to ascertain the trustworthiness of its own state.
3. Storage of Endorsement Key (EK) (which is optional in MTM) and/or Attestation Identification Keys (AIKs).
4. Key migration.

We can further dissect abstract engines as components of different services as shown in Fig. 2. The non-trusted services in an engine cannot access the trusted resources directly. They have to use the Application Programming Interfaces (APIs) implemented by the trusted services. The trusted resources, including reporting, verification and enforcement, are new concepts that are introduced in the MTM specifications. The MTM measurement and storage services shown

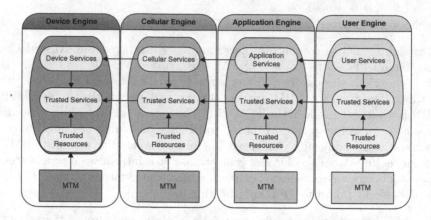

Fig. 1. Possible (Generic) architecture of mobile trusted platform

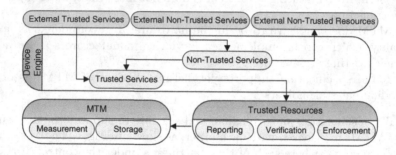

Fig. 2. Generic architecture of an abstract engine

in Fig. 2 are similar to the TPMs discussed in previous sections. The MTM specification defines two variants of the MTM profile depending upon who is the owner of a particular MTM. They are referred as Mobile Remote Ownership Trusted Modules (MRTMs) and Mobile Local Ownership Trusted Modules (MLTMs). The MRTM supports the remote ownership, which is held either by the device manufacturer or the mobile network operator, while the MLTM supports the user ownership. The roots of trust in the MTM include those discussed in TPM, including Root of Trust for Storage (RTS), Root of Trust for Measurement (RTM), and Root of Trust for Reporting (RTR); however, the MTM introduces two new roots of trust known as Root of Trust for Verification (RTV) and Root of Trust for Enforcement (RTE) (Fig. 3). During MTM operations on a trusted mobile platform, we can logically group different roots of trust; for example, RTM and RTV are grouped together to perform an efficient measure-verify-extend operation illustrated in Fig. 5. Similarly, RTS and RTR can be grouped together to deal with secure storage and trustworthiness of the mobile platform. The MTM operations as shown in Fig. 5 begin when a process starts execution, and they are:

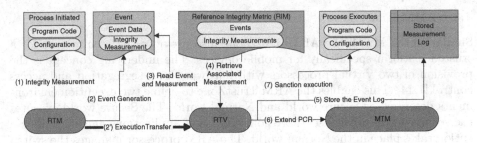

Fig. 3. MTM measurement and verification process

1. The RTM performs integrity measurements on the initiated process.
2. The RTM registers an event that includes the event data (application/process identifier) and associated integrity measurement. The RTM then transfers the execution to the RTV.
3. The RTV reads the event registered by the RTM.
4. The RTV then searches the event details via the Reference Integrity Metric (RIM). This includes the trusted integrity measurements associated with individual events, populated by the engine owner. This operation makes the MTM different from the TPM, as the latter does not make any decision regarding the trustworthiness of the application or process. However, MTM does so via the comparison performed by the RTV to verify that the integrity measurement performed by the RTM matches the one stored in the RIM. If the integrity measurement does not match, the MTM terminates the execution or disables the process. If the verification is successful then it proceeds with steps 5 and 6 along with sanctioning the execution (step 7).
5. The RTV registers the event in the measurement logs. These logs give the order in which the measurements were made to generate the final (present) value of the associated PCR.
6. The RTV extends the associated PCR value that is stored in the MTM.
7. If verification is successful, the execution of the process is sanctioned.

4.2 M-Shield

Texas Instruments has designed the M-Shield as a secure execution environment for the mobile phone market [5]. Unlike ARM TrustZone, the M-Shield is a stand-alone secure chip, and it provides secure execution and limited non-volatile memory. It also has internal memory (on-chip memory) to store runtime execution data [13] and this makes it less susceptible to attacks on off-chip memory or communication buses[1] [12].

---

[1] The memory or communication buses mentioned are between a TPM and other components on a motherboard, rather than the on-chip memory and communication buses.

4.3   ARM TrustZone

Similar to the MTM, the ARM TrustZone also provides the architecture for a trusted platform specifically for mobile devices. The underlying concept is the provision of two virtual processors with hardware-level segregation and access control [7,14]. This enables the ARM TrustZone to define two execution environments described as Secure world and Normal world. The Secure world executes the security- and privacy-sensitive components of applications and normal execution takes place in the Normal world. The ARM processor manages the switch between the two worlds. The ARM TrustZone is implemented as a security extension to the ARM processors (e.g. ARM1176JZ(F)-S, Cortes-A8, and Cortex-A9 MPCore) [7], which a developer can opt to utilise if required (Fig. 4).

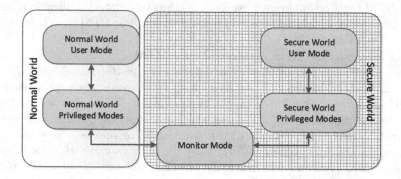

Fig. 4. Generic architectural view of ARM TrustZone

4.4   GlobalPlatform Trusted Execution Environment (TEE)

The TEE is GlobalPlatform's initiative [3,4,8] for mobile phones, set-top boxes, utility meters, and payphones. GlobalPlatform defines a specification for interoperable secure hardware, which is based on GlobalPlatform's experience in the smart card industry. It does not define any particular hardware, which can be based on either a typical secure element or any of the previously discussed tamper-resistant devices. The rationale for discussing the TEE as one of the candidate devices is to provide a complete picture. The underlying ownership of the TEE device still predominantly resides with the issuing authority, which is similar to GlobalPlatform's specification for the smart card industry [1].

4.5   Secure Elements

A secure element is an electronic chip which can securely store and execute programs. Examples are the Universal Integrated Circuit Card (UICC), the Embedded Secure Element, and Secure Memory Cards. Secure elements available on most of the Google Android supported devices conform to the Java Card specifications [2]. A generic framework to use the secure elements (or even Subscriber

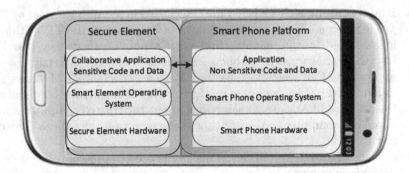

Fig. 5. Generic architectural view of secure element-based framework

Identity Module: SIM card) is shown in Fig. 5 and discussed below. An application installed on a smart phone platform can have a collaborative application available on the secure element. The collaborative application has the responsibility for executing and storing security- and/or privacy-preserving functionality and data. The application, once installed and executing on the smart phone platform, provides a feature-rich interface to the user, while communicating with collaborative applications when required.

4.6   TPM MOBILE

The TPM chip, whose specification is defined by the Trusted Computing Group [10], is known as a hardware root-of-trust into the trusted computing ecosystem. Currently it is deployed to laptops, PCs, and mobiles and is produced by manufacturers including Infineon, Atmel and Broadcom. At present, the TPM is available as a tamper-resistant security chip that is physically bounded to the computers motherboard and controlled by software running on the system using well-defined commands. The TPM MOBILE with Trusted Execution Environment has recently emerged; its origin lies in the TPM v1.2 a with some enhancements for mobile devices [9]. The TPM provides:

1. The **Roots of trust** include hardware/software components that are intrinsically trusted to establish a chain of trust that ensures only trusted software and hardware can be used (see the MTM, Sect. 4.1).
2. The **Platform Configuration Register "PCR"** in the most modern TPM includes 24 registers. It is used to store the state of system measurements. These measurements are represented normally by a cryptographic hash computed from the hash values (SHA-1) of components (applications) running on the platform. PCRs cannot be written directly; data can only be stored by a process called extending the PCR.
3. The **RSA keys**: There are two types of RSA keys that TPM generates and which are considered as *root keys* (they never leave the TPM):

a. **Endorsement Key (EK)**: This key is used in its role as a *Root of Trust for Reporting*. During the installation of an owner in the TPM, this key is generated by the manufacturer with a public/private key pair built into the hardware. The public component of the EK is certified by an appropriate CA, which assigns the EK to a particular TPM. Thus, each individual TPM has a unique platform EK. For the private component of the EK, the TPM can sign assertions about the trusted computer's state. A remote computer can verify that those assertions have been signed by a trusted TPM.

b. **Storage Root Key (SRK)**: This key is used to protect other keys and data via encryption.

c. **Attestation Identity Keys (AIKs)**: The AIK is used to identify the platform in transactions such as platform authentication and platform attestation. Because of the uniqueness of the EK, the AIK is used in remote attestation by a particular application. The private key is non-migratable and protected by the TPM and the public key is encrypted by a storage root key (or other key) outside the TPM with the possibility to be loaded into the TPM. The security of the public key is bootstrapped from the TPM's EK. The AIK is generally used for several roles: signing/reporting user data; storage (encrypting data and other keys); and binding (decrypting data, used also for remote parties).

4.7   Overseeing the Overseer

In the proposals discussed in this chapter, the burden of secure application execution is moved to the trusted execution environment in one way or another. The security and reliability of the trusted execution environment has to be not only adequate, but in certain cases provable. We need to build a trusted environment that can ensure all application code being executed on it will be protected from any runtime tampering by a potential malicious entity. In the subsequent sections, we address the security and reliability of the trusted execution environment and how we can ensure a trusted application execution.

5   Remaining Security Challenges of Application Execution

Before we begin a detailed discussion of this section we summarise what has been presented so far. Mobile devices are composed of hardware, operating system and applications. Techniques such as code hardening and centralised vetting try to protect mobile applications from malicious intruders by inserting clues, such as redundant statements, into the application executables and verifying them centrally before they are installed. However, they cannot protect against attacks targeting the operating system or the underlying hardware. To counteract such attacks, device attestation is needed. Device attestation such as TPM ensures only that the necessary components of the operating system are started securely during device booting. However, this does not provide any protection against attacks that can take place after the operating system is up and running. Manufacturers try to tackle this challenge by using various techniques including MTM, ARM TrustZone, M-Shield and GlobalPlatforms TEE. The common theme of these protections is to provide a secure execution space for critical applications, for example PIN verification, which is segregated from the main execution space. In spite of all the efforts to secure embedded systems, there still remain significant threats and vulnerabilities that can be exploited by dedicated attackers. The questions one may ask regarding the security of embedded systems are:

1. How do we make sure that the hardware processor is secure and free of malicious entities such as hardware Trojans?
2. If we only execute selected applications/programs inside the secure zone, what happens to the other applications?

In the subsequent sections we discuss these security challenges and their possible solutions.

5.1   Pre-deployment/Post-production Device Verification

Recent economic conditions have forced embedded system manufacturers to outsource their production processes to cheaper cost structure countries. While this significantly reduces the total production cost, it also makes it much easier for an attacker to compromise the supply chain for components used in critical business and military applications, and replace them with defective components. This threat to the electronic components supply chain is already a cause for alarm in some countries [18,20]. For this reason, some governments have been subsidising high-cost local foundries to produce components used in military applications [19]. However, this is not an affordable solution for most developing countries and commercial applications. According to [23], the incidence of defective components increased from 3,868 in 2005 to 9,356 in 2008. Such defective electronic components have at least the following ramifications: (1) original component providers incur an irrecoverable loss due to the sale of often cheaper counterfeit components; (2) low performance of defective products (that are often of lower quality and/or cheaper older generations of a chip family) affects the overall efficiency of the integrated systems that unintentionally use them, which could in turn harm the reputation of authentic providers; (3) unreliability of defective devices could render the integrated systems that unknowingly use the parts unreliable, potentially affecting the performance of weapons, airplanes, cars or other crucial applications [24]; and (4) untrusted defective components may have intentional malware or some backdoor for spying, remotely controlling critical objects and/or leaking secret information. These ramifications and their growing presence in the market make them important problems to address. Traditionally, the integrity of software codes on personal computers and other platforms is verified by using hash values and digital signatures. The software developer hashes the entire software code and signs it with his private key. Later, the person using it verifies the signature before installing it. This scheme, however, suffers from a major drawback in embedded devices. The reason is that hashing the entire program memory is often impossible due to the read protection countermeasures that embedded systems implement. In certain scenarios the software developer can provide users with the source code so the users can manually check it before using it. However, for commercial and intellectual property reasons this is not possible in many cases. Sometimes it may be necessary to verify the hardware before installing the software. In this case the easiest way of doing it would be to verify the integrity of the netlist[2] of the target device. A definition of the term netlist can also be found in [35]. However, as with software codes this is generally impossible as companies do not reveal such information for commercial and intellectual property reasons. Therefore, to verify an embedded system before it is deployed/inserted into larger electronic equipment we need to find alternative but reliable methods that can help us verify its integrity. In [28] Paul et al. demonstrated that side channel information, such as power consumption, carries information about the data processed at runtime. Furthermore, it is possible that the same information can reveal much more information about the internal state of the device than just runtime data. In [29–31] the authors demonstrated that the side channel leakage of an embedded device contains information about the executed instructions and that it can be used to partially reverse engineer them. In [32] Mehari et al. have improved the recognition rate to fully reverse engineer them. The authors of [25] also demonstrate that side channel information can be used to spot additional modules that were not part of the original design of the device, such as hardware Trojans. From the above work it is reasonable to conclude that side channel information can be effectively used to verify embedded devices before they are deployed. Mehari et al. have demonstrated the possibility of software integrity verification, in the context of embedded systems, in their paper [33].

5.2 Runtime Security Protection

As discussed in the previous sections, several techniques have been proposed and deployed to secure embedded systems. However, they still remain vulnerable to a range of attacks. This is true partly because security was not the main criterion of the original processor design and it has not changed much since then. On some occasions researchers have tried to address this problem by integrating security into the processor design. Integrated hardware protections are implemented by hardware manufacturers. One of the hardware protections is hardware block redundancy, in which selected or all hardware blocks on the embedded chip are implemented more than once. During runtime the program is executed by all blocks and a comparator compares the results. In [16], several varieties of this protection are discussed in detail. Figure 6 illustrates a simple duplicate of a hardware block. The decision block either resets the device or

---

[2] A list of logic gates and a textual description of their interconnections which make up an electronic circuit.

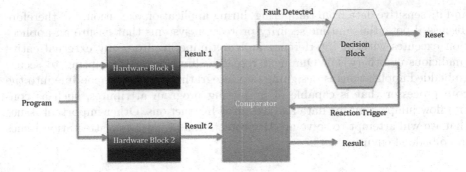

Fig. 6. A simple hardware redundancy with two identical blocks.

invokes a specifically designed reaction algorithm when a fault is detected by the comparator. In another approach Arora et al. [26] demonstrated that the control flow jumps and instruction integrity of embedded programs can be verified on the fly with minimal overhead by integrating a security module into the core design. They discussed the idea that if the security attributes of the program can be extracted during compilation, then these attributes can be used at runtime to ensure the program is behaving correctly. If problems are detected, either shutdown or reset signals will be generated. Krutartha et al. [27] discussed a similar approach, designing a security module as part of the processor code, to secure multiprocessors against code injection attacks. They introduced a new module called the monitor processor that monitors communication between the individual processors. In an N-processor core the individual processors communicate with each other through a First In First out (FIFO) queue structure. In their approach the program is broken down to basic blocks. The basic blocks are then attributed with two FIFO instructions that notify the monitor processor of the start and finish of each basic block. Although these approaches show some success in securing embedded system application at runtime; however, they require extensive analysis before they could be considered a commercially viable solutions.

6   Conclusion

In this chapter, we discussed the importance of SAE for mobile devices, especially smart phones. The chapter also briefly described the Apple iOS and Google Android ecosystem, along with how they secure not only their respective platforms but also the applications running on them. Different proposals that provide a secure and trusted environment for execution and data-storage of sensitive applications were discussed. These proposals included MTM, TPM MOBILE, M-Shield, GlobalPlatform TEE, ARM TrustZone and Secure Elements. One thing in common to most of these proposals is a secure and trusted hardware-based execution environment that serves the smart phone platform and applications. These trusted execution environments have to protect the application and its sensitive data from tampering during application execution. We therefore discussed potential runtime security protection systems that ensure an application executes without interference and/or tampering from any external entity (malicious or otherwise). Our next research direction in attempting to secure embedded applications is designing and integrating a hardware module into the core processor that is capable of protecting program attributes, such as control flow jumps, runtime data and executed instructions. Other important issues that we will attempt to solve are IP protection and hardware attestation issues in embedded environments.

Acknowledgement. Mehari G. Msgna is sponsored by the Information Network Security Agency, Addis Ababa, Ethiopia.

References

1. GlobalPlatform: GlobalPlatform Card Specification, Version 2.2 (2006)
2. Java Card Platform Specification: Application Programming Interface, Runtime Environment Specification, Virtual Machine Specification (2006). http://java.sun. com/javacard/specs.html
3. Device, G.: GPD/STIP Specification Overview, Specification Version 2.3, GlobalPlatform (2007)
4. GlobalPlatform Device Technology: Device Application Security Management - Concepts and Description Document Specification. Online (2008)
5. M-Shield Mobile Security Technology: Making Wireless Secure. Whilte Paper, Texas Instruments (2008). http://focus.ti.com/pdfs/wtbu/ti_mshield_whitepaper. eps
6. TCG Mobile Trusted Module Specification. Online (2008)
7. ARM Security Technology: Building a Secure System using TrustZone Technology. White Paper PRD29-GENC-009492C, ARM (2009)
8. GlobalPlatform Device Technology: TEE System Architecture. Specification Version 0.4, GlobalPlatform (2011)
9. Trusted Platform Module Main Specification
10. Trusted Computing Group, Online (2011)
11. Brickell, E., Camenisch, J., Chen, L.: Direct anonymous attestation. In: Proceedings of the 11th ACM Conference on Computer and Communications Security (CCS 2004), pp. 132–145. ACM, New York (2004). http://doi.acm.org/10.1145/ 1030083.1030103, doi:10.1145/1030083.1030103
12. Halderman, J.A., Schoen, S.D., Heninger, N., Clarkson, W., Paul, W., Calandrino, J.A., Feldman, A.J., Appelbaum, J., Felten, E.W.: Lest we remember: cold boot attacks on encryption keys. In: Proceedings of the 17th Conference on Security Symposium, pp. 45–60. USENIX Association, Berkeley, CA, USA (2008)
13. Kostiainen, K., Ekberg, J.E., Asokan, N., Rantala, A.: On-board credentials with open provisioning. In: Proceedings of the 4th International Symposium on Information. Computer, and Communications Security (ASIACCS 2009), pp. 104–115. ACM, New York (2009). http://doi.acm.org/10.1145/1533057.1533074
14. Wilson, P., Frey, A., Mihm, T., Kershaw, D., Alves, T.: Implementing embedded security on dual-virtual-CPU systems. IEEE Des. Test Comput. **24**, 582–591 (2007)

15. Muchnick, S.S.: Advanced Compiler Design and Implementation. Morgan Kaufmann, San Francisco (1997)
16. Bar-El, H., Choukri, H., Naccache, D., Tunstall, M., Whelan, C.: The sorcerer's apprentice guide to fault attacks. In: IACR Cryptology ePrint Archive (2004). http://eprint.iacr.org/2004/100
17. Maebe, J., De Keulenaer, R., De Sutter, B., De Bosschere, K.: Mitigating smart card fault injection with link-time code rewriting: a feasibility study. In: Sadeghi, A.-R. (ed.) FC 2013. LNCS, vol. 7859, pp. 221–229. Springer, Heidelberg (2013)
18. Defense Advanced Research Projects Agency: DARPA BAA06-40, A TRUST for Integrated Circuits Visited, September 2014
19. Defense Science Board Task Force: High Performance Microchip Supply. http://www.acq.osd.mil/dsb/reports/ADA435563.eps. Accessed September 2014
20. Lieberman, J.I.: The national security aspects of the global migration of the U.S. semiconductor industry. http://www.fas.org/irp/congress/2003_cr/s060503.html. Accessed September 2014
21. Diablo: Diablo is a better link-time optimizer. https://diablo.elis.ugent.be/. Accessed October 2014
22. Oxford Dictionaries: Definition of obfuscate. http://www.oxforddictionaries.com/definition/english/obfuscate
23. U.S. Department Of Commerce: Defense Industrial Base Assessment: Counterfeit Electronics. Bureau of Industry and Security, Office of Technology Evaluation. http://www.bis.doc.gov/defenseindustrialbaseprograms/osies/defmarketresearchrpts/final_counterfeit_electronics_report.eps. Accessed January 2010
24. Koushanfar, F., Sadeghi, A.-R., Seudie, H.: EDA for secure and dependable cybercars: Challenges and opportunities. In: 49th ACM/EDAC/IEEE Design Automation Conference (DAC), pp. 220–228 (2012)
25. Agrawal, D., Baktir, S., Karakoyunlu, D., Rohatgi, P., Sunar, B.: Trojan detection using IC fingerprinting. In: IEEE Symposium on Security and Privacy (SP 2007), pp. 296–310 (2007)
26. Arora, D., Ravi, S., Raghunathan, A., Jha, N.K.: Secure embedded processing through hardware-assisted run-time monitoring. In: Design, Automation and Test in Europe, vol. 1, pp. 178–183 (2005). doi:10.1109/DATE.2005.266
27. Patel, K., Parameswaran, S., Shee, S.L.: Ensuring secure program execution in multiprocessor embedded systems: a case study. In: IEEE/ACM/IFIP International Conference on Hardware/Software Codesign and System Synthesis (CODES+ISSS), pp. 57–62 (2007)
28. Kocher, P.C., Jaffe, J., Jun, B.: Differential power analysis. In: Wiener, M. (ed.) CRYPTO 1999. LNCS, vol. 1666, p. 388. Springer, Heidelberg (1999)
29. Vermoen, D., Witteman, M., Gaydadjiev, G.N.: Reverse engineering java card applets using power analysis. In: Sauveron, D., Markantonakis, K., Bilas, A., Quisquater, J.-J. (eds.) WISTP 2007. LNCS, vol. 4462, pp. 138–149. Springer, Heidelberg (2007)
30. Quisquater, J.-J., Samyde, D.: Automatic code recognition for smartcards using a kohonen neural network. In: CARDIS, USENIX 21–22 November, San Jose, CA, USA (2002)
31. Eisenbarth, T., Paar, C., Weghenkel, B.: Building a side channel based disassembler. In: Gavrilova, M.L., Tan, C.J.K., Moreno, E.D. (eds.) Transactions on Computational Science X. LNCS, vol. 6340, pp. 78–99. Springer, Heidelberg (2010)

32. Msgna, M., Markantonakis, K., Mayes, K.: Precise instruction-level side channel profiling of embedded processors. In: Huang, X., Zhou, J. (eds.) ISPEC 2014. LNCS, vol. 8434, pp. 129–143. Springer, Heidelberg (2014). doi:10.1007/978-3-319-06320-1_11

33. Msgna, M., Markantonakis, K., Naccache, D., Mayes, K.: Verifying software integrity in embedded systems: a side channel approach. In: Prouff, E. (ed.) COSADE 2014. LNCS, vol. 8622, pp. 261–280. Springer, Heidelberg (2014). doi:10.1007/978-3-319-10175-0_18

34. What is SHA-1. https://en.wikipedia.org/wiki/SHA-1

35. Netlist Definition. Xilinx. http://www.xilinx.com/itp/xilinx10/help/iseguide/mergedProjects/constraints_editor/html/ce_d_netlist.htm

36. iOS Security Sandbox white paper. https://www.cs.auckland.ac.nz/courses/compsci702s1c/lectures/rs-slides/6-iOS-SecuritySandbox.eps

37. https://www.apple.com/privacy/docs/iOS_Security_Guide_Oct_2014.eps

38. http://en.wikipedia.org/wiki/XNU

39. http://en.wikipedia.org/wiki/Android

40. http://developer.android.com/tools/publishing/app-signing.html

41. http://developer.android.com/guide/topics/security/permissions.html

42. What is MAC/DAC. https://www.internetsociety.org/sites/default/files/02_4.eps

43. http://www.tclouds-project.eu/downloads/factsheets/tclouds-factsheet-07-attestation.eps

44. Zeller, T.: The ghost in the CD; Sony BMG stirs a debate over software used to guard content, The New York Times, c1, November 14 (2005)

45. http://en.wikipedia.org/wiki/CIH_(computer_virus)

46. Gratzer, V., Naccache, D.: Alien vs. quine, the vanishing circuit and other tales from the industry's crypt. In: Vaudenay, S. (ed.) EUROCRYPT 2006. LNCS, vol. 4004, pp. 48–58. Springer, Heidelberg (2006)

47. Chevallier-Mames, B., Naccache, D., Paillier, P., Pointcheval, D.: How to disembed a program? In: Joye, M., Quisquater, J.-J. (eds.) CHES 2004. LNCS, vol. 3156, pp. 441–454. Springer, Heidelberg (2004)

48. Bellare, M., Garay, J.A., Rabin, T.: Fast batch verification for modular exponentiation and digital signatures. In: Nyberg, K. (ed.) EUROCRYPT 1998. LNCS, vol. 1403, pp. 236–250. Springer, Heidelberg (1998)

49. Benaloh, J.C., de Mare, M.: One-way accumulators: a decentralized alternative to digital signatures. In: Helleseth, T. (ed.) EUROCRYPT 1993. LNCS, vol. 765, pp. 274–285. Springer, Heidelberg (1994)

Hardware-Enforced Protection Against Buffer Overflow Using Masked Program Counter

Jean-Luc Danger[1,2], Sylvain Guilley[1,2], Thibault Porteboeuf[1,2], Florian Praden[1(✉)], and Michaël Timbert[1]

[1] Telecom ParisTech, Institut Mines-Télécom, Paris, France
florian.praden@telecom-paristech.fr
[2] Secure-IC S.A.S., Threat Protection Business Line, Rennes, France

Abstract. The threat based on Buffer Overflow is one of the main software vulnerability which is exploited by many viruses and cyber attacks. A buffer overflow overwrites the return address to the parent program of a subroutine. To counter it, we propose in this paper to mask on-the-fly this return address by slightly modifying the processor architecture. We show that the hardware overhead, as well as software modification, is very small. The efficiency has been demonstrated on a bare metal program running on a Leon 3 processor. This paper also shows the limitation when using a real OS.

1 Introduction

Some sneaky cyber-attacks are those which exploit software bugs. They can basically apply to all implementations which run the buggy software [1–6], without being detected if programmed properly. CVE statistics (see Table 1) show that stack smashing remains an important proportion of reported software vulnerabilities. Many different attack paths are made possible by such computer state alteration.

Data corruption is one possibility. Another option is control flow hijacking. It is achieved by overwriting return addresses which are stored on the stack frames, with a crafted address where the attacks aims at deviating the program control flow to.

In this article, we are interested by a method to deceive control flow hijacking, especially suitable for embedded systems.

1.1 State-of-the-Art

Processors used in information technologies (IT) services, like personal desktop or laptop computers, servers, routers, etc. have some builtin protection against attacks which exploit software bugs. Some protections do not prevent from smashing the stack. For instance, the memory management unit (MMU), the execution prevention measures (NX bit, W xor X, etc.), TrustZone, Trusted Execution Environment (TEE), etc. cannot prevent stack smashing. Some protections however specifically prevent stack smashing attacks [9–12] One exemple

© Springer-Verlag Berlin Heidelberg 2016
P.Y.A. Ryan et al. (Eds.): Kahn Festschrift, LNCS 9100, pp. 439–454, 2016.
DOI: 10.1007/978-3-662-49301-4_27

Table 1. CVE for *buffer overflows* (B.O.) (Data aggregated from https://web.nvd. nist.gov)

Year	B.O.	Total	Percent	Year	B.O.	Total	Percent
1989	1	3	33.33%	1990	1	11	9.09%
1991	0	15	0.00%	1992	0	13	0.00%
1993	0	13	0.00%	1994	0	25	0.00%
1995	4	25	16.00%	1996	15	75	20.00%
1997	63	252	25.00%	1998	47	246	19.11%
1999	157	894	17.56%	2000	187	1020	18.33%
2001	254	1677	15.15%	2002	358	2156	16.60%
2003	287	1527	18.80%	2004	311	2451	12.69%
2005	514	4931	10.42%	2006	486	6608	7.35%
2007	653	6514	10.02%	2008	488	5632	8.66%
2009	496	5732	8.65%	2010	360	4639	7.76%
2011	333	4150	8.02%	2012	371	5288	7.02%
2013	309	5186	5.96%	2014	318	7937	4.01%
2015	81	1644	4.93%				

is stack canaries. Memory layout obfuscation (e.g., thanks to ASLR)[15] can also help mitigated stack smashing attacks. However, some attacks [7,14] manage to bypass those protections. Therefore, a complementary protection would be welcomed. Such defense in depth strategy would make attacks more complicated.

In the field of embedded systems, processors are more simple, and an operating system is not always ran. In these conditions, a protection against stack smashing attacks needs to be made from scratch [8]. Such systems include soft-core processors, like LEON (SPARC v8), LowRISC (open-source RISC 64 bits), MicroBlaze (32 bit from Xilinx), Nios II (32 bit from Altera), Mico (32 bit from Lattice), Atmega 103 (available from http://www.opencores.org), ARM Cortex M0, etc.

1.2   Contributions

In this article, we implement and discuss a full hardware protection against return address overwriting. One important advantage of 100 % hardware solutions is that they cannot be bypassed. Also, the rationale of the protection being kept simple, it is is a priori not flawed; anyway they cannot be exploited because not exposed to the attacker (only parts of the memory is). A second advantage is that the protection acts in real-time, that is, the exploitation triggers an error as soon as it is perpetrated.

The protection consists in masking the return address, which is indeed vulnerable when stored on the stack. The proposed approach is shown very convenient when used on firmware, i.e., code compiled once for all for the platform. It is also shown to work when there is an operating system, although with more pitfalls to be taken into consideration.

1.3   Outline

The paper is structured as follows. The principle of the countermeasure is given in Sect. 2. Then, the hardware implementation is described in Sect. 3. The use with software is detailed in Sect. 4. Finally, Sect. 5 concludes the paper.

2   Return Address Masking: Theory

2.1   Motivation

A common way to program on computer is dividing program in small block of code. Each block calls multiple other block. To do that, a processor has a specific opcode to call a function and return in the parent function. Usually, the CALL opcode goes to that sub-function and RET opcode returns to the parent. As we can see, the processor offers a way to store the pointer to the parent function used by the RET opcode. In sparc processor, the %i7 register (or r31) is used to save this pointer. In x86 or amd64, the CALL save the pointer in the stack. A classical way to disrupt the flow of a program is to override this saved value by a attacker's value pointing to a shellcode. Multiple protections (canaries, boundaries, memory protection) and counter-protection (specific addresses overwriting, ROP and JOP) exist. Another way to protect the saved program counter is to mask it with a random values not known by the attacker. Different approaches exist:

– software method: like canaries in the stacks, after each call, a little function is used to replace the value by a masked one.
– hardware method: the PC is masked all the times in hardware or masked when saved.

Like canaries, software methods slow down the program, because at each call and ret, the saved value are altered. An example in x86 could be the Listing 1.1:

Listing 1.1. fun function with software PC masking in x86

```
1   fun:
2           mov eax,[mask]
3           pop ebx
4           xor eax,ebx
5           push eax
6           [...]
7           mov eax,[mask]
8           pop ebx
9           xor eax,ebx
10          push eax
11          ret
```

As we can see, the overhead for one call is rather big. The strengthening by PC masking is done by the compiler, so it could be bypassed by replacing the host program, thus creating another trust problem.

2.2   Model and Goal of the Attacker

To fully qualify the threat and the countermeasure, the model of the attacker is the following:

- it has access to the binary code and source code,
- it has access to the input/output offered by the program,
- but it can not use side channel attacks or physical attacks in order to extract some information leakage about the running code or the state of the processor,
- it can not access the internal registers or debugger features of the processor (e.g. the DSU in LEON is deactivated) or software debugger like gdb when use against the real target.

In other words, it could perform some learning pentests with full debugging support, but has restricted access to the host device in real condition. It is the classical model for cyber-attackers.

2.3   Rationale of the Protection in Hardware

To avoid software overhead and misuse by programmers, the masking could be done in hardware. The main advantage is the independence of protection and highest speed. In short, we use the special PC register and transform the stored value by masking it (see Fig. 1).

The construction of modern processor include pipelining to increase the performance level. There are many types of hardware architecture and pipelines. ARM, Intel and SPARC pipelines are very different. Hence this protection must be adapted to each processor type, including specificities like register windows in SPARC.

Fig. 1. Masking the PC with a XOR

2.4   Others Works

The theory is well covered. In [13], Papadogiannakis and al. included the PCX protection in their protected LEON3. But in his term, "As the calling conventions are not always strictly obeyed in several legacy applications and libraries, the use of return address encryption may not be always possible.". To mitigate these words, we have implemented the protection on the same processor using the same method describes in his paper. Calling convention are not in fact the critical problem, as we will see in Sect. 4.2.

3   Implementation on a LEON3 Processor

3.1   Hardware Description

For this implementation, the LEON3 processor is chosen. It is a compact processor implementing the SPARC v8 instruction set including multiply and divide instructions and a 7-stage pipeline. Our configuration includes a debug support unit (DSU), a 32 × 32 multiplier, data and instruction caches with MMU and 8 register windows. The LEON3 is integrated on a Virtex 5 (XC5VLX110) FPGA. The Fig. 2 summarizes the architecture of the processor and Fig. 3 for a view of the real prototype.

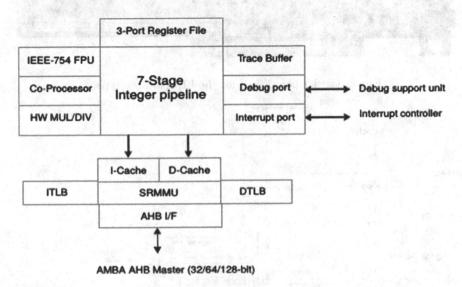

Fig. 2. LEON 3 internal

3.2   Pipeline

As we said, the LEON3 has a 7-stage pipeline: **FETCH, DECODE, REGISTER ACCESS, EXECUTE, MEMORY, EXCEPTION, WRITEBACK** (see Fig. 4). In SPARC, two conventional methods is used to jump on a subfunction:

- CALL: an absolute address is used to jump to the subfunction and %o7 is used to save the CALL address for the return.
- JMPL: a jump in a register-saved address with an offset given in the opcode. the JMPL address is also saved in a register. Since the %o7 is used to save the return address, the JMPL is used like `jmpl <register+offset>,%o7` for calling subfunction.

Fig. 3. Gaisler board used for the LEON3 prototype

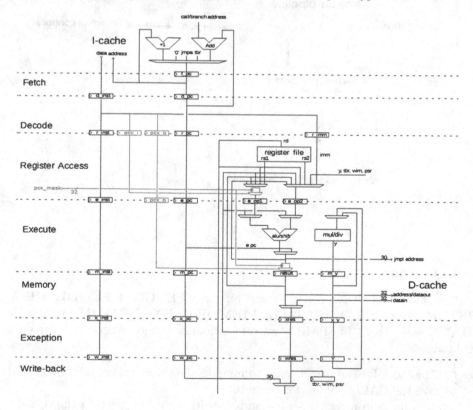

Fig. 4. LEON 3 pipeline with PCX (in blue) (Color figure online)

There is no RET function but it can done by using a JMPL opcode. Depending of the function type, the RET synthetic opcode is:

- in a leaf-function (no register window sliding): jmpl %o7+8,%g0
- in a normal function (with register window sliding): jmpl %i7+8,%g0

In SPARC, a delay-slot is introduced to optimize the pipeline, so the instruction after each branch is executed (an exception: to also give an option to optimize the code size, conditional branch could avoid the execution of the next instruction by setting the annul bit in the opcode, saving the space of the next opcode). The synthetic RET opcode take that in consideration to jump over 2 opcodes: the jump opcode and the delay-slot opcode.

3.3   Pitfall

The optimization done by the pipeline makes the implementation of the masking a little more complex. The signal of each stage is propagated at each clock cycle. The write-back in register file is done in the **WRITE-BACK** stage, and the saved value in the register file could be out-of-sync when the pipeline access it. An example could be seen in Listing 1.2

Listing 1.2. dependance between opcode: When the RET opcode is exectuted, the %o7 (return address) is in the EXCEPTION stage

```
1    xs   call __test
2      nop
3
4      ( ... )
5
6    __test:
7      ( ... )
8      mov %o7,%l1  ; save of register %o7 in %l1
9      ( ... )
10     mov %l1,%o7  ; restore the register %o7 from %l1
11     ret          ; synthetic function : jump to %o7+8
12     nop          ; delay-slot : we do nothing
```

To overcome this, the pipeline uses values in all stage to compute an up-to-date result. In particular, we could not wiretap the register-access bus to perform the masking of the program counter saved in %o7. We have to mask the program counter deep into the pipeline.

3.4   Pipeline Modification

In order to mask the program counter, we modify the pipeline bus at each stage to include two signals:

- pcx_i: the input must be unmasked
- pcx_o: the output must be masked

These two signals are computed in the **DECODE** stage.

In the **REGISTER ACCESS**, the pcx_i is used to unmask the first register. It is this first register that the RET opcode use to jump back to the parent function. In the **EXECUTE**, the return address is computed and saved in case of a branch opcode. The pcx_o is used to mask this computed value.

All this is resumed in the modified pipeline diagram (see Fig. 4).

As we can see, the return address is masked deeply in the pipeline. A drawback is the arithmetical operation on this value. It is impossible to use arithmetical operation on the saved program counter before an RET instruction for instance. We will see how bad is this drawback and how we could modify this implementation to overcome this limitation (see Results and limitation, Solutions in Sect. 4.2).

3.5   Hardware Glue

To control this module, an AMBA AHB wrapper is used to permit the communication with the code. This AHB wrapper could be discover this the AMBA Plug and Play protocol. By default the base address is 0xfff00000. The configuration for the AMBA Plug and Play is the following:

– VENDOR_ID: $0xFF$
– DEVICE_ID: $0x001$

The configuration includes two words (2 × 32 bits):

– control (base address): flags including
  • MAGIC_WORD [31:24] = $0xabc$ (RO): fixed read-only value,
  • RESERVED [23:21] : reserved for future,
  • PCX_AVAIL [20] (RO): equal to 1 if the masking of the program counter is available,
  • RESERVED [19:1] : reserved for future,
  • PCX_ENABLE [0] (RW): equal to 1 if the masking must be used.
– PCX_MASK (base address + 4) (RW): the 32-bits mask used in the protection.

4   Software with PCX

There is two kind of software :

– bare metal: a single program run into the SPARC processor
– OS: an operating system is used to run multiple programs with multiple users

Each kind of software has his own restriction. In baremetal, we could control each instruction run by the processor but a single program and no user exist on the device. In OS, we could not control what the processor does or executes, but we could run multiple programs.

With this protection, we will see that the OS restriction is not compatible with the current implementation of the masking.

4.1   Baremetal

In case of a firmware or baremetal program, the modification to run with the protection are minimal:

- a code to enable the protection: see Listing 1.3
- a code to disable the protection: see Listing 1.4

Listing 1.3. C code to enable PCX protection

```
1  #ifdef PCX
2  {
3     unsigned int pcx_ctrl=0x1;
4     unsigned int pcx_mask=0x12345678; // PCX mask value
5     unsigned int pcx_ba  =0xfff00000; // PCX base address
6     // Write mask
7     __asm__ (''sta %0,[%1]0x1c'' : // no output
8     : ''r''(pcx_mask), ''r''(pcx_ba+4)
9     );
10    // Write control register
11    __asm__ (''sta %0,[%1]0x1c'' : // no output
12    : ''r''(pcx_ctrl), ''r''(pcx_ba)
13    );
14 }
15 #endif
```

Listing 1.4. C code to disable PCX protection

```
1  #ifdef PCX
2  {
3     unsigned int pcx_ctrl=0x0;
4     unsigned int pcx_ba  =0xfff00000;
5     // Write control register
6     __asm__ (''sta %0,[%1     ]0x1c'' : // no output
7     : ''r''(pcx_ctrl), ''r''(pcx_ba)
8     );
9  }
10 #endif
```

If the protection is activated inside a function, the programmer must disable the function before the RET instruction. If not, the processor will try to unmask the clear program counter, which is the same as returning to the masked value of the program counter because the XOR masking function is an involution.

4.2   Linux

On a Linux kernel, we try to link the hardware protection with each userland process. A new process will have a random mask and a flag set to one if the protection is activated. When the processor enter in kernelland, the protection must be disable and once the kernel tasks are done, it must be reactivated with the correct values depending of the next-to-be-run process.

Three modifications must be done:

- the modification of the task_struct, to include the protection like the mask
- the modification of userland ⇒ kernelland entry point
- the modification of the kernelland ⇒ userland out point

Task Structure. Each process is scheduled by the Linux scheduler. It uses a chained list describe in the task_struct structure (see Listing 1.5).

Listing 1.5. the task_struct structure(partial) that is used by the linux scheduler

```
1  struct task_struct {
2      volatile long state;/* −1 unrunnable, 0 runnable, >0
           stopped */
3      void *stack;
4      atomic_t usage;
5      unsigned int flags;/* per process flags, defined below */
6      unsigned int ptrace;
7      /* (...) */
8      unsigned int cyber_ctrl;
9      unsigned int pcx_mask;
10 };
```

To permit the debugging of the protection, an entry for each process in the / proc is created by adding some code dumping the states of the protection.

We can obtain the status of a process using the virtual filesystem.

The modified version of the task_struct in schematized in Fig. 5.

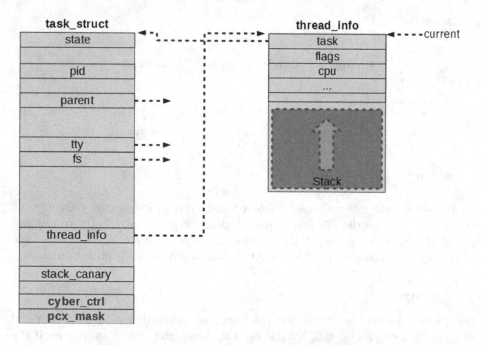

Fig. 5. Linux task_struct structure with PCX fields

Kernelland − Userland Transition. Since the PCX protection is used in userland only, it must be deactivated and activated at each transition, if the process is protected (see Fig. 6 for an example). The process goes to kernelland if and only if:

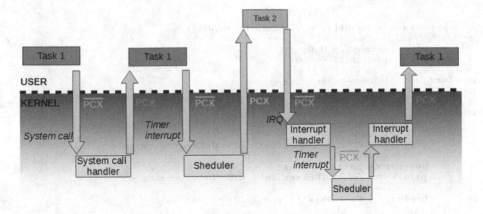

Fig. 6. Linux kernelland/userland transition in the scheduler with PCX implementation

- a syscall is performed,
- an error (trap) is raised,
- an hardware interrupt (also trap) is raised.

All this mechanism go thru the trap table, which is hardware dependant. Each trap redirect the call to a kernel handler. Two case should be considered:

- we are in a kernel to kernel transition: before the trap, we are in kernelland. It is possible because the kernel is mostly reentrant.
- we are in a user to kernel transition: before the trap, we are in userland. It is the main case.

At each return-from-trap, we could return in kernelland or userland, depending the case.

When we return from a trap, if we go to userland and the process has activated the masking protection, we saved the current values of the protection in the task structure of the current process and restore the values of the protection for the next program that the Linux kernel scheduler will executes.

Creation of a New Process. The creation of new task is done in the do_execve_common function. For now, we modify the function to initialize the protection depending of the environment variable PCX. At the end, we will save the state of the protection in the elf header. This modification could be seen in Listing 1.6

Listing 1.6. Modification of the linux execve function which is responsible of the creation of a new task

```
1  static int do_execve_common( const char *filename,
2  struct user_arg_ptr argv,
3  struct user_arg_ptr envp)
```

```
4   [...]
5   bprm->envc = count(envp, MAX_ARG_STRINGS);
6   /* default value */
7   current->pcx_mask = 0x0;
8   current->cyber_ctrl = 0x0;
9
10  for( i=0 ; i<bprm->envc ; i++)
11  {
12    if( strncmp( get_user_arg_ptr(envp,i), ''PCX='', 4) == 0 )
13    {
14      sscanf( get_user_arg_ptr(envp,i),''PCX=%x\n'',&(current->
              pcx_mask));
15      printk(''CYBER PCX mask set to : 0x%X\n'', current->
              pcx_mask);
16      current->cyber_ctrl=0x1;
17      printk(''CYBER CTRL set to : 0x%X\n'', current->
              cyber_ctrl);
18      break; // Dont need to parse other env vars
19    }
20  }
```

Results and Limitation. The modification of the hardware and the kernel did not affect the Linux OS and the userland programs running without the protection activated. But the use of this protection impose the masking of the program counter. By that, it is impossible for the program to know it. The main advantage of OS is the dynamics libraries, but this libraries are position-independant compiled. As we can see in Listing 1.7

Listing 1.7. Call of a dynamic linked library: **printf** from stdio.

```
1   00011a54 <__sparc_get_pc_thunk.l7 >:
2      retl
3      add  %o7, %l7, %l7      ! arithmetical operation on %o7
4   00011a5c <__GI_printf >:
5      save  %sp, -104, %sp
6      sethi  %hi(0x17400), %l7
7      call  11a54 <__sparc_get_pc_thunk.l7 >
8      add  %l7, 0x190, %l7
9      ! 17590 <_fpadd_parts+0x214>
10     ! %l7 have the offset to localize
11     ! position-dependant object
12     ! Here it is the GOT (0x17590+0x11a64)
13     st  %i1, [ %fp + 0x48 ]
14     st  %i2, [ %fp + 0x4c ]
15     st  %i3, [ %fp + 0x50 ]
16     st  %i4, [ %fp + 0x54 ]
17     st  %i5, [ %fp + 0x58 ]
18     sethi  %hi(0), %g1
19     xor  %g1, 0xb4, %g1
20     ! add offset of the object to the GOT
21     add  %l7, %g1, %g1
22     ! loading the object from the  GOT
23     !    (segfault in case of PCX)
24     ld  [ %g1 ], %o0
25     add  %fp, 0x48, %o2
```

This same limitation is the reason of the use in userland only because the kernel use a lot of construction that saved the program counter on a spare register and jump using it (see Listing 1.8 for an example).

Listing 1.8. Little example of kernel code that do ugly stuff with the return pointer

```
1   kernelfun:
2       (...)
3       mov %i7,%13
4       (...)
5       add %g3,212,%12
6       jmpl %12,%o7 ;  call from
7       (...)
8       jmpl %13+8,%g0 ;  ret
9       nop
```

Arguing that not respecting the calling convention as [13] does is not correct. **gcc** use a lot of optimization that just save the program counter to another register, and position-independant code is clearly incompatible with this current implementation of the protection.

Solutions. To overcome the limitation we built scripting tools that detect code that break calling convention. In a baremetal program, restoring the calling convention is possible since it is possible to move and jump from the **%o7** register by restoring **%o7** just before the synthetic opcode **RET**.

The only limitation is the impossible use of position independant code.

The first solution is to use a specific instruction to read the real program counter. Since the attacker must disrupt the program flow before executing his own code. The program code could be changed to include this function to get the real program counter (_sparc_get_pc_thunk.l7).

Another solution is the change of the masking function to be compatible with classical PC arithmetic operation. We can see that the couple *add/sub* masking function is in fact like ASLR protection.

The other solution is obtained from the following observation: the attacker use the rewriting of the saved program counter located into the stack to disrupt the program flow. It is not an obligation to mask the register inside the pipeline. We could just mask the value when it go out of the pipeline to the memory (stack for instance) or when the register window slides (SPARC specifics). Hooking the **RESTORE** and **SAVE** opcode outside the trap handler, we could mask the %o7 register. On SPARC specifically, the value is saved or restored when the processor executes a window overflow or underflow trap. The hardware protection could be done by adding one instruction to each trap, and since the trap are in the trusted part of the code, it is secure. But it is SPARC specific because on x86, the saved value could be done in userland, since the value is pushed onto the stack directly. The same modification could be made in others architectures. For x86 and amd64, the **push/pop** operation just after the call could be hack in hardware to store encrypted value of the program counter.

4.3   Baremetal Program and Exploit

To test the protection and to try an exploit, we use a test program which test an user password and write a "ACCESS GRANTED" if the password is good. The user send the password thru a serial line using a function which did not check the length of the user password and save the value in a static allocated buffer onto the stack.

At each function, gcc reserves some space onto the stack in case of a window-overflow trap and for stack variables, done by the SAVE opcode.

The purpose of the shellcode is to exploit a buffer overflow to dump the program secret key, which is randomly generated, and to resume the normal operation. It could be done by generating a new stack with correct PC/SP register for doing a ROP or by executing a little shellcode which does exactly the same.

Using a shellcode, we are able to dump the secret key by using a classical buffer overflow.

Activating the PCX protection with 0xFFFFFFFF as the mask, we obtained a memory alignment error trap (see Listing 1.7) when using the buffer overflow vulnerability (%i7 is masked: 0xBFFFDF9B and %o7 (buffer address containing the shellcode) is not : 0x407FFE88) (Fig. 7).

```
IU in error mode (tt = 0x07, mem address not aligned)
   0x40002a4c: 81c3e008  retl     <check_me+68>

INS          LOCALS     OUTS       GLOBALS
0:  00000000  4000F800  00000000  00000000
1:  4000ECEC  4000ED40  66646464  00000000
2:  00000000  00000000  E8384C2D  00000001
3:  00000000  00000000  57C7E393  000000C9
4:  00000000  00000000  57C7DFAB  4000F8F0
5:  00000000  00000000  E839097D  00000003
6:  407FFF70  00000000  407FFF10  BFFF2A5B
7:  BFFFDF9B  00000000  407FFE88  00000000

psr: F30000E5   wim: 00000040   tbr: 40001060   y: 053F499F

pc:   40002A4C  retl
npc:  40002A50  nop
```

Fig. 7. Register after the modification of the return pointer: a trap error

5 Conclusions and Perspectives

Protection against control flow hijacking can be ascertained at hardware level, by simply "encoding" the vulnerable return addresses. We show how to implement this solution within a pipelined processor, and how to use it in software. There are multiple way to implement the same theory and we saw that changing the way the protection is implemented permit the use of an real OS with position independant code, which is not possible with the naive way of implementing the masking. In hardware, the overhead is limited, since only a couple of multiplexers and exclusive-or gates are added on the integer unit datapath. In particular, the fastest operation frequency is negligibly affected (a few percent is lost) but the maximum frequency of the processor is not changed since the critical path is in the cache module. The overhead during the software execution is equal to exactly 0: as a matter of fact, only some configuration is required when starting the new process, and afterwards, the countermeasure works transparently.

Our study is validated by a successful detection of an attack attempt on a bugged software code, which can otherwise be exploited by a buffer overrun.

However, some pitfalls are to be expected with relocatable code, as is the case when the protected code is load and run by an operating system. These issues can be dealt with at compile time and with a modified version of the initial protection.

Nonetheless, our study highlight that hardware-level protections are very attractive, in that they have no (or little) influence on the performances (this is the characteristic of hardware), while systematically achieving protection (no single function return address is pushed on the stack with being masked).

In the future, we envision to augment the platform with other protections, such as a code real-time integrity check, and a data tainting strategy to protect against data manipulation.

Acknowlegments. These developments have been supported by the Directorate General of Armaments and the General Directorate for Enterprises through the RAPID "CyberCPU" project. We thank the positive feedback from the French DGA/MI (Information Superiority) who helped improve this paper and our work in general.

References

1. Linux kernel remote buffer overflow vulnerabilities (2006). http://secwatch.org/advisories/1013445/
2. Openbsd ipv6 mbuf remote kernel buffer overflow (2007). http://www.securityfocus.com/archive/1/462728/30/0/threaded
3. Microsoft security bulletin ms08-067 – critical (2008). http://www.microsoft.com/technet/security/Bulletin/MS08-067.mspx
4. Microsoft windows tcp/ip igmp mld remote buffer overflow vulnerability (2008). http://www.securityfocus.com/bid/27100
5. Microsoft security advisory (975191): Vulnerabilities in the ftp service ininternet information services (2009). http://www.microsoft.com/technet/security/advisory/975191.mspx
6. Microsoft security advisory (975497): Vulnerabilities in smb could allow remotecode execution (2009). http://www.microsoft.com/technet/security/advisory/975497.mspx
7. Bletsch, T., Jiang, X., Freeh, V.W., Liang, Z.: Jump-oriented programming: a new class of code-reuse attack. In: Proceedings of the 6th ACM Symposium on Information, Computerand Communications Security, pp. 30–40. ACM (2011)

8. Buchanan, E., Roemer, R., Shacham, H., Savage, S.: When good instructions go bad: Generalizing return-orientedprogramming to risc. In: Proceedings of the 15th ACM Conference on Computer and Communications Security, pp. 27–38. ACM (2008)

9. Cowan, C., Calton, P., Maier, D., Walpole, J., Bakke, P., Beattie, S., Grier, A., Wagle, P., Zhang, Q., Hinton, H.: Stackguard: Automatic adaptive detection and prevention of buffer-overflow attacks. Usenix Secur. **98**, 63–78 (1998)

10. Cowan, C., Beattie, S., Johansen, J., Wagle, P.: Pointguard TM: protecting pointers from buffer overflow vulnerabilities. In: Proceedings of the 12th Conference on USENIX SecuritySymposium, vol. 12, pp. 91–104 (2003)

11. Dalton, M., Kannan, H., Kozyrakis, C.: Real-world buffer overflow protection for userspace and kernelspace. In: USENIX Security Symposium, pp. 395–410 (2008)

12. Frantzen, M., Shuey, M.: Stackghost: Hardware facilitated stack protection. In: USENIX Security Symposium, vol. 112 (2001)

13. Papadogiannakis, A., Loutsis, L., Papaefstathiou, V., Ioannidis, S.: Asist: Architectural support for instruction set randomization. In: Proceedings of the 2013 ACM SIGSAC conference on Computer & Communications Security, pp. 981–992. ACM (2013)

14. Pincus, J., Baker, B.: Beyond stack smashing: Recent advances in exploiting buffer overruns. Secur. Priv. IEEE **2**(4), 20–27 (2004)

15. Shacham, H., Page, M., Pfaff, B., Goh, E.J., Modadugu, N., Boneh, D.: On the effectiveness of address-space randomization. In: Proceedings of the 11th ACM Conference on Computer and Communications Security, pp. 298–307. ACM (2004)

Public-Key Cryptography

Hierarchical Identities from Group Signatures and Pseudonymous Signatures

Julien Bringer[1], Hervé Chabanne[1,2,3(✉)], Roch Lescuyer[1], and Alain Patey[1,2,3]

[1] Morpho, 11 Boulevard Galliéni, 92130 Issy-les-Moulineaux, France
herve.chabanne@morpho.com
[2] Télécom ParisTech, Identity and Security Alliance (The Morpho and Télécom ParisTech Research Center), Paris, France
[3] Identity and Security Alliance (The Morpho and Télécom ParisTech Research Center), Paris, France

Abstract. The use of group signatures has been widely suggested for authentication with minimum disclosure of information. In this paper, we consider an identity management system, where users can access several group signatures, managed by different authorities. These authorities follow a hierarchy that impacts key issuing and revocation, but we still enforce that anonymity within a group is preserved towards authorities of other groups. We thus define *cross-unlinkable hierarchical group signatures*, for which we give a generic instantiation based on VLR group signatures and domain-specific pseudonymous signatures.

1 Introduction

Group signatures [13] enable registered users to anonymously sign on behalf of a group. Dynamic group signature schemes allow for revocation, *i.e.* for preventing some previously registered users from further issuing group signatures. In this paper, we focus on *verifier-local* revocation (VLR) [5], in which the revocation is dealt with using revocation lists. In the VLR setting, revocation does not impact the actions of the signers but only the ones of the signature verifiers. In the VLR case, a single authority, called the *group manager*, deals with key issuing, user revocation and signature opening. VLR Group signatures have been, *e.g.*, considered for application to anonymous authentication [10].

In this paper, we consider a scenario where users have access to several groups, equipped with group signatures, that have some dependencies between them: the set $\mathcal{G}$ of these groups is partially ordered and can be represented as a tree. When one wants to apply for new signing keys in a group $\mathcal{G}_l$, one has to own valid signing keys for the parent group $\mathcal{G}_k$ in the tree $\mathcal{G}$. This organization also requires that it should be possible to revoke automatically across different groups. To this aim, the new signing key is derived from the key of the same member for $\mathcal{G}_k$ in order to maintain a link. One important issue in our model is then to ensure the privacy of this link.

P.Y.A. Ryan et al. (Eds.): Kahn Festschrift, LNCS 9100, pp. 457–469, 2016.
DOI: 10.1007/978-3-662-49301-4_28

This scenario and the associated security properties are particularly adapted to identity management systems. In this setting, a user owns several identities derived from a strong identity (*e.g.,* the national identity) while maintaining privacy and unlinkability between the different identities, even towards the providers of the other identities.

We address this problem of derivation of group signatures keys from other group signature keys with privacy properties in mind. In particular we want to ensure that a given group manager cannot retrieve – except in case of revocations – the link between a signature in his group and a signature, issued by the same user, in any of his children groups. Our goal is to put in parallel several instances of VLR group signatures while fulfilling the following additional requirements.

- A user registered into a given group should be able to sign anonymously on behalf of this group.
- When a user asks for registering to a new group, he has to prove that he can sign on behalf of the parent group.
- The derivation process should be compatible with a revocation process that echoes downwards, *i.e.* when a user i is revoked from a given group $\mathcal{G}_l$, he must also be revoked from all the groups that are below $\mathcal{G}_l$ in the tree $\mathcal{G}$.
- Despite these revocation and derivation processes, only the manager of a given group $\mathcal{G}_l$ (and the signer) can learn information on the signer when looking at a signature for the group $\mathcal{G}_l$, provided this signer is not revoked from $\mathcal{G}_l$. Particularly, the other group managers learn nothing more than any observer and thus cannot link the signer to the members of their groups. This property, that we name *Cross-Unlinkability*, is an essential feature of our proposal.

For instance, consider the group tree described in Fig. 1. We assume that a science faculty sets up a system using groups signatures, used for instance for access control. In this example, applying for a key for the BioInformatics Team requires to previously own a key for the Computer Science Department. We also wish that, when one signs on behalf of, *e.g.,* the Mechanics Department, anonymity of the signer is guaranteed against the managers of all other groups, including the managers of the parent group (Science Faculty), the children groups (Fluid Dynamics and Solid Mechanics) or the sibling groups (Computer Science Dept.).

Domain-specific pseudonymous signatures (DSPS) have recently been introduced by Bender *et al.* [3]. They can be seen as a variant of VLR group signatures with some anonymity relaxations. In the DSPS setting, signatures depend on a domain (*e.g.,* a service to which the user authenticates). Each registered user holds a unique pseudonym per domain that is required to check every signature he issues. Consequently, signatures of the same user for the same domain are linkable using pseudonyms. Anonymity properties however guarantee that signatures of the same user for different domains are unlinkable (except for the issuing authority).

We suggest to use DSPS for the derivation process of our hierarchical group signatures. The "domain" for which a signature is issued is the edge of the group

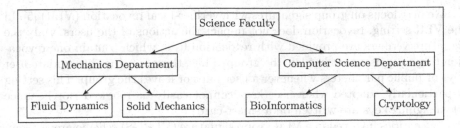

Fig. 1. An example of a group tree $\mathcal{G}$

tree related to the current key derivation. Since derivation is done at most once per edge, linkability using pseudonyms is not an issue in our scheme.

In the process described in this chapter, we need to use a VLR group signature scheme and a DSPS scheme that use the same parameters. We can for instance use the schemes described in [19, Part1] and introduced in [6,9,11,14].

Related works. Other settings with several parallel group signatures have already been introduced. Multi-group signatures [1,4] enable a user to sign on behalf of either a single group or several groups to which he belongs. The notion of hierarchy between group signatures has been introduced in [18], where having a key for an upper group allows to sign on behalf of lower groups. Hierarchical Group Signatures [21] define a group organization that is close to ours: the managers are organized in a tree structure, but all of them do not manage signers, some only manage groups of managers; anonymity and (a weaker notion of) unlinkability between the users of different groups are considered but there is no possibility of revocation. Attribute-based group signatures [16,17], anonymous proxy signatures [15] and delegatable anonymous credentials [2] are also related notions. None of the above constructions however considers at the same time group hierarchy, unlinkability across the groups and revocation through the groups.

Outline of the paper. This paper expands on our precedent works [7,8,19], where VLR group signatures with Backward Unlinkability are used for derivation, instead of DSPS [6]. In Sect. 2 we introduce the cryptographic building blocks, namely VLR group signatures and domain-specific pseudonymous signatures. Then in Sect. 3 we present our generic construction of cross-unlinkable hierarchical group signatures.

2   VLR Group Signatures and Domain-Specific Pseudonymous Signatures

2.1   VLR Group Signatures

Group signatures [13] enable registered users to sign on behalf of a group while remaining anonymous within the group, except towards an opening authority. In the case of dynamic group signatures, users can join or leave the group at any time, there are consequently procedures to revoke users.

We here focus on group signatures with verifier-local revocation (VLR) [5]. In the VLR setting, revocation does not impact the actions of the users. Only the signature verifiers are provided with revocation lists, which contain one revocation token per user that has left the group. Thus, there is no need to update user keys or public parameters whenever a user joins or leaves the group. This setting is particularly adapted when user keys cannot easily be renewed (for instance when signing keys are written on a smart-card).

The entities involved in a VLR group signature (VLRGS) scheme are: a group manager $\mathcal{GM}$ that deals with key issuing and signature opening, a set $\mathcal{U}$ of users that possess keys to sign messages on behalf of the group, and a set $\mathcal{V}$ of verifiers that are given the group public parameters to check signatures. A VLR group signature scheme consists of the following algorithms[1]:

KeyGen(1^λ), run by $\mathcal{GM}$, outputs the public parameters gpk, the master secret key msk and an empty revocation list RL;

Join(gpk) $\leftrightarrow$ Issue(gpk, msk), run by, resp., a user i applying to join the group and $\mathcal{GM}$, outputs, resp. user i's secret key sk$_i$ and a revocation token rt$_i$;

Sign(gpk, sk$_i$, m), run by a user i, outputs a signature σ on m;

Verify(gpk, m, σ, RL), run by a verifier, outputs a decision d on the validity of the signature and the non-revocation of its signer ($d \in \{\text{valid}, \text{invalid}\}$);

Revoke(gpk, RL, rt$_i$), run by $\mathcal{GM}$, outputs an updated revocation list RL, preventing user i from further making valid signatures.

An implicit tracing algorithm Open [5] can be run by the GM, applying the revocation check part of the Verify algorithm using the revocation tokens of every registered user. Namely, to open a valid signature σ on a message m: for all $i \in \mathcal{U}$, $\mathcal{GM}$ computes RL = Revoke(gpk, $\{\}$, rt$_i$) and $d \leftarrow$ Verify(gpk, m, σ, RL); if $d = \text{invalid}$, then i is designated as the signer. We now define the security requirements that are awaited from such a scheme.

Correctness. The scheme is *correct* if every signature created by an unrevoked member is verified as valid and every signature made by a revoked user is verified as invalid. Formally, a scheme is correct if for all large enough λ, all (gpk, msk, RL) = KeyGen(1^λ), all sk$_i$ $\leftarrow$ Join(gpk) $\leftrightarrow$ Issue(gpk, msk) $\rightarrow$ rt$_i$, all $m \in \{0,1\}^*$, all σ = Sign(gpk, sk$_i$, m), all RL $\ni$ rt$_i$, Verify(gpk, m, σ, $\{\}$)= valid and Verify(gpk, m, σ, RL) = invalid.

Selfless-Anonymity. A group signature is selfless-anonymous if no one, except the signer and the group manager, is able to learn information about the signer of a given signature.

Selfless-Anonymity$_{\mathcal{A}}^{\text{VLRGS}}(\lambda)$

- (gpk, msk) $\leftarrow$ VLRGS.KeyGen(1^λ) ; $\mathcal{HU}, \mathcal{CU}, \mathcal{CH} \leftarrow \{\}$; $b \xleftarrow{\$} \{0,1\}$

---

[1] Sometimes, additional algorithms to verify openings are suggested, *e.g.*, the DProve and DVerify algorithms of [11,14].

- $\mathcal{O} \leftarrow \{\texttt{AddHonestUser}(\cdot), \texttt{Corrupt}(\cdot), \texttt{AddCorruptedUser}(\cdot, \cdot), \texttt{Revoke}(\cdot, 0),$
    $\texttt{Open}(\cdot, 0, \cdot, \cdot), \texttt{GSSign}(\cdot, 0, \cdot), \texttt{SAChallenge}(b, \cdot, \cdot, \cdot, \cdot)\}$
- $b' \leftarrow A^{\mathcal{O}}(\text{gpk})$
- Return 1 if $b' == b$, and return 0 otherwise.

A VLR-GS scheme achieves *selfless-anonymous* if the probability for a polynomial adversary $\mathcal{A}$ to win the Selfless-Anonymity$_{\mathcal{A}}^{\text{VLRGS}}$ game is negligible.

Traceability. A group signature is *traceable* if the group manager is able to open any valid signature.

Traceability$_{\mathcal{A}}^{\text{VLRGS}}(\lambda)$

- $(\text{gpk}, \text{msk}) \leftarrow \text{VLRGS.KeyGen}(1^{\lambda})$; $\mathcal{D}, \mathcal{HU}, \mathcal{CU}, \mathcal{CH} \leftarrow \{\}$; $b \xleftarrow{\$} \{0, 1\}$
- $\mathcal{O} \leftarrow \{\texttt{AddHonestUser}(\cdot), \texttt{CorruptUser}(\cdot), \texttt{AddCorruptedUser}(\cdot, \cdot) \texttt{Revoke}(\cdot, 0),$
    $\texttt{Open}(\cdot, 0, \cdot, \cdot), \texttt{GSSign}(\cdot, 0, \cdot)\}$
- $(m^*, \sigma^*) \leftarrow A^{\mathcal{O}}(\text{gpk})$
- Return 1 if $\texttt{Verify}(\text{gpk}, m^*, \sigma^*, \{\text{rt}_i \mid i \in \mathcal{CU} \cup \mathcal{HU}\})$, and return 0 otherwise.

A VLR-GS scheme achieves *traceability* if the probability for a polynomial adversary $\mathcal{A}$ to win the Traceability$_{\mathcal{A}}^{\text{VLRGS}}$ game is negligible.

Exculpability. A group signature is exculpable if no one, including the group manager, is able to sign on behalf of an honest user.

Exculpability$_{\mathcal{A}}^{\text{VLRGS}}(\lambda)$

- $(\text{gpk}, \text{msk}) \leftarrow \text{VLRGS.KeyGen}(1^{\lambda})$; $\mathcal{D}, \mathcal{HU}, \mathcal{CU}, \mathcal{CH} \leftarrow \{\}$; $b \xleftarrow{\$} \{0, 1\}$
- $\mathcal{O} \leftarrow \{\texttt{SendToUser}(\cdot), \texttt{CorruptUser}(\cdot), \texttt{Sign}(\cdot, \cdot, \cdot)\}$
- $(m^*, \sigma^*, i^*) \leftarrow A^{\mathcal{O}}(\text{gpk}, \text{msk})$
- Return 1 if $i^* \in \mathcal{HU}$, m^* was not queried, $\texttt{Verify}(\text{gpk}, m^*, \sigma^*, \{\}) = \texttt{valid}$,
    $\texttt{Verify}(\text{gpk}, m^*, \sigma^*, \{\text{rt}_{i^*}\}) = \texttt{invalid}$, and return 0 otherwise.

A VLR-GS scheme achieves *exculpability* if the probability for a polynomial adversary $\mathcal{A}$ to win the Exculpability$_{\mathcal{A}}^{\text{VLRGS}}$ game is negligible.

2.2   Domain-Specific Pseudonymous Signatures

Domain-specific pseudonymous signatures have been introduced by Bender *et al.* in [3] as a tool to extend the *Restricted Identification* protocol [12] that can be run between an e-ID document and a service provider. Domain-specific pseudonymous signatures relax the anonymity properties of group signatures. Indeed, there are several *domains* for which a user can sign. For each domain, a user owns a unique pseudonym, derived from his secret key and some domain parameters. The signatures issued by a user for a domain come with the related pseudonym. The pseudonym enables to link the signatures. In the sequel we summarize the model for domain-specific pseudonymous signatures of [6], that corrects the models of [3,9].

A *dynamic domain-specific pseudonymous signature scheme* is given by an issuing authority IA, a set of users $\mathcal{U}$, a set of domains $\mathcal{D}$, and the functionalities $\{\texttt{KeyGen}, \texttt{DomainKeyGen}, \texttt{Join}, \texttt{Issue}, \texttt{NymGen}, \texttt{Sign}, \texttt{Verify}, \texttt{DomainRevoke}, \texttt{Revoke}\}$ as described below. By convention, users are enumerated here with indices $i \in \mathbb{N}$ and domains with indices $j \in \mathbb{N}$.

KeyGen. On input a security parameter λ, this algorithm computes global parameters gpk and an issuing secret key msk. The sets $\mathcal{U}$ and $\mathcal{D}$ are initially empty. The global parameters gpk are implicitly given to all algorithms, if not explicitly specified. We note $(\text{gpk}, \text{msk}) \leftarrow \text{KeyGen}(1^\lambda)$.

DomainKeyGen. On input the global parameters gpk and a domain $j \in \mathcal{D}$, this algorithm outputs a public key dpk_j for j. Together with the creation of a public key, an empty revocation list RL_j associated to this domain j is created. We note $(\text{dpk}_j, RL_j) \leftarrow \text{DomainKeyGen}(\text{gpk}, j)$.

Join $\leftrightarrow$ Issue. This protocol involves a user $i \in \mathcal{U}$ and the issuing authority IA. Join takes as input the global parameters gpk. Issue takes as input the global parameters gpk and the issuing secret key isk. At the end of the protocol, the user i gets a secret key usk_i and the issuing authority IA gets a revocation token rt_i. We note $\text{usk}_i \leftarrow \text{Join}(\text{gpk}) \leftrightarrow \text{Issue}(\text{gpk}, \text{isk}) \rightarrow \text{rt}_i$.

NymGen. On input the global parameters gpk, a public key dpk_j for a domain $j \in \mathcal{D}$ and a secret key usk_i of a user $i \in \mathcal{U}$, this *deterministic* algorithm outputs a pseudonym nym_{ij} for the user i usable in the domain j. We note $\text{nym}_{ij} \leftarrow \text{NymGen}(\text{gpk}, \text{dpk}_j, \text{usk}_i)$.

Sign. On input the global parameters gpk, a public key dpk_j of a domain $j \in \mathcal{D}$, a user secret key usk_i of a user $i \in \mathcal{U}$, a pseudonym nym_{ij} for the user i and the domain j and a message $m \in \{0,1\}^*$, this algorithm outputs a signature σ. We note $\sigma \leftarrow \text{Sign}(\text{gpk}, \text{dpk}_j, \text{usk}_i, \text{nym}_{ij}, m)$.

Verify. On input the global parameters gpk, a public key dpk_j of a domain $j \in \mathcal{D}$, a pseudonym nym_{ij}, a message $m \in \{0,1\}^*$, a signature σ and the revocation list RL_j of the domain j, this algorithm outputs a decision $d \in \{\text{accept}, \text{reject}\}$. We note $d \leftarrow \text{Verify}(\text{gpk}, \text{dpk}_j, \text{nym}_{ij}, m, \sigma, RL_j)$.

DomainRevoke. On input the global parameters gpk, a public key dpk_j of a domain $j \in \mathcal{D}$, a revocation token rt_i of a user $i \in \mathcal{U}$ and the revocation list RL_j of the domain j, this algorithm outputs an updated revocation list RL_j'. We note $RL_j' \leftarrow \text{DomainRevoke}(\text{gpk}, \text{dpk}_j, \text{rt}_i, RL_j)$.

We consider the dynamic case where both users and domains may be added to the system. Users might also be revoked. Moreover, the global revocation may concern all the domains at a given point, or a subset of them. A global revocation protocol enabling to revoke the user i from every domain is implicit here: it suffices to publish rt_i. Using rt_i and public parameters, anyone can revoke user i, even for domains that will be added later. Pseudonyms are deterministic. This implies the existence of an implicit Link algorithm to link signatures inside a specific domain. On input a domain public key dpk and two triples (nym, m, σ) and $(\text{nym}', m', \sigma')$, this algorithm outputs 1 if $\text{nym} = \text{nym}'$ and outputs 0 otherwise. This also gives implicit procedures for the service providers to put the users on a white list or a black list, without invoking the Revoke or DomainRevoke algorithms: it suffices to publish the pseudonym of the concerned user.

Seclusiveness. Informally, a DSPS scheme achieves seclusiveness if, by similarity with the traceability property of the group signatures, an adversary $\mathcal{A}$ is unable to forge a valid signature that cannot "trace" to a valid user. In the group signature case, there is an opening algorithm, which enables to check if a valid user produced a given signature. However, there is no opening here, so one might ask how to define "tracing" users. Nevertheless, the management of the revocation tokens allows to correctly phrase the gain condition, as in VLR group signatures [5], providing that we take into account the presence of the pseudonyms. At the end of the game, we revoke all users on the domain supplied by the adversary. If the signature is still valid, then the adversary has won the game. Indeed, in this case, the signature does not involve any existing user. (This is an analogue of "the opener cannot conclude" in the group signature case).

Seclusiveness$_A^{DSPS}(\lambda)$

- $(\mathbf{gpk}, \mathbf{isk}) \leftarrow \mathrm{DSPS.KeyGen}(1^\lambda)$; $\mathcal{D}, \mathcal{HU}, \mathcal{CU} \leftarrow \{\}$
- $\mathcal{O} \leftarrow \{\mathtt{AddDomain}(\cdot), \mathtt{AddUser}(\cdot), \mathtt{CorruptUser}(\cdot), \mathtt{UserSecretKey}(\cdot), \mathtt{Sign}(\cdot, \cdot, \cdot),$
    $\mathtt{ReadRegistrationTable}(\cdot), \mathtt{SendToIssuer}(\cdot, \cdot)\}$
- $(\mathrm{dpk}_*, \mathrm{nym}_*, m_*, \sigma_*) \leftarrow A^{\mathcal{O}}(\mathbf{gpk})$
- Find $j \in \mathcal{D}$ such that $\mathrm{dpk}_* := \mathbf{dpk}[j]$. If no match is found, then return 0.
- Return 1 if for all $i \in \mathcal{U}$, either $\mathbf{rt}[i] = \perp$ or $\mathrm{DSPS.Verify}(\mathbf{gpk}, \mathrm{dpk}_*, \mathrm{nym}_*, m_*, \sigma_*,$
    $RL)=$ accept where $RL := \mathrm{DSPS.DomainRevoke}(\mathbf{gpk}, \mathrm{dpk}_*, aux, \mathbf{RL}[j])$ and aux
    $:= \mathrm{DSPS.Revoke}(\mathbf{gpk}, \mathbf{rt}[i], \{\mathrm{dpk}_*\}).$

A DSPS scheme achieves *seclusiveness* if the probability for a polynomial adversary A to win the Seclusiveness$_A^{DSPS}$ game is negligible.

Unforgeability. Informally, we want that a corrupted authority and corrupted owners of the domains cannot sign on behalf of an honest user.

Unforgeability$_A^{DSPS}(\lambda)$

- $(\mathbf{gpk}, \mathbf{isk}) \leftarrow \mathrm{DSPS.KeyGen}(1^\lambda)$; $\mathcal{D}, \mathcal{HU}, \mathcal{CU} \leftarrow \{\}$
- $\mathcal{O} \leftarrow \{\mathtt{AddDomain}(\cdot), \mathtt{WriteRegistrationTable}(\cdot, \cdot), \mathtt{Sign}(\cdot, \cdot, \cdot), \mathtt{SendToUser}(\cdot, \cdot)\}$
- $(\mathrm{dpk}_*, \mathrm{nym}_*, m_*, \sigma_*) \leftarrow A^{\mathcal{O}}(\mathbf{gpk}, \mathbf{isk})$
- Return 1 if all the following statements hold.
  - There exists $j \in \mathcal{D}$ such that $\mathrm{dpk}_* = \mathbf{dpk}[j]$
  - There exists $i \in \mathcal{HU}$ such that $\mathrm{nym}_* = \mathbf{nym}[i][j]$, $\mathbf{usk}[i] \neq \perp$ and $\mathbf{rt}[i] \neq \perp$
  - $m_* \notin \mathbf{\Sigma}[(i,j)]$
  - $\mathrm{DSPS.Verify}(\mathbf{gpk}, \mathrm{dpk}_*, \mathrm{nym}_*, m_*, \sigma_*, \{\}) =$ accept
  - $\mathrm{DSPS.Verify}(\mathbf{gpk}, \mathrm{dpk}_*, \mathrm{nym}_*, m_*, \sigma_*, L) =$ reject
    where $L := \mathtt{DomainRevoke}(\mathbf{gpk}, \mathrm{dpk}_*, \mathrm{DSPS.Revoke}(\mathbf{gpk}, \mathbf{rt}[i], \{\mathrm{dpk}_*\}), \{\})$

A DSPS scheme achieves *unforgeability* if the probability for a polynomial adversary A to win the Unforgeability$_A^{DSPS}$ game is negligible.

Cross-domain anonymity. Informally, a DSPS scheme achieves cross-domain anonymity if an adversary is not able to link users across domains. We formalize this intuition thanks to a *left-or-right* challenge oracle. Given two users i_0 and i_1 and two domains j_A and j_B, the challenger picks two bits $b_A, b_B \in \{0, 1\}$ and returns $(\mathrm{nym}_0, \mathrm{nym}_1)$ where nym_0 is the pseudonym of i_{b_A} for the first domain and nym_1 the pseudonym of i_{b_B} for the second domain. The adversary wins if he correctly guesses the bit $(b_A == b_B)$, in other words if he correctly guesses that underlying users are the same user or not.

Cross-Domain-Anonymity$_{\mathcal{A}}^{\text{DSPS}}(\lambda)$

- $(\text{gpk}, \text{isk}) \leftarrow \text{DSPS.KeyGen}(1^{\lambda})$; $\mathcal{D}, \mathcal{HU}, \mathcal{CU}, \mathcal{CH} \leftarrow \{\}$; $b_A, b_B \xleftarrow{\$} \{0, 1\}$
- $\mathcal{O} \leftarrow \{\text{AddDomain}(\cdot), \text{AddUser}(\cdot), \text{CorruptUser}(\cdot), \text{UserSecretKey}(\cdot), \text{Revoke}(\cdot, \cdot),$
    $\text{DomainRevoke}(\cdot, \cdot), \text{Nym}(\cdot, \cdot), \text{NymDomain}(\cdot), \text{NymSign}(\cdot, \cdot, \cdot), \text{SendToIssuer}(\cdot, \cdot),$
    $\text{CDChallenge}(b_A, b_B, \cdot, \cdot, \cdot, \cdot)\}$
- $b' \leftarrow \mathcal{A}^{\mathcal{O}}(\text{gpk})$
- Return 1 if $b' == (b_A == b_B)$, and return 0 otherwise.

A DSPS scheme achieves *cross-domain anonymity* if the probability for a polynomial adversary $\mathcal{A}$ to win the Cross-Domain-Anonymity$_{\mathcal{A}}^{\text{DSPS}}$ game is negligible[23].

3   A Model and a Generic Construction for Cross-Unlinkable Hierarchical Group Signatures

In this section, we describe our model for cross-unlinkable hierarchical group signatures (Sect. 3.1) and the security requirements we expect from such schemes, in particular the *cross-unlinkability* property (Sect. 3.2). We then describe a generic protocol fitting this model, based on group signatures and pseudonymous signatures (Sect. 3.3).

3.1   Our Model

We now describe our model for cross-unlinkable hierarchical group signatures (CUHGS). The involved entities are: a set $\mathcal{G}$ of group managers (organized as a tree), a set $\mathcal{U}$ of users, and a set $\mathcal{V}$ of verifiers. We denote by $k \dashv l$ the fact that a group $\mathcal{G}_k$ is a parent of a group $\mathcal{G}_l$ in $\mathcal{G}$. A CUHGS scheme is composed of the following procedures.

KeyGen$(1^{\lambda}, \mathcal{G})$. On input a security parameter λ and a group tree $\mathcal{G}$, this algorithm run by all $\mathcal{GM}_l \in \mathcal{G}$, outputs, for every group $\mathcal{G}_l \in \mathcal{G}$ public parameters gpk^l, a master secret key msk^l, an empty revocation list RL^l and C_l empty revocation lists $(\text{RL}^{l \dashv m})_{l \dashv m}$, where $C_l := |\{m \mid l \dashv m\}|$ is the number of children of l in $\mathcal{G}$. We note $(\text{gpk}^l, \text{msk}^l, \text{RL}^l, (\text{RL}^{l \dashv m})_{l \dashv m})_{\mathcal{G}_l \in \mathcal{G}} \leftarrow \text{KeyGen}(1^{\lambda}, \mathcal{G})$.

Join$(\text{gpk}^0) \leftrightarrow$ Issue$(\text{gpk}^0, \text{msk}^0)$. This is an interactive protocol between the group manager $\mathcal{GM}_0$ and a user i. Group manager $\mathcal{GM}_0$ inputs his secret key msk^0 and the public parameters gpk^0, user i inputs the public parameters. In the end, i outputs a secret key sk_i^0 for the group signature of $\mathcal{G}_0$. Group manager $\mathcal{GM}_0$ gets a revocation token rt_i^0. We note

$$\text{sk}_i^0 \leftarrow \text{Join}(\text{gpk}^0) \leftrightarrow \text{Issue}(\text{gpk}^0, \text{msk}^0) \rightarrow \text{rt}_i^0.$$

---

[2] The SendToIssuer oracle might be surprising here. But, contrary to group signatures, the issuing authority IA is not corrupted. This assumption is minimal since the IA may trace all honest users. Hence we must give the adversary the ability to interact as a corrupted user with the honest issuer.

[3] Our model takes into account the case where pseudonyms leak from the network. To this aim, the NymDomain oracle gives the adversary a collection of pseudonyms.

$\mathtt{DeriveUser}(\mathtt{gpk}^k, \mathtt{gpk}^l, \mathtt{sk}_i^k) \leftrightarrow \mathtt{DeriveGM}(\mathtt{gpk}^k, \mathtt{RL}^{k\dashv l}, \mathtt{gpk}^l, \mathtt{msk}^l)$ is an interactive protocol between a group manager $\mathcal{GM}_l$ and a user i, asking for a group signature key for the group $\mathcal{G}_l$, such that $k \dashv l$. Group manager $\mathcal{GM}_l$ inputs his secret key $\mathtt{msk}^l$ and the public parameters $\mathtt{gpk}^k, \mathtt{gpk}^l, \mathtt{RL}^{k\dashv l}$, user i inputs the public parameters and his secret key $\mathtt{sk}_i^k$ for the parent group $\mathcal{G}_k$ of $\mathcal{G}_l$ in $\mathcal{G}$. At the end, if i successfully proves to $\mathcal{GM}_l$ that he is a non revoked member of $\mathcal{G}_k$, i outputs a secret key $\mathtt{sk}_i^l$ for the group signature of $\mathcal{G}_l$. Group manager $\mathcal{GM}_l$ gets the revocation token $\mathtt{rt}_i^l$ of i and a registration information $\mathtt{reg}_i^l$ (that can be used for revocation, see below). We note

$$\mathtt{sk}_i^l \leftarrow \mathtt{DeriveUser}(\mathtt{gpk}^k, \mathtt{gpk}^l, \mathtt{sk}_i^k) \leftrightarrow$$
$$\mathtt{DeriveGM}(\mathtt{gpk}^k, \mathtt{RL}^{k\dashv l}, \mathtt{gpk}^l, \mathtt{msk}^l) \rightarrow (\mathtt{rt}_i^l, \mathtt{reg}_i^l).$$

$\mathtt{Sign}(\mathtt{gpk}^l, m, \mathtt{sk}_i^l)$. This algorithm, run by a user i, takes as inputs the public parameters $\mathtt{gpk}^l$, i's secret $\mathtt{sk}_i^l$ for group $\mathcal{G}_l$ and a message m. It outputs a signature σ. We note $\sigma \leftarrow \mathtt{Sign}(\mathtt{gpk}^l, m, \mathtt{sk}_i^l)$.

$\mathtt{Verify}(\mathtt{gpk}^l, \sigma, m, \mathtt{RL}^l)$. This algorithm, run by a verifier, takes as input a message m, a signature σ, the revocation list $\mathtt{RL}^l$ for group $\mathcal{G}_l$ and the public parameters $\mathtt{gpk}^l$. It checks if the message has been signed by a member of group $\mathcal{G}_l$ that is not revoked, without revealing the signer's identity. The possible outputs are $\mathtt{valid}$ and $\mathtt{invalid}$. We note $d \leftarrow \mathtt{Verify}(\mathtt{gpk}^l, \sigma, m, \mathtt{RL}^l)$.

$\mathtt{Revoke}(\mathtt{gpk}^l, \mathtt{rt}_i^l, \mathtt{RL}^l, (\mathtt{RL}^{l\dashv m})_{l\dashv m})$. This recursive algorithm is run by the group manager $\mathcal{GM}_l$ of $\mathcal{G}_l$ who wants to revoke a member i of $\mathcal{G}_l$. It takes as input the revocation token of user i and the revocation lists maintained by $\mathcal{GM}_l$. User i is also recursively globally revoked from the whole subtree of $\mathcal{G}$ whose root is $\mathcal{G}_l$. It outputs updated revocation lists. We note

$$(\mathtt{RL}^l, (\mathtt{RL}^{l\dashv m})_{l\dashv m}) \leftarrow \mathtt{Revoke}(\mathtt{gpk}^l, \mathtt{rt}_i^l, \mathtt{RL}^l, (\mathtt{RL}^{l\dashv m})_{l\dashv m}).$$

The upwards revocation algorithm $\mathtt{UpRevoke}$ is there to give the possibility for a group manager to report to the parent group manager that a user i has been revoked. For this algorithm to be launched, $\mathcal{GM}_l$ has to provide $\mathcal{GM}_k$ with the registration information $\mathtt{reg}_i^l$ obtained when user i joined $\mathcal{G}_l$. After executing $\mathtt{UpRevoke}$, $\mathcal{GM}_k$ is able, if he wishes, to revoke i from $\mathcal{G}_k$ using the $\mathtt{Revoke}$ algorithm.

$\mathtt{UpRevoke}(\mathtt{reg}_i^l, (\mathtt{rt}_i^l)_{i \in \mathcal{G}_k})$. This algorithm, run by $\mathcal{GM}_k$, enables to retrieve the identity of a misbehaving user i signaled by $\mathcal{GM}_l$. Group manager $\mathcal{GM}_k$ gets the identity of user i. We note $i \leftarrow \mathtt{UpRevoke}(\mathtt{reg}_i^l, (\mathtt{rt}_i^l)_{i \in \mathcal{G}_k})$.

As for usual VLR group signatures, an opening procedure is implicit, independently of the actual construction:

$\mathtt{Open}(\mathtt{gpk}^l, \{\mathtt{rt}_i^l\}_{i \in \mathcal{G}_l}, \sigma, m)$
   1: If $\mathtt{Verify}(\mathtt{gpk}^l, \sigma, m, \{\}) = \mathtt{invalid}$, abort.
   2: Return $\{i \mid \mathtt{Verify}(\mathtt{gpk}^l, \sigma, m, \{\mathtt{rt}_i^l\}) = \mathtt{invalid}\}$.

3.2 Security Requirements

We here describe the security properties that we expect from cross-unlinkable group signatures. Correctness is the same property as in the mono-group setting. Traceability and exculpability are similar to the namesake properties of the VLR group signatures described in Sect. 2. Cross-Unlinkability strengthens Selfless-Anonymity by enforcing that anonymity should even hold towards other group managers.

Correctness. The scheme is correct if every signature created by a non revoked member is verified as valid and every signature made by a revoked user is verified as invalid. We also include the fact that incorrect openings should be disputable while correct openings should not. Formally, it is *correct* if for all large enough λ, all group trees $\mathcal{G}$, all $(\text{gpk}^l, \text{msk}^l, \text{RL}^l, (\text{RL}^{l \dashv m})_{l \dashv m})_{\mathcal{G}_l \in \mathcal{G}} = \text{KeyGen}(1^\lambda, \mathcal{G})$, all $\mathcal{G}_l \in \mathcal{G}$, all $(\text{sk}_i^l, \text{rt}_i^l)$ obtained using honest Join $\leftrightarrow$ Issue and DeriveUser $\leftrightarrow$ DeriveGM executions, all $m \in \{0,1\}^*$, all $\sigma = \text{Sign}(\text{gpk}^l, m, \text{sk}_i^l)$, all $\text{RL}^l \ni \text{rt}_i^l$, $\text{Verify}(\text{gpk}^l, \sigma, m, \{\}) = \text{valid}$ and $\text{Verify}(\text{gpk}^l, \sigma, m, \text{RL}^l) = \text{invalid}$.

Cross-Unlinkability. The Cross-Unlinkability property is an extension of the Selfless-Anonymity property to the hierarchical group setting. The CU property ensures that a signature issued for the group $\mathcal{G}_l$ remains anonymous even for the GMs of other groups, for instance the parent or the sibling groups of $\mathcal{G}_l$ in $\mathcal{G}$. We also insist on the fact that, in case of a revocation, if $\mathcal{GM}_l$ does not inform, using UpRevoke, the manager $\mathcal{GM}_k$ of the parent group $\mathcal{G}_k$ of $\mathcal{G}_l$ that a given user is revoked from $\mathcal{G}_l$, the manager of $\mathcal{G}_k$ is not able to know about the identity of this user.

Cross-Unlinkability$_{\mathcal{A}}^{\text{CUHGS}}(\lambda, \mathcal{G})

- $(\text{gpk}^l, \text{msk}^l, \text{RL}^l, (\text{RL}^{l \dashv m})_{l \dashv m})_{\mathcal{G}_l \in \mathcal{G}} \leftarrow \text{KeyGen}(1^\lambda, \mathcal{G})$
     $\mathcal{HU}, \mathcal{CU}, \mathcal{HGM}, \mathcal{CGM}, \mathcal{CH} \leftarrow \{\}$; $b \xleftarrow{\$} \{0,1\}$
- $\mathcal{O} \leftarrow \{\text{AddHonestUser}(\cdot), \text{CorruptUser}(\cdot), \text{AddCorruptedUser}(\cdot), \text{Revoke}(\cdot, \cdot),$
     $\text{Open}(\cdot, \cdot, \cdot), \text{Sign}(\cdot, \cdot, \cdot), \text{CorruptGM}(\cdot), \text{DeriveHonestUser}(\cdot, \cdot, \cdot),$
     $\text{DeriveCorruptedUser}(\cdot, \cdot, \cdot), \text{CUChallenge}(b, \cdot, \cdot, \cdot, \cdot)\}$
- $b' \leftarrow A^{\mathcal{O}}(\text{gpk})$
- Return 1 if $b' == b$, and return 0 otherwise.

A CUHGS scheme achieves *cross-unlinkability* if the probability for a polynomial adversary $\mathcal{A}$ to win the Cross-Unlinkability$_{\mathcal{A}}^{\text{CUHGS}}$ game is negligible.

3.3   A Generic Construction Based on VLR Group Signatures and Pseudonymous Signatures

We assume that there exist a group signature scheme G and a domain-specific pseudonymous signature D that share the same parameters, *i.e.* the same KeyGen algorithm and the same Join $\leftrightarrow$ Issue protocol, and consequently a user i can use the same key sk_i for signing using the G or the D scheme. One can for instance use the [14] group signature (patched as in [11,19]) as the G scheme and one of the pseudonymous signatures schemes of Bringer *et al.* [6,9] as the D scheme.

Key generation. The C1.KeyGen algorithm consists of one invocation of the G.KeyGen algorithm per group manager. Every group manager $\mathcal{GM}_l$ also adds C_l domains.

C1.KeyGen($1^\lambda, \mathcal{G}$)
1: $[(\mathcal{GM}_l)_{\mathcal{G}_l \in \mathcal{G}}]$ Compute and output $(\text{gpk}^l, \text{msk}^l) = \text{G/D.KeyGen}(1^\lambda)$.
2: $[(\mathcal{GM}_l)_{\mathcal{G}_l \in \mathcal{G}}]$ For all m such that $l \dashv m$, compute and output $(\text{dpk}^{l \dashv m}, \text{RL}^{l \dashv m}) = \text{D.DomainKeyGen}(\text{gpk}^l, m)$.

Join. The join procedure simply consists in an execution of the G/D.Join $\leftrightarrow$ G/D.Issue algorithm between i and $\mathcal{GM}_0$.

C1.Join(gpk^0) $\leftrightarrow$ C1.Issue($\text{gpk}^0, \text{msk}^0$)
1: Run and output $\text{sk}_i^0 \leftarrow \text{G/D.Join}(\text{gpk}^l) \leftrightarrow \text{G/D.Issue}(\text{gpk}^l, \text{msk}^l) \rightarrow \text{rt}_i^0$.

Key derivation. We now explain how to derive signing keys. Let $\mathcal{G}_k$ be the parent group of $\mathcal{G}_l$ in $\mathcal{G}$ and let us assume that a user i owns keys for $\mathcal{G}_k$ and wants to acquire keys for the group $\mathcal{G}_l$. i has to engage a specific authentication process with the group manager $\mathcal{GM}_l$ of $\mathcal{G}_l$. First, the user authenticates to $\mathcal{GM}_l$ by signing on behalf of $\mathcal{G}_k$, parent of $\mathcal{G}_l$ in $\mathcal{G}$, to prove that he is allowed to join $\mathcal{G}_l$. This signature is a pseudonymous signature associated to the domain "$k \dashv l$", dedicated to the derivation from $\mathcal{G}_k$ to $\mathcal{G}_l$. In addition, i sends his pseudonym $\text{nym}_i^{k \dashv l}$ associated to the "$k \dashv l$" domain. The group manager $\mathcal{GM}_l$ then acts as a verifier for the pseudonymous signature of $\mathcal{G}_k$ and checks the validity of the signature. The fact that i is not revoked from $\mathcal{G}_k$ is done by checking if $\text{nym}_i^{k \dashv l} \notin \text{RL}^{k \dashv l}$ and ensured by the C1.Revoke protocol, see below. The fact that the pseudonymous signature is checked as valid ensures the legitimacy of the user. Once $\mathcal{GM}_l$ is sure that i is a non revoked member of $\mathcal{G}_k$, i and $\mathcal{GM}_l$ can run the Join $\leftrightarrow$ Issue procedure for the group $\mathcal{G}_l$, and $\text{nym}_i^{k \dashv l}$ is kept by $\mathcal{GM}_l$ as an auxiliary information for revocation.

C1.DeriveUser($\text{gpk}^k, \text{gpk}^l, \text{sk}_i^k$) $\qquad\qquad\qquad\qquad\qquad\qquad\qquad$ $\leftrightarrow$
$\quad$C1.DeriveGM($\text{gpk}^k, \text{RL}^{k \dashv l}, \text{gpk}^l, \text{msk}^l$)

1: $[\mathcal{GM}_l]$ Pick $m \xleftarrow{\$} \{0,1\}^*$ (of reasonable length) and send it to i.
2: $[i]$ Compute $\text{nym}_i^{k \dashv l} = \text{D.NymGen}(\text{gpk}^k, \text{dpk}^{k \dashv l}, \text{sk}_i^k)$
3: $[i]$ Compute $\sigma = \text{D.Sign}(\text{gpk}^k, \text{dpk}^{k \dashv l}, \text{sk}_i^k, \text{nym}_i^{k \dashv l}, m)$.
4: $[i]$ Send σ and $\text{nym}_i^{k \dashv l}$ to $\mathcal{GM}_l$.
5: $[\mathcal{GM}_l]$ Check $\text{D.Verify}(\text{gpk}^k, \text{dpk}^{k \dashv l}, \text{nym}_i^{k \dashv l}, m, \sigma, \text{RL}^{k \dashv l}) = \text{valid}$, otherwise abort.
6: If all checks succeed, $\mathcal{GM}_l$ and i run an issuing protocol:
$\quad$ G/D.Join(gpk^l) $\leftrightarrow$ G/D.Issue($\text{gpk}^l, \text{msk}^l$).
7: $[\mathcal{GM}_l]$ Register $\text{reg}_i^l = \text{nym}_i^{k \dashv l}$.

Signature generation and verification. The Sign and Verify algorithms are direct applications of the G scheme algorithms.

$\mathtt{C1.Sign}(\mathtt{gpk}^l, m, \mathtt{sk}_i^l)$

   1: Compute and output $\sigma = \mathtt{G.Sign}(\mathtt{gpk}^l, \mathtt{sk}_i^l, m)$.

$\mathtt{C1.Verify}(\mathtt{gpk}^l, \sigma, m, \mathtt{RL}^l)$

   1: Compute and output $d = \mathtt{G.Verify}(\mathtt{gpk}^l, m, \sigma, \mathtt{RL}^l)$.

Revocation. The $\mathtt{C1.Revoke}$ algorithm is a combined application of the DSPS revocation $\mathtt{D.DomainRevoke}$ and the VLRGS $\mathtt{G.Revoke}$ algorithms, followed by a recursive call to $\mathtt{C1.Revoke}$ in the children groups of $\mathcal{G}_l$.

$\mathtt{C1.Revoke}(\mathtt{gpk}^l, \mathtt{rt}_i^l, \mathtt{RL}^l, (\mathtt{RL}^{l\dashv m})_{l\dashv m})$

   1: Compute and output $\mathtt{RL}^l = \mathtt{G.Revoke}(\mathtt{gpk}^l, \mathtt{rt}_i^l, \mathtt{RL}^l)$.

   2: For each $\mathcal{G}_m$ such that $l \vdash m$, compute and output
     $\mathtt{RL}^{l\dashv m} = \mathtt{D.DomainRevoke}(\mathtt{gpk}^l, \mathtt{dpk}^{l\dashv m}, \mathtt{nym}_i^{l\dashv m}, \mathtt{RL}^{l\dashv m})$

   3: $[(\mathcal{GM}_m)_{l\dashv m}]$ If there exists $j \in \mathcal{G}_m$ such that $\mathtt{reg}_j^m = \mathtt{nym}_i^{l\vdash m}$, run
     $\mathtt{C1.Revoke}(\mathtt{gpk}^m, \mathtt{rt}_i^m, \mathtt{RL}^m, (\mathtt{RL}^{m\dashv n})_{m\dashv n})$

4 Conclusion

In this paper we considered hierarchical group signatures, in which users have access to several groups, each of them being equipped with a group signature scheme. The groups are organized in a tree. A user must belongs to a parent node before joining a children node. If a user is revoked at a particular node, it is possible to revoke across the groups in the subtree. However, signatures for non revoked users stay unlinkable. This notion is of particular interest for the privacy of users in identity management systems, since in practice users often access to different areas. We also propose a construction of such a notion based on VLR group signatures. The derivation process from a parent to a children uses domain-specific pseudonymous signatures, the domain being the edge of the group tree related to the key derivation.

References

1. Ateniese, G., Tsudik, G.: Some open issues and new directions in group signatures. In: Franklin, M.K. (ed.) FC 1999. LNCS, vol. 1648, pp. 196–211. Springer, Heidelberg (1999)
2. Belenkiy, M., Camenisch, J., Chase, M., Kohlweiss, M., Lysyanskaya, A., Shacham, H.: Randomizable proofs and delegatable anonymous credentials. In: Halevi, S. (ed.) CRYPTO 2009. LNCS, vol. 5677, pp. 108–125. Springer, Heidelberg (2009)
3. Bender, J., Dagdelen, Ö., Fischlin, M., Kügler, D.: Domain-specific pseudonymous signatures for the German identity card. In: Gollmann, D., Freiling, F.C. (eds.) ISC 2012. LNCS, vol. 7483, pp. 104–119. Springer, Heidelberg (2012)
4. Benjumea, V., Choi, S.G., Lopez, J., Yung, M.: Fair traceable multi-group signatures. In: Tsudik, G. (ed.) FC 2008. LNCS, vol. 5143, pp. 231–246. Springer, Heidelberg (2008)

5. Boneh, D., Shacham, H.: Group signatures with verifier-local revocation. In: Atluri, V., Pfitzmann, B., McDaniel, P.D. (eds.) ACM Conference on Computer and Communications Security, pp. 168–177. ACM (2004)

6. Bringer, J., Chabanne, H., Lescuyer, R., Patey, A.: Efficient and strongly secure dynamic domain-specific pseudonymous signatures for ID documents. In: Financial Cryptography and Data Security (FC) (2014)

7. Bringer, J., Chabanne, H., Patey, A.: An application of a group signature scheme with backward unlinkability to biometric identity management. In: Samarati et al. [20], pp. 421–425 (2012)

8. Bringer, J., Chabanne, H., Patey, A.: Cross-unlinkable hierarchical group signatures. In: De Capitani di Vimercati, S., Mitchell, C. (eds.) EuroPKI 2012. LNCS, vol. 7868, pp. 161–177. Springer, Heidelberg (2013)

9. Bringer, J., Chabanne, H., Patey, A.: Collusion-resistant domain-specific pseudonymous signatures. In: Lopez, J., Huang, X., Sandhu, R. (eds.) NSS 2013. LNCS, vol. 7873, pp. 649–655. Springer, Heidelberg (2013)

10. Bringer, J., Chabanne, H., Pointcheval, D., Zimmer, S.: An application of the Boneh and Shacham group signature scheme to biometric authentication. In: Matsuura, K., Fujisaki, E. (eds.) IWSEC 2008. LNCS, vol. 5312, pp. 219–230. Springer, Heidelberg (2008)

11. Bringer, J., Patey, A.: VLR group signatures - how to achieve both backward unlinkability and efficient revocation checks. In: Samarati et al. [20], pp. 215–220 (2012)

12. BSI: advanced security mechanisms for machine readable travel documents. Part 2 extended access control version 2 (EACv2), password authenticated connection establishment (PACE), and restricted identification (RI). Technical report TR-03110-2, BSI, version 2.10, March 2012

13. Chaum, D., van Heyst, E.: Group signatures. In: Davies, D.W. (ed.) EUROCRYPT 1991. LNCS, vol. 547, pp. 257–265. Springer, Heidelberg (1991)

14. Chen, L., Li, J.: VLR group signatures with indisputable exculpability and efficient revocation. In: Elmagarmid, A.K., Agrawal, D. (eds.) SocialCom/PASSAT, pp. 727–734. IEEE Computer Society (2010)

15. Fuchsbauer, G., Pointcheval, D.: Anonymous proxy signatures. In: Ostrovsky, R., De Prisco, R., Visconti, I. (eds.) SCN 2008. LNCS, vol. 5229, pp. 201–217. Springer, Heidelberg (2008)

16. Khader, D.: Attribute based group signature with revocation. IACR Cryptology ePrint Archive 2007, 241 (2007)

17. Khader, D.: Attribute based group signatures. IACR Cryptology ePrint Archive 2007, 159 (2007)

18. Kim, S., Park, S., Won, D.: Group signatures for hierarchical multigroups. In: Okamoto, E. (ed.) ISW 1997. LNCS, vol. 1396. Springer, Heidelberg (1998)

19. Patey, A.: Techniques cryptographiques pour l'authentification et l'identification biométriques respectant la vie privée. Ph.D. thesis, Télécom ParisTech (2014)

20. Samarati, P., Lou, W., Zhou, J. (eds.): SECRYPT 2012 - Proceedings of the International Conference on Security and Cryptography, Rome, Italy, 24–27, SECRYPT is part of ICETE - The International Joint Conference on e-Business and Telecommunications. SciTePress (2012), July 2012

21. Trolin, M., Wikström, D.: Hierarchical group signatures. In: Caires, L., Italiano, G.F., Monteiro, L., Palamidessi, C., Yung, M. (eds.) ICALP 2005. LNCS, vol. 3580, pp. 446–458. Springer, Heidelberg (2005)

Secure ElGamal-Type Cryptosystems Without Message Encoding

Marc Joye[✉]

Technicolor, 175 S. San Antonio Road, Los Altos, CA 94022, USA
marc.joye@technicolor.com

Abstract. ElGamal cryptosystem is one of the oldest public-key cryptosystems. It is known to be semantically secure for arbitrary messages in the random oracle model under the decisional Diffie-Hellman assumption. Semantic security also holds in the standard model when messages are encoded as elements in the group for which the decisional Diffie-Hellman assumption is defined. This paper introduces a setting and companion cryptosystem where semantic security can be proved in the standard model *without* message encoding. Extensions achieving security against chosen-ciphertext attacks are also provided.

1 Introduction

The classical ElGamal cryptosystem [7,8] is closely related to the Diffie-Hellman key exchange protocol. It was introduced by Taher ElGamal in 1984. In retrospect, it is somewhat surprising that this scheme was not discovered before the RSA cryptosystem.

The original scheme goes as follows. Let p be a large prime and let g be a primitive element modulo p, that is, g generates all of $\mathbb{F}_p^*$. The public key is $\mathsf{pk} = \{g, y, p\}$ where $y = g^x \bmod p$ for a random integer r with $0 \leq x < p$. The secret key is $\mathsf{sk} = \{x\}$. The encryption of a message m, with $1 \leq m < p$, is given by the pair (c_1, c_2) where $c_1 = g^r \bmod p$ and $c_2 = m\, y^r \bmod p$ for a random integer $0 \leq r < p$. Message m is then recovered using secret key x as $m = c_2 \cdot c_1^{-x} \bmod p$.

As already pointed out in [7], breaking the above scheme and the Diffie-Hellman key exchange protocol are equally difficult. Using modern terminology, ElGamal showed that his cryptosystem is *one-way* against chosen-plaintext attacks (OW-CPA) under the *computational Diffie-Hellman (CDH) assumption.* Informally, the CDH assumption says that given two random elements $A = g^a$ and $B = g^b$ in $\mathbb{F}_p^*$ the value of $g^{ab} \in \mathbb{F}_p^*$ cannot be recovered. It is now easy to see that an attacker against the one-wayness of the ElGamal cryptosystem can be used to solve a CDH problem in $\mathbb{F}_p^*$; namely, obtaining $g^{ab} \pmod{p}$ from (p, g, g^a, g^b). One gives the attacker the public key $\mathsf{pk} = \{g, g^a, p\}$ and the challenge ciphertext $c = (g^b, c_2)$ for some random value $c_2 \in \mathbb{F}_p^*$. The attacker answer with the corresponding message $m = c_2 \cdot (g^b)^{-a} \pmod{p}$, which yields the value of g^{ab} as $c_2/m \pmod{p}$. The other direction is immediate.

Semantic security [10] captures a stronger notion of data privacy. Basically, it requires that an adversary should not learn anything about a plaintext given

© Springer-Verlag Berlin Heidelberg 2016
P.Y.A. Ryan et al. (Eds.): Kahn Festschrift, LNCS 9100, pp. 470–478, 2016.
DOI: 10.1007/978-3-662-49301-4_29

its encryption beyond the length of the plaintext. An equivalent notion is that of indistinguishable encryptions. ElGamal cryptosystem is known to meet the IND-CPA security level (i.e., *indistinguishability against chosen-plaintext attacks*) under the *decisional Diffie-Hellman (*DDH*) assumption* [15]. Formal definitions are given in the next section.

Unfortunately, the DDH assumption does not hold in $\mathbb{F}_p^*$. If $\mathbb{F}_p^* = \langle g \rangle$ (that is, g is a generator of $\mathbb{F}_p^*$) then it follows that $\left(\frac{g}{p}\right) = -1$, where $\left(\frac{g}{p}\right)$ denotes the Legendre symbol of g modulo p. Hence, for any $0 \leq x < p-1$, $\left(\frac{g^x}{p}\right) = (-1)^x$ leaks the value of $x \bmod 2$. A more sophisticated attack against the original ElGamal cryptosystem is presented in [3, Sect. 4].

These issues can easily be circumvented by working in a (large) prime-order subgroup $\mathbb{G}$ of $\mathbb{F}_p^*$. The ElGamal encryption proceeds exactly in the same way except that g is now an element of order q where q is a large prime factor of $p-1$. Messages being encrypted must also be elements of the subgroup generated by g; i.e., the message space is $\mathcal{M} = \mathbb{G}$ with $\mathbb{G} = \langle g \rangle$. Representing messages as group elements is known as *message encoding*.

In [15], Tsiounis and Yung propose the following message encoding when $\mathbb{G}$ is the subgroup of quadratic residues modulo p and $(p-1)/2$ is prime. Let ε be a security parameter (typically $\varepsilon = 64$). A κ-bit message m (with $\kappa = |p|_2 - \varepsilon$) is encoded as $\widehat{m} = \rho \, 2^\kappa + m$ for $\rho = 0, 1, 2, \ldots$ until $\widehat{m}$ is a quadratic residue so that $\widehat{m} \in \mathbb{G}$. Note that message m can be obtained from $\widehat{m}$ as $m = \widehat{m} \bmod 2^\kappa$. There are several drawbacks in this approach. First, it requires computing Legendre symbols to test the quadratic residuosity. Second, the potential message space is not fully exploited as several bits are provisioned to store ρ. Third, as presented, the message encoding is not time-constant and so may reveal information on m (timing attack).

An alternative message encoding for the previous setting is mentioned in [6, Sect. 5.1]. The messages being encrypted are restricted to be elements in the set $\{1, \ldots, q\}$ with $q = (p-1)/2$ prime. A message m is then encoded by squaring it modulo p, yielding $\widehat{m} = m^2 \bmod p$ in $\mathbb{G}$. For the decryption, message m can be recovered from its encoding $\widehat{m}$ by computing its unique square root in the set $\{1, \ldots, q\}$ —observe that since q is an [odd] prime, it follows that $p \equiv 3 \pmod 4$. On the down side, the total decryption time to get plaintext (decoded) message m is longer.

In [5], Chevallier-Mames *et al.* suggest a modification to the classical ElGamal cryptosystem so as to avoid message encoding. The semantic security of the resulting cryptosystem relies on a new, specifically introduced assumption; namely, the *decisional class Diffie-Hellman assumption*. However, its connection with the standard DDH assumption is unclear and was left as an open problem in [5].

Another way to avoid message encoding is to invoke the random oracle model [1] when proving the security. The second part of an ElGamal ciphertext is modified as $c_2 = m \oplus \mathcal{H}(y^r \bmod p)$, where $\mathcal{H} : \mathbb{G} \to \mathcal{M}$ and $\mathcal{M} = \{0, 1\}^\kappa$. The random oracle model assumes that the hash function $\mathcal{H}$ behaves as a random function. While the resulting cryptosystem can be shown to achieve semantic security, the security proof only stands in the idealized random-oracle model. In particular, there are no guarantees that the proof holds in the standard model when function $\mathcal{H}$ is concretely instantiated, as demonstrated by Canetti et al. [4].

This paper presents a variation of the ElGamal cryptosystem meeting the IND-CPA security notion without message encoding, nor random oracles. Extensions to deal with stronger scenario attacks are also presented. Unlike [15] the message space is optimal and unlike [6] the decryption time is roughly the same as for the original ElGamal cryptosystem. Further, the ciphertext components are one bit shorter, which can be useful for super-encryption. The security of all presented schemes relies on a standard DDH assumption.

2   Background

In this section, we review well-known definitions and notions for public-key encryption. We also introduce some useful notation.

Public-Key Encryption. A *public-key encryption scheme* [10] is a tuple of three algorithms (KeyGen, Enc, Dec):

Key generation. The key generation algorithm KeyGen is a randomized algorithm that takes as input some security parameter 1^λ and returns a matching pair of public key and secret key for some user: $(\mathsf{pk}, \mathsf{sk}) \xleftarrow{R} \mathsf{KeyGen}(1^\lambda)$. The message space is denoted by $\mathcal{M}$.

Encryption. The encryption algorithm Enc is a randomized algorithm that takes as input a public key pk and a plaintext $m \in \mathcal{M}$, and returns a ciphertext c. We write $c \leftarrow \mathsf{Enc}_{\mathsf{pk}}(m)$.

Decryption. The decryption algorithm Dec takes as input secret key sk (matching pk) and ciphertext c and returns the corresponding plaintext m or a special symbol $\bot$ indicating that the ciphertext is invalid. We write $m \leftarrow \mathsf{Dec}_{\mathsf{sk}}(c)$ if c is a valid ciphertext and $\bot \leftarrow \mathsf{Dec}_{\mathsf{sk}}(c)$ if it is not.

We require that $\mathsf{Dec}_{\mathsf{sk}}(\mathsf{Enc}_{\mathsf{pk}}(m)) = m$ for any message $m \in \mathcal{M}$, where $(\mathsf{pk}, \mathsf{sk}) \xleftarrow{R} \mathsf{KeyGen}(1^\lambda)$.

Complexity Assumptions. Let $\mathbb{G} = \langle g \rangle$ denote a (multiplicatively written) cyclic group of order q. Given $g^a, g^b \xleftarrow{R} \mathbb{G}$, the *computational* Diffie-Hellman (CDH) problem is to compute g^{ab}. Likewise, the *decisional* Diffie-Hellman (DDH) problem is to distinguish between the two distributions (g, g^a, g^b, g^{ab}) and (g, g^a, g^b, g^c) for $a, b, c \xleftarrow{R} \mathbb{Z}/q\mathbb{Z}$.

More formally, the DDH assumption is defined as follows.

Definition 1. *The* DDH *assumption in* $\mathbb{G}$ *requires that for any probabilistic polynomial-time adversary* $\mathcal{A}$ *the advantage*

$$\left| \Pr\left[\mathcal{A}(\mathbb{G}, q, g, g^a, g^b, g^{ab}) = 1 \right] - \Pr\left[\mathcal{A}(\mathbb{G}, q, g, g^a, g^b, g^c) = 1 \right] \right|$$

is negligible in the security parameter λ, *where the probabilities are taken over the experiment of generating a group* $\mathbb{G} = \langle g \rangle$ *of order* q *on input* 1^λ *and choosing* $a, b, c \xleftarrow{R} \mathbb{Z}/q\mathbb{Z}$.

Examples of groups $\mathbb{G}$ for which the DDH problem is hard include a prime-order subgroup of $\mathbb{F}_p^*$ or a prime-order subgroup of the points of an elliptic curve over a finite field. An excellent survey on the DDH problem is provided in [2].

Security Notions. In order to properly define the notion of *indistinguishability of encryptions*, we view an adversary $\mathcal{A}$ as a pair $(\mathcal{A}_1, \mathcal{A}_2)$ of probabilistic algorithms. This corresponds to adversary $\mathcal{A}$ running in two stages. In the "find" stage, algorithm $\mathcal{A}_1$ takes as input a public key pk and outputs two equal-size messages m_0 and $m_1 \in \mathcal{M}$ and some state information s. In the "guess" stage, algorithm $\mathcal{A}_2$ receives a challenge ciphertext c which is the encryption of m_b under pk and where b is chosen at random in $\{0, 1\}$. The goal of $\mathcal{A}_2$ is to recover the value of b from s and c.

A public-key encryption scheme is said *indistinguishable* (or *semantically secure*) if

$$\Pr\left[\begin{matrix} (\mathsf{pk}, \mathsf{sk}) \xleftarrow{R} \mathsf{KeyGen}(1^\lambda), (m_0, m_1, s) \leftarrow \mathcal{A}_1(\mathsf{pk}), \\ b \xleftarrow{R} \{0, 1\}, c \leftarrow \mathsf{Enc}_{\mathsf{pk}}(m_b) \end{matrix} : \mathcal{A}_2(s, c) = b \right] - \frac{1}{2}$$

is negligible in the security parameter for any polynomial-time adversary $\mathcal{A}$; the probability is taken over the random coins of the experiment according to the distribution induced by KeyGen and over the random coins of the adversary.

As we are in the public-key setting, the adversary $\mathcal{A} = (\mathcal{A}_1, \mathcal{A}_2)$ is given the public key pk and so can encrypt any message of its choice. In other words, the adversary can mount chosen-plaintext attacks (CPA). Hence, we write IND-CPAthe security notion achieved by a semantically secure encryption scheme.

A stronger scenario is to give the adversary an adaptive access to a decryption oracle. The previous definition readily extends to this model. Adversary $\mathcal{A} = (\mathcal{A}_1, \mathcal{A}_2)$ is allowed to submit any ciphertext of its choice and receives the corresponding plaintext (or $\perp$); the sole exception is that $\mathcal{A}_2$ may not query the decryption oracle on challenge ciphertext c [14]. We write IND-CCA2 the corresponding security notion; it stands for indistinguishability under *adaptive* chosen-ciphertext attacks. A weaker security notion is when only $\mathcal{A}_1$ is given access to the decryption oracle [13]. The corresponding security notion is written IND-CCA1 and stands for indistinguishability under *non-adaptive* chosen-ciphertext attacks.

3 A DDH-type Group

Let $q \neq 2$ be a Sophie Germain prime; that is, both q and $2q + 1$ are prime. We let $p = 2q + 1$. Consider the set $\{1, 2, \dots, q\}$. This set can be endowed with the structure of a group under the group law $\star$ given by

$$a \star b = |ab \bmod p|$$

where $ab \bmod s\, p$ represents the absolute smallest residue of ab modulo p (namely, the complete set of absolute smallest residues are: $-(p-1)/2, \ldots, -1, 0, 1, \ldots, (p-1)/2$), and where $|ab \bmod s\, p|$ represents the absolute value of $ab \bmod s\, p$. We let $\mathbb{H}_q$ denote the set $\{1, \ldots, q\}$ equipped with the group law $\star$. A similar setting was considered in [9,11] for RSA composites.

Let g be a generator of $(\mathbb{Z}/p\mathbb{Z})^*$ (i.e., $\langle g \rangle = (\mathbb{Z}/p\mathbb{Z})^*$) and $h = |g \bmod s\, p|$. It is easily verified that h generates the group $\mathbb{H}_q$:

$$\mathbb{H}_q = \left\{ |h^j \bmod s\, p| \text{ for } 0 \le j < q \right\} .$$

Indeed, we have $h^q \bmod s\, p = -1$ and thus $|h^q \bmod s\, p| = 1$. Further, for $0 \le j_1, j_2 < q$, $|h^{j_1} \bmod s\, p| = |h^{j_2} \bmod s\, p|$ implies $h^{2j_1} \equiv h^{2j_2} \pmod{p}$, which in turn implies $j_1 \equiv j_2 \pmod{q}$ and thus $j_1 = j_2$.

Remarkably, as will be stated, the DDH assumption in $\mathbb{H}_q$ is equivalent to the DDH in the subgroup of quadratic residues in $\mathbb{F}_p^*$, which is believed to be hard when $p = 2q + 1$ for some prime q. This latter assumption is a standard intractability assumption that has been used in proving the security of a variety of cryptographic schemes.

Theorem 1. *Let $q \ne 2$ be a Sophie Germain prime and let $p = 2q + 1$. Let also g be a generator of $(\mathbb{Z}/p\mathbb{Z})^*$, $s = g^2 \bmod p$, and $h = |g \bmod s\, p|$. Define the groups $\mathrm{QR}(p) = \left\{ s^j \bmod p \text{ for } 0 \le j < q \right\}$ and $\mathbb{H}_q = \left\{ |h^j \bmod s\, p| \text{ for } 0 \le j < q \right\}$. Then the groups $\mathrm{QR}(p)$ and $\mathbb{H}_q$ are isomorphic; we have*

$$\psi : \mathrm{QR}(p) \overset{\sim}{\longrightarrow} \mathbb{H}_q, x \longmapsto |\sqrt{x} \bmod s\, p|$$

and

$$\psi^{-1} : \mathbb{H}_q \overset{\sim}{\longrightarrow} \mathrm{QR}(p), y \longmapsto y^2 \bmod p .$$

Proof. Note that the map ψ is well defined. Since q is odd, it follows that $p \equiv 3 \pmod{4}$ and thus $-1 \notin \mathrm{QR}(p)$. Hence square roots exist and are unique in $\mathrm{QR}(p)$: if $x \in \mathrm{QR}(p)$ then $\sqrt{x}$ denotes the unique element $z \in \mathrm{QR}(p)$ such that $z^2 \equiv x \pmod{p}$ —observe that $-z \notin \mathrm{QR}(p)$.

Consider two arbitrary elements $x_1, x_2 \in (\mathbb{Z}/p\mathbb{Z})^*$. For $i \in \{1, 2\}$, letting $z_i = \sqrt{x_i} \in \mathrm{QR}(p)$, we have $\psi(x_i) = |z_i \bmod s\, p|$.

Define $x_3 = x_1 x_2 \bmod p$ and let $z_3 = \sqrt{x_3} \in \mathrm{QR}(p)$. Then we obtain $\psi(x_3) = |z_3 \bmod s\, p| = |z_1 z_2 \bmod s\, p| = \psi(x_1) \star \psi(x_2)$. Map ψ is a group homomorphism.

We have to show that ψ is bijective. Suppose that $\psi(x_1) = \psi(x_2)$. This means that $|z_1 \bmod s\, p| = |z_2 \bmod s\, p|$ and thus $z_1 \equiv \pm z_2 \pmod{p}$. This implies $z_1 = z_2$ since they are both elements of $\mathrm{QR}(p)$. Moreover, for each $y \in \mathbb{H}_q$, there exists an $x \in \mathrm{QR}(p)$; namely, $x = \psi^{-1}(y)$, and $\psi(\psi^{-1}(y)) = \psi(y^2 \bmod p) = |(\frac{y}{p}) y \bmod s\, p| = y$. □

Corollary 1. *The DDH in $\mathbb{H}_q$ is equivalent to the DDH in $\mathrm{QR}(p)$.*

Proof. Let $\mathbb{H}_q = \langle h \rangle$ and $\mathrm{QR}(p) = \langle s \rangle$ with $s = \psi(h)$. Since the isomorphisms between $\mathbb{H}_q$ and $\mathrm{QR}(p)$ are efficiently computable, it is easy to transform a DDH challenge $(h, |h^a \bmod s\, p|, |h^b \bmod s\, p|, |h^c \bmod s\, p|) \in \mathbb{H}_q{}^4$ into a DDH challenge $(s, s^a \bmod p, s^b \bmod p, s^c \bmod p) \in \mathrm{QR}(p)^4$ as $s = \psi(h)$, $s^a \bmod p = \psi(|h^a \bmod s\, p|)$, $s^b \bmod p = \psi(|h^b \bmod s\, p|)$, $s^c \bmod p = \psi(|h^c \bmod s\, p|)$; and vice-versa using ψ^{-1}. $\qquad\qquad\qquad\qquad\qquad\qquad\qquad\qquad\qquad\qquad\qquad$ □

4 A Variant of ElGamal Cryptosystem

From Corollary 1, we obtain an ElGamal-type cryptosystem that is IND-CPA secure under the standard DDH assumption in $\mathrm{QR}(p)$.

Key generation. On input some security parameter 1^λ the key generation algorithm generates a Sophie Germain prime q. It also defines $p = 2q + 1$, a generator g of $(\mathbb{Z}/p\mathbb{Z})^*$, and $h = |g \bmod s\, p|$. Finally it picks at random an element x in $\mathbb{Z}/q\mathbb{Z}$ and computes $y = |h^x \bmod s\, p|$. The public key is $\mathsf{pk} = \{h, p, q, y\}$ while the secret key is $\mathsf{sk} = \{x\}$. The message space is $\mathcal{M} = \{1, \ldots, q\}$.

Encryption. The encryption of a message $m \in \mathcal{M}$ is given by $c = (c_1, c_2)$ where

$$c_1 - |h^r \bmod s\, p| \quad \text{and} \quad c_2 = |m\, y^r \bmod s\, p| \ .$$

Decryption. Given a ciphertext $c = (c_1, c_2) \in \mathbb{H}_q{}^2$, the corresponding plaintext message m can be recovered using secret key x as

$$m = |c_2/c_1{}^x \bmod s\, p| \ .$$

5 Chosen-Ciphertext Security

The previous cryptosystem is "malleable". Given the encryptions of messages m and m' in $\mathcal{M}$, say (c_1, c_2) and (c_1', c_2'), anyone can derive the encryption of message $m'' = m \star m' \in \mathcal{M}$ as $(c_1'', c_2'') = (c_1 \star c_1', c_2 \star c_2')$.

While malleability is sometimes useful for certain applications (e.g., for blind decryption), it also rules out the security against chosen-ciphertext attacks. From Corollary 1 and [6, Sect. 5.4], it is possible to get an ElGamal-type cryptosystem that is IND-CCA1 secure under the standard DDH assumption in $\mathrm{QR}(p)$.

Key generation. On input some security parameter 1^λ the key generation algorithm generates a Sophie Germain prime q. It also defines $p = 2q+1$, two generators g and $\bar{g}$ of $(\mathbb{Z}/p\mathbb{Z})^*$, and sets $h = |g \bmod s\, p|$ and $\bar{h} = |\bar{g} \bmod s\, p|$. Finally it picks at random three elements $x, \xi, \bar{\xi}$ in $\mathbb{Z}/q\mathbb{Z}$ and computes $y = |h^x \bmod s\, p|$ and $X = |h^\xi \bar{h}^{\bar{\xi}} \bmod s\, p|$. The public key is $\mathsf{pk} = \{h, \bar{h}, p, q, y, X\}$ while the secret key is $\mathsf{sk} = \{x, \xi, \bar{\xi}\}$. The message space is $\mathcal{M} = \{1, \ldots, q\}$.

Encryption. The encryption of a message $m \in \mathcal{M}$ is given by $c = (c_1, \bar{c}_1, c_2, v)$ where

$$c_1 = |h^r \bmod s\, p| \ , \quad \bar{c}_1 = |\bar{h}^r \bmod s\, p| \ , \quad c_2 = |m\, y^r \bmod s\, p| \ ,$$
$$\text{and } v = |X^r \bmod s\, p| \ .$$

Decryption. Given a ciphertext $c = (c_1, \bar{c}_1, c_2, v) \in \mathbb{H}_q{}^4$, the decryption algorithm first checks whether $v = |c_1{}^\xi\, \bar{c}_1{}^{\bar{\xi}} \bmod{s}\, p|$. If so, the corresponding plaintext message m can be recovered using secret key x as

$$m = |c_2/c_1{}^x \bmod{s}\, p| \ ;$$

otherwise the decryption algorithm returns $\perp$.

Security against *adaptive* chosen-ciphertext attacks can be achieved by assuming in addition the existence of a hash function $\mathcal{H}$ chosen from a universal one-way family [12]. We note that this requirement is weaker than that of collision-resistance. Doing so, we obtain from Corollary 1 and [6, Section 4] a Cramer-Shoup like cryptosystem that is IND-CCA2 under the standard DDH assumption in QR(p).

Key generation. On input some security parameter 1^λ the key generation algorithm generates a Sophie Germain prime q. It also defines $p = 2q + 1$, two generators g and $\bar{g}$ of $(\mathbb{Z}/p\mathbb{Z})^*$, and sets $h = |g \bmod{s}\, p|$ and $\bar{h} = |\bar{g} \bmod{s}\, p|$. It picks at random five elements $x, \xi, \bar{\xi}, \eta, \bar{\eta}$ in $\mathbb{Z}/q\mathbb{Z}$ and computes $y = |h^x \bmod{s}\, p|$, $X = |h^\xi\, \bar{h}^{\bar{\xi}} \bmod{s}\, p|$ and $Y = |h^\eta\, \bar{h}^{\bar{\eta}} \bmod{s}\, p|$. Finally it selects a hash function $\mathcal{H}$ from a family of universal one-way hash functions that map bit string to elements of $\mathbb{Z}/q\mathbb{Z}$. The public key is $\mathsf{pk} = \{h, \bar{h}, p, q, y, X, Y, \mathcal{H}\}$ while the secret key is $\mathsf{sk} = \{x, \xi, \bar{\xi}, \eta, \bar{\eta}\}$. The message space is $\mathcal{M} = \{1, \ldots, q\}$.

Encryption. The encryption of a message $m \in \mathcal{M}$ is given by $c = (c_1, \bar{c}_1, c_2, v)$ where

$$c_1 = |h^r \bmod{s}\, p| \ , \quad \bar{c}_1 = |\bar{h}^r \bmod{s}\, p| \ , \quad c_2 = |m\, y^r \bmod{s}\, p| \ ,$$
$$\text{and } v = |X^r\, Y^{r\alpha} \bmod{s}\, p| \quad \text{where } \alpha = \mathcal{H}(c_1, \bar{c}_1, c_2) \ .$$

Decryption. Given a ciphertext $c = (c_1, \bar{c}_1, c_2, v) \in \mathbb{H}_q{}^4$, the decryption algorithm first computes $\alpha = \mathcal{H}(c_1, \bar{c}_1, c_2)$. Next, using α, it checks whether $v = |c_1{}^{\xi+\eta\alpha}\, \bar{c}_1{}^{\bar{\xi}+\bar{\eta}\alpha} \bmod{s}\, p|$. If so, the corresponding plaintext message m can be recovered using secret key x as

$$m = |c_2/c_1{}^x \bmod{s}\, p| \ ;$$

otherwise the decryption algorithm returns $\perp$.

From Corollary 1 and [6, Sect. 5.3], it is also possible to obtain a Cramer-Shoup like cryptosystem that is IND-CCA2 under the *sole* standard DDH assumption in QR(p). Hash function $\mathcal{H}$ is eliminated, at the expense of longer keys and slightly increased processing time.

Key generation. On input some security parameter 1^λ the key generation algorithm generates a Sophie Germain prime q. It also defines $p = 2q + 1$, two generators g and $\bar{g}$ of $(\mathbb{Z}/p\mathbb{Z})^*$, and sets $h = |g \bmod{s}\, p|$ and $\bar{h} =$

$|\bar{g} \bmod s\, p|$. Finally it picks at random nine elements $x, \xi, \bar{\xi}, \eta_1, \bar{\eta}_1, \eta_2, \bar{\eta}_2, \eta_3, \bar{\eta}_3$ in $\mathbb{Z}/q\mathbb{Z}$ and computes $y = |h^x \bmod s\, p|$, $X = |h^\xi \bar{h}^{\bar{\xi}} \bmod s\, p|$, $Y_1 = |h^{\eta_1} \bar{h}^{\bar{\eta}_1} \bmod s\, p|$, $Y_2 = |h^{\eta_2} \bar{h}^{\bar{\eta}_2} \bmod s\, p|$ and $Y_3 = |h^{\eta_3} \bar{h}^{\bar{\eta}_3} \bmod s\, p|$. The public key is $\mathsf{pk} = \{h, \bar{h}, p, q, y, X, Y_1, Y_2, Y_3, \mathcal{H}\}$ while the secret key is $\mathsf{sk} = \{x, \xi, \bar{\xi}, \eta_1, \bar{\eta}_1, \eta_2, \bar{\eta}_2, \eta_3, \bar{\eta}_3\}$. The message space is $\mathcal{M} = \{1, \ldots, q\}$.

Encryption. The encryption of a message $m \in \mathcal{M}$ is given by $c = (c_1, \bar{c}_1, c_2, v)$ where

$$c_1 = |h^r \bmod s\, p|\,, \quad \bar{c}_1 = |\bar{h}^r \bmod s\, p|\,, \quad c_2 = |m\, y^r \bmod s\, p|\,,$$
$$\text{and } v = |X^r Y_1^{r c_1} Y_2^{r \bar{c}_1} Y_3^{r c_2} \bmod s\, p|\,.$$

Decryption. Given a ciphertext $c = (c_1, \bar{c}_1, c_2, v) \in \mathbb{H}_q{}^4$, the decryption algorithm first checks whether $v = |c_1{}^{\xi + \eta_1 c_1 + \eta_2 \bar{c}_1 + \eta_3 c_2}\, \bar{c}_1^{\bar{\xi} + \bar{\eta}_1 c_1 + \bar{\eta}_2 \bar{c}_1 + \bar{\eta}_3 c_2} \bmod s\, p|$. If so, the corresponding plaintext message m can be recovered using secret key x as

$$m = |c_2/c_1{}^x \bmod s\, p|\,;$$

otherwise the decryption algorithm returns $\perp$.

6 Conclusion

This paper described a simple modification to the classical ElGamal cryptosystem which, at the same time,

- provably meets the IND-CPA security notion (a.k.a. semantic security) in the standard model under the standard DDH assumption, and
- enables the encryption of messages without prior encoding as group elements.

Efficient extensions meeting the stronger security notions of IND-CCA1 and IND-CCA2 (security against chosen-ciphertext attacks) were also presented.

References

1. Bellare, M., Rogaway, P., Random oracles are practical: a paradigm for designing efficient protocols. In: 1st ACM Conference on Computer and Communications Security, pp. 62–73. ACM Press (1993)
2. Boneh, D.: The decision Diffie-Hellman problem. In: Buhler, J.P. (ed.) ANTS 1998. LNCS, vol. 1423, pp. 48–63. Springer, Heidelberg (1998)
3. Boneh, D., Joux, A., Nguyên, P.Q.: Why textbook ElGamal and RSA encryption are insecure. In: Okamoto, T. (ed.) ASIACRYPT 2000. LNCS, vol. 1976, pp. 30–43. Springer, Heidelberg (2000)
4. Canetti, R., Goldreich, O., Halevi, S.: The random oracle methodology, revisited. J. ACM 51(4), 557–594 (2004)
5. Chevallier-Mames, B., Paillier, P., Pointcheval, D.: Encoding-free ElGamal encryption without random oracles. In: Yung, M., Dodis, Y., Kiayias, A., Malkin, T. (eds.) PKC 2006. LNCS, vol. 3958, pp. 91–104. Springer, Heidelberg (2006)

6. Cramer, R., Shoup, V.: A practical public key cryptosystem provably secure against adaptive chosen ciphertext attack. In: Krawczyk, H. (ed.) CRYPTO 1998. LNCS, vol. 1462, pp. 13–25. Springer, Heidelberg (1998)

7. El Gamal, T.: A public key cryptosystem and a signature scheme based on discrete logarithms. In: Blakely, G.R., Chaum, D. (eds.) CRYPTO 1984. LNCS, vol. 196, pp. 10–18. Springer, Heidelberg (1985)

8. ElGamal, T.: A public key cryptosystem and a signature scheme based on discrete logarithms. IEEE Trans. Inf. Theory 31(4), 469–472 (1985)

9. Fischlin, R., Schnorr, C.P.: Stronger security proofs for RSA and Rabin bits. J. Cryptology 13(2), 221–244 (2000)

10. Goldwasser, S., Micali, S.: Probabilistic encryption. J. Comput. Syst. Sci. 28(2), 270–299 (1984)

11. Hofheinz, D., Kiltz, E.: The group of signed quadratic residues and applications. In: Halevi, S. (ed.) CRYPTO 2009. LNCS, vol. 5677, pp. 637–653. Springer, Heidelberg (2009)

12. Naor, M., Yung, M.: Universal one-way hash functions and their cryptographic applications. In: 21st Annual ACM Symposium on Theory of Computing, pp. 33–43. ACM Press (1989)

13. Naor, M., Yung, M.: Public-key cryptosystems provably secure against chosen ciphertext attacks. In: 22nd Annual ACM Symposium on Theory of Computing, pp. 427–437. ACM Press (1990)

14. Rackoff, C., Simon, D.R.: Non-interactive zero-knowledge proof of knowledge and chosen ciphertext attack. In: Feigenbaum, J. (ed.) CRYPTO 1991. LNCS, vol. 576, pp. 433–444. Springer, Heidelberg (1992)

15. Tsiounis, Y., Yung, M.: On the security of ElGamal based encryption. In: Imai, H., Zheng, Y. (eds.) PKC 1998. LNCS, vol. 1431, pp. 117–134. Springer, Heidelberg (1998)

Safe-Errors on SPA Protected Implementations with the Atomicity Technique

Pierre-Alain Fouque[1], Sylvain Guilley[2,3],
Cédric Murdica[2], and David Naccache[4](✉)

[1] Institut Universitaire de France, Université de Rennes 1, Rennes, France
`Pierre-Alain.Fouque@ens.fr`
[2] Secure-IC S.A.S., 80 avenue des Buttes de Coësmes, 35700 Rennes, France
`{sylvain.guilley,cedric.murdica}@secure-ic.com`
[3] Département COMELEC, Institut TELECOM,
TELECOM ParisTech, CNRS LTCI, Paris, France
`sylvain.guilley@telecom-paristech.fr`
[4] Département d'informatique, École normale supérieure,
45, rue d'Ulm, 75230 Paris Cedex 05, France
`david.naccache@ens.fr`

Abstract. ECDSA is one of the most important public-key signature scheme, however it is vulnerable to lattice attack once a few bits of the nonces are leaked. To protect Elliptic Curve Cryptography (ECC) against Simple Power Analysis, many countermeasures have been proposed. Doubling and Additions of points on the given elliptic curve require several additions and multiplications in the base field and this number is not the same for the two operations. The idea of the atomicity protection is to use a fixed pattern, *i.e.* a small number of instructions and rewrite the two basic operations of ECC using this pattern. Dummy operations are introduced so that the different elliptic curve operations might be written with the same atomic pattern. In an adversary point of view, the attacker only sees a succession of patterns and is no longer able to distinguish which one corresponds to addition and doubling. Chevallier-Mames, Ciet and Joye were the first to introduce such countermeasure. In this paper, we are interested in studying this countermeasure and we show a new vulnerability since the ECDSA implementation succumbs now to C Safe-Error attacks. Then, we propose an effective solution to prevent against C Safe-Error attacks when using the Side-Channel Atomicity. The dummy operations are used in such a way that if a fault is introduced on one of them, it can be detected. Finally, our countermeasure method is generic, meaning that it can be adapted to all formulæ. We apply our methods to different formulæ presented for Side-Channel Atomicity.

Keywords: Elliptic Curve Cryptography · Side-channel atomicity · Fault attacks · Infective countermeasure · Lattice attack

© Springer-Verlag Berlin Heidelberg 2016
P.Y.A. Ryan et al. (Eds.): Kahn Festschrift, LNCS 9100, pp. 479–493, 2016.
DOI: 10.1007/978-3-662-49301-4_30

1   Introduction

As well as most of cryptosystems, Elliptic Curve Cryptography (ECC) is vulnerable to side-channel attacks. One of the first reported attack on ECC was the Simple Side-Channel Analysis (SSCA) [6]. It consists in analyzing a single trace of the execution of the Elliptic Curve Scalar Multiplication and attempts to distinguish the power consumption between a doubling and an addition of elliptic curve points.

Numerous countermeasures exist against the SSCA. The side-channel Atomicity is one of them and was proposed by Chevallier-Mames, Ciet, Joye in 2004 [4]. It consists in writing the different elliptic curve operations, such as doubling and addition, with identical block of field operations, which makes SSCA infeasible. Inspired from this paper [4], different formulæ that are more efficient, or more suitable for particular scalar multiplications, have been proposed [7,10,15]. Up to now, all these formulæ contain at least one dummy operation.

One of the most popular elliptic curve cryptographic scheme is the signature scheme ECDSA and it is well-known that this scheme is sensible to lattice attacks once some information on the most significant bits of the nonces k are known. Many attacks have been proposed since [3,8,12,13].

It is possible to use C Safe-Errors on the dummy operations added purportedly for the atomicity formulae as Yen *et al.* proposed against the CRT-RSA implementation in [18]. The attacker introduces a fault during a possibly dummy field operation. If the result is still correct, the operation was indeed dummy and the elliptic curve operation can be deduced. As a consequence, the current target bit of the secret scalar can be learned. However, such way of attacking discloses only a small number of bits of the nonce per ECSM if we allow multiple faults. Liu and Nguyen at CT-RSA 2013 in [9] show that it is possible to recover the secret key on DSA as soon as we have at least 2 bits of the nonces for 160-bit modulus. This lower bound has been proven in [14]. The number of bits increases with the size of the modulus and for 192-bit and 256-bit moduli we do not know how many bits are required. Thus, C safe errors must be improved, otherwise not enough information is collected to extract the secret key. Another alternative to lattice-based attacks consists in using Bleichenbacher attack that has been recently proposed by De Mulder *et al.* at CHES 2013 [11]. This attack allows in theory to recover the secret key as soon as a few bits of the nonces is known and according to the modulus size, it could be preferable to use this attack in comparison with lattice attacks. The main drawback of this attack is that if we want to use a very small number of bits, then the number of needed signature becomes quite large. For instance, in order to attack ECDSA on 160-bit finite field knowing only one bit of the nonce, the number of signatures is about 2^{33}. We use an interesting idea introduced in [1] to reduce the number of faulty signatures to 2^{26} if one bit is known for 160-bit moduli and to 2^{19} if two bits are known and in this case we can attack 160-bit and 192-bit moduli by increasing the time and memory complexity. When more bits are available, it is not easy to tell which one of lattice attacks and Bleichenbacher attacks is the most efficient as shown in [11] since lattice attack can also be used to makes Bleichenbacher attack more efficient.

In this paper, we also present a countermeasure against this attack for the atomicity implementations. The formulæ are rewritten such that the dummy operations no longer occur. We define some processes such that every fault induced will inevitably be detected.

The rest of the paper is organized as follows. In Sect. 2, we recall background on ECC, side-channel attacks, and the side-channel atomicity countermeasures. The attacks on protected implementations are given in Sect. 3. The classical C safe-errors when the exponent is static and our new attack when the exponent is ephemeral using previous algorithms [1,11]. Section 4 presents our proposed solution that can be applied to any formulæ. Finally, we conclude in Sect. 5.

2   Background

In this section, we present the required background to understand the attack on the Side-Channel Atomicity and the protection that we suggest.

2.1   Elliptic Curve Cryptography

An elliptic curve over a finite prime field $\mathbb{F}_p$ of characteristic $p > 3$ can be described by its reduced Weierstraß form:

$$E\colon y^2 = x^3 + ax + b. \tag{1}$$

We denote by $E(\mathbb{F}_p)$ the set of points $(x, y) \in \mathbb{F}_p^2$ satisfying Eq. (1), plus the point at infinity $\mathcal{O}$.

The points on $E(\mathbb{F}_p)$ define an additive Abelian group given by the following addition law. Let $P = (x_1, y_1) \neq \mathcal{O}$ and $Q = (x_2, y_2) \notin \{\mathcal{O}, -P\}$ be two points on $E(\mathbb{F}_p)$. Point addition $R = (x_3, y_3) = P + Q$ is defined by the formula:

$$
\begin{aligned}
x_3 &= \lambda^2 - x_1 - x_2 \\
y_3 &= \lambda(x_1 - x_3) - y_1
\end{aligned}
\quad \text{where } \lambda =
\begin{cases}
\frac{y_1 - y_2}{x_1 - x_2} & \text{if } P \neq Q, \\
\frac{3x_1^2 + a}{2y_1} & \text{if } P = Q.
\end{cases}
$$

The inverse of point P is defined as $-P = (x_1, -y_1)$.

To avoid modular inversions, implementers frequently work in the Jacobian projective coordinates system. The equation of an elliptic curve in the Jacobian projective coordinates system in the reduced Weierstraß form is:

$$E^{\mathcal{J}}\colon Y^2 = X^3 + aXZ^4 + bZ^6.$$

The projective point (X, Y, Z) corresponds to the affine point $(X/Z^2, Y/Z^3)$. The point (X, Y, Z) is equivalent to any point (r^2X, r^3Y, rZ) with $r \in \mathbb{F}_p^*$.

Let $P_1 = (X_1, Y_1, Z_1), P_2 = (X_2, Y_2, Z_2)$ be two points on $E^{\mathcal{J}}(\mathbb{F}_p)$ with $P_1 \neq \mathcal{O}, ord(P_1) > 2$ and $P_2 \notin \{\mathcal{O}, -P_1\}$. Point doubling and points addition are defined by the following formulæ:

– **ECDBL.** $P_3 = (X_3, Y_3, Z_3) = 2P_1$ can be computed as:
$X_3 = T$, $Y_3 = -8Y_1^4 + M(S - T)$, $Z_3 = 2Y_1 Z_1$, where
$S = 4X_1 Y_1^2$, $M = 3X_1^2 + aZ_1^4$, $T = -2S + M^2$
– **ECADD.** $P_3 = (X_3, Y_3, Z_3) = P_1 + P_2$ can be computed as:
$X_3 = -H^3 - 2U_1 H^2 + R^2$, $Y_3 = -S_1 H^3 + R(U_1 H^2 - X_3)$, $Z_3 = Z_1 Z_2 H$,
where
$$U_1 = X_1 Z_2^2, \ U_2 = X_2 Z_1^2, \ S_1 = Y_1 Z_2^3, \ S_2 = Y_2 Z_1^3, \ H = U_2 - U_1, \ R = S_2 - S_1$$

2.2   Elliptic Curve Digital Signature Algorithm

The Elliptic Curve Digital Signature Algorithm (ECDSA) is a signature scheme. It has been standardized in [17]. Given the following curve parameters:

– E, an elliptic curve over a prime field $\mathbb{F}_p$,
– G, a generator of a subgroup of E of order t,

the signature process is as follows:

Algorithm 1. ECDSA Signature

Input: private key d, an encoded integer $m \in \{0, p - 1\}$ representing a message
Output: Signature (r, s)
1: $k \xleftarrow{\mathcal{R}} \{1, \ldots, t - 1\}$
2: $Q \leftarrow [k]G$
3: $r \leftarrow x_Q \mod t$
4: **if** $r = 0$ **then**
5:      **go to** line 1
6: **end if**
7: $s \leftarrow k^{-1}(dr + m) \mod t$
8: **if** $s = 0$ **then**
9:      **go to** line 1
10: **end if**
11: **return** (r, s)

2.3   Side-Channel Atomicity

In ECC, one has to compute scalar multiplications, *i.e.* compute $[k]P$, given P and an integer k. The Left-to-Right Double-and-Add and Right-to-Left algorithms (Algorithms 2 and 3) are ways of doing so.

Algorithm 2. Left-to-Right Double-and-Add

Input: a point P and an integer $k = (1, k_{n-2}, \ldots, k_0)_2$
Output: $[k]P$
  $R_0 \leftarrow P$
  for $i = n - 2$ **downto** 0 **do**
    $R_0 \leftarrow 2R_0$ $\triangleright R_0 = [(k_{n-1}, \ldots, k_{i+1}, 0)_2]P$
    if $k_i = 1$ **then** $R_0 \leftarrow R_0 + P$ $\triangleright R_0 = [(k_{n-1}, \ldots, k_{i+1}, k_i)_2]P$
  end for
  return R_0

Algorithm 3. Right-to-Left Double-and-Add

Input: $k = (k_{n-1}, \ldots, k_1, 1)_2, P$
Output: $[k]P$
  $R_0 \leftarrow P$
  $R_1 \leftarrow 2P$
  for $i = 1$ **to** $n - 1$ **do**
    if $k_i = 1$ **then** $R_0 \leftarrow R_0 + R_1$ $\triangleright R_0 = [(k_i, \ldots, k_0)_2]P$
    $R_1 \leftarrow 2R_1$ $\triangleright R_1 = [2^{i+1}]P$
  end for
  return R_0

Both algorithms exist when the scalar is given by its Non-Adjacent Form (NAF) representation. They are given in Appendix A.

If an adversary is able to distinguish the power consumption of an addition and a doubling during the execution of such algorithm, then she is able to recover the secret scalar k [6]. In order to prevent this attack called the Simple-Power Analysis, Chevallier-Mames, Ciet and Joye suggest to write the elliptic curve formulæ with sequences of identical *atomic patterns*. An atomic pattern is defined in [4] as the sequence of the following (possibly dummy) operations:

1. modular multiplication or square
2. modular addition
3. modular opposite
4. modular addition

A point doubling requires 10 of these atomic patterns, while an addition requires 16 in the Jacobian coordinates systems. It has been later improved several times by Longa in [10], Giraud and Verneuil in [7] and Rondepierre in [15]. Hereafter, we recall Giraud and Verneuil's pattern, the state-of-the-art best atomic pattern when applied with the Right-to-Left Double-and-Add, and Rondepierre's pattern, the state-of-the-art best atomic pattern when applied with the Left-to-Right Double-and-Add.

2.4 Giraud and Verneuil's pattern [7]

Giraud and Verneuil suggest a pattern composed of two squares, six multiplications, six additions and four subtractions. An addition of points requires two patterns while a doubling requires only one. The points are given in modified Jacobian coordinates: $P = (X_1, Y_1, Z_1, W_1 = aZ_1^4)$, for faster doubling [5]. These coordinates are suitable for the Right-to-Left Double-and-Add algorithms (Algorithms 3 and 5). We recall the formulæ in Fig. 1. From $P = (X_1, Y_1, Z_1)$ and $Q = (X_2, Y_2, Z_2)$, one can compute $P + Q = (X_3, Y_3, Z_3)$ and $2P = (X_3, Y_3, Z_3, W_3 = aZ_3^4)$.

1.	$T_1 \leftarrow Z_2^2$	$T_1 \leftarrow T_6^2$	$T_1 \leftarrow X_1^2$
2.	$\star \leftarrow \star + \star$	$\star \leftarrow \star + \star$	$T_2 \leftarrow Y_1 + Y_1$
3.	$T_2 \leftarrow Y_1 \times Z_2$	$T_4 \leftarrow T_5 \times T_1$	$Z_3 \leftarrow T_2 \times Z_1$
4.	$\star \leftarrow \star + \star$	$\star \leftarrow \star + \star$	$T_4 \leftarrow T_1 + T_1$
5.	$T_5 \leftarrow Y_2 \times Z_1$	$T_5 \leftarrow T_1 \times T_6$	$T_3 \leftarrow T_2 \times Y_1$
6.	$\star \leftarrow \star + \star$	$\star \leftarrow \star + \star$	$T_6 \leftarrow T_3 + T_3$
7.	$T_3 \leftarrow T_1 \times T_2$	$T_1 \leftarrow Z_1 \times T_6$	$T_2 \leftarrow T_6 \times T_3$
8.	$\star \leftarrow \star + \star$	$\star \leftarrow \star + \star$	$T_1 \leftarrow T_4 + T_1$
9.	$\star \leftarrow \star + \star$	$\star \leftarrow \star + \star$	$T_1 \leftarrow T_1 + W_1$
10.	$T_4 \leftarrow Z_1^2$	$T_6 \leftarrow T_2^2$	$T_3 \leftarrow T_1^2$
11.	$T_5 \leftarrow T_5 \times T_4$	$Z_3 \leftarrow T_1 \times Z_2$	$T_4 \leftarrow T_6 \times X_1$
12.	$\star \leftarrow \star + \star$	$T_1 \leftarrow T_4 + T_4$	$T_5 \leftarrow W_1 + W_1$
13.	$T_2 \leftarrow T_2 - T_3$	$T_6 \leftarrow T_6 - T_1$	$T_3 \leftarrow T_3 - T_4$
14.	$T_5 \leftarrow T_1 \times X_1$	$T_1 \leftarrow T_5 \times T_3$	$W_3 \leftarrow T_2 \times T_5$
15.	$\star \leftarrow \star - \star$	$X_3 \leftarrow T_6 - T_5$	$X_3 \leftarrow T_3 - T_4$
16.	$\star \leftarrow \star - \star$	$T_4 \leftarrow T_4 - X_3$	$T_6 \leftarrow T_4 - X_3$
17.	$T_6 \leftarrow X_2 \times T_4$	$T_3 \leftarrow T_4 \times T_2$	$T_4 \leftarrow T_6 \times T_1$
18.	$T_6 \leftarrow T_6 - T_5$	$Y_3 \leftarrow T_3 - T_1$	$Y_3 \leftarrow T_4 - T_2$

Fig. 1. Addition and doubling operations written with Giraud and Verneuil's pattern ($\star$ represents a dummy operand). Each column is an atomic pattern.

2.5 Rondepierre's pattern [15]

Rondepierre suggests a pattern composed of two squares, eight multiplications, five additions and five subtractions. An addition of points requires one pattern, as well as a doubling. From $P = (X_1, Y_1, Z_1, Z_1^2, Z_1^3), Q = (X_2, Y_2, 1)$ and $I = \sqrt{-a3^{-1}}$, Rondepierre proposes formulæ to compute $P + Q = (X_3, Y_3, Z_3, Z_3^2, Z_3^3), P - Q = (X_3, Y_3, Z_3, Z_3^2, Z_3^3)$ or $2P = (X_3, Y_3, Z_3, Z_3^2, Z_3^3)$. The subtraction of points is suitable for the Right-to-Left method (Algorithms 3 and 5). The formulæ are suitable for the Right-to-Left Double-and-Add algorithms (Algorithms 3 and 5). They are given in Fig. 2.

1.	$T_1 \leftarrow X_2 \times Z_1^2$	$T_1 \leftarrow X_2 \times Z_1^2$	$T_0 \leftarrow I \times Z_1^2$
2.	$T_1 \leftarrow T_1 - X_1$	$T_1 \leftarrow T_1 - X_1$	$T_1 \leftarrow X_1 - T_0$
3.	$\star \leftarrow \star + \star$	$Z_1^2 \leftarrow Y_1 + Y_1$	$T_2 \leftarrow Y_1 + Y_1$
4.	$T_2 \leftarrow T_1 \times T_1$	$T_2 \leftarrow T_1 \times T_1$	$Z_3^2 \leftarrow Y_1 \times T_2$
5.	$\star \leftarrow \star + \star$	$\star \leftarrow \star + \star$	$Y_3 \leftarrow Z_3^2 + Z_3^2$
6.	$T_3 \leftarrow X_1 \times T_2$	$T_3 \leftarrow X_1 \times T_2$	$T_3 \leftarrow T_2 \times Z_1$
7.	$T_0 \leftarrow Y_2 \times Z_1^3$	$T_0 \leftarrow Y_2 \times Z_1^3$	$T_2 \leftarrow Y_3 \times X_1$
8.	$\star \leftarrow \star + \star$	$T_0 \leftarrow Z_1^2 + T_0$	$X_3 \leftarrow X_1 + T_0$
9.	$Z_1^3 \leftarrow T_1 \times T_2$	$Z_1^3 \leftarrow T_1 \times T_2$	$T_0 \leftarrow T_1 \times X_3$
10.	$T_2 \leftarrow Z_1 \times T_1$	$T_2 \leftarrow Z_1 \times T_1$	$T_1 \leftarrow Z_3^2 \times Y_3$
11.	$X_3 \leftarrow T_3 + T_3$	$X_3 \leftarrow T_3 + T_3$	$T_2 \leftarrow T_0 + T_0$
12.	$X_3 \leftarrow Z_1^3 + X_3$	$X_3 \leftarrow Z_1^3 + X_3$	$T_0 \leftarrow T_0 + T_2$
13.	$Z_3^2 \leftarrow (T_0)^2$	$Z_3^2 \leftarrow (T_0)^2$	$X_3 \leftarrow (T_0)^2$
14.	$T_0 \leftarrow T_0 - Y_1$	$T_0 \leftarrow T_0 - Y_1$	$X_3 \leftarrow X_3 - T_2$
15.	$T_1 \leftarrow (T_0)^2$	$T_1 \leftarrow (T_0)^2$	$Z_3^2 \leftarrow (T_3)^2$
16.	$X_3 \leftarrow T_1 - X_3$	$X_3 \leftarrow T_1 - X_3$	$X_3 \leftarrow X_3 - T_2$
17.	$T_1 \leftarrow T_3 - X_3$	$T_1 \leftarrow T_3 - X_3$	$T_2 \leftarrow T_2 - X_3$
18.	$T_3 \leftarrow T_1 \times T_0$	$T_3 \leftarrow T_1 \times T_0$	$Z_3^2 \leftarrow Z_3^2 \times T_3$
19.	$T_0 \leftarrow Y_1 \times Z_1^3$	$T_0 \leftarrow Y_1 \times Z_1^3$	$Y_3 \leftarrow T_0 \times T_2$
20.	$Y_3 \leftarrow T_3 - T_0$	$Y_3 \leftarrow T_3 - T_0$	$Y_3 \leftarrow Y_3 - T_1$
21.	$Z_3 \leftarrow T_2$	$Z_3 \leftarrow T_2$	$Z_3 \leftarrow T_3$

Fig. 2. Addition, subtraction and doubling operations written with Rondepierre's pattern ($\star$ represents a dummy operand). Each column is an atomic pattern.

3 Attacks on Side-Channel Atomicity

3.1 C Safe-Error

The C Safe-Error attack was first published by Yen, Kim, Lim and Moon [18]. They target an RSA implementation which contains dummy operations to prevent the SPA. A fault is introduced during an operation which is possibly a dummy one. If the result of the cryptographic operation is correct, the operation was indeed a dummy operation and some information on the private key can be deduced.

C Safe-Error on the side-channel atomicity countermeasure for ECC relies on the same principle.

C Safe-Error on Giraud and Verneuil's Pattern. Suppose that the Right-to-Left Double-and-Add (Algorithm 3) is used, with the patterns of Fig. 1. Regarding the Right-to-Left Double-and-Add, the last pattern is necessarily a doubling. However, regarding the trace during the execution of the penultimate pattern, the attacker cannot deduce that it is a doubling or the second part of an addition.

Suppose that the attacker injects a fault on the arithmetic module unit during the execution of the first addition of the penultimate pattern (line 6 of Fig. 1).

If the pattern is indeed the second part of an addition, the error has no effect on the result. The fault is *safe*. In this case, the most significant bit of the scalar is 1.

On the other hand, if the result is incorrect, the pattern was a doubling and the most significant bit is 0.

The attacker can repetitively perform this attack during several ECDSA signature generations. She can collect several signatures and keep only the correct ones (the ones where the error was safe). She then got several signatures knowing that the most significant bit of the ephemeral scalar is 1.

C Safe-Error on Rondepierre's Pattern. The attack on this pattern is analogous to the previous one.

Suppose that the Left-to-Right Double-and-Add (Algorithm 2) is used, with the patterns of Fig. 2. Regarding the trace during the execution of the last pattern, the attacker cannot deduce that it is a doubling an addition.

Suppose that the attacker injects a fault on the arithmetic module unit during the execution of the first subtraction of the last pattern (line 3 of Fig. 2). If the pattern is indeed an addition, the error has no effect on the result. The fault is *safe*. In this case, the least significant bit of the scalar is 1.

On the other hand, if the result is incorrect, the pattern was a doubling and the least significant bit is 0.

The attacker can repetitively performs this attack during several ECDSA signature generations. She can collect several signatures and keep only the correct ones (the ones where the error was safe). Hence she has got several signatures such that the least significant bit is 1.

Extension to Several Bits. Of course, the attacker can inject several faults at different times during the algorithm.

For Giraud and Verneuil's patterns, two patterns are required for the addition. The attacker can inject one fault on the penultimate pattern and one fault on the fifth last pattern. If the result is correct, it means that the last patterns are $\mathcal{A}1; \mathcal{A}2; \mathcal{D}; \mathcal{A}1; \mathcal{A}2; \mathcal{D}$, thus the two most significant bits are 1.

For Rondepierre's patterns, the attacker can inject a fault on the last pattern and on the third last pattern. If the result is correct, it means that the last patterns are $\mathcal{A}; \mathcal{D}; \mathcal{A}$, thus the two least significant bits are 1.

Injecting the Fault at the Right Time. We describe here the issue of injecting the fault at the right time. As a matter of fact, we said before that the attacker needs to inject a fault on the last or penultimate pattern. How does she know that this is the last or penultimate pattern before the end of the ECSM? Indeed, a fault cannot be injected retrospectively, i.e., after noticing that the ECSM is finished.

In fact, she can suppose that the Hamming weight of the n-bit scalar is $n/2$ which happens with high probability. In this case, there will be n doubling and

$n/2$ additions. This gives a total of $2n$ Giraud and Verneuil's pattern (because two patterns are required for the addition) and $n + n/2$ Rondepierre's pattern. The last pattern is thus the $2n^{th}$ pattern (Giraud and Verneuil) and the $(n + n/2)^{th}$ pattern (Rondepierre).

The attacker can verify afterwards that the Hamming weight of the scalar was is indeed $n/2$ counting the patterns by SPA. If it is not the case, she throws out the signature[1].

3.2 Lattice Attacks Knowing only Two Bits per Value of the Ephemeral Nonces

The attack works as follows: in a first step, a small number of bits ℓ (e.g., $\ell = 1, 2, 3, 4, 5$, or 6) is gathered about the nonce k used in ECDSA. Namely, one bit is tested through the effectiveness (or not) of an injection at a given field operation in one ECDBL or ECADD atomic pattern. Then, a lattice attack is launched using only these ℓ bits of information about the ephemeral nonce per ECSM.

There are basically two different strategies to recover the secret key d. The first one consists in solving the Hidden Number Problem (HNP), which can be described as follows: given (t_i, u_i) pairs of integers such that

$$|dt_i - u_i|_q \le q/2^{\ell+1},$$

where ℓ denotes the number of bits we recovered by C Safe-Errors, d denotes the hidden number we are looking for and $|\cdot|_q$ denotes the distance to $q\mathbb{Z}$, i.e. $|z|_q = \min_{a \in \mathbb{Z}} |z - aq|$. Such problem can be cast as a Closest Vector Problem (CVP) in a lattice and the LLL algorithm can be used to solve it in practice very efficiently. We recall the basic attack in Appendix 5 and its extensive presentation can be found in [14]. The main advantage of this technique is that the number of signatures required is usually very small, but it cannot be used all the time when the number of bits becomes very small. Indeed, in this case for 160-bit modulus for instance, Liu and Nguyen used BKZ 2.0 to solve such lattice and the dimension becomes very high for lattice algorithms [9].

When the number of bits is very small, which is the case here if we try to reduce the number of faults, another technique due to Bleichenbacher can be used. This technique has been described in [11] for attacking a smartcard using ECDSA on 384-bit modulus. The idea is that there is a bias on distribution of the nonces k_j. If we correctly guess the value of the secret d is large and all other biases are small (close to 0) according to the correct definition of bias $B_q(D) = E(\exp^{2i\pi D/q})$ where E is the expectation of the random variable $\exp^{2i\pi D/q}$ and D is the random variable representing the choice of d. We can approximate this bias experimentally using many signatures by computing $B_q(d) = (1/m) \cdot \sum_{j=0}^{m-1} \exp^{2i\pi(h_j + c_j d)/q}$ where $h_j = H(m_j)/s_j \mod q$ and $c_j = r_j/s_j \mod q$ for

---

[1] Notice that the atomicity countermeasure does not execute in constant time. However, the only information that is leaked is the Hamming weight of the scalar, which is not enough to design an attack (at least with state-of-the-art knowledge).

signature (r_j, s_j) of message m_j and m the number of such signatures. The idea is just to compute all the bias $B_q(d)$ for all possible values of d and pick the largest one. Due to the special form of the bias, it is possible to perform all these computations using Fast Fourier Transform, however the time complexity of this task is out of reach since there are 2^{160} different values for d. Bleichenbacher proposes a first phase which consists in reducing the range of the value d (we are looking for the, say 32 most significant bits of d, by reducing the bias of d. This operation will also widen the width of the pick of the bias d in the frequence domain. In the first stage of this attack, we are looking for a linear combination of the values c_j which is small, less than 32 bits. In this case, it has been shown in [11] that we can recover the 32 most significant bits of d. However, the number of required signatures becomes very high and De Mulder *et al.* use a lattice reduction technique to reduce the number of signature contrary to Bleichenbacher original attack which uses more Generalized Birthday Paradox (GBP) ideas [16]. For instance, given (h_j, c_j) such that $h_j + dc_j = k_j$, if c_j and $c_{j'}$ have 32 bits in common, then $h_j - h_{j'} + d(c_j - c_{j'}) = k_j - k_{j'}$ is a new relation where the new value $(c_j - c_{j'})$ has been reduced by 32 bits and since we add the k_js, the initial bias b is increased to b^2 according to the Piling-up lemma. In [1], the authors show that it is possible to recover a 160-bit secret value with only *one bit* of the nonces. However, the number of required signatures grows up to 2^{33}. They also show that it is possible to reduce the number of signatures required in Bleichenbacher algorithm by using time-memory/signature tradeoff.

The idea is that the first iteration will allow us to make many signature samples (h_j, c_j) by increasing the bias. For instance, given m signatures, we can generate m^2 samples by performing addition and subtraction mod q of the initial signatures.

In Fig. 3, we give the minimal number m of signatures required for number of known bits ℓ of the nonce.

q	160 bits			192 bits	256 bits
ℓ	1	2	2	2	3
m	2^{26}	2^{14}	200	2^{16}	2^{16}
Tech.	Bleich.	Bleich.	Latt.	Bleich.	Bleich.
Compl.	2^{40}	2^{28}	Few hr	2^{33}	2^{33}

Fig. 3. Minimal number of signatures d required depending on the number of bits ℓ using Brainpool curves.

4   Our Protection

We propose in this section our protection. It consists in using the dummy operations to perform a check at the end of the ECSM.

4.1   Generalized Protection

In the patterns of all known atomic side-channel protections, the dummy operations are either field additions or field subtractions and are only on patterns of the addition and subtraction of points. The underlying reason is that those operations are more furtive than multiplications. Thus, it is unlikely that an attacker manages to distinguish between dummy and functional operations in the patterns.

Our idea is to perform a check at the end of the ECSM such that if an error occurred, the circuit detects it and no result is returned.

Let addition and doubling formulæ using some patterns such that an addition of points contains l dummy field additions and m dummy subtractions. This means that, at the end of the ECSM, there are (l times the number of additions of points) dummy field additions and (m times the number of additions of points) dummy field subtractions.

We propose to add two temporary registers T_{add} and T_{sub} first initialized with $T_{add} \leftarrow r_{add}$, $T_{sub} \leftarrow -r_{sub}$; r_{add}, r_{sub} being two random integers. Every dummy addition $\star \leftarrow \star + \star$ is replaced by $T_{add} \leftarrow T_{add} + r_{add}$ and every subtraction $\star \leftarrow \star - \star$ is replaced by $T_{sub} \leftarrow T_{sub} - r_{sub}$. In this way, at the end of the ECSM, T_{add} should be equal to $l \times r_{add}$ times the number of additions performed during the ECSM and T_{sub} should be equal to $m \times r_{sub}$ times the number of additions.

A counter is added for each pattern to count the number of additions and doubling performed. Another method is that the number of patterns is related to the Hamming weight (HW) of the scalar used.

The protection consists in verifying that the equality is satisfied at the end of the ECSM.

4.2   The Protection with Giraud and Verneuil's Pattern

With those formulæ, there are 11 dummy additions and 2 dummy subtractions for the addition of points. The number of addition of points is $\mathrm{HW}(k)$ for the Right-to-Left Double-and-Add algorithm (Algorithms 3), k being the scalar.

Thus the protection consists in verifying that T_{add} is equal to $11 \times \mathrm{HW}(k) \times r_{add}$ and T_{sub} is equal to $2 \times \mathrm{HW}(k) \times r_{sub}$ at the end of the ECSM.

4.3   The Protection with Rondepierre's Pattern

With those formulæ, there are 3 dummy additions for the addition of points. The number of addition of points is $\mathrm{HW}(k)$ for the Left-to-Right Double-and-Add algorithm (Algorithm 2), k being the scalar.

Thus the protection consists in verifying that T_{add} is equal to $3 \times \mathrm{HW}(k) \times r_{add}$.

5   Conclusion

In this paper, we show how to use C Safe-Errors on the atomicity side-channel countermeasure to recover a few bits of ephemeral scalars used during ECDSA signatures. With only two bits of the scalar, we are able to recover the secret key.

Then, we propose a protection to thwart C Safe-Errors that target the atomicity countermeasure. The method consists in replacing the dummy operations of the atomic patterns by chained secret operations that are verified in a final check. In this case, the C Safe-error is no longer applicable.

References

1. Aranha, D.F., Fouque, P.-A., Gérard, B., Kammerer, J.-G., Tibouchi, M., Zapalowicz, J.-C.: GLV/GLS decomposition, power analysis, and attacks on ECDSA signatures with single-bit nonce bias. In: Sarkar, P., Iwata, T. (eds.) ASIACRYPT 2014. LNCS, vol. 8873, pp. 262–281. Springer, Heidelberg (2014)
2. Boneh, D., Venkatesan, R.: Hardness of computing the most significant bits of secret keys in Diffie-Hellman and related schemes. In: Koblitz, N. (ed.) CRYPTO 1996. LNCS, vol. 1109, pp. 129–142. Springer, Heidelberg (1996)
3. Brumley, B.B., Tuveri, N.: Remote timing attacks are still practical. In: Atluri, V., Diaz, C. (eds.) ESORICS 2011. LNCS, vol. 6879, pp. 355–371. Springer, Heidelberg (2011)
4. Chevallier-Mames, B., Ciet, M., Joye, M.: Low-cost solutions for preventing simple side-channel analysis: side-channel atomicity. IEEE Trans. Comput. **53**(6), 760–768 (2004)
5. Cohen, H., Miyaji, A., Ono, T.: Efficient elliptic curve exponentiation using mixed coordinates. In: Ohta, K., Pei, D. (eds.) ASIACRYPT 1998. LNCS, vol. 1514, pp. 51–65. Springer, Heidelberg (1998)
6. Coron, J.-S.: Resistance against differential power analysis for elliptic curve cryptosystems. In: Koç, Ç.K., Paar, C. (eds.) CHES 1999. LNCS, vol. 1717, pp. 292–302. Springer, Heidelberg (1999)
7. Giraud, C., Verneuil, V.: Atomicity improvement for elliptic curve scalar multiplication. In: Gollmann, D., Lanet, J.-L., Iguchi-Cartigny, J. (eds.) CARDIS 2010. LNCS, vol. 6035, pp. 80–101. Springer, Heidelberg (2010)
8. Howgrave-Graham, N., Smart, N.P.: Lattice attacks on digital signature schemes. Des. Codes Cryptogr. **23**(3), 283–290 (2001)
9. Liu, M., Nguyen, P.Q.: Solving BDD by enumeration: an update. In: Dawson, E. (ed.) CT-RSA 2013. LNCS, vol. 7779, pp. 293–309. Springer, Heidelberg (2013)
10. Longa, P.: Accelerating the scalar multiplication on elliptic curve cryptosystems over prime fields. Master's thesis, School of Information and Engineering, University of Ottawa, Canada (2007)
11. De Mulder, E., Hutter, M., Marson, M.E., Pearson, P.: Using Bleichenbacher's solution to the hidden number problem to attack nonce leaks in 384-bit ECDSA: extended version. J. Cryptogr. Eng. **4**(1), 33–45 (2014)
12. Naccache, D., Nguyên, P.Q., Tunstall, M., Whelan, C.: Experimenting with faults, lattices and the DSA. In: Vaudenay, S. (ed.) PKC 2005. LNCS, vol. 3386, pp. 16–28. Springer, Heidelberg (2005)

13. Nguyen, P.Q., Shparlinski, I.: The insecurity of the elliptic curve digital signature algorithm with partially known nonces. Des. Codes Cryptogr. **30**(2), 201–217 (2003)

14. Nguyen, P.Q., Tibouchi, M.: Lattice-based fault attacks on signatures. In: Joye, M., Tunstall, M. (eds.) Fault Analysis in Cryptography. Information Security and Cryptography, pp. 201–220. Springer, Heidelberg (2012)

15. Rondepierre, F.: Revisiting atomic patterns for scalar multiplications on elliptic curves. In: Francillon, A., Rohatgi, P. (eds.) CARDIS 2013. LNCS, vol. 8419, pp. 171–186. Springer, Heidelberg (2014)

16. Wagner, D.: A generalized birthday problem. In: Yung, M. (ed.) CRYPTO 2002. LNCS, vol. 2442, pp. 288–303. Springer, Heidelberg (2002)

17. ANSI X9.62. Public key cryptography for the financial services industry: the elliptic curve digital signature algorithm (ECDSA). ANSI, USA (1998)

18. Yen, S.-M., Kim, S., Lim, S., Moon, S.-J.: A countermeasure against one physical cryptanalysis may benefit another attack. In: Kim, K. (ed.) ICISC 2001. LNCS, vol. 2288, pp. 414–427. Springer, Heidelberg (2002)

Reminder About the Lattice-Based Attack on ECDSA

Using the ℓ least significant bits of k (the attack also works with the most significant bits), we can write $k = 2^\ell(k \gg \ell) + \mathrm{lsb}_\ell\, k = 2^\ell b + \mathrm{lsb}_\ell\, k$ for some integer $b \geq 0$. We then get from $dr = sk - h \mod q$:

$$dr \cdot 2^{-\ell} s^{-1} = b - h \cdot 2^{-\ell} s^{-1} + \mathrm{lsb}_\ell\, k \cdot 2^{-\ell} \mod q.$$

Now let t and u two values which can be computed from known or retrieved information, such as:

$$t = r \cdot 2^{-\ell} s^{-1} \mod q, \quad u = -h \cdot 2^{-\ell} s^{-1} + \mathrm{lsb}_\ell\, k \cdot 2^{-\ell} \mod q.$$

The inequality $b < q/2^\ell$ can be expressed in terms of t and u as:

$$0 \leq dt - u \mod q < q/2^\ell.$$

Therefore, if we denote by $|\cdot|_q$ the distance to $\mathbb{Z}/q\mathbb{Z}$, i.e. $|z|_q = \min_{a \in \mathbb{Z}} |z - aq|$, we have:

$$|dt - u - q/2^{\ell+1}|_q \leq q/2^{\ell+1},$$
$$|dt - v/2^{\ell+1}|_q \leq q/2^{\ell+1},$$

where v is the integer $2^{\ell+1}u + q$. Given a number of faulty signatures (r_i, s_i) of various messages, say m of them, the same method yields pairs of integers (t_i, v_i) such that

$$|dt_i - v_i/2^{\ell+1}|_q \leq q/2^{\ell+1}. \tag{2}$$

The goal is to recover d from this data. The problem is very similar to the hidden number problem considered by Boneh and Venkatesan in [2], and is approached by transforming it into a lattice closest vector problem.

More precisely, consider the $(m + 1)$-dimensional lattice L spanned by the rows of the following matrix:

$$\begin{pmatrix} 2^{\ell+1}q & 0 & \cdots & 0 & 0 \\ 0 & 2^{\ell+1}q & \ddots & \vdots & \vdots \\ \vdots & \ddots & \ddots & 0 & \vdots \\ 0 & \cdots & 0 & 2^{\ell+1}q & 0 \\ 2^{\ell+1}t_1 & \cdots & \cdots & 2^{\ell+1}t_m & 1 \end{pmatrix}$$

Inequality (2) implies the existence of an integer c_i such that:

$$|2^{\ell+1}dt_i - v_i - 2^{\ell+1}c_i q| \le q. \tag{3}$$

Now note that the row vector, called *hidden vector*,

$$\mathbf{c} = (2^{\ell+1}dt_1 + 2^{\ell+1}c_1 q, \cdots, 2^{\ell+1}dt_m + 2^{\ell+1}c_m q, d)$$

belongs to L and $\mathbf{c}$ is very close to the row vector $\mathbf{v} = (v_1, \cdots, v_m, 0)$. Indeed, by (3), the distance from $\mathbf{c}$ to $\mathbf{v}$ is bounded as:

$$\|\mathbf{v} - \mathbf{c}\| \le q\sqrt{m + 1}.$$

We thus have a CVP to solve. In practice, we use an embedding technique to reduce CVP to SVP. This technique consists in computing the $(m + 2)$-dimensional lattice L' spanned by the rows of the matrix

$$\begin{pmatrix} L & 0 \\ \mathbf{v} & 1 \end{pmatrix}$$

The row vector $(\mathbf{v} - \mathbf{c}, 1)$ is short, belongs to L' and we hope this is the shortest vector of L'. This assumption implies a condition on the required number of signatures depending on the parameter ℓ and the modulus. An estimate which makes it possible to recover the private key is:

$$m \gtrsim \frac{n}{\ell - \log_2 \sqrt{\pi e/2}}.$$

The above estimate is heuristic, but it is possible to give parameters for which attacks of this kind can be proved rigorously [13].

A Elliptic Curve Scalar Multiplications in NAF

We recall the definition and the NAF of integers.

Definition 1. *A non-adjacent form (NAF) of a positive integer k is an expression $k = \sum_{i=0}^{l-1} k_i 2^i$ where $k_i \in \{-1, 0, 1\}$, $k_{l-1} \ne 0$, and no two consecutive digits k_i are nonzero. The length of the NAF is l. The NAF of an integer k is denoted $NAF(k)$ or $(k_{l-1}, \ldots, k_0)_{NAF}$.*

Algorithm 4. Left-to-Right NAF scalar multiplication

Input: $k = (1, k_{l-2}, \ldots, k_0)_{\text{NAF}}, P$
Output: $[k]P$
  $Q \leftarrow P$
  $i \leftarrow l - 2$
  while $i \geq 0$ **do**
    $Q \leftarrow 2Q$
    if $k_i = 1$ **then** $Q \leftarrow Q + P$
    if $k_i = -1$ **then** $Q \leftarrow Q - P$
    $i \leftarrow i - 1$
  end while
  return Q

The following algorithm computes the width NAF representation of the scalar on the fly.

Algorithm 5. Right-to-Left NAF scalar multiplication

Input: $k = (k_{n-1}, \ldots, k_0)_2, P$
Output: $[k]P$
  $R \leftarrow P$
  $Q \leftarrow \mathcal{O}$
  while $k \geq 1$ **do**
    if $k_0 = 1$ **then**
      $u \leftarrow (k \mod 4)$
      $k \leftarrow k - u$
      if $u = 1$ **then**
        $Q \leftarrow Q + R$
      else
        $Q \leftarrow Q - R$
      end if
    end if
    $R \leftarrow 2R$
    $k \leftarrow k/2$
  end while
  $Q \leftarrow Q + R$
  return Q

Models and Protocols

Clever Arbiters Versus Malicious Adversaries
On the Gap Between Known-Input Security and Chosen-Input Security

Serge Vaudenay[✉]

EPFL, 1015 Lausanne, Switzerland
serge.vaudenay@epfl.ch
http://lasec.epfl.ch

Abstract. When moving from known-input security to chosen-input security, some generic attacks sometimes become possible and must be discarded by a specific set of rules in the threat model. Similarly, common practices consist of fixing security systems, once an exploit is discovered, by adding a specific rule to thwart it. To study feasibility, we investigate a new security notion: security against undetectable attacks. I.e., attacks which cannot be ruled out by any specific rule based on the observable behavior of the adversary. In this model, chosen-input attacks must specify inputs which are indistinguishable from the ones in known-input attacks. Otherwise, they could be ruled out, in theory.

Although non-falsifiable, this notion provides interesting results: for any primitives based on symmetric encryption, message authentication code (MAC), or pseudorandom function (PRF), known-input security is equivalent to this restricted chosen-input security in Minicrypt. Otherwise, any separation implies the construction of a public-key cryptosystem (PKC): for a known-input-secure primitive, any undetectable chosen-input attack transforms the primitive into a PKC.

In this paper, we develop the notion of security based on open rules. We show the above results. We revisit the notion of related-key security of block ciphers to illustrate these results. Interestingly, when the relation among the keys is specified as a black box, no chosen-relation security is feasible. By translating this result to non-black box relations, either no known-input security is feasible, or we can recognize any obfuscated relation by a fixed set of rules, or we can build a PKC. Any of these three results is quite interesting in itself.

1 Preamble

Children often use adaptive rules in their games. Indeed, ruling a game is usually the result of a learning process. There are also common practices to motivate games with adaptive rules. Irrespective on whether this is good or bad, computer security often relies on security patches, or new signatures in anti-virus systems, which appear once an exploit is known.

In cryptography, security definitions followed a similar learning process. We often have to rule out some specific attacks once we realize that no security is

© Springer-Verlag Berlin Heidelberg 2016
P.Y.A. Ryan et al. (Eds.): Kahn Festschrift, LNCS 9100, pp. 497–517, 2016.
DOI: 10.1007/978-3-662-49301-4_31

feasible because there exists *generic* attacks. For instance, to model resistance to chosen-ciphertext attack (CCA), we define a game where the adversary can query a ciphertext to a decryption oracle. As he must distinguish whether a given ciphertext c encrypts a message m_0 or a message m_1, a first rule says that he cannot query the decryption oracle after c is determined. This is the security against "lunchtime attack" [27]. Another rule allows further queries, conditioned to that they are not equal to c. This is the standard CCA security [13,14]. Clearly, no security is feasible without this rule.

A more complicated case is the one of related-key attacks (RKA) [5,6,25]. In this model, the adversary can query a plaintext and a transformation of the key. There are many attacks based on some weird transformations. In Appendix A.1, we describe the attacks by Biham [7], Bellare and Kohno [3], Harris [20,21], and Bernstein [4]. These attacks show that no RKA security is feasible without some specific rules making these attacks forbidden. To rule them out, the easy way is to add some drastic rules such as the transformation must be of the form $k \mapsto k \oplus \Delta$. But the question of a minimal set of rules allowing any random-looking transformation remains.

In this work, we describe the security with adaptive rules as a game, with a challenger, an adversary, and a ruler trying to catch the malicious behavior of the adversary. The game consists of playing with an oracle to evaluate a keyed primitive f_K. So, we distinguish known-input security, where the inputs to the oracle are random, to chosen-input security, where the adversary selects the input. Ruling out malicious behaviors means to restrict to adversaries making chosen inputs indistinguishable from known inputs.

The Paper At A Glance

Setting. We consider a keyed primitive denoted $f_K(q)$. This primitive is set up with a key K and one bit b (which is supposed to be a hard-core bit of K, as we will explain later). An example to consider is given by $f_K(q) = \mathsf{Enc}_{\varphi(K)}(x)$ for $q = (\varphi, x)$, where Enc is some encryption function. In this case, the input φ is referred to as *relation* φ (in reminiscence of *related*-key security) and x as a plaintext.

We further consider the problem of guessing whether the coin b is a Head Or a Tail, i.e., the HOT *game*. In this game, the adversary ignores the key but he can make oracle queries to f_K. We distinguish between the case where q is chosen by the adversary and the case where q is selected based on a random distribution D, i.e., chosen-input attack vs. known-input attack.

On finding a minimal set of rules for related-key security. In related-key security, the adversary must provide a relation to the challenger. In a black-box model, this relation is provided in terms of access to an oracle (i.e., the inner structure of the relation is not visible). Otherwise, relations must be specified in terms of an executable code (or Turing machine). Since there is a double-exponential number of relations, we must consider only relations that can be implemented by a short code and specify a distribution for known-relation security. Alternatively, we must substantially restrict the set of relations, e.g., by taking the set T_+ of all translations $\varphi(K) = K + \Delta$, given a group law "+" over the key-space. Even in that case, a separation between known-relation security and chosen-relation security induces a public-key cryptosystem.

Defining a sound model for related-key security appears to be challenging as many "trivial attacks" using convoluted relations have been discovered, e.g., [5,6]. For this reason, we introduce the notion of game with rules which could be updated incrementally. Indeed, our security game comprises an adversary, a challenger, and a ruler who performs a checking on that the adversary did not select unauthorized relations. This model is particularly useful to show the nonexistence of rules making security feasible.

Our focus. In this paper, we consider a restricted chosen-input model. Thus, we look at chosen inputs that are indistinguishable from the random ones present in known-input models.

Known-input security vs. certain chosen-input security. We observe that having a separation between known-input security and restricted chosen-input security yields the ability to construct a public-key cryptosystem. I.e., if we have a primitive secure against known-input attacks but vulnerable to some chosen-input attack, the cryptosystem's design is based on the primitive and it exploits the attack. In the Minicrypt world [24], public-key cryptography does not exist but symmetric cryptography does. So, therein we cannot have any separation. So, known-input security implies our restrictive chosen-input security.

Black-box vs. non black-box related-key security. We further show that the separation actually holds for related-key security when relations are considered as black-boxes. To remove black-box relations, we consider obfuscated white boxes. Since it is unlikely that one could build a cryptosystem from a block cipher and an adversary, we deduce that either no known-relation security is possible, or there is a generic way to break obfuscation schemes for relations.

Our contribution concisely. In this paper we formalize the notion of ruler/arbiter of a security game and the security notions linked to this. We prove that a gap between known-input security and permissive chosen-input security implies public-key cryptography. We show that the gap exists for related-key security in a black-box model. When removing the black-boxes using an obfuscation scheme, we deduce that either no known-relation security is feasible, or any obfuscation scheme is weak, or it makes a public-key cryptosystem.

Structure of this paper. In Sect. 2, we introduce some meta-security notions via the (formal) concepts of game, ruler, permissive ruler, known-input attack, and chosen-input attack. In Sect. 3 we show that a gap between known-input security and permissive chosen-input security implies public-key cryptography. In Sect. 4 we extend the Harris attack to break any cipher using related keys and we show that no permissive ruler can detect it when the relations used are black-boxes.

We further discuss on extending this with obfuscation and on the difficulty to identity the exact rules to make related-key security sound.

Related work. Related-key attacks independently appeared in Biham's [5,6] and Knudsen's [25]. Basically, an adversary has access to some encryption/decryption black boxes which relate to each other by some known- or chosen-relations by the adversary. Concretely, the adversary makes (φ, x) queries for a relation φ and a plaintext x and gets back $\mathsf{Enc}_{\varphi(K)}(x)$, i.e., the encryption of x under key $\varphi(K)$. (In chosen ciphertext attacks, the adversary can query (φ, y) to get back $\mathsf{Enc}^{-1}_{\varphi(K)}(y)$.) In the literature, cryptanalysts have looked for relations φ such that the adversary could get an advantage in this model. Although the relevance of this model has been controversial, it is widely admitted that, for some applications, these attacks can pose a real threat. Indeed, in some applications, keys can be updated in a way which might be known (or influenced) by an adversary. To make the attack model as general as possible, it is tempting to allow *any* relation. Unfortunately, we can then show that no security is feasible without more restrictions.

Bellare and Kohno [3] studied a formal model for related-key security. Their model had to be relative to a set of authorized permutations. It works in the ideal cipher model (that is, when the block cipher is random and only usable through specific oracle accesses) and when the relations selected by the adversary are not cipher-dependent (that is, to evaluate a relation, we shall not have any access to the encryption or decryption oracles). They proposed some sufficient conditions for identifying authorized relations. These results were extended by Farshim, Paterson, Albrecht, and Watson [16] by allowing relations to depend on the ideal cipher but obeying extra conditions.

Lucks [26] studied related-key security based on partial transformations, i.e., relations modifying only a part of the key. Another approach by Goldenberg and Liskov [17] shows that related-key security can be achieved by (and can make) a related-key pseudorandom bit. Bellare and Cash [2] constructed one by using public-key cryptography techniques.

Other similar existential results exist. For instance, Pietrzak [28] shows that for any $k \geq 2$, either there exists a secure key agreement protocol working with k messages, or the sequential composition of $(k-1)$-adaptively secure PRF is a k-adaptively secure PRF. (k-adaptive security refers to adversaries allowed to make up to k round of queries where queries in the same round as selected at the same time.) So, in the Minicrypt world where we have no key agreement protocol, sequential composition transform non-adaptive security into adaptive security.

Notations. In what follows, we will consider asymptotic security notions.[1] That is, cryptographic algorithms and parameters shall depend on a security parameter λ. Specifically, these algorithm run in time which is polynomial in λ.

---

[1] Exact, i.e., not asymptotic, security could also be considered, but it would require heavier notations.

Adversaries defeating the security requirements do so via computations that are polynomial in terms of λ. For readability, the parameter λ will be omitted from certain notations.

A function negl is *negligible* if for any integer d we have $\mathsf{negl}(\lambda) \in \mathcal{O}(\lambda^{-d})$. A function whose inverse is polynomially bounded is not negligible.

We will be using the Hoeffding bound [22]: for $X_1, \ldots, X_n$ independent identically distributed (i.i.d.) Bernoulli random variables of expected value p and $t \geq 0$,

$$\Pr\left[\frac{1}{n}\sum_{i=1}^{n}X_i \geq p + t\right] \leq e^{-2nt^2} \quad , \quad \Pr\left[\frac{1}{n}\sum_{i=1}^{n}X_i \leq p - t\right] \geq e^{-2nt^2}$$

In the special case where $t = |p - \frac{1}{2}|$, we obtain that the majority of $X_1, \ldots, X_n$ does not correspond to the most likely value of X_1 with probability at most $e^{-2n(p-\frac{1}{2})^2}$. This will be referred to as the Chernoff bound [9].

2   Ruler-Based Security Models

We define here some meta-security notions, encapsulated in the security game $\Gamma_{\mathcal{F}}(\mathcal{A}, \lambda)$ for a primitive $\mathcal{F}$. These notions comprise the adversary $\mathcal{A}$, the challenger $\mathcal{C}$, the advantage that $\mathcal{A}$ may have at winning this game, and a special measure of the latter called *uniform advantage*.

Keyed Primitive. Throughout this paper, we consider a "keyed primitive" $\mathcal{F}$ defined by the following: 1. a generator Gen generating a coin $b \in \{0, 1\}$ and some $K \in \mathcal{K}$, i.e., $(b, K) \leftarrow$ Gen; 2. an algorithm $f_K(q)$ taking as input a key K, a "query" $q \in \mathcal{D}$. The function f_K may be probabilistic. Again, a natural choice for related-key security would be to consider $f_K(q) = \mathsf{Enc}_{\varphi(K)}(x)$ for $q = (\varphi, x)$, where Enc is some encryption function. Here, φ is called a "relation".

Definition 1 (The $\Gamma_{\mathcal{F}}(\mathcal{A}, \lambda)$ Security Game). *Given a keyed primitive $\mathcal{F}_\lambda$ depending on some security parameter λ, we consider a game $\Gamma_{\mathcal{F}}(\mathcal{A}, \lambda)$ between two principles called an* adversary $\mathcal{A}$ *and a* challenger $\mathcal{C}$. *The adversary is arbitrary. The challenger is specified in the game. Both are probabilistic interactive Turing machines running with expected polynomial time in terms of λ. The game consists of setting up both $\mathcal{A}$ and $\mathcal{C}$ with some independent random coins ρ and $\rho_{\mathcal{C}}$ (respectively), then running an interactive protocol between them and waiting for a final outcome $\Gamma_{\mathcal{F}}(\mathcal{A}, \lambda) = 0$ or 1. If the outcome is 0, we say that the adversary wins.*

The advantage *of the adversary is*

$$\mathsf{Adv}_{\Gamma_{\mathcal{F}}}(\mathcal{A}, \lambda) = \Pr_{\rho, \rho_{\mathcal{C}}}\left[\Gamma_{\mathcal{F}}(\mathcal{A}, \lambda) = 0\right] - \Pr_{\rho, \rho_{\mathcal{C}}}\left[\Gamma_{\mathcal{F}}(\mathcal{A}, \lambda) = 1\right]$$

where the probability goes over all random coins. We say that $\mathcal{F}$ is Γ-secure if for any $\mathcal{A}$, $\mathsf{Adv}_{\Gamma_{\mathcal{F}}}(\mathcal{A}, \lambda)$ is negligible in terms of λ. The uniform advantage *of the adversary is*

$$\mathsf{UAdv}_{\Gamma_{\mathcal{F}}}(\mathcal{A}, \lambda) = \min_{\rho_{\mathcal{C}}}\left(\Pr_{\rho}[\Gamma_{\mathcal{F}}(\mathcal{A}, \lambda) = 0] - \Pr_{\rho}[\Gamma_{\mathcal{F}}(\mathcal{A}, \lambda) = 1]\right)$$

In the definition, the advantage is the difference between the probability to win and the probability to lose. We could have taken $\Pr_\rho[\Gamma_\mathcal{F}(\mathcal{A}, \lambda) = 0] - \frac{1}{2}$ as a definition. We prefer our formalism since it facilitates the extension to games producing a third possible outcome. And, indeed, we are going to consider games which can abort, so the outcome could be 0, 1, or abort.

We also defined the notion of *uniform advantage* as it is easy to amplify (as shown in Lemma 2 below). It captures high advantages whatever the coins used by the challenger.

Head-Or-Tail game. We consider the following Head-Or-Tail game (HOT), which we denote by $\mathsf{HOT}_\mathcal{F}(\mathcal{A})$:

1. Using fresh coins from $\rho_\mathcal{C}$, run Gen to generate b and K.
2. Run $\mathcal{A}(\rho)$ iteratively and answer its queries q_i by $y_i = f_K(q_i)$. I.e., $q_1 = \mathcal{A}(\rho)$, $q_2 = \mathcal{A}(y_1; \rho)$, $q_3 = \mathcal{A}(y_1, y_2; \rho)$, ... If f_K is probabilistic, running $y_i = f_K(q_i)$ assumes independent coins which are taken from $\rho_\mathcal{C}$.
3. Whenever $\mathcal{A}$ stops making queries and outputs a bit γ, stop and yield $b \oplus \gamma$. I.e., $\mathcal{A}$ wins if $\gamma = b$.

The primitive is stateless in the sense that queries $f_K(q)$ produce a distribution which only depends on q throughout the execution of the game. The last output of the adversary is a bit denoted by γ. The primitive $\mathcal{F}$ is secure if no adversary can guess b by playing with f_K. Later, we use b set as a function of K (a hard-core bit of K).

Amplification of uniform advantages. The notion of uniform advantage relates to advantages that do not depend on the random coins of the challenger. This notion is convenient for amplifying an advantage of λ^{-d} to $1 - \mathsf{negl}$. The following lemma shows this exactly.

Lemma 2 (Amplification Lemma). *If a polynomial adversary $\mathcal{A}$ has a uniform advantage ε in the $\mathsf{HOT}_\mathcal{F}$ game, where $\varepsilon = \Omega(\lambda^{-d})$ for some d, then we can build a polynomial adversary with uniform advantage $1 - \mathsf{negl}(\lambda)$ in the $\mathsf{HOT}_\mathcal{F}$ game.*

This extends to any other game in which the following holds: 1. the challenger is stateless (that is, its state before any query is fully determined by its random tape $\rho_\mathcal{C}$); 2. the outcome of the game is a function $g(\gamma, \rho_\mathcal{C})$, with $\rho_\mathcal{C}$ being the random coins of $\mathcal{C}$ and γ being the bit eventually produced by the adversary.

Proof. Due to the assumptions, the adversary has two possible choices for the output γ. Furthermore, for any $\rho_\mathcal{C}$, $\mathcal{A}$'s choice γ leads to $b \oplus \gamma = 0$ with probability $p \geq \frac{1+\varepsilon}{2}$ over ρ. We define an adversary who simulates the adversary $\mathcal{A}$ repeatedly $k = \lambda^{2d+1}$ times and who finally outputs $\bar{\gamma}$ to be the majority of $\mathcal{A}$'s outputs γ. Since the challenger is stateless and the advantage is uniform, whatever the key and the unique coins used by the challenger, every iteration of the adversary makes independent γs such that $b \oplus \gamma = 0$ with probability p. Due to the Chernoff bound [9], with probability less than $e^{-2k(p-\frac{1}{2})^2} \leq e^{-\frac{k\varepsilon^2}{2}} \leq e^{-\Omega(\lambda)} = \mathsf{negl}(\lambda)$, the majority $\bar{\gamma}$ of all γs is such that $b \oplus \bar{\gamma} \neq 0$. $\qquad \square$

Known-input security. We now define the notion of known-input security. For that, we need to specify the distribution of randomly selected relations.

Definition 3 (D-Known-Input (KI) Security). *Consider a distribution D over $\mathcal{D}$ which is polynomially samplable. We say that the adversary $\mathcal{A}$ in the $\mathsf{HOT}_{\mathcal{F}}(\mathcal{A})$ game is D-KI if each of his queries q is either identical to a previous query[2] or a freshly sampled random query following the distribution D. These queries are sampled independently.*

We say that $\mathcal{F}$ is HOT-KI-secure for D if for all D-KI adversary the advantage in the corresponding HOT game is negligible.

Rulers. When defining restricted chosen-input security, we will introduce some new rules in the game which will be enforced by an extra process called "ruler". Typically, we will require that inputs chosen by the adversary are indistinguishable from inputs sampled in a known-input attack.

Given a keyed primitive $\mathcal{F}$ as in the HOT game, we will define the RHOT game involving a ruler. A *ruler* is a probabilistic polynomial time Turing machine $\mathcal{R}$ which produces a bit given a possible view of the challenger.

Definition 4 (Rulers and Ruled Games). *Given the list $q_1, \ldots, q_n$ of queries from the adversary and the random coins $\rho_{\mathcal{C}}$ of the challenger in the HOT game, ruler $\mathcal{R}$ computes a bit denoted $\tilde{b} = \mathcal{R}(q_1, \ldots, q_n, \rho_{\mathcal{C}}; \rho_{\mathcal{R}})$. The ruled-game RHOT runs as follows:*

Game $\mathsf{RHOT}_{\mathcal{F}}(\mathcal{A}, \mathcal{R})$:

1: *pick $\rho_{\mathcal{R}}$ at random*
2: *run the HOT game as before until γ is set, denote $q_1, \ldots, q_n$ the queries from $\mathcal{A}$ and $\rho_{\mathcal{C}}$ the coins of the challenger*
3: $\tilde{b} \leftarrow \mathcal{R}(q_1, \ldots, q_n, \rho_{\mathcal{C}}; \rho_{\mathcal{R}})$
4: **if** $\tilde{b} = 1$ **then**
5:     return abort
6: **else**
7:     return $b \oplus \gamma$
8: **end if**

When $\tilde{b} = 0$, we say that $\mathcal{A}$ follows the rules of $\mathcal{R}$. Otherwise, we say that $\mathcal{R}$ rules over $\mathcal{A}$.

The advantage of $\mathcal{A}$ for ruler $\mathcal{R}$ is

$$\mathsf{Adv}_{\mathsf{RHOT}_{\mathcal{F}}}(\mathcal{A}, \mathcal{R}) = \Pr[\mathsf{RHOT}_{\mathcal{F}}(\mathcal{A}, \mathcal{R}) = 0] - \Pr[\mathsf{RHOT}_{\mathcal{F}}(\mathcal{A}, \mathcal{R}) = 1]$$

We say that $\mathcal{F}$ is RHOT-secure for a class of rulers if for all $\mathcal{A}$ there is a ruler $\mathcal{R}$ in this class such that $\mathsf{Adv}_{\mathsf{RHOT}_{\mathcal{F}}}(\mathcal{A}, \mathcal{R})$ is negligible.

The ruler captures the common practice of encompassing known threats in a model for attack-detection. I.e., in related-key security, some "trivial attacks" breaking any cipher can be deployed. (See Appendix A.1.) However, these attacks

---

[2] Since $\mathcal{F}$ may be probabilistic, it may be useful to repeat a query.

use specific relations which can be added to the security model, i.e., for the ruler to check on the fly if such "trivial attacks" are taking place.

The advantage is

$$\mathsf{Adv}_{\mathsf{RHOT}_{\mathcal{F}}}(\mathcal{A}, \mathcal{R}) = \Pr[\mathsf{RHOT}_{\mathcal{F}}(\mathcal{A}, \mathcal{R}) = 0] - \Pr[\mathsf{RHOT}_{\mathcal{F}}(\mathcal{A}, \mathcal{R}) = 1]$$
$$= \Pr[\tilde{b} = 0](\Pr[\gamma = b | \tilde{b} = 0] - \Pr[\gamma \neq b | \tilde{b} = 0])$$

That is, this is the advantage given that the game follows the rules defined by the ruler, multiplied by the probability to follow the rules. It is necessary to consider the probability to follow the rules since an adversary with high advantage but almost never in the legal case would certainly be insignificant for security.

The HOT game can be seen as a RHOT game in which the ruler would always output 0, i.e., $\mathcal{R}$ would allow every "behavior" of $\mathcal{A}$. Conversely, a ruler answering 1 too often would make $\mathcal{F}$ trivially secure, i.e., if all is forbidden, then no attack is possible. Thus, to make security non-trivial we require rulers that are, in some sense, permissive, i.e., they allow the adversary to play as long as we cannot see any malicious behavior.

Definition 5 (Permissive Ruler). *Given a keyed primitive $\mathcal{F}$ and a polynomially samplable distribution D over the set $\mathcal{D}$ of inputs, we say that a ruler $\mathcal{R}$ is permissive for D if for any D-KI adversary $\mathcal{A}$, the probability that $\mathcal{R}$ rules over $\mathcal{A}$ in the RHOT game is negligible.*

The above definition says that D-permissive rulers allow adversaries to select inputs by sampling D. Clearly, the AND/OR of a polynomial number of permissive rules is also a permissive rule.

Chosen-input security. We now give a restricted notion of chosen-input (CI) security called PCI.

Definition 6 (D-Permissive Chosen-Input (PCI) Security). *Given a keyed primitive $\mathcal{F}$, consider a polynomially samplable distribution D over the set $\mathcal{D}$ of inputs. We say that $\mathcal{F}$ is RHOT-PCI-secure for D if it is RHOT-secure for the class of all permissive rulers for D. I.e., for any adversary $\mathcal{A}$, there is a D-permissive ruler $\mathcal{R}$ such that $\mathsf{Adv}_{\mathsf{RHOT}}(\mathcal{A}, \mathcal{R})$ is negligible.*

So, we only rule out CI attacks whose behavior can be distinguished from the one of KI attacks.

3   The PCI/KI Gap Includes Public-Key Cryptography

3.1   Our Result

We show that if there exists a non-adaptive CI-adversary $\mathcal{A}$ successfully attacking a keyed primitive in front of any D-permissive ruler $\mathcal{R}$ and if the primitive resists KI attacks, then we can construct a cryptosystem from $\mathcal{F}$ and $\mathcal{A}$.

Lemma 7. *Consider a keyed primitive $\mathcal{F}$ over the key domain $\mathcal{K}$ in which the generator* Gen *produces balanced coin b. Assume that $\mathcal{F}$ is* HOT-KI-*secure for a distribution D. If there is a non-adaptive adversary $\mathcal{A}$ in the* RHOT *game with advantage $1 - \mathsf{negl}(\lambda)$ for all permissive rulers for D, then we have a public-key cryptosystem defined by the following:*

- *The key generation: pick a secret key ρ and the public key $q = (q_1, \ldots, q_n) \leftarrow \mathcal{A}(\rho)$, the non-adaptive queries by $\mathcal{A}$.*
  We write $(\rho, q) = \mathsf{PKGen}(\rho)$. I.e., ρ is the secret key and q is the public one.
- *The encryption of a bit β: pick $\rho_C = (\rho_C^0, \rho_C^1, \ldots)$ randomly and do: $(b, K) \leftarrow$ Gen(ρ_C^0), $y \leftarrow (f_K(q_i; \rho_C^i))_{i=1,\ldots,n}$, and $e \leftarrow \beta \oplus b$.*
  We write $(y, e) = \mathsf{PKEnc}_q(\beta; \rho_C)$.
- *The decryption of (y, e): do $b' \leftarrow \mathcal{A}(y; \rho) \oplus e$.*
  We write $b' = \mathsf{PKDec}_\rho(y, e)$.

This cryptosystem is correct and secure.

This lemma uses an adversary $\mathcal{A}$ producing its set of queries q non-adaptively, which is the public key. Then, the encryption of β is the answers to the queries (with a fresh (b, K) and some fresh coins for f_K) together with $\beta \oplus b$. The bit b can be guessed by $\mathcal{A}$ for decryption. The high advantage of $\mathcal{A}$ makes the cryptosystem correct. Any decryption algorithm $\mathcal{E}$ would imply a permissive ruler to detect the behavior of $\mathcal{A}$. Since $\mathcal{A}$ cannot be ruled over, the cryptosystem is secure.

Proof. Let us assume that an adversary as above exists. Let q and y be the vectors of query-inputs and query-outputs to and from the challenger, respectively.

$\mathsf{PKDec}_\rho(y, e) = \beta$ is equivalent to $b = \mathcal{A}(y; \rho)$, i.e., to $\mathcal{A}$ winning in the HOT game. By definition, for any permissive ruler $\mathcal{R}$, we have

$$1 - \mathsf{negl}(\lambda) = \mathsf{Adv}(\mathcal{A}, \mathcal{R}) = \Pr[\mathcal{R} \text{ accepts}] (1 - 2 \Pr[\mathsf{PKDec}_\rho(y, e) \neq \beta | \mathcal{R} \text{ accepts}])$$

We apply this to the ruler $\mathcal{R}$ who always accepts. We obtain that the probability that (y, e) does not decrypt to β is negligible. This holds for any β. So, the cryptosystem satisfies correctness. So, what remains to be proven is its security.

Consider some algorithm $\mathcal{E}(q, y, e)$ trying to decrypt (y, e) given a public key q, and let $\varepsilon_q = \Pr[\mathcal{E}(q, \mathsf{PKEnc}_q(\beta; \rho_C)) = \beta] - \frac{1}{2}$ over a random ρ_C and β, for the public key q fixed. We want to show that $E(\varepsilon_q)$ is negligible over ρ, for $q = \mathcal{A}(\rho)$.

We construct rulers $\mathcal{R}_d(q, \rho_C; \rho_R)$ based on $\mathcal{E}$ as follows. For a number of $k = \lambda^{2d+1}$ random $\rho_C(j)$ and β_j, encrypt β_j under coins $\rho_C(j)$ with public key q and get the ciphertext $(y_j, e_j) = \mathsf{PKEnc}_q(\beta_j; \rho_C(j))$. Then, count for how many j's we have $\beta_j = \mathcal{E}(q, y_j, e_j)$. If this number is above the threshold $t = k(\frac{1}{2} + \lambda^{-d})$, then rule over $\mathcal{A}$. Note that this ruler makes no use of ρ_C. It is just testing the public key q and it aborts if $\mathcal{E}(q, ., .)$ breaks this with an advantage that is too large. We will show that $\mathcal{R}_d$ is permissive and deduce that it rules over $\mathcal{A}$ with negligible probability. Consequently, $E(\varepsilon_\rho) \leq \lambda^{-d} + \mathsf{negl}(\lambda)$. As it holds for all d, we conclude that $E(\varepsilon_\rho)$ is negligible.

We first show that $\mathcal{R}_d$ is permissive. We consider an arbitrary D-KI adversary $\mathcal{A}'$ generating n KI queries $q' = (q_1', \ldots, q_n')$, receiving the responses y' based on some coins ρ_C, and producing a final bit γ'. We want to show that $\Pr[\mathcal{R}_d(q'; \rho_C) = 1] = \mathsf{negl}(\lambda)$. (We recall that the outcome γ'' is not provided to the ruler.) To do so, we must estimate $\varepsilon_{q'}$.

For this, we construct another adversary $\mathcal{A}''$ who makes the same queries q' as $\mathcal{A}'$ but computes his final γ'' in a special way. We define $\mathcal{A}''$ as follows: $\mathcal{A}''(\rho'')$ simulates $\mathcal{A}'(\rho')$ with some fresh coins ρ' taken from ρ'', sets $q'' = q'$ and gets the responses $y'' = y'$ based on some coins ρ_C. Then, it picks some random bit e and computes $\gamma_1 = \mathcal{E}(q', y', e) \oplus e$. Note that for q' fixed, if b is the bit generated by Gen from ρ_C we have $\gamma_1 = b$ with probability $\frac{1}{2} + \varepsilon_{q'}$. In addition to this, $\mathcal{A}''$ picks a random β and computes $\gamma_2 = \mathcal{E}(q', \mathsf{PKEnc}_{q'}(\beta)) \oplus \beta$. For q' fixed, we have $\gamma_2 = 0$ with probability $\frac{1}{2} + \varepsilon_{q'}$. The final answer is $\gamma'' = \gamma_1 \oplus \gamma_2$. So, we have $\gamma'' = b$ with probability $\frac{1}{2} + 2\varepsilon_{q'}^2$, which is the probability for $\mathcal{A}''$ to win the $\mathsf{HOT}_{\mathcal{F}}(\mathcal{A}'')$ game. Clearly, $\mathsf{Adv}_{\mathsf{HOT}_{\mathcal{F}}}(\mathcal{A}'') = 4E(\varepsilon_{q'}^2)$ over the random choice of ρ' and $q' = \mathcal{A}'(\rho')$. Since $\mathcal{A}''$ is a D-KI adversary, due to D-KI security, we obtain that $E(\varepsilon_{q'}^2)$ is negligible.

Let B be the event that $\varepsilon_{q'}^2 \leq \lambda^{-2d-2}$ for d fixed. Since $\Pr[\neg B] \leq \lambda^{2d+2} E(\varepsilon_{q'}^2)$, we have that $\Pr[\neg B]$ is negligible. So, B holds except in negligible cases. When B holds, we have $\varepsilon_{q'} \leq \lambda^{-d-1}$. The Hoeffding bound [22] deduces that $\mathcal{R}_d$ aborts with a probability bounded by $e^{-2\lambda(1-\lambda^{-1})^2}$, which is negligible. So, the overall probability that $\mathcal{R}_d$ aborts on queries q' is negligible when B holds, and other cases are negligible. So, $\mathcal{R}_d$ aborts on queries made by an arbitrary KI adversary $\mathcal{A}'$ with negligible probability. Therefore, $\mathcal{R}_d$ is permissive.

We now go back to the adversary $\mathcal{A}$ using the permissive ruler $\mathcal{R}_d$. Due to our assumptions, $\mathcal{R}_d$ rules over $\mathcal{A}$ with negligible probability. If $\varepsilon_\rho \geq \lambda^{-d}$, then by applying same reasoning as above, we obtain that the probability for the adversary $\mathcal{A}$ to pass the ruler's test is less than $e^{-2\lambda(\varepsilon_\rho \lambda^d - 1)^2}$, which is negligible. Since $\mathcal{R}_d$ rules over $\mathcal{A}$ with negligible probability, the probability that $\varepsilon_\rho \geq \lambda^{-d}$ is negligible. So, we must have $E(\varepsilon_\rho) \leq \lambda^{-d} + \mathsf{negl}(\lambda)$. We deduce then that $\Pr[\mathcal{E}(q, y, \beta \oplus b) = \beta] - \frac{1}{2} = \mathcal{O}(\lambda^{-d})$ for a random public key q, a random K, and a random β.

We apply this result for every d and obtain that $\Pr[\mathcal{E}(q, \mathsf{PKEnc}_q(\beta; \rho_C)) = \beta] - \frac{1}{2}$ is negligible for any β and any polynomial $\mathcal{E}$. Therefore, the cryptosystem is secure.   □

Extension to adaptive adversaries. Clearly, this result extends to adaptive adversaries but with a cryptosystem replaced by a public cryptography protocol [29]. Namely, the encryption becomes interactive, but it can still be carried out with public information. I.e., Alice starts with a message m and a public key; Bob starts with a secret key and ends with m, but m remains private. We conclude this part as follows.

Theorem 8. *Consider a keyed primitive $\mathcal{F}$. Assume that $\mathcal{F}$ is HOT-KI-secure for a given distribution D. If there exists an adversary $\mathcal{A}$ in the RHOT game with advantage $1 - \mathsf{negl}(\lambda)$ for the class of D-permissive rulers, then we can construct a public cryptography protocol based on $\mathcal{F}$ and $\mathcal{A}$.*

The Minicrypt case. Using the Minicrypt hypothesis [24] that public-key cryptosystems do not exist but one-way functions do, security in the known-relations model implies security in the chosen-relations model with permissive rulers in the following two cases:

- in a weak form in the sense that it is ensured that no adversary has an advantage $1 - \mathsf{negl}(\lambda)$;
- in a uniform form in the sense that it is ensured that no adversary has a uniform advantage $1/\mathsf{Poly}(\lambda)$ (due to Lemma 2).

Assuming that doing public-key cryptography from symmetric cryptography is impossible (which is supported by Rudich [29]), we obtain that known-input security implies permissive chosen-input (weak or uniform) security, for all $\mathcal{F}$ based on symmetric cryptography. If we do have known-input security, for any CI adversary, there must be a permissive ruler making its advantage negligible.

3.2   Concrete Constructions of Cryptosystems

As a nice example of application of Lemma 7, we show that we can obtain the ElGamal cryptosystem by this result.

Let a family $(G, g, n, h)_\lambda$ of tuples, with G being a finite Abelian group, g being an element of prime order n, and h being a Boolean function such that $\Pr[h(g^x) = 0] - \frac{1}{2}$ is negligible when $x \in \{0, \ldots, n-1\}$. We assume the following facts: 1. there exist algorithms which are polynomially bounded and compute products and inverses in G; 2. $\log n$ is polynomially bounded; 3. there is a polynomially bounded algorithm to compute $h(x)$, for x in the subgroup $\langle g \rangle$ generated by g.

We define $\mathcal{F}$ as follows: Gen picks K and defines $b = h(g^K)$. Then, $f_K(q) = q^K$. We consider the uniform distribution D over $\langle g \rangle$. A chosen input attack could select $q = g$ and deduce b from the response $f_K(q)$ but this can be ruled out by the rule saying that $q = g$ is not allowed (indeed, it does not look like random). Later, we will randomize q so that it cannot be detected by permissive rules. In relation to Sect. 3.1, we have the following result.

Lemma 9. *If the decisional Diffie-Hellman problem is hard in $(G, g, n)_\lambda$, then f is HOT-secure against D-KI attacks.*

Proof. In KI attack settings, the adversary gets random (q_i, q_i^K) pairs.

When n is prime, it reduces to the case where a single pair is given. This is so since the adversary could sample other pairs with the same distribution by simply raising the unique pair to some random power. If the decisional Diffie-Hellman problem is hard in G, then —given (g, q, q^K)— it is hard to infer $h(g^K)$. So, f resists to D-known-relation attacks.   □

After referring to known-input security, we now elaborate on chosen-input attack. A CI adversary choosing $q = g^\rho$ with ρ random is indistinguishable from the KI case. However, such adversary can easily compute $b = h(y^{\frac{1}{\rho}})$ given $y =$

q^K. So, we are in the situation where we can construct a public-key cryptosystem, following Lemma 7. (The public key is one q. The secret key is ρ such that $q = g^\rho$. To encrypt β, we pick a random K and compute both $y = q^K$ and $e = \beta \oplus b$. To decrypt (y, e), we compute $e \oplus h(y^{\frac{1}{\rho}})$.) So, we obtain a kind of ElGamal cryptosystem [15], or some hybrid construction based on the Diffie-Hellman key exchange [12].

4 Related-Key Security

We apply here our approach to model (in)security for the case of related-key attacks. We first present previous approaches to this. We then extend our model to black-box relations to support related-key attacks. Next, we show that we cannot reach security in this model for the uniform distribution among all permutations over $\mathcal{K}$. Finally, we discuss on obfuscation.

Similar results would hold for Key-Dependent Input (KDI) security. For this, we would define $f_K(\varphi, x) = \mathsf{Enc}_K(\varphi(K))$ (See Appendix B). Also, these are special cases for leakage-resilience as defined by $f_K(\varphi, x) = \varphi(K, x)$.

4.1 The Black-Box Approach

In this section, we consider a black-box model, in which relations are provided by the adversary in terms of a black-box oracle access.

Definition 10 (Black-Box Adversary, Black-Box Ruler). *A black-box adversary $\mathcal{A}$ for the RHOT game, denoted as a BBRHOT-adversary, is an adversary who provides relations φ_i in terms of a stateless oracle access. The challenger (and the ruler) can freely query each oracle defined by the adversary. A primitive $\mathcal{F}$ is BBRHOT-PCI-secure for D if for any CI-adversary there is a D-permissive ruler making the advantage negligible.*

We define $\mathcal{F}$ by $f_K(\varphi, x) = e_{\varphi(K)}(x)$ for a keyed function e and $b = b(K)$ for a nonzero linear function b. The domain $\mathcal{D}$ of (φ, x) queries is $\mathcal{S}_\mathcal{K} \times \mathcal{M}$, the product of the set $\mathcal{S}_\mathcal{K}$ of permutations φ over $\mathcal{K}$ and the domain $\mathcal{M}$ of x. We show that BBRHOT-PCI-security for the uniform distribution over $\mathcal{D}$ is not possible. For this, we show that there is a CI-adversary which can break any keyed function e in the HOT game, and that this adversary passes any permissive ruler in the black-box model. That is, by extending the Harris attack [20,21], we mount a key-bit recovery attack in the black-box relation model.

Theorem 11. *Given a keyed function $e_K(x)$ and a nonzero linear function $b(K)$ over the domain $\mathcal{K}$ of K and the domain $\mathcal{M}$ of x, we define a keyed primitive $\mathcal{F}$ via $(K, b) \leftarrow \mathsf{Gen}$ and $f_K(\varphi, x) = e_{\varphi(K)}(x)$, with $K \in \mathcal{K}$, $b = b(K)$, and $\varphi \in \mathcal{S}_\mathcal{K}$ a permutation over $\mathcal{K}$. We assume that $(k \mapsto e_k(x))_{x \in \mathcal{M}}$ is a collision-resistant family of functions over $\mathcal{K}$.*[3]

---

[3] I.e., given a random x, it is hard to find $k \neq k'$ such that $e_k(x) = e_{k'}(x)$. This could be the case, e.g., when $\mathcal{M}$ is much larger than $\mathcal{K}$.

If one-way functions exist, there is a non-adaptive polynomially bounded PCI-adversary $\mathcal{A}$ in the BBRHOT game for the uniform distribution D over $\mathcal{D}$, $\mathcal{A}$ having a uniform advantage of $1 - \mathsf{negl}(\lambda)$.

This theorem shows that some attacks exist for this distribution D. They cannot be detected by analyzing the chosen-relations in a black-box manner. Therefore, permissive related-key security is not possible in a black-box setting.

Proof. Lemma 12 below shows that there is one adversary $\mathcal{A}$, using a single query (φ, x), with uniform advantage in the HOT game being $\frac{1}{2} - \mathsf{negl}(\lambda)$. So, we can use the Amplification Lemma 2 with $k = \lambda$ iterations. Lemma 12 further says that for ρ_C fixed, φ selected by $\mathcal{A}$ is a PRP while x is uniform and independent. The amplification uses independent queries with same distribution. So, a permissive ruler in the black box model cannot rule over the amplified adversary.   □

Lemma 12. *We assume a keyed primitive e such that $(k \mapsto e_k(x))_{x \in \mathcal{M}}$ is a collision-resistant family of functions over $\mathcal{K}$. Let b be a nonzero linear function from $\mathcal{K}$ to $\{0, 1\}$. If one-way functions exist, there is a polynomially bounded adversary $\mathcal{A}$ using a single query (φ, x) in the HOT game with uniform advantage $\frac{1}{2} - \mathsf{negl}(\lambda)$.*

Furthermore, φ and x are independent, φ is a PRP, and x is uniform.

Proof. Essentially, we construct an adversary by using the Harris [20,21] attack, but we obfuscate the relation and the leaking information. This latter adversary is using a single CI (φ, x) and a linear bit $b(K)$. This simplifies the HOT game as follows:

Game $\mathsf{HOT}_{\mathcal{F}}(\mathcal{A})$:
1: initialize $\mathcal{A}$ with some random coins ρ
2: set $K \in \mathcal{K}$ at random
3: $(\varphi, x) \leftarrow \mathcal{A}(\rho)$
4: $y \leftarrow e_{\varphi(K)}(x)$
5: $\gamma \leftarrow \mathcal{A}(y; \rho)$
6: return $\gamma \oplus b(K)$

The uniform advantage $\mathsf{UAdv}_{\mathsf{HOT}_{\mathcal{F}}}(\mathcal{A})$ of $\mathcal{A}$ is $\mathsf{UAdv}_{\mathsf{HOT}}(\mathcal{A}) = \min_K 2 \Pr[\gamma = b(K)] - 1$.

We define $g_x(K) = e_K(x)$. Let ε be a fixed vector such that $b(\varepsilon) = 1$.

Given $\sigma \in \mathcal{S}_{\mathcal{K}}$, a Boolean function F over $\mathcal{M}$, and $x \in \mathcal{M}$, we define $\mathsf{bit}_{\sigma, F, x}(K) = F \circ g_x \circ \sigma(K)$, a Boolean function extracting a bit of K and

$$\varphi_{\sigma, F, x}(K) = \begin{cases} \sigma(K') \text{ for } K' \in \{K, K \oplus \varepsilon\} \text{ s.t.} \\ \qquad \mathsf{bit}_{\sigma, F, x}(K') = b(K) & \text{if } \mathsf{bit}_{\sigma, F, x}(K) \neq \mathsf{bit}_{\sigma, F, x}(K \oplus \varepsilon) \\ \sigma(K) & \text{otherwise} \end{cases}$$

Note that $\varphi_{\sigma, F, x}$ is a permutation. Indeed, given $y = \varphi_{\sigma, F, x}(K)$ we can recover the pair $\{K, K \oplus \varepsilon\}$ by computing $\sigma^{-1}(y)$ and its XOR to ε. Then, we can figure out whether $\mathsf{bit}_{\sigma, F, x}(K) = \mathsf{bit}_{\sigma, F, x}(K \oplus \varepsilon)$ by computing the two bits. If they are equal, then $K = \sigma^{-1}(y)$. If they are different, K is the only one such that $\mathsf{bit}_{\sigma, F, x}(\sigma^{-1}(y)) = b(K)$.

Let σ_{ρ_1} be a pseudorandom permutation (PRP) over $\mathcal{K}$, and let F_{ρ_2} be a Boolean pseudorandom function (PRF) with domain $\mathcal{M}$.

We define the adversary $\mathcal{A}$ for the game $\mathsf{HOT}_{\mathcal{F}}$. $\mathcal{A}$ picks ρ_1, ρ_2, x from ρ and defines $\varphi = \varphi_{\sigma_{\rho_1}, F_{\rho_2}, x}$. The only query made by $\mathcal{A}$ is (φ, x). Then, using the response $y = e_{\varphi(K)}(x) = g_x(\varphi(K))$, we define $\gamma = \mathcal{A}(y; \rho) = F_{\rho_2}(y) = F_{\rho_2} \circ g_x(\varphi(K))$ as the final output.

Since ρ_1 resp. ρ_2 are only used inside σ_{ρ_1} resp. F_{ρ_2} within the algorithm of $\mathcal{A}$, then the computations of σ and F can be outsourced to some oracle and $\mathcal{A}$ needs not ρ any more. Since σ is a PRP and F is a PRF, the outcome of the (polynomially bounded) game is indistinguishable from the resulting outcome if we were to use a random pair (σ, F) with uniform distribution. We can thus make the assumption that σ is a uniformly distributed permutation and that F is a randomly distributed function, and assume that $\varphi_{\sigma, F, x}$ is defined from σ and F instead of σ_{ρ_1} and F_{ρ_2}.

In Lemma 13, we show that for any x, the relation $\varphi_{\sigma, F, x}$ is a PRP. So, φ is a PRP independent from the uniform x. Furthermore, Lemma 13 shows that $\gamma = b(K)$ with probability close to $\frac{3}{4}$ when K is fixed. So, the uniform advantage is close to $\frac{1}{2}$.   □

Lemma 13. *Let $(g_x)_{x \in \mathcal{M}}$ be a collision-resistant family of functions over $\mathcal{K}$, $\varepsilon \in \mathcal{M}$, and b be a linear form over $\mathcal{M}$ such that $b(\varepsilon) = 1$. Let σ be a random Boolean permutation and F be a random function on $\mathcal{M}$. Given x, we define $\varphi(K) = \sigma(K')$ where $K' \in \{K, K \oplus \varepsilon\}$ is such that $F \circ g_x \circ \sigma(K') = b(K)$ if $F \circ g_x \circ \sigma(K) \neq F \circ g_x \circ \sigma(K \oplus \varepsilon)$ and $K' = K$ otherwise.*

Given a fixed key x, φ is indistinguishable from a uniformly distributed permutation.

Given $k \in \mathcal{K}$ fixed and x uniformly distributed. $\Pr[F \circ g_x(\varphi(k)) = b(k)] = \frac{3}{4} - \mathsf{negl}(\lambda)$.

Proof. Given x fixed, we consider a distinguisher $\mathcal{R}$ playing with the φ oracle. Let E be the event that $\mathcal{R}$ queries φ with two keys K and K' such that $K \neq K'$, $K \neq K' \oplus \varepsilon$, and $g_x(\sigma(K)), g_x(\sigma(K \oplus \varepsilon)), g_x(\sigma(K')), g_x(\sigma(K' \oplus \varepsilon))$ are not pairwise different. Clearly, this adversary translates to a polynomial algorithm to find collisions on g with success probability $\Pr[E]$. But, by underlying assumptions, this must be negligible. So, we assume that E does not occur in the execution of $\mathcal{R}$. Let S denote the union of all $\{K, K \oplus \varepsilon\}$ of all K's which are queried by $\mathcal{R}$ to φ. We obtain that $g_x \circ \sigma$ is injective on S.

We say that two permutations π and π' are equivalent if for all K in S, the two unordered pairs $\{\pi(K), \pi(K \oplus \varepsilon)\}$ and $\{\pi'(K), \pi'(K \oplus \varepsilon)\}$ are the same. We note that φ is always equivalent to σ. We will show that if we select σ in a given equivalence class Class and pick F at random, then φ restricted to S will be a uniformly distributed element of Class. Indeed, the ordering of a pair for φ is locally defined by the ordering of σ on the same pair and the values of F related to this pair. In addition to this, if we flip the order for σ and we complement the two related bits in F on this pair, then we obtain the inverse order for φ. (Since $g_x \circ \sigma$ is injective on S, note that the F values to flip are independent from the others.) Therefore the mapping $(\sigma, F) \mapsto \varphi$ is balanced for $\sigma \in \mathsf{Class}$ and F random. So, it is balanced over the permutation set. Therefore, φ is uniformly distributed.

The φ construction is such that $F \circ g_x(\varphi(K)) = b(K)$ when $F \circ g_x \circ \sigma(K) \neq F \circ g_x \circ \sigma(K \oplus \varepsilon)$ and only for half of the K's in the other case. Given a fixed k, let E_k be the event that $g_x(\sigma(k)) = g_x(\sigma(k \oplus \varepsilon))$. Since σ transforms the $(k, k \oplus \varepsilon)$ pair into a random pair of different keys, we have $\Pr[E_k] = p_{\mathsf{coll}}$ where $p_{\mathsf{coll}} = \Pr[g_x(K) = g_x(K')|K \neq K']$ when K and K' are independent and uniformly distributed. If E_k does not occur, the probability over F that $F \circ g_x(\varphi(k)) = b(k)$ corresponds to the case where the pair is mapped by F to different bits or to two bits equal to $b(k)$, so

$$\Pr[F \circ g_x(\varphi(k)) = b(k)|\neg E_k] = \frac{3}{4}$$

Similarly,

$$\Pr[F \circ g_x(\varphi(k)) = b(k)|E_k] = \frac{1}{2}$$

So,

$$\Pr[F \circ g_x(\varphi(k)) = b(k)] = \frac{3}{4}(1 - p_{\mathsf{coll}}) + \frac{1}{2}p_{\mathsf{coll}} = \frac{3}{4} - \frac{1}{4}p_{\mathsf{coll}}$$

$\square$

4.2   On Obfuscation

Theorem 11 relies on obfuscating the Harris attack behind pseudorandom permutations and functions so that no ruler would recognize the structure of the relation in a black-box manner. In this construction, we have $\varphi = \varphi_{\sigma_{\rho_1}, F_{\rho_2}, x}$. When moving to a non-black-box model, relations must be specified in terms of a code which could try to obfuscate the relation as well. Namely, the adversary could provide some code $\mathsf{Obf}(\varphi)$ obfuscated by some algorithm Obf so that there is an execution algorithm Exe such that for all x, $\mathsf{Exe}(\mathsf{Obf}(\varphi), x) = \mathsf{Exe}(\varphi, x)$.

Assuming that $\mathsf{Obf}(\varphi_{\sigma_{\rho_1}, F_{\rho_2}, x})$ and $\mathsf{Obf}(\varphi)$ for φ random cannot be distinguished, then Theorem 8 says that we can construct a public-key cryptosystem based on $\mathcal{F}$ and $\mathsf{Obf}(\varphi_{\sigma_{\rho_1}, F_{\rho_2}, x})$. Namely, a public key would be the obfuscated relation and the secret key would consist of the ρ values. Since this construction is unlikely to be feasible due to the separation between symmetric cryptography and public-key cryptography, we deduce that for any Obf, there must be a ruler to tell $\mathsf{Obf}(\varphi_{\sigma_{\rho_1}, F_{\rho_2}, x})$ and $\mathsf{Obf}(\varphi)$ apart.

We could try to obfuscate φ using white-box cryptography [10, 11] or any obfuscation mechanism [1, 23]. Our result shows that there must be a generic way to defeat these techniques in that case. So, it is likely to be a hard task to find the appropriate ruler.

5   Conclusion

We have formalized security notions in which the adversary tries to win against a challenger while a ruler is watching him. This gave definitions for known-input and permissive chosen-input security. We have shown that a gap between these notions implies a public cryptography protocol construction. As for related-key security, we have shown that the gap exists when providing relations in terms of black-boxes. When removing black-boxes, we deduced that all obfuscation schemes can be defeated by a ruler, or we can construct a public-key cryptosystem from a block cipher, pseudorandom permutations, and the obfuscation scheme, or no known-relation security exists.

Acknowledgements. We thank Jorge Nakahara, Martijn Stam, and Ioana Boureanu for many valuable remarks in earlier versions of this paper.

References

1. Barak, B., Goldreich, O., Impagliazzo, R., Rudich, S., Sahai, A., Vadhan, S.P., Yang, K.: On the (Im)possibility of obfuscating programs. In: Kilian, J. (ed.) CRYPTO 2001. LNCS, vol. 2139, pp. 1–18. Springer, Heidelberg (2001)
2. Bellare, M., Cash, D.: Pseudorandom functions and permutations provably secure against related-key attacks. In: Rabin, T. (ed.) CRYPTO 2010. LNCS, vol. 6223, pp. 666–684. Springer, Heidelberg (2010)
3. Bellare, M., Kohno, T.: A theoretical treatment of related-key attacks: RKA-PRPs, RKA-PRFs, and applications. In: Biham, E. (ed.) EUROCRYPT 2003. LNCS, vol. 2656, pp. 491–506. Springer, Heidelberg (2003)
4. Bernstein, D.J.: Private communication (2010)
5. Biham, E.: New types of cryptanalytic attacks using related keys. In: Helleseth, T. (ed.) EUROCRYPT 1993. LNCS, vol. 765, pp. 398–409. Springer, Heidelberg (1994)
6. Biham, E.: New types of cryptanalytic attacks using related keys. J. Cryptol. **7**, 229–246 (1994)
7. Biham, E.: How to decrypt or even substitute DES-encrypted messages in 228 steps. Inf. Process. Lett. **84**, 117–124 (2002)
8. Black, J., Rogaway, P., Shrimpton, T.: Encryption-scheme security in the presence of key-dependent messages. In: Nyberg, K., Heys, H.M. (eds.) SAC 2002. LNCS, vol. 2595. Springer, Heidelberg (2003)
9. Chernoff, H.: A measure of asymptotic efficiency for tests of a hypothesis based on the sum of observations. Ann. Math. Stat. **23**(4), 493–507 (1952)
10. Chow, S., Eisen, P., Johnson, H., Van Oorschot, P.C.: White-box cryptography and an AES implementation. In: Nyberg, K., Heys, H.M. (eds.) SAC 2002. LNCS, vol. 2595. Springer, Heidelberg (2003)
11. Chow, S., Eisen, P., Johnson, H., van Oorschot, P.C.: A white-box DES implementation for DRM applications. In: Feigenbaum, J. (ed.) DRM 2002. LNCS, vol. 2696, pp. 1–15. Springer, Heidelberg (2003)
12. Diffie, W., Hellman, M.E.: New directions in cryptography. IEEE Trans. Inf. Theory **IT–22**, 644–654 (1976)

13. Dolev, D., Dwork, C., Naor, M.: Non-malleable cryptography. In: Proceedings of the 23rd ACM Symposium on Theory of Computing, New Orleans, pp. 542–552. ACM Press (1991)
14. Dolev, D., Dwork, C., Naor, M.: Non-malleable cryptography. SIAM J. Comput. **30**, 391–437 (2000)
15. ElGamal, T.: A public-key cryptosystem and a signature scheme based on discrete logarithms. IEEE Trans. Inf. Theory **IT–31**, 469–472 (1985)
16. Albrecht, M.R., Farshim, P., Paterson, K.G., Watson, G.J.: On cipher-dependent related-key attacks in the ideal-cipher model. In: Joux, A. (ed.) FSE 2011. LNCS, vol. 6733, pp. 128–145. Springer, Heidelberg (2011)
17. Goldenberg, D., Liskov, M.: On related-secret pseudorandomness. In: Micciancio, D. (ed.) TCC 2010. LNCS, vol. 5978, pp. 255–272. Springer, Heidelberg (2010)
18. Haitner, I., Holenstein, T.: On the (Im)Possibility of key dependent encryption. In: Reingold, O. (ed.) TCC 2009. LNCS, vol. 5444, pp. 202–219. Springer, Heidelberg (2009)
19. Halevi, S., Krawczyk, H.: Security under key-dependent inputs. In: 14th ACM Conference on Computer and Communications Security, Alexandria, pp. 466–475. ACM Press (2007)
20. Harris, D.G.: Generic ciphers are more vulnerable to related-key attacks than previously thought. In: Presented at WCC 2009 (2009)
21. Harris, D.G.: Critique of the related-key attack concept. Des. Codes Crypt. **59**, 159–168 (2011)
22. Hoeffding, W.: Probability inequalities for sums of bounded random variables. J. Am. Stat. Assoc. **58**, 13–30 (1963)
23. Hofheinz, D., Malone-Lee, J., Stam, M.: Obfuscation for cryptographic purposes. In: Vadhan, S.P. (ed.) TCC 2007. LNCS, vol. 4392, pp. 214–232. Springer, Heidelberg (2007)
24. Impagliazzo, R.: A personal view of average-case complexity. In: Structure in Complexity Theory Conference SCT 1995, Minneapolis, pp. 134–147. IEEE (1995)
25. Knudsen, L.R.: Cryptanalysis of LOKI 91. In: Zheng, Y., Seberry, J. (eds.) AUSCRYPT 1992. LNCS, vol. 718. Springer, Heidelberg (1993)
26. Lucks, S.: Ciphers secure against related-key attacks. In: Roy, B., Meier, W. (eds.) FSE 2004. LNCS, vol. 3017, pp. 359–370. Springer, Heidelberg (2004)
27. Naor, M., Yung, M.: Public-key cryptosystems provably secure against chosen ciphertext attacks. In: Proceedings of the 22nd ACM Symposium on Theory of Computing, Baltimore, pp. 427–437. ACM Press (1990)
28. Pietrzak, K.: Composition implies adaptive security in minicrypt. In: Vaudenay, S. (ed.) EUROCRYPT 2006. LNCS, vol. 4004, pp. 328–338. Springer, Heidelberg (2006)
29. Rudich, S.: The use of interaction in public cryptosystems. In: Feigenbaum, J. (ed.) CRYPTO 1991. LNCS, vol. 576, pp. 242–251. Springer, Heidelberg (1992)

A On Related-Key Security

A.1 Some Attacks to Be Ruled Over

We list here some non-dedicated attacks in related-key settings. The purpose of this list is to keep in mind some necessary rules to be considered when developing a feasible security model.

In a folklore attack, the adversary uses ℓ queries (φ_i, x_i), $i = 0, \ldots, \ell - 1$, where ℓ is the key length and $\varphi_i(K) = K \text{ AND } 1^{\ell-i}0^i$. That is, $\varphi_i(K)$ consists of the first $\ell - i$ bits of K padded with zeroes. Clearly, by getting one known plaintext/ciphertext pair per black-box, an adversary can recover all bits of K sequentially by exhaustive search with complexity $\mathcal{O}(\ell)$.

In 2003, Bellare and Kohno [3] proposed another similar attack in this model. Essentially, they use ℓ related keys again (ℓ being the key length). The permutation φ_i for $i > 0$ was defined as follows: if the ith bit of x is 1, then $\varphi_i(K)$ is obtained from K by flipping the least significant bit, otherwise $\varphi_i(K) = K$. (Assume that the least significant bit $\mathsf{lsb}(K)$ is 0.) Additionally, $\varphi_0(K) = K$. In a chosen plaintext attack, one could get $y_i = \mathsf{Enc}_{K_i}(x)$ for all i. If $y_i \neq y_0$, it means that the ith bit of K_0 is 1. Clearly, we recover again all bits in linear time.

Recently, Harris [20,21] proposed another attack which is similar to the Bellare-Kohno [3] attack. Here, $\varphi_{i,x}(K)$ is either K or $K \oplus e_i$ for $e_i = 0^{\ell-i-1}10^i$ (i.e., $K \oplus e_i$ is K with its ith bit flipped), depending on some condition related to the least significant bits (lsb) $y = \mathsf{lsb}(\mathsf{Enc}_K(x))$ and $y' = \mathsf{lsb}(\mathsf{Enc}_{K \oplus e_i}(x))$. Namely, if $y = y'$, then $\varphi_{i,x}(K) = K$. Otherwise, either y or y' is equal to the ith bit of K. If this is y then $\varphi_{i,x}(K) = K$. Otherwise, $\varphi_{i,x}(K) = K \oplus e_i$. It is not hard to realize that this defines a permutation $\varphi_{i,x}$. The nice property is that $\mathsf{lsb}(\mathsf{Enc}_{\varphi_{i,x}(K)}(x))$ equals the ith bit of K with probability $\frac{3}{4}$ over the random choice of x. So, by statistical analysis, we can infer every bit by using several related keys.

Even more recently, Bernstein [4] proposed a generic related-key distinguisher using a single related key. The proposed relation is $K' = \mathsf{Enc}_K(0)$. Although it is not a permutation, one can admit that it is still a one-way transformation for which finding collisions is hard. The attack consists of encrypting 0 with key K (say $y_0 = \mathsf{Enc}_K(0)$) and any plaintext x with key K' (say $y = \mathsf{Enc}_{K'}(x)$) then comparing $\mathsf{Enc}_{y_0}(x)$ with y. The distinguisher has essentially an advantage of 1. So far, it is not clear how this attack can be turned into a key recovery attack.

All these attacks could be seen as devastating in theory although they do not seem to mean any endemic weakness for any cipher. What is in common between all these attacks is that they are generic and they use some intricate relations. Consequently, these relations must be explicitly forbidden by ad hoc rules, i.e., arbiters should rule them over.

If the set of authorized permutations makes it possible to define r related keys, one could use a tradeoff attack as proposed by Biham [7]. Essentially, one could collect $y_i = \mathsf{Enc}_{K_i}(x)$ for all i then perform a multi-target exhaustive search to recover one key out of r. This works with complexity $\mathcal{O}(2^\ell/r)$. For $r = 2^{\frac{\ell}{2}}$, this is $\mathcal{O}(2^{\frac{\ell}{2}})$. For instance, if the transformations $\varphi(x) = x \oplus c$

are allowed for all c, we can mount a key recovery attack against any ℓ-bit key cipher with complexity $\mathcal{O}(2^{\frac{\ell}{2}})$. As another example, if only the transformation $\varphi(x) = x + 1 \bmod 2^\ell$ and its iterations are allowed, we obtain the same result. In general, allowing r permutations and related keys makes it possible to use the previous attack with space complexity $\mathcal{O}(r)$ and time complexity $\mathcal{O}(2^\ell/r)$. Fortunately, this attack has a super-polynomial complexity. So, in practice, we are not threatened by this attack.

A.2 Previous Approaches for Related-Key Security

Due to the existence of related-key attacks breaking all ciphers by using special relations (see Appendix A.1), sound security models for related-key security must rule over attackers using these relations. Bellare-Kohno [3] devised an exhaustive list of criteria including such allowed relations but his criteria only work in the ideal cipher model. These relations must be in a set D such that the following aspects are the case.

- **Output unpredictability**: For any subset P of a (polynomially) large set D and for any set X of keys of (polynomially) bounded size, the probability over $K \in_U \mathcal{K}$ that $\{\varphi(K); \varphi \in P\} \cap X \neq \emptyset$ is negligible.
- **Collision resistance**: For any subset P of a (polynomially) large set D, the probability over $K \in_U \mathcal{K}$ that $\#\{\varphi(K); \varphi \in P\} < \#P$ is negligible.

Output unpredictability rules over attackers working with functions which cancel too many bits. Since $\varphi(K) = K$ for many relations, collision resistance eliminates the Bellare-Kohno attack and the Harris attack (see Appendix A.1). So, these criteria eliminate *all threats* except the Bernstein [4] attack.[4] (See Appendix A.1.) Bellare and Kohno prove that these two criteria are sufficient to prove security in the PRP-RKA$_{\mathsf{Enc}}^D$ game *in the ideal cipher model*. This model by itself discards Bernstein's attack, since relations cannot call the cipher itself. What is satisfactory about their approach is that all polynomial attacks mentioned in Appendix A.1 are eliminated. As per [3], therein we could indeed show that some secure block ciphers exist. What is not satisfactory about their approach is that all dedicated attacks in the literature are also eliminated because they attack a cipher which is not in the ideal cipher model.

In [21], Harris proposed to define related-key security in the standard model but for tweakable encryption, in which the adversary would have to commit to a set of allowed relations before he learns which tweak τ is being used. Of course, this set must be polynomially bounded. Otherwise, the adversary could decide to allow $\varphi_{i,x,\tau}$ for all τ. Still, the relevance of this model to practice is debatable. In [16], relations can invoke Enc and Enc^{-1} but there is the extra condition, called

---

[4] What is in common between the Harris attack [20,21] and the Bernstein one [4] is that the relation is defined using the encryption itself. We could consider a related-key attack in the ideal cipher model (a.k.a. the Shannon model), where the encryption/decryption would be given as an oracle-access. Having encryption/decryption circumvented in an oracle makes it possible to prevent from using it in the definition of elements of D.

oracle independence. It means that the adversary shall not produce (φ_1, x) and φ_2 such that $(\varphi_1(K), x)$ was queried to Enc or Enc^{-1} during the computation of $\varphi_2(K)$. This condition rules over the Bernstein attack (due to $\varphi_1(K) = K$, $x = 0$, and $\varphi_2(K) = \mathsf{Enc}_K(0)$). It also eliminates the improved Harris attack (due to $\varphi_1(K) = K \oplus e_i$ and $\varphi_2 = \varphi_{i,x}$). However, oracle independence inherently relies on the ideal cipher model: any instantiation may hide the fact that $(\varphi_1(K), x)$ is queried during the computation of $\varphi_2(K)$; this is done by not querying it but doing the computation locally instead.

In order to rule over the above improvement of the Harris attack in the standard model (i.e., with no cipher oracle), we shall use our security model based on rulers.

A.3 Using Rulers for Related-Key Security

The Bellare-Kohno [3] conditions for output unpredictability and collision resistance could also cast as a class Jury of rulers. Indeed, we make Jury contain two types of rulers, as follows.

– For output unpredictability:
  For each $k \in \mathcal{K}$, and for each integers d and i, we define $\mathcal{R}_{k,d,i}$ as follows. Let φ_i be the relation in the ith query by $\mathcal{A}$. The ruler ought to make statistics to estimate whether $\Pr[\varphi_i(K) = k] \geq \lambda^{-d}$ (taken over random K), and it ought to reject if this holds. (If there is no ith query, just output 0.)
– For collision resistance:
  For each d, i, j such that $i < j$, we define $\mathcal{R}_{d,i,j}$ as follows. Let φ_i be the relation in the ith query of $\mathcal{A}$ and φ_j be the relation in jth query of $\mathcal{A}$. The ruler ought to make statistics to estimate whether $\Pr[\varphi_i(K) = \varphi_j(K)] \geq \lambda^{-d}$ (taken over random K) and it ought to reject, if this holds. (If there is no ith query, just output 0.)

Namely, for output unpredictability, using $n = \lambda^{2d+1}$ samples $K_1, \ldots, K_n$, the ruler $\mathcal{R}_{k,d,i}$ aborts if the number of js such that $\varphi_i(K_j) = k$ goes beyond $\frac{n}{2}\lambda^{-d}$. By using the Hoeffding bound [22], we obtain that —if $\Pr[\varphi_i(K) = k] \geq \lambda^{-d}$— then, with probability at most $e^{-\frac{\lambda}{2}}$, the ruler $\mathcal{R}_{k,d,i}$ does not abort. If $\Pr[\varphi_i(K) = k] \leq \frac{1}{4}\lambda^{-d}$, the ruler aborts with probability at most $e^{-\frac{\lambda}{8}}$. If the set of relations satisfies output unpredictability, then we know that $\Pr[\varphi_i(K) = k] = \mathcal{O}(\lambda^{-d-1})$. So, there is a λ_0 such that for all $\lambda > \lambda_0$ and we have $\Pr[\varphi_i(K) = k] < \frac{1}{4}\lambda^{-d}$. Therefore, $\mathcal{R}_{k,d,i}$ aborts with negligible probability. This holds for all k, d, i. Conversely, if the set does not satisfy output unpredictability, there must be some k, d, and i such that $\Pr[\varphi_i(K) = k] \geq \lambda^{-d}$ for infinitely many λ's. So, $\mathcal{R}_{k,d,i}$ aborts with a probability which is not negligible.

The same arguments hold for collision resistance.

We note that all these rulers are polynomially bounded and permissive. In this fashion, we rule over most of polynomial attacks from Appendix A.1 except the Bernstein one. To rule over the Bernstein attack, we can use a ruler $\mathcal{R}$ who looks whether there exists an (i, j)-pair such that $y_i = \mathcal{A}_1(c_j, K; \rho)$ (i.e., one encryption-result equals one related key). This ruler rejects if this is the case. Again, this is also polynomially bounded and permissive. So, we can rule over all polynomial attacks from Appendix A.1 without using the Shannon model.

B Related-Key Model Versus Key-Dependent Input Model

As we can see, the problem with the Harris attack [20,21] lies in the way the adversary makes the relation depends on the message to encrypt. Somehow, this is a reminiscent of the key-dependent input (KDI) model. In the KDI model, a query φ returns $\mathsf{Enc}_K(\varphi(K))$.

Indeed, the Harris attack translates to our model in a straightforward way. We define $\varphi_i(K) = x$ as the smallest number such that $\mathsf{lsb}(\mathsf{Enc}_K(x))$ is the ith bit of K. By making the φ_i query to a KDI challenger, we obtain a ciphertext whose least significant bit is equal to the ith bit of K. This was already noticed in Black-Rogaway-Shrimpton [8].

This could be even worse: when the key is smaller than the message block, the $\varphi(K) = \mathsf{Enc}_K^{-1}(K)$ query would yield K, as noticed by Halevi-Krawczyk [19]. They further observed that no deterministic encryption can be KDI-secure with respect to every set of allowed relations of cardinality 1. This is essentially due to the Bernstein attack: setting $\varphi(K) = \mathsf{Enc}_K(0)$, we can query φ, 0 and its result and check consistency of the outputs to mount a distinguisher.

Halevi-Krawczyk [19] then showed that for any well-spread function φ (i.e. preimages are not too big), we can construct a deterministic encryption which is KDI-secure with respect to the class $\{\varphi\}$. We note that the well-spread condition reminds our previous condition on colliding relations.

Halevi-Krawczyk [19] observed that we can achieve KDI-secure deterministic encryption in the ideal cipher model by preventing key-dependent input functions to depend on the ideal cipher. This is the same situation as in the related-key model in Bellare-Kohno [3].

As we can see, the related-key attacks and key-dependent input attacks share similar properties. Of course, we could combine them and propose a more general framework. In this paper, we were rather inspired by the results on KDI-security and want to see how to address related-key attacks.

In a recent result, Haitner-Holenstein [18] proved that if relations are treated as black-boxes, there is no KDI-secure encryption based on a one-way permutation. We took this approach and look at what happens if related-key permutations were treated like black-boxes.

Security Analysis of the Modular Enhanced Symmetric Role Authentication (mERA) Protocol

Jean-Sébastien Coron[(✉)]

Tranef, Luxembourg, Luxembourg
jscoron@tranef.com

Abstract. We provide a security analysis of the Modular Enhanced Symmetric Role Authentication ($mERA$) protocol. We prove that mERA is secure in the Bellare-Rogaway model, the standard model for analyzing the security of cryptographic protocols.

1 Introduction

The $mERA$ Protocol. The $mERA$ protocol [1] is a symmetric-key authentication protocol involving two parties: a smart card (or integrated circuit card) called ICC, and a smart card reader called IFD. The ICC owns a master secret key mk. This master key is shared by a large number of ICCs for user-privacy purpose, i.e. in order to prevent the identification by an IFD of a specific ICC within the group of ICCs sharing the same master key mk.

Every IFD owns a specific secret key sk_i which can also be computed on the ICC side from both the master key mk and the IFD identifier id_i. In addition, every IFD is equipped with a long-term Diffie-Hellman pair (x_i, g^{x_i}) and a pseudo-certificate σ_i in order to prevent ICCs from impersonating an IFD.

The $mERA$ protocol is modular, which means that it can be used in two different ways called $mERA_{1-3}$ and $mERA_{1-7}$. The security goal of $mERA_{1-3}$, which is executed between an ICC and an IFD identified with id_i, is to store on the ICC side some data that is authenticated by the IFD while protecting against replay attacks. The security goal of $mERA_{1-7}$, which is also executed between an ICC and an IFD identified with id_i, is to establish a *forward-secure* shared secret between the ICC and the IFD, thus providing a mutual authentication between the ICC and the IFD.

Informally the main security requirements for $mERA_{1-3}$ and $mERA_{1-7}$ are the following:

1. Data authenticity and confidentiality in $mERA_{1-3}$: it should be impossible for a coalition of malicious IFDs to authenticate an application payload *data* as coming from an IFD with id_i, without knowing the IFD's secret key sk_i (authenticity). It should also be impossible for such coalition to learn any information about *data* (confidentiality).

This work has been supported by Gixel and ANTS.

P.Y.A. Ryan et al. (Eds.): Kahn Festschrift, LNCS 9100, pp. 518–542, 2016.
DOI: 10.1007/978-3-662-49301-4_32

2. Secrecy and authentication in $mERA_{1-7}$: the session-key established between an ICC and an IFD should remain secure against a coalition of malicious IFDs and also against a malicious ICC (secrecy). It should be impossible for a coalition of IFDs to impersonate the ICC or another IFD (authentication). The mutually established session key should remain secure against future compromise of the IFD and ICC long-term secrets (forward security).

The Bellare-Rogaway Model. To prove the security of a key-exchange protocol such as mERA one must develop a formal model and define security notions for the task of setting up a common secret value (a session key). In [2] Bellare and Rogaway described a formal model in which the players are modeled via oracles and the protocol execution is controlled by the attacker via queries to these oracles. The model guarantees that the session-key will remain secure even in the presence of active adversaries who can modify and inject messages between the protocol participants. More precisely the indistinguishability approach of [6] is used to defining the security of the session-key: a key-exchange protocol is called secure if the adversary cannot distinguish the value of the session-key generated by the protocol from an independent random value.

The Bellare-Rogaway model was later extended by Canetti and Krawczyk [3] with modeling the leakage of the internal state of a protocol participant. Such information might be for example the exponent x used by a party to compute a value g^x used in a Diffie-Hellman key-exchange protocol. The property of forward secrecy guarantees that the leakage of long term secrets does not give information about the previously generated session-keys. The Canetti-Krawczyk model was later extended by LaMacchia et al. [9] to encompass more attacks based on the leakage of the session state and/or the long-term secrets. Canetti and Krawczyk also described in [4] an extension of the CK model for protocols in which the peer identities are not necessarily known at the beginning of the protocol, such as in the Internet Key Exchange (IKE) standard [7]; they call this model the "post-specified peer" model.

In this article we follow the original approach in [2]. Namely we do not consider the leakage of session-specific states as in [3]; as in [2] we only consider the leakage of session-keys. We also consider a notion of forward secrecy analogous to the weak Perfect Forward Secrecy (wPFS) notion in [8]: informally speaking a session-key established without the active intervention of the attacker (passive attack) is guaranteed to be irrecoverable by the attacker, even if the attacker knew the long term secrets of both parties when the session key was established. Our model is similar to the model used in [5] to prove the security of the EAC protocol.

Security of the $mERA_{1-3}$ and $mERA_{1-7}$ Protocols. In this article we show that the $mERA_{1-3}$ and $mERA_{1-7}$ are secure in the Bellare-Rogaway model. For the $mERA_{1-3}$ protocol we prove that the protocol ensures the authenticity and confidentiality of *data* that is eventually stored in the ICC. Informally, it should be infeasible for an adversary to authenticate *data* as coming from an IFD identified with *id* without knowing the IFD's secret key *sk*, even if the adversary has obtained the secret keys from other IFDs; additionally the adversary should not learn any information about *data*. We stress that in the Bellare-Rogaway model the adversary can perform an active attack: he can intercept and replace any message by its own.

For $mERA_{1-7}$ we prove that the protocol ensures both the secrecy of the mutually established session-key and the mutual authentication of the ICC and the IFD. The secrecy property ensures that the session key established between an ICC and an IFD should remain secure against a coalition of malicious IFDs and also against a malicious ICC. Additionally the mutually established session key should remain secure against future compromise of the IFD and ICC long-term secrets (forward security).

More precisely, in $mERA_{1-7}$ the adversary should learn no information about a session-key established between an ICC and an IFD when neither the ICC nor the IFD have been corrupted, even under an active attack. Moreover even if the ICC or the IFD have been corrupted, previous session-keys and future session-keys computed without the active participation of the adversary are still secure (forward security). And even if the ICC has been corrupted, future session-keys computed by the legitimate ICC are still secure, even under an active attack.

Finally we show that $mERA_{1-7}$ ensures the authentication of both the IFD and the ICC in the Bellare-Rogaway model. We show that an adversary cannot impersonate the ICC when interacting with an IFD: more precisely if the IFD has generated a session-key then the legitimate ICC must also have generated a session-key with this IFD, except with negligible probability. Similarly we show that the adversary cannot impersonate an IFD when interacting with an ICC: more precisely the adversary cannot make the ICC generate a session-key with an IFD without involving (or corrupting) the legitimate IFD, except with negligible probability.

2   The Bellare-Rogaway Model for Authenticated Key Exchange Protocols

In this article the security of the $mERA_{1-3}$ and $mERA_{1-7}$ protocols will be analyzed in the Bellare and Rogaway model [2], which has become the standard model for analyzing the security of Authenticated Key Exchange (AKE) protocols. In this section we first provide a general description of the Bellare-Rogaway model in the context of the $mERA_{1-7}$ protocol. The model will be adapted to the analysis of the $mERA_{1-3}$ protocol in Sect. 5.

Protocol Participants. Every participant in the protocol is either an IFD of identity *id* or the ICC. We denote by $\mathcal{U}$ the set of all participants.

Long-Lived Keys. Every IFD of identity *id* holds a secret-key *sk* and a private exponent x_i corresponding to its public-key g^{x_i}. The ICC holds the master-key mk.

Protocol Execution. The interaction between the adversary $\mathcal{A}$ and the protocol participants occurs only via oracle queries from the adversary. This is to model the capabilities of the adversary in a real attack, in which the adversary can modify the messages exchanged by the protocol participants.

Several instances of the same participant may be created by the adversary during the execution of the protocol. In the *concurrent model* several instances of a given participant can be active at the same time. In the *non-concurrent model*, only one active user instance is allowed. In this article we are working in the concurrent model.

We denote by U^j the j-th instance of a participant U. Initially the adversary receives all public-keys of the users along with their certificates. As in [5] these users are called *honest* whereas the users whose public-key is chosen and registered by the adversary, are called *adversarially controlled*. The following oracles are available to the adversary:

- $Send(U^j, m)$: this oracle query sends the message m to the participant instance U^j. The oracle outputs the message generated by the participant instance upon receipt of m. The $Send$ oracle is used to model an active attack, in which the adversary may tamper with the messages being sent to the participants.
- $Execute(U^j, U^k)$: outputs the set of messages exchanged during an honest execution of the protocol between the participant instance U^j and the participant instance U^k. This is used to model a passive attack in which the adversary gets the messages exchanged by two protocol participants.
- $Reveal(U^j)$: this query returns the session key held by the instance U^j, if U is not adversarially controlled. If the instance has no such session key, then $\perp$ is returned.
- $Corrupt(U)$: the adversary obtains the long term key of user U. If U is the IFD of identity id_i, the adversary obtains the corresponding sk_i and the secret exponent x_i. If U is the ICC, the adversary obtains the master-key mk.
- $Test(U^j)$: if the session key for instance U^i is defined, then the oracle flips a bit b, and returns the session-key defined for instance U^i if $b = 1$, and a random key of the same size if $b = 0$. The adversary's goal is then to guess the value of b.
- $Register(U^*, pk^*)$: the adversary registers a public-key pk^* in the name of a new user U^*. The user is then considered as adversarially controlled.

Informal Security Goals. We first consider the secrecy of the mutually established session-key. The session key established between an ICC and an IFD should remain secure against a coalition of malicious IFDs and also against a malicious ICC. Additionally the mutually established session key should remain secure against future compromise of the IFD and ICC long-term secrets (forward security). A little bit more precisely the security goals for secrecy are the following:

1. The adversary should learn no information about a session-key established between an ICC and an IFD of identity id_i when no *Corrupt* query has been

issued against the ICC and the IFD, and the IFD's public-key has not been registered by the adversary; this should hold even under an active attack.

2. Even if the ICC or the IFD of identity id_i has received a *Corrupt* query or the IFD's public-key has been registered by the adversary, previous session-keys and future session-keys passively generated by *Execute* are still secure (forward security).

3. Even if the ICC has received a *Corrupt* query, future session-keys computed by the legitimate ICC are still secure, even under an active attack[1].

Partnering. Following [2], two instances U_1^i and U_2^j are said to be partners if the following conditions are met:

1. Both instances U_1^i and U_2^j are in the accept state;
2. Both U_1^i and U_2^j share the same session identifications *sid*. The *sid* can be taken as the transcript of the conversation between the two instances before they are in the accept state;
3. The partner identification for U_1^i is U_2^j and conversely; and
4. No instance other than U_1^i and U_2^j is in the accept state with a partner identification equal to U_1^i or U_2^j.

Freshness. The goal of the freshness notion is to avoid cases in which the adversary already knows the session-key and must not be allowed to perform the *Test* query. This happens for example if a *Reveal* query has been issued to this instance or its partner.

We say that an instance U^i is *opened* if a query $Reveal(U^i)$ has been made by the adversary, or if a query $Corrupt(U)$ has been made by the adversary with $U \neq ICC$, or if U's public-key has been registered by the adversary. We say that an instance is *unopened* if it is not *opened*. We say that an instance has *accepted* if it goes into an accept mode. Finally, we say that an instance U^i is *fresh* if it has *accepted* and if both U^i and its partner are *unopened*.

AKE Security. We consider an execution of the key exchange protocol P by an adversary $\mathcal{A}$ who is given access to the *Send, Execute, Reveal, Corrupt, Register* oracles, and asks a single *Test* query to a fresh instance, and outputs a guess bit b'. We say that the adversary is successful if $b' = b$, where b is the hidden bit used by the *Test* oracle.

We define the advantage an adversary $\mathcal{A}$ in violating the semantic security of the protocol P by:

$$\mathsf{Adv}_P^{\mathsf{ake}}(\mathcal{A}) = 2 \cdot \Pr[b' = b] - 1$$

---

[1] This means that although the adversary knowing mk can authenticate as an IFD of identity id_i, without a *Corrupt* query to this IFD the adversary cannot recover the session-key computed the legitimate ICC. In other words even when knowing mk the adversary cannot impersonate an IFD interacting with the legitimate ICC.

We define $\mathsf{Adv}_P^{\mathsf{ake}}(t, q_s, q_c, q_h)$ as the maximum advantage over all adversaries running in time at most t, and making at most q_s *Send* and *Execute* queries, q_c corrupt queries, and q_h hash queries.

Definition 1 (AKE Semantic Security). *We say that a key exchange protocol is* $(t, q_s, q_c, q_h, \varepsilon)$-*semantically secure if* $\mathsf{Adv}_P^{\mathsf{ake}}(t, q_s, q_c, q_h) \leq \varepsilon$.

Authentication. We consider an execution of the key exchange protocol P by the adversary. We say that the adversary is successful in impersonating the ICC if an IFD instance U_i^j of identity id_i and index j has accepted but the legitimate ICC is not in accept mode, and no *Corrupt* query was issued against this IFD nor against the ICC. We denote by $\mathsf{Adv}_P^{\mathsf{ICC-auth}}(\mathcal{A})$ the success probability of such adversary. We define $\mathsf{Adv}_P^{\mathsf{ICC-auth}}(t, q_s, q_c, q_h)$ as the maximum advantage over all adversaries running in time at most t, and making at most q_s *Send* and *Execute* queries, q_c corrupt queries, and q_h hash queries.

Similarly we say that the adversary is successful in impersonating an IFD of identity id_i if the ICC is in the accept mode with the j-th instance of the IFD of identity id_i while such instance was never issued a *Send* query, an *Execute* query or a *Corrupt* query, nor did the ICC receive a *Corrupt* query. We denote by $\mathsf{Adv}_P^{\mathsf{IFD-auth}}(\mathcal{A})$ the success probability of such adversary. We define $\mathsf{Adv}_P^{\mathsf{IFD-auth}}(t, q_s, q_c, q_h)$ as the maximum advantage over all adversaries running in time at most t, and making at most q_s *Send* and *Execute* queries, q_c corrupt queries, and q_h hash queries. Finally we let $\mathsf{Adv}_P^{\mathsf{auth}}(t, q_s, q_c, q_h) = \max(\mathsf{Adv}_P^{\mathsf{IFD-auth}}(t, q_s, q_c, q_h), \mathsf{Adv}_P^{\mathsf{ICC-auth}}(t, q_s, q_c, q_h))$

Definition 2 (AKE Authentication). *We say that a key exchange protocol is* $(t, q_s, q_c, q_h, \varepsilon)$-*authentic if* $\mathsf{Adv}_P^{\mathsf{auth}}(t, q_s, q_c, q_h) \leq \varepsilon$.

3   Description of $mERA$

The modular Enhanced Symmetric Role Authentication (mERA) protocol is a two-party protocol played between an ICC and an IFD. In this section, we first define the cryptographic primitives used in the $mERA$ protocol. Next, we define the generic algorithms of $mERA$ which are based on these cryptographic primitives. Finally, we describe the protocols $mERA_{1-3}$ and $mERA_{1-7}$.

3.1   Cryptographic Primitives

In the following, we denote by κ the general security parameter. The $mERA$ protocol is built upon the following cryptographic primitives:

1. A key derivation function:

$$\mathsf{KDF} : \{0,1\}^\alpha \times \{0,1\}^\beta \rightarrow \{0,1\}^\gamma$$

with α, β and γ, three security parameters that should be defined according to the general security parameter κ.

2. A deterministic symmetric encryption scheme with encryption function:

$$\mathsf{Enc} : \{0,1\}^\gamma \times \{0,1\}^{\lambda \cdot \delta} \to \{0,1\}^{\lambda \cdot \delta}$$

with δ a security parameter that should be defined according to the general security parameter κ, and λ a positive integer. The encryption function Enc is associated with the decryption function:

$$\mathsf{Dec} : \{0,1\}^\gamma \times \{0,1\}^{\lambda \cdot \delta} \to \{0,1\}^{\lambda \cdot \delta}$$

3. A MAC function:

$$\mathsf{Mac} : \{0,1\}^\gamma \times \{0,1\}^{\lambda \cdot \delta} \to \{0,1\}^\theta$$

with θ a security parameter that should be defined according to the general security parameter κ.

4. Five hash functions:

$$H_1, H_2, H_3 : \{0,1\}^{2\delta} \to \{0,1\}^\gamma$$
$$H_4, H_5 : \{0,1\}^* \to \{0,1\}^\eta$$

with η a security parameter that should be defined according to the general security parameter κ.

3.2   Algorithms

We describe the $mERA$ protocol with the following seven algorithms: ICCKey-Gen, IFDIdGen, IFDKeyDF, IFDKeyDHGen, SessionKDF, AuthResp and Verif-AuthResp.

1. ICCKeyGen is a probabilistic algorithm which takes as input a security parameter κ and outputs a master key $\mathsf{mk} \in \{0,1\}^\alpha$.
2. IFDIdGen is a probabilistic algorithm which takes as input the list of previously delivered identifiers id's. It outputs a new identifier $id_i \in \{0,1\}^\beta$.
3. IFDKeyDF is a deterministic algorithm which takes as input a master key mk, and an identifier id_i. It outputs the secret key sk_i. Given a master key $\mathsf{mk} \in \{0,1\}^\alpha$ and an identifier $id_i \in \{0,1\}^\beta$, it computes $sk_i \in \{0,1\}^\gamma$ as follows:

$$sk_i = \mathsf{KDF}(\mathsf{mk}, id_i)$$

4. IFDKeyDHGen is a probabilistic algorithm which takes as input a security parameter κ and outputs a private Diffie-Hellman element x, a public Diffie-Hellman element g^x, and a certificate σ. Then (x, g^x, σ) is securely transmitted to the IFD.

Here, we implicitly assume that the DH parameters, i.e. (p, q, g) or (p, a, b, G, n), have been chosen according to the general security parameter κ.

5. SessionKDF is a deterministic algorithm which takes as input a secret key sk_i, an input message m and outputs three session keys k_a, k_b and k_c:

$$(k_a, k_b, k_c) \leftarrow \text{SessionKDF}(sk_i, m)$$

Given a secret key $sk_i \in \{0,1\}^\gamma$, a message $m \in \{0,1\}^{2\delta}$, it computes $k_a \in \{0,1\}^\gamma$, $k_b \in \{0,1\}^\gamma$ and $k_c \in \{0,1\}^\gamma$ as follows:

$$zz = \text{Enc}(sk_i, m); \quad k_a = H_1(zz); \quad k_b = H_2(zz); \quad k_c = H_3(zz).$$

6. AuthResp is a deterministic algorithm which takes as input an ephemeral encryption key k_1, an ephemeral MAC key k_2, and a message m. It outputs a pair (E, M) where E is the encryption of the plaintext message m under the key k_1 and M is the MAC value of E under the key k_2:

$$(E, M) \leftarrow \text{AuthResp}(k_1, k_2, m)$$

Given an ephemeral encryption key $k_1 \in \{0,1\}^\gamma$, an ephemeral MAC key $k_2 \in \{0,1\}^\gamma$, and a message $m \in \{0,1\}^{\lambda \cdot \delta}$ with $\lambda \geq 1$, it computes a pair (E, M) with $E \in \{0,1\}^{\lambda \cdot \delta}$ and $M \in \{0,1\}^\theta$ as follows:

$$E = \text{Enc}(k_1, m), \quad M = \text{Mac}(k_2, E)$$

7. VerifAuthResp is a deterministic algorithm which takes as input a pair (E, M), an ephemeral encryption key k_1, an ephemeral MAC key k_2, and a message m. It checks the validity of (E, M). If it is not valid, it outputs $\perp$. Else it outputs the plaintext message $m = \text{Dec}(k_1, E)$:

$$Output \leftarrow \text{VerifAuthResp}(E, M, k_1, k_2, m)$$

Given $E \in \{0,1\}^{\lambda \cdot \delta}$, $M \in \{0,1\}^\theta$, $k_1 \in \{0,1\}^\gamma$, $k_2 \in \{0,1\}^\gamma$, and $m \in \{0,1\}^{\lambda \cdot \delta}$, it computes $M' = \text{Mac}(k_2, E)$ and $res = \text{Dec}(k_1, E)$. If $M' \neq M$ or if $res \neq m$, it outputs $\perp$. Else it outputs $res = m$.

Remark 1. The message m does not necessarily represent a unique message. Indeed, a message m can be of the form $m = *^\lambda || m'$ or $m = m' || *^\lambda$ where $*^\lambda$ represents any λ-bit string. Thus, in this case the matching test is performed on the value m'.

3.3   Key Setup

The general security parameter κ is fixed. In the following description, we omit the parameter κ in the inputs of the algorithms. The setup of the system is the following.

- The master key mk $\in \{0,1\}^\alpha$ is generated using the probabilistic algorithm ICCKeyGen().
- For every IFD in the system:

- a new identifier id_i is generated using the probabilistic algorithm IFDId-Gen($pastIDs$);
- the corresponding secret key sk_i is computed according to the deterministic algorithm IFDKeyDF(mk, id_i);
- the probabilistic algorithm IFDKeyDHGen is executed to get a private Diffie-Hellman element x_i, a public Diffie-Hellman element g^{x_i}, and also a certificate σ_i.

The secret values are (sk_i, x_i) and the public values are $(id_i, g^{x_i}, \sigma_i)$.

The master key mk is securely transmitted to any legitimate ICC of the system. Every IFD in the system securely receives its personal secret values (sk_i, x_i) and its personal public values $(id_i, g^{x_i}, \sigma_i)$.

3.4 The $mERA_{1-3}$ protocol

The protocol is played between an ICC with secret key mk and an IFD with secret key sk_i and public identifier id_i; see Fig. 1 for an illustration.

1. The IFD generates a random value $r_1 \in \{0,1\}^\delta$ and sends (r_1, id_i) to the ICC.
2. The ICC:
   - computes the IFD secret key sk_i following the computation steps of IFDKeyDF(mk, id_i);
   - generates a random value $r_2 \in \{0,1\}^\delta$;
   - computes the session keys k_a, k_b and k_c using of SessionKDF($sk_i, r_2 \| r_1$);
   - sends r_2 to the IFD.
3. The IFD:
   - computes the session keys k_a, k_b and k_c using SessionKDF($sk_i, r_2 \| r_1$);
   - computes (E, M) following the computation steps of AuthResp($k_a, k_c, r_2 \| data$) where $data$ is an application-specific payload;
   - sends (E, M) to the ICC.
4. The ICC:
   - checks the validity of (E, M) following the computation steps of VerifAuthResp($E, M, k_a, k_c, r_2 \| *^\lambda$) where λ is a positive integer. If the output is different from $\perp$, then it stores the application specific payload $data$.

3.5 The $mERA_{1-7}$ Protocol

The protocol is played between an ICC with secret key mk and an IFD with secret keys (sk_i, x_i) and public values $(id_i, g^{x_i}, \sigma_i)$. See Fig. 2 for an illustration.

1. The IFD generates a random value $r_1 \in \{0,1\}^\delta$ and sends (r_1, id_i) to the ICC.
2. The ICC:
   - computes the IFD secret key sk_i following the computation steps of IFDKeyDF(mk, id_i);

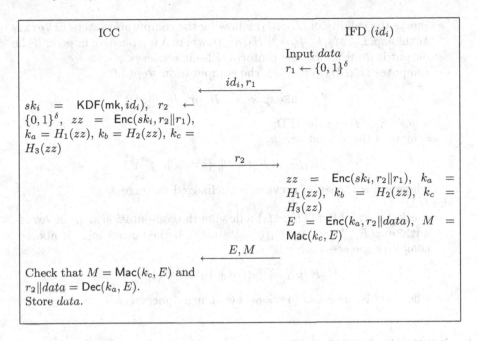

Fig. 1. The $mERA_{1-3}$ protocol, played between an ICC and an IFD of identity id.

- generates a random value $r_2 \in \{0,1\}^\delta$;
- computes the session keys k_a, k_b and k_c following the computation steps of $\mathtt{SessionKDF}(sk_i, r_2\|r_1)$;
- sends r_2 to the IFD.

3. The IFD:
   - computes the session keys k_a, k_b and k_c following the computation steps of $\mathtt{SessionKDF}(sk_i, r_2\|r_1)$;
   - generates a random value $r_3 \in \{0,1\}^\delta$ and sends it to the ICC;

4. The ICC:
   - generates an ephemeral DH pair (y, g^y)
   - computes (E_1, M_1) following the computation steps of $\mathtt{AuthResp}(k_b, k_c, r_3\|g^y)$
   - sends (E_1, M_1) to the IFD.

5. The IFD:
   - checks the validity of (E_1, M_1) following the computation steps of $\mathtt{VerifAuthResp}(E_1, M_1, k_b, k_c, r_3\|*^\lambda)$ with λ a positive integer. If the output is $\bot$, it aborts the protocol. Else it retrieves g^y.
   - generates an ephemeral DH pair $(x', g^{x'})$ and computes (E_2, M_2) following the computation steps of $\mathtt{AuthResp}(k_a, k_c, g^{x'}\|H_4(g^{x_i}))$;
   - sends $(g^{x_i}, \sigma_i, E_2, M_2)$ to the ICC.

6. The ICC:
   - checks the certificate σ_i of g^{x_i};

- checks the validity of (E_2, M_2) following the computation steps of Verif-AuthResp$(E_2, M_2, k_a, k_c, *^\lambda || H_4(g^{x_i}))$, where λ is a positive integer. If the output is $\perp$, it aborts the protocol. Else it retrieves $g^{x'}$.
- computes (E_3, M_3) following the computation steps of:

$$\text{AuthResp}(k_b, k_c, H_4(g^{x'} || g^{x_i} || g^y))$$

- sends (E_3, M_3) to the IFD;
- computes the session key

$$K_{ICC} = H_5(sid \,||\, (g^{x_i})^y \,||\, (g^{x'})^y)$$

where sid is the set of previously exchanged messages.
7. The IFD:
- checks the validity of (E_3, M_3) following the computation steps of Verif-AuthResp$(E_3, M_3, k_b, k_c, H_4(g^{x'} || g^{x_i} || g^y))$. If the output is $\perp$, it aborts.
- computes the session-key

$$K_{IFD} = H_5(sid \,||\, (g^y)^{x_i} \,||\, (g^y)^{x'})$$

where sid is the set of previously exchanged messages.

4   Security Assumptions

In this section we formulate the security assumptions for proving the security of the $mERA$ protocol.

4.1   Diffie-Hellman Assumptions

The security of the $mERA$ protocol is based on the Gap Diffie-Hellman (GDH) assumption. We first recall the CDH assumption.

Definition 3 (CDH Assumption). *Let κ be a security parameter. Let p, q be primes, where q is of length κ bits and $q|p-1$. Let g be of order q in $\mathbb{Z}_p^*$. We say that CDH is (t, ε)-hard if no algorithm given as input (g, g^a, g^b) where $a, b \leftarrow \mathbb{Z}_q$ can compute g^{ab} is time at most t.*

The GDH assumption states that the CDH problem remains hard even if the adversary has access to a DDH oracle.

Definition 4 (DDH Oracle). *Let κ, p, q, g as in Definition 3. A DDH oracle takes as input (g, g^a, g^b, z) and returns 1 if $z = g^{ab}$ and 0 otherwise.*

Definition 5 (GDH Assumption). *Let κ, p, q, g as in Definition 3. We say that GDH is (t, q_d, ε)-hard if no algorithm given as input (g, g^a, g^b) where $a, b \leftarrow \mathbb{Z}_q$ can compute g^{ab} is time at most t while making at most q_d queries to the DDH oracle.*

We denote by $\text{Adv}^{\text{GDH}}(t, q_d)$ the maximum success probability of solving the GDH problem over algorithms running in time at most t and making at most q_d queries to the DDH oracle.

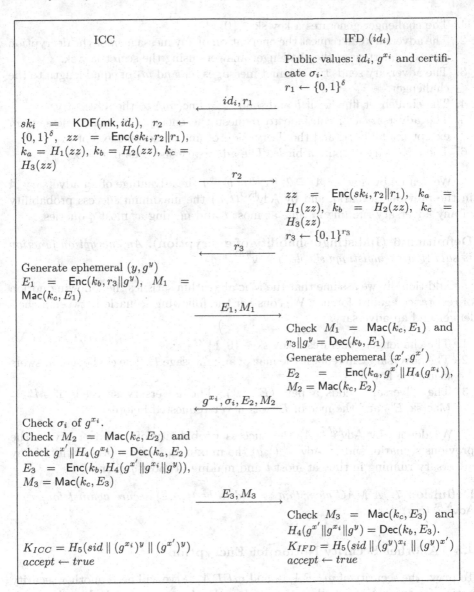

ICC	IFD (id_i)
	Public values: id_i, g^{x_i} and certificate σ_i.
	$r_1 \leftarrow \{0,1\}^\delta$
$\xleftarrow{\quad id_i, r_1 \quad}$	
$sk_i = \mathsf{KDF}(\mathsf{mk}, id_i)$, $r_2 \leftarrow \{0,1\}^\delta$, $zz = \mathsf{Enc}(sk_i, r_2 \| r_1)$, $k_a = H_1(zz)$, $k_b = H_2(zz)$, $k_c = H_3(zz)$	
$\xrightarrow{\quad r_2 \quad}$	
	$zz = \mathsf{Enc}(sk_i, r_2 \| r_1)$, $k_a = H_1(zz)$, $k_b = H_2(zz)$, $k_c = H_3(zz)$
	$r_3 \leftarrow \{0,1\}^{r_3}$
$\xleftarrow{\quad r_3 \quad}$	
Generate ephemeral (y, g^y) $E_1 = \mathsf{Enc}(k_b, r_3 \| g^y)$, $M_1 = \mathsf{Mac}(k_c, E_1)$	
$\xrightarrow{\quad E_1, M_1 \quad}$	
	Check $M_1 = \mathsf{Mac}(k_c, E_1)$ and $r_3 \| g^y = \mathsf{Dec}(k_b, E_1)$
	Generate ephemeral $(x', g^{x'})$ $E_2 = \mathsf{Enc}(k_a, g^{x'} \| H_4(g^{x_i}))$, $M_2 = \mathsf{Mac}(k_c, E_2)$
$\xleftarrow{\quad g^{x_i}, \sigma_i, E_2, M_2 \quad}$	
Check σ_i of g^{x_i}. Check $M_2 = \mathsf{Mac}(k_c, E_2)$ and check $g^{x'} \| H_4(g^{x_i}) = \mathsf{Dec}(k_a, E_2)$ $E_3 = \mathsf{Enc}(k_b, H_4(g^{x'} \| g^{x_i} \| g^y))$, $M_3 = \mathsf{Mac}(k_c, E_3)$	
$\xrightarrow{\quad E_3, M_3 \quad}$	
	Check $M_3 = \mathsf{Mac}(k_c, E_3)$ and $H_4(g^{x'} \| g^{x_i} \| g^y) = \mathsf{Dec}(k_b, E_3)$.
$K_{ICC} = H_5(sid \| (g^{x_i})^y \| (g^{x'})^y)$ accept $\leftarrow$ true	$K_{IFD} = H_5(sid \| (g^y)^{x_i} \| (g^y)^{x'})$ accept $\leftarrow$ true

Fig. 2. The $mERA_{1-7}$ protocol.

4.2 Encryption and MAC

We assume that the encryption function Enc satisfies the following notion of indistinguishability under a chosen ciphertext attack. We consider the following scenario between a challenger and an adversary.

1. The challenger generates a key $sk \in \{0, 1\}^\gamma$
2. The adversary can request the encryption of any message m or the decryption of any ciphertext c; the challenger answers using the secret key sk.
3. The adversary sends two distinct messages m_0 and m_1 of equal length to the challenger.
4. The challenger flips a bit b and sends $c = \mathsf{Enc}(m_b)$ to the adversary.
5. The adversary can continue to request the encryption of any message m except m_0 and m_1, and the decryption of any ciphertext except c;
6. The adversary outputs a bit b'. The adversary succeeds if $b' = b$.

We denote by $\mathsf{Adv}^{\mathsf{IND}}(\mathcal{A}) = 2 \cdot \Pr[b' = b] - 1$ the advantage of an adversary $\mathcal{A}$ in the previous scenario, and by $\mathsf{Adv}^{\mathsf{IND}}(t, q)$ the maximum success probability of any adversary running in time at most t and making at most q queries.

Definition 6 (Indistinguishability of encryption). *An encryption function is said (t, q, ε)-indistinguishable if $\mathsf{Adv}^{\mathsf{IND}}(t, q) \leq \varepsilon$.*

Additionally we assume that the Mac algorithm satisfies the following notion of resistance against forgery. We consider the following scenario between a challenger and an adversary:

1. The challenger generates a key $sk \in \{0, 1\}^\gamma$.
2. The adversary can request the mac of any message E. The challenger answers using the key sk.
3. The adversary sends a pair (E', M'). The adversary succeeds if $M' = \mathsf{Mac}(sk, E')$ and the mac of E' was never requested before.

We denote by $\mathsf{Adv}^{\mathsf{MAC}}(\mathcal{A})$ the success probability of an adversary in the previous scenario, and by $\mathsf{Adv}^{\mathsf{MAC}}(t, q)$ the maximum success probability of any adversary running in time at most t and making at most q queries.

Definition 7. *A MAC algorithm is said to be (t, q, ε)-secure against forgery if $\mathsf{Adv}^{\mathsf{MAC}}(t, q) \leq \varepsilon$.*

4.3 Another Security Notion for Encryption

To prove the security of $mERA_{1-3}$ and $mERA_{1-7}$ we will need another security notion for encryption; we show that such notion is actually implied by the previous indistinguishability notion. More precisely we consider the following notion of chosen plaintext security between a challenger and an adversary:

1. The challenger generates a key $sk \in \{0, 1\}^\gamma$.
2. The adversary can request the encryption of any message m; the challenger answers using the secret key sk.
3. Step 2 is repeated at most q times.
4. The adversary sends a pair (m', c') to the challenger. The adversary succeeds if $c' = \mathsf{Enc}(sk, m')$ and m' was never queried at step 2.

We denote by $\mathsf{Adv}_{\mathsf{Enc}}^{\mathsf{CPA}}(\mathcal{A})$ the success probability of an adversary in the previous scenario, and by $\mathsf{Adv}_{\mathsf{Enc}}^{\mathsf{CPA}}(t, q)$ the maximum success probability of any adversary running in time at most t and making at most q queries.

Definition 8 (Chosen Plaintext Security). *An encryption function is said (t, q, ε)-chosen plaintext secure if* $\mathsf{Adv}_{\mathsf{Enc}}^{\mathsf{CPA}}(t, q) \leq \varepsilon$.

We show in Appendix A that this later security notion is implied by the previous indistinguishability notion.

Lemma 1. *If an encryption function if (t, q, ε)-indistinguishable, then it is (t, q, ε) chosen-plaintext secure.*

4.4 Security of Certificates

The security of the $mERA_{1-7}$ protocol is also based on the security of the certificates provided by the certification authority. We assume that the certification authority checks that the public-key is a well-formed group element. We denote by $\mathsf{Adv}_{\mathcal{CA}}^{\mathsf{forge}}(\mathcal{A})$ the probability that an adversary produces a valid certificate not generated by the certification authority and by $\mathsf{Adv}_{\mathcal{CA}}^{\mathsf{forge}}(t, q)$ the maximum probability over all adversaries running in time at most t and requesting at most q certificates.

4.5 Random Oracle Model

We are working in the random oracle model for the key derivation function KDF and the five hash functions H_1, H_2, H_3, H_4 and H_5. Although it is better to obtain security results that do not rely on the random oracle model, security proofs in the random oracle model are generally believed to provide a reasonable security guarantee.

5 Security of $mERA_{1-3}$

In this section, we prove that the $mERA_{1-3}$ protocol ensures the authenticity and confidentiality of *data* that is eventually stored in the ICC. Informally, it should be infeasible for an adversary to authenticate *data* as coming from an IFD identified with *id* without knowing the IFD's secret key *sk*, even if the adversary has obtained the secret keys from other IFDs; additionally the adversary should not learn any information about *data*. We stress that in the Bellare-Rogaway model the adversary can perform an active attack: he can intercept and replace any message by its own.

5.1   Authenticity in the BR Model

In this section we formalize the authenticity notion in the Bellare-Rogaway model, and we show that the $mERA_{1-3}$ protocol satisfies this notion. We assume that in the protocol the IFD of identity id receives as input $data$ that is be stored in the memory of the ICC at the end of the $mERA_{1-3}$ protocol. In the Bellare-Rogaway model the adversary controls the communication between the protocol participants; therefore we let the adversary provide $data$ as input to the IFD. Informally the adversary succeeds if the ICC eventually stores $data$ is memory as coming from an IFD of identity id_i and such IFD was neither corrupted nor started with $data$.

Formally the Bellare-Rogaway model is simplified as follows to model the authenticity of the protocol. The adversary gets access to the following oracles:

- $Send(U^j, m)$: as in Sect. 2 this oracle query sends the message m to the participant instance U^j, and outputs the message generated by the participant upon receipt of m. Additionally the adversary can issue a $Send(IFD^j, \text{start} \| data)$ that initiates the j-th instance of an IFD with $data$ as input.
- $Corrupt(id_i)$: the adversary receives the secret-key sk_i of the IFD of identity id_i. Note that there is no corrupt query to the ICC, as given mk the adversary could trivially break the scheme.

We say that the adversary is successful if the following conditions are met: (1) at the end of the protocol the ICC stores $data$ as coming from the j-th instance of an IFD of identity id_i, and (2) no $Corrupt$ query was issued against this IFD and (3) the j-th instance of this IFD was not started with $data$. Note that our security model prevents replay attacks in which the same $data$ would be stored more often than resulting from the interaction with the legitimate IFD.

We denote by $\mathsf{Adv}_P^{\mathsf{auth}}(\mathcal{A})$ the success probability of an adversary $\mathcal{A}$ in the above scenario. We define $\mathsf{Adv}_P^{\mathsf{auth}}(t, q_s, q_c, q_h)$ as the maximum advantage over all adversaries running in time at most t, and making at most q_s $Send$ and $Execute$ queries, q_c corrupt queries, and q_h hash queries.

Definition 9 (Authenticity in the BR model). *We say that a protocol is* $(t, q_s, q_c, q_h, \varepsilon)$*-authentic if* $\mathsf{Adv}_P^{\mathsf{auth}}(t, q_s, q_c, q_h) \leq \varepsilon$.

The following theorem shows that the $mERA_{1-3}$ achieves the authenticity property in the Bellare-Rogaway model.

Theorem 1 ($mERA_{1-3}$ Authenticity). *The $mERA_{1-3}$ protocol is $(t, q_s, q_c, q_h, \varepsilon)$-authentic with:*

$$\varepsilon = \frac{2(q_s)^2}{2^\delta} + q_h \cdot 2^{-\alpha} + q_h \cdot \mathsf{Adv}_{\mathsf{Enc}}^{\mathsf{CPA}}(t + \mathcal{O}(\kappa), q_s) + q_s \cdot \mathsf{Adv}^{\mathsf{MAC}}(t + \mathcal{O}(\kappa), q_s)$$

5.2   Proof of Theorem 1

We show how to break the chosen-plaintext security of the encryption function Enc or the security of the mac scheme Mac using an adversary who breaks the authenticity of the $mERA_{1-3}$ protocol. The hash functions H_i and the key derivation function KDF are viewed as random oracles.

We use a sequence of games; we denote by S_i the event that the attacker succeeds in $Game_i$. We recall the Difference Lemma [10]:

Lemma 2 (Difference Lemma). *Let A, B, F be events defined in some probability distribution, and suppose that $A \wedge \neg F \Leftrightarrow B \wedge \neg F$. Then $|\Pr[A] - \Pr[B]| \leq \Pr[F]$.*

$Game_0$: this is the original attack scenario. The oracles *Send* and *Corrupt* can be perfectly simulated given knowledge of the master key mk. More precisely the *Corrupt* oracle is simulated as follows: given query id_i, the corresponding secret-key sk_i is answered using $sk_i \leftarrow \mathsf{KDF}(\mathsf{mk}, id)$.

$Game_1$: we abort if the random r_1 generated by the IFD was previously generated by the same or another IFD, or if the random r_2 generated by the ICC was previously generated. By the Difference Lemma we get:

$$|\Pr[S_1] - \Pr[S_0]| \leq \frac{2 \cdot q_s^2}{2^\delta}$$

$Game_2$: we modify the way the secret keys sk are generated; instead of letting $\mathsf{sk} \leftarrow \mathsf{KDF}(\mathsf{mk}, id)$, we use a private random oracle H_p and let $\mathsf{sk} \leftarrow H_p(id)$ for every new identity. Similarly the *Corrupt* oracle is modified so that $\mathsf{sk} \leftarrow H_p(id)$ is returned instead.

Let G be the event that the adversary makes a random oracle query to $\mathsf{KDF}(\mathsf{mk}, id)$ for some id. It is clear that games 1 and 2 proceed identically unless event G happens; this gives:

$$|\Pr[S_2] - \Pr[S_1]| \leq \Pr[G]$$

Since mk is generated at random in $\{0,1\}^\alpha$ and there are at most q_h hash oracle queries to KDF, we have:

$$\Pr[G] \leq q_h \cdot 2^{-\alpha}$$

$Game_3$: we select a random target identity id^* among the possible identities; note that there are at most q_s such possible identities. Informally the identity id^* is our guess of which IFD will be targeted by the adversary. We modify the *Send* oracle as follows. For the IFD of identity id^* we change the way the value k_c is generated at the second round of the protocol. Instead of letting $k_c = H_3(zz)$ where $zz = \mathsf{Enc}(\mathsf{sk}, r_1 \| r_2)$ and sk corresponding to id^*, we simply generate k_c at random in $\{0,1\}^\gamma$. Note that this is done for any instance corresponding to the IFD of identity id^*, where such instances are possibly run concurrently. We proceed similarly for the value k_a.

We denote by F the event that the adversary makes a H_1 or H_3 query to zz where $zz = \mathsf{Enc}(\mathsf{sk}, r_1 \| r_2)$ and sk corresponding to id^*. It is clear that games 2 and 3 proceed identically unless F occurs; therefore by the Difference Lemma:

$$|\Pr[S_3] - \Pr[S_2]| \leq \Pr[F]$$

Lemma 3. *The following holds.*

$$\Pr[F] \leq q_h \cdot \mathsf{Adv}_{\mathsf{Enc}}^{\mathsf{CPA}}(t + \mathcal{O}(\kappa), q_s) \tag{1}$$

Proof. Given an adversary $\mathcal{A}$, we construct an algorithm C_{Enc} breaking the chosen-plaintext security of Enc as follows. Note that algorithm C_{Enc} has oracle access to the function $\mathsf{Enc}(\mathsf{sk}^*, \cdot)$ where sk^* is unknown. It must output a pair (m, c) such that $c = \mathsf{Enc}(\mathsf{sk}^*, m)$ and m was never queried to the $\mathsf{Enc}(\mathsf{sk}^*, \cdot)$ oracle before.

The *Send* oracle is modified again as follows. For the IFD of identity id^* instead of generating $\mathsf{sk}^* = H_p(id^*)$ we use the encryption oracle $\mathsf{Enc}(\mathsf{sk}^*, \cdot)$ to simulate the authentication protocol.

If event F occurs then the pair (zz, k_c) appears in the history of H_1 or H_3, where $zz = \mathsf{Enc}(\mathsf{sk}^*, r_1 \| r_2)$. Since at least r_1 has been generated by the IFD or r_2 has been generated by the ICC, and from Game 1 such r_1 or r_2 has never appeared before, the string $r_1 \| r_2$ has never been queried to the $\mathsf{Enc}(sk^*, \cdot)$ oracle; therefore the pair $(r_1 \| r_2, zz)$ is a valid output for C_{Enc}.

However our algorithm C_{Enc} cannot determine which element of the history of H_1 or H_3 is zz. Therefore algorithm C_{Enc} outputs a random input query in the history of H_1 or H_3 and succeeds with probability at least $1/q_h$, where q_h is the number of hash queries. Denoting by $\Pr[C_{\mathsf{Enc}}]$ the success probability of algorithm C_{Enc}, we have:

$$\Pr[C_{\mathsf{Enc}}] \geq \Pr[F] \cdot \frac{1}{q_h}$$

Since $\Pr[C_{\mathsf{Enc}}] \leq \mathsf{Adv}_{\mathsf{Enc}}^{\mathsf{CPA}}(t + \mathcal{O}(\kappa), q_s)$ this gives inequality (1).   □

Lemma 4. *The following holds:*

$$\Pr[S_3] \leq q_s \cdot \mathsf{Adv}^{\mathsf{MAC}}(t + \mathcal{O}(\kappa), q_s) \tag{2}$$

Proof. Given an adversary $\mathcal{A}$, we construct an algorithm C_{Mac} that breaks the mac algorithm Mac as follows. Note that algorithm C_{Mac} must output a forgery for algorithm Mac with unknown key k_{Mac}. We modify the *Send* oracle in Game 3 as follows: for the IFD of identity id^* under a given instance (there are at most q_s possible choices of identities and instances under a given identity), instead of generating k_c at random we simply let $k_c = k_{mac}$; this does not change the distribution of k_c. We note that our algorithm C_{Mac} does not need to know k_{Mac}. Then to generate $M = \mathsf{Mac}(k_c, E)$ for such instance we make a MAC oracle query for the message E.

Eventually the adversary sends a pair (E', M') to the ICC. If E' is not the encryption of $data$ with which the IFD instance was initially started, then (E', M') is a valid MAC forgery. Recall that we must have selected the right identity and the right instance under this identity, which happens with probability at least $1/q_s$; therefore our algorithm C_{Mac} succeeds with probability at least $\Pr[S_3]/q_s$; this gives inequality (2). □

Finally, combining the previous inequalities, we obtain:

$$\Pr[S_0] \leq \frac{2(q_s)^2}{2^\delta} + q_h \cdot 2^{-\alpha} + q_h \cdot \mathsf{Adv}_{\mathsf{Enc}}^{\mathsf{CPA}}(t + \mathcal{O}(\kappa), q_s) + q_s \cdot \mathsf{Adv}^{\mathsf{MAC}}(t + \mathcal{O}(\kappa), q_s)$$

which terminates the proof of Theorem 1.

5.3 Confidentiality in the Bellare-Rogaway Model

In this section we consider the confidentiality property of the $mERA_{1-3}$ protocol in the Bellare-Rogaway model recalled in Sect. 2. Formally the Bellare-Rogaway model is simplified as follows to model the confidentiality of the protocol. A hidden random bit b is flipped at the beginning of the attack scenario. The adversary's goal is to guess the bit b.

The adversary gets access to the following oracles:

- $Send(U^j, m)$: as in Sect. 2 this oracle query sends the message m to the participant instance U^j, and outputs the message generated by the participant upon receipt of m. As in Sect. 5.1 the adversary can issue a $Send(IFD^j, \mathsf{start}\|data)$ that initiates the j-th instance of an IFD with $data$ as input.

  Additionally the adversary can issue a $Send(IFD^j, \mathsf{start}'\|data_0\|data_1)$ query to the j-th instance of an IFD, where $data_0$ and $data_1$ are two messages of equal length; the output of a regular $Send(IFD^j, \mathsf{start}\|data_b)$ is then returned corresponding to the IFD being started with $data_b$. Such query can appear multiple times in the protocol execution.
- $Corrupt(id_i)$: as in Sect. 5.1 the adversary receives the secret-key sk_i of the IFD of identity id_i. Note that there is no corrupt query to the ICC, as the adversary could trivially break the scheme when knowing the master-key.

Eventually the adversary outputs a guess b' of the hidden bit b, and succeeds if $b' = b$ and no $Corrupt$ query was issued against any of the IFD's for which a $Send(IFD^j, \mathsf{start}'\|data_0\|data_1)$ was issued. As in Sect. 2 we define the advantage of an adversary $\mathcal{A}$ in violating the confidentiality of the protocol P by:

$$\mathsf{Adv}_P^{\mathsf{ind}}(\mathcal{A}) = 2 \cdot \Pr[b' = b] - 1$$

We define $\mathsf{Adv}_P^{\mathsf{ind}}(t, q_s, q_c, q_h)$ as the maximum advantage over all adversaries running in time at most t, and making at most q_s *Send* and *Execute* queries, q_c corrupt queries, and q_h hash queries.

Definition 10 (Protocol Confidentiality). *We say that a protocol P provides* $(t, q_s, q_c, q_h, \varepsilon)$-*indistinguishability if* $\mathsf{Adv}_P^{\mathsf{ind}}(t, q_s, q_c, q_h) \leq \varepsilon$.

The following theorem shows that $mERA_{1-3}$ achieves the confidentiality property.

Theorem 2 (Confidentiality of $mERA_{1-3}$). *The* $mERA_{1-3}$ *provides* $(t, q_s, q_c, q_h, \varepsilon)$-*indistinguishability, with:*

$$\varepsilon = \frac{2(q_s)^2}{2^{\delta}} + q_h \cdot 2^{-\alpha} + q_h \cdot \mathsf{Adv}_{\mathsf{Enc}}^{\mathsf{CPA}}(t + \mathcal{O}(\kappa), q_s) + q_s \cdot \mathsf{Adv}^{\mathsf{IND}}(t + \mathcal{O}(\kappa), q_s) \quad (3)$$

5.4 Proof of Theorem 2

The proof is essentially the same as the proof of Theorem 1. The only difference is that in Game 3 in order to bound $\Pr[S_3]$ we construct a distinguisher for the Enc function instead of a Mac forger. Therefore using a hybrid argument the term $\mathsf{Adv}^{\mathsf{MAC}}(t + \mathcal{O}(\kappa), q_s)$ is replaced by $\mathsf{Adv}^{\mathsf{IND}}(t + \mathcal{O}(\kappa), q_s)$ in Eq. (3).

6 Security of $mERA_{1-7}$

In this section we show that the $mERA_{1-7}$ protocol is secure in the Bellare-Rogaway model recalled in Sect. 2. We first consider the secrecy property of the session-key.

Theorem 3. *The $mERA_{1-7}$ protocol is (t, q_s, q_c, q_h)-semantically secure in the random oracle model, where:*

$$\varepsilon = \mathsf{Adv}_{\mathcal{CA}}^{\mathsf{forge}}(t + \mathcal{O}(\kappa), q_s) + 3 \cdot q_s \cdot \mathsf{Adv}^{\mathsf{GDH}}(t + \mathcal{O}(\kappa), q_h) + \frac{2 \cdot q_s^2}{2^{\delta}} +$$
$$q_h \cdot 2^{-\alpha} + q_s \cdot q_h \cdot \mathsf{Adv}_{\mathsf{Enc}}^{\mathsf{CPA}}(t + \mathcal{O}(\kappa), q_s) + q_s \cdot \mathsf{Adv}^{\mathsf{MAC}}(t + \mathcal{O}(\kappa), q_s)$$

6.1 Proof of Theorem 3

As previously we use a sequence of games; we denote by S_i the event that the attacker succeeds in Game_i.

Game_0: this is the attack scenario. We can perfectly simulate the oracles *Send*, *Execute*, *Reveal*, *Corrupt* and *Test* using our knowledge of the master key mk and the exponents x_i.

$Game_1$: we abort if the adversary sends to the ICC a certificate σ_i for public-key g^{x_i} corresponding to identity id_i, where the public-key g^{x_i} has not been registered to the certification authority before.

$$|\Pr[S_1] - \Pr[S_0]| \leq \mathsf{Adv}_{\mathcal{CA}}^{\mathsf{forge}}(t + \mathcal{O}(\kappa), q_s)$$

$Game_2$: we modify our simulation of the *Send* oracle as follows. For any IFD of identity id_i which has not received a *Corrupt* query and whose public-key was not registered by the adversary, instead of computing $K_{ICC} = H_5(sid \parallel (g^{x_i})^y \parallel (g^{x'})^y)$, we generate a random K_{ICC} in $\{0,1\}^\eta$ and let $K_{IFD} = K_{ICC}$ for the partner IFD instance. Note that this is done for all ICC instances, where such instances are possibly run concurrently.

Let F_2 be the event that the adversary makes a H_5 hash query for $\cdot \parallel (g^{x_i})^y \parallel \cdot$ where y has been computed by the ICC in an interaction with an IFD of identity id_i which is not adversarially controlled. It is clear that games 1 and 2 proceed identically unless event F_2 happens, therefore:

$$|\Pr[S_2] - \Pr[S_1]| \leq \Pr[F_2]$$

Lemma 5. *The following holds:*

$$\Pr[F_2] \leq q_s \cdot \mathsf{Adv}^{\mathsf{GDH}}(t + \mathcal{O}(\kappa), q_h) \tag{4}$$

Proof. We show how to construct from the adversary $\mathcal{A}$ an algorithm C_{GDH} to solve the GDH problem. We receive as input a GDH instance (g, g^a, g^b) and we must compute g^{ab}. We select a target identity id^* at random among the possible identities; note that there are at most q_s possible identities. We let the public-key $g^{x_{i^*}}$ be equal to the DDH instance g^a for this identity id^*. Moreover instead of generating the g^y elements from the ICC by first randomly selecting a random y in $\mathbb{Z}_q$ and then computing g^y, for every such element we generate a random $\beta \in \mathbb{Z}_q$ and use the GDH instance g^b by letting $g^y = (g^b)^\beta$, which implicitly defines $y = \beta \cdot b \pmod q$.

If event F_2 occurs for identity id, we abort if $id \neq id^*$. Then given the H_5 query part $(g^{x_i})^y = (g^a)^{\beta b}$ we can compute g^{ab} and solve the GDH challenge. The right H_5 query is selected by querying the DDH oracle available for solving the GDH problem. More precisely, for any H_5 query part z, we query the DDH oracle with $(g, g^a, (g^b)^\beta, z)$ to test whether $z = (g^a)^{\beta b}$ and recover the value $(g^a)^{\beta b}$ among the H_5 queries.

Since we must have guessed the correct identity id^*, the success probability of our C_{GDH} algorithm is at least $\Pr[F_2]/q_s$. This gives inequality (4). $\square$

$Game_3$: we abort if the random r_1 generated by the IFD was previously generated by the IFD or if the random r_2 generated by the ICC was previously generated by the ICC. By the Difference Lemma we get:

$$|\Pr[S_3] - \Pr[S_2]| \leq \frac{2 \cdot q_s^2}{2^\delta}$$

Game_4: we modify the way the secret keys sk are generated; instead of letting sk $\leftarrow$ KDF(mk, id), we use a private random oracle H_p and let sk $\leftarrow H_p(id)$ for every new identity. Similarly the $Corrupt$ oracle is modified so that $sk \leftarrow H_p(id)$ is returned instead.

Let G be the event that the adversary makes a random oracle query to KDF(mk, id) for some id. It is clear that games 3 and 4 proceed identically unless event G happens; this gives:

$$|\Pr[S_4] - \Pr[S_3]| \leq \Pr[G]$$

Since mk is generated at random in $\{0,1\}^\alpha$ and there are at most q_h hash oracle queries to KDF, we have:

$$\Pr[G] \leq q_h \cdot 2^{-\alpha}$$

Game_5: we modify the $Send$ oracle as follows. We change the way the values k_a, k_b and k_c are generated at the second round of the protocol. Instead of letting $k_c = H_3(zz)$ where $zz = \mathsf{Enc}(\mathsf{sk}, r_1 \| r_2)$ and sk corresponding to an IFD of identity id, we simply generate k_c at random in $\{0,1\}^\gamma$; we proceed similarly for k_a and k_b. This is done for any ICC instance and IFD instance, where such instances are possibly run concurrently. This implies that the values k_a, k_b and k_c are generated independently for every distinct AKE sessions, even run concurrently.

We denote by F the event that the adversary makes a H_1, H_2 or H_3 query to zz where $zz = \mathsf{Enc}(\mathsf{sk}, r_1 \| r_2)$ and sk corresponding to id. It is clear that games 4 and 5 proceed identically unless F occurs; therefore by the Difference Lemma:

$$|\Pr[S_5] - \Pr[S_4]| \leq \Pr[F]$$

Lemma 6. *The following holds.*

$$\Pr[F] \leq q_s \cdot q_h \cdot \mathsf{Adv}_{\mathsf{Enc}}^{\mathsf{CPA}}(t + \mathcal{O}(\kappa), q_s) \tag{5}$$

Proof. The proof is similar to the proof of Lemma 3 and is therefore omitted. □

Game_6: the $Send$ simulation is modified as follows: the session is aborted if the values (E_1, M_1) sent by the adversary to an IFD instance of identity id at the second round of the protocol has not been generated by the legitimate ICC, $i.e.$ we abort if (E_1, M_1) is not the output of a previous $Send$ oracle query to the ICC instance, when the ICC and the corresponding IFD have not received a $Corrupt$ query. Let denote by F_6 the corresponding event. We have:

$$|\Pr[S_6] - \Pr[S_5]| \leq \Pr[F_6]$$

Lemma 7. *The following holds:*

$$\Pr[F_6] \leq q_s \cdot \mathsf{Adv}^{\mathsf{MAC}}(t + \mathcal{O}(\kappa), q_s)$$

Proof. The proof is similar to the proof of Lemma 4 and is therefore omitted. $\square$

Note that since from Game 5 the keys k_a, k_b and k_c are generated independently for every distinct AKE sessions, the adversary engaged in concurrent executions of the protocol cannot use a pair (E_1, M_1) obtained from one session into another session.[2] Note also that in game 6 the value g^y that is used by the IFD of identity id is the same as the one generated by the ICC.

Game$_7$: we modify our simulation of the *Send* oracle as follows. For any IFD of identity id_i which has not received a *Corrupt* query and whose public-key was not registered by the adversary, instead of computing $K_{IFD} = H_5(sid \parallel (g^y)^{x_i} \parallel (g^y)^{x'})$, we generate a random K_{IFD} in $\{0,1\}^n$.

Let F_7 be the event that the adversary makes a H_5 hash query for $\cdot \parallel (g^y)^{x_i} \parallel \cdot$ where g^y is the value received by the IFD of identity id_i and the IFD of identity id_i did not receive a *Corrupt* query. We have:

$$|\Pr[S_7] - \Pr[S_6]| \leq \Pr[F_7]$$

Lemma 8. *The following holds:*

$$\Pr[F_7] \leq q_s \cdot \mathsf{Adv}^{\mathsf{GDH}}(t, q_h) \tag{6}$$

Proof. From Game 6 the value g^y has been computed by the legitimate ICC in an interaction with an IFD which is not adversarially controlled. Therefore we can proceed as in the proof of Lemma 5 to obtain inequality (6). $\square$

Game$_8$: we modify again our simulation of the *Send* oracle as follows. For any interaction between the ICC and an IFD obtained through an *Execute* query, instead of computing $K_{IFD} = H_5(sid \parallel (g^y)^{x_i} \parallel (g^y)^{x'})$ and $K_{ICC} = H_5(sid \parallel (g^{x_i})^y \parallel (g^{x'})^y)$, we generate a random K_{IFD} in $\{0,1\}^n$ and let $K_{ICC} = K_{IFD}$.

Let F_8 be the event that the adversary makes a H_5 hash query for $\cdot \parallel (g^{x'})^y$ where $g^{x'}$ and g^y have been generated during a passive *Execute* query between the ICC and an IFD of identity id. We have as previously:

$$|\Pr[S_8] - \Pr[S_7]| \leq \Pr[F_8]$$

Lemma 9. *The following holds:*

$$\Pr[F_8] \leq q_s \cdot \mathsf{Adv}^{\mathsf{GDH}}(t, q_h) \tag{7}$$

---

[2] For example the attacker could run two sessions in parallel between ICC^i and IFD^j, and $ICC^{i'}$ and $IFD^{j'}$, and send (E_1, M_1) from ICC^i to $IFD^{j'}$ instead of IFD^j. However from Game 5 the value k_c generated between ICC^i and IFD^j is independent from the value k'_c generated between $ICC^{i'}$ and $IFD^{j'}$; therefore the pair (E_1, M_1) sent to $IFD^{j'}$ would either be rejected (as not verifying the MAC equation) or be a MAC forgery (where the probability of such forgery is bounded in Lemma 7).

Proof. The proof is similar to the proof of Lemma 5 and is therefore omitted. □

Finally we have that in Game_8 the adversary has not made a H_5 query for any key $(g^{x_i})^y\|(g^{x'})^y$ computed by the ICC or the IFD. Therefore the adversary's view is independent of any session-key computed between the ICC and the IFD which can not be obtained through a *Reveal* or *Corrupt* query. This implies:

$$\Pr[S_8] = \frac{1}{2}$$

Combining the previous inequalities, we obtain:

$$\left|\Pr[S_0] - \frac{1}{2}\right| \leq \mathsf{Adv}_{CA}^{\text{forge}}(t + \mathcal{O}(\kappa), q_s) + 3 \cdot q_s \cdot \mathsf{Adv}^{\text{GDH}}(t + \mathcal{O}(\kappa), q_h) + \frac{2 \cdot q_s^2}{2^\delta} +$$

$$q_h 2^{-\alpha} + q_s q_h \cdot \mathsf{Adv}_{\text{Enc}}^{\text{CPA}}(t + \mathcal{O}(\kappa), q_s) + q_s \cdot \mathsf{Adv}^{\text{MAC}}(t + \mathcal{O}(\kappa), q_s)$$

which terminates the proof of Theorem 3.

6.2   Authentication Property of $mERA_{1-7}$

In this section we show that the $mERA_{1-7}$ protocol satisfies the authenticity property.

Theorem 4. *The $mERA_{1-7}$ protocol is $(t, q_s, q_e, q_h, \varepsilon)$-authentic in the random oracle model, where:*

$$\varepsilon = \frac{2(q_s)^2}{2^\delta} + q_h \cdot 2^{-\alpha} + q_s \cdot q_h \cdot \mathsf{Adv}_{\text{Enc}}^{\text{CPA}}(t + \mathcal{O}(\kappa), q_s) + q_s \cdot \mathsf{Adv}^{\text{MAC}}(t + \mathcal{O}(\kappa), q_s)$$

Proof. The proof is essentially the same as the proof of Theorem 1. Therefore we present only the main ideas and omit the technical details.

The authentication of the IFD with respect to the ICC is ensured by the elements (E_2, M_2) sent by the IFD in the 3-rd round of the protocol. As in the proof of Theorem 1, one can show that the adversary can not provide a pair (E_2, M_2) not computed during the same session between the ICC and the IFD instance; as in the proof of Theorem 1, this is based on the freshness of the $r_2\|r_1$ string, the secrecy of mk, the chosen plaintext security of the function Enc, and the unforgeability of the Mac function. Therefore we obtain that for any adversary running in time at most t and making at most q_s *Send* and *Execute* queries, q_c *Corrupt* queries and q_h hash queries:

$$\mathsf{Adv}_{mERA1-7}^{\text{IFD-auth}}(\mathcal{A}) \leq \frac{2(q_s)^2}{2^\delta} + q_h \cdot 2^{-\alpha} + q_s \cdot q_h \cdot \mathsf{Adv}_{\text{Enc}}^{\text{CPA}}(t + \mathcal{O}(\kappa), q_s)$$

$$+ q_s \cdot \mathsf{Adv}^{\text{MAC}}(t + \mathcal{O}(\kappa), q_s)$$

Similarly the authentication of the ICC with respect to the IFD is ensured by the elements (E_3, M_3) sent by the ICC at the end of the protocol. As in the proof of Theorem 1, one can show that the adversary can not provide a pair (E_3, M_3) without the legitimate ICC being in accept mode; as in the proof of Theorem 1, this is based on the freshness of the $r_2 \| r_1$ string, the secrecy of mk, the chosen plaintext security of the function Enc, and the unforgeability of the Mac function. Therefore we obtain for any adversary running in time at most t and making at most q_s Send and Execute queries, q_c Corrupt queries and q_h hash queries:

$$\mathsf{Adv}^{\mathsf{ICC-auth}}_{\mathsf{mERA1-7}}(\mathcal{A}) \leq \frac{2(q_s)^2}{2^\delta} + q_h \cdot 2^{-\alpha} + q_s \cdot q_h \cdot \mathsf{Adv}^{\mathsf{CPA}}_{\mathsf{Enc}}(t + \mathcal{O}(\kappa), q_s)$$
$$+ q_s \cdot \mathsf{Adv}^{\mathsf{MAC}}(t + \mathcal{O}(\kappa), q_s)$$

Combining the two previous inequalities, this proves Theorem 4.

7   Conclusion

We have provided a security analysis of the Modular Enhanced Symmetric Role Authentication (mERA) protocol, showing that mERA is secure in the Bellare-Rogaway model, the standard model for analyzing the security of cryptographic protocols.

References

1. AFNOR. Modular enhanced symmetric role authentication (mERA). Technical report (2010)
2. Bellare, M., Rogaway, P.: Entity authentication and key distribution. In: Stinson, D.R. (ed.) CRYPTO 1993. LNCS, vol. 773, pp. 232–249. Springer, Heidelberg (1994)
3. Canetti, R., Krawczyk, H.: Analysis of key-exchange protocols and their use for building secure channels. In: Pfitzmann, B. (ed.) EUROCRYPT 2001. LNCS, vol. 2045, pp. 453–474. Springer, Heidelberg (2001)
4. Canetti, R., Krawczyk, H.: Security analysis of IKE's signature-based key-exchange protocol. In: Yung, M. (ed.) CRYPTO 2002. LNCS, vol. 2442, pp. 143–161. Springer, Heidelberg (2002)
5. Dagdelen, Ö., Fischlin, M.: Security analysis of the extended access control protocol for machine readable travel documents. In: Burmester, M., Tsudik, G., Magliveras, S., Ilić, I. (eds.) ISC 2010. LNCS, vol. 6531, pp. 54–68. Springer, Heidelberg (2011)
6. Goldwasser, S., Micali, S.: Probabilistic encryption. J. Comput. Syst. Sci. **28**(2), 270–299 (1984)
7. Harkins, D., Carrel, D.: The internet key exchange (IKE). RFC 2409, November 1998
8. Krawczyk, H.: HMQV: a high-performance secure Diffie-Hellman protocol. In: Shoup, V. (ed.) CRYPTO 2005. LNCS, vol. 3621, pp. 546–566. Springer, Heidelberg (2005)
9. LaMacchia, B.A., Lauter, K., Mityagin, A.: Stronger security of authenticated key exchange. In: Susilo, W., Liu, J.K., Mu, Y. (eds.) ProvSec 2007. LNCS, vol. 4784, pp. 1–16. Springer, Heidelberg (2007)
10. Shoup, V., Sequences of games: a tool for taming complexity in security proofs. Cryptology ePrint Archive, Report 2004/332 (2004). http://eprint.iacr.org/

A Proof of Lemma 1

The proof is based on the fact that Enc is a deterministic encryption scheme. We consider an attacker against the chosen plaintext security of Enc who succeeds with probability at least ε, and we must break the indistinguishability of Enc. We forward the encryption queries of the attacker to the indistinguishability challenger. Eventually the attacker submits a pair (m', c') where m was not queried before for encryption. We select another message m'' of the same length and set $m_0 = m'$ and $m_1 = m''$. The indistinguishability challenger returns an encryption c of message m_b. If $c' = c$ we return $b' = 0$, otherwise we return $b' = 1$. It is easy to see that our new adversary's advantage is at least ε, which proves Lemma 1.

Crypto Santa

Peter Y.A. Ryan[✉]

University of Luxembourg, Kirchberg, Luxembourg
peter.ryan@uni.lu

1 Introduction

Secret Santa, also known as Kris Kindle etc., is a ceremony widely enacted in various countries, notably the Netherlands, on or around the 6th of December. The idea is to create a secret allocation of presents in such a way that each participant learns to whom their present will go but nobody learns from whom they received their present. Traditionally this is done with a drawing of names from a hat: each participant's name is written on a slip of paper, these are placed in a hat and shaken. Then each player in turn draws a slip from the hat. If the slip has her own name she announces this and replaces it and draws again after shaking the hat. If it is the name of another player then she retains it and takes this to be her designated recipient. Now there are online sites that provide the service, e.g. https://www.drawnames.com/secret-santa-generator.

To a cryptographer of course, Secret Santa provides an irresistible challenge, and an opportunity to show off the power of modern cryptography. In this little chapter we present a way for a group of people to run their own Secret Santa ceremony without resorting to such outdated 20th century devices as hats and slips of paper, and without resorting to anything as unsavoury as a trusted third party.

The challenge is to devise a cryptographic ceremony that allows the players to generate a secret permutation without fixed points, i.e. a *derangement*, in such a way that the only thing each player learns is the identity of the person to whom they will give their present. Furthermore, we would like a solution that will foil any attempt by a player to undermine the goals of the ceremony. This of course immediately begs certain questions: what precisely are the goals? In what way might a player want to undermine these goals, and what capabilities do we attribute to the players? What can a coalition of malicious players achieve?

The topic may seem rather frivolous, and indeed this chapter is intended as a light-hearted tribute to David Kahn, but there are arguably some serious points to the exercise. The author, along with some colleagues, investigated Secret Santa originally in [5]. The motivation for this stemmed from the observation that the process of designing and analysing a security protocol never seems to run true: it always appears to be a process of trial and error. An initial design is later discovered to be vulnerable to an unforeseen style of attack, necessitating a revision of the protocol and, typically, the requirements.

It would be nice to think that we would write down the security requirements at the outset, design a protocol and prove that it satisfies these requirements in

© Springer-Verlag Berlin Heidelberg 2016
P.Y.A. Ryan et al. (Eds.): Kahn Festschrift, LNCS 9100, pp. 543–549, 2016.
DOI: 10.1007/978-3-662-49301-4_33

a given threat environment, i.e. assumptions about the attacker's capabilities. In practice, our initial set of requirements invariably seems to be incomplete, and we later uncover new styles of attack that force us to revise or enlarge the set of requirements and redesign the protocol. Thus, threats and attacks drive the security requirements. For more discussion of such matters we refer the reader to [5], for now we will just regard Secret Santa as an enticing crypto-mathematical problem.

A number of crypto protocols were presented in [5], but here we present a simpler, and we think more elegant, solution exploiting a rather powerful, but apparently little known, construction know as *exponentiation mixes*.

2   The Secret Santa Protocol

At its core, the Secret Santa ceremony calls for the generation of a secret derangement of the set $\{1, 2, ..., N\}$. The only information leaks that are permitted are that the ith player should learn to whom they will donate their present. No other information should leak, in particular no player should learn from whom their present came. Of course, players might exchange information about their allocations using channels outside the protocol we describe here. We cannot prevent this and we will not be concerned about it. What concerns us is that the protocol itself not leak any further information.

We further require that no player can influence the final permutation in a predictable way. More precisely, we require that for each player the final permutation is indistinguishable from a random derangement. We achieve this by ensuring that each player contribute his or her own secret, random permutation and that the final permutation be a product of all of these.

To start with, we describe the protocol assuming that all the players are honest. Later, in Sect. 5, we will introduce some elaborations designed to ensure that no player can cheat undetectably.

3   Related Work

The Secret Santa protocol problem was first described in the scientific literature by Crépeau and Kilian [1] in 1994. They propose a solution using only a deck of playing cards. Later, in 2002, Gerard Tel uses the problem as an example in his text book [7]. He describes a probabilistic, decentralized solution. One of his students studied the problem in more detail and developed implementations of different solutions [8]. Liberti and Raimondi studied the problem from a different point of view. They do not propose a protocol but an algorithm to determine if a solution exists under certain constraints, including an anonymity requirement [4]. Recently, Heather, Schneider, and Teague [2] proposed a solution with physical objects only.

The solution proposed by Crépeau and Kilian [1] assumes an honest but curious party who is responsible for picking the permutation using a deck of cards only. Participants are represented by specific sequences of cards in the deck.

The protocol consists of N rounds. The ith round consists of a random cyclic shift of the cards, after which the participant represented by the topmost sequence of cards is assigned to participant i. The encoding of participants through card sequences and the card sequences separating these encodings are designed in such a way that the boundaries of such a sequence can be blindly determined and it can be verified blindly whether a participant's sequence is assigned to himself. If such a self-assignment is detected, the algorithm is repeated from scratch, making this a probabilistic solution.

Heather, Schneider, and Teague [2] describe a simple, centralized solution, requiring nothing further than envelopes, cards, and pens. Their solution is guaranteed to produce a cyclic permutation. Thus no donor will need to buy a gift for himself. However, their solution cannot produce derangements which are not cyclic permutations. Thus, every donor also knows that he will not receive a gift from his recipient.

4   A Cryptographic Ceremony for Secret Santa

We propose a solution using the rather elegant *exponentiation mix* construct from [6]. We assume the usual ElGamal set up: a group G of large prime order q with generator g in which the discrete log problem is considered to be hard. Let us assume that each player is equipped with a public key pair (PK_i, SK_i), where: $PK_i = g^{SK_i}$. For notational simplicity we will denote SK_i by x_i. We arrange the PKs in a list:

$$\langle g^{x_1}, g^{x_2}, \ldots, g^{x_N} \rangle$$

The players take it in turns to put these terms through a sequence of exponentiation mixes: The first player P_1 takes the original list of PKs, generates a fresh, random $s_1 \in \{0, \ldots, q-1\}$ and raises each term to this power s_1. P_1 then subjects the resulting terms to a secret shuffle π_1 and posts the result to the WBB. P_1 also appends the term g^{s_1} to this list.

$$\langle g^{x_{\pi_1(1)} \cdot s_1}, g^{x_{\pi_1(2)} \cdot s_1}, \ldots, g^{x_{\pi_1(N)} \cdot s_1}, g^{s_1} \rangle$$

The ith player P_i takes the batch of outputs from the previous player P_{i-1} raises each of the first N terms, to a secret common power s_i, subjects the resulting first N terms to a secret shuffle π_i and outputs the result to the WBB. P_i also appends g^{s_i} to the list and passes $g^{\hat{s}_i} := g^{\hat{s}_{i-1} \cdot s_i}$ over a private channel to P_{i+1}. Note that the generator terms g^{s_i} are not permuted but stay fixed at the $N+1$ position in the lists. The final output is a list:

$$\langle g^{x_{\pi(1)} \cdot s}, g^{x_{\pi(2)} \cdot s}, \ldots, g^{x_{\pi(N)} \cdot s}, g^{s_N} \rangle$$

The last player also publishes the final generator g^s. Where:

$$\pi = \prod_{i=1}^{N} \pi_i, \ \hat{s}_{i+1} = \prod_{i=1}^{i} \hat{s}_i \ and \ s = \hat{s}_N = \prod_{i=1}^{N} s_i$$

Now each player P_i can identify her pseudo-PK, PK^* in the list by computing $(g^s)^{x_i}$ and finding the match. Suppose that P_i finds her pseudo-PK in the jth position in the list, then she will present her present to P_j.

But we are not quite done because this list generated in this fashion might not be a derangement as required. We could at this point simply require a player to announce that she has found herself at a fixed point of π, and we could even then require her to provide a Zero-Knowledge proof of this, by showing knowledge of the x_i such that $PK_i^* = (g^s)^{x_i}$. This would prevent players falsely claiming to be at a fixed point to avoid giving their present to someone they dislike for example. Our construction so far does not however prevent a player who happens to find herself at a fixed point and likes the idea of giving herself her present from not owning up.

Now it is debatable as to whether this is a real problem. One might argue that the odds that someone will find themselves at a fixed point and be totally anti-social is pretty low and who cares anyway. But the crypto-purist would want to eliminate even such an arguably innocuous misbehaviour.

4.1   Detecting Fixed Points

In order to detect the presence of a fixed point in the permutation π in a manner that does not reveal anything about π but is verifiable by all the players, we pair off the elements of the original list of PKs and the final shuffled list of pseudo-PKs to form a list of N pairs of the form:

$$(g^{x_i}, g^{x_{\pi(i)} \cdot s})$$

We will think of these as ElGamal encryptions with respect to the public key: g^s, i.e. with secret key s. Now the players will take it in turns to subject these pairs to a randomisation operation. The first player will take in the list above and for the ith pair it will generate a random $r_{1,i}$ and raise both components to this power and he posts the results to the WBB:

$$(g^{x_i}, g^{x_{\pi(i)} \cdot s}) \rightarrow (g^{x_i \cdot r_{1,i}}, g^{x_{\pi(i)} \cdot s \cdot r_{1,i}})$$

The second player takes the transformed list output by first player and applies his own transformation, using his own randoms, and so on until the last player.

Notice that, in contrast to the exponentiation mixes we used previously, here each term is raised to an independent random value. Once they have all the players have performed their transformations we will have a list of pairs:

$$(g^{x_i \cdot r_i}, g^{x_{\pi(i)} \cdot s \cdot r_i})$$

where $r_i = \prod_{j=1}^{N} r_{j,i}$.

The players now take it in turns to perform a partial decryption of these terms using their s_j share of the secret key s. Thus, P_j will perform the following transformation on each term:

$$(g^{x_i \cdot r_i}, g^{x_{\pi(i)} \cdot s \cdot r_i}) \rightarrow (g^{x_i \cdot r_i}, \frac{g^{x_{\pi(i)} \cdot s \cdot r_i}}{g^{x_i \cdot r_i \cdot s_j}})$$

The result will be a list of decryptions:

$$\Delta_i := \frac{g^{x_{\pi(i)} \cdot s \cdot r_i}}{g^{x_i \cdot r_i \cdot s}}$$

The Δ_ith term will equal 1 if and only if $i = \pi(i)$, i.e. i is a fixed point of π. Otherwise the result is a pure random value. Thus, if all N terms are $\neq 1$ then π is a derangement, and no further information is revealed about the permutation. If π turns out not to be a derangement they perform a further shuffle or shuffles and check again. The odds of a random permutation being a derangement tends to e^{-1} as $N \rightarrow \infty$ so it should only require a few iterations to reach a derangement.

The procedure above of course reveals where any fixed points are in π, if they exist, but this does not matter as we will discard any permutations with fixed points. When π turns out to have no fixed points, no information about it is revealed aside from the fact that it is a derangement. This is because each term will be ratio of a PK and a PK^* raised to a random element of $r_i \in Z_q$.

5   Detecting Cheating Players

So far we have assumed that all the players have been honest, i.e. behaved according to the protocol rules. In particular we have been assuming that each player performs their exponentiation mix correctly, i.e. they raise all the terms to the same exponent and they perform a genuine shuffle. Similarly we have assumed that they all perform the randomisations of the $(g^{x_i}, g^{x_{\pi(i)} \cdot s})$ terms correctly, i.e. for each such pair they raise both components to the same, random exponent. Finally we have been assuming that they all perform their partial decryption steps correctly.

In fact we can dispense with such assumptions by including extra mechanisms to detect any dishonesty.

For the exponentiation mixes we can introduce Zero-Knowledge proofs of correct shuffles based on those proposed in [9]. Alternatively we could use partial random checks in the manner of [3]: after a player has committed to a mix he is challenged to reveal some of the links and required to prove in zero-knowledge that he used the same exponent.

A possible audit strategy is to chose a random sub-set of the output terms and require the player who performed the mix to reveal the corresponding source sub-set. Now we take the product of the terms in the input sub-set, call this ϕ, and the product of the terms of the output sub-set, call this ψ. The player should now be able to prove in zero-knowledge that he knows the Discrete log of ψ w.r.t. ϕ.

For the randomisation of the $(g^{x_i}, g^{x_{\pi(i)} \cdot s})$ terms we can simply require the player to provide, for each pair, a ZK proof of knowledge of the common $r_{i,j}$ exponent. For the partial decryption steps we can again use standard ZK proofs of correct decryption with respect to the g^{s_j} terms.

6   The Surrounding Ceremony

As is so often the case with such security protocols, we need also to consider the surrounding context in which the cryptographic protocol exists. We now have a elegant solution for generating a secret derangement and revealing to donors the identity of the person to whom they will assign their gift. But if we expand the scope of the system we can ask: by what mechanism do the recipients collect their presents in a way that preserves the anonymity of the donor but also prevents ways of cheating?

We might imagine for example that P_i should attach a card to his present with P_j's identity. But we now have the difficulty that P_i might cheat and put a different identity than the one assigned by the protocol. We can counter this is by also requiring P_i to provide a Zero-Knowledge proof of the x_i such that:

$$(g^s)^{x_i} = PK_j^*$$

i.e. a ZK proof of knowledge of the discrete log of PK_j^* w.r.t. the base g^s.

7   Doubly Anonymous Allocations

The protocol above can be extended to make the donations doubly anonymous: even the donor does not know to whom he is assigning his present. Whether this is desirable is questionable, but it is amusing that we can do it if we wish. The trick is simply to introduce a second exponentiation shuffle and hence a second set of pseudonyms:

$$\langle \{g^{\rho(1) \cdot s'}\}, \{g^{\rho(2) \cdot s'}\}, \ldots, \{g^{\rho(N) \cdot s'}\}, \{g^s\} \rangle$$

Let's denote this second set of pseudonyms by $PK^\sharp$. Now P_i finds his position in the first list and finds the corresponding $g^{\rho(j) \cdot s}$ in the same position in the second list. He writes this pseudonym on the card that he attaches to his present. He thus does not know the real identity associated with $g^{\rho(j) \cdot s}$ but P_j can find the label with his pseudo-$PK^\sharp$.

8   Conclusions

We have seen how the tools of modern cryptography can be used to devise a simple, distributed protocol for the Secret Santa game. We have further seen how this construction can be extended to provide double anonymity, i.e. even the donor not does not learn to whom he assigns his gift.

References

1. Crépeau, C., Kilian, J.: Discreet solitary games. In: Stinson, D.R. (ed.) CRYPTO 1993. LNCS, vol. 773, pp. 319–330. Springer, Heidelberg (1994)
2. Heather, J., Schneider, S., Teague, V.: Cryptographic protocols with everyday objects. Formal Aspects Comput. 26(1), 37–62 (2014)
3. Jakobsson, M., Juels, A., Rivest, R.L.: Making mix nets robust for electronic voting by randomized partial checking. In: Proceedings of the 11th USENIX Security Symposium, San Francisco, CA, USA, 5–9 August 2002, pp. 339–353 (2002)
4. Liberti, L., Raimondi, F.: The secret santa problem. In: Fleischer, R., Xu, J. (eds.) AAIM 2008. LNCS, vol. 5034, pp. 271–279. Springer, Heidelberg (2008)
5. Mauw, S., Radomirović, S., Ryan, P.Y.A.: Security protocols for secret santa. In: Christianson, B., Malcolm, J. (eds.) Security Protocols 2010. LNCS, vol. 7061, pp. 175–184. Springer, Heidelberg (2014)
6. Haenni, R., Spycher, O.: Secure internet voting on limited devices with anonymized DSA public keys. In: Proceedings of the 2011 Conference on Electronic Voting Technology/Workshop on Trustworthy Elections, EVT/WOTE 2011. USENIX Association (2011)
7. Tel, G.: Cryptografie - Beveiliging van de Digitale Maatschappij. Addison Wesley, Reading (2002)
8. Verelst, J.: Secure computing and distributed solutions to the Secret Santa problem. Master's thesis, Computer Science Dept., University of Utrecht (2003)
9. Wikström, D.: A sender verifiable mix-net and a new proof of a shuffle. In: Roy, B. (ed.) ASIACRYPT 2005. LNCS, vol. 3788, pp. 273–292. Springer, Heidelberg (2005)

Author Index

Printed in the United States
By Bookmasters